D1431835

THESE ARE UNCORRECTED ADVANCE PROOFS
BOUND FOR YOUR REVIEWING CONVENIENCE

In quoting from this book for reviews or any other
purpose, it is essential that the final printed book be
referred to, since the author may make changes on these
proofs before the book goes to press.

An ambitious yet accessible work that embraces *all* of the prophecies in the Bible that deal directly or tangentially with the end times.

At the last millennial change, the entire nation of Iceland converted to Christianity in fear that the end was near. Today, even if our daily preoccupation as we approach 2000 has as much to do with computer bugs as with the end of the world as we know it, the inevitable growing public interest in prophecies of all kinds will undoubtedly focus on the rich, complex, and enigmatic prophetic writings of the Bible.

Arranged topically according to their apparent chronology, this comprehensive book provides a context in which these prophecies can be examined. It opens with the first signs of the times and climaxes with the utopian visions of a new heaven and a new earth. The author has allowed the original text to speak for itself, providing pertinent interpretation, cross-references, explanations, and transitions from one section to another that are essential to the understanding of the text.

While eschewing a didactic or an alarmist approach to the subject, Haggith reinforces the notion that the grand purpose of prophecy is "not to provide a road map to the future but to enable willing listeners to recognize the working of God in times of danger and uncertainty." What emerges is an engrossing and sometimes baffling view of the world—or at least the world that biblical chroniclers perceived through the prism of divine inspiration. Scholars and skeptics, believers and agnostics alike will come away from this book with a renewed appreciation for the human and spiritual dramas that unfold throughout the scriptures.

David Haggith has contributed articles, mostly on contemporary religious issues and matter of faith, to The Lutheran, Presbyterian Record, The Baptist Leader, Christian Living *and* Our Sunday Visitor. *He lives in Seattle.*

End-Time Prophecies of the Bible

DAVID HAGGITH

G.P. Putnam's Sons
New York

End-Time

Prophecies of

the Bible

Haggith, David.
    End-time prophecies of the Bible / by David Haggith.
      p.   cm.
    Includes bibliographical references and index.
    ISBN 0-399-14532-X (alk. paper)
    1. Bible—Prophecies—End of the world.   2. End of the world—Biblical teaching.
    I. Title.
BS649.E63H34   1999
236'.9—dc21   99-20654 CIP

Acknowledgments

TK

more acknowledgments???

Dedicated to

EVELYΠ HAGGIᵗH

for her lifelong interest

in prophecy

Contents

The Church at Pergamos 00

The Church at Thyatira 00

The Church at Sardis 00

The Church at Philadelphia 00

The Church at Laodicea 00

9.   VISIONS: MYSTICAL ENCOUNTERS OF
     GOD AND HEAVEN 00

     Prophetic Technique 00

     A Vision of Paradise 00

     The Mysterious Sealed Scroll 00

     The Revealed Messiah 00

10. SORROWS: THE SEVEN SEALS AND THE
     BEGINNING OF THE END 00

     The Four Horsemen of the Apocalypse 00

     The Martyrs of Righteousness 00

     A Prelude to the End 00

11. SALVATION: TRIUMPH OVER TRIBULATION 00

     Sealing the Servants of God 00

     The Dilemma of Evil 00

     The 144,000 00

     Marked for Martyrdom or Their Fate is Sealed? 00

     The Great White Hope 00

12. TRIBULATION: THE SEVENTH SEAL AND THE
     SEVEN TRUMPETS 00

     When the Heavens Shall Fall 00

     What Are the Odds? 00

     When Fire Falls Like Rain 00

     Woe to the Earth: World War 00

13. MYSTERY: THE SEVENTH TRUMPET AND THE
     GREAT REVELATION 00

     The Mystery of God Revealed 00

     The Mystery of the Lost Temple 00

     The Two Witnesses 00

     The Seventh Trumpet 00

End-Time
Prophecies of
the Bible

introduction

To the fullest extent possible, the goal of this book is to collect all that the Bible has to say about the ultimate destiny of earth.

Humans are attracted to mystery like air toward a vacuum. We yearn for meaning to fill our void of knowledge as we yearn for light to fill in the dark. So when a new millennium opens a vast unknown before us, prophets of all kinds will emerge to help us fill the void; and great profits of the other kind will be made in the process.

Inevitably the Bible will be one of the prophetic books of greatest interest. No other book sweeps through the epochs of human history with such poetry, brutality, embrace of humanity, and glorious promise as this ancient library of Hebrew and Greek manuscripts. Whether taken literally or symbolically, its mythologic language stirs our souls with tales of our ancient beginnings, and its poetry of apocalypse envisions our spectacular end. Between its covers, we make love and war. It is full of humanity and God. Like the Christ of the New Testament, the Bible is a very human body of writings imbued with an utterly divine spirit.

With so many modern prophets quoting the Bible to substantiate their particular beliefs about "end-time" events, it seemed there should be—for the first time—a book that pulls together *all* of the biblical prophecies regarded as "end-time" revelations. This book also tries to make some sense of how these mysterious words have been understood through history, shaped by history, and especially how they have shaped history itself.

Humanity's intensive effort to record events for posterity demonstrates that humans believe history gives meaning to the future. We have a sense of destiny with a hope for progress and, at the same time, an aversion for predestination. We yearn to know the future yet fear losing our freedom if the future can really be told.

Many of the Jewish prophets were historians as well. By weaving their futuristic perspectives into the history of Israel as they recorded it, they introduced the concept of destiny and gave the world a new way to think of history. Their words shattered earlier beliefs that history was an endless cycle—a wheel that goes round and round but never moves ahead. For the first time, history became a time line—a road moving from a humble beginning toward a divinely ordained and perfect future. Past events had future implications; they shaped destiny.

The Jewish prophets also introduced the idea that all the nations of earth form a single history, because their visions of the future revealed that all nations were headed on a path that converged at Israel while one God presided over all. Prior to these ancient Jews, not much thought had been given by humans about the future of the entire earth. Pagan prophets were only concerned with immediate events: Will the king win this next war?

Recent historians have combined the concepts of historic cycles and time lines, comparing the patterns of history to a coil—like the back of a spiral notebook. Human events come in cycles, but they never come full circle; instead, they spiral along, creating a line of human progress. Or, as the British historian Arnold Toynbee said, "The wheel goes around, but the wagon moves forward."

A better metaphor for understanding the complex patterns between history and future (as seen by the prophets) may be derived from the recent mathematical discovery of fractals. Fractals are complex patterns formed by simple patterns that repeat at multiple scales. A good example is a snowflake. It starts crystallizing at the center and branches out according to fairly simple rules. But the rules are affected by the near-infinite number of environments it floats through on its gradual descent—stronger wind, a fractional drop in temperature, suddenly no wind and then a gust, more moisture, then less moisture—until the snowflake becomes a story of the micro-environments through which it has traveled. In the end, every snowflake is immediately identifiable as a snowflake because of the fairly simple rules of water crystallization. Yet every one is unique because of the infinite combination of environments working on those rules.

History builds like a snowflake. It is not simply a two-dimensional time line. Like the snowflake, history evolves within four dimensions—three physical dimensions plus the dimension of time. History still offers a sense of progress because it had a beginning and all growth is outward from that center. Like the snowflake, certain patterns in the formation of history repeat on different scales and with different frequency. This gives us the sense that there are cycles. Yet, each time history repeats itself, it's within a slightly different environment, and so the pattern is not exactly the same as the time before. The snowflake has a destiny predetermined by the rules of snowflakes, yet with infinite possibilities. Likewise with history.

With fractals, the slightest variation at the beginning of an event can have enormous consequences later. When fractal mathematics is used in weather prediction, this is referred to as the butterfly effect: If a butterfly flaps its wings in Brazil, will it set off a tornado in Texas two weeks later? Because of this extreme sensitivity to innumerable influences, knowing the fractal rules under which a snowflake or cloud formation is developing only allows general predictions.

Prophecy faces a similar problem. The prophet receives divine insight into how destructive evil will work against the creative good. He sees the overarching pattern, but there are too many variables for his readers to predict history in advance. The prophet sees a catastrophic end to evil but does not predict names and faces. As the eminent scientist Stephen Hawking has said, the most minute change of the tiniest event at the beginning of the universe would have resulted in a vastly different universe.

When Jesus said, "I tell you before it come, that, when it is come to pass, ye may believe that I am" (John 13:19), he indicated the purpose of prophecy is not to provide a road map to the future but to enable willing listeners to recognize the working of God in times of danger and uncertainty. He implies his words are predictive yet can only be understood in hindsight. Seeing his words come to pass will help people believe when the time comes. Prophetic words turn unfolding dangers into evidence of truth for those times when hope is most absent.

Does the Change of a Millennium have any Real Significance?

Certainly the change of a millennium affects human behavior. At the turn of the last millennium, the entire nation of Iceland converted to Christianity. Major calendar changes have even tempted some people to give away all their earthly goods and climb onto house tops, expecting the return of Christ—only to climb back down again a day or two later considerably poorer. Even a change as small as one year causes us to celebrate with parties and fireworks and lots of noise. So the awareness of time, in itself, affects history because of how it influences human behavior.

Generally, the bigger the unit of time, the more important it is to us. We use decades to classify recent history into periods: We talk of the roaring twenties or the Great Depression of the thirties. The sixties are remembered for the sexual revolution, anti-war demonstrations, rock 'n' roll, and domestic upheaval. The seventies are forgotten. And so on.

We use centuries to measure the epochs of history. For the United States, the 1700s was the revolutionary period. The 1800s were the years of westward expansion. The 1900s became the Industrial Revolution and then the "modern" century. The concept of the modern century created an important shift in how we think. For the first time, the future became more important to our culture than the past. Until recently, cultures were built much more upon heritage than upon anticipation.

But what are millennia for? Too much happens in a thousand years for a millen-

nium to form any meaningful classification of human events. A single millennium en-
compasses more than 10 percent of recorded human history. It dwarfs our existence, so
its change feels cosmic in significance. We almost expect something big—like the end of
the world—to happen at such monumental changes of time. When it doesn't—when we
find ourselves still doing laundry on day two of 2001—we may even feel disappointed.

Of course most historians believe the modern calendar, known as the "Gregorian
Calendar," misplaces the date of Christ's birth by four to six years, which means that
technically the millennium has already changed. When Pope Gregory XIII commissioned the calendar five hundred years ago, his advisors perpetuated a mistake made a
thousand years prior by a monastic mathematician named Dionysius Exiguus, who created the A.D. (*anno Domini,* "year of our Lord") dating system.

But, no matter how arbitrary a millennium may be, simply passing such a mam-
moth milepost will irrevocably change the emerging patterns of history because of its
importance to the human psyche. What kind of movement of the masses will occur
when the millennium's gravitational field passes over us? Will individual concerns aggregate as mass hysteria—a sort of millennial madness? Or will there be a deepening and
strengthening of the social and spiritual fabric of our society as we make the ultimate
New Year's resolutions?

I hope this book will contribute more to the second response than the first.

How the Book Is Laid Out

To facilitate a better overall understanding of the grand-scale events foretold in the
Bible, this book groups the prophecies according to the events to which they seem to relate and combines them with historic records and a narrative that offers an overview of
historic interpretations, which suggesting other possible interpretations. The narrative
linking the prophetic texts is a tour guide, giving points of interest along the way. The
reader is encouraged to explore and come to his or her own conclusions. In some cases,
there are so many prophecies on a particular subject that a number of them have been
grouped under Appendix A in the back of the book for the reader who wants to explore
the full extent of biblical end-times prophecy.

To make the reader's exploration easier, *prophetic* Bible quotes are distinguished
from all other quotes by italics. Words within square brackets [ ] are not part of the Bible
but are added for clarification where something is quoted out of its context. *All* biblical
quotes have the reference directly following the text for easy indentification.

Of course, even the arrangement is an act of interpretation that requires choices as
to which prophecies actually parallel each other and, for that matter, which statements
in the Bible should be understood as having future implications. Even when it is clear

that a biblical passage refers to the future, there is often a question as to whether it has been fulfilled since it was written.

A Little About Prophecy Itself

Some prophecies may even be intended to be fulfilled during more than one period of history: Take for example an Old Testament prophecy (Joel 2: 28–32) quoted by the Apostle Peter in the New Testament as being fulfilled during his own lifetime:

And it shall come to pass in the last days, saith God, I will pour out of my Spirit upon all flesh: and your sons and your daughters shall prophesy, and your young men shall see visions, and your old men shall dream dreams: And on my servants and on my handmaidens I will, in those days, pour out of my Spirit; and they shall prophesy: And I will show wonders in heaven above, and signs on the earth beneath; blood, and fire, and vapour of smoke: The sun shall be turned into darkness, and the moon into blood, before that great and notable day of the Lord come: And it shall come to pass, that whoever shall call on the name of the Lord shall be saved. (Acts 2:17–21)

Much of this was, indeed, fulfilled during the lives of Jesus' disciples. Yet, the moon did not turn red. It did not turn out to be the "last days" for earth, though it did turn out to be the last days for ancient Israel, which happened with tremendous "blood and fire and billows of smoke." Perhaps the images of the moon and the sun were just figurative language, or perhaps the prophecy has a greater fulfillment to come. There's always a question as to whether the "last days" means the end of an age or the end of the world.

Time seems rather liquid in biblical prophecies. It undulates, lapses back on itself, reflects what is behind and what is ahead—all like a reflection on rippling water. Mystical experiences, by nature, transcend time like a dream. Peter, who likely knew such experiences firsthand, tells how even the prophet may not understand the chronology of his vision or its meaning—in the same way that many people do not understand the meanings of their own dreams:

Of this salvation the prophets have enquired and searched diligently, who prophesied of the grace that should come to you: Searching what, or what manner of time the Spirit of Christ who was in them did signify, when he testified beforehand the sufferings of Christ, and the glory that should follow. To whom it was revealed, that not to themselves, but to us they ministered the things, which are now reported to you by them that have preached the gospel to you with the Holy Spirit sent down from heaven; which things the angels desire to look into. (1 Peter 1:10–12)

If those who preached these visions sent by God's Holy Spirit did not understand the time or circumstances of their own visions, then we may not be able to understand all of them yet either. As Peter indicates, some prophecies are intended to be understood only by those who will be living during the time foreseen by the prophecy.

God even commands some of his prophets to seal their prophecies so that people may be "ever hearing, but never understanding":

And he [God] said, Go, and tell this people, Hear ye indeed, but understand not; and see ye indeed, but perceive not. Make the heart of this people fat, and make their ears heavy, and shut their eyes; lest they see with their eyes, and hear with their ears, and understand with their heart, and be converted, and be healed. Then said I, [the prophet Isa- *iah] Lord, how long? And he answered, Until the cities shall be wasted without inhabitant, and the houses without man, and the land be utterly desolate, And the LORD shall have removed men far away, and there be a great forsaking in the midst of the land.*

(Isaiah 6:9–12)

At first, it seems odd that God would ask his prophets to speak words that no one could understand. Apparently, some prophecies would be self-defeating if people understood them ahead of time. If, for example, a prophecy clearly stated something like "Nineteen hundred years after Jesus Christ, the Antichrist will come and his name would be 'Adolph Hitler,'" who in the 1900s would name their child "Adolph Hitler"? The prophecy, because it is present in the future it predicts, would change that future. Sealing the prophecy so that it cannot be understood until after it is fulfilled is a way of avoiding what some refer to as the time conundrum. If predicting the future, changes the future, how can you predict the future?

Apparently, then, prophecies were not intended to impart insider knowledge of the future or help us create time lines of future events. Prophecies were spoken in advance in order to give light to dark times when they come. In that day, the reader will feel assured that the prophet saw by a true light because his foresight was not humanly possible:

We have also a more sure word of prophecy; to which ye do well that ye take heed, as to a light that shineth in a dark place, until the day dawn, and the day star arise in your hearts: Knowing this first, that no prophecy of the scrip- *ture is of any private interpretation. For prophecy came not in old time by the will of man: but holy men of God spoke as they were moved by the Holy Spirit.*

(2 Peter 1:19–21)

Because true prophecy is not divined through private interpretation by throwing bones or reading the stars or feeling the innards of chickens, God set the highest standard for prophets who were going to work in his name: Anyone claiming their prophecies are divinely inspired must be 100 percent accurate in everything he or she foretells or be killed:

I will raise up to them [the Jews] a prophet from among their brethren, like thee, and will put my words in his mouth; and he shall speak to them all that I shall command him. And it shall come to pass, that whoever will not hearken to my words which he shall speak in my name, I will require it of him. But the prophet, who shall presume to speak a word in my name, which I have not commanded him to speak, or that shall speak in the name of other gods, even that prophet shall die. And if thou shalt say in thy heart, How shall we know the word which the LORD hath not spoken? When a prophet speaketh in the name of the LORD, if the thing doth not follow, nor come to pass, that is the thing which the LORD hath not spoken, but the prophet hath spoken it presumptuously: thou shalt not be afraid of him.

(DEUTERONOMY 18:18–22)

Then the LORD said to me, The prophets prophesy lies in my name: I have not sent them, neither have I commanded them, neither spoken to them: they prophesy to you a false vision and divination, and a thing of nought, and the deceit of their heart. Therefore thus saith the LORD . . . they say, Sword and famine shall not be in this land; By sword and famine shall those prophets be consumed. And the people to whom they prophesy shall be cast out in the streets of Jerusalem because of the famine and the sword; and they shall have none to bury them—them, their wives, nor their sons, nor their daughters: for I will pour their wickedness upon them.

(JEREMIAH 14:14–16)

Even those who pay attention to such prophets were to be killed. Let it suffice to say prophecy was a high-stakes venture for the Jews. Words spoken with so much at stake are usually worth listening to.

PROPHECY AND THE MODERN MIND

Reading the prophecies in this book, one should expect questions too great to be answered, words that push forward through time like a shockwave, turning over everything in their path. Uncertainty. Hope. Discomfort. Strengthening of faith. Raising of doubts. An untamed God with fire in his eyes. The Good Shepherd. Death. Rebirth. Heaven and hell. Fractal-like patterns recycling through time, instead of straight lines to the truth. Mystery. Revelation. Apocalypse.

The terms "revelation" and "apocalypse" share the same meaning. An apocalypse is a prophetic revelation of truth. Apocalyptic writing is highly poetic. In fact, prophets and poets were once regarded as the same breed. Poets will load as many meanings upon a single phrase as they wish to—and often a few meanings they didn't foresee but would agree with if they were pointed out. That's one of the reasons both poetry and prophecy seem obscure to some people. (Of course some false prophets, like some false poets, simply sound obscure so you'll think they're profound.)

Narrowly insisting that prophets speak only to the events of their own times, or only to one particular future event, places a constraint on apocalyptic writing that no literate reader would place on other poetic writings. It denies the potency and mystery of mystical experience and gives time more substance than it deserves. On the other hand, by looking for layers of meaning that are not intended, one can imagine chariots in ordinary clouds and devils in ink blots.

The best guide for how far to go in interpreting poetry *and* prophecy is found in the language itself. If it lures you to look beyond the next bend, the writer probably intended to draw his readers to greater vistas. Apocalyptic language presses like a race horse against the gate. It runs better if you give it some rein. It's poetry, not prose.

One modern writer astutely sums up the problem for the modern mind. Walter Brueggemann, in his book *Finally Comes the Poet,* writes:

> Our technical way of thinking reduced mystery to problem, transforms assurance to rigid certitude, revises quality into quantity, and so takes the categories of biblical faith and represents them in manageable shapes. . . . There is then no danger, no energy, no possibility, no opening for newness. . . . Truth is greatly reduced. To address the issue of a truth greatly reduced requires us to be poets who speak against a prose world.[1]

To appreciate prophecy one has to be willing to live with mystery. Humility is often lacking in prophetic interpretation—the willingness to admit there are many things in the Bible we don't fully understand and some things we don't understand at all.

On one extreme, some scholars flatly deny the predictive quality of biblical prophecies, interpreting images like "a third of the waters turned to blood" as metaphors for spiritual insight. Though spiritual insight is to be derived from all parts of the Bible, reading everything as a spiritual metaphor is often simply a refusal to allow the possibility of supernatural knowledge. It ignores the fact that many prophecies in the Old Testament were fulfilled quite literally according to later archaeological finds.

If the plagues in the Book of Revelation (The Apocalypse) are spiritual metaphors, what should one make of similar plagues which Moses brought against Egypt? Would Pharaoh have let the slaves of Israel go free over a few aptly chosen metaphors?

On the other extreme, some see the Book of Revelation as a coded text for predicting the future. They leap over a great deal of spiritual insight in a madcap search for encrypted messages that almost always prove wrong with time. Or they are so literal they become bothered if someone even suggests that "a third of the waters turned to blood" may be a metaphor meaning that a third of the life in the sea will die. It has to be literal blood, flowing in rivers, pooling in lakes, and dissipating into the sea.

The truth is likely in the balance: Biblical prophecies are layered with spiritual meanings derived from genuinely anticipated events. Jesus' miracles are the perfect example: Jesus never did a miracle that wasn't a metaphor for spiritual truth, yet *all* of his miracles are presented as real physical events. Whether past, present, or predicted, real physical events abound in spiritual implications. In the fractal view of history, that is because physical reality is patterned on spiritual reality.

The most fulfilling way to journey through exotic terrain is to take the guided tour first, then go back to your favorite places and explore awhile. Those who only take the tour never experience the culture. Since the Old Testament was written by Jews, all of its prophecies have some connection with Israel. Likewise, the New Testament, written mostly, if not entirely, by Christian Jews, also has strong connection to Israel. The future of other people and nations is seen in terms of their connection to Israel or Christianity. The future has a history, and so this prophetic tour starts with the most cataclysmic event in Israel's past, which changed the future of the world forever.

Blessed is he that readeth, and they that hear the words of this prophecy,
and keep those things which are written in it: for the time is at hand.
INTRODUCTION TO THE APOCALYPSE OF ST. JOHN

DESOLATION:

THE DESTRUCTION OF ISRAEL AND DIASPORA OF THE JEWS

THE JEWISH STRUGGLE

It's one of the most peculiar stories in the Bible, written by one of the earliest Jewish prophets. Moses told of a man named Jacob, who got in a wrestling match that lasted through the night. When morning came, his opponent merely touched Jacob's hip and dislocated it. Though Jacob did not ask for this wrestling match (the man came to him), Jacob would not let go until the man agreed to bless him. The man finally blessed Jacob by giving him a new name: "Israel," which means "struggles with God." They parted company, and Jacob limped away. He named the place of his struggle "Face of God," saying, "I saw God face to face, and yet my life was spared."

This story and the name "Israel" summarize what it means to be a Jew. These are the people who saw God in the wilderness, and their relationship with him has been one of struggle. God and man join in an impassioned human relationship with flashes of anger, bursts of affection, and occasional dry spells in between. God shows a human face because he desires relationship with human beings.

The Jews' record of this relationship honestly displays their own shortcomings, again and again in stories filled with epic heroes and pathetic cowards and a menagerie of ordinary people. God has called, and they have sometimes resisted. In their struggles to be free of God, God has touched them, and they have known pain. He has even dislocated them from their homes. As Tevye says in *Fiddler on the Roof* during his own struggle with God, "I'm tired of being one of the chosen. Could you choose someone else for a while?"

The tenacity of Jacob and the blessing of God have made the Jews indestructible in the face of the world's greatest empires. Their first encounter with a great empire began when the man named Israel and his children moved to Egypt, where their descendants were made slaves. A few centuries later, the prophet Moses enters the story. He calls down plagues from heaven. The Nile River turns to blood; the land is covered with darkness; all firstborn male Egyptians die. The plagues continue relentlessly until Pharaoh has had enough and lets God's people go. Moses then leads the descendants of Israel out of Egypt, but Pharaoh changes his mind and pursues them. He dies in battle by a miracle of God when the waters of the Red Sea crash over the armies of Egypt.

Having escaped Egypt, Moses prophesied that God would bless the children of Israel by making them into a prosperous nation—so long as they continued to live under the authority of their God. This was God's covenant with them. Under King David and then his son, King Solomon, this group of slaves from Egypt became a dominant nation in the Mediterranean. Eventually, even Egypt paid tribute to the land of Israel.

But Moses also prophesied formidable doom to the children of Israel if they turned away from the God who delivered them from slavery in Egypt—the God who had created a nation out of one man, naming him "Israel."

MOSES PREDICTS THE DESOLATION OF ISRAEL

But if ye will not hearken to me [God], and will not do all these commandments; And if ye shall despise my statutes, or if your soul shall abhor my judgments, so that ye will not do all my commandments, but that ye break my covenant: I also will do this to you; I will even appoint over you terror, consumption, and the burning fever, that shall consume the eyes, and cause sorrow of heart: and ye shall sow your seed in vain, for your enemies shall eat it. And I will set my face against you, and ye shall be slain before your enemies: they that hate you shall reign over you; and ye shall flee when none pursueth you. And if ye will not yet for all this hearken to me, then I will punish you seven times more for your sins. And I will break the pride of your power; and I will make your heaven as iron, and your earth as brass. . . . And if ye shall [still] walk contrary to me, and will not hearken to me; I will bring seven times more plagues upon you ac-

cording to your sins. I will also send wild beasts among you, which shall rob you of your children, and destroy your cattle, and make you few in number; and your high ways shall be desolate. And if ye will not be reformed by me by these things, but will walk contrary to me; Then will I also walk contrary to you, and I will punish you yet seven times for your sins. And I will bring a sword upon you, that shall avenge the quarrel of my covenant: and when ye are gathered together within your cities, I will send the pestilence among you; and ye shall be delivered into the hand of the enemy. And when I have broke the staff of your bread, ten women shall bake your bread in one oven, and they shall deliver you your bread again by weight: and ye shall eat, and not be satisfied. And if ye will not for all this hearken to me, but walk contrary to me; Then I will walk contrary to you also in fury; and I, even I, will chastise you seven times for your sins. And ye shall eat the flesh of your sons, and the flesh of your daughters shall ye eat. And I will destroy your high places, and cut down your images, and cast your remains upon the remains of your idols, and my soul shall abhor you. And I will make your cities waste, and bring your sanctuaries to desolation, and I will not smell the savour of your sweet odours [of sacrifice]. And I will bring the land into desolation: and your enemies who dwell in it shall be astonished at it. And I will scatter you among the nations, and will draw out a sword after you: and your land shall be desolate, and your cities waste. Then shall the land enjoy its sab-

baths [meaning "day of rest"] . . . because it did not rest in your sabbaths, when ye dwelt upon it. And upon them that are left alive of you I will send a faintness into their hearts in the lands of their enemies; and the sound of a shaken leaf shall chase them; and they shall flee, as fleeing from a sword; and they shall fall when none pursueth. . . . And ye shall perish among the nations, and the land of your enemies shall eat you up. And they that are left of you shall pine away in their iniquity [sin] in your enemies' lands; and also in the iniquities of their fathers shall they pine away with them. (LEVITICUS 26:14–39)

Thy sons and thy daughters shall be given to another people, and thy eyes shall look, and fail with longing for them all the day long. . . . So that thou shalt be mad for the sight of thy eyes which thou shalt see. . . . And thou shalt become an astonishment, a proverb, and a byword, among all nations where the LORD shall lead thee. . . . Thou shalt beget sons and daughters, but thou shalt not enjoy them; for they shall go into captivity. . . . The stranger that is within thee shall rise above thee very high; and thou shalt come down very low. He . . . shall be the

head, and thou shalt be the tail. Moreover all these curses shall come upon thee, and shall pursue thee, and overtake thee, till thou art destroyed; because thou didst hearken not to the voice of the LORD thy God, to keep his commandments and his statutes which he commanded thee: And they shall be upon thee for a sign and for a wonder, and upon thy seed [offspring] for ever. Because thou didst not serve the LORD thy God with joyfulness, and with gladness of heart, for the abundance of all things. (DEUTERONOMY 28:32–47)

Given human nature, the reader of these prophecies knows the good times would not last forever. Some Jewish kings who came along after the death of King Solomon were rebels who usurped the throne and ruled with terror. Some of the kings encouraged Israel to worship the idols of neighboring nations. One king even went so far as to sacrifice his own children by fire to such an idol god.[1]

Many prophets arose in the midst of these evil kings and gave warnings that were similar to those spoken by Moses. But most of the kings did not listen, nor did the people. Rather than overthrow their evil king or change their own evil ways, the people often ridiculed or occasionally killed the prophet who spoke against them.

Finally, came the prophet Isaiah, one of the greatest prophets in Old Testament times, who made good on Moses' earlier warnings:

> Then said Isaiah to Hezekiah [the reigning king], Hear the word of the LORD of hosts: Behold, the days come, that all that is in thy house, and that which thy fathers have laid up in store until this day, shall be carried to Babylon: nothing shall be left, saith the LORD. And of thy sons that shall issue from thee, which thou shalt beget, shall they take away; and they shall be eunuchs in the palace of the king of Babylon.
>
> (ISAIAH 39:5–7)

Because Hezekiah was a good king, this prophecy was not fulfilled in his lifetime. But other kings after him were as vile as those before, and many other prophets rose up to warn them:

> And the LORD God of their fathers sent to them by his messengers, rising up early, and sending; because he had compassion on his people, and on his dwelling place: But they mocked the messengers of God, and despised his words, and misused his prophets, until the wrath of the LORD arose against his people, till there was no remedy. Therefore he brought upon them the king of the Chaldees [another name for Babylonians], who slew their young men with the sword in the house of their sanctuary, and had no compassion upon young man or maiden, old man, or him that stooped for age: he gave them all into his hand.
>
> (2 CHRONICLES 36:15–17)

And so the Southern Kingdom of Israel (called Judah) was conquered by Babylon in 586 B.C. under the reign of King Nebuchadnezzar and, subsequently, taken into slavery. The Northern Kingdom of Israel, which had divided off during an earlier civil war, had already been conquered by Assyria (precursor to modern day Syria) in about 722 B.C., and the Jews from that part of Israel had already been relocated to the north to become slaves of the Assyrians. So the land was now drained of its Jews.

KING NEBUCHADNEZZAR'S PROPHETIC DREAM

After Israel had been conquered by Babylon, a new prophet told the king of Babylon the entire imperial future of Israel until the end of earth:

> In the third year of the reign of Jehoiakim king of Judah came Nebuchadnezzar king of Babylon to Jerusalem, and besieged it. And the Lord gave Jehoiakim king of Judah into his hand. . . .
>
> And in the second year of the reign

of Nebuchadnezzar, Nebuchadnezzar dreamed dreams, by which his spirit was troubled, and his sleep broke from him. Then the king commanded to call the magicians, and the astrologers, and the sorcerers, and the Chaldeans, to show the king his dreams. So they came and stood before the king. And the king said to them, I have dreamed a dream, and my spirit was troubled to know the dream. Then the Chaldeans spoke to the king in Syrian, O king, live for ever: tell thy servants the dream, and we will show the interpretation. The king answered and said to the Chaldeans, The thing is gone from me: if ye will not make known to me the dream, with the interpretation of it, ye shall be cut in pieces, and your houses shall be made a refuse heap. . . . if ye will not make known to me the dream, there is but one decree for you: for ye have prepared lying and corrupt words to speak before me . . . therefore tell me the dream, and I shall know that ye can show me the interpretation of it. The Chaldeans answered before the king, and said, There is not a man upon the earth that can reveal the king's matter: therefore there is no king, lord, nor ruler, that hath asked such things of any magician, or astrologer, or Chaldean. . . . For this cause the king was angry and very furious, and commanded to destroy all the wise men of Babylon. . . .

Then was the secret revealed to Daniel [one of the Jews that Nebuchadnezzar had taken captive during his siege of Jerusalem] in a night vision. Then Daniel blessed the God of heaven. Daniel answered and said, Blessed be the name of God for ever and ever: for wisdom and might are his: And he changeth the times and the seasons: he removeth kings, and setteth up kings: he giveth wisdom to the wise, and knowledge to them that know understanding: He revealeth the deep and secret things: he knoweth what is in the darkness, and the light dwelleth with him. I thank thee, and praise thee, O thou God of my fathers, who hast given me wisdom and might, and hast made known to me now what we desired of thee: for thou hast now made known to us the king's matter.

Therefore Daniel went in to Arioch, whom the king had ordained to destroy the wise men of Babylon: he went and said thus to him; Destroy not the wise men of Babylon: bring me in before the king, and I will reveal to the king the interpretation. Then Arioch brought in Daniel before the king in haste, and said thus to him, I have found a man of the captives of Judah, that will make known to the king the interpretation. The king answered and said to Daniel . . . Art thou able to make known to me the dream which I have seen, and the interpretation of it? Daniel answered in the presence of the king, and said, The secret which the king hath demanded the wise men, the astrologers, the magicians, the soothsayers, cannot reveal to the king; But there is a God in heaven that revealeth secrets, and maketh known to the king Nebuchadnezzar what shall be in the latter days. Thy dream, and the visions of thy head upon thy bed, are these. . . .

Thou, O king, sawest, and behold a great image. This great image, whose brightness was excellent, stood before thee; and its form was terrible. The head of this image was of fine gold, his breast and his arms of silver, his belly and his thighs of brass, His legs of iron, his feet part of iron and part of clay. Thou sawest till a stone was cut out without hands, which smote the image upon his feet that were of iron and clay, and broke them to pieces. Then was the iron, the clay, the brass, the silver, and the gold, broken to pieces together, and became like the chaff of the summer threshing floors; and the wind carried them away, that no place was found for them: and the stone that smote the image became a great mountain, and filled the whole earth. This is the dream; and we will tell the interpretation of it before the king. Thou, O king, art a king of kings: for the God of heaven hath given thee a kingdom, power, and strength, and glory. And wherever the children of men dwell, the beasts of the field and the fowls of the heaven hath he given into thy hand, and hath made thee ruler over them all. Thou art this head of gold. And after thee shall arise another kingdom inferior to thee, and another third kingdom of brass, which shall bear rule over all the earth. And the fourth kingdom shall be strong as iron: forasmuch as iron breaketh in pieces and subdueth all things: and as iron that breaketh all these, shall it [the fourth kingdom] break [others] in pieces and bruise. And though thou sawest the feet and toes, part of potters' clay, and part of iron, the kingdom shall be divided; but there shall be in it of the strength of the iron, forasmuch as thou sawest the iron mixed with the miry clay. And as the toes of the feet were part of iron, and part of

clay, so the kingdom shall be partly strong, and partly broken. And though thou sawest iron mixed with miry clay, they shall mingle themselves with the seed of men: but they shall not join one to another, even as iron is not mixed with clay. And in the days of these kings shall the God of heaven set up a kingdom, which shall never be destroyed: and the kingdom shall not be left to other people, but it shall break in pieces and consume all these kingdoms, and it shall stand for ever. Forasmuch as thou sawest that the stone was cut out of the mountain without hands, and that it broke in pieces the iron, the brass, the clay, the silver, and the gold; the great God hath made known to the king what shall come to pass after this: and the dream is certain, and the interpretation of it sure.

Then the king Nebuchadnezzar fell upon his face, and worshipped Daniel, and commanded that they should offer an oblation and sweet odours to him. The king answered to Daniel, and said, Of a truth it is, that your God is the God of gods, and the Lord of kings, and a revealer of secrets, seeing thou couldest reveal this secret. Then the king made Daniel a great man, and gave him many great gifts, and made him ruler over the whole province of Babylon, and chief of the governors over all the wise men of Babylon.

(Dᴀɴɪᴇʟ 1:1–2; 2:1–6, 9, 10, 12, 19–28, 31–48)

Babylon turned out, as prophesied, to be an empire in a golden age. The Hanging Gardens of Babylon, created by Nebuchadnezzar, became one of the seven wonders of the world. The empire, however, was short lived. The prophecy of Daniel began coming true just twenty-three years after Nebuchadnezzar died. The Persians pushed up from what is now called the Persian Gulf into what is now Iraq and conquered Babylon. Like the part of the body in Nebuchadnezzar's statue that had two arms, this new empire had two parts. Cyrus, the king of Persia, placed a Mede named Darius as the ruler over Babylon, forming what historians refer to as the Medo-Persian empire.

About two years after Babylon was conquered, the Babylonian Jews were released from their slavery to return to Jerusalem so they could rebuild their temple, and soon after that, they were allowed to rebuild the city walls. Nevertheless, all of Israel was still ruled by the Medo-Persian empire, and many of the Jews who had been conquered earlier by Assyria—who, therefore, were not among the Babylonian Jews—remained scattered as slaves among other nations.

Next, the Greeks, under Alexander the Great, conquered the Medes and the Persians. Their conquest fulfilled what was predicted by the third part of the statue—the belly and thighs of bronze.

Finally, the Romans conquered the Greeks. The iron legs of the statue represent the iron empire. As with the two arms of the statue, the two legs also represent a divided empire, for Rome eventually divided into the Eastern and Western Roman Empires.

Each succeeding empire represented in the statue brought a certain loss of aesthetic fineness but an increase of brute strength, just as the minerals represented in each section of the statue represent a loss in fineness but an increase in strength.

THE ROMAN CONFLICT

The first Roman conqueror of Israel was General Pompey. This wasn't so much a conquering of Israel as a conquering of the Greeks who already occupied Israel. From then on, Israel never escaped Roman dominion. The great *Pax Romana,* the Roman Peace, was always tenuous at best. The Romans not only had to constantly defend their possession against Jewish uprisings, but they also had to fend off invading forces from outlying empires.

Herod the Great, who was appointed King of the Jews by Caesar Augustus, won the faith of many Jews when he staked his own life in battle against their enemies. He ruled with an iron grip, but defused tensions by paying respect to the religion of the Jews. To this end, he helped them rebuild their temple after the ravages that had come to it under the Greeks. He erected great cloisters around it and walls of protection around the cloisters and endowed its treasury with considerable wealth. Most of the glory that belonged to Jerusalem at this time was built by Herod because this was his capital. Jerusalem became the jewel of Israel once again.

In the end, however, Herod became a cruel tyrant. Endlessly deceived by every member of his family, he became hopelessly paranoid and cynical, which weighed heavily on the people he ruled. In fact, so certain was he that the Jews would rejoice upon his death, that he determined a bitter way to make sure they wouldn't. Days before his death, he ordered all the highest and most respected Jews—the finest minds in the land—to be locked into an arena. Then he ordered that, upon his death, they were all to be immediately killed. This would guarantee mourning throughout the land when Herod died. (Fortunately, his sister countermanded the order when he died, and the Jews were spared.)

About seventy years after the reign of Herod the Great, the Jews rebelled, and Rome conquered Israel a second time. This second devastating conquest was described centuries earlier in another prophecy by Moses about a nation that would swoop down on Israel like an eagle (the eagle was Rome's national crest):

The LORD shall bring a nation against thee from far, from the end of the earth, as swift as the eagle flieth; a nation whose language thou shalt not understand; A nation of fierce countenance, which shall not regard the person of the old, nor show favour to the young: And he shall eat the fruit of thy cattle, and the fruit of thy land, until thou art destroyed: which also shall not leave thee either grain, wine, or oil, or the increase of thy cattle, or flocks of thy sheep, until he hath destroyed thee. And he shall besiege thee in all thy gates, until thy high and fortified walls come down, in which thou didst trust, throughout all thy land . . . which the LORD thy God hath given thee. And thou shalt eat the fruit of thy own body, the flesh of thy sons and of thy daughters, which the LORD thy God hath given thee, in the siege, and in the distress, by which thy enemies shall distress thee: So that the man that is tender among you, and very delicate, his eye shall be evil toward his brother, and toward the wife of his bosom, and toward the remnant of his children whom he shall leave: So that he will not give to any of them of the flesh of his children whom he shall eat: because he hath nothing left him in the siege, and in the distress, by which thy enemies shall distress thee in all thy gates. The tender and delicate woman among you, who would not venture to set the sole of her foot upon the ground for delicateness and tenderness, her eye shall be evil toward the husband of her bosom, and toward her son, and toward her daughter, And toward her young one her own offspring, and toward her children which she shall bear: for she shall eat them for lack of all things secretly in the siege and distress, by which thy enemy shall distress thee in thy gates.

. . . And ye shall be left few in number, though ye were as the stars of heaven for multitude; because thou wouldest not obey the voice of the LORD thy God.

. . . And the LORD shall scatter thee among all people, from the one end of the earth even to the other. . . . And among these nations shalt thou find no ease. . . . And thy life shall hang in doubt before thee; and thou shalt fear day and night, and shalt have no assurance of thy life: . . . And the LORD shall bring thee into Egypt again with ships, by the way of which I have said to thee, Thou shalt see it no more again: and there ye shall be sold to your enemies for male and female slaves, and no man shall buy you.

(DEUTERONOMY 28:49–57, 62, 64–66, 68)

ISRAEL'S LAST PROPHET

Prior to the second conquest by Rome, God brought Israel one final prophet from its own people. Among other things, he predicted destruction of the glorious temple Herod had just rebuilt. This temple, to the Jews, was a place so holy that the people were only allowed by God to enter its courtyards. Even the priests could not enter the holiest part of the temple—except for the high priest, and he could only enter it once a year. The temple was the glory of Israel.

But this prophet, like some prophets before his time, was killed for relentlessly saying things Israel did not want to hear about its need for reformation. His name was Jesus. One day, as Jesus was walking past the temple with his disciples, they marvelled at how the temple was adorned with beautiful stones and with gifts dedicated to God. This gave rise to a prophecy by Jesus:

And Jesus went out, and departed from the temple: and his disciples came to him to show him the buildings of the temple. And Jesus said to them, See ye not all these things? Verily I say to you, There shall not be left here one stone upon another, that shall not be thrown down. And as he sat upon the mount of Olives, the disciples came to him privately, saying, Tell us, when shall these things be? and what shall be the sign of thy coming, and of the end of the world? And Jesus answered and said to them, Take heed that no man deceive you. For many shall come in my name, saying, I am Christ; and shall deceive many. And ye shall hear of wars and rumours of wars: see that ye be not troubled: for all these things must come to pass, but the end is not yet. For nation shall rise against nation, and kingdom against kingdom: and there shall be famines, and pestilences, and earthquakes, in various places. All these are the beginning of sorrows. Then shall they deliver you up to be afflicted, and shall kill you: and ye shall be hated by all nations for my name's sake. And then shall many be offended, and shall betray one another, and shall hate one another. And many false prophets shall rise, and shall deceive many. And because iniquity shall abound, the love of many shall become cold. But he that shall endure to the end, the same shall be saved. And this gospel of the kingdom shall be preached in all the world for a testimony to all nations; and then shall the end come. When therefore ye shall see the abomination of desolation, spoken of by Daniel the prophet, stand in the holy place (whoever readeth, let him understand), Then let them who are in Judaea flee to the mountains: Let him who is on the housetop not come down to take any thing out of his house: Neither let him who is in the field return back to take his clothes. And woe to them that are with child, and to them that nurse infants in those days! But pray ye that your flight may not be in the winter, neither on the sabbath: For then shall be great tribulation, such as hath not been since the beginning of the world to this time, no, nor ever shall be. And except those days should be shortened, there should no flesh be saved: but for the elect's sake those days shall be shortened. Then if any man shall say to you, Lo, here is Christ, or there; believe it not. For false Christs will arise, and false prophets, and shall show great signs and wonders; so that, if it were possible, they would deceive the very elect. Behold, I have told you before. Therefore if they shall say to you, Behold, he is in the desert; go not forth: behold, he is in the secret chambers; believe it not. For as the lightning cometh out of the east, and shineth even to the west; so shall also the coming of the Son of man be. For wherever the carcass is, there will the eagles be gathered together. Immediately after the tribulation of those days shall the sun be darkened, and the moon shall not give her light, and the stars shall fall from heaven, and the powers of the heavens shall be shaken: And then shall appear the sign of the Son of man in heaven: and then shall all the tribes of the earth mourn, and they shall see the Son of man coming in the clouds of heaven with power and great glory. And he shall send his angels with a great sound of a trumpet, and they shall gather together his elect from the four winds, from one end of heaven to the other. (MATTHEW 24:1–31)

THE ROMAN DESTRUCTION OF ISRAEL

Although the prophecies had said that Israel would return to freedom only when the people returned to God, many Jews hoped to take their land back by military force. As a result, in A.D. 70, Titus, who was Caesar under his father Vespasian (who was High Caesar), destroyed Jerusalem and numerous other Jewish towns. Jews fled to whatever nations they could for refuge. This was the first stage of what historians refer to as the great diaspora.

One historian Josephus, himself a Jew, lived when the heat of revolt smoldered through the people of Israel. He was, in fact, a commander over many Jewish fighters during that revolt, and he gives a compelling story about the severity of distress during those times.

Josephus was a priest in Jerusalem—a member of an elite group called the Pharisees, who ruled the Jewish people off and on during the time their land was occupied by Romans. (Limited self-rule by the priests was allowed under Herod the Great because Herod, in his earlier years, had become a convert to the Jewish faith—though his conversion may have been nothing more than a political façade.)

Josephus didn't want the Jews to rebel. During his own travels to Rome, on a mission to gain the release of some priests who had been wrongfully imprisoned on a minor offense, he had witnessed the might of Rome, and he did not believe the Jews could succeed. He also felt Jerusalem was doing pretty well under Roman rule—until the rebellion:

Our city had arrived at a higher degree of felicity than any other city under the Roman government, and yet at last fell into the sorest of calamities again. Accordingly it appears to me, that the misfortunes of all men, from the beginning of the world, if they be compared to these of the Jews are not so considerable.[2]

It should be noted that some scholars believe Josephus' account of the war is biased against his own people. The fact that Josephus changed sides in the middle of the war when his city fell is one reason for questioning his loyalties. The fact that he saved himself by trickery is one reason to question his honesty. And the fact that his patron while he wrote his history of the war was none other than Roman General Titus, who later became Caesar, is another reason to question his bias. But the assumption that these facts add up to a bias against his own people is still speculation.

There are no *primary* historical records of the war that contradict Josephus, nor any histories written by others in his time that contradict him. (Josephus does tend to exaggerate his numbers when talking about people involved in an event, or it may be that others have underestimated the numbers involved.) Neither is there any archaeological evidence dug up in later years that contradicts Josephus, though several things have been found at Masada that corroborate what he says.

While it is almost certainly true that Josephus presents his Roman patron Titus in a *better* light than he deserves and that Josephus fails to mention some of the atrocities of Rome, it would be dissimilar to all of Josephus' other writings for him to cast his own people in a more *negative* light than the truth demanded. In one of his other works written for a Roman audience, *History of the Jews,* Josephus presents an affirmative picture of his people; and in another book, *Against Apion,* he ardently defends the Jews against Egyptian anti-Semitism, yielding no ground to the adversaries of his people. Concerned that similar anti-Semitism in Rome would turn against him for taking the Jewish side as much as he did in his history, he even uses his introduction to ask his Roman readers not to begrudge him for telling how the Jews fought with valor. He employs the argument that there is greater victory to the Romans in defeating a great enemy than a weak one.

First a Jewish general during the war and later a resident of Rome, Josephus presents the most balanced history written in his time. The Roman historian Tacitus also briefly described the Jewish rebellion, but Tacitus is an anti-Semite through and through. The fall of Jerusalem is one of those rare occasions where history was actually recorded by a member of the losing side, rather than by the victor. One contemporary rabbi, Joseph Telushkin, writes in his book *Jewish Literacy:* "Jews still passionately debate whether [Josephus] was a loyal Jew or a traitor. Even his detractors, however, concede that Josephus' writings are the most important historical source on the Great Revolt against Rome." {Rabbi Joseph Telushkin, *Jewish Literacy* (New York: William Morrow and Company, 1991), p. 139}

The flames of revolt, which Josephus describes, broke out when Nero appointed a new procurator over Judea (roughly that part of Israel that had once been the southern kingdom conquered by Babylon). The procurator, Gessius Florus, was a rabid anti-Semite. He deliberately antagonized the Jews at every opportunity. He created anarchy among the Jews by encouraging organized crime. Any robber who shared his Jewish spoils with Florus was given complete liberty throughout the land to pillage all he pleased. Florus even pillaged the temple treasury—the act that lit the match to the rebellion. As a result, Josephus says,

> His greediness of gain was the occasion that entire toparchies [regions of government] were brought to desolation; and a great many of the people left their own country, and fled to foreign provinces.[3]

(Hear the echo of the prophets: "They that hate you shall reign over you; and ye shall flee when none pursueth you," and "Ye shall perish among the nations, and the land of your enemies shall eat you up.")

This initial exodus into self-exile by those who would rather flee than fight left a greater concentration of people who wanted to rebel, and these were stirred to war by false prophets:

> These were such men as deceived and deluded the people under pretence of divine inspiration, but were for procuring innovations and changes of the government, and these prevailed with the multitude to act like madmen, and went before them into the wilderness, as pretending that God would there show them the signals of liberty.[4]

(Again the prophet's voice echoes: "False Christs will arise, and false prophets, and shall show great signs. . . . Therefore if they shall say to you, Behold, he is in the desert; go not forth" and "ye shall hear of wars and rumours of wars.")

When the murmurings of war finally broke out in open rebellion, Nero appointed Vespasian as head of the war effort and promoted Titus, Vespasian's son, to be general under Vespasian. Vespasian and Titus conquered every Jewish town and city before finally coming to Jerusalem three years later. They conquered all other cities first in order to make certain there would be no uprisings to distract them when they set about the ultimate battle of regaining control of Jerusalem. ("He shall besiege thee in all thy gates, until thy high and fortified walls come down . . . throughout all thy land. . . .")

Once the Romans began conquering the towns and villages, old bad blood between the resident Greeks, who were the former conquerors, and the Jews came to the surface. People were made to pay for the sins of their fathers or even their great-grandfathers.

On one occasion, after Josephus was captured by the Romans, the Greeks came after him in the beautiful seaside city of Caesarea:

The [Greek] citizens here received both the Roman army and its general with all sorts of acclamations and rejoicings, and this partly out of the good-will they bore to the Romans, but principally out of the hatred they bore to those [the Jews] that were conquered by them: on which account they came clamoring against Josephus in crowds and desired that he might be put to death.[5]

So, now the Jews were not only lower than the Romans who occupied Israel, they were also lower than the Greeks. ("The stranger that is within thee shall rise above thee very high; and thou shalt come down very low.") Even the Greeks who lived in distant Roman cities outside Israel, such as Alexandria in Egypt, saw the opportunity for their hatred and rose up against the Jews:

Conflicts perpetually arose with the Grecians; and although the governors did every day punish many of them, yet did the sedition grow worse; but at this time especially . . . the disorders among them were put into a greater flame. . . . They [the Greeks] rushed out and laid violent hands upon them [the Jews]; and as for the rest, they were slain as they ran away; but there were three men whom they caught, and hauled them along, in order to have them burnt alive.[6]

("Among these nations shalt thou find no ease, neither shall the sole of thy foot have rest: but the LORD shall give thee there a trembling heart, and failing of eyes, and sorrow of mind. . . . And thy life shall hang in doubt before thee, and thou shalt fear day and night, and shalt have none assurance of thy life.")

After being captured by Titus, Josephus offers a prophecy of his own, which saves his life: He predicts that Vespasian will soon be made Caesar. Vespasian holds him as a captive, believing Josephus is just flattering him to save his life but he keeps him alive, just in case what he says comes true. It does.

The first time armies gathered around Jerusalem, many, whether they knew it or not, heeded another warning given by Jesus Christ:

And when ye shall see Jerusalem surrounded by armies, then know that her desolation is near. Then let them who are in Judaea flee to the mountains; and let them who are in the midst of it depart from it; and let not them that are in the countries enter into it. For these are the days of vengeance, that all things which are written may be fulfilled. But woe to them that are with child, and to them that nurse infants, in those days! for there shall be great distress in the land, and wrath upon this people. And they shall fall by the edge of the sword, and shall be led away captive into all nations: and Jerusalem shall be trodden down by the Gentiles, until the times of the Gentiles shall be fulfilled. (LUKE 21:20–24)

Josephus records in his history that as the armies were approaching:

> . . . Many of the most eminent of the Jews swam away from the city, as from a ship when it was going to sink.[7]

Josephus mentions on several occasions how people fled from the cities and villages of Judea into the mountains, but they weren't always fleeing the Romans. The Jews' decision to revolt created a power vacuum among themselves. If the Romans were no longer in power, who was? According to Josephus, the war took a vile turn toward anarchy with the Jews attacking themselves, as different parties vied for ascendancy. The most notorious parties were the organized bands of thieves who had been given free reign under Florus:

> The captains of these troops of robbers, being satiated with [plundering] in the country, got all together from all parts and became a band of wickedness, and all together crept into Jerusalem, which was now become a city without a governor. . . . [They] omitted no kind of barbarity . . . but proceeded as far as murdering men . . . openly in the day-time, and began with the most eminent persons in the city. . . . And every one contented himself with taking care of his own safety, as they would do if the city had been taken in war.[8]

The one area in which Josephus probably presents some Jews in a more negative light than they deserved is his coloration of some of the rebels known as "Zealots." While he is probably accurate regarding the facts of their actions, he casts a dark cloud over them by referring to them as robbers, etc., without thinking through the reason for their thievery. One has to read between the lines to recognize that the Jewish Zealots emerge, in Josephus account, *after* most of the peasantry had been run out of their villages by Romans. The Romans practiced a "scorched earth" policy, destroying everything around a village, leaving those who fled with nothing. To make matters worse, Judea was coming out of a famine and had long lived under heavy Roman taxation. So, it's not hard to infer that many of Josephus' thieves may have come from the peasantry who had been driven from their livelihood and had joined the Zealots, turning to rob certain members of their wealthier countrymen who cooperated with Rome. Josephus, a member of the wealthier class, has only the harshest words for the Zealots because he had predicted their rebellion was a futile cause, and he blamed the Zealots for pressing for a war that, in the end, cost Israel everything it had and cost him his comfortable life in Israel.

As a result of this social conflict, the siege of Jerusalem did not begin from the outside with attacks from Titus; it began on the inside between the rebels—before Titus even arrived. The nation that had once been governed by a priesthood was now governed by thieves, thanks to Florus's approval. Though the people had courage enough to take on the entire Roman army, for some reason they lacked courage to take on their own thieves. Even the priesthood cowered before those Josephus describes as thieves, allowing them to ordain certain ignoble people who would assist them in their rebellion.

In the absence of Roman governance, the priesthood had become the government by default, which is why the rebellious wanted to make sure they controlled the priesthood. The temple in Jerusalem, which was considered by Jews, and even by a small number of God-fearing Romans, to be the most holy place on earth, became a citadel for the Zealots. Most Romans had given the temple such reverential respect—in deference to Jewish beliefs, as well as to their own belief in holy places—that they never set foot in it, yet contributed vast wealth to its construction and treasuries. There were, of course, a few Romans like Florus who had deliberately defied this tradition in brazen ways. The sanctuary, now, became "a shop of tyranny."

The Zealots gave the rank of high priesthood to a village idiot who did not even know what the high priesthood was. They adorned him and hailed him as though he were king and placed sacred garments on him. Of course, because he did not know what a priest did, they told him on every occasion what to do. To the Zealots, this was a pastime, but to the defrocked priests, the dissolution of that office with all its sacred dignity was to be lamented with tears:

> Ananus [who had been high priest] stood in the midst of [the people], and casting his eyes frequently at the temple, and having a flood of tears in his eyes he said, "Certainly, it had been good for me to die before I had seen the house of God full of so many abominations, or these sacred places . . . filled with the feet of these blood-shedding villains. . . . But why do I complain of the tyrants? Was it not you [the citizens of Jerusalem] and your sufferance of them, that have nourished them? Was it not you that overlooked those that . . . were . . . but a few, and by your silence made them grow to be many? . . . When houses were pillaged, nobody said a word, which was . . . why they carried off the owners of those houses. Will you bear, therefore—will you bear to see your sanctuary trampled on? . . . Shall we not bear the lords of the habitable earth to be lords over us, and yet bear tyrants of our own country?"[9]

The high priest's referral to the house of God being full of so many abominations recalls part of that prophecy Jesus had given to his disciples forty years prior: "When therefore ye shall see the abomination of desolation, spoken of by Daniel the prophet, stand in the holy place . . . Then let them who are in Judaea flee to the mountains."

The "abomination that causes desolation" to which Jesus referred is a crucial prophecy given in the Old Testament Book of Daniel that was to mark the downward turn in the affairs of the people of Jerusalem—a certain sign that destruction was imminent:

... And after sixty and two weeks shall Messiah be cut off, but not for himself: and the people of the prince that shall come shall destroy the city and the sanctuary; and its end shall be with a flood, and to the end of the war desolations are determined. And he shall confirm the covenant with many for one week: and in the midst of the week he shall cause the sacrifice and the oblation to cease, and for the overspreading of abominations he shall make it desolate, even until the consummation, and that determined shall be poured upon the desolate. . . .

And forces shall stand on his part, and they shall pollute the sanctuary of strength, and shall take away the daily sacrifice, and they shall place the abomination that maketh desolate.

(DANIEL 9:26, 27; 11:31)

The desecration of the most holy place in the world was a prophecy well-known to the high priest and others. Ananus was right in thinking he would have been better off to die than to see this moment. So Ananus resolved to undergo whatever sufferings came upon him and roused the people to revolt against the Zealots. The citizens of Jerusalem found the courage they should have shown earlier, and with great passion they rose against the Zealots, who were superior in their armaments. A great slaughter ensued between Jews, which resulted in further desecration of the temple:

> When any of the zealots were wounded, he went up into the temple and defiled that sacred floor with his blood, insomuch that one may say it was their blood alone that polluted our sanctuary.[10]

The shedding of human blood within the holy sanctuary was considered so sacrilegious that women were not even allowed to enter its courtyard when they were menstruating, nor were people with bleeding wounds allowed to enter. These laws were established to clearly distinguish the Jews from the nations around, whose pagan practices often included human sacrifice to idols. God would have no human blood in his holy temple.

The zealots continued to use the temple as a fortress. Its courtyard walls and gates, which had been financed by Herod, barred the people from entering, and Ananus did not think it fitting to destroy the gates of God's temple, nor to slaughter men inside of it. Now the citizens of Jerusalem were forced to hold their own temple under siege, and Ananus had his own bonds put on the gates, for with the Romans advancing toward the city, they could hardly fight a battle both within and without.

The zealots, however, managed to slip a message out to the Idumeans, distant cousins of the Jews who lived in an area south of Jerusalem and who always wanted a good fight. Their message stated that they, the *good* people of the city, were being held hostage inside the temple by a band of thieves. The Idumeans believed this reversal of the truth and came to attack Jerusalem.

The Romans had not yet arrived, so when the Idumeans arrived and found the gates of the city closed, they were all the more certain the message was correct. They camped around the city, making Jerusalem a city of outlaws surrounded by ordinary citizens surrounded by feisty cousins who had believed a lie. This meant the ordinary citizens were really the ones who were surrounded on both sides. No amount of persuasion by Ananus from the top of one of the towers could dissuade the Idumeans, and meanwhile the zealots, according to Josephus, desecrated the holy temple even more by drinking its sacramental wine until they were drunk. Thus, Ananus called out to the Idumeans:

> This place [the temple] which is adored by the habitable world, and honored by such as only know it by report, as far as the ends of the earth, is trampled upon by these wild beasts born among ourselves. They now triumph in the desperate condition they are already in, when they hear . . . that your nation has gotten an army together against its own bowels.[11]

His words did not prevail, and the Idumeans remained camped about the city. A storm came that night, as fierce as though the wrath of God were pouring down upon Jerusalem for the desecration of his temple and because Jews were fighting Jews:

> There broke out a prodigious storm in the night, with the utmost violence, and very strong winds, with the largest showers of rain, with continual lightnings, terrible thunderings, and amazing concussions and bellowings of the earth, that was in an earthquake. These things were a manifest indication that some destruction was coming upon men, when the system of the world was put into this disorder; and any one would guess that these wonders foreshowed some grand calamities that were coming.[12]

Who could not help but hear the echoes of the prophets in the storm that night? ("Nation shall rise against nation [Rome against Jews], and kingdom against kingdom [Idumeans against Jews]: and there shall be famines, and pestilences, and earthquakes, in various places. . . . the beginning of sorrows.")

Whether or not the voice of the prophets echoed in the storm, the noise of the wind and thunder that night obscured the sound of saws at the temple gate—saws that were kept in the temple, most likely for carving up animal sacrifices. The zealots, under cover of darkness and rain, broke free of the temple and crept through the streets to open the city gates and let the Idumeans enter.

Those citizens of Jerusalem who woke from their sleep to the shrieks of dying guards, discovered themselves so outnumbered that all they could do was echo the cry of the guards with their own wails of lament—all under the continuing crash of thunder. The people pled with the Idumeans, reminding them that they were relations, but the

Idumeans spared none they got their hands on. They plundered every house and slew everyone they met until the corpses lay in heaps along the darkened streets. With great zeal they chased down the high priests and killed them, including Ananus. Then they stood upon the corpses and jeered at the living. People fled to the temple courts and were even slaughtered there:

> And now the outer [court] of the temple was all of it overflowed with blood; and that day, as it came on, saw eight thousand five hundred dead bodies there. . . . I should not mistake if I said that the death of Ananus was the beginning of the destruction of the city, and that from this very day may be dated the overthrow of her wall, and the ruin of her affairs. . . . [13]

To add to the abomination of thousands of dead bodies lying around a temple that was never supposed to have human blood in it, the people simply threw the dead away, rather than bury them—probably out of fear of being killed while burying them. But Jews were a people who, as Josephus says:

> . . . used to take so much care of the burial of men, that they took down those that were condemned and crucified, and buried them before the going down of the sun. [14]

A dead body was an unclean thing according to the religion of the Jews and, therefore, was to be immediately buried. Those who handled it had to go through a period of ritualistic cleansing afterward before they could enter the temple. No such period of cleansing was observed now:

> . . . Those that a little before had worn the sacred garments, and had presided over the public worship . . . were cast out naked, and seen to be the food of the dogs and wild beasts. . . . The terror that was upon the people was so great that no one had courage enough either to weep openly for the dead man that was related to him, or bury him; but those that were shut up in their own houses could only shed tears in secret, and durst not even groan without great caution. [15]

Another twelve thousand died by the sword in the following days. Meanwhile, the Romans heard about the anarchy in Jerusalem, and Vespasian decided to take his time, claiming,

> The providence of God is on our side; by setting our enemies at variance against one another . . . the Jews are vexed to pieces every day by their civil wars and dissensions. [16]

Many of the rich purchased their salvation with money and fled the city, only to flee, unfortunately, into the arms of the advancing Romans, who—according to Josephus—showed them more mercy than they could find in the city. The poor, however, had no choice but to die. The living were taken into the prisons of Jerusalem and tortured, and the dead rotted under the sun, which brought a pestilence to the city, fulfilling more of the prophecies.

> These men, therefore, trampled upon all the laws of man, and laughed at the laws of God; and for the oracles of the prophets, they ridiculed them as the tricks of jugglers; yet did these prophets foretell many things . . . which when these zealots violated, they occasioned the fulfilling of those very prophecies belonging to their own country.[17]

("I will bring a sword upon you, that shall avenge the quarrel of my covenant: and when ye are gathered together within your cities, I will send the pestilence among you.")

It was at this time that Nero died and Vespasian was made Caesar, just as Josephus had prophesied. Vespasian went to Rome and left his son, Titus, in charge of the war. As a result of this change in powers, the Romans were considerably delayed in getting to Jerusalem.

By the time winter came upon Jerusalem, a new band of zealots that had been raiding the countryside made its way to the city. According to Josephus, the thieves in Jerusalem thought the "thieves" outside Jerusalem a worse lot than they, and so they sallied forth and attacked them.

The new band, headed by a renegade named Simon, drove the original band, headed by a rogue named John, back into the city, where they sealed themselves off in their temple fortress. John felt his group could hold out well in the temple with its courtyard walls as fortification and a plentiful stock of food that was consecrated for sacred use. Of course, that meant Simon had to attack the temple, which he was not at all reluctant to do.

Since the Romans still had not attacked Jerusalem, Josephus describes this new turn in the war within Jerusalem as,

> . . . a wild beast grown mad, which for want of food from abroad [Romans], fell now upon eating its own flesh.[18]

The peculiar thing was that during the time John and his men had been ravaging the city, he had continued to allow some people to go to the temple and offer sacrifices and to allow a few priests to officiate. Now, as Simon and his men began heaving rocks into the temple courtyards and hurling javelins over the walls, these priests were slaughtered alongside John's men. And so the blood of priests and "thieves" mixed in pools upon the temple floor:

> . . . insomuch that any persons who came [there] with great zeal from the ends of the earth, to offer sacrifices at this celebrated place, which was esteemed holy by all mankind, fell down before their own sacrifices . . . and sprinkled the altar . . . with their own blood . . . and the blood of dead carcasses stood in lakes in the holy courts themselves.[19]

The temple, by such a slough of abominations, was utterly defiled, and the Holy City became a sepulchre for the bodies of its own people. (And the words of the prophets echoed, "And I will destroy your high places, and cut down your images, and cast your remains upon the remains of your idols, and my soul shall abhor you. And I will make your cities waste, and bring your sanctuaries to desolation, and I will not smell the savour of your sweet odours [of sacrifice].")

Now, because John and his men took refuge in their temple citadel, which had its own supply of food, he sent out sallies to destroy the food stores of the city, which Simon depended upon. They set fire to the houses that were full of corn and to all other provisions, which only played into the hands of the Romans who were finally arriving on the scene:

> The noise of those that were fighting was incessant, both by day and by night; but the lamentation of those that mourned exceeded the other . . . they were inwardly tormented, without daring to open their lips in groans. Nor was any regard paid to those that were still alive by their relations . . . but, for the seditions themselves, they fought against each other, while they trod upon the dead bodies as they lay heaped one upon another.[20]

("Wherever the carcass is, there will the eagles be gathered together.")

By this time nearly all vestiges of humanity had been stripped from the people. Those who had longtime differences with each other began to kill each other out of their buried hatred. If one person had offended another some years before, the offended party now devised ways to turn the other over to the zealots, so they were led like lambs to the slaughter. ("And then shall many be offended, and shall betray one another, and shall hate one another . . . And because iniquity shall abound, the love of many shall become cold.")

Meanwhile, Titus was outside preparing to make real war. His armies destroyed all the gardens, groves, and hedges around the city to set up camps for their thousands of troops and to build battering rams and siege ramps. But the ramps and battering rams were successfully burned by the Jews, and the Roman soldiers had to travel to more distant forests to bring back more timbers. And all the while, Titus offered the Jews his "right hand of security" if they would surrender, for he hoped to make the city his own capital someday soon, and did not want to see it destroyed. But the people would not surrender, or could not because the zealots would kill anyone who did.

While Titus took his time in building his war machine, in hopes that the siege would starve the Jews out or intimidate them by a show of force into surrendering, famine began to cut into the population. Many sold all they had to buy a single measure of wheat, and if they were rich, they could buy a measure of barley; thus fulfilling the words of another one of their prophets, Ezekiel:

They shall cast their silver in the streets, and their gold shall be removed: their silver and their gold shall not be able to deliver them in the day of the wrath of the LORD: they shall not satisfy their souls, neither fill their stomachs: because it is the stumblingblock of their iniquity.

(EZEKIEL 7:19)

When those with money had purchased what little wheat they could from the city's sparse stores, they shut themselves away in the inner-most rooms of their houses to grind the wheat and to bake it into bread:

A table was nowhere laid for a distinct meal, but they snatched the bread out of the fire, half-baked and ate it very hastily. . . . Children pulled the very morsels that their fathers were eating out of their very mouths, and, what was still more to be pitied, so did the mothers do as to their infants; and when those that were most dear were perishing under their hands, they were not ashamed to take from them the very last drops that might preserve their lives . . . but the seditious everywhere came upon them immediately, and snatched away from them what they had gotten from others. . . . The old men who held their food fast were beaten; and if the women hid what they had within their hands, their hair was torn. . . . They also invented terrible methods of torment to discover where any food was. . . .[21]

(And, so, the words of the prophets kept echoing: "And when I have broke the staff [supply] of your bread, ten women shall bake your bread in one oven, and they shall deliver you your bread again by weight: and ye shall eat, and not be satisfied.")

In a parallel account to the prophecy given by Jesus earlier in this chapter, the Gospel of Mark recorded him as also saying:

Now the brother shall betray the brother to death, and the father the son; and children shall rise up against their parents, and shall cause them to be put to death. And ye shall be hated by all men for my name's sake: but he that shall endure to the end, the same shall be saved.

(MARK 13:12–13)

Josephus continues:

> Then did the famine widen its progress, and devoured the people by whole houses
> and families; the upper rooms were full of women and children that were dying by
> famine, and the lands of the city were full of the dead bodies of the aged; the chil-
> dren also and the young men wandered about the market-places like shadows, all
> swelled with the famine and fell down dead. . . . Many died as they were burying
> others.[22]

Others lay alive on the ground and begged to die, but the zealots refused to dispatch
them with their swords, preferring to let them die in suffering. Others managed to escape to the Romans where they ate too much:

> When they came first to the Romans, they were puffed up by the famine . . . after
> which they all of the sudden over-filled those bodies that were before empty, and
> so burst asunder.[23]

While the average citizens starved, the thieves who holed up in the temple dined
well on temple food. John told his men that it was proper for them to use the divine elements because they were fighting a holy war against the Romans. Not only did they eat
from the temple's stores, they melted down its sacred articles (presumably into instruments of war), many of which had been donated to the temple by the Romans.

Josephus, himself a priest, laments:

> I cannot but speak my mind. . . . I suppose that had the Romans made any longer
> delay in coming against these villains, the city would either have been swallowed
> up by the ground . . . or been overflowed by water, or else been destroyed by such
> thunder as the country of Sodom perished by, for it had brought forth a genera-
> tion of men much more atheistical than were those [in the Old Testament] that
> suffered such punishments; for by their madness it was that all the people came to
> be destroyed.[24]

So, it was not just the land that was becoming desolate; it was the people.

By now, the body count at Jerusalem, according to Titus, was no fewer than 115,000.
The hills that were once forested and the valleys that were gardens had become a desert.
It's interesting to note that in certain parts of the Bible, forests are mentioned in Israel
where today one can see only desert. What was once described as "the promised land—
a land flowing with milk and honey" had become a wasteland under the ravages of war
as the Romans had moved from city to city. Josephus says:

... Those places which were before adorned with trees and pleasant gardens were now become a desolate country every way, and its trees were all cut down; nor could any foreigner that had formerly seen Judea and the most beautiful suburbs of the city, and now saw it as a desert, but lament ... at so great a change; for the war had laid all signs of beauty quite waste; nor if any one that had known the place before, had come on a sudden to it now, would he have known it again. ... Though he were in the city itself, yet would he have inquired for it.[25]

("And I will bring the land into desolation: and your enemies who dwell in it shall be astonished at it.")

The "sanctuary of strength" had been used for its strength and desecrated, and the sacrifices in the temple had ceased because of the presence of Titus's forces—just as Daniel's prophecy about "the abomination that maketh desolate" had predicted. The sanctuary had been "polluted" by the Jewish rebels, and the entire city and the land as far as the eye could see lay desolate. Still, the final destruction of Jerusalem lay heavy against its wall in the form of Titus's battering rams.

After many weeks of waiting for the famine to work, Titus ordered his battering rams into action. They eventually smashed their way through three successive walls of the city until they came against the walls of the temple courtyard. While many of the citizens had surrendered themselves to Titus, both bands of zealots had retreated, again, into their temple fortress, the "sanctuary of strength."

The rams stopped when they came to the walls of the temple. Titus, according to Josephus, wished to spare the temple. So, he ordered Josephus to earnestly plead with the hold-outs to quit using the temple as a fortress. The rebels scoffed at Josephus as a worthless sell-out to the Roman cause. Josephus quoted prophecies at them, stating the ruin spread out before them had been predicted, but they only scoffed more. When Josephus failed, Titus, himself, stepped forward, and Josephus translated:

Have not you, vile wretches that you are, by our [Roman] permission, put up this partition-wall before your sanctuary? [a wall the Jews had requested in order to keep Gentiles out] Have not you been allowed ... to engrave in Greek, and in your own letters, this prohibition, that no foreigner should go beyond that wall? Have not we given you leave to kill such as go beyond it, though he were Roman? And what do you do now? ... Why do you trample upon dead bodies in this temple? and why do you pollute this holy house with the blood both of foreigners and Jews themselves? I appeal to the gods of my own country, and to every god that ever had any regard to this place (for I do not suppose it to be now regarded by any of them); I also appeal to my own army ... and even to you yourselves, that I do not force you to defile this sanctuary; and if you will but change the place whereon you will fight, no Roman shall either come near your sanctuary, or offer any affront to it. ..."[26]

But the zealots would not trust Titus to allow them to move their war to different grounds. And so the Roman soldiers breached the wall, and some stood on the cloisters that were on the other side. The zealots who remained then set fire to the temple cloisters and engulfed the Romans in flames. The siege lasted several more days, and, with the temple finally depleted of its stores, the famine finally engulfed the zealots.

There, within the temple wall, the greatest abomination of all occurred:

[A certain woman could not find any more food] while the famine pierced through her very bowels and marrow. . . . She then tempted a most unnatural thing; and snatching up her son, who was a child sucking from her breast, she said, "O, thou miserable infant! for whom shall I preserve thee in this war . . ." As soon as she had said this she slew her son; and then roasted him, and ate the one half of him, and kept the other half by her concealed. Upon this the seditious came in presently, and smelling the horrid scent of this food, they threatened her, that they would cut her throat immediately if she did not show them what food she had gotten ready. She replied, that she had saved a very fine portion of it for them; and withal uncovered what was left of her son. . . . "Do not you pretend to be either more tender than a woman, or more compassionate than a mother." . . . After which, those men went out trembling. . . . So those that were thus distressed by the famine were very desirous to die; and those already dead were esteemed happy, because they had not lived long enough either to hear or to see such miseries.[27]

And so the most unlikely of prophecies came true. ("Thou shalt eat the fruit of thy own body, the flesh of thy sons and of thy daughters . . . in the siege, and in the distress, by which thy enemies shall distress thee. . . . The tender and delicate woman among you, who would not venture to set the sole of her foot upon the ground for delicateness and tenderness, her eye shall be evil toward the husband of her bosom, and toward her son, and toward her daughter . . . for she shall eat them for lack of all things secretly in the siege and distress. . . .") And because it happened in the temple courts, the temple was utterly defiled by a child sacrifice.

When all else failed in trying to get the zealots to surrender—even offering them immunity if they would—Titus, according to Josephus, remained unwilling to destroy so vast and beautiful a structure as the temple since it would be an ornament to the Romans if they retained it. He resolved, instead, to storm its walls with his whole army the next day and camp around the holy house, itself. Josephus recounts that when the fight broke out inside the courtyard walls, one of the Roman soldiers took a section of the cloisters that was still burning and set fire to the temple through one of the golden windows. As chance or providence would have it, the day was the very day when the former temple had been burned by the king of Babylon centuries earlier.

Titus was told of the fire while back in his headquarters, and he ran to have it extinguished, but the clamor of fighting and the growing roar of the flames was so loud no one could hear him. (Or the Romans' passion for revenge was so inflamed that they pretended not to hear in order to fight on.) It's interesting that a literal reading of the prophecy in Daniel said, "and the *people* of the prince that shall come shall destroy the city and the sanctuary." Titus was quite literally a prince, for his father had just become Caesar. Literally true to the prediction, it was the *people* of the prince, acting against his orders, who destroyed the sanctuary. Acting *upon* his order, they would soon destroy the city.

The zealots now were in too much distress with their fighting, which was life or death, to attend to the fire. The rest of the people were too weak from starvation and sickness, and those that could move had their throats slit as soon as they were discovered. Around the altar lay dead bodies in heaps with trails of blood leading up to the altar, where they had been slaughtered. And behind the altar, the smoke and flames rose to the heavens.

Titus, himself, entered the holiest inner room of the temple before the flames had reached it. Titus penetrated its virginal space with his commanders and marvelled at its splendor, which he later described as being everything the priests had imagined it to be. To the Jews this was the holiest ground on earth—so holy that even priests were forbidden to enter on pain of death. Even the high priest could enter only once a year. In this room, the spirit of God dwelled within the ark of the covenant. The final pollution of the sanctuary had happened: a warrior and his specatators had violated the inner sanctum.

Titus left in haste and, according to Josephus, endeavored again to get the soldiers to stop their fighting and quench the fire. He even ordered one of his centurions to beat the renegade soldiers into cooperation, but their fired-up passions had been too long restrained outside the walls to relent now that they had broken through. Now that they had the long-hunted enemy within their grasp, they wouldn't let go:

> The flame was also carried a long way, and made an echo, together with the groans of those that were slain; and because this hill was high, and the works at the temple were very great, one would have thought the whole city had been on fire.... One would have thought that the hill itself, on which the temple stood, was seething-hot, as full of fire on every part of it, that the blood was larger in quantity than the fire, and those that were slain more in number than those that slew them; for the ground did nowhere appear visible.[28]

In spite of this massacre, a considerable number of zealots still managed to escape to other parts of the city. Titus, weary of it all, finally ordered the entire city destroyed in search of them—all its walls to come down, including what was left of the temple. The great palace of Herod was also to be destroyed. The only thing to be left were a few of its greatest towers—as a monument to what had been built there and what had been destroyed. ("See ye not all these things? [Jesus asked his disciples regarding the temple] Verily I say to you, There shall not be left here one stone upon another, that shall not be thrown down.") As for the temple, of which Jesus spoke, his prediction came literally true. Not a single one of its stones is left standing.

The city was set on fire, and housefulls of dead bodies were given a natural cremation. The remaining people were herded away, and the youngest and most beautiful (of those who had not surrendered earlier) were taken away to Rome to be part of the triumph celebration as food for the gladiators' sword. ("Thy sons and thy daughters shall be given to another people, and thy eyes shall look, and fail with longing for them all the day long.")

As for many of the older ones, Josephus says: He put them into bonds, and sent them to the Egyptian mines.[29]

(As the prophet had said, "And the LORD shall bring thee into Egypt again with ships, by the way of which I have said to thee, Thou shalt see it no more again.") They returned to the country from which they had first entered the promised land.

Titus also sent a great number into the provinces, as a present to them, that they might be destroyed upon their theatres, by the sword and by the wild beast.[30]

("And I will scatter you among the nations, and will draw out a sword after you.")

The number of captives taken from Jerusalem alone was 97,000. Because they were so many and so wasted from famine, those sold as slaves were sold for a pittance. Some were given away to whomever would take them. ("And there ye shall be sold to your enemies for male and female slaves, and no man shall buy you.")

By the end of the Jerusalem holocaust, the dead count was 1,100,000, and the land of promise had become a desert. Josephus describes what was left:

But as for the rest of the wall, it was so thoroughly laid even with the ground by those that dug it up to the foundation, that there was left nothing to make those that came thither believe it had ever been inhabited.[31]

("And I will bring the land into desolation: and your enemies who dwell in it shall be astonished at it. And . . . your land shall be desolate, and your cities waste. Then shall the land enjoy its sabbaths [meaning "day of rest"] . . . because it did not rest in your sabbaths, when ye dwelt upon it.")

The abominations had spread across the entire city, and desolations had occurred until the "end of the war" as predicted. Blood covered the land like a flood. And so the prophecy of Daniel regarding a future prince came literally true in every way. It had warned that "because of the overspreading of abomination, he [the prince] shall make desolate even until the consummation." The land of Israel remained a desolate wasteland for two thousand years. Only in this century has its restoration begun as the sovereign homeland of the Jews. Did the prophecy mean that Israel's desolation would last *until* the consummation of human history was about to occur? (In which case, the end is near.) Or did it merely mean that the prince would continue making the land desolate until all of Israel was consumed? Perhaps the phrase was intentionally ambiguous so that it could mean both.

Chapter 2

ABOMINATION:

THE SIGNATURE OF EVIL TIMES

D id the prophet Daniel see far enough into time to foresee an end for Israel that might include the final era on earth?

Daniel was one of Babylon's most outstanding scholars. He was educated in all the ancient knowledge Babylon had to offer, as well as in all Jewish literature. His visions often began with prayer and fasting. Fasting and mortification of the flesh (self-inflicted suffering or deprivation) were methods used by ancient mystics to release the body's attachment to life and free the spirit for spiritual communion. Prayer and fasting is the path to holy visions, rather than visions into the dark side of the spiritual realm. Daniel saturated himself in both prayer and scripture:

... I Daniel understood by books the number of the years, concerning which the word of the LORD came to Jeremiah the prophet, that he would accomplish seventy years in the desolations of Jerusalem. And I set my face to the Lord God, to seek by prayer and supplications, with fasting, and sackcloth, and ashes: ... Yea, while I was speaking in prayer, even the man Gabriel, whom I had seen in the vision at the beginning, being caused to fly swiftly, touched me about the time of the evening oblation. And he informed me, and talked with me, and said, O

Daniel, I am now come forth to give thee skill and understanding. At the beginning of thy supplications the commandment came forth, and I am come to show thee; for thou art greatly beloved: therefore understand the matter, and consider the vision. Seventy weeks are determined upon thy people and upon thy holy city, to finish the transgression, and to make an end of sins, and to make reconciliation for iniquity, and to bring in everlasting righteousness, and to seal up the vision and prophecy, and to anoint the most Holy. (DANIEL 9:2, 3, 21–24)

Daniel's prophecy will clearly demonstrate that prophetic numbers can have both figurative and literal meanings at the same time. His prophecy is based on an earlier revelation by the prophet Jeremiah, who predicted Israel, once conquered by the Babylonian king Nebuchadnezzar, would remain desolate for seventy years:

And this whole land shall be a desolation, and an astonishment; and these nations shall serve the king of Babylon seventy years. And it shall come to pass, when seventy years are accomplished, that I will punish the king of Babylon, and that nation, saith the LORD, for their iniquity, and the land of the Chaldeans, and will make it perpetual desolations. (JEREMIAH 25:11–12)

Near the end of these seventy years, an angel revealed to the prophet Daniel that it would be seventy *weeks* of years (i.e., *seventy times seven* years) before Israel's salvation would come, starting from the decree to restore Jerusalem.

Why the coded meaning? Jeremiah's prophecy used poetic shorthand to encapsulate two events into a single prediction. As prophesied, the Babylonian empire was defeated in seventy years when the Medes and Persians moved in. The Medes conquered Babylon, and it gradually wasted away into utter desolation. It has remained desolate ever since, proving a literal meaning also for the "perpetual desolations" that Babylon would experience when God punished it for conquering Israel.

The round number seventy had symbolic significance and allowed the text a double meaning. Numbers based on seven are used in numerous biblical prophecies and dates to signify the completion of events between God and humanity, usually in the form of justice. The conquest of Babylon brought divine justice against that empire's evil ways. Being even greater in wickedness than Israel, Babylon could not go unpunished for walking all over Israel. Divine justice seemed to require that nations so eager to become God's agent of discipline against Israel would be disciplined for their own evil ways.

Anyone reading Jeremiah, however, would have thought Israel would be completely free once Babylon was conquered. To a large degree it did become free. Within a year of Babylon's fall to the Medes, the Jews were released by the new emperor to return to Jerusalem and rebuild their city and its sanctuary, but they remained under the emperor's imperial thumb.

After the literal seventy years of Babylonian captivity had ended, then the figurative seventy weeks of years began. From the decree to restore Jerusalem it would be 490 years to the anointing of the most holy or "holy of holies," which could mean Israel's temple sanctuary or their long-awaited Messiah (Hebrew for "anointed one"). Throughout those 490 years the Jews would endure continued times of trouble under the other imperial regimes that had been envisioned in Nebuchadnezzar's dream of the statue.

"Messiah" is more the likely interpretation for anointing of the most hold since the next verse of Daniel's prophecy speaks of "Messiah the Prince":

Know therefore and understand, that from the going forth of the command-ment to restore and to build Jerusalem to the Messiah the Prince shall be seven weeks, and sixty and two weeks: the street shall be built again, and the wall, even in troublous times. And after sixty and two weeks shall Messiah be cut off, but not for himself: and the people of the prince that shall come shall destroy the city and the sanctuary; and its end shall be with a flood, and to the end of the war desolations are determined.

(DANIEL 9:25, 26)

The time given until the Messiah is actually only sixty-nine of the seventy weeks (or 483 of the 490 years). The first seven weeks (forty-nine years) predicted are likely the time it actually took to rebuild the walls and temple. According to the biblical books of Nehemiah and Ezra, that reconstruction did take place during "troublous times." The re-maining 434 years would be the number of years from the completion of the temple un-til the coming of the Anointed One.

After the Messiah came he was to be "cut off." A strange statement because the Mes-siah was supposed to save Israel from its oppressors. But the prophecy indicates he would be cut off almost as soon as he arrived (for he comes after the sixty-two weeks of years, and he's cut off after sixty-two weeks). It's strongly implied that the cutting off of the Messiah would be connected with the end of Jerusalem and the temple by war.

THE COMING OF THE MESSIAH

How does the end as it was described by Josephus fit with Daniel's statements about the coming of the Messiah and his cutting off?

The sixty-nine weeks (483 years) was to begin with the decree to restore Jerusalem from its first destruction under Babylon. Three decrees are recorded in various years for the reconstruction of the *temple* in Jerusalem, but there is only one known decree that specifically calls for the reconstruction of Jerusalem itself. (For the three decrees to re-build the temple, see Ezra 1:1–4; 6:1–12; 7:1–26. For the decree to rebuild Jerusalem, see Nehemiah 2:1–8.) That decree was made in 444 B.C. when Artaxerxes I, Emperor of Per-sia, issued a letter authorizing the reconstruction of Jerusalem.

Counting 483 years from 444 B.C. would give an arrival date for the Messiah of A.D. 40 (since the *anno Domini* ("year of our Lord") dating system has no "zero" year). Daniel, however would have been using the Babylonian calendar, which was five days shorter than the modern calendar year. So, subtracting five days for each of Daniel's Babylonian years brings the date back to match with A.D. 33 on the modern calendar. That's the year many scholars say Jesus Christ rode with great fanfare into Jerusalem as his Jewish followers proclaimed him king. Only a few days later he was pronounced

"King of the Jews" by Pilate and was crucified (i.e., "cut off"). Though Pilate's pronouncement may have been mocking Jesus, his words had ironic significance. These events in Jesus' life all took place on the very month Artaxerxes' decree had been written (the first month of the Jewish year during the celebration of Passover).

Many scholars now believe Christ was born four to six years earlier than the modern calendar indicates. So, some scholars start counting Daniel's years from an earlier decree to rebuild the *temple* in 457 B.C. There is some evidence from the biblical Book of Ezra (7:6 and 9:9) that this decree was broad enough to allow rebuilding the city walls, even though the city was not specified where the decree is first mentioned (crucial to remaining faithful to the wording of Daniel's prophecy). From this starting date, a straightforward accounting in regular solar years still yields an interesting date for the arrival of the Messiah ("the Anointed One")—A.D. 27. Those who hold that Jesus was born about four years earlier than the modern calendar indicates usually place his death in A.D. 30. In that case, A.D. 27 would have been the year Jesus was "anointed" for his ministry through baptism since his ministry lasted about three years. It was at this inaugural event that John the Baptist announced Jesus' arrival to the world: "Behold, the Lamb of God!"

Obviously, there is enough uncertainty in the modern calendar to make placement of an *exact* year for any of these events impossible. Still, one has to ask how it happens that no matter which of the two decrees you start from, reasonable methods of calculation yield plausible dates for the two most significant years of Jesus' ministry.

If this is a coincidence, it must be the most extraordinary coincidence in history: Daniel's prophecy was well known among Jews long before Jesus was born, so the timing couldn't have been made to order by Christians. In fact, because of this prophecy many Jews expected the Messiah to come during the years of Jesus' life. That's why people kept asking Jesus if he was the Messiah. (Because he wanted them to recognize this for themselves, he never gave them a direct answer, which is all the more indication that he wasn't simply trying to fit their expectations. Most false messiahs are self-proclaiming. Also, if Jesus were a self-anointed messiah, he would have had to plan his death to fit Daniel's "cutting off." What would be the point?)

Because many Jews—especially a sect known as the Essenes, who collected or wrote the Dead Sea scrolls—did expect the Messiah to arrive at this time, many self-proclaimed messiahs did show up before and after Jesus. But they all left little impact on the world. Given the hundreds of generations humans have dwelled on earth, what are the odds that the *only* prophecy in the Bible that gives a method to calculate the arrival of the Messiah should fall *anywhere* within the life of the single human being who had the greatest impact on world history? What more does it take to fulfill messianic prophecy: a Jew, descended from the line of King David, quite possibly arriving in Jerusalem on the exact month and year predicted by Daniel, hailed as a king by his Jewish followers, mockingly proclaimed "King of the Jews" by a high Roman official, and "cut off" from life shortly after his arrival?

Interestingly, the *Tanakh* (the Jewish Bible) translates Daniel's "cutting off" of the Messiah as "the Anointed One will disappear and vanish." Christians, of course, do not believe Jesus remained dead. They believe he was resurrected and then ascended into heaven—vanished not to be seen again until "the end."

Perhaps the *Tanakh* is a better translation.

Is there anyone else whose life falls within the timing stated in Daniel's prophecy who can be said "to make an end of sins, and to make reconciliation for iniquity, [wickedness] and to bring in everlasting righteousness"? It can also be said that Jesus "seal[ed] up vision and prophecy," for there have been no recorded Jewish prophets after him (except those who wrote about him). One does not have to agree with Christian theology to recognize there is no one else near Daniel's predicted time that remotely fulfills any of these rolls.

THE MESSIAH'S CONNECTION TO THE END OF JERUSALEM

Daniel predicted that the cutting off of the Messiah would not be for himself (in some translations "he shall have nothing"): At Jesus' death, all of his disciples deserted him, even Peter, who swore he never would. There is also no question from an historic standpoint that shortly after Jesus was "cut off" or "disappeared," there came a prince whose people destroyed the city. Within the lifetime of Jesus' followers, death washed over the city like a flood, leaving behind bodies piled upon an altar dripping with human blood.

It is at this point that Daniel's prophecy said,

> And he shall confirm the covenant with many for one week: and in the midst of the week he shall cause the sacrifice and the oblation to cease, and for the overspreading of abominations he shall make it desolate, even until the consummation, and that determined shall be poured upon the desolate.
>
> (DANIEL 9:27)

This verse is ambiguous as to whether the "he" is the Messiah or the prince. One traditional way of understanding the verse is that Jesus confirmed the laws (the covenant) of Moses with the Jews, for he said that he did not come to abolish the law, but to "fulfill it," i.e., confirm it. Jesus also ended sacrifice for his followers, who gradually discontinued the practice, believing it was no longer necessary because of his death.

Jesus' death, resurrection, and ascension from earth came about three and a half years after his anointing, which would be seen as the middle of a the final week of years during which his ministry was exclusively to the Jews. Three and a half years after his ascension, Jesus appeared one more time to a Jewish Pharisee who had attended the stoning of a young Christian man. Because of Jesus' appearance, the Pharisee converted to Christianity and took a new name—Paul. Paul shifted the major focus of Christianity toward the Gentiles (anyone who's not Jewish by race); and Christianity began its split from Judaism.

The "he" in this verse seems more likely, however, to refer to the emperor Titus. Because the second week appears disconnected from the first sixty-nine, it's reasonable to assume some discontinuity in time. Practically speaking, Titus ended sacrifice for *all* Jews. Jewish law requires sacrifices to be done in the temple. No temple, no sacrifice. (Reformed Judaism no longer believes sacrifice is God's way *even if* the temple should someday be restored.) The verse quoted above has a possible counterpart later in Daniel, which makes it much more clear that the sacrifice is taken away by military forces:

> And forces shall stand on his part, and they shall pollute the sanctuary of strength, and shall take away the daily sacrifice, and they shall place the abomination that maketh desolate.
>
> (DANIEL 11:31)

Josephus, in fact, records how it came about that Titus's forces inadvertently caused the daily sacrifice to cease and added to the abominations that had already begun by the rebels:

> Those darts [spears or arrows] that were thrown by the engines came with that force, that they . . . reached as far as the altar and the temple itself, and fell upon the priests and those that were about the sacred offices; insomuch that in any persons who came . . . to offer sacrifices at this celebrated place . . . fell down before their own sacrifices themselves and sprinkled that altar . . . with their own blood; till the dead bodies of strangers were mingled together with . . . those of the priests and the blood of all sorts of dead carcasses stood in lakes in the holy courts.[1]

Josephus, in fact, precisely records the day the sacrifice permanently ended under Titus. While the soldiers of Titus were digging under the walls to make their final assault on the temple stronghold, Titus ordered Josephus brought to him because he still hoped to avert destroying or desecrating the holy temple. According to Josephus, Titus was concerned because,

> he had been informed on that very day, which was the seventeenth day of Panemus [Tamuz], the sacrifice called "the daily sacrifice" had failed and had not been offered to God for want of men to offer it, and that the people were grievously troubled at it.[2]

Titus declared that he would allow the rebels free egress from the temple to another part of town so the Jews could offer their sacrifices. Titus ordered Josephus to speak to the leader of the band holed up in the temple and implore him to come with his men out of the temple,

> in order to fight, without the danger of destroying either his city or temple . . . [for Titus] desired he would not defile the temple, nor thereby offend against God.[3]

The leader of the rebels responded that he, the leader, was not concerned about the city. Because it was God's holy city, God would protect it. Josephus reproached him sarcastically:

> To be sure thou has kept this city wonderfully pure for God's sake! the temple also continues entirely unpolluted! Nor hast thou been guilty of any impiety against him, for whose assistance thou hopest! He still receives his accustomed sacrifices! Vile wretch that thou art! . . . Thou hopest to have that God for thy support in this war whom thou hast deprived of his everlasting worship! It is God therefore, it is God himself who is bringing on this fire, to purge [this] city and temple by means of the Romans, and is going to pluck up this city, which is full of your pollutions.[4]

Because the rebels did not trust Titus's offer, they did not yield ground, and the rest happened as Josephus declared. The date given for the ceasing of the daily sacrifice is especially interesting. It was exactly three and one half years from the date when Vespasian began this war against the Jews in A.D. 66. Even more interesting is the fact that the total war lasted a week of years, placing the date the sacrifice was ceased in the middle of this week of years, as Daniel indicated. Officially, the Romans celebrated their triumph right after the fall of Jerusalem, but their triumph was not complete, for the same rebels who began the war escaped Jerusalem and holed up in the high desert fortress called Massada. After one of the most gruelling and famous sieges in military history, the Romans finally breached the impenetrable fortress, moments after the last of the original Jewish rebels committed suicide. It was A.D. 73, seven years after the war had begun. So, the war between Titus and the Jews fits Daniel's seventieth week predicted to be the end time for ancient Israel.

Ironically, Titus's victory arch still stands in Rome, but the Romans do not, and the Jews have returned to Jerusalem.

TITUS CONFIRMS A COVENANT

Daniel had also foretold that the prince would confirm a covenant with many in the middle of this final week of years. When Titus had broken through the first two walls, he entreated the people to surrender by offering them a covenant:

> When therefore he came in, he did not permit his soldiers to kill any of those they caught, nor to set fire to their houses neither; nay he gave leave to the seditious, if they had a mind, to fight without any harm to the people, and promised to restore the people's effects to them; for he was very desirous to preserve the city for his own sake and the temple for the sake of the city. . . .
>
> A resolution was now taken by Titus to relax the siege for a little while, and to afford the seditious an interval for consideration, and to see whether the demolishing of their second wall would not make them a little more compliant. . . . Titus, . . . being sensible that exhortations are frequently more effectual than arms, . . . persuaded them to surrender the city, now in a manner already taken, and thereby to save themselves.[5]

Josephus implored the people on Titus's behalf, asking them how they could hope to win, considering their two strongest walls had already been destroyed. Now all that remained was the weakest wall near the temple. He reminded them that their escape from Egypt had not come by military effort. God had become their General and delivered them miraculously. Likewise, they were not delivered from Babylon by war, but God had softened the heart of the Babylonian emperor so that he simply released them. If they had escaped their previous oppressors without rebellion, why did they insist on rebelling now, instead of waiting upon God?

Apparently still speaking for Titus, Josephus says,

> The Romans do demand no more than that accustomed tribute which our father paid to their fathers; and if they may but once obtain that, they neither aim to destroy this city, nor to touch this sanctuary. . . .[6]

The Jews did not, at first, back down, so the battle pressed hard against them. When the daily sacrifice ended because the temple was under such duress, some finally began to surrender:

> Many also of the . . . nobility went over to the Romans, together with the high priests. Now Caesar not only received these men very kindly in other respects, but knowing they would not willingly live after the customs of other nations, he sent

them to Gophna . . . and told them, that when he was gotten clear of this war, he would restore each of them to their possessions again; so they cheerfully retired to that small city which was allotted them, without fear of any danger. . . .

When Titus [later] recalled those men from Gophna, he gave orders that they should go round the wall [of the temple, still under siege], together with Josephus, and show themselves to the people [as being unharmed by their surrender]; upon which a great many fled to the Romans.[7]

Even at the last moment, when the gates of the temple were burning, Titus continued to hold out terms of surrender:

In the meantime there deserted to him . . . the most bloody of all the [rebel] guards . . . hoping to be still forgiven. . . . [Titus] told them they were only driven to this desertion because of the utmost distress they were in. . . . However, the security he had promised deserters overcame his resentments, and he dismissed them accordingly, though he did not give them the same privileges that he had afforded to others.[8]

As a result, many were spared by the covenant of surrender Titus offered. If a few of the original rebels had not held out, even the temple and the city could have been saved. Thus, every detail of Daniel's prophecy was fulfilled in the two events of Jesus' life and Titus's destruction of Jerusalem and the temple. A small astrologic detail occurs during Josephus' description of the final days, which ties the prince's destruction of city and the temple to the earlier Messiah:

A star resembling a sword [or cross?] stood over the city, and a comet, that continued a whole year.[9]

The star sounds strikingly familiar to the one recorded in the Gospels that shone over Bethlehem seventy years earlier when Jesus was born. As though to say, what had begun then, has ended now. In that respect, the discontinuity between Daniel's first sixty-nine weeks and the final seventieth week may represent more than the break in time between Jesus and Titus. It could hint that the *seventieth* week also implies another kind of week—a week of decades that began with the birth of Jesus and closed with the destruction of the old Jewish temple.

The old form of Judaism that the temple stood for hasn't been practiced since. Jesus' death, resurrection, and ascension, which occurred in the middle of those seventy years, created a new *covenant* or new religion that opened worship of the God of the Jews to a broader Gentile public. Thus there may be layers upon layers of meaning in prophetic shorthand.

Because modern Judaism is as different from its Judaic roots as Christianity is, and because *both* have Jewish members and *neither* practices all of the old laws, neither has an intrinsically better claim to the original religion. Both also had Jewish founders.

The small band of Jews who followed Christ did not join in Israel's military exchange with the Romans, yet they changed the world. The devastating failure of the Jewish military struggle against Rome, on the other hand, is pretty convincing evidence that Jesus' way of peace may have been the truest messianic approach—though it made little sense to many who wanted war. Certainly, it was distinctive from what all other "messiahs" were preaching. For years, Christians suffered right alongside other Jews under Roman rule, but in the end, who wound up ruling Rome?

Even though Titus fulfills every detail of Daniel's prophecy, within the last one hundred fifty years some Christians have come to believe that the seventieth week in Daniel represents a quantum leap through time to a different "prince who shall come." This prince, called the Antichrist, is viewed as another great destroyer of Jerusalem at the end of the world. Under this view, the "consummation" referred to is not just the end of Israel but the end of history as it has run for the past six thousand or so years on record. This pseudo-messiah supposedly will establish a false covenant with the Jews—maybe even with the whole world. To fit Daniel's description, he must reign for seven years, which will be a time of great tribulation upon the earth.

It would be peculiar, however, for biblical prophecy to skip over the decimation of Israel around A.D. 70 in order to talk about the end of earth. This was beyond any doubt the most significant crisis in Israel's national history. Also, there is no hint throughout the rest of biblical prophesy of any covenant being made during the end times of earth. Some quote Isaiah 28:14–22 to support the idea of a false covenant with the Antichrist in the middle of his seven-year reign, but the context of that passage regards an ancient covenant made in Isaiah's own time between king Hezekiah of Israel and the invading king of Assyria. Also, applying Daniel's prophecy to the ultimate "end times" would require that the temple be rebuilt in Jerusalem and sacrifice be reinitiated. Otherwise, the false messiah cannot end sacrifice and destroy the city and the temple as described.

This view takes the most poetic license with Daniel's numbers by leaping across millennia in a way that is completely disjoined from the context of the first sixty-nine weeks. Ironically, this figurative approach is taken for granted by those who, otherwise, insist upon the most literal reading of prophecy; and it is scoffed at by those who usually prefer figurative interpretations. Even the most literal teachers will be figurative where it suits their interests, and the most liberal are willing to be literal when it suits theirs. Perhaps the irony illustrates well how people would be best off to retain a little latitude in their prophetic views and a little poetry in their thinking.

Though Titus has already fulfilled Daniel's prophecy to a "T," an echo of the pattern recurring near the end of time is not outside the possibilities of poetic interpretation.

Having already been perfectly and *literally* fulfilled, however, it's not necessary for the pattern to repeat itself completely. It's not *necessary* for it to repeat at all. The *possibility* for repetition with variation, however, can be seen even in Titus, who was a larger echo of an earlier and lesser prince predicted elsewhere in Daniel. History is a great recycler of trash, even as it advances.

The Evil Prince Antiochus Epiphanes

Therefore the male goat became very great: and when he was strong, the great horn was broken; and in its stead came up four notable ones toward the four winds of heaven. And out of one of them came forth a little horn, which became exceeding great, toward the south, and toward the east, and toward the pleasant land. And it grew great, even to the host of heaven; and it cast down some of the host and of the stars to the ground, and stamped upon them. (DANIEL 8:8–10)

The image of the one-horned goat in Daniel represented Alexander the Great who overthrew the Persian empire after the Jews restored Jerusalem. True to history, Daniel described Alexander as being cut off at the height of his power ("the great horn was broken"). Alexander died young, and the empire held together in a fractured state for a number of years under divided leadership. Eventually, four of Alexander's former generals (the four horns) grew in strength and claimed four regions of the former empire as their own kingdoms.

Horns, for an obvious reason, symbolize power. The little horn that became great represented a weasel named Antiochus, though some think it represents Titus because the two, by their actions, are sometimes difficult to distinguish, which is exactly the point in terms of historic patterns repeating with variation.

In 170 B.C., 200 years before Titus, Antiochus conquered Jerusalem long after it had been restored from Babylon, killing forty thousand Jews. The significance of this event is that it appears to be the first conquest in human history rooted in religious persecution. Previous empires had been established solely for acquisition of power. Antiochus, however, made his attack directly against the religion of the Jews. (In that respect he was much different than Titus, who had no motivation against the Judaism, though he caused great changes in it by his war.)

The Greek Antiochus wanted all of his region to be Greek in culture—especially in religion. His evil attack against the religion of the Jews lowers him to the level of symbolizing Satan incarnate in Daniel's prophecy. The Book of Revelation (The Apocalypse) and Jesus both allude to the image of Antiochus reaching for the heavens and casting down the host (the many inhabitants) of heaven as a symbol of Satan's defeat and his fallen angels. (As will be described later in the book.)

The images in The Apocalypse and Daniel are so closely tied that it is as though Antiochus were possessed by the devil. So that what is said later of the devil is true of the spirit within the man Antiochus. His satanic nature is revealed through his deliberate desecration of God's temple on earth—much different from the abominations that occurred under Titus, which were a casualty of war. Within the context of Antiochus' own life, the "starry host" probably signify the Jewish saints of God, thrown down to earth in the sense that forty thousand of them were slaughtered and buried. The reach of the language, however, seems to beg for an interpretation that ascends to the heavens for its ultimate cosmic fulfillment:

> *Yea, he magnified himself even to the prince of the host, and by him the daily sacrifice was taken away, and the place of his sanctuary was cast down.*
>
> (DANIEL 8:11)

The Prince of the host is sometimes understood as a reference to the predicted Messiah. The name "Epiphanes," a moniker Antiochus IV chose for himself, means "God made visible." It reveals his delusion of messianic grandeur. Another section of Daniel gives further insight into his delusions:

> *And the king shall do according to his will; and he shall exalt himself, and magnify himself above every god, and shall speak marvelous things against the God of gods, and shall prosper till the indignation be accomplished: for that which is determined shall be done. Neither shall he regard the God of his fathers, nor the desire of women, nor regard any god: for he shall magnify himself above all. But in his estate shall he honour the God of forces: and a god whom his fathers knew not shall he honour with gold, and silver, and with precious stones, and pleasant things. Thus shall he do in the strongest fortresses with a foreign god, whom he shall acknowledge and increase with glory: and he shall cause them to rule over many, and shall divide the land for gain.*
>
> (DANIEL 11:36–39)

The "desire of women" is probably better translated as "the one desired by women," referring to the Greek god Apollo. Until the time of Antiochus, the god Zeus had dominated Greek culture. Appropriately to his nature, Antiochus raised Apollo, the Destroyer (or god of forces), to prominence. Above all, however, Antiochus honored himself almost as though he were one of the gods.

The Jewish conflict with Antiochus is told in one of the books of the Apocrypha (a disputed section of the Bible that was originally part of the King James version but later removed because of questions about the authenticity of certain books). The book of 1 Maccabees says:

[Antiochus] went up against Israel and came to Jerusalem with a strong force. He arrogantly entered the sanctuary and took the golden altar, the lampstand for the light, and all its utensils. He took also the table for the bread of the Presence, the cups for the drink offerings . . . also the hidden treasures which he found. Taking them all he departed to his own land. He committed deeds of murder, and spoke with great arrogance . . .

Then the king [Antiochus] wrote to his whole kingdom that all should be one people, and that each should give up his customs. Many even from Israel gladly adopted his religion; they sacrificed to idols and profaned the sabbath. And the king sent letters by messengers to Jerusalem and the cities of Judah; he directed them to . . . forbid burnt offerings and sacrifices . . . , to profane sabbaths and feasts, to defile the sanctuary and the priests, to build altars and sacred precincts and shrines for idols, to sacrifice swine and unclean animals, and to leave their sons uncircumsized. They were to make themselves abominable by everything unclean and profane.

. . . they erected a desolating sacrilege upon the altar of burnt offering. They also built altars in the surrounding cities of Judah. . . . The books of the [religious] law [of Moses] which they found they tore to pieces and burned with fire. . . . If anyone adhered to the law, the decree of the king condemned him to death. . . . they put to death the women who had their children circumcised, and their families . . . and they hung the infants from their mothers' necks. . . . And very great wrath came upon Israel.

Jerusalem was uninhabited like a wilderness; not one of her children went in or out. The sanctuary was trampled down, and the sons of aliens held the citadel; it was a lodging place for the Gentiles. Joy was taken from Jacob; the flute and the harp ceased to play.[10]

All of this fulfills another part of Daniel's prophecy, which was applied earlier to Titus:

And forces shall stand on his [Antiochus'] part, and they shall pollute the sanctuary of strength, and shall take away the daily sacrifice, and they shall place the abomination that maketh desolate. (DANIEL 11:31)

Thus, Antiochus did not bring down the sanctuary literally as Titus later did, but he brought it down in honor by corrupting it and vandalizing it. Its altar later had to be destroyed and rebuilt and reconsecrated because of the abominations that had been committed on it, such as sacrificing swine and possibly standing a statue of Zeus on top of it.[11] Antiochus *deliberately* ended Jewish sacrifice in order to begin his own mockery of it. Titus, *inadvertently* ended sacrifice when he brought the war to the temple stronghold. Titus's military effort was aided by the help of a wicked band among the Jewish citizenry that cared nothing about desecrating its own temple. This, too, is an echo of

Antiochus, who found a ready number of Jews to join his cause in corrupting the nation's religion:

> And an host was given him against the
> daily sacrifice by reason of transgression,
> and it cast down the truth to the ground;
> and it continued, and prospered.
>
> (DANIEL 8:12)

> And such as do wickedly against the covenant shall he corrupt by flatteries: but the people that know their God shall be strong, and do exploits. And they that understand among the people shall instruct many: yet they shall fall by the sword, and by flame, by captivity, and by spoil, many days. Now when they shall fall, they shall be helped with a little help: but many shall join with them with flatteries. And some of them of understanding shall fall, to try them, and to purge, and to make them white, even to the time of the end: because it is yet for a time appointed. (DANIEL 11:32–35)

Those who did "wickedly against the covenant" of God were the Jews who joined Antiochus in his efforts to Hellenize (bring Greek culture into) Jerusalem, but another group of Jews resisted firmly under a heroic leader named Judas Maccabeus. The Book of Maccabees describes how Antiochus managed to get a number of Jews to corrupt their own temple:

> In those days lawless men came forth from Israel, and misled many, saying, 'Let us go and make a covenant with the Gentiles round about us, for since we separated from them many evils have come upon us.' This proposal pleased them, and some of the people eagerly went to the king [Antiochus]. He authorized them to observe the ordinances of the Gentiles. So they built a gymnasium in Jerusalem, according to Gentile custom [where there would be nude games, which those Jews who remained true to their religion abhorred], and removed the marks of circumcision [a sign of Jewishness], and abandoned the holy covenant. They joined with the Gentiles and sold themselves to do evil. [Then] Antiochus saw that his kingdom was established. . . .[12]

The kingdom of Antiochus Epiphanes was established because a majority of Jews felt that the Gentiles generally had a better life than they did. The pattern of Jews desecrating their own temple repeated with variation when Titus came two hundred years later. In his case, a lawless minority of Jews brought havoc on the city and decimated it before he even arrived. The variation is that the lawless people were on the side of Antiochus, but were against Titus.

Titus more closely echoes Antiochus in another respect: both rulers terrorized Israel with three and a half years of conflict—only Antiochus started by desecrating the temple and Titus finished by destroying it:

Judas [the heroic leader who liberated Jerusalem from Antiochus] set the rededication of the temple exactly three years after its pollution . . . and three and a half years after Antiochus' capture of Jerusalem.[13]

This also appears to fit Daniel's prophecy about Antiochus:

Then I heard one saint speaking, and another saint said to that certain saint who spoke, How long shall be the vision concerning the daily sacrifice, and the transgression of desolation, to give both the sanctuary and the host to be trodden under foot? And he said to me, Until two thousand and three hundred days; then shall the sanctuary be cleansed.

(DANIEL 8:13–14)

The prophecy, literally translated, says it will be 2,300 "evenings and mornings." Some scholars have suggested that the 2,300 evenings and mornings be understood as the sum of 1,150 evenings plus 1,150 mornings—in other words, 1,150 complete days, which is almost equal to the three and a half years that Jerusalem lay desolate. It's still a rough match, but that could be due to the ambiguity regarding the date of the event that starts the clock ticking—even though the event that stops the clock (the reconsecration of the temple) is precisely named and dated in history. In other words, it may have been exactly 1,150 days.

The desolation was ended by Judas Maccabeus and his men. They fought off the king's men while Antiochus was busy with other campaigns outside of Israel. They didn't wait for Antiochus to return before restoring the city and its temple:

They saw the sanctuary desolate, the altar profaned, and the gates burned. In the courts they saw bushes sprung up as in a thicket. . . . They saw also the chambers of the priests in ruins. . . . [Judas] chose blameless priests devoted to the law, and they cleansed the sanctuary and removed the defiled stones [of the altar]. . . . Then they took unhewn stones, as the law directs, and built a new altar like the former one. They also rebuilt the sanctuary and the interior of the temple, and consecrated the courts. . . . Early in the morning on the twenty-fifth day of the ninth month, which is the month of Chislev, in the one hundred and forty-eighth year, they rose and offered sacrifice, as the law directs, on the new altar of burnt offering which they had built. At the very season and on the very day that the Gentiles had profaned it, it was dedicated with songs and harps and lutes and cymbals.[14]

Thus, the timing was exactly *three* years from the date the temple was profaned, but about *three and a half* from the time Antiochus took Jerusalem.

But if Daniel's 2,300 "evenings and mornings" meant 1,150 days, why didn't he just come right out and say it? The ambiguity of the expression has left many to speculate that the prophecy is intended to have a meaning larger than the original event. It may foreshadow certain events in the end times of human history.

The only other place in the Bible that the words "evening" and "morning" are joined as an expression to represent a day is in Genesis where they divide the events of creation—"days" of indeterminate length in the creation story (indeterminate because the sun was not created to "rule over the length of the day") until the fourth "day" of creation. Why should Daniel's prophecy be clouded with an ambiguous phrase like "evenings and mornings" when the word "day" could easily have been used—unless poetic ambiguity was necessary to broaden the meaning? Could these "evenings and mornings" have another reference beyond the time of Antiochus?

Because the method of making literal sense out of the 2,300 "evenings and mornings" (as representing 1,150 complete days) seems contrived, many people have tried to crunch this number like a code to predict when the end will come. (Counting 2,300 *years* from Antiochus Epiphanes' conquest of Jerusalem, for example, could yield a date for the end of the world of approximately A.D. 2130. Usually, however, the code cracker tries to work out a date that will be within his own lifetime: "2,300 years, which reckoned from the time Alexander [the Great] invaded Asia, B.C. 334, will be A.D. 1966." Obviously, that one didn't happen.)

No one who has calculated a date for the end has been right yet. Most of them are dead, and the world goes on. So maybe it's best to keep the application of the 2,300 evenings and mornings to the events of Antiochus Epiphanes, and let the future reveal any encrypted meaning when the future becomes the present. Trying to create charts or time lines of the future can easily become an obsession that distracts one from the more interesting insights biblical prophecies offer into the relationships between the spiritual realm and our own physical world and to the meaning of earth's history, which is always at their heart and soul.

Even the prophet did not understand all that was revealed:

And it came to pass, when I, even I Daniel, had seen the vision, and sought for the meaning, then, behold, there stood before me one having the appearance of a man. And I heard a man's voice between the banks of Ulai, which called, and said, Gabriel, make this man to understand the vision. So he came near where I stood: and when he came, I was afraid, and fell upon my face: but he said to me, Understand, O son of man: for at the time of the end shall be the vision. Now as he was speaking with me, I was in a deep sleep on my face toward the ground: but he touched me, and set me upright. And he said, Behold, I will make thee know what shall be in the last end of the indignation: for at the time appointed the end shall be. . . .

And the vision of the evening and the morning which was told is true: therefore shut thou up the vision; for it shall be for many days. And I Daniel fainted, and was sick certain days; afterward I rose, and did the king's business; and I was astonished at the vision, but none understood it. (DANIEL 8:15–19, 26, 29)

"The time of the end" would seem to indicate a legitimate basis for looking for a second meaning in the prophecy because Antiochus did not come at "the time of the end" for anything. When he died, Israel went on just as before. Outside of Israel's history he is completely insignificant. Nor do any of the measurements of time involved match with the end of ancient Israel. The end of "indignation" mentioned could refer to the days of God's final judgment on earth, the ultimate consummation. The fact that Daniel is told to "shut up" the vision, that is, "seal its meaning," is especially strong evidence that it does hold encrypted meanings, but it also means no one will figure them out until the time is right. For who can presume to solve a mystery God has chosen to conceal? The vision that follows, even though it still applies to Antiochus, uses language that leans in the direction of end-time events, perhaps anticipating the final destruction of the spirit that filled Antiochus:

And in the latter time of their kingdom, when the transgressors are come to the full, a king of fierce countenance, and understanding dark sentences, shall stand up. And his power shall be mighty, but not by his own power: and he shall destroy wonderfully, and shall prosper, and continue, and shall destroy the mighty and the holy people. And through his policy also he shall cause deceit to prosper in his hand; and he shall magnify himself in his heart, and by peace shall destroy many: he shall also stand up against the Prince of princes; but he shall be broken without hand. (DANIEL 8:23–25)

It is not hard to see the death of Antiochus Epiphanes in the prophecy that he would "be broken without [human] hands." Having experienced defeat in his campaigns abroad, when Antiochus heard how Jerusalem had been retaken by the Jews and how the "abomination" he had erected on the altar had been torn down, he

took to his bed and became sick from grief, because things had not turned out for him as he had planned. He lay there for many days . . . and he concluded that he was dying. So he called all his friends and said to them . . . "I remember the evils I did in Jerusalem. . . . I know that it is because of this that these evils have come upon me. . . . Thus Antiochus the king died.[15]

A more elaborate account explains the evils that came upon him:

But the all-seeing Lord, the God of Israel, struck him an incurable and unseen blow. . . . He was seized with pain in his bowels for which there was no relief. . . . Yet he did not in any way stop his insolence, but was even more filled with arrogance, breathing fire in his rage against the Jews, and giving orders to hasten [his] journey [home from his campaigns]. And so it came about that he fell out of his chariot as it was rushing along, and the fall was so hard as to torture every limb of his body. Thus he who had just been thinking that he could command the waves of the sea, in his superhuman arrogance, and imagining that he could weigh the high mountains in a balance, was brought down to earth and carried in a litter, making the power of God manifest to all. And so the ungodly man's body swarmed with worms, and while he was still living in anguish and pain, his flesh rotted away, and because of his stench the whole army felt revulsion at his decay. Because of his intolerable stench no one was able to carry the man who a little while before had thought that he could touch the stars of heaven. . . . So the murderer and blasphemer . . . came to the end of his life.[16]

Of course, the writer of this section from 2 Maccabees was well aware of the prophecies in Daniel and may have embellished his tale.

Thus, Antiochus was broken "without [human] hands," but could the prophetic description of a prince that would be broken "without [human] hands" also relate to king Nebuchadnezzar's dream where all the imperial governments represented in the statue are destroyed by "the stone [that] was cut out of the mountain without hands"? Antiochus Epiphanes may have foreshadowed this divine end on a smaller scale, but the remainder of what is said in the sections about Antiochus doesn't fit the end he came to at all, making it seem the prophet's vision has, in fact, leaped ahead to another time:

And at the time of the end shall the king of the south push at him: and the king of the north shall come against him like a whirlwind, with chariots, and with horsemen, and with many ships; and he shall enter into the countries, and shall overflow and pass through. He shall enter also into the glorious land [Israel], and many countries shall be overthrown: but these shall escape out of his hand, even Edom, and Moab [countries east of Israel], and the chief of the children of Ammon. He shall stretch forth his hand also upon the countries: and the land of Egypt shall not escape. But he shall have power over the treasures of gold and of silver, and over all the precious things of Egypt: and the Libyans and the Cushites [Ethiopians] shall be at his steps. But tidings out of the east and out of the north shall trouble him: therefore he shall go forth with great fury to destroy, and utterly to sweep away many. And he shall plant the tabernacles [tents] of his palace between the seas in the glorious holy mountain; yet he shall come to his end, and none shall help him. And at that time shall Michael stand up, the great prince who standeth for the children of thy people: and there shall be a time of trouble, such as never was since there was a nation even to that same time: and at that time thy people shall be delivered, every one that shall be found written in the book.

(DANIEL 11:40–45; 12:1)

The location mentioned for the prince's tents is Mount Zion, between the Dead Sea and the Mediterranean, the site of Jerusalem. The prince's temporary dwelling in tents indicates he is there at war. He has not conquered Jerusalem, or he would have a palace. Nor will he conquer, for the children of Israel will be delivered.

Even Jesus did not see Antiochus Epiphanes as the ultimate fulfillment of these prophecies. In his discourse with the disciples about the destruction of the temple he says:

When therefore ye shall see the abomination of desolation, spoken of by Daniel the prophet, stand in the holy place, (whoever readeth, let him understand:) Then let them who are in Judaea flee to the mountains: (MATTHEW 24:15, 16)

He refers to the "abomination of desolation" (quoted in the above prophecies about Antiochus) as an event yet to watch out for. At least some elements in the prophecy about Antiochus, then, looked further ahead—perhaps only to Titus or perhaps to the consummation of history.

Chapter 3

COVENANTS:

WHO ARE THE CHOSEN PEOPLE?

W hy did Israel fall to Babylon, then rise to fall again?

According to the prophets, God's original purpose in choosing the Jews was to a establish a single monotheistic nation that would become a light in the midst of a world full of pantheistic darkness. To make that light shine brightly, God promised to bless Israel with unparalleled prosperity, health, goodness, knowledge, and wisdom—so long as they worshipped him. Then all the nations of the world would be drawn to the truth by virtue of its superior evidence in lives built on faith in the one God. There was, of course, more than allure involved. If entire nations lived by good principles, how could things not go well for them on the whole?

THE CHOSEN FEW

Long before there was a Jew in Jerusalem, God began working out his plan by choosing one righteous man named Abram out of a land filled with pagan rituals that included human sacrifice. He came from the motherland of Babylon:

Now the LORD had said to Abram, Depart from thy country, and from thy kindred, and from thy father's house, to a land that I will show thee: And I will make of thee a great nation, and I will bless thee, and make thy name great. . . . And I will bless them that bless thee, and curse him that curseth thee: and in thee shall all families of the earth be blessed. . . . To thy seed [offspring] will I give this land: and there he built an altar to the LORD, who appeared to him.

(GENESIS 12:1–3, 7)

And the LORD said to Abram . . . Lift up now thine eyes, and look from the place where thou art northward, and south-ward, and eastward, and westward: For all the land which thou seest, to thee will I give it, and to thy seed for ever. And I will make thy seed as the dust of the earth: so that if a man can number the dust of the earth, then shall thy seed also be numbered. (GENESIS 13:14–16)

Because Abram and his wife Sarai were both about a hundred years old and with-out children, they didn't have much hope for an heir to make this promise come true. Abram naturally wondered about this, but God promised Abram and Sarai a son. So Abram believed even though he didn't understand how it could happen.

And, behold, the word of the LORD came to him, saying . . . He that shall come forth out of thy own loins shall be thy heir. . . . Look now toward heaven, and count the stars, if thou art able to number them: . . . So shall thy seed be. And he [Abram] believed in the LORD; and he [the LORD] counted it to him for righteousness. And he said to him, I am the LORD that brought thee out of Ur of the Chaldees [Babylonians], to give thee this land to inherit it.

. . . In that same day the LORD made a covenant with Abram, saying, To thy seed have I given this land, from the river of Egypt to the great river, the river Eu-phrates. (GENESIS 15:4–7, 18)

It would be a full millennium until all of the promise was inherited. (Some argue that it still has not been completely fulfilled because the promised land was never fully occupied, even though it was controlled by Abram's descendants. That may be splitting hairs.) God sealed his covenant with Abram (which means "exalted father") by giving him a new name, *Abraham* (which means "father of a multitude"). God placed no con-ditions on his permanent covenant, except that he asked Abraham to seal it with all his descendants and household staff by a private physical sign of belonging:

. . . Kings shall come forth from thee. And I will establish my covenant be-tween me and thee and thy seed after thee in their generations for an everlast-ing covenant, to be a God to thee, and to thy seed after thee. . . . And God said to Abraham, . . . This is my covenant, which ye shall keep, between me and you and thy seed after thee; Every male among you shall be circumcised . . . and it shall be a sign of the covenant between me and you. . . . And the uncircumcised male . . . shall be cut off from his people; he hath broken my covenant. (GENESIS 17:6–11, 14)

This sign marked Abraham, all the male members of his household and his descen-dants as God's chosen, but individuals who refused to cut their flesh would cut them-selves off from inheriting the everlasting covenant.

God also renamed Sarai (which means "princess"), giving her the new name *Sarah* ("noblewoman.") This was to show that she was just as much a part of his new creation as was Abraham, for God was establishing his new creation through her. And God promised her, "She shall be a mother of nations; kings of people shall come from her." Soon, Sarah gave birth to a son, whom God named *Isaac* (which means "laughter"), for Abraham and Sarah both laughed to think that a couple so old could give birth to a child. God restated the promise to Isaac when he matured and to Isaac's son whose name was *Jacob* (the one God renamed *Israel*).

While Israel was in the land that would someday bear his name, he had a dream in which God handed down the promise he had given to Israel's father and grandfather. Israel revered the holy land on which his head had rested while he dreamed of a connection between heaven and earth.

> And Jacob awoke from his sleep, and he said, Surely the LORD is in this place; and I knew it not. And he was afraid, and said, How dreadful is this place! this is no other but the house of God, and this is the gate of heaven.
>
> (GENESIS 28:16, 17)

So, Jacob (or Israel) saw this holy land as a portal, or a nexus, between heaven and earth. Here God would enter human history.

A SECOND COVENANT UNDER MOSES

The promise God had given to Abraham, Isaac, and Israel would always be held open to those descendants who shared Abraham's faith in God and who received the mark of circumcision. There was an interim period, however, in which the children of Israel were enslaved in Egypt. Later, when Moses led God's people out of the Egyptian Empire, God set specific conditions for retaining what they were about to receive. In stating these conditions, he also revealed his spiritual purpose of establishing a place on earth suitable for his presence to be experienced:

> *Now therefore, if ye will obey my voice indeed, and keep my covenant, then ye shall be a special treasure to me above all people: for all the earth is mine: And ye shall be to me a kingdom of priests, and an holy nation. . . .* (EXODUS 19:5, 6)
>
> *If ye walk in my statutes, and keep my commandments . . . I will give peace in the land. . . . For I will have respect to you, and make you fruitful, and multiply you, and establish my covenant with you. . . . And I will walk among you, and will be your God, and ye shall be my people.* (LEVITICUS 26:3, 6, 9, 12)

The human nature of any people chosen by God could lead them to become arrogant or chauvinistic about their special calling. This, of course, would hamper God's effort to create an example to the nations of a bountiful relationship with the creator. So God reminded the descendants of Abraham, Isaac, and Jacob that he had only chosen them because of his promise to their faithful fathers. It had nothing to do with merit. God chose ordinary people because ordinary people make the most extraordinary examples of transformation. Nevertheless, the promise would be theirs if they adhered to a second covenant that God was about to make through Moses:

And because he [God] loved thy fathers, therefore he chose their seed after them, and brought thee out of Egypt; in his sight with his mighty power; To drive out nations from before thee greater and mightier than thou art, to bring thee in, to give thee their land for an inheritance, as it is this day. Know therefore . . . that the LORD he is God in heaven above, and upon the earth beneath: there is none else. Thou shalt keep therefore his statutes, and his commandments, which I command thee this day, that it may be well with thee, and with thy children after thee, and that thou mayest prolong thy days upon the earth, which the LORD thy God giveth thee, for ever.

(DEUTERONOMY 4:37–40)

For thou art an holy people to the LORD thy God: the LORD thy God hath chosen thee to be a special people to himself, above all people that are upon the face of the earth. The LORD did not set his love upon you, nor choose you, because ye were more in number than any people; for ye were the fewest of all people: . . .
. . . Thou shalt be blessed above all people. . . .
. . . Not for thy righteousness, or for the uprightness of thy heart, dost thou go to possess [the land now occupied by others]: but for the wickedness of these nations the LORD thy God doth drive them out from before thee, and that he may perform the word which the LORD swore to thy fathers, Abraham, Isaac, and Jacob. Understand therefore, that the LORD thy God giveth thee not this good land to possess it for thy righteousness; for thou art a stiffnecked people.

(DEUTERONOMY 7:6, 7, 14; 9:5–6)

God carved out a land and placed a new people within it in order to establish a place for monotheism to **develop.** It would be counterproductive for God to bless Israel if they ignored his truth. That would only allure other nations down the same path. Therefore, if Israel, having so great a destiny given to it, turned from God, the downside would be as low as the upside was high. This was elementary religious education: Do good and follow the one true God, and paradise will be restored; do evil and serve yourselves or false gods, and death follows. God made it clear to Moses from the beginning that he was under no delusion this simple pattern would succeed without evolving to greater complexity, but there were mysteries within God's plan he had not yet revealed:

Is not this laid up in store with me, and
sealed up among my treasures?

(DEUTERONOMY 32:34)

And the LORD said to Moses, Behold,
thou shalt sleep [rest in peace] with thy
fathers; and this people will rise up, and
play the harlot with the gods of the
strangers of the land . . . and will forsake
me, and break my covenant which I have
made with them. Then my anger shall be
kindled against them in that day, and I
will forsake them, and I will hide my face
from them, and they shall be devoured,
and many evils and troubles shall befall
them; so that they will say in that day,
Have not these evils come upon us, be-
cause our God is not among us?

. . . And it came to pass . . . that Moses
commanded the Levites, . . . saying, . . .
I know thy rebellion, and thy stiff neck:
behold, while I am yet alive with you this
day, ye have been rebellious against the
LORD; and how much more after my
death? . . . For I know that after my death
ye will utterly corrupt yourselves, and
turn aside from the way which I have
commanded you; and evil will befall you
in the latter days; because ye will do evil
in the sight of the LORD. . . .

(DEUTERONOMY 31:16, 17, 24, 25, 27, 29)

So, Israel prospered at first as promised. Yet, instead of attracting the surrounding nations from the darkness into their light, the children of Israel become captivated by the darkness and reverted to their wild Babylonian roots.

But Jeshurun [Israel] grew fat, and
kicked . . . then he forsook God who
made him, and lightly esteemed the Rock
of his salvation. . . . Of the Rock that be-
gat thee thou art unmindful, and hast
forgotten God that formed thee. And
when the LORD saw it, he abhorred
them. . . . And he said, I will hide my
face from them, I will see what their end
shall be: for they are a very perverse gen-
eration, children in whom is no faith.
They have moved me to jealousy with
that which is not God; they have pro-
voked me to anger with their vanities:
and I will move them to jealousy with
those who are not a people; I will provoke

them to anger with a foolish nation. For
a fire is kindled in my anger, and shall
burn to the lowest hell, and shall con-
sume the earth with her increase, and set
on fire the foundations of the mountains.
I will heap mischiefs upon them; I will
spend my arrows upon them. . . . I said, I
would scatter them into corners, I would
make the remembrance of them to cease
from among men. . . . For they are a na-
tion void of counsel, neither is there any
understanding in them. O that they were
wise, that they understood this, that they
would consider their latter end!

(DEUTERONOMY 32:15, 17–23, 26, 28, 29)

EARLY MESSIANIC PROPHECIES

Because the great empires around them had kings and Israel longed for the imperial road to greatness, the children of Israel demanded a king. They chose their first king based on his appearance of physical power, and things did not turn out too well. God, then, guided them to a second king and followed his pattern of choosing the ordinary— a mere shepherd boy. But this shepherd had a heart for God, so the little nation of Israel blossomed. God, then, extended the promises of Abraham's covenant to the new king, whose name was David:

And it shall come to pass, when thy days shall be ended that thou must go to be with thy fathers, that I will raise up thy seed after thee, who shall be of thy sons; and I will establish his kingdom. He shall build me an house [temple], and I will establish his throne for ever. I will be his father, and he shall be my son: and I will not take my mercy away from him, as I took it from him [the first king] that was before thee: But I will settle him in my house and in my kingdom for ever: and his throne shall be established for evermore. (1 CHRONICLES 17:11–14)

For I have said, Mercy shall be built up for ever: thy faithfulness shalt thou establish in the very heavens. I have made a covenant with my chosen, I have sworn to David my servant, Thy seed will I establish for ever, and build up thy throne to all generations. Selah [a word probably meaning something like "Amen"]. . . . Also I will make him my firstborn, higher than the kings of the earth. My mercy will I keep for him for evermore, and my covenant shall stand fast with him. His seed also will I make to endure for ever, and his throne as the days of heaven. . . . Nevertheless my lovingkindness will I not utterly take from him, nor allow my faithfulness to fail. My covenant will I not break, nor alter the thing that hath gone out of my lips. Once have I sworn by my holiness that I will not lie to David. His seed shall endure for ever, and his throne as the sun before me. It shall be established for ever as the moon, and as a faithful witness in heaven. Selah. (PSALM 89:2–4, 27–29, 33–37)

God's plan still worked within the human choice to have a king, so free will was not abrogated by God's destiny. Destiny merely reshaped around the new events. The extended promise began its fulfillment through David's son Solomon when he built the temple, but the eternal language of the promise looked ahead either to an unending line of succession or to a single immortal being who would occupy the throne of Israel. Neither David nor Solomon were firstborn children, so it is unlikely that either one was the prophesied king who would be made higher than all the kings of earth. Yet, they were both the highest kings Israel ever had.

Things took a sharp downturn after Solomon, however, because later kings returned the nation to paganism. As the budding empire dropped its bloom, bigger competitors began to trample upon it. As a result, promises given to King David were looked to for the first time with raised messianic expectations of salvation from Israel's enemies.

A New Age of Prophecy

An age of prophecy began in which God tried enlightening the thoughts and religious practices of his people by emphasizing justice and mercy over the religious laws and rituals established earlier by Moses. In a world filled with human sacrifice, God had introduced Moses to show the Jews a better form of sacrifice: One did not kill one's children to prove to God how much one was willing to sacrifice. Even killing animals in order to eat was imbued with religious significance when the slaughtering was done by a priest. Life had to be respected. One could not drink blood as the Babylonians did, for example, because the blood contained the life, and the life of the animal belonged to God. Now God began to hint through his prophets that he did not really desire animal sacrifices either. What he really desired was virtue. Sacrifice was primarily a daily reminder that evil living had a cost—that human sins were the source of suffering in the world, for they diminished God's presence. Since God cannot abide evil, he does not dwell among those who persist in it. That is a loss for all of creation brought on by humans alone:

> For I desired mercy, and not sacrifice;
> and the knowledge of God more than
> burnt offerings.   (HOSEA 6:6)

What God really wanted to see in his people was transformation toward justice, humility, generosity—love. Virtue defined holy living more than sacrifice or ritual, and paganism had nothing to offer with regard to virtue. Unlike idols, God did not need to be fed daily sacrifices to still a ravenous belly and rapacious temperament.

Instead of becoming a vehicle for respecting the life they ate or a reminder of the cost of evil, the practice of sacrifices as begun by Moses had become an excuse for continuing to sin: We can sin today, and sacrifice tomorrow to keep God happy. They had become a form of indulgence. So God reminded his little nation that he is quite capable of preparing his own sacrifice—if sacrifice were really what he wanted—and that he would do exactly that if they persisted in their foolishness:

> I will utterly consume all things from off the land, saith the LORD. I will consume man and beast; I will consume the fowls of the heaven, and the fishes of the sea, and the stumblingblocks with the wicked; and I will cut off man from off

the land, saith the LORD. I will also stretch out my hand upon Judah, and upon all the inhabitants of Jerusalem; and I will cut off the remnant of Baal [pagan god of Babylon] from this place, and the name of the Chemarims [pagan priests] with the priests; And them that worship the host of heaven [stars or angelic spirits] upon the housetops; and them that worship and that swear by the LORD, and that swear by Malcham [another of the pagan gods]; And them that have turned back from the LORD; and those that have not sought the LORD, nor enquired for him.

Hold thy peace at the presence of the Lord GOD: for the day of the LORD is at hand: for the LORD hath prepared a sacrifice, he hath invited his guests. And it shall come to pass in the day of the LORD'S sacrifice, that I will punish the princes, and the king's children, and all such as are clothed with foreign apparel. In the same day also will I punish all those that leap on the threshold, who fill their masters' houses with violence and deceit. And it shall come to pass in that day, saith the LORD, that there shall be the noise of a cry from the fish gate [one of the entrances to Jerusalem], and a wailing from the second, and a great crashing from the hills. Wail, ye inhabitants of Maktesh [a valley in Jerusalem],

for all the merchant people are cut down; all they that bear silver are cut off. And it shall come to pass at that time, that I will search Jerusalem with lamps, and punish the men that are settled on their lees: that say in their heart, The LORD will not do good, neither will he do evil. Therefore their goods shall become a booty, and their houses a desolation: they shall also build houses, but not inhabit them; and they shall plant vineyards, but not drink the wine of them.

The great day of the LORD is near, it is near, and hasteneth greatly, even the voice of the day of the LORD: the mighty man shall cry there bitterly. That day is a day of wrath, a day of trouble and distress, a day of wasting and desolation, a day of darkness and gloominess, a day of clouds and thick darkness, A day of the trumpet and alarm against the fortified cities, and against the high towers. And I will bring distress upon men, that they shall walk like blind men, because they have sinned against the LORD: and their blood shall be poured out as dust, and their flesh as the dung. Neither their silver nor their gold shall be able to deliver them in the day of the LORD'S wrath; but the whole land shall be devoured by the fire of his jealousy: for he shall make even a speedy riddance of all them that dwell in the land.   (ZEPHANIAH 1:2–18)

How can a God who is loving, who is perfect, and who is unchanging because he is perfect, get so emotional? Emotions seem highly changeable, unstable, even unpredictable and dangerous. One answer may be that human emotions reflect divine nature just as much as human intellect does. Another may be that God communicates in language that human listeners should be able to understand. He lowers himself to state his case in human terms. And how could a wake-up call be more plain? One would think such dire predictions would have brought immediate reform, but they usually fell on deaf ears.

GOD THE JILTED LOVER

God's emotional pleas were even plaintive. The creator of the universe seemed to humiliate himself before his creation by *begging* for their affections. This was not likely because God felt unfulfilled without their affection, so it must have been because God would lower himself even to pleading *if* that's what it took to guide humanity toward their fulfillment in him. It speaks volumes for the virtue of humility that God was willing to speak in such humanly comprehensible terms because of his love. In one striking passage of utterly human passion, God speaks of himself as a lover jilted by his bride. He reminds his bride, Israel, that he had transformed her into a princess, though she began from the common clay of the nations around her. The Jews had come out of the land of Babylon into Jerusalem, but Babylon would be their destiny again if they continued in its ways:

Again the word of the LORD came to me, saying, Son of man, cause Jerusalem to know her abominations, And say, Thus saith the Lord GOD to Jerusalem; Thy birth and thy nativity is of the land of Canaan [the name of Abraham's promised land before it became Israel's land]. . . . In the day thou wast born thy navel was not cut, neither wast thou washed in water to cleanse thee. . . . No eye pitied thee, to do any of these to thee, to have compassion upon thee; but thou wast cast out in the open field, to the lothing of thy person, in the day that thou wast born.

And when I passed by thee, and saw thee polluted in thy own blood, I said to thee . . . Live. . . . I have caused thee to multiply as the bud of the field, and thou hast increased and become great, and thou art come to excellent ornaments: thy breasts are fashioned, and thy hair is grown, though thou wast naked and bare. Now when I passed by thee, and looked upon thee, behold, thy time was the time of love; and I spread my skirt over thee [a euphemism for sexual relations], and covered thy nakedness: yea, I swore to thee, and entered into a covenant with thee, saith the Lord GOD, and thou becamest mine. Then I washed thee with water; yea, I thoroughly washed away thy blood from thee, and I anointed thee with oil. I clothed thee also with embroidered work . . . and I girded thee with fine linen, and I covered thee with silk. I decked thee also with ornaments, and I put bracelets upon thy hands, and a chain on thy neck. And I put a jewel on thy forehead, and earrings in thy ears, and a beautiful crown upon thy head. . . . Thou didst eat fine flour, and honey, and oil, thou wast exceeding beautiful, and thou didst prosper into a kingdom. And thy renown went forth among the nations for thy beauty: for it was perfect through my comeliness, which I had put upon thee, saith the Lord GOD. . . .

(EZEKIEL 16:1–14)

Having used the language of a marriage covenant, this love poem takes a sudden turn. The bride that had begun as nothing and had been transformed by God's own beauty prostitutes her beauty by giving her devotion to other gods. God describes himself as a cuckolded husband. The marriage between God and the people of Jerusalem is broken by their unfaithfulness. In practical terms, the people of Israel did this by building temples in high places to pagan gods. The metaphor of prostitution is particularly appropriate because many of these temples required temple prostitutes to carry out their fertility rites before pagan gods. In that respect these pagan temples were nothing more than religious brothels, and the priests nothing more than pimps, making a living off the temple prostitutes.

But thou didst trust in thy own beauty, and didst play the harlot because of thy renown, and didst pour out thy harlotries on every one that passed by. . . . And of thy garments thou didst take, and didst deck thy high places with various colours, and didst play the harlot upon them: . . . Thou hast also taken thy fair jewels of my gold and of my silver, which I had given thee, and hast made to thyself images of men, and hast committed harlotry with them, And . . . thou hast set my oil and my incense before them. My food also which I gave thee, fine flour, and oil and honey, with which I fed thee, thou hast even set before them for a sweet savour. . . . Moreover thou hast taken thy sons and thy daughters, whom thou hast borne to me, and these hast thou sacrificed to them to be devoured. Is this . . . a small matter, That thou hast slain my children, and delivered them to cause them to pass through the fire? . . . (EZEKIEL 16:15–21)

Instead of using the material wealth with which God had blessed them to build a monotheistic nation, the people of Israel had reverted to the pagan ways of the Babylonians—even to human sacrifice. A few Jews at this time were not above killing the greatest blessing that had come out of their marriage with God—the children they had made together.

And in all thy abominations and thy harlotries thou hast not remembered the days of thy youth, when thou wast naked and bare, and wast polluted in thy blood. . . . Thou hast built thy high place [shrine] at every head of the way, and hast made thy beauty to be abhorred, and hast offered thyself to every one that passed by. . . . How weak is thy heart, saith the Lord GOD, seeing thou doest all these things, the work of an imperious harlot. . . . But as a wife that committeth adultery, who taketh strangers instead of her husband! They give gifts to all harlots: but thou givest thy gifts to all thy lovers, and hirest them, that they may come to thee on every side for thy harlotry. And thou art the opposite from other women . . . in that thou givest a reward, and no reward is given to thee. . . .

(EZEKIEL 16:22, 25, 30, 32–34)

Because the Jews were unwanted, God says, they had to humiliate themselves by paying others to commit prostitution with them (perhaps meaning they had to pay tribute to those nations whose imperial strength had impressed them):

Behold, therefore I will gather all thy lovers [the surrounding nations], with whom thou hast taken pleasure, and all them that thou hast loved, with all them that thou hast hated; I will even gather them on every side against thee, and will uncover thy nakedness to them, that they may see all thy nakedness. And I will judge thee, as women that break wedlock and shed blood are judged; and I will give thee blood in fury and jealousy. And I will also give thee into their hand, and they shall throw down thy eminent place, and shall break down thy high places: they shall strip thee also of thy clothes, and shall take thy fair jewels, and leave thee naked and bare. They shall also bring up a company against thee, and they shall stone thee with stones, and thrust thee through with their swords. And they shall burn thy houses with fire, and execute judgments upon thee in the sight of many women: and I will cause thee to cease from playing the harlot, and thou also shalt give no hire any more. So will I make my fury toward thee to rest, and my jealousy shall depart from thee, and I will be quiet, and will be no more angry. Because thou hast not remembered the days of thy youth, but hast provoked me in all these things; behold, therefore I also will recompense thy way upon thy head, saith the Lord GOD: and thou shalt not commit this lewdness above all thy abominations.

Behold, every one that useth proverbs shall use this proverb against thee, saying, As is the mother [Babylon or Canaan], so is her daughter. Thou art thy mother's daughter, that loatheth her husband and her children. . . . For thus saith the Lord GOD; I will even deal with thee as thou hast done, who hast despised the oath in breaking the covenant.

Nevertheless I will remember my covenant with thee in the days of thy youth, and I will establish to thee an everlasting covenant. Then thou shalt remember thy ways, and be ashamed, when thou shalt receive thy sisters [neighboring nations]. . . . thou also, who hast judged thy sisters, bear thy own shame for thy sins that thou hast committed more abominable than they: they are more righteous than thou. . . . when thy sisters, Sodom and her daughters, shall return to their former state, and Samaria and her daughters shall return to their former state, then thou and thy daughters shall return to your former state. For thy sister Sodom was not mentioned by thy mouth in the day of thy pride. . . . I will give them to thee for daughters, but not by thy covenant. And I will establish my covenant with thee; and thou shalt know that I am the LORD: That thou mayest remember, and be confounded, and never open thy mouth any more because of thy shame, when I am pacified toward thee for all that thou hast done, saith the Lord GOD.

(EZEKIEL 16:37–45, 52, 59–63)

Thus, the prophet Ezekiel predicted Jerusalem's first destruction at the hands of the Babylonians because the people had broken the covenant established by Moses, but he also made predictions of a new covenant to come. How appropriate, since Jerusalem turned to the pagan gods of Babylon, that Babylon should have its way with her. She would get the lover she had seduced and would be raped by him. She would, then, find her *former* lover was no longer there to protect her and would discover her illicit lover's true domineering nature. Jerusalem did what came natural to her, and Babylon would do what came natural to it in the state of human affairs.

God expressed the ramifications of Jewish idolatry in terms of a jealous human lover so the people of Jerusalem could feel their shame and change, but they did not. The resulting punishment came about entirely by human will carried out by human hands (Babylonian plans carried out by Babylonian hands). At the same time, God spoke as though he was the one bringing these things about because he chose to allow them to happen.

The destruction that eventually came upon Jerusalem was not God's way of evening the score. The only way the Jews of that time were going to understand the error of trusting in Babylon's religion was to *experience* how misplaced that trust was. Books of words had failed to turn them around, but reality communicates when words have failed. That God is not a vindictive lover is shown by how quickly he is ready to restore Jerusalem— even before Jerusalem has done anything to show change.

Because the Gentile nations had in some cases been better than God's own people, he promised to make them prosper. Their prosperity, however, would not be based on the same covenant God had with the Jews since the days of Moses. God promised a new covenant that would include the Gentile nations. Thus, the Jews will never open their mouths to speak proudly over their Gentile sisters as they had done in the past, for the Gentiles would also become a chosen people.

God Divorces His Bride

God continued to try to make his marriage with Israel work, but she repeatedly turned to her other loves. Early on, God used one his prophets, who had a similar problem with his own wife, to give Israel an official certificate of divorce as a warning. The time would soon come when God would take that certificate and sign on the dotted line:

> Plead with your mother, plead: for she is not my wife, neither am I her husband: let her therefore put away her whoredoms out of her sight, and her adulteries from between her breasts; Lest I strip her naked, and set her as in the day that she was born, and make her as a wilderness, and set her like a dry land, and slay her with thirst. And I will not have mercy upon her children; for they be the children of whoredoms. . . .
>
> (HOSEA 2:2–4)

When Israel's destruction would come, God would cease to treat her descendants as his own children. Yet, even as he described the destruction that would befall Israel under Assyria, Babylon and, finally, Rome, he spoke as a lover who cannot bear the results. He promised to call Israel back to himself someday and restore his vows, when his relationship with the Jews will be more intimate than before, but on different grounds.

> *Therefore, behold, I will allure her, and bring her into the wilderness, and speak comfortably unto her. And I will give her her vineyards from thence, and the valley of Achor for a door of hope: and she shall sing there, as in the days of her youth, and as in the day when she came up out of the land of Egypt. And it shall be at that day, saith the LORD, that thou shalt call me Ishi ["man" or "husband"]; and shalt call me no more Baali ["my Lord" but also a variation on the name of the pagan god of Babylon]. . . .*
>
> (HOSEA 2:14–16)

Under the covenant with Moses (Mosaic Covenant), God was Israel's master—the Lord God. The new covenant would be a more intimate human relationship in which God's communion with humanity would raise the stature of all the earth:

> *And in that day will I make a covenant for them with the beasts of the field, and with the fowls of heaven, and with the creeping things of the ground: and I will break the bow and the sword and the battle out of the earth, and will make them to lie down safely. And I will betroth thee unto me for ever; yea, I will betroth thee unto me in righteousness, and in judgment, and in lovingkindness, and in mercies. I will even betroth thee unto me in faithfulness: and thou shalt know the LORD. And it shall come to pass in that day, I will hear, saith the LORD, I will hear the heavens, and they shall hear the earth; And the earth shall hear the corn, and the wine, and the oil; and they shall hear Jezreel. And I will sow her unto me in the earth; and I will have mercy upon her that had not obtained mercy; and I will say to them which were not my people, Thou art my people; and they shall say, Thou art my God. . . .*
>
> (HOSEA 2:18–23)

To many Christians, God's words here express a double meaning that was not understood at the time. On the first level, God would restore the Jews, who, while they were in Babylon, were no longer his people. That's history. On a deeper level, he will take people that *never* were his chosen people and make them his people, too. God next gives real flesh to his words by asking his prophet Hosea to marry a woman who turns out to be as unfaithful to Hosea as Israel was to God. Through his love for his wife and his own loss, the prophet understands the nature of God. When Hosea's wife prostitutes herself, Hosea winds up having to buy her back from her lover, indicating that in chasing other lovers she had become enslaved—just as Israel did with Babylon. There was a cost to restoring the relationship:

Then said the LORD unto me, Go yet, love a woman beloved of her friend, yet an adulteress, according to the love of the LORD toward the children of Israel, who look to other gods, and love flagons of wine. So I bought her to me for fifteen pieces of silver, and for an homer of barley, and an half homer of barley: And I said unto her, Thou shalt abide for me many days; thou shalt not play the harlot, and thou shalt not be for another man: so will I also be for thee. For the children of Israel shall abide many days without a king, and without a prince, and without a sacrifice, and without an image, and without an ephod [a priestly garment], and without teraphim [idols— all describing the Jew's condition in Babylon]: Afterward shall the children of Israel return, and seek the LORD their God, and David their king; and shall fear the LORD and his goodness in the latter days. . . . (HOSEA 3:1–5)

In the last part of Hosea, some Christians see early hints of the messianic king predicted to come from David's line. They see within the writing the foreshadowing of later events that happened to Jesus, who rose from the dead on the third day of his death:

Come, and let us return unto the LORD: for he hath torn, and he will heal us; he hath smitten, and he will bind us up. After two days will he revive us: in the third day he will raise us up, and we shall live in his sight. Then shall we know, if we follow on to know the LORD: his going forth is prepared as the morning; and he shall come unto us as the rain, as the latter and former rain unto the earth. O Ephraim [the northern kingdom of Israel conquered by Assyria], what shall I do unto thee? O Judah [the southern kingdom conquered by Babylon], what shall I do unto thee? for your goodness is as [fleeting as] a morning cloud, and as the early dew it goeth away. Therefore have I hewed them by the prophets; I have slain them by the words of my mouth: and thy judgments are as the light that goeth forth. . . .

Set the trumpet to thy mouth. He shall come as an eagle [perhaps meaning swiftly and fiercely or perhaps also alluding further ahead to the insignia of Rome carried before the armies of Titus] against the house of the LORD, because they have transgressed my covenant, and trespassed against my law. Israel shall cry unto me, My God, we know thee. Israel hath cast off the thing that is good: the enemy shall pursue him. . . . Israel is swallowed up: now shall they be among the Gentiles as a vessel wherein is no pleasure. (HOSEA 6:1–5; 8:1–2)

I the LORD have called thee in righteousness, and will hold thy hand, and will keep thee, and give thee for a covenant of the people, for a light of the Gentiles; To open the blind eyes, to bring out the prisoners from the prison, and them that sit in darkness out of the prison house. (ISAIAH 42:6, 7)

Because some were faithful to God's calling, the words of the prophets continue to enlighten the world today. But the majority of the nation was not productive in fulfilling God's purpose:

As a woman with child, that draweth
near the time of her delivery, is in pain,
and crieth out in her pangs; so have we
been in thy sight, O LORD. We have
been with child, we have been in pain,

we have as it were brought forth wind;
we have not wrought any deliverance
on the earth; neither have the inhabitants of the world fallen.

(ISAIAH 26:17, 18)

Because the majority of God's people failed to see the truth, God said that the
people who had been called to be a light would be left in spiritual darkness for awhile
themselves. They would fail to comprehend the words of their own prophets:

*Stay yourselves, and wonder; cry ye out,
and cry: they are drunk, but not with
wine; they stagger, but not with strong
drink. For the LORD hath poured out
upon you the spirit of deep sleep, and
hath closed your eyes: the prophets and
your rulers, the seers hath he covered.
And the vision of all is become to you as
the words of a book that is sealed, which
men deliver to one that is learned, saying, Read this, I pray thee: and he saith, I
cannot; for it is sealed: And the book is
delivered to him that is not learned, saying, Read this, I pray thee: and he saith, I
am not learned. Therefore the Lord said,*

*Forasmuch as this people draw near me
with their mouth, and with their lips do
honour me, but have removed their
heart far from me, and their fear toward
me is taught by the precept of men:
Therefore, behold, I will proceed to do a
marvelous work among this people, even
a marvelous work and a wonder: for the
wisdom of their wise men shall perish,
and the understanding of their prudent
men shall be hid. And in that day shall
the deaf hear the words of the book, and
the eyes of the blind shall see out of obscurity, and out of darkness.*

(ISAIAH 29:9–14, 18)

After many centuries of failing to rise to their national calling, God eventually let
Assyria have its way with the northern half of the Israel. When the southern half did not
learn by watching, he let Babylon finish their destruction.

GOD ESTABLISHES A NEW COVENANT
AND A NEW PEOPLE

Having divorced Israel, God spoke through another prophet, foretelling a new covenant:

*Behold, the days come, saith the LORD,
that I will make a new covenant with the
house of Israel [captured by Assyria],
and with the house of Judah [captured
later by Babylon]: Not according to the
covenant that I made with their fathers
in the day that I took them by the hand*

*to bring them out of the land of Egypt;
which my covenant they broke, although
I was an husband to them, saith the
LORD: But this shall be the covenant
that I will make with the house of Israel;
After those days, saith the LORD, I will
put my law in their inward parts, and*

write it in their hearts; and will be their God, and they shall be my people. And they shall teach no more every man his neighbour, and every man his brother, saying, Know the LORD: for they shall all know me, from the least of them to the greatest of them, saith the LORD: for I will forgive their iniquity, and I will remember their sin no more. Thus saith the LORD, who giveth the sun for a light by day, and the ordinances of the moon and of the stars for a light by night, who divideth the sea when its waves roar; The LORD of hosts is his name: If those ordinances depart from before me, saith the LORD, then the seed of Israel also shall cease from being a nation before me for ever. Thus saith the LORD; If heaven above can be measured, and the foundations of the earth searched out beneath, I will also cast off all the seed of Israel for all that they have done, saith the LORD.

(JEREMIAH 31:31–37).

The New Covenant would not be according to the one handed down to Moses, which contained more than five hundred laws. The New Covenant is described as a covenant of conscience, written upon each individual's heart. Therefore, all of Israel will become faithful to God because they will be guided to truth from within. The words "they shall teach no more every man his neighbour" imply a time will come when it will no longer be necessary to teach people about God, for everyone will be guided within their own spirits—not by religious laws.

Incline your ear, and come to me: hear, and your soul shall live; and I will make an everlasting covenant with you [Israel], even the sure mercies of David. Behold, I have given him for a witness to the people, a leader and commander to the people. Behold, thou shalt call a nation that thou knowest not [a Gentile people], and nations that knew not thee shall run to thee because of the LORD thy God, and for the Holy One of Israel; for he hath glorified thee.

(ISAIAH 55:3–5)

The following passage indicates that it will be God, not the Jews, who will establish another people as his own, along with the Jews under a new eternal covenant:

Neither let the son of the foreigner [Gentile], that hath joined himself to the LORD, speak, saying, The LORD hath utterly separated me from his people: neither let the eunuch say, Behold, I am a dry tree. For thus saith the LORD to the eunuchs that keep my sabbaths, and choose the things that please me, and take hold of my covenant; Even to them will I give in my house and within my walls a place and a name better than of sons and of daughters: I will give them an everlasting name, that shall not be cut off. Also the sons of the foreigner, that join themselves to the LORD, to serve him, and to love the name of the LORD, to be his servants, every one that keepeth the sabbath from profaning it, and taketh hold of my covenant; Even them will I bring to my holy mountain, and

make them joyful in my house of prayer: for all people. The Lord GOD who gath-
their burnt offerings and their sacrifices ereth the outcasts of Israel, Yet will I
shall be accepted upon my altar; for my gather others to him, besides those that
house shall be called an house of prayer are gathered to him. (ISAIAH 56:3–8)

This second passage is especially clear as to just how far God is willing to go to bring Gentiles into his new covenant. Under the Mosaic Covenant, Jewish religious law did not allow eunuchs to enter the temple of worship (Deut. 23:1). Their emasculation was considered an abomination, especially if it was done as a rite of some pagan religion. Here God clearly reveals he is changing the old laws to make way for lowest of the Gentiles to be considered his people—with a stature even higher than the Jews had under the Mosaic Covenant ("a place and a name better than of sons and of daughters")—regardless of their past. All they will need to do to be considered a part of his newly chosen people is to honor his sabbath and bond themselves to him and live justly. This describes the new revelation the prophecies had been leading toward. Like Abraham, Isaac, and Jacob, the Gentile who lives for God will be given a new name by God and a place in his temple. Since Solomon's temple was destroyed by Babylon, this could refer to the temple that was rebuilt in its place (though that was destroyed by Titus) or, by analogy, to spiritual existence in God's presence (heaven), symbolized in the temple architecture. The prophecy contains the seeds of a huge reformation that would sweep over the Jewish religion—something greater than Israel had before, which will extend to *all* people.

The promises in the covenant that came through Moses were always conditional, but the first covenant with Abraham was called "everlasting." Just as the blessings under the Mosaic Covenant fulfilled the immediate promise of the Abrahamic Covenant, so the New Covenant will fulfill the everlasting promises of the Abrahamic Covenant, in broader terms that will include a people that was not even seeking God:

I am sought by them that asked not for number you to the sword, and ye shall all
me; I am found by them that sought me bow down to the slaughter: because
not: I said, Behold me, behold me, to a when I called, ye did not answer; when I
nation that was not called by my name. spoke, ye did not hear; but did evil before
And I will bring forth a seed out of Jacob, my eyes, and did choose that in which I
and out of Judah an inheritor of my delighted not. Therefore thus saith the
mountains: and my elect shall inherit it, Lord GOD, Behold, my servants shall
and my servants shall dwell there. And eat, but ye shall be hungry: behold, my
Sharon [a coastal plain in Israel] shall be servants shall drink, but ye shall be
a fold of flocks, and the valley of Achor a thirsty: behold, my servants shall rejoice,
place for the herds to lie down in, for my but ye shall be ashamed: Behold, my ser-
people that have sought me. But ye are vants shall sing for joy of heart, but ye
they that forsake the LORD, that forget shall cry for sorrow of heart, and shall
my holy mountain. . . . Therefore will I wail for vexation of spirit. And ye shall

leave your name for a curse to my cho-
sen: for the Lord GOD shall slay thee,
and call his servants by another name:
That he who blesseth himself in the earth
shall bless himself in the God of truth;

and he that sweareth in the earth shall
swear by the God of truth; because the
former troubles are forgotten, and be-
cause they are hid from my eyes.

(ISAIAH 65:1, 9–16)

Two groups of people are mentioned here—one that was not looking for God but will find him, another that was unfaithful and knew better and will perish. The second group represents the ancient Jews, who frequently turned away from God. The first group may represent the Jews that God restored from Babylon or it may represent a people that truly was not looking for the God of the Jews at all—the Gentile nations around Israel. A single seed—a single offspring—is predicted to rise from the Jewish tribe of Judah (King David's lineage), and the people are called to behold him—to look upon him. This one seed could refer collectively to the generation of Jews who came back from Babylon. If that's the case, it's odd that the only tribe mentioned is Judah, for two tribes are known to have returned—Judah and Levi. Alternately, the "seed" could re- fer to the leader from the line of King David described in other prophecies as a seed from Judah. In other words, the Messiah.

This prophecy and the previous one each mention the giving of a new name by God. When this renaming first happened with Abraham, Isaac, and Jacob, it marked the establishment of a covenant that became part of the individual's identity. Jacob's new name, "Israel," became the identity of God's chosen people. Reading each of the three prophecies above in the light of the others would favor an understanding where God's new people includes the Gentiles, a people not searching for the Jewish God yet finding him through a Messiah from the tribe of Judah.

The New Testament, which Christians see as the expression of the New Covenant, says that when Jesus was born in the same city as King David, God gave him his name— just as God had named the man Israel. As God had recommitted Abraham's covenant to his descendent David, God recommits his covenant with David to David's descendant, Jesus, showing the Jewish lineage through which the original promise was made true.

And the angel said to her, Fear not,
Mary: for thou hast found favour with
God. And, behold, thou shalt conceive in
thy womb, and bring forth a son, and
shalt call his name JESUS. He shall be
great, and shall be called the Son of the

Highest: and the Lord God shall give to
him the throne of his father David: And
he shall reign over the house of Jacob for
ever; and of his kingdom there shall be
no end. (LUKE 1:31–33)

For unto you is born this day in the city
of David a Saviour, which is Christ the
Lord. (LUKE 2:11)

Years later, when Jesus was anointed for his ministry by baptism, one of his future disciples immediately believed Jesus was the long-awaited Christ (Greek for "Messiah"):

He [the disciple Andrew] first findeth his own brother Simon [shortly renamed Peter], and saith unto him, We have found the Messiah, which is, being interpreted, the Christ.

(JOHN 1:41)

Perhaps this is the new name the prophets had foretold for God's new people—"Christ" as in "Christians," a name and a people that did not exist until the Jewish seed (offspring) of David walked the earth. Under the New Covenant, belonging is not by race but by faithfulness to the God of the Jews, who has become the God of all who have faith in him. One of the prophecies above even stated that the name of God's first chosen people would become a curse in the world. That may be simply a prophecy of fact, not a statement of how things ought to be. Certainly, the name "Jew" has been treated with scorn throughout the world, and not just by Christians. Again, that does not by any means justify such treatment, but if that is what the prophecy meant, it certainly came true. It has always been incomprehensibly difficult for people to be called "Jews" in this world.

Because the Abrahamic Covenant was everlasting, the New Covenant broadens its terms to include Gentiles. God promised his love for his first people would never cease. The New Covenant emerged from the Jews and certainly is intended to embrace all Jews.

The covenant that began through Abraham's faith became a religion of blood during the days of Moses—a religion of sacrifice and racial membership, where God dwelled physically in a temple made of stone. Gentiles were always separated from Jews in worship by a physical barrier that gave them an inferior position. Ancient Judaism, being so strongly tied to racial belonging, did not have true universality.

In order for Abraham's covenant to become universal so that Abraham could truly be considered "a blessing to all nations," it had to move from being a covenant in blood (race) to a covenant in faith (spirit). Because Abraham received his covenant by faith alone, the New Covenant is also received by faith alone. This makes it more inclusive than the covenant of laws given to Moses, even though all people (Jew or Gentile) must participate by faith—just like Abraham.

Abraham's grandson, Israel, was prophesied to become the father of "a nation," which he became through his twelve sons, the patriarchs of the twelve tribes of Israel. He was *also* prophesied to become the father of "a company of nations." Jacob's descendent, Jesus, could easily be said to have fulfilled this promise by making Jacob the spiritual father of a vast people who come from *all* nations—a community of nations joined in one faith.

Chapter 4

C⊙nfLiCT:

†HE RiSE OF ĴESVS AnD †HE FALL OF ĴERVSALEm

Did Daniel's prophecy regarding the "Anointed One" and the "abomination that causes desolation" connect the arrival of the Messiah with the destruction of Jerusalem under Titus, and did it have anything to do with Jesus?

When Jesus' followers proclaimed him king as he arrived at the Holy City, he mourned the desolation he foresaw:

And when he had come near, even now at the descent of the mount of Olives, the whole multitude of the disciples began to rejoice and praise God with a loud voice for all the mighty works that they had seen; Saying, Blessed be the King that cometh in the name of the Lord: peace in heaven, and glory in the highest. And some of the Pharisees from among the multitude said to him, Master, rebuke thy disciples. And he answered and said to them, I tell you that, if these should hold their peace, the stones would immediately cry out.

And when he had come near, he beheld the city, and wept over it, Saying, If thou hadst known, even thou, at least in this thy day, the things which belong to thy peace! but now they are hid from thy eyes. For the days shall come upon thee, that thy enemies shall cast a trench about thee, and surround thee, and keep thee in on every side, And shall lay thee even with the ground, and thy children within thee; and they shall not leave in thee one stone upon another; because thou knewest not the time of thy visitation. (LUKE 19:37–44)

The Pharisees had to be concerned about what the Romans would do to their city if a Jew rode in on a major holiday like Passover with a large throng proclaiming him king. Their positions of wealth and security depended on Roman favor. This was not the kind of celebration Romans were fond of:

Then the chief priests and the Pharisees gathered a council, and said, What do we? for this man performeth many miracles. If we let him thus alone, all men will believe on him: and the Romans shall come and take away both our place and nation. And one of them, named Caiaphas, being the high priest that same year, said to them, Ye know nothing at all, Nor consider that it is expedient for us, that one man should die for the people, and that the whole nation perish not. And this he spoke not of himself: but being high priest that year, he prophesied that Jesus should die for that nation; And not for that nation only, but that also he should gather together in one the children of God that were scattered abroad. Then from that day forth they took counsel together to put him to death.

(JOHN 11:47–53)

On the fateful day of his entry into Jerusalem, Jesus also foresaw his own death, stretching down the road ahead like his own shadow:

And Jesus going up to Jerusalem took the twelve disciples aside in the way, and said to them, Behold, we go up to Jerusalem; and the Son of man shall be betrayed to the chief priests and to the scribes, and they shall condemn him to death, And shall deliver him to the Gentiles to mock, and to scourge, and to crucify him: and the third day he shall rise again. (MATTHEW 20:17–19)

As a prophet, Jesus had good reason to expect rejection. According to their own writings, the ancient Jews had a tradition of rejecting their prophets—something they had been warned of by their very first prophet:

For Moses truly said to the fathers, A prophet shall the Lord your God raise up to you of your brethren, like me; him shall ye hear in all things whatever he shall say to you. And it shall come to pass, that every soul, who will not hear that prophet, shall be destroyed from among the people. Yea, and all the prophets also from Samuel and those that follow, as many as have spoken, have likewise foretold these days.

(ACTS 3:22–24 [QUOTING DEUTERONOMY 18:15–19])

In vain I punished your people; they did not respond to correction. Your sword has devoured your prophets like a ravening lion. (JEREMIAH 2:30)

And the Spirit of God came upon Zechariah the son of Jehoiada the priest, which stood above the people, and said unto them, Thus saith God, Why transgress ye the commandments of the LORD . . . because ye have forsaken the LORD, he hath also forsaken you. And they conspired against him, and stoned him with stones at the commandment of the king in the court of the house of the LORD. (2 CHRONICLES 24:20–21)

JESUS: THE FIRST REFORMED JUDAISM

Jesus' own ministry was almost exclusively to the Jews, but his reforms of the blood religion were too great for the established hierarchy to contain. The relationship between Jesus and the religious leaders (from the tribe of Levi mentioned below) was antagonistic right from the beginning—exactly as messianic prophecy said it would be:

Behold, I will send my messenger, and he shall prepare the way before me: and the Lord, whom ye seek, shall suddenly come to his temple, even the messenger of the covenant, whom ye delight in: behold, he shall come, saith the LORD of hosts. But who may abide the day of his coming? and who shall stand when he appeareth?

for he is like a refiner's fire, and like fullers' soap: And he shall sit as a refiner and purifier of silver: and he shall purify the sons of Levi, and purge them as gold and silver, that they may offer to the LORD an offering in righteousness.

(MALACHI 3:1–3)

The messenger that came before Jesus was John the Baptist, who prepared the way by direct confrontation for Jesus' introduction of the New Covenant with its controversial reforms:

But when he [John the Baptist] saw many of the Pharisees and Sadducees [the religious leaders] come to his baptism, he said to them, O generation of vipers, who hath warned you to flee from the wrath to come? Bring forth therefore fruits worthy of repentance: And think not to say within yourselves,

We have Abraham for our father: for I say to you, that God is able of these stones to raise up children to Abraham. And now also the axe is laid to the root of the trees: therefore every tree which bringeth not forth good fruit is hewn down, and cast into the fire.

(MATTHEW 3:7–10)

The New Covenant was under way, laying its axe to the roots of the old Judaism by challenging the sacrosanct notion that one could be considered the chosen of God only by birthright. John proclaimed that only those who lived righteous lives of true faith would remain standing.

When Jesus began his own ministry, he made it clear that he had not come to abolish the laws of Moses but to fulfill the spirit of that law:

Think not that I am come to destroy the law, or the prophets: I am not come to destroy, but to fulfil. For verily I say to you, Till heaven and earth shall pass

away, one jot or one tittle [i.e., the tiniest pen strokes] shall by no means pass from the law, till all be fulfilled. Whoever therefore shall break one of these least

commandments, and shall teach men so, *teach them, the same shall be called great*
he shall be called the least in the king- *in the kingdom of heaven.*
dom of heaven: but whoever shall do and (MATTHEW 5:17–19)

Nevertheless, Jesus did not find a receptive audience among the leaders. In his own words, one "cannot put new wine into old wineskins." Because the old wineskins have lost their ability to stretch, they will burst when the new wine begins to ferment. The watershed moment in Jesus' ministry arrived when the religious leaders burst out against him declaring he had a demonic spirit because he could cast out demons.

Jesus, knowing that the Spirit within him was God's Holy Spirit, said:

He that is not with me is against me; and *men. And whoever speaketh a word*
he that gathereth not with me scattereth *against the Son of man, it shall be for-*
abroad. Therefore I say to you, All man- *given him: but whoever speaketh against*
ner of sin and blasphemy shall be for- *the Holy Spirit, it shall not be forgiven*
given to men: but the blasphemy against *him, neither in this world, neither in the*
the Holy Spirit shall not be forgiven to *world to come.* (MATTHEW 12:30–32)

The importance of this message is often misunderstood. What Jesus was saying was that anyone could say anything they wanted about him as a *man*, and it did not matter. By claiming his spirit was demonic, however, they failed to recognize his *divinity*. He was stating that everyone must recognize the true spirit of the Messiah to be included in the New Covenant:

[A non-Jewish] woman saith to him, Sir, *cometh, and now is, when the true wor-*
I perceive that thou art a prophet. Our *shippers shall worship the Father in*
fathers worshipped in this mountain; *spirit and in truth: for the Father seeketh*
and ye [the Jews] say, that in Jerusalem *such to worship him. God is a Spirit: and*
is the place where men ought to worship. *they that worship him must worship him*
Jesus saith to her, Woman, believe me, *in spirit and in truth. The woman saith*
the hour cometh, when ye shall neither *to him, I know that Messiah cometh,*
in this mountain, nor yet at Jerusalem, *who is called Christ: when he is come, he*
worship the Father. Ye worship ye know *will tell us all things. Jesus saith to her, I*
not what: we know what we worship: for *that speak to thee am he.*
salvation is from the Jews. But the hour (JOHN 4:19–26)

The unforgivable sin was failure to recognize Jesus' divine Spirit, for the New Covenant was based solely on spiritual membership. One's spirit cannot commune with the Divine Spirit if it cannot even recognize Him.

From the moment the Pharisees accused him of being demonic, Jesus began to speak to the Jews in parables. Though his ministry was still to the Jews, only those who really wanted truth could understand his words. This, too, was a fulfillment of Old Testament prophecies, where God had told his prophets a time was coming when the Jews would be ever listening but never understanding his message. This watershed in Jesus' ministry is evident by the disciples' surprise at the way he was now speaking:

And the disciples came, and said to him, Why speakest thou to them in parables? He answered and said to them, Because it is given to you to know the mysteries of the kingdom of heaven, but to them it is not given. For whoever hath, to him shall be given, and he shall have more abundance: but whoever hath not, from him shall be taken away even that which he hath. Therefore I speak to them in parables: because they seeing see not; and hearing they hear not, neither do they understand. And in them is fulfilled the prophecy of Isaiah, which saith, By hearing ye shall hear, and shall not understand; and seeing ye shall see, and shall not perceive: For this people's heart has become dull, and their ears are hard of hearing, and their eyes they have closed; lest at any time they should see with their eyes, and hear with their ears, and should understand with their heart, and should be converted, and I should heal them. . . . That it might be fulfilled which was spoken by the prophet, saying, I will open my mouth in parables; I will utter things which have been kept secret from the foundation of the world.

(MATTHEW 13:10–15)

Jesus was saying that those who have a little understanding of who he is, such as his disciples, will be given more because they want the truth, but he speaks in parables so that those who have rejected him will not be able to see the truth. One must genuinely want the truth to find it in a parable.

The reason for this goes back to the time when God foretold through an earlier parable that he would reject his people because, after all the blessings he had given to their tiny nation, they remained unfaithful and fruitless as a nation:

Now will I sing to my wellbeloved a song of my beloved concerning his vineyard. My wellbeloved hath a vineyard in a very fruitful hill: And he dug it, and removed its stones, and planted it with the choicest vine, and built a tower in the midst of it, and also made a winepress in it: and he expected that it should bring forth grapes, and it brought forth wild grapes. And now, O inhabitants of Jerusalem, and men of Judah, judge, I pray you, between me and my vineyard. What more could have been done to my vineyard, that I have not done in it? Why, when I expected that it should bring forth grapes, brought it forth wild grapes? And now come; I will tell you what I will do to my vineyard: I will take away its hedge, and it shall be eaten up; and break down the wall of it, and it shall be trodden down: And I will lay it waste: it shall not be pruned, nor dug; but there shall come up briers and thorns: I will also command the clouds that they rain no rain upon it. For the vineyard of the LORD of hosts is the house of Israel, and the men of Judah his pleasant plant: and he looked for judgment [justice], but behold oppression; for righteousness, but behold a cry. Therefore my people have gone into captivity, because they have no knowledge: and their honourable men are famished, and their multitude dried up with thirst. Therefore hell hath enlarged herself, and opened her mouth without measure: and their glory, and their multitude, and their pomp, and he that rejoiceth, shall descend into it.

(ISAIAH 5:1–7, 13, 14)

When God removed his protection (his "hedge") from around Israel so that Babylon could destroy it, he rejected them. Then, as Hosea had prophesied, God called his people again into the desert to speak love to them, and he restored them. Again, the pattern of unfaithfulness began to repeat itself. Many individual Jews had been paramount in their faithfulness, bringing a tremendous gift of spiritual knowledge into the world with elegant poetry and enduring words, but the nation's leadership regularly steered away from God, taking the majority of the people with them. The faithful were usually a remnant of the total nation.

In Jesus' view, the pattern of leadership that could not see the importance of justice over law, mercy over justice, love over all, was happening again. If he was the Messiah, as he claimed to the non-Jewish woman, then they had even failed to recognize their Messiah. So his change toward speaking in parables marked his rejection of the establishment for rejecting him. He even declared his rejection of them in a parable that alluded to the vineyard story of Isaiah, in which the vinedressers represent the religious leaders to whom God had entrusted the spiritual care of Israel (the vineyard), and the servants represent the Jewish prophets:

Then he began to speak to the people this parable; A certain man planted a vineyard, and let it out to vinedressers, and went into a far country for a long time. And at the season he sent a servant to the vinedressers, that they should give him of the fruit of the vineyard: but the vinedressers beat him, and sent him away empty. And again he sent another servant: and they beat him also, and treated him shamefully, and sent him away empty. And again he sent the third: and they wounded him also, and cast him out. Then said the lord of the vineyard, What shall I do? I will send my beloved son: it may be when they see him they will reverence him. But when the vinedressers saw him, they reasoned among themselves, saying, This is the heir: come, let us kill him, that the inheritance may be ours. So they cast him out of the vineyard, and killed him. What therefore shall the lord of the vineyard do to them?

(LUKE 20:9–15)

. . . [The people responded to Jesus], He will miserably destroy those wicked men, and will let out his vineyard to other vinedressers, who shall render him the fruits in their seasons. Jesus saith to them, Did ye never read in the scriptures, The stone which the builders rejected, the same is become the head of the *corner: this is the Lord's doing, and it is marvelous in our eyes? Therefore I say to you, The kingdom of God shall be taken from you, and given to a nation bringing forth the fruits of it. And whoever shall fall on this stone shall be broken: but on whomever it shall fall, it will grind him to powder. And when the chief priests and Pharisees had heard his parables, they perceived that he spoke of them. But when they sought to lay hands on him, they feared the multitude, because they [the multitude] regarded him as a prophet.* (MATTHEW 21:41–46)

Because the Jewish leaders had frequently rejected the prophets in the past and now rejected Jesus, God would entrust his truth to another nation, meaning the Gentiles. Here began the "community of nations" promised to Abraham from the very beginning—a community of faith pulled together from many nations

The cornerstone Jesus alludes to is the best rock in the pile. In construction, the cornerstone is selected for its perfection in order to be set into the wall, engraved with the name of the building, perhaps the names of the principal builders, and the construction date. So the very stone the builders of the Jewish nation rejected turned out to be the most important one—the Messiah.

Jesus made a similar prediction in abrupt terms when a Roman (Gentile) official showed more faith in him than he had seen from his own people:

When Jesus heard it [the Roman's statement of faith], he marvelled, and said to them that followed, Verily I say to you, I have not found so great faith, no, not in Israel. And I say to you, That many shall come from the east and the west, and shall sit down with Abraham, and Isaac, and Jacob, in the kingdom of heaven. But the children of the kingdom shall be cast out into outer darkness: there shall be weeping and gnashing of teeth. (MATTHEW 8:10–12)

Being a descendant of "Abraham, and Isaac, and Jacob" is the precise definition of a Jew. In other words, those from Gentile nations will be united with the fathers of the Jews (be joined to the very essence of Jewishness) while those who had long considered themselves God's children of the kingdom would be cast out in torment. This could mean cast out of the land, as happened later under Titus, or cast out of the heavenly kingdom. The key to inclusion in the new "nation" is not race but faith, for it was the faith of the Roman official that led to Jesus' prophecy.

Jesus' rejection of the nation of Israel was not a rejection of Jews as individuals. It was a rejection of any special claims based on Jewish nationality. His ministry continued to be almost exclusively to the Jews, giving every individual opportunity, but he immediately told his disciples to reject any Jewish individual that did not welcome them and their message:

These twelve Jesus sent forth, and commanded them, saying, Go not into the way of the Gentiles, and enter ye not into any city of the Samaritans [distant cousins of the Jews]: But go rather to the lost sheep of the house of Israel [i.e., Jews only]. And as ye go, preach, saying, The kingdom of heaven is at hand. . . . And whoever shall not receive you, nor hear your words, when ye depart from that house or city, shake off the dust of your feet. Verily I say to you, It shall be more tolerable for the land of Sodom and Gomorrah [pagan cities] in the day of judgment, than for that city.

(MATTHEW 10:5–7, 14, 15)

Jews told them the kingdom of heaven was near because he was near. Citizenship in his kingdom was as near as their willingness to receive him, and if all received him, perhaps the end would have come in that generation.

But the end came another way, as later described by Peter:

The God of Abraham, and of Isaac, and of Jacob, the God of our fathers, hath glorified his Son Jesus; whom ye [Peter's fellow Jews] delivered up, and denied him in the presence of Pilate, when he was determined to let him go. But ye denied the Holy One and the Just, and desired a murderer to be granted to you; And killed the Prince of life, whom God hath raised from the dead; to which we are witnesses. . . . And now, brethren, I know that through ignorance ye did it, as did also your rulers. But those things, which God before had shown by the mouth of all his prophets, that Christ should suffer, he hath so fulfilled. Repent ye therefore, and be converted, that your sins may be blotted out, when the times of refreshing shall come from the presence of the Lord; And he shall send Jesus Christ, who before was preached to you: Whom the heaven must receive until the times of restitution of all things, which God hath spoken by the mouth of all his holy prophets since the world began. . . . Ye are the children of the prophets, and of the covenant which God made with our fathers, saying to Abraham, And in thy seed shall all the kindreds of the earth be blessed.

(ACTS 3:13–15, 17–21, 25)

There is an interesting thought buried within Peter's accusation against the Jews for Jesus' crucifixion: He implies that Jesus will return when the Jews are willing to accept him fully. He refers to Jesus' second coming as a time of restitution.

Though the crucifixion was carried out by Roman hands, Peter did not absolve his countrymen for their complicity in it. On the other hand, he *does* allow that they acted out of ignorance, implying their actions were not due to a mean spirit. Though he is accusing them, he is not bitter. Because he was speaking at the temple to the very people involved, his criticism is measured and appropriate.

Peter was a Jew and spent his whole life preaching a message of reconciliation to the Jews. Like Jesus, however, he stated the truth of a situation in a forthright manner, and if someone doesn't like the truth, they're liable to hate the message bearer. The result was inevitable alienation, which Jesus himself had prophesied to his followers:

> *Remember the word that I said to you, The servant is not greater than his lord. If they have persecuted me, they will also persecute you; if they have kept my say-ing, they will keep yours also. But all these things will they do to you for my name's sake, because they know not him that sent me.* (JOHN 15:20, 21)

THE PERSECUTED

Because the nation rejected Jesus and his reformed Judaism to the point of seeking his death, his truth was finally given to the Gentiles. As a nation, the Jews had rejected Jesus:

> *Then Paul and Barnabas became bold, and said, It was necessary that the word of God should first be spoken to you [Jews]: but seeing ye reject it, and judge yourselves unworthy of everlasting life, lo, we turn to the Gentiles. For so hath the Lord commanded us, saying, I have set thee to be a light of the Gentiles, that thou shouldest be for salvation to the ends of the earth. . . . But the Jews stirred up the devout and honourable women, and the chief men of the city, and raised persecution against Paul and Barnabas, and expelled them from their region.* (ACTS 13:46, 47, 50)

Paul became the chief proponent of the New Covenant as it went out to the Gentiles, clarifying the latent meanings that were layered in the Old Testament prophecies quoted earlier regarding the Jews being a light to the Gentiles. He narrowed the focus of the prophecies to show that what they really promised was that a few specific Jews—those who followed the Messiah—would be a light to the Gentiles:

> For the scripture saith, Whoever believeth on him shall not be ashamed. For there is no difference between the Jew and the Greek: for the same Lord over all is rich to all that call upon him. For whoever shall call upon the name of the Lord shall be saved. (ROMANS 10:11–13)

> . . . Those who are led by the Spirit of God are sons of God. . . . you received the Spirit of sonship. And by him we cry, "Abba [Papa], Father." . . . Now if we are children, then we are heirs—heirs of God and co-heirs with Christ, if indeed we share in his sufferings in order that we may also share in his glory. (ROMANS 8:14–17)

Paul taught that the inheritance promised to Abraham's seed was now mutually shared by those who join the New Covenant through spiritual membership as sons and daughters of God. God no longer drew distinctions between Jews and Gentiles. As long as the nation of Israel remained in existence, however, Paul continued taking his message to the Jews first. In most cases the Jews in a city rejected him, at which point he would speak almost exclusively to the Gentiles of the city.

Understandably, many Jews felt the Christian sect of Judaism was preempting their religion, leaving no place for them in God's plan. This conflict led to lethal persecution. A writer named Hegesippus lived in the time of the apostles and wrote about the martyrdom of Jesus' brother James (one of the New Testament writers and the first Christian bishop of Jerusalem). James died at the hands of Jewish Pharisees who threw him from the temple parapet:

> So they went up and threw down the Righteous one. Then they said to each other "Let us stone James the Righteous," and began to stone him, as in spite of his fall he was still alive. But he turned and knelt, uttering the words; "I beseech Thee, Lord God and Father, forgive them; they do not know what they are doing." While they pelted him with stones, one . . . called out: "Stop! what are you doing? the Righteous one is praying for you." Then one of them . . . took the club . . . and brought it down on the head of the Righteous one. . . .
>
> . . . Immediately after this Vespasian began to besiege them.[1]

James could ask for forgiveness on behalf of his countrymen while he was being killed, just as Jesus had done on the cross, because he knew that in their own minds they were ardently defending the truth of their religion. He had been there. The New Testament records that in his own past James had been unable to believe his brother was the Messiah. An appearance of the resurrected Jesus seems to have changed James' mind. Now he died because he did believe. Hegesippus' account of the death of James is also corroborated by the Jewish historian Josephus.

(It should be noted that some scholars believe "Hegesippus" was just a wildly embellished plagiarism of Josephus along with a bad name translation. Josephus's account of James's accusers mentions nothing about a fall from the tower and leaves the question hanging as to whether or not James actually was stoned to death. It also mentions a number of good Jews who tried to save James from the high priest. In either account, however, the religious leaders were out to get him.) At least two other Christians had been killed by their fellow Jews before James, but James was the last Christian known to have his blood flow onto the stones of Jerusalem before it was destroyed. The small rift between Jews widened into a chasm when Christians saw the writing on the wall for Jerusalem and surrounding Judea (part of ancient Israel) and began to flee. The great diaspora of the Jews in 586 B.C. had spread Jews and Jewish beliefs across the planet. The original Jews for Jesus fleeing Jerusalem and Judea just ahead of the spreading fire of Roman troops now further spread Jewish ideas. Because their message had already found more fertile ground among the Greeks, who always loved a new philosophy, many migrated to parts of the former Greek empire. Thus, the coming winds of war helped blow the seeds of messianic belief farther afield.

THE END IS NEAR

Whether by coincidence or not, the Jewish troubles with Rome that led to the fall of Jerusalem began escalating right after Jesus was killed. Ironically, they had begun as a result of a Roman decree carried out by Jesus' executioner, Pilate. Pilate had been ordered by Tiberius Caesar to set up images of the divine Caesar in the Holy City of Jerusalem. This was an act intolerable to the Pharisees who, in their wish for security within the city, had conspired to plot Jesus' death.

Early Christian historians saw Pilate's involvement as a sign of poetic (and divine) justice. As Peter indicated above, a mob of Jews had demanded Jesus' death. Because Jesus was inconsequential to Pilate, he reluctantly gave in to quell the mob. Josephus, the Pharisee who recorded the entire scope of Jewish troubles, corroborates the New Testament's account of Jesus' death:

> Now there was about this time Jesus, a wise man, if it be lawful to call him a man, for he was a doer of wonderful works—a teacher of such men as receive the truth with pleasure. He drew over to him both many of the Jews, and many of the Gentiles. He was [the] Christ; and when Pilate, at the suggestion of the principal men amongst us, had condemned him to the cross, those that loved him at the first did not forsake him, for he appeared to them alive again the third day, as the divine prophets had foretold these and ten thousand other wonderful things concerning him; and the tribe of Christians, so named from him, are not extinct at this day.[2]

Modern Jewish skeptics have maintained words were added to Josephus' history by Christians in later years because a Pharisee would never have written such things, which is a plausible argument. There is, however, no evidence to support it. All known ancient manuscripts contain the account of Jesus Christ and his crucifixion (though one Arabic version says Jesus "was *perhaps* the messiah," rather than "he was the Christ").

Other secular evidence, besides that of Josephus, lends support to the New Testament view of religious persecution against Jesus by his fellow Jews. The archives of Edessa, a Mesopotamian city several hundred miles north of Jerusalem, document a letter from the king of Edessa to Jesus. Eusebius, the bishop of Caesarea (circa A.D. 300), claimed to have seen the record of this letter and translated it word for word in his *History of the Church:*

> Abgar Uchama, the Toparch, to Jesus, who has appeared as a gracious saviour in the region of Jerusalem—greeting.
>   . . . I have heard about you and about the cures you perform without drugs or herbs. . . . When I heard all this about you, I concluded that one of two things must be true—either you are God and came down from heaven to do these things, or you are God's Son doing them. Accordingly, I am writing to get you to come to me, whatever the inconvenience, and cure the disorder from which I suffer. I may add that I understand the Jews are treating you with contempt and desire to injure you: my city is very small, but highly esteemed, adequate for both of us.[3]

According to this document, Jesus dictated a response, which was returned by messenger to Edessa:

> Happy are you who believed in me without having seen me! For it is written of me that those who have seen me will not believe in me, and that those who have not seen will believe and live. As to your request that I should come to you, I must complete all that I was sent to do here, and on completing it must at once be taken up to the One who sent me. When I have been taken up I will send you one of my disciples to cure your disorder and bring life to you and those with you.[4]

As with the Josephus account, this sounds like an early Christian fabrication (being too good to be true). Yet, the record Eusebius quoted from still survives in its original Syriac language (according to footnotes by his recent translator, who claims to have travelled to see it and to have gained possession of a copy). Whether or not the original letters existed as recorded cannot be proven, but the document that records them appears authentically Mesopotamian. Since Josephus states (almost two hundred years before Eusebius lived) that regular contact existed between Jerusalem and the Jews of northern Mesopotamia, such an interchange is plausible.

Another irony of history was that the siege of Jerusalem began during Passover—the holiday when Jesus was executed. The most interesting aspect of its timing, however, is that the Roman siege began forty years after Jesus' death.

Forty, to the Jews, was a mystical number: It was the number of days specified for mourning the embalmed dead while they were in Egypt. It was the number of days God punished the earth with rain during Noah's flood. It was the number of days Moses waited on Mt. Sinai for God to give him the new Jewish religion. It was the number of years the Jews wandered in the wilderness as punishment for rejecting the promised land because they lacked faith. Forty was the maximum number of lashings allowed as punishment under Jewish law. The prophet Elijah fasted forty days before God revealed himself. Forty was the number of years Israel suffered under the Philistines when they finally went to occupy the promised land, and it was the number of years King David reigned over Israel after defeating the Philistines. It was also the number of days the Philistine giant, Goliath, persecuted Israel before David killed him. To Christian Jews, forty years was the perfect number of years for mourning the death of their rejected Messiah until the punishment of Jerusalem drove the infant religion out of the land.

The beginning of the siege is well established as A.D. 70. Usually Christ's death is placed at A.D. 33, but there's enough uncertainty about that date that Eusebius, living much closer to the event, could be right in placing it at the equivalent of A.D. 30. Even if Jesus' death was in A.D. 33, the war against the Jews did not really end until Masada in A.D. 73. So, there are *exactly* forty years between the death of Jesus and the destruction of Jerusalem, *or* there are forty years (within a few months) between his death and the end of the war.

As though under divine protection, Jesus' followers escaped the Jerusalem holocaust entirely. They had been forewarned in his final prophecy to flee to the mountains as soon as they saw signs of armies in the area around Jerusalem. According to Eusebius, all Christians in Jerusalem fled to Pella, a city right at the edge of the mountains that remained just outside the area of Roman military action.

DID JERUSALEM FALL BY DIVINE JUDGMENT?

Perhaps the strongest witness that the destruction of Jerusalem was a judgment by God came from the lips of Eleazar, commander of the Jewish rebels. After Jerusalem fell and the original rebels escaped to the high fortress Masada, Eleazar gave the following speech just before the Romans breached the fortress walls:

> We were the very first that revolted [against the Romans], and we are the last that fight against them. . . . It is very plain that we shall be taken within a day's time. . . . Nor can we propose any more to fight them and beat them:
>
> . . . God, who had of old taken the Jewish nation into his favor, had now condemned to destruction; for had he either continued favorable, or been but in a lesser degree displeased with us, he had not overlooked the destruction of so many men, or delivered his most holy city to be burnt and demolished by our enemies.
>
> . . . Wherefore, consider how God hath convinced us that our hopes were in vain, by bringing such distress upon us in the desperate state we are now in, and which is beyond all our expectations; for the nature of this fortress, which was in

itself unconquerable, hath not proved a means of our deliverance.... We are openly deprived by God himself of all hope of deliverance; for that fire which was driven upon our enemies did not, of its own accord, turn back upon the wall which we had built: this was the effect of God's anger against us for our manifold sins, which we have been guilty of in a most insolent manner with regard to our own countrymen.

...And where is now that great city, the metropolis of the Jewish nation, which was fortified by so many walls round about, which had so many fortresses and large towers to defend it, which could hardly contain the instruments prepared for war, and which had so many ten thousands of men to fight for it? Where is this city that was believed to have God himself inhabiting therein? It is now demolished to the very foundations; and hath nothing but that monument of it preserved, I mean the camp of those that have destroyed it, which still dwells upon its ruins.... And I cannot but wish that we had all died before we had seen that holy city demolished by the hands of our enemies, or the foundations of our holy temple dug up after so profane a manner.... Let us pity ourselves for we are born to die.[5]

In the Jewish mind, the land of Israel had been guaranteed by God as an eternal inheritance. To have lost the entire land and then the world's most impregnable fortress could only mean that God's favor no longer rested with the Jews. This was a desolation vastly greater than anything any Jews had ever experienced. If Babylon had once been God's agent of punishment for Jewish unfaithfulness, then what was this, being ten times greater?

After their leader's speech, the last of the zealots committed suicide, first killing their own wives and children to spare them of a worse fate at the hands of the Romans, then killing each other. Of course, the only record of these words comes from the historian Josephus, whom many Jews regard as a traitor even today. (Though it should be pointed out that his counsel to surrender to Rome was no different than that of the hero Rabbi Yochanan ben Zakkai, who is credited with the survival of Judaism after the fall of Jerusalem. Nor was Josephus' method of saving himself by prophesying that Vespasian would become Caesar any different.) Josephus received the story from a woman who survived by hiding in a cave with five children and another woman. Obviously, he lent his own eloquence to their tale:

...because the reasoning they went upon appeared to them to be very just ... the husbands tenderly embraced their wives, and took their children into their arms, and gave the longest parting kisses to them, with tears in their eyes. Yet at the same time did they complete what they had resolved on, as if they had been executed by the hands of strangers.[6]

Thus ended the seven-year revolt.

ANOTHER MESSIAH BRINGS THE END
OF THE END FOR ISRAEL

As pledged in his covenant of surrender, Titus allowed those who surrendered to remain in the land, and some Christians undoubtedly returned from Pella. In later years, around A.D. 130, a Jew named Simon Bar Kochba proclaimed himself Messiah. He insisted all Christian Jews confess that he was the true Messiah. Bar Kochba was not a man of peace as Jesus had been. So, when Jesus' followers refused to confess him as Messiah, he tried torturing them into denying Jesus. After all, there could not be two Messiahs.

Justin Martyr, who eventually became a Christian and was killed as his name implies, wrote as a contemporary of Bar Kochba:

> In the recent Jewish war, Bar Cochba, leader of the Jewish insurrection, ordered the Christians alone to be sentenced to terrible punishments if they did not deny Jesus Christ and blaspheme Him.[7]

But hadn't Jesus warned his followers this would happen?

Then shall they deliver you up to be afflicted, and shall kill you: and ye shall be hated by all nations for my name's sake. And then shall many be offended, and shall betray one another, and shall hate one another. And many false prophets shall rise, and shall deceive many. . . .

Then if any man shall say to you, Lo, here is Christ, or there; believe it not.

For false Christs will arise, and false prophets, and shall show great signs and wonders; so that, if it were possible, they would deceive the very elect. Behold, I have told you before. Therefore if they shall say to you, Behold, he is in the desert; go not forth: behold, he is in the secret chambers; believe it not.

(MATTHEW 24:9–11, 23–26)

For a second time, the words of Jesus' prophecy must have given strength and guidance to his followers, especially as Bar Kochba became popular with a vast number of the Jews of his day. Bar Kochba's strong leadership, coupled with the support of one of the most celebrated rabbis of all time, made him one of the more prominent figures in Jewish history. Rabbi Akiva, who is still considered one of the greatest scholars of the Talmud, officially validated Bar Kochba's messianic claim. Whatever fellowship had remained in the synagogues between Jesus' followers and their fellow Jews disintegrated under this new alliance.

In A.D. 132 Bar Kochba, with the spiritual support of Akiva, staged another revolt against Rome. When Bar Kochba's insurrection failed, the Romans drove the last of the Jews out of Judea and made Jewish presence upon the ashes of Jerusalem illegal. To remove the last sound of Judaism from the land, they even changed the name of the land from "Judea" to "Syria Philistina" (hence Palestine). A new Roman city was built upon the ashes of Jerusalem and named "Aelia Capitalina" after a Roman emperor, and new temples were built to Roman gods. The new city was completely pagan.

As Eleazar, the leader at Masada, had said seventy years before, it was as though the Jews were fighting against their own destiny. It would seem God had delivered them into the hands of an enemy they could not defeat no matter how bravely they tried.

THE MESSIAH CONNECTION

Early Christians referred to their times as the "last days" because they saw thousands of years of Old Testament prophecies come to fulfillment within a single generation. They looked upon the destruction of the Jerusalem temple as the end of an old covenant, creating a space for the new. It was an apocalyptic time beyond anything they had imagined in their childhood days.

All of these events that were part of ancient Israel's end times had been foreseen, according to the New Testament, by Jesus during the last days of his life. On the day that he foretold the destruction of Jerusalem and its temple, he openly declared his rejection of the Jewish leadership for what he knew was on their minds. He held the leaders guilty of all the innocent blood shed in the pages of the Jewish Bible from its beginning to its end because they were acting in the same spirit as their forefathers. He also predicted the future persecutions that would be carried out by the leadership against his own followers, as described in this chapter. Finally, he linked all of these events to his death and the impending judgment upon the city he loved and upon the generation that killed him a few days later:

> Woe to you, scribes and Pharisees, hypocrites! for ye pay tithe of mint and anise and cummin, and have omitted the weightier matters of the law, justice, mercy, and faith: these ye ought to have done, and not to leave the others undone. Ye blind guides, who strain out a gnat, and swallow a camel. . . . Woe to you, scribes and Pharisees, hypocrites! because ye build the tombs of the prophets, and garnish the sepulchres of the righteous, And say, If we had been in the days of our fathers, we would not have been partakers with them in the blood of the prophets. Therefore ye are witnesses against yourselves, that ye are the children of them who killed the prophets. Fill ye up then the measure of your fathers. Ye serpents, ye generation of vipers, how can ye escape the damnation of hell?
>
> Therefore, behold, I send to you prophets, and wise men, and scribes: and some of them ye shall kill and crucify; and some of them ye shall scourge in your synagogues, and persecute them from city to city: That upon you may

come all the righteous blood shed upon the earth, from the blood of righteous Abel to the blood of Zachariah son of Barachias, whom ye slew between the temple and the altar. Verily I say to you, All these things shall come upon this generation. O Jerusalem, Jerusalem, thou that killest the prophets, and stonest them who are sent to thee, how often would I have gathered thy children together, even as a hen gathereth her chickens under her wings, and ye would not! Behold, your house [the Holy House] is left to you desolate. For I say to you, Ye shall not see me henceforth, till ye shall say, Blessed is he that cometh in the name of the Lord. . . . And Jesus went out, and departed from the temple.

. . . Verily I say to you, This generation shall not pass, till all these things shall be fulfilled.

(MATTHEW 23:23, 24, 29–39; 24:1, 34)

Chapter 5

RESTORATION:

A Land and People
Reunited in Modern Times

One of the modern ironies in the destruction of the Jerusalem temple was that Christians had been persecuted by their Jewish countrymen for breaking away from some of the religious laws. Most notably, the Christians claimed animal sacrifices were no longer essential for forgiveness of sins. Because the temple was the only place sacrifice was allowed by Jewish custom, once it was gone, *all* Jews broke away from the same religious laws.

After the fall of the temple, but prior to Bar Kochba's final rebellion, Rabbi Yochanan ben Zakkai began to reform Judaism to fit the needs of the people in the diaspora. He reminded his countrymen that the prophets had said on God's behalf, "I desire mercy, not sacrifice." Ben Zakkai taught that loving-kindness superseded sacrifice as the way to honor God.

This was the same message that had brought Christian Jews into disrepute. Of course, the Christians said more than love your enemies and forget about animal sacrifices. There was the acceptance of Jesus as the Messiah. With the arrival of Bar Kochba, however, almost all Jews believed in a messiah. The gap between the Christian sect and the rest of the Jews in terms of actual religious practice was closing. Perhaps, because Bar Kochba came as a great warrior against the hated Romans, he seemed more like a messiah.

The Christian Jews had also caused considerable upset by claiming that it was no longer necessary to follow Jewish dietary laws in order to please God. Now, in the twentieth century, many Reformed Jews are saying the same thing. Like Christianity, Reformed Judaism has moved toward becoming a religion of ethics instead of a religion of laws. It would almost seem Jesus was a man ahead of his times. He had moved toward the prophets' emphasis on justice, charity, and love for God two thousand years before many were ready to hear it.

All of this brings Reformed Judaism and Christianity nearer in the present time, except for the defining question of whether or not Jesus is the Messiah and what it means to be the Messiah. The crushing defeats of Bar Kochba and the earlier rebels are a good example of why a warrior messiah was not God's way for Israel. Under Bar Kochba, the entire nation was destroyed because one man honored himself and war. In Jesus, one man lost his life honoring others and love. In Bar Kochba, the entire movement ended with his death. In Jesus, the movement came to life through his death.

The statue in Nebuchadnezzar's prophetic dream revealed that human politics would never lead to an eternal kingdom for Israel. One kingdom would always conquer another until all kingdoms would someday be conquered by something "not cut out by [human] hands"—in other words, something divine. The only sword used to establish God's eternal kingdom would be the sword of truth, grasped by those who voluntarily submit to it. As though to illustrate the point, one of Jesus' disciples pulled out a real sword and cut off someone's ear on the night the Jewish leaders and Roman officials came to capture Jesus, but Jesus healed the ear and told his disciple to leave the sword alone.

THE RESTORATION OF ISRAEL: A MODERN SIGN?

If the *destruction* Jesus predicted for Israel was connected with his departure, then it would seem very likely that the *restoration* of Israel in the twentieth century would be connected with his return—especially since Jesus himself spoke of both events in the same context when he rejected the Jewish leaders and walked out of the temple.

There is, in fact, a messianic prophecy in the Old Testament that implies the same connections, linking the siege of Jerusalem with the Messiah's rejection of Israel and the Messiah's return with Israel's restoration. The Messiah is described as one who is born in Bethlehem yet has been around forever; and the prophecy indicates he will reject the children of Israel until the land is reborn and the scattered remant of Jews returns to it:

> *Now gather thyself in troops, O daughter of troops: he hath laid siege against us: they shall smite the judge of Israel with a rod upon the cheek. But thou, Bethlehem Ephratah, though thou art little among the thousands of Judah [the tribe of King David], yet out of thee shall he come forth to me that is to be ruler in Israel; whose goings forth have been from of old, from everlasting. Therefore will he give them up, until the time that she who travaileth [a phrase used in another prophecy predicting the restoration of Israel] hath brought forth: then the remnant of his brethren shall return to the children of Israel.* (MICAH 5:1–3)

The restoration of Israel was a highly prophesied event. Just as numerous prophecies said God would scatter the Jews to the four winds for their unfaithfulness, many more prophecies predicted God would bring the dispersed Jews back into the land of Israel:

> *If they shall confess their iniquity, and the iniquity of their fathers, with their trespass which they trespassed against me, and that also they have walked contrary to me; And that I also have walked contrary to them, and have brought them into the land of their enemies; if then their uncircumcised hearts shall be humbled, and they then accept of the punishment of their iniquity: Then will I remember my covenant with Jacob, and also my covenant with Isaac, and also my covenant with Abraham will I remember; and I will remember the land. The land also shall be left by them, and shall enjoy her sabbaths, while she lieth desolate without them: and they shall accept of the punishment of their iniquity: because, even because they despised my judgments, and because their soul abhorred my statutes.*
>
> (LEVITICUS 26:40–43)

About two thousand years of human history preceded Abraham. Following that age of paganism, God and Israel went through their strained marriage for another two thousand years. Then came the great divorce, and the Jews were driven out of the land, and for nearly two thousand years the land has enjoyed its sabbath rest, lying fallow and sparsely populated. During the entire time of the diaspora, the prophets also have enjoyed their rest because God discontinued speaking to Israel through prophets—as he had forewarned.

After so long a time, most of the world thought the prophecies that foretold the restoration of the Jewish homeland would never prove true. The Jews had lived out of Israel for so many centuries, and many had set up good businesses for themselves. Would they even want to return to such a barren wasteland? Meanwhile, the Arabs had occupied the land for so many centuries, they would never give it up. But the prophecies, themselves, kept the Zionist hope alive.

Following the longest divine silence in Jewish history, some of these ancient prophecies appear to have begun their dark and mysterious turnings again:

> *Since thou hast been precious in my sight, thou hast been honourable, and I have loved thee: therefore will I give men for thee, and people for thy life. Fear not: for I am with thee: I will bring thy seed from the east, and gather thee from the west; I will say to the north, Give up; and to the south, Keep not back: bring my sons from far, and my daughters from the ends of the earth; Even every one that is called by my name: for I have created him for my glory, I have formed him; verily, I have made him. Bring forth the blind people that have eyes, and the deaf that have ears. Let all the nations be gathered together, and let the people be assembled: who among them can declare this, and show us former things? let them bring forth their witnesses, that they may be justified: or let them hear, and say, It is truth.*
>
> (ISAIAH 43:4–9)

The time Israel was restored from Babylon following Isaiah's writing hardly fits the breadth of his description. The prophecy predicts the Jews would return from "the ends of the earth." Even if one diminishes "the ends of the earth" to mean "the ends of the *known* earth," that doesn't explain how they would return from the west. To the west of Israel there was only the sea. No Jews were exiled in the west until the diaspora of A.D. 70, when when Jews began gradual migration throughout the world. Therefore, no Jews returned from the west prior to the diaspora.

This prophecy hints that the spiritual blindness the prophets had predicted and Jesus had affirmed will be brought to an end during the time of Israel's restoration. It also states that all the nations would be gathered together to witness the restoration of Israel.

After World War I, in 1917, the Balfour Declaration by Great Britain gave Jews the right to return to Palestine and live there under British rule. This breath of air gave life to the small flame of Zionism. Following World War II, the recently formed United Nations assembled with murmurings that the Palestine Jews were about to declare statehood.

Fifty hours before the still unnamed nation was declared on May 14, 1948, President Truman asked Special Counsel Clark Clifford to make the case for U.S. recognition to the presidential cabinet, should the Jews in Palestine officially declare independence. The centerpiece of Clifford's appeal to a reluctant and, at points, hostile cabinet was a line from a prophecy in Deuteronomy in which God promised the Palestinian strip of land to Moses and his people (probably the following passage, since Clifford does not give a reference):

And the LORD thy God will bring thee into the land which thy fathers possessed, and thou shalt possess it; and he will do thee good, and multiply thee above thy fathers. (DEUTERONOMY 30:5)

The preceding part of this prophecy runs like this:

And it shall come to pass, when all these things have come upon thee, the blessing and the curse [being the desolation that was predicted], which I have set before thee, and thou shalt call them to mind among all the nations, where the LORD thy God hath driven thee, And shalt return to the LORD thy God, and shalt obey his voice according to all that I command thee this day, thou and thy children, with all thy heart, and with all thy soul; That then the LORD thy God will turn thy captivity, and have compassion upon thee, and will return and gather thee from all the nations, where the LORD thy God hath scattered thee. If any of thine shall be driven out to the outmost parts of heaven, from there will the LORD thy God gather thee, and from there will he bring thee. (DEUTERONOMY 30:1–4)

Clifford's speech was successful, and the U.S. decided to vote in favor of statehood if the Palestine Jews made such a declaration. On the afternoon of May 14, with all the nations of the earth gathered together at the United Nations general assembly, the prophecies of Isaiah and Deuteronomy were fulfilled. The remnant of a people that had almost died from the face of the earth during World War II was reborn.

The great irony of World War II was that Hitler's brutal attempt to annihilate the Jews left the survivors without a home, creating a greater need for a Jewish homeland. His brutality also garnered enough world sympathy for the Jews to make such a dream politically viable. As for Hitler, himself, the very same prophecy continues,

And the LORD thy God will put all these curses upon thy enemies, and on them that hate thee, who persecuted thee. And thou shalt return and obey the voice of the LORD, and do all his commandments which I command thee this day.
(DEUTERONOMY 30:7,8)

After the destroyer of the Jews was destroyed, the Jews exchanged their prison rags of mourning for white wedding dresses in the middle of their refugee camps. They returned to Israel in couples and replenished the barren land with children, while those Germans who had risen out of hatred to destroy them grieved over their own wasted land:

And the LORD thy God will make thee to abound in every work of thy hand, in the fruit of thy body, and in the fruit of thy cattle, and in the fruit of thy land, for good: for the LORD will again rejoice over thee for good, as he rejoiced over thy fathers: If thou shalt hearken to the voice of the LORD thy God, to keep his commandments and his statutes which are written in this book of the law, and if thou shalt turn to the LORD thy God with all thy heart, and with all thy soul. For the LORD shall judge his people, and repent for his servants, when he seeth that their power is gone, and there is none shut up, or left.
(DEUTERONOMY 30:9, 10; 32:36)

With more than one million dispossessed Jews flooding into the new Israel, the politically compromised land settlement quickly proved too small to contain them. Within a decade, another million arrived from all continents. Jewish independence and the demand for more land led to wars between Jews and the previous occupants. During the War of Independence, 700,000 Arabs lost their land and homes. At its lowest point, the Arab population dropped to about 69,000. The need for more land also fits the restoration that had been predicted for Israel:

Thy children shall make haste; thy destroyers and they that made thee waste shall go forth from thee. Lift up thy eyes all around, and behold: all these [the

children of Israel] gather themselves to-gether, and come to thee. As I live, saith the LORD, thou shalt surely clothe thee with them all, as with an ornament, and bind them on thee, as a bride doeth. For thy waste and thy desolate places, and the land of thy destruction, shall even now be too narrow by reason of the in-habitants, and they that swallowed thee up [the nations they entered in the dias-pora] shall be far away. The children who thou shalt have, after thou hast lost the other, shall say again in thy ears, The place is too small for me: give place to me that I may dwell. Then shalt thou say in thy heart, Who hath begotten these [new children] for me, seeing I have lost my children, and am desolate, a captive, and moving to and fro [in the diaspora]? and who hath brought up these? Behold, I was left alone; these, where have they been? (ISAIAH 49:17–21)

Finally, after the Six-Day War in 1967, the process of reclaiming the land was rela-tively complete. Israel gained control of Judea (the area around Jerusalem), East Jeru-salem, the Gaza strip, and the West Bank of the Jordan River, and most of the rest of what is considered "Israel" today. Next began the process of restoring the land that was re-claimed:

And they shall build the old wastes, they shall raise up the former desolations, and they shall repair the waste cities, the des-olations of many generations. And for-eigners shall stand and feed your flocks, and the sons of the alien shall be your plowmen and your vinedressers. (ISAIAH 61:4, 5)

The last line of this prophecy describes the unfortunate situation that exists today for the Palestinians. Most Arabs are Muslim, some are Christian. They live in segregated neighborhoods or in refugee camps that are not much better than the refugee camps Jews were relegated to after World War II. The situation is the worst for the Palestinian Arabs. More than 30 percent are unemployed. Those who have jobs are the equivalent of plowmen and vinedressers. For the most part, they have the lowest labor jobs in the na-tion, and they're completely dependent upon the Jews.

The declaration of certain situations in prophecy does not necessarily indicate how things *ought* to be; often it is simply a statement of the way things will turn out.

RESTORATION: PEOPLE TO LAND, PEOPLE TO GOD, AND PEOPLE TO PEOPLE?

Does all of this mean the great divorce between God and his people is coming to an end? The prophecies of restoration foretell much more than just recovering the land. They also speak of the relationship between God and his people being restored:

But if from there thou shalt seek the LORD thy God, thou shalt find him, if thou shalt seek him with all thy heart and with all thy soul. When thou art in tribulation, and all these things have come upon thee, even in the latter days, if thou shalt turn to the LORD thy God,

and shalt be obedient to his voice; (For the LORD thy God is a merciful God;) he will not forsake thee, neither destroy thee, nor forget the covenant of thy fathers which he swore to them.

(DEUTERONOMY 4:29–31)

And the LORD thy God will circumcise thy heart, and the heart of thy seed, to love the LORD thy God with all thy

heart, and with all thy soul, that thou mayest live. (DEUTERONOMY 30:6)

Modern Israel remains a primarily secular state. Many of its people observe holidays, but do not go to synagogue on a regular basis. But the prophecies above speak of a process, not an instant change, even implying this process of spiritual renewal will take place "in the latter days" during times of tribulation. What Ezekiel wrote during exile under Babylon would appear to have much greater application for the diaspora and the recent restoration of Israel, revealing that the Jews would be brought back to the land *first* and *then* would be brought into God's New Covenant:

. . . These are the people of the LORD, and are gone forth out of his land. But I had pity for my holy name, which the house of Israel had profaned among the nations, where they went. Therefore say to the house of Israel, Thus saith the Lord GOD; I do not this for your sakes, O house of Israel, but for my holy name's sake, which ye have profaned among the nations, where ye went. And I will sanctify my great name, which was profaned among the nations, which ye have profaned in the midst of them; and the nations shall know that I am the LORD, saith the Lord GOD, when I shall be sanctified in you before their eyes. For I

will take you from among the nations, and gather you out of all countries, and will bring you into your own land. Then will I sprinkle clean water upon you, and ye shall be clean: from all your filthiness, and from all your idols, will I cleanse you. A new heart also will I give you, and a new spirit will I put within you: and I will take away the stony heart out of your flesh, and I will give you an heart of flesh. And I will put my spirit within you, and cause you to walk in my statutes, and ye shall keep my judgments, and do them.

(EZEKIEL 36:20–27)

In language matching that of the New Covenant, this prophecy states that God will put a new spirit in the Jews that return to Israel. Their *hearts* will be circumcised (marked for God) and not just their *bodies*. They will walk according to God's statutes, not because they have a religion of laws but because God's own Holy Spirit will dwell in their hearts.

WILL JEWS AND CHRISTIANS BECOME ONE PEOPLE?

Restoration could also mean modern Judaism and its sister, Christianity (neither one is the original/mother Judaism) could soon become reconciled in this remarriage under the New Covenant. The gap between Jews and Christians has never been narrower in two millennia. Throughout the rebirth of Israel, evangelical Christians were strong proponents of Zionism. The Jewish homeland probably would not have been tenable without some British support for small Jewish occupations in Palestine and subsequent U.S. support. During the nineteenth and twentieth centuries, evangelical Christians in both countries sponsored conferences in support of Zionist ideals, almost entirely due to their beliefs regarding end-time prophecies. Some prominent Christian evangelists were advocates of the Jewish hope, including J. Hudson Taylor, Dwight L. Moody and A. B. Simpson.

Several of the British diplomats whose work helped lead toward the Balfour Declaration were also Christians motivated by prophetic beliefs—notables such as James Finn, the British Consul at Jerusalem (1845–1862) and Lord Shaftesbury. Renowned financier Henry Drummond sponsored conferences advocating Zionism based on his zeal to bring on the second coming of Christ before the millennium. It would appear to some that the nineteenth century was drunk on millennialism.

In Germany, William Hechler, chaplain to the British embassy, persuaded Kaiser Wilhelm II to support Zionism because he believed a Jewish state was necessary for the fulfillment of prophecy. Hechler became a traveling companion of Theodore Herzl, the first president of the World Zionist Organization.

In later years, the goodwill has also run the other way. Christian pilgrimages play a major part in Israel's tourist economy—one of Israel's biggest industries.

It would seem God now has two chosen people—having added the Gentiles as He professed—and that he is bringing his children closer together, but the crucial question remains: "Is Jesus the Jewish Messiah?" The possibility of these two people being joined into one by a messianic king may be the deeper meaning of another prophecy that was given by Ezekiel. The original prophecy spoke of the split kingdoms of the ancient Jews coming together. (Israel split into northern and southern halves, after which the northern half was conquered and taken into exile by Assyria and the southern by Babylon.) It's not too hard to see a similar split between Christian Jews and non-Christian Jews after which the second and greater exile known as the diaspora began.

In the following prophecy, think of "Judah" as representing Christians (since Christ descended from the tribe of Judah and, in Christian thought, fulfilled the promises made to Judah), and interpret "Joseph" as representing non-Christian Jews. Then interpret King David (who died long *before* the prophecy was written) as representing Jesus

Christ, David's "seed." The prophecy, then, becomes a striking promise that two peoples who split long ago will be bound together by a messianic king from the line of David, all in the context of a new covenant—a new religion for the Jews (but the same God):

The word of the LORD came again to me, saying, Moreover, thou son of man, take thee one stick, and write upon it, For Judah, and for the children of Israel his companions: then take another stick, and write upon it, For Joseph, the stick of Ephraim, and for all the house of Israel his companions: And join them one to another into one stick; and they shall become one in thy hand. And when the children of thy people shall speak to thee, saying, Wilt thou not show us what thou meanest by these? Say to them, Thus saith the Lord GOD; Behold, I will take the stick of Joseph, which is in the hand of Ephraim, and the tribes of Israel his companions, and will put them with him, even with the stick of Judah, and make them one stick, and they shall be one in my hand. And the sticks on which thou writest shall be in thy hand before their eyes. And say to them, Thus saith the Lord GOD; Behold, I will take the children of Israel from among the nations, where they are gone, and will gather them on every side, and bring them into their own land: And I will make them one nation in the land upon the mountains of Israel; and one king shall be king to them all: and they shall be no more two nations, neither shall they be divided into two kingdoms any more at all: Neither shall they defile themselves any more with their idols, nor with their detestable things, nor with any of their transgressions: but I will save them out of all their dwellingplaces, in which they have sinned, and will cleanse them: so shall they be my people, and I will be their God. And David my servant shall be king over them; and they all shall have one shepherd: they shall also walk in my judgments, and observe my statutes, and do them. And they shall dwell in the land that I have given to Jacob my servant, in which your fathers have dwelt; and they shall dwell in it, even they, and their children, and their children's children for ever: and my servant David shall be their prince for ever. Moreover I will make a covenant of peace with them; it shall be an everlasting covenant with them: and I will place them, and multiply them, and will set my sanctuary in the midst of them for evermore. My tabernacle also shall be with them: yea, I will be their God, and they shall be my people. And the nations shall know that I the LORD sanctifieth Israel, when my sanctuary shall be in the midst of them for evermore.

(EZEKIEL 37:15–28)

Perhaps the shared occupation of Jerusalem by Jews, Christians, and Muslims is a sign that God is bringing all the "seed of Abraham" together.

CONNECTING THE RESTORATION OF ISRAEL
TO THE "END TIMES"

One prophecy, recorded in Isaiah 66, describes the restoration of Israel after its fall to Babylon, showing events identical to those described for the end times in the Book of Revelation and other apocalyptic prophecies. It begins by pointing out that the temple no longer exists and connects the disappearance of the temple with a time when sacrifice has become an abomination because what God really wants from his people is a contrite heart. The times, then, are similar to the present:

Thus saith the LORD, The heaven is my throne, and the earth is my footstool: where is the house that ye build to me? and where is the place of my rest? For all these things hath my hand made, and all these things have been, saith the LORD: but to this man will I look, even to him that is poor and of a contrite spirit, and trembleth at my word. He that killeth an ox [as sacrifice] is as if he slew a man; he that sacrificeth a lamb, as if he cut off a dog's neck; he that offereth an oblation, as if he offered swine's blood; he that burneth incense, as if he blessed an idol. Yea, they have chosen their own ways, and their soul delighteth in their abominations. I also will choose their delusions, and will bring their fears upon them; because when I called, none did answer; when I spoke, they did not hear: but they did evil before my eyes, and chose that in which I delighted not. . . .

The prophecy goes on to say that when Israel's restoration came, it would happen practically overnight. It would come upon the world like a birth without the forewarning of labor pains. That's how the restoration from Babylon happened, and that's how the modern nation of Israel was reborn. Following the sudden birth, God clearly says, he would not have produced such a political miracle if he did not intend to raise his new child all the way to maturity:

. . . Hear the word of the LORD, ye that tremble at his word; Your brethren that hated you, that cast you out for my name's sake, said, Let the LORD be glorified: but he shall appear to your joy, and they shall be ashamed. A voice of noise from the city, a voice from the temple, a voice of the LORD that rendereth recompence to his enemies. Before she travailed, she brought forth; before her pain came, she was delivered of a son. Who hath heard such a thing? who hath seen such things? Shall the earth be made to bring forth in one day? or shall a nation be born at once? for as soon as Zion travailed, she brought forth her children. Shall I bring to the birth, and not cause to bring forth? saith the LORD: shall I cause to bring forth, and shut the womb? saith thy God. Rejoice ye with Jerusalem, and be glad with her, all ye that love her: rejoice for joy with her, all ye that mourn

for her: That ye may nurse, and be satis-fied with the breasts of her consolations; that ye may draw milk, and be delighted with the abundance of her glory. For thus saith the LORD, Behold, I will extend peace to her like a river, and the glory of the Gentiles like a flowing stream: then shall ye be nursed, ye shall be borne upon her sides, and be dandled upon her knees. As one whom his mother com-forteth, so will I comfort you; and ye shall be comforted in Jerusalem. And when ye see this, your heart shall rejoice, and your bones shall flourish like an herb: and the hand of the LORD shall be known toward his servants, and his in-dignation toward his enemies.

There was no peace for Jerusalem after it was restored from Babylon, however; nor did the glory of the Gentile nations flow into her like a stream. So perhaps the prophecy has the present restoration in view. Undoubtedly, a large part of the money that has flowed into Israel to help it sustain itself militarily has been Gentile money from the U.S. From here, the prophecy connects the newborn nation's maturity to a time that matches end-time prophecies regarding the destruction of people who continue to reject God and his ways. All is predicted to happen in the context of the Lord's coming through events that will encompass the lands of the Middle East and distant shores:

. . . For, behold, the LORD will come with fire, and with his chariots like a whirlwind, to render his anger with fury, and his rebuke with flames of fire. For by fire and by his sword will the LORD plead with all flesh: and the slain of the LORD shall be many. They that sanctify themselves, and purify themselves in the gardens behind one tree in the midst, eating swine's flesh, and the abomina-tion, and the mouse, shall be consumed together, saith the LORD. For I know their works and their thoughts: it shall come, that I will gather all nations and tongues; and they shall come, and see my glory. And I will set a sign among them, and I will send those that escape of them to the nations, to Tarshish, Pul, and Lud, that draw the bow, to Tubal, and Javan, [lands around the Middle East] to the isles afar off [can also be translated dis-tant shores], that have not heard my fame, neither have seen my glory; and they shall declare my glory among the Gentiles. And they shall bring all your brethren for an offering to the LORD out of all nations upon horses, and in chari-ots, and in litters, and upon mules, and upon swift beasts, to my holy mountain Jerusalem, saith the LORD, as the chil-dren of Israel bring an offering in a clean vessel into the house of the LORD. . . .

Although the Jews were not brought to modern Israel by the ancient transportation methods described, they were brought on Gentile ships and Gentile airplanes by the mil-lions, some of it sponsored with Gentile money, most with Jewish money. Beyond the time of Israel's restoration, the prophecy speaks of the creation of a new heaven and new earth just as the Book of Revelation predicts. It connects the restoration of Israel to a fu-ture time when all the earth will worship the same God, following a time of holocaust:

...*And I will also take of them for priests and for Levites, saith the LORD. For as the new heavens and the new earth, which I will make, shall remain before me, saith the LORD, so shall your seed and your name remain. And it shall come to pass, that from one new moon to another, and from one sabbath to an-other, shall all flesh come to worship be-fore me, saith the LORD. And they shall go forth, and look upon the dead bodies of the men that have transgressed against me: for their worm shall not die, neither shall their fire be quenched; and they shall be an abhorrence to all flesh.*

(ISAIAH 66:1–24)

THE CLOCK IS TICKING

The present restoration of Israel is a unique event in human history, and it came about under both Christian and Jewish influence. Never before has a nation resurrected from its ashes millennia after being thoroughly destroyed, with its people utterly dispersed and its land completely occupied by others. Has this monumental event started the prophetic clock ticking again? Or is it, as others claim, merely a peculiar artifact of history?

In the words of the renowned archeologist William F. Albright, who knew his artifacts:

No other phenomenon in history is quite so extraordinary as the unique event represented by the Restoration of Israel. At no other time in world history, so far as it is known, has a people been destroyed, and then come back after a lapse of time and reestablished itself. It is utterly out of the question to seek a parallel for the recurrence of Israel's restoration. . . . [1]

Christianity and Islam both teach that *Jesus* will return to Jerusalem. Judaism teaches the *Messiah* will come to Jerusalem. Christianity, Islam, *and* Judaism, all contain end-time prophecies about an Antichrist/Antimessiah figure who will be destroyed by the coming Messiah. All three religions trace their roots to Abraham from whom the Messiah is to descend. For the first time in history, all three religions occupy the Holy City where Jesus or the Messiah is prophesied to return. Does this unique convergence set the stage for the Holy One to be revealed and to bring, perhaps, all three of these disparate groups together?

Given that one of the most significant and unlikely prophecies in the Bible—the restoration of the Jews to their own land—began in the twentieth century, perhaps there is a basis for thinking that the prophetic clock, long silent, has begun ticking again.

Chapter 6

SIGNS:

IS THE END NEAR?

With so many of the prophecies by Jesus and certain Old Testament prophets already proven true to the very word, does anything remain for the future? Or were the "end times" of ancient Israel the only "end times" the prophets had in mind? History and prophecy show that patterns do repeat. On the other hand, they do not *have to* repeat, which leaves little room for dogmatism when it comes to interpreting the future.

Some of the things Jesus prophesied, however, were not fulfilled in the fall of Jerusalem. The famines and earthquakes mentioned in Josephus' history were localized around Jerusalem, not "in various places" as Jesus had predicted. The "gospel of the kingdom"—the message of New Testament—had not been "preached in all the world for a testimony to all nations." Also, Jesus had said, "If these days had not been cut short, *no one* would survive." He could have meant "no one in Jerusalem," but the days for Jerusalem were not cut short; they dragged on to the bitter end. His words often sound as though he was predicting something on a global scale. Most of all, Jesus did not appear "in the clouds of heaven with power and great glory" as predicted in the section of Matthew's Gospel that deals with the fall of Jerusalem. Nor did he "send his angels with a great sound of a trumpet."

There were, however, signs in the heavens near the time of the fall of Jerusalem, as already described by Josephus, and there were many false prophets, just as Jesus had prophesied:

> Now, there was then a great number of false prophets suborned by the tyrants to impose upon the people. . . . This was in order to keep them from deserting.[1]

And there were later false prophets, culminating in the days of Bar Kochba, but there is no record that any of them displayed "great signs and wonders," as Jesus' prophecy had predicted.

Neither was Nebuchadnezzar's dream about the imperial statue completely fulfilled by the conquests of the Roman empire. The legs of iron in the statue—Rome—continued to rule the western world five centuries after Jerusalem was destroyed, and the eastern half of the Roman empire continued in power for nearly fifteen centuries. The climax of Nebuchadnezzar's dream still has not been realized, which is the stone that becomes a mountain, as though from out of nowhere, and destroys all empires.

Since God's prophets were supposed to be accurate 100 percent of the time, did these prophets miss the mark, in spite of how accurate they were on so many details? Or did their predictions of past events include latent prophecies yet to be fulfilled?

The answer lies in the question to which Jesus was responding when he foretold the disasters of Jerusalem. His prophecy was made in response to the disciples' question regarding when the temple would be thrown down, so it's natural to think that everything would take place at that time. Yet, was that all the disciples asked? Without realizing it, they asked a loaded question. Within their question regarding when the temple would be torn down, they also asked, ". . . and what shall be the sign of thy coming, and of the end of the world?" (Matthew 24:3b).

Their question was loaded with the assumption that all three events—the destruction of the temple, the coming of Christ, and the end of the world—would happen together. So did Jesus give their loaded question a loaded answer? Obviously, his first concern would be with the events that would happen within the disciples' own lifetime. They had asked an honest question, even if it was a bit confused, and Jesus would not have played games with their safety in the perilous times he knew lay ahead for them.

Their question, however, may also have been fortuitous for Jesus. In the desolations that would follow his rejection of the Jewish leaders, Jesus may have seen numerous parallels to events that would begin to swirl up again around his return. The disciples' question gave Jesus the opportunity to link Jerusalem's destruction with his return—implying the two events were inextricably connected across time.

Poets and prophets often talk about something straight-forward at one level, while talking about something deeper on another. For example, Alfred Lord Tennyson's poem "Crossing the Bar" talks about crossing a sand bar at the mouth of a river by boat. It makes perfect sense on that level alone, and if that's all the reader gets out of it, he or she can still enjoy the poem. Yet, the language pulls the reader toward a deeper and more significant awareness, where "crossing the bar" refers to the poet's death and his soul's crossing to the other side:

> *Sunset and evening star,*
> *And one clear call for me!*
> *And may there be no moaning of the bar*
> *When I put out to sea . . .*

> *. . . For though from out our bourne of Time and Place*
> *The flood may bear me far,*
> *I hope to see my Pilot face to face*
> *When I have crossed the bar.*[2]

If a reader only understood the pilot as being the skipper of a boat, he or she would not be wrong but would have missed a much deeper insight where the pilot is the speaker's maker. Poets usually try to say as much as possible with the fewest words, raising the power of each word. The overlay of meanings upon a single image gives the poem more potency. Prophets, who would speak of major events in vastly different times, also need economy of language. Because patterns do repeat in history, the superimposing of parallel events from different times reveals a connection in the meaning behind those events.

So while Jesus gave his followers warnings that would help them escape the imminent destruction of Jerusalem, his prophecy also looked to the consummation of all prophecy at the far end of time.

Jesus' Imminent Return

The Apostles often spoke as if the end were going to happen within their own lifetime:

> *But the end of all things is at hand. . . .*
> (1 PETER 4:7)

> *Little children, it is the last time: and as*
> *ye have heard that antichrist cometh,*
> *even now are there many antichrists; by*
> *which we know that it is the last time.*
> (1 JOHN 2:18)

It is almost two thousand years since Peter said, "The end of all things is near," yet the world goes on. And, similar to the Apostle John, some declared during World War II that Hitler was the "Antichrist" and that World War II was the last times, but the end did not come then, either. What end did the apostles have in mind?

Will the statement that "the end is near" ever be said and be right? Each time it is wrong, people grow more doubtful about the prophecies altogether. If the year 2001 passes by and the world keeps going on as before—which is quite likely—the Bible's prophecies about the end of the world will seem even more faint. Then people will be tempted to ignore what the Bible says.

The prophets and apostles and Jesus, himself *wanted* each generation to think the end might come in their own time so they would not ignore what the Bible says. They wanted their readers to remain attentive to their words. They weren't being deceitful. They believed in the end, and they believed it *could* come at any time, and certainly the one end that was most important to all their listeners *did* come in their own time—the end of Israel.

When Jesus' own disciples asked him when the end would come, he did not answer them with a specific time. Instead, he gave them the *signs* they asked for, followed by a couple of warnings in the form of parable:

. . . Watch therefore: for ye know not what hour your Lord cometh. But know this, that if the master of the house knew in what watch the thief would come, he would have watched, and would not have allowed his house to be broken into. Therefore be ye also ready: for in such an hour as ye think not the Son of man cometh. Who then is a faithful and wise servant, whom his lord hath made ruler over his household, to give them food in due season? Blessed is that servant, whom his lord when he cometh shall find so doing. Verily I say to you, That he shall make him ruler over all his goods. But if that evil servant shall say in his heart, My lord delayeth his coming; And shall begin to beat his fellowservants, and to eat and drink with the drunken; The lord of that servant shall come in a day when he looketh not for him, and in an hour that he is not aware of, And shall cut him asunder, and appoint him his portion with the hypocrites: there shall be weeping and gnashing of teeth.

Then shall the kingdom of heaven be likened to ten virgins, who took their lamps, and went forth to meet the bridegroom. And five of them were wise, and five were foolish. They that were foolish took their lamps, and took no oil with them: But the wise took oil in their vessels with their lamps. While the bridegroom tarried, they all slumbered and slept. And at midnight there was a cry made, Behold, the bridegroom cometh; go ye out to meet him. Then all those virgins arose, and trimmed their lamps. And the foolish said to the wise, Give us of your oil; for our lamps are gone out. But the wise answered, saying, Not so; lest there be not enough for us and you: but go ye rather to them that sell, and buy for yourselves. And while they were going to buy, the bridegroom came; and they that were ready went in with him to the marriage: and the door was shut. Afterward came also the other virgins, saying, Lord, Lord, open to us. But he answered and said, Verily I say to you, I know you not. Watch therefore, for ye know neither the day nor the hour when the Son of man cometh.

(MATTHEW 24:42–51 AND 25:1–13)

If Jesus had told his disciples he wouldn't return for two thousand years—or three thousand—they might have grown slack in their living. There's more than a hint of that concern in both parables, which make the point that, because no one knows the hour of the master's return, *everyone* should be ready all the time.

It's significant that the verse quoted above from Peter, which says, "The end of all things is near," continues by saying, "Therefore, be clear minded and self-controlled so that you can pray." Peter, too, allowed his disciples to believe the end was very near in order to keep them living diligently. That Peter appears to have suspected, on the other hand, that the end of world would not come for some time—in terms of how most of us think of time—is evident in another one of his writings:

> Knowing this first, that there shall come in the last days scoffers, walking after their own lusts, And saying, Where is the promise of his coming? for since the fathers fell asleep, all things continue as they were from the beginning of the creation. For this they willingly are ignorant of, that by the word of God the heavens were of old [came into being], and the earth standing out of the water and in the water [i.e., the land masses rose out of the deep]: By which the world that then was, being overflowed with water, perished [Noah's flood]: But the heavens and the earth, which are now, by the same word are kept in store, reserved to fire for the day of judgment and perdition of ungodly men. But, beloved, be not ignorant of this one thing, that one day is with the Lord as a thousand years, and a thousand years as one day. The Lord is not slack concerning his promise, as some men count slackness; but is long-suffering toward us, not willing that any should perish, but that all should come to repentance. But the day of the Lord will come as a thief in the night; in which the heavens shall pass away with a great noise, and the elements shall melt with fervent heat, the earth also and the works that are in it shall be burned up.
>
> (2 PETER 3:3–10)

When Peter said, "The end of all things is near," he would be quite right in geologic time—even if the end did not come until five thousand years after he spoke. Geologic time is the most reasonable chronometer to use in measuring the life span of the earth. It would also seem appropriate that God's chronometer runs at geologic speed. And yet, as soon as people think the end will take forever, it will come as a thief in the night—according to the warnings above. For the apostles to speak in terms of the immediacy of the end was just good counsel, following the approach Jesus himself had taken when he described the destruction of Jerusalem:

> Verily I say to you, that this generation shall not pass, till all these things shall be done. Heaven and earth shall pass away: but my words shall not pass away. But of that day and that hour knoweth no man, no, not the angels which are in heaven, neither the Son, but the Father. Take ye heed, watch and pray: for ye know not when the time is. (MARK 13:30–33)

With regard to his second coming, Jesus used examples of past judgments against the earth to show that the world would be caught completely off guard:

And he said to his disciples, The days will come, when ye shall desire to see one of the days of the Son of man, and ye shall not see it. And they shall say to you, See here; or, see there: go not after them, nor follow them. For as the lightning, that lighteneth from the one part under heaven, shineth to the other part under heaven; so shall also the Son of man be in his day. But first he must suffer many things, and be rejected by this generation. And as it was in the days of Noah, so shall it be also in the days of the Son of man. They ate, they drank, they married wives, they were given in marriage, until the day that Noah entered into the ark, and the flood came, and destroyed them all. Likewise also as it was in the days of Lot; they ate, they drank, they bought, they sold, they planted, they built; But the same day that Lot went out of Sodom it rained fire and brimstone from heaven, and destroyed them all. Even thus shall it be in the day when the Son of man is revealed. In that day, he who shall be upon the housetop, and his furniture in the house, let him not come down to take it away: and he that is in the field, let him likewise not return back. Remember Lot's wife [who looked back in fleeing Sodom and was turned to a pillar of salt]. Whoever shall seek to save his life shall lose it; and whoever shall lose his life shall preserve it.

(LUKE 17:22–33)

The stories of Noah and Lot have two implications. The first is fairly clear: People on earth will be carrying on as usual when destruction comes suddenly upon them. The other is that Jesus' followers may be "taken out" of the world immediately before the last cataclysm that destroys all others. That's inferred from the fact that Noah got safely on his ark the same day the rains began when the waters rose to flood the earth. Lot walked out of the city just before it was incinerated. But the essential message is that when Jesus comes and reveals himself to the world, there will be no time to change one's ways. The door of the ark will already be closed. The fire from heaven will already be falling.

There is another sense in which the Bible says the coming of Christ is imminent. His coming is always as close as one's own soul: In that sense, the kingdom of God comes immediately, but slowly. It comes to the world through the hearts of those who choose to believe and gradually spreads from individual to individual:

And when he was asked by the Pharisees, when the kingdom of God should come, he answered them and said, The kingdom of God cometh not with observation: Neither shall they say, Lo here! or, lo there! for, behold, the kingdom of God is within you.

(LUKE 17:20, 21)

Signs of the Times

So, what are the tickings of God's chronometer—signs that may click by with increasing speed and volume until Christ returns to reveal the truth about himself to all the world?

The Gospel of Luke (21:7–33) has a parallel passage to the one in Matthew where Jesus answers the disciples' question regarding the destruction of the temple and his second coming. It has a few nuances of its own that help sort out which events applied to the destruction of Jerusalem and which apply to Jesus' return:

And they asked him, saying, Master, but when shall these things be? and what sign will there be when these things shall come to pass? And he said, Take heed that ye be not deceived: for many shall come in my name, saying, I am Christ; and the time draweth near: therefore go ye not after them. But when ye shall hear of wars and commotions, be not terrified: for these things must first come to pass; but the end is not yet. . . .

The first thing Jesus lets the disciples know is that the wars and rumors of wars they will hear of in the next few decades of their lives are not signs of the end. Wars are a condition of humanity that will always be present. Although wars play a significant role in the final events of human history, Jesus implies they cannot be looked to as signs.

Like the coming of Christ, the next world war is always imminent. Without a doubt, the twentieth century was one of the bloodiest in history: the Soviet Revolution, two world wars, the Korean War, the Vietnam War, the Persian Gulf War, the numerous Soviet wars during the middle of the century to seize control of satellite nations, the manifold wars of independence fought by those satellite nations during the last quarter of the century. Clearly, humans are no closer to learning how to live in peaceful coexistence than the ancients were.

Modern history does not leave much hope that humanity will evolve into peaceful co-existence. The human race seems further from that scenario now than ever. The threat by Russian President Boris Yeltzin in January 1998 that the U.S. should not risk starting WW III by attacking Iraq is an all-too-clear reminder that the threat of war, even between the old superpowers, is not dead. War is not a trustworthy sign because it is an always-present human condition.

. . . Then said he to them, Nation shall rise against nation, and kingdom against kingdom: And great earthquakes shall be in various places, and famines, and pestilences; and fearful sights and great signs shall there be from heaven. . . .

The frequency of these "natural" events throughout earth's history make their reliability as signs also questionable. Jesus may simply be grouping these things along with war as some of the many things that happen, "but the end is not yet." He seems to have anticipated that people would see such events as omens of the world's final doom. To allay their concerns in advance, he pointed out that these things are only the beginning of the world's sorrows.

The Bible does provide some basis, however, for thinking these common catastrophes will increase in the end—*more* earthquakes, *more* famines, *more* pestilence. The Book of Revelation is full of such images, especially fearful and great signs in the heavens, and it has much to say about Christ's second coming. But these things are part of the end, not necessarily things preceding it.

Both Josephus and the Roman historian Tacitus record significant earthquakes and astrological signs during the last years of Nero's reign. Jesus may have been pointing to these things as specific signs for the siege. That seems the most likely interpretation because Jesus does move directly to talking about the events the disciples would experience during those years, beginning with the persecutions that preceded the signs of the siege:

> . . . *But before all these, they shall lay their hands on you, and persecute you, delivering you up to the synagogues, and into prisons, being brought before kings and rulers for my name's sake. And it shall turn to you for a testimony. Settle it therefore in your hearts, not to meditate before what ye shall answer: For I will give you a mouth and wisdom, which all your adversaries shall not be able to speak against nor withstand. And ye shall be betrayed both by parents, and brethren, and kinsmen, and friends; and some of you shall they cause to be put to death. And ye shall be hated by all men for my name's sake. But there shall not an hair of your head perish. In your patience possess ye your souls. . . .*

Then he moves to talking about the siege, to which the signs relate:

> . . . *And when ye shall see Jerusalem surrounded by armies, then know that her desolation is near. Then let them who are in Judaea flee to the mountains; and let them who are in the midst of it depart from it; and let not them that are in the countries enter into it. For these are the days of vengeance, that all things which are written may be fulfilled. But woe to them that are with child, and to them that nurse infants, in those days! for there shall be great distress in the land, and wrath upon this people. And they shall fall by the edge of the sword, and shall be led away captive into all nations: and Jerusalem shall be trodden down by the Gentiles, until the times of the Gentiles shall be fulfilled. . . .*

Even here, there is a hint that Jerusalem would not be oppressed forever. Jerusalem would remain destroyed as a Jewish city *until* the times of the Gentiles are over (meaning God had determined a certain period through which it would be occupied by Gentiles). Having described Jerusalem's destruction, Jesus now moves to the time of its restoration—at the other end of history.

> *. . . And there shall be signs in the sun, and in the moon, and in the stars; and upon the earth distress of nations, with perplexity; the sea and the waves roaring; Men's hearts failing them for fear, and for expectation of those things which are coming on the earth: for the powers of heaven shall be shaken. And then shall they see the Son of man coming in a cloud with power and great glory. And when these things begin to come to pass, then look up, and lift up your heads; for your redemption draweth near. . . .*

Once Jesus starts talking about horrific signs in the sky, he moves into events that are less common and that have traditionally been associated with times of cataclysm in many ancient cultures—like the comet over Jerusalem during the time of the Jerusalem siege. It would seem that *during* the time of the end the kinds of astrological signs and earth movements that occurred when Jerusalem fell will recur on a much greater scale— to the point that they will cause people's hearts to fail. The political or economic stress of nations will grow to where the world is perplexed over how to solve its problems. The roaring of the sea waves indicates an increase in the ferocity of storms, such as hurricanes. One key to distinguishing between these signs and the kind of turmoil present in any century might be their concurrence after the restoration of Israel:

> *. . . And he spoke to them a parable; Behold the fig tree, and all the trees; When they now shoot forth, ye see and know of your own selves that summer is now near at hand. So likewise ye, when ye see these things come to pass, know that the kingdom of God is near at hand. Verily I say to you, This generation shall not pass away, till all be fulfilled. Heaven and earth shall pass away: but my words shall not pass away.* (LUKE 21:7–33)

Right after Jesus entered Jerusalem on the fateful day he prophesied its destruction, he saw a fig tree that did not bear fruit. Because he hungered and the tree did not bear fruit, he cursed the tree and it died—perhaps as a sign of what would happen to Israel for similar reasons. It was right after he cursed the fig tree that Jesus went into the temple and rejected the religious leaders, saying, "Therefore I say to you, the kingdom of God shall be taken from you, and given to a nation bringing forth the fruits of it."

The languishing of the fig tree was frequently used in Old Testament prophecies of Israel's demise, whereas prophecies of earth's utopian age frequently repeated the promise that "every man shall sit under his own fig tree." So the flourishing of the fig tree meant good times for Israel. After Jesus walked out of the temple, he used this example of a budding fig tree as a sign that the end would be near when Israel came back to life after its long winter.

Of course, Jesus is also using the fig tree as a straight-forward illustration that when the confluence of cosmic, environmental, and political signs he has just given occurs, then the time is near, just as summer is near when the trees begin to grow leaves.

Jesus statement that "this generation shall not pass away, till all be fulfilled" certainly meant the generation in which his disciples lived would not pass until everything related to the fall of Jerusalem was fulfilled. Whether or not it means the same thing for the generation that will be living at the other end of time when Jerusalem is restored is less certain. The word "generation" can also be translated "race," so Jesus may have only been saying that the Jewish race would not pass away until all the events of his prophecy were fulfilled. He may have meant all three.

Although Jesus indicates signs of warning will herald the last days, he says there will be no signs to forewarn of his coming. Because he will come quickly, unexpectedly, and universally, his followers will know better than to fall for the false prophets and false messiahs that will inevitably arise during any time of great duress.

The Apostle Peter warned of such pretenders though not necessarily in connection with the end times:

> *But there were false prophets also among the people, even as there shall be false teachers among you, who will secretly bring in damnable heresies, even denying the Lord that bought them, and bring upon themselves swift destruction. And many shall follow their pernicious ways; by reason of whom the way of truth shall be evil spoken of. And through covetousness they shall with deceptive words exploit you: whose judgment now of a long time lingereth not, and their destruction slumbereth not.* (2 Peter 2:1–3)

Overall, it would seem the times of Jesus' departure and the times of his return have much in common.

The Spirit of the Age

This increase in false teachers and false messiahs is a sign that fits other prophecies of global spiritual deception in the end times. These New Testament prophecies describe the spiritual climate that will precede the return of Jesus Christ. Germans call it the *zeitgeist*—the spirit of the age.

Now the Spirit speaketh expressly, that in the latter times some shall depart from the faith, giving heed to seducing spirits, and doctrines of devils. (1 TIMOTHY 4:1)

This could easily be a description of today's New Age movement. What is called "New Age" is, in fact, very old age. The modern practice of "channeling spirit guides," is called "demonic possession" in the Bible. One who channels for personal guidance of future predictions is simply allowing another spirit to possess their mind. The angels seen by New Age mystics are referred to in the Bible as "fallen angels"—celestial beings who have coveted the opportunity to guide the course of human actions from the beginning of history. The Apostle Paul drew a pointed connection between false prophets and these fallen celestial beings:

For such are false apostles, deceitful workers, transforming themselves into the apostles of Christ. And no marvel; for Satan himself is transformed into an angel of light. Therefore it is no great thing if his ministers also be transformed as the ministers of righteousness; whose end shall be according to their works.

(2 CORINTHIANS 11:13–14)

In assessing the spirit of the present age, one should ask who or what is the spirit of the New Age? Being spiritual does not necessarily mean being true. Looking good isn't the same as being good.

This spiritual awakening to the dark side has a counterpart in another sign of the times Jesus gave:

And this gospel of the kingdom shall be preached in all the world for a testimony to all nations; and then shall the end come. (MATTHEW 24:14)

Most international Christian missionary agencies have forecasted that by the year 2000 the Gospel will have been preached—for the first time—to every group of people on earth. There will be no society that has not heard of Jesus Christ. So at the beginning of the millennium the first part of Jesus' statement will finally become true.

The *zeitgeist* not only takes into account the religious climate of the end times, it also describes the people of that time:

This know also, that in the last days perilous times shall come. For men shall be lovers of their own selves, covetous, boasters, proud, blasphemers, disobedient to parents, unthankful, unholy, Without natural affection, trucebreakers, false accusers, incontinent, fierce, despisers of those that are good, Traitors,

*heady, highminded, lovers of pleasures
more than lovers of God; Having a form
of godliness, but denying its power: from
such turn away. . . . Ever learning, and
never able to come to the knowledge of
the truth. . . . men of corrupt minds, rejected as concerning the faith. But they
shall proceed no further: for their folly
shall be evident to all men, as theirs also
was. . . . And, all indeed that will live
godly in Christ Jesus shall suffer persecution. But evil men and seducers shall become worse and worse, deceiving, and
being deceived.*

(2 TIMOTHY 3:1–5, 7–9, 12, 13)

Such people have existed in all ages, but the last line indicates they will increase sig-
nificantly in the final age. The last two or three decades of the twentieth century saw
more people into self-exploration, self-actualization, self-fulfillment, and self-esteem;
more multi-billionaires and millionaires than any other time. The Bible does not speak
against money or success, but it does speak against becoming absorbed by money or by
one's own interests. How many other generations have read so much news about children killing parents and children killing children, drive-by-shootings, and unwed mothers who dump their babies in garbage dumpsters? One is hardly a social worrywart to
question the spirit of such an age.

Cultural shifts are likely to be accepted as the norm by a generation that has known
nothing else. Liars believe everyone is lying to them; adulterers believe all people commit adultery. The emotionally disconnected don't care if anyone cares. People become
"despisers of those that are good" because they do not believe in goodness.

HURRICANES AND EARTHQUAKES

Not so long ago, many of the prophets of doom and gloom were radio preachers whose
tirades were the only disturbances in the air. But for the past two decades scientists
across the globe have been the harbingers of doom. World councils of both science and
industry have convened to discuss the seriousness of global threats. One only has to look
through recent newspaper headlines to see the tide has changed:

> Every disaster story must have a Jeremiah; Bill Gray is this one's. He's the leading
> forecaster of hurricane trends, a meteorologist at Colorado State University in
> Fort Collins. . . . For ten years he's been predicting a dramatic upswing in the fre-
> quency of Atlantic hurricanes. Sadly, he's looking better every year. . . . Says Gray:
> "It looks like we're going to see hurricane damage like we've never previously
> seen."
>
> FORTUNE MAGAZINE[3]

The world insurance business fears that erratic weather induced by global warming could deal it a crippling financial blow any time soon, industry executives say. "Disaster losses will continue to rise drastically in dimension and frequency," said Dr. Gerhard Berz, head of Geoscience Research at the company Munich Reinsurance.

. . . The experts were speaking at a conference entitled "The Impact of Climate Change on Business and Industry," held recently in Brussels.

. . . Berz said the overwhelming danger to the industry's future is climate change. "It is to be feared that climate change will produce in nearly all regions of the world . . . natural disasters of unprecedented severity and frequency. . . ."

REUTERS BUSINESS REPORT[4]

. . . More and more homeowners across the U.S. are running into problems getting and keeping affordable coverage. . . .

. . . Even after adjusting for inflation, four out of five of the costliest natural disasters of the past 40 years have occurred since 1989, including hurricanes Andrew, Hugo and Iniki.

. . . The devastating natural disasters of the past five years have persuaded many insurers who do business in coastal states to sharply curtail writing new homeowners policies. . . .

MONEY MAGAZINE[5]

. . . The current decade is unprecedented in terms of the disasters that have occurred: the most costly earthquake and hurricane; record tornado seasons; the worst floods; the worst blizzards and ice storms; the costliest wildfire damage.

LOS ANGELES TIMES[6]

. . . There's little doubt global temperatures are rising. Europe's alpine glaciers have lost half their volume since 1850. . . . The number of frosty winter days in Queensland, Australia, has dropped by half since 1900.

. . . Scientists are fairly confident that further warming, caused by humans or not, will make certain weather extremes more common.

FORTUNE MAGAZINE[7]

Jesus indicated that wars, storms, and earthquakes are not reliable signs. What's being seriously discussed by science and business officials now, however, is not the occasional event but an accumulation of *all* types of disasters on a global scale that appears to be unprecedented in human history. That these things should begin happening (and are predicted to become much worse) right after the restoration of Israel and right at the change of a millennium proves nothing, but it does give pause, especially given the following global conversations.

THE POLITICAL-ECONOMIC CLIMATE

In the last couple of decades, global economics have become as hot an issue as global warming. Globalization was the political buzz-word of the nineties, and it certainly fits the scenario described in one of the most famous passages of the Book of Revelation, which describes the times when the Antichrist will be revealed:

> *And he causeth all, both small and great, rich and poor, free and bond, to receive a mark in their right hand, or in their fore-heads: And that no man might buy or sell, except him that had the mark, or the name of the beast, or the number of his name. Here is wisdom. Let him that hath understanding count the number of the beast: for it is the number of a man; and his number [is] Six hundred and sixty [and] six.* (REVELATION 13:16–8)

The ability of one individual to have financial control over everyone almost has to imply a global economy. For forty years those old-time radio preachers have proclaimed that the requirement of a personal identification code including the number 666 for all financial transactions indicates a future cashless society. Now those who shape world finances and technology are publicly announcing the same thing:

> Rather than holding paper currency, the new wallet will store unforgeable digital money. . . . Tomorrow the wallet PC will make it easy for anyone to spend and accept digital funds. Your wallet will link into a store's computer to allow money to be transferred. . . .
>
> When wallet PCs are ubiquitous, we can eliminate the bottlenecks that now plague airport terminals, theaters, and other locations. . . . As you pass through an airport gate, for example, your wallet PC will connect to the airport's computers and verify that you have paid for a ticket. . . . Your wallet PC will identify you to the computer. . . .
>
> As cash and credit cards begin to disappear, criminals may target the wallet PC, so there will have to be safeguards. . . . Automatic teller machines ask you to provide a personal identification number, which is just a very short password. Another option, which would eliminate the need for you to remember a password, is the use of biometric measurements. . . . a physical trait, such as a voice print or a fingerprint. . . .
>
> . . . Smart cards, the most basic form of the wallet PC, look like credit cards and are popular now in Europe. Their microprocessors are embedded within the plastic. The smart card of the future will identify its owner and store digital money. . . .[8]

That statement from Bill Gates's book *The Road Ahead* is identical with the kinds of predictions made by radio prophecy preachers forty years ago. When such predictions are stated by an industrial leader who, reportedly, bought $2–billion-worth of banking stock in the nineties, it should be taken seriously.

The next logical question—since the chips can be imbedded in small plastic cards—is why not imbed the identification number under a person's skin? That would make it difficult to steal and impossible to lose or forget. Such identification implants are already used on pets. Once the system became universal, people who refused to participate would, by default, be shut out.

For the consumer, such a system means total convenience. For banks, it means huge efficiency gains over paper transactions. For political leaders, it may mean perfect financial control and automatic, instantaneous tax transfers on every sale. For police, it may mean financial trails to each individual's whereabouts.

With the consolidation of national economies in Europe, globalization of the world may not be far away. The biggest driver in globalization and cashless financial transactions is the computer itself, as the following comments by Bill Gates indicate:

> The global information market will be huge and will combine all the various ways human goods, services, and ideas are exchanged. . . . In short, just about everything will be done differently, I can hardly wait for this tomorrow, and I'm doing what I can to help make it happen. . . .
>
> . . . The information highway will extend the electronic marketplace and make it the ultimate go-between, the universal middleman. . . . [Computer] servers distributed worldwide will accept bids, resolve offers into completed transactions, control authentication and security, and handle all other aspects of the marketplace. . . . It will be a shopper's heaven. . . .
>
> This idea will scare a lot of people . . . and I expect dramatic changes in the business of retailing as commerce flows across the highway. But, as with so many changes, I think once we get used to it we'll wonder how we did without it. . . .
>
> . . . When the information highway makes geography less important, we will see electronic, on-line banks that have no branches—no bricks, no mortar, and low fees. These low-overhead electronic banks will be extremely competitive and transactions will be made through computer appliances.[9]

Gates calls this "friction-free capitalism." Or is it the electronic Tower of Babel? The rapid increase in financial transactions over the Internet is creating high demand for a single electronic currency that will work worldwide and a universal language of commerce. If human inertia and fear prevent a fully automated cashless economy at first, the next worldwide economic crash may provide the perfect impetus for implementing such globalization as part of the recovery.

As for the mysterious number 666, here's an interesting piece of trivia: Almost every universal product code (UPC) on nearly every grocery item sold already has this number. In UPC language, one way to represent the number six is with two thin bars. Every grocery UPC has two extended thin bars at the beginning of the code, two extended thin bars in the middle of the code and two extended thin bars at the end of the code. In that sense, every code has a six at the beginning, a six in the center, and a six at the end. These extended bars, called "guard bars," are used by the computer scanner to bracket two sets of numbers that each code is composed of so the computer can lock onto the product code. While the computer does not read these *extended* lines for their numeric value, they appear like sixes would elsewhere in the code, which may be all that matters in terms of locking onto them with biblical prophecy. Maybe it's just a short matter of time until people scan the same way groceries do. So people, too, become a part of the electronic Tower of Babel.

With the world getting so complicated so fast, one has to wonder what will happen to people who are slow on the technical learning curve.

THE TIMES, THEY ARE A CHANGIN'

It's commonly accepted that our sense of time is relative to how much of one's life one has used up. If human history is measured by the ticking of world events, then its chronometer is buzzing; which may indicate that humanity as a whole is reaching its end. The developments of new discoveries and new technologies reached atomic speed in the twentieth century. As also happens with age, the human world is shrinking. The rapid increase in travel and global communication within the last generation is greater than the increase in all previous generations combined. Once a planet of vast unexplored space, earth has shrunk into a village.

This acceleration of travel and increase of knowledge fits the description of the end given to the prophet Daniel:

> *But thou, O Daniel, shut up the words, and seal the book, even to the time of the end: many shall run to and fro, and knowledge shall be increased.... And I heard, but I understood not: then said I, O my Lord, what shall be the end of these things? And he said, Go thy way, Daniel: for the words are closed up and sealed till the time of the end.* (DANIEL 12:4, 8–9)

According to the prophets, however, the specific time of the end is a mystery not to be revealed:

> *But of the times and the seasons, brethren, ye have no need that I write to you. For yourselves know perfectly that the day of the Lord so cometh as a thief*

in the night. For when they shall say, Peace and safety; then sudden destruction cometh upon them, as travail upon a woman with child; and they shall not escape. (1 THESSALONIANS 5:1–3)

If anyone tries to predict specific dates for Christ's return, they're defying prophesy, not illuminating it. A few prognosticators have tried to find a loophole by claiming that Jesus only stated no one would "know the day nor the hour," but that does not preclude knowing the month and the year. That's being hyperliteral.

Nevertheless, the apostles always encouraged belief in the unpredictable but imminent return of Jesus Christ. The resurrection of the Jewish state, the anomalous surge of environmental disasters, the globalization of politics and economics, and the astronomical speed in human developments—all at the turn of a millennium—heighten the sense that the ultimate climax of human history may be close.

Chapter 7

A P⊙C A L Y P S E:

†HE ΠESSiAH REVEALED

INTRODUCTION TO THE APOCALYPSE

The Revelation of Jesus Christ, which God gave to him, to show to his servants things which must shortly come to pass; and he sent and signified it by his angel to his servant John: Who bore witness of the word of God, and of the testimony of Jesus Christ, and of all things that he saw. (REVELATION 1:1–2)

The remainder of this book follows The Apocalypse of John, better known as the Book of Revelation. (Other prophecies of the Bible will tie in where appropriate.) Containing as much Old Testament as it does new revelation, the Apocalypse is the climax of the Bible and the last biblical prophecy written. It marries the Old Testament to the New Testament—the Old Covenant to the New Covenant. The peak of prophetic literature, John's scroll has given its name to all other "apocalyptic" writings.

The word "apocalypse" does not mean "holocaust" as it has come to mean in modern cinema and literature, which has borrowed the book's images. It simply means "revelation" and can refer to any truth that might be revealed, not just to future predictions. John's apocalypse is a specific revelation. It is the "revelation of Jesus Christ." It both comes from Jesus Christ and reveals who he is. Ultimately, it claims to come from God *to* Jesus Christ and *through* his angel *to* John.

John's Apocalypse holds a place in history unlike any other book. No book—even from the Bible—has inspired more dreams of utopia or nightmares of doom than the Book of Revelation. Its vivid imagery and symbolism and its stark warnings have inspired endless paintings and books, television shows, and Hollywood movies. It is a book that transcends time.

John's peculiar symbolism is full of ambiguity, which some readers find frustrating because they want to narrow the images to one specific meaning. Sometimes the best answer to "Does John mean this . . . or that?" may be "yes." Sometimes his prophecy may be intentionally obscure in order to encrypt its meanings from Roman officials; but, for the most part, it is probably ambiguous because it *does* intend more than one meaning. This comes back to economy of language—using one image to cover more than one event.

The desire to solidify the fluid language of the Apocalypse has led to numerous conflicting interpretations from John's commentators, often condemning those who disagree to the nether regions of John's hell. This led Catholic writer G. K. Chesterton to quip, "Though St. John the Evangelist saw many strange monsters in his vision, he saw no creature so wild as one of his own commentators."[1]

APOCALYPTIC TIME

Blessed is he that readeth, and they that hear the words of this prophecy, and keep those things which are written in it: for the time is at hand. (REVELATION 1:3)

When John said "the time is at hand," to what time was he referring? Most scholars believe the destruction of Jerusalem had already happened by the time John wrote the Apocalpyse, but if he was referring to the time of Jesus' return, wasn't he off the mark by, at least, a couple of millennia?

John's Apocalypse defies time. Its eternally potent images weave through the book like a dream, unconscious of time. The process of writing mandates putting one section before another, which may cause the reader to think of them as being sequential. Yet, the dreamscapes described in one section of the book could be overlapping or even lapse back to precede events described earlier in the book.

More than any other book in the Bible, the Apocalypse displays the complex patterns of a fractal, repeating in nonlinear ways. No clear time line emerges. Instead, one gets the unsettled feeling that time is merely a human concern. Modern historians are obsessed with time lines, but the Apocalypse, being concerned with the eternal, looks not for time but for patterns that reflect meaning. It is a bridge between the spiritual, eternal realm and the physical, temporal world.

Parts of the Apocalypse may foreshadow the fall of Rome or later events of the Holy Roman Empire. Recently, many people saw in its predictions a portrayal of the Third Reich, bringing on the end of the world. Some parts, however, have no apparent parallel in history, which indicates the book has yet to be fulfilled.

Throughout all the dire events it predicts, its purpose is to comfort the persecuted people of God in any age. Its nightmarish images bring no fear to those who already live in one of the world's darker corners. For them, the nightmares of the Apocalypse describe the truth they already live. Instead, they see the hope of victory flooding the background of the Apocalypse between every sketch of evil. Perhaps it is by design that the book has been understood by people in every period of historic persecution as being written specifically for their time. Since John borrows most of his images from previous Old Testament writings and reworks them to his contemporary purposes, he would not likely object to his readers doing the same. Because the book is timeless, every generation that reads it is encouraged to believe Jesus is coming in their time.

APOCALYPTIC NUMEROLOGY

The first thing that becomes apparent to many readers of the Apocalypse is that numbers have importance far beyond simple counting. Numeric symbolism is integrated throughout John's vision.

The number three had obvious importance to Christians in representing the triune nature of God—the Father, Son, and Holy Spirit. The human image of the divine nature is reflected in mind, body, and spirit. But the association of the number three with God goes back to the ancient Jews, predating the concept of the trinity.

In an extraordinary encounter, Abraham saw God in the appearance of three men:

And the LORD appeared to him in the plains of Mamre: and he [Abraham] sat in the tent door in the heat of the day; And he lifted up his eyes and looked, and, lo, three men stood by him: and when he saw them, he ran to meet them from the tent door, and bowed himself toward the ground, And said, My Lord, if now I have found favour in thy sight, pass not away, I pray thee, from thy servant: Let a little water, I pray you, be brought, and wash your feet, and rest yourselves under the tree: (GENESIS 18:1–4)

Abraham has a meal prepared while they rested. As they dine together, the text jumps from referring to three men to referring simply to one God, moving confusingly from "they" to "he." Finally, the text seems to call these three, or one of them, "the Lord":

And they said to him, Where is Sarah thy wife? And he [Abraham] said, Behold, in the tent. And he [the other] said, I will certainly return to thee according to the time of life; and, lo, Sarah thy wife shall have a son. And Sarah heard it in the tent door, which was behind him. . . . Therefore Sarah laughed within herself, saying, After I am become old shall I have pleasure, my lord [Abraham] being old also? And the LORD said to Abraham, Why did Sarah laugh, saying, Shall I certainly bear a child, who am old? Is any thing too hard for the LORD? At the time appointed I will return to thee, according to the time of life, and Sarah shall have a son. (GENESIS 18:9, 10, 12–14)

Later in the conversation Abraham refers to these three "men" as the "Judge of all the earth." Christians have seen in this visionary encounter the first hint of the triune nature of God.

Other connections in Jewish literature between the number three and divinity come more by analogy. During the times of Moses, the typical journey into the wilderness to encounter the divine was a three-day journey. In similar fashion, it was three months after the children of Israel fled Egypt that they encountered God at Mt. Sinai on the third day when Moses went up to receive the Ten Commandments. God instituted three holy feasts during the days of Moses and commanded that his altar be built three cubits high. Three days were required after touching a dead body before one could begin the ritual cleansing that would make one pure—the human counterpart to holiness. So, *three* is associated with God and holiness, the primary attribute of God.

Numbers that are *multiples* of three or *divisions* of it are also significant in Jewish symbolism: The number of Israel's chosen men for bringing the ark of the covenant (God's dwelling place) into the city of Jerusalem (making Jerusalem a holy dwelling place) is thirty-thousand. Solomon used three thousand, three hundred chief officers during the building of God's temple as the resting place for the ark. The temple he built was thirty cubits high, divided in three stories. It was built upon three rows of pillars with a hall thirty cubits wide and the whole building was surrounded by a court with walls built in three courses of stone. In the temple was a large basin, thirty cubits in circumference that was supported by twelve bronze oxen, three facing north, three facing south, and it held three thousand measures of water. Solomon offered sacrifices in the temple three times per year in accordance with the holy days ordained under Moses. The wise King Solomon spoke three thousand proverbs during his life. So three is a number associated with holy articles and holy words.

God's judgments are often associated with the number three as well. It is said, God must judge evil *because* he is holy. Judgment is a way of bringing the earth back to a holy standard. The prophet Zechariah was paid thirty pieces of silver for a flock of sheep that was to be slaughtered, symbolizing God's rejection of Israel and the annulment of his covenant with them. This exchange was referred to as "the lordly price at which I was paid off by them." Centuries later Judas is paid off with thirty pieces of silver when he betrays Jesus. The Zekhariah prophecy is quoted, and Israel is finally rejected.

Jesus prayed three times on the night he was betrayed. Peter denies that he knows Jesus three times on the night Jesus is betrayed. Jesus' death from the time he was betrayed spans three days. The *third* time Jesus appears to his disciples after his resurrection from the dead is the last appearance recorded before he ascends into the heavens. At this appearance, he asks Peter three times to take care of his "sheep," meaning his people the Jews, bringing the story full circle to Zechariah's sheep that were sold off to slaughter.

Unusual numeric coincidences happen all the time because the universe is full of numbers. John's Apocalypse, however, seems clearly to intend numeric symbolism. It consistently and emphatically repeats certain numbers, as though to drive the reader's attention toward them. In addition, John writes during an age when certain mystical sects of Judaism were steeped in numerology. It was the right kind of language for a prophet to use.

The second number John repeats frequently is four. In most ancient cultures, including ancient Jewish culture, the number four was a universal symbol (an archetype) representing the earth. The earth has four seasons. For Jews, it was on the fourth day of the creation story that the sun and the moon were created to rule over those seasons and over time itself. This was, in effect, the establishment of time. Four rivers emerged from the paradise of Eden and flowed out to the natural world. Four cardinal points on the compass cover all the directions of earth. As a result, people of all cultures have spoken of the "four winds" or metaphorically of the "four corners of the earth." By extension from the earth, four also represents the created cosmos. So four is the number of creation, that is, of the physical, temporal realm.

The sum of three and four represents the union of the divine and holy one with earth and nature. Seven is John's favorite number. It is where eternity and time meet. It is the immortal joined to mortality. It represents God and nature in totality. Accordingly, the story of God creating the world covers seven days. The *seventh* day of the week, the sabbath, is holy because it represents the fulness of time during which man dwells on earth while God rests from his creative work. (Human civilization would not be possible if the world were not resting from the dynamic forces of creation—extreme volcanism, upheavals of the earth's crust, etc. Humanity dwells under the laws of entropy—the time in which God's creation is coasting, winding down. It is in that sense, that God is at rest.)

Seven carries this distinction of unity between the divine and nature even outside of Jewish writings. In music, there are seven notes on the major scale, thus perfection, harmony. In ancient mythology there were seven divine beings represented by the seven luminaries of the sky—the sun, the moon, and the visible planets.

Because God and nature often meet in holy judgment, God's judgment comes in sevens. (At least, it does for John.) Such periods are also referred to as "the day of the Lord." For God to join with nature, nature must first be purged and perfected. God purges evil, according to the prophets, in order to restore unity between human and human, as well as between human and God. Thus Noah brought *seven* animals of specified kinds for sacrifice when the world, mankind and God were restored in relationship after the flood. If Israel broke its covenant with God, God warned he would punish them *seven* times over if they did not return to him on their own. The final result? They would flee from their enemies in *seven* directions (Deut 28:25).

The Apocalypse repeats this Old Testament cause and effect of divine justice in seven worldwide plagues, where God gives repeated opportunities for the world to repent. Three different parts of Revelation refer to seven plagues, perhaps only because there is more than one series of events, or perhaps to show that collectively their purpose is to bring the world into God's holiness.

Finally, there is the number twelve, which is highly significant in Jewish and Christian history. Twelve is the product of three and four. It is what is produced when there is unity between God and humanity (or creation). Twelve is the number of Jewish patriarchs who descended from Abraham under the first covenant, and it is the number of apostles chosen by Jesus under the New Covenant. The patriarchs fathered the twelve tribes of God's people, Israel. The apostles "fathered" the Church. Genesis also prophesied twelve rulers would descend from Abraham's other son, Ishmael, the forefather of the Islamic nations.

Because Israel was made up of twelve tribes, the number twelve came to represent Israel, itself. This made great sense of the number's symbolic value: Israel was the product of the union between God and humanity. Many of the temple's religious articles were made in twelves, so there would be one to represent each tribe. Just as twelve represents the *fulness* of Israel, it has the meaning of fulness in other cultures. Astrologically, twelve is a complete year—twelve signs of the zodiac and twelve months. Even today, twelve connotes fulness to most people. That's why packagers more often group goods by the dozen than by ten, even though tens are easier to add.

THE ETERNAL SCOPE OF APOCALYPTIC VISION

The numerology in John's vision is introduced right from the beginning:

> *John to the seven churches which are in Asia: Grace be to you, and peace, from him who is, and who was, and who is to come; and from the seven Spirits who are before his throne; And from Jesus Christ, who is the faithful witness, and the first begotten of the dead, and the prince of the kings of the earth. To him that loved us, and washed us from our sins in his own blood, And hath made us kings and priests to God and his Father; to him be glory and dominion for ever and ever. Amen.* (REVELATION 1:4–6)

The vision John receives hints right from the beginning at its overall theme—the coming together of God, humanity, and nature. The things that will be revealed in this book encompass eternity. God is God of the present, the past, and the future. God is the Eternal Creator; God is Spirit; and God is Jesus Christ. Jesus Christ is the faithful witness, the first human resurrected from the dead, and the ruler over all rulers. This *three*-beat cadence is typical of John's style, where the form always fits the symbolic function.

This background beat echoes the number three, like a musical signature of God over all that happens.

Just a couple paragraphs later in his book, the divine being in John's vision tells him to "Write the things which thou hast seen, and the things which are, and the things which shall be after this." The visions described in the book will go back to the birth of Christ (the past that John, himself, "had seen"). Throughout, they will encourage the churches of John's present day in the face of persecution by Rome and perhaps by certain Jews, who saw Christianity as an heretical cult (the things "which are"). And they will give hope to Jesus' followers in future ages, who will also face persecution for their beliefs (the "things which shall be").

The vivid images of the Apocalypse will describe the cosmic battle that led to the fall of Lucifer (the devil) and his angels from heaven. Such events may even be past, on-going, *and* future. They happen, at least in part, outside of our time and space (universe) yet somehow intersect with it. John's book is about this intersection between the eternal and the temporal. Ultimately, John's visions will look toward the far extent of human history, starkly contrasting preliminary scenes of doom with a final "aquarian" age of peace. Finally, everything, climaxes in the creation of a new universe.

No single time in history has ever served as a lens sufficient for bringing the events described in the Apocalypse into clear focus. To try to flatten the contours of this mystical and poetic drama into a two-dimensional chart of events is to reduce a Van Gogh or a surrealist masterpiece into a paint-by-numbers. If it's intended as a book for all times, there may not be an exact match of events with any *one* time, because what has been created is a complexity of rhythms that will repeat in different ways in different times.

The imagery has a vibrancy and force of life that is much more than a coded history written in future tense. It is not a time line for specific events. Historically, those who have tried to box it up with formulaic interpretations that extrapolate dates for events they believe will happen in their own times have all been wrong. Not one of them completely agrees with another. The Apocalypse is a wild creature that will not be tamed by the human mind. Although it describes future scenarios, its relationship to the future is dynamic. It even has the strength to shape the future it describes, as will be demonstrated repeatedly in the remainder of this book.

The Apocalypse is a *living word,* written to embolden and revive those who struggle against evil in the pits of death. Thus, the book began, "Blessed is he that readeth, and they that hear the words of this prophecy, and keep those things which are written in it."

THE REVEALED MESSIAH

The revelation of Messiah, "the revelation of Jesus Christ," is the primary theme of John's book. Everything written in it reveals the Messiah as God's entrance into humanity—past, present and future—and the guarantee of victory over evil:

> *Behold, he cometh with clouds; and every eye shall see him, and they also who pierced him: and all kindreds of the earth shall wail because of him. Even so, Amen.* (REVELATION 1:7)

Writing to an audience that was mostly Gentile Christians but included some Jewish Christians, John began by saying that Christ had made *all* his followers into kings and priests before God. He makes no distinctions based on race. But with this last line, he focuses on a particular prophecy to the Jews because of their historic role:

> *And I [God] will pour upon the house of David, and upon the inhabitants of Jerusalem, the spirit of grace and of supplications: and they shall look upon me whom they have pierced, and they shall mourn for him, as one mourneth for his only son, and shall be in bitterness for him, as one that is in bitterness for his firstborn. In that day shall there be a great mourning in Jerusalem, as the mourning of Hadadrimmon [a place where a national lamentation was held for the death of Jewish king] in the valley of Megiddon [Armageddon]. And the land shall mourn, every family apart; the family of the house of David apart, and their wives apart; the family of the house of Nathan apart, and their wives apart; The family of the house of Levi apart, and their wives apart; the family of Shimei apart, and their wives apart; All the families that remain, every family apart, and their wives apart.* (ZECHARIAH 12:10–14)

The description of Jesus' trial and death in the Gospels of Matthew and John explains the connection John is forging between the Messiah and these citizens of Jerusalem who will look upon the one they have pierced and mourn his death as the death of a firstborn son:

> . . . And the high priest . . . said to him, I adjure thee by the living God, that thou tell us whether thou art the Christ, the Son of God. Jesus saith to him, Thou hast said: nevertheless I say to you, *After this shall ye see the Son of man sitting on the right hand of power, and coming in the clouds of heaven. . . .* Then they spat in his face, and buffeted him; and others smote him with the palms of their hands, Saying, Prophesy to us, thou Christ, Who is he that smote thee? . . .

> . . . When the morning was come,

all the chief priests and elders of the people took counsel against Jesus to put him to death: And when they had bound him, they led him away, and delivered him to Pontius Pilate the governor. . . .

. . . When Pilate saw that he could not prevail at all [against the intentions of the angry Jewish leadership], but that rather a tumult was made, he took water, and washed his hands before the multitude, saying, I am innocent of the blood of this just person: see ye to it. Then answered all the people, and said, His blood be on us, and on our children. . . .

(MATTHEW 26:63–64, 67, 68; 27:1, 2, 24, 25)

John completes the story in his Gospel. Claiming to have been an eyewitness to the crucifixion, he tells that, because the next day was a special day during the passover holidays, the Jewish leaders did not want bodies hanging around Jerusalem left on crosses. Therefore, they asked the Romans to speed up the deaths of everyone crucified that day so they could bury them. In a sense, the following implicates Gentiles as much as Jews:

Then came the soldiers, and broke the legs of the first, and of the other who was crucified with him. But when they came to Jesus, and saw that he was dead already, they broke not his legs: But one of the soldiers with a spear pierced his side, and immediately came out blood and water . . . For these things were done, that the scripture should be fulfilled, A bone of him shall not be broken. And again another scripture saith, They shall look on him whom they pierced.

(JOHN 19:32–34, 36, 37)

Only hours before this, Jesus had walked out of the temple and rejected the priests and leaders, saying,

Behold, your house is left to you desolate: and verily I say to you, Ye shall not see me, until the time shall come when ye shall say, Blessed is he that cometh in the name of the Lord. (LUKE 13:35)

Like many of the older prophecies previously quoted, John's Apocalypse links the return of Jesus to the days when the Jewish leaders rejected him and he rejected them. Hence, the meaning of his statement, "Every eye shall see him, and they also who pierced him." The implication is that everything between his crucifiction and his return happened because of that rejection. The intervening time had to last however long it took until every group of Gentile people had the opportunity to receive the New Covenant that the Jewish leaders had rejected. Once every Gentile people has had that opportunity, Jesus the Messiah will return to bring the Jews into the New Covenant he had offered to them first. Thus, "the first shall be last", but, in the end, all shall be one. Jesus' return is described as being so glorious there will be no question as to who he is. Jews at that future event will accept him with mixed feelings—mourning the past but rejoicing in their final reunion:

Every valley shall be exalted, and every mountain and hill shall be made low: and the crooked shall be made straight, and the rough places plain: And the glory of the LORD shall be revealed, and all flesh together shall see it: for the mouth of the LORD hath spoken it. . . . O Zion, that bringest good tidings, go up upon the high mountain; O Jerusalem, that bringest good tidings, lift up thy voice with strength; lift it up, be not afraid; say to the cities of Judah, Behold your God! Behold, the Lord GOD will come with strong hand, and his arm shall rule for him: behold, his reward is with him, and his work before him.

(ISAIAH 40:4, 5, 9, 10)

In that day there shall be a fountain opened to the house of David and to the inhabitants of Jerusalem for sin and for uncleanness. (ZECHARIAH 13:1)

The broader picture drawn is that Jews and Gentiles will all see the Messiah's return and recognize who he is. John's vision uses the same eternal description for the coming Messiah as it did to describe God:

I am Alpha and Omega, the beginning and the ending, saith the Lord, who is, and who was, and who is to come, the Almighty. (REVELATION 1:8)

And Jesus said, I am: and ye shall see the Son of man sitting on the right hand of power, and coming in the clouds of heaven. (MARK 14:62)

Chapter 8

PERSECUTION:

SEVEN LETTERS FOR SEVEN CHURCHES

Behold, I send you forth as sheep in the midst of wolves: be ye therefore wise as serpents, and harmless as doves. But beware of men: for they will deliver you to the councils, and they will scourge you in their synagogues; And ye shall be brought before governors and kings for my sake, for a testimony against them [the Jews of the synagogues] and the Gentiles.

MATTHEW 10:16–18)

And, all indeed that will live godly in Christ Jesus shall suffer persecution.

(2 TIMOTHY 3:12)

Jesus made it clear to his disciples that the people of Israel would treat them no better than they had treated him. The persecution they would certainly receive would be a testimony against both Jews and Gentiles. Because he cared about what he knew they'd suffer, Jesus reminded them before the event to recall his words of warning as a form of assurance that all of this was a part of what had to be endured if his kingdom was to spread:

Remember the word that I said to you, The servant is not greater than his lord.   *If they have persecuted me, they will also persecute you. . . .*   (JOHN 15:20)

CHRISTIANS UNDER FIRE

By the time John wrote the Apocalypse, he had become intimately familiar with both religious and political persecution. But the abuse early Christians received from their fellow Jews hardly compares to the savagery they received from the Romans.

Everyone is familiar with the story of how Nero fiddled while Rome burned. According to the Roman historian Tacitus, a contemporary of both John and Josephus, rumor had it that Nero was out of town while Rome burned. While the temples of the gods burned like Hades, Nero was at Antium singing on a stage—singing about the destruction of Troy. Strangely, while some Romans tried to extinguish the flames, others stopped them, claiming a higher authority.

As the rebuilding of the city commenced in grand style with broad promenades, public places, gardens, and waterworks, many Romans became suspicious that Nero ordered the fire as a way to prepare for his new construction. It seemed the fires had broken out in the area central to his building scheme. Hadn't Nero spoken of founding a new city named after himself?

Nero badly needed a scapegoat. He blamed the fire on Christians, a convenient group because most Romans already disliked them. Christians openly disapproved of a society that lived for no higher value than entertainment at any cost. Reading the secular historian Tacitus, it's not hard to imagine why Christians were so critical of Nero's self-indulgence:

> Nero . . . prepared banquets in the public places, and used the whole city, so to say, as his private house. Of these entertainments the most famous for their notorious profligacy were those . . . which I will describe as an illustration that I may not have again and again to narrate similar extravagance. He had a raft constructed on Agrippa's lake, put the guests on board and set it in motion by other vessels towing it. These vessels glittered with gold and ivory; the crews were arranged according to age and experience in vice. Birds and beasts had been procured from remote countries, and sea monsters from the ocean. On the margin of the lake were set up brothels crowded with noble ladies, and on the opposite bank were seen naked prostitutes with obscene gestures and movements. . . . Nero, who polluted himself by every lawful and lawless indulgence, had not omitted a single abomination which could heighten his depravity.[1]

Nero hoped to end two of his biggest problems by blaming Christians for the fire. He'd remove the heat of the fire from his own reputation, and he'd get rid of his largest group of critics. Even Tacitus, who despised Christians as beneath contempt, found their persecution by Nero abominable:

> Nero fastened the guilt and inflicted the most exquisite tortures on a class hated for their abominations, called Christians by the populace. Christus, from whom the name had its origin, suffered the extreme penalty during the reign of Tiberius at the hands of one of our procurators, Pontius Pilatus, and a most mischievous superstition, thus checked for the moment, again broke out not only in Judea, the first source of the evil, but even in Rome, where all things hideous and shameful from every part of the world find their centre and become popular. Accordingly, an arrest was first made of all who pleaded guilty [of being Christian]; then, upon

their information, an immense multitude was convicted, not so much of the crime of firing the city, as of hatred against mankind. Mockery of every sort was added to their deaths. Covered with the skins of beasts, they were torn by dogs and perished, or were nailed to crosses, or were doomed to the flames and burnt, to serve as a nightly illumination, when daylight had expired.

Nero offered his gardens for the spectacle, and was exhibiting a show in the circus, while he mingled with the people in the dress of a charioteer or stood aloft on a car. Hence, even for criminals who deserved extreme and exemplary punishment, there arose a feeling of compassion; for it was not, as it seemed, for the public good, but to glut one man's cruelty, that they were being destroyed.[2]

Tacitus also reports that at the close of Nero's persecutions, a comet appeared as an omen against the empire. There had never been more lighting storms, and a number of two-headed births occurred of both animals and humans. People began to talk about the evil presaged by these events. All of these signs occurred just before Nero's war against the Jews, which ended in Jerusalem's destruction. Josephus' history, as already reported, recorded similar bizarre cosmic signs around this time.

Nero, by his insane evil, made himself a natural target of blame for these ill omens, and conspiracies began to mount against him. A failed assassination plot fueled Nero's carefully cultivated paranoia and resulted in the death of a number of Roman officials. His childhood teacher and political counselor, Seneca, also became embroiled in Nero's suspicion. Seneca knew that one who had killed his own mother and brother to secure his crown would not stop at killing his aged teacher. To avoid a worse death by Nero, Seneca slit his wrists and the veins in his legs and lay in a pool of warm water.

A letter supposedly written by Seneca to St. Paul describes the times well. That Seneca appears by the letter to have become a Christian would explain his falling out with Nero. Perhaps Seneca was one of the "saints" who "belong[ed] to Caesar's household," referred to by Paul at the end of his epistle to the Philippians. (Given Nero's extreme hatred of Christians, Paul obviously would have been careful not to mention someone so close to Nero by name, just in case his epistle to the Philippians was intercepted by one of the king's men.) As with many ancient documents, it's difficult to establish for certain whether Seneca actually wrote the following letter, but St. Jerome, who translated the first Bible from Hebrew into Latin, believed in it implicitly:

Annaeus Seneca to Paul, Greeting:
All happiness to you, my dearest Paul. Do you not suppose I am extremely concerned and grieved that your innocence should bring you into sufferings? And that all the people should suppose you (Christians) so criminal, and imagine all the misfortunes that happen to the city, to be caused by you? But let us bear the charge with a patient temper, appealing (for our innocence) to the court (above),

which is the only one our hard fortune will allow us to address to, till at length our misfortunes shall end in unalterable happiness. . . .

. . . As to the frequent burnings of the city of Rome, the cause is manifest; and if a person in my mean circumstances might be allowed to speak, and one might declare these dark things without danger, every one should see the whole matter. The Christians and the Jews are indeed commonly punished for the crime of burning the city; but that impious miscreant, who delights in murders and butcheries, and disguises his villainies with lies, is appointed to, or reserved till, his proper time. And as the life of every excellent person is now sacrificed instead of that one person (who is the author of the mischief) so this one shall be sacrificed for many, and he shall be devoted to be burnt with fire instead of all.

One hundred and thirty-two houses, and four whole squares (or islands) were burnt down in six days: the seventh put an end to the burning. I wish you all happiness.[3]

Seneca's misfortunes, and possibly Paul's, did not end in "unalterable happiness" on this side of death. (Eusebius records that at about this time Nero had the Apostle Paul beheaded and Peter crucified upside down.) It could be this letter never made it to Paul. Since it has Seneca's name on it, it could have been the very cause of Nero's suspicion— if it was intercepted.

Others, besides Seneca, chose suicide to escape the tortures of Nero. The final memoirs of Nero's life are written in the blood of his confidants, political enemies, and former friends. Rome became a temple of human sacrifice, a city of funerals. Talk grew around the capital that Nero had killed many innocent people out of rank jealousy and fear. Not long after these general terrors, he killed his own pregnant wife in a flare of rage by killing her with a kick.

All the while, Tacitus records, heaven continued to mark these evil deeds "by storms and pestilence." A hurricane destroyed country houses and crops, "sweeping away all classes of human beings":

Houses were filled with lifeless forms and the streets with funerals. . . . Wives and children . . . were often consumed on the very funeral pile of their friends by whom they had been sitting and shedding tears. Knights and senators perished indiscriminately, and yet their deaths were less deplored because they seemed to forestall the emperor's cruelty by an ordinary death.[4]

Even if I had to relate foreign wars and deaths encountered in the service of the State with such a monotony of disaster, I should myself have been overcome by disgust, while I should look for weariness in my readers, sickened as they would be by the melancholy and continuous destruction of our citizens . . . so much wanton bloodshed at home fatigue the mind and paralyze it with grief. The only indulgence I would ask . . . is that I be not thought to hate men . . . Such was the wrath of heaven against the Roman State that one may not pass over it with a single mention.[5]

Nero's inflamed heart engulfed him in a hatred that burned throughout the city of Rome, and he eventually ended by taking his own life in order to prevent others from doing it for him—just as his victims had ended theirs.

In summarizing the state of Rome during the siege of Jerusalem, which followed the death of Nero, Tacitus says,

> I am entering on the history of a period rich in disasters, frightful in its wars, torn by civil strife, and even in peace full of horrors. . . . Besides the manifold vicissitudes of human affairs, there were prodigies in heaven and earth, the warning voices of thunder and other intimations of the future. . . . Never surely did more terrible calamities of the Roman People, or evidence more conclusive, prove that the Gods take no thought for our happiness, but only for our punishment.[6]

Given all the things Rome was doing against the people of God's two covenants, perhaps it was not the *Roman* gods who were speaking.

Rome fell into civil war and famine for more than a year as three pretenders to the throne killed each other in quest of power. This convinced Vespasian, who was fighting the Jews, that it was in the state's best interest and his own that he leave Judea in the hands of his son Titus in order to consolidate his power and move his armies to Rome to claim the throne. With Vespasian's success, Christians, who had fled Israel because of prophetic warnings, enjoyed a brief period of reprieve from persecution, which now focused solely on the Jews.

It was a short reprieve. After Vespasian died, his son Titus took over as Caesar, but he was killed by his brother Domitian. Eusebius describes life under this fratricide and indicates how all of these events connected to John's writing of the Apocalypse:

> Many were the victims of Domitian's appalling cruelty. At Rome great numbers of men were executed without a fair trial, and countless other eminent men were for no reason at all banished from the country. . . . He showed himself the successor of Nero in enmity and hostility to God. He was, in fact, the second to organize persecution against us. . . .
> . . . There is ample evidence that at that time the apostle and evangelist John was still alive, and because of his testimony to the word of God was sentenced to confinement on the island of Patmos.[7]

Because Jesus was a descendent of King David, Domitian ordered the execution of everyone who was a descendent of David's line, right down to the grandsons of Jesus' brother Jude. Again, history was repeating itself, for Caesar Augustus had done a similar thing when Jesus was born. The same beast of Roman imperialism drove both emperors to deluded attempts at preserving their power by austere persecution. When Domitian saw, however, that these grandsons were common laborers, he released them as unlikely rivals to his throne.

It seems few Christians died a natural death during the first two centuries of the new faith. Regarding his own times in the second century, Justin Martyr writes of his life before becoming a Christian:

> I . . . used to hear the Christians abused, but when I found them fearless in the face of death and all that men think terrible, it dawned on me that they could not possibly be living in wickedness and self-indulgence. For how could a self-indulgent person . . . greet death with a smile, as if he wanted to be deprived of the things he loved most?[8]

These were the storms during which the Apocalypse was written. One has to wonder whether Christianity would have spread at all if Jesus had not died and risen from the dead as reported. How would so many hundreds of people have found the courage to brave their own deaths as the cost for enlightening the darkness of Rome? In that respect, the death of Jesus, instead of ending the movement he had begun, became the fuel that burned in the hearts of thousands of his followers. Jesus' death and resurrection was the one hope they clung to as they endured the cost of spreading his words. If he was willing to die, so were his disciples. If they were willing to die, so were their disciples.

The Christians Nero placed on stakes to illuminate the nights of his cinder city burned an inextinguishable image into the retinas of the Roman populous. The light of their death revealed Nero's evil for what it was and caused thousands of Romans to wonder what consolation was worth so great a cost to these Christians.

Throughout these times the followers of Jesus did not return fire for fire. The kingdom of the Messiah was to be different from all earthly kingdoms, which had come by conquest, war, human suffering and inflicted death. If the Kingdom of Heaven was to overcome the numerous kingdoms of earth it would do so by being true to its own values.

GOD'S PROMISE OF JUSTICE

Whether or not the followers of Jesus who live near the time of his predicted return will endure sufferings like those endured under Rome is often a matter of contentious debate. That they would bear such suffering in John's day, however, is clearly a major theme of the Apocalypse, starting with the letters to the seven churches. Since the Apocalypse also relates to the future, perhaps similar times should be expected again.

I John, who also am your brother, and companion in tribulation, and in the kingdom and patience of Jesus Christ, was in the isle that is called Patmos, for the word of God, and for the testimony of Jesus Christ. I was in the Spirit on the Lord's day, and heard behind me a great voice, as of a trumpet, Saying, I am Al- pha and Omega, the first and the last: and, What thou seest, write in a book, and send it to the seven churches which are in Asia; to Ephesus, and to Smyrna, and to Pergamos, and to Thyatira, and to Sardis, and to Philadelphia, and to Laodicea. (REVELATION 1:9–11)

The Apocalypse is addressed to seven local churches in John's day, probably churches over which he was bishop. The word "church" actually means a gathering or congregation. ("Church" with a capital "C" indicates *all* followers of Christ or a major grouping, such as the "Catholic Church," rather than a local congregation.) Even in the small provence of Asia Minor, referred to here simply as "Asia," there were more churches than the seven mentioned. That the vision selects only seven, which form a circle among the many, indicates seven were chosen for the symbolic value of the number, fitting the book's major themes of divine justice and divine interaction with the natural world.

Epistles or letters had become the accepted form of Christian expression by the time John wrote the Apocalypse. These letters, however, are much more literary in their precise use of symbolism than most—symbols that are repeated throughout the book. The seven letters are clearly one unified expression, illustrating in detail the various symbols that occur in John's first vision. They are even unified in form.

At least six of the seven churches that are described in the first few chapters of the Apocalypse endured persecution, often severe, and the seventh was promised it would soon receive its share too. All are told how they can be overcomers. One of the first things revealed about the prophet writing this book is that he is among his churches in their suffering, even if he is not among them in person, as he would like to be. John has been exiled to the Roman version of Alcatraz for his religious beliefs. Patmos was a penal colony where prisoner slaves quarried marble for Roman palaces. John was probably placed there by Domitian, though one or two scholars think he was exiled earlier under Nero.

The Apocalypse is, above all, a promise that those followers of Christ who withstand the flames of Rome (or of any regime in any time) will receive justice. For spiritual endurance in the face of great evil, it promises rewards that human language is inadequate to describe.

A Vision of Jesus Christ after Death

The prophet Daniel once had a vision of the Messiah that depicted him as being like a human ("like a son of man") but also as having divinely appointed eternal dominion over all nations:

I saw in the night visions, and, behold, one like the Son of man came with the clouds of heaven, and came to the Ancient of days, and they brought him near before him. And there was given him dominion, and glory, and a kingdom, that all people, nations, and languages, should serve him: his dominion is an everlasting dominion, which shall not pass away, and his kingdom that which shall not be destroyed.

(DANIEL 7:13, 14)

Presumably Daniel's envisioned Messiah would fulfill the role in Nebuchadnezzar's dream of the stone that was not cut out with hands, which became a mountain that destroyed all kingdoms and dominated the earth forever. John's vision of the Son of Man is closely patterned on a description of the Book of Daniel (see Daniel 10:5–12 for the comparison):

And I turned to see the voice that spoke with me. And having turned, I saw seven golden lampstands; And in the midst of the seven lampstands one like the Son of man, clothed with a garment down to the foot, and girt about the breasts with a golden band. His head and his hairs were white like wool, as white as snow; and his eyes were as a flame of fire; And his feet like fine brass, as if they burned in a furnace; and his voice as the sound of many waters. And he had in his right hand seven stars: and out of his mouth went a sharp two-edged sword: and his countenance was as the sun shineth in his strength. And when I saw him, I fell at his feet as dead. And he laid his right hand upon me, saying to me, Fear not; I am the first and the last: I am he that liveth, and was dead; and, behold, I am alive for evermore, Amen; and have the keys of hell and of death. Write the things which thou hast seen, and the things which are, and the things which shall be after this; The mystery of the seven stars which thou sawest in my right hand, and the seven golden lampstands. The seven stars are the angels of the seven churches: and the seven lampstands which thou sawest are the seven churches.

(REVELATION 1:12–20)

Nearly every element of John's vision of the divine being exists for its symbolic value and will be used in each of the letters to the churches—even the attributes of the being himself. Lampstands represent the churches because they are like the people of God—designed to hold a burning lamp, which represents the Spirit of God, who gives light to the world through each church. The sword extended from the mouth of the being in this vision is not likely a literal description of Jesus Christ in heaven. Like the Sacred Heart image of Jesus of Catholic piety, it is not intended to be taken literally, but rather one use the image to find meaning.

Thus, the sword indicates this is the one who fights his battles with the truth that comes from his mouth, not with the weapons of war. The image is in keeping with other New Testament passages such as Ephesians: 6:17—"And take the helmet of salvation, and the sword of the Spirit, which is the word of God"—or Hebrews 4:12—"For the word of God is living, and powerful, and sharper than any twoedged sword, piercing even to the dividing asunder of soul and spirit, and of the joints and marrow, and is a discerner of the thoughts and intents of the heart."

The one seen by John is likely white because he is pure. His eyes are radiant like fire because they melt away our masks and pretenses, penetrating to the thoughts and attitudes of the heart: "Neither is there any creature that is hidden in his sight: but all things are naked and opened to the eyes of him with whom we have to do" (Hebrews 4:13). His voice roars like the surf or like a great waterfall because his word has overwhelming power. He holds the seven stars that represent the seven angels of the seven churches in his right hand as a sign that he holds the churches securely in his grasp—that every church has angelic protection. The right hand repeatedly symbolizes authority in the Bible. It is the hand that bestows blessings and covenants. In all, Christ reveals himself through an image (or angelic representative), showing glory and majesty, purity and truth, power and authority.

The virtues and power ascribed to this being are held by one who is also compassionate, one who lays his hand upon John's shoulder and says to him, "Do not be afraid." Words that seem to echo through time to all who would face persecution.

THE CHURCH AT EPHESUS

The seven churches seem to have been chosen because they exemplify problems that can be found in churches today. Because the letters are written in a single document (a scroll) to be circulated among *all* the churches, it's clear that each church was intended to learn from what had been written to the all the others. In this way, each "church" that John describes represents virtues to be emulated and imperfections to be avoided by anyone during any time—at the "end time" or otherwise.

One school of prophecy, called Fundamentalism or Dispensationalism sees the seven churches as figuratively representing seven stages of church history from the time of Christ's ascension until his return.

John's first letter is to the church at Ephesus. Ephesus was the closest city to John's exile and was the capital of Asia Minor (now Turkey), a city of international renown.

The most significant city in Asia Minor also contained one of the most significant churches in Asia Minor. There's fairly strong agreement in historic testimony that John probably lived in Ephesus before and after his exile. Because it was the center of his ministry, the Christians there may have held a special place in his heart. The emphasis of the first letter John is asked to write is on love.

The city is also a good example of the religious environment John encountered on a daily basis. It was the seat of emperor worship in Asia Minor with a temple dedicated apparently to Vespasian, Titus, and his brother Domitian. This temple had such regional significance that there are inscriptions honoring it in several other cities. Another temple appears to have been dedicated to the deified Julius Caesar. Obviously, Ephesus was also the capital of imperial cults. The book John is about to write will easily be understood by his followers as denouncing this entire system of worshiping human beings. The refusal of Christians to worship emperors at a seat of emperor worship could not go unpunished—as John apparently found out before writing the Apocalypse.

Ephesus also had an ancient temple to the mysteries of Artemis (the goddess Diana) that predated emperor worship. Represented with a turreted head and multiple breasts, Artemis was served by temple prostitutes. This great temple was a source of major civic pride and a significant economic center because of the manufacture of silver talismans, shrines, and souvenirs, as well as prostitution. If Christianity challenged this religion, it was threatening the local economy and pride. (Such a confrontation is recorded in the New Testament Book of Acts.)

One of the primary functions of all prophets was to be a critic of their own society, speaking the words of God. John begins his perilous critique with this instruction from the spiritual being in his vision, which starts with elements from John's earlier vision of the son of man, and which emphasize Ephesus' centrality among the seven churches:

> To the angel of the church of Ephesus write; These things saith he that holdeth the seven stars in his right hand, who walketh in the midst of the seven golden lampstands; I know thy works, and thy labour, and thy patience, and that thou canst not bear them who are evil: and thou hast tried them who say they are apostles, and are not, and hast found them liars: And hast borne [held up], and hast patience, and for my name's sake hast laboured, and hast not fainted. Nevertheless I have somewhat against thee, because thou hast left thy first love. Remember therefore from which thou hast fallen, and repent, and do the first works; or else I will come to thee quickly, and will remove thy lampstand out of its place, except thou repent. But this thou hast, that thou hatest the deeds of the Nicolaitans, which I also hate. He that hath an ear, let him hear what the Spirit saith to the churches; To him that overcometh will I give to eat of the tree of life, which is in the midst of the paradise of God. (REVELATION 2:1–7)

Rather than being like those described by the Old Testament prophets as "ever hearing but never understanding," John's listeners are counseled to listen with spiritual ears to understand spiritual truths. In essence, the message is that it doesn't much matter if you do all the right things and stand up for good and against evil, if you do it without love.

The message echoes familiar words spoken by Jesus when he walked the earth: When a religious leader asked him what was essential for eternal life, the answer was ". . . Thou shalt love the Lord thy God with all thy heart, and with all thy soul, and with all thy strength, and with all thy mind; and thy neighbour as thyself" (Luke 10:27). The "first love" for the Ephesians should be their love for God. Love for God, however, cannot be separated from love for neighbor. The Apostle Paul also affirmed that love is higher than any religious act: "And though I have the gift of prophecy, and understand all mysteries, and all knowledge; and though I have all faith, so that I could remove mountains, and have not charity [love], I am nothing" (1 Corinthians 13:2).

This church is commended for its firm stand against evil and false people and for enduring hardships. They have gained personal refinement as a result of persecution—turning evil to good. According to early church traditions, the false doctrines this church stood against came about by a misunderstanding of a church deacon named Nicolaus. The Book of Acts says he was a convert to Judaism who became a Christian and was later appointed as a church deacon by the apostles. According to St. Clement of Alexandria, this man had an attractive young wife, and the apostles accused Nicolaus of jealousy because of her beauty. To prove he was not a jealous man, Nicolaus offered his wife to any one of them who would have her, and he became one of the first ascetic Christians (a case of misguided zeal). Of course, they did not take him up on the offer or they would have been worse than what they accused him of.

After this, according to tradition, Nicolaus began preaching that "the flesh must be treated with contempt." He renounced all desire in the belief that yielding to pleasure was a distraction from serving God. The sect that claimed his name, however, deliberately misinterpreted this famous statement as a license to get fat, get drunk, and practice promiscuity. After all, if this body of flesh wasn't important, what did it matter what you did with it?[9]

This church is commended for standing against such materialism, yet, without love, good doctrinal theology degenerates into anger between those who differ in their beliefs. And there is a stiff warning taken from the vision of the divine being: this one who walks among the seven golden lampstands will remove their lampstand (their church) from its place if they do not restore the love they have lost. Those who love, even in spite of their persecutions, will find themselves in paradise forever.

Removal from their place was a vivid warning to this particular church: The entire port city of Ephesus had been moved more than once in its history because of its drifting coastline. Perhaps the church did not heed the warning, however, for today, one could not even guess which building may have once contained the church that was the center of Asian ministry.

THE CHURCH AT SMYRNA

And to the angel of the church in Smyrna write; These things saith the first and the last, who was dead, and is alive; I know thy works, and tribulation, and poverty, (but thou art rich) and I know the blasphemy of them who say they are Jews, and are not, but are the synagogue of Satan. Fear none of those things which thou shalt suffer: behold, the devil shall cast some of you into prison, that ye may be tried; and ye shall have tribulation ten days: be thou faithful to death, and I will give thee a crown of life. He that hath an ear, let him hear what the Spirit saith to the churches; He that overcometh shall not be hurt by the second death. (REVELATION 2:8–11)

As with Ephesus, the persecution in Smyrna came about mostly because of emperor worship. Smyrna had a temple dedicated to Tiberius Caesar and the Roman Senate. Pressed in on one side by Romans who would kill them for not worshiping the emperor and on the other by Jewish persecution, this little band of Jesus' followers had much to fear. So the letter to this church starts with an encouraging reminder from John's first vision that the one speaking in John's vision has overcome death.

All of this can be seen in a letter from the church of Smyrna to the other churches around it, which describes the number of martyrdoms they had to endure, the most notable of which is that of their bishop, Polycarp, who was a young man when the Apocalypse was written and, in fact, was appointed to his position by John. He died an old man as described in the following abridgement of the letter, which shows things did not change much after John's time. John may even have been predicting these very events:

The hour for departure had come . . . and they brought him [Polycarp] to the city. The day was a Great Sabbath [Passover Saturday, as when Jesus had died]. . . . He set off happily and at a swinging pace for the stadium. There the noise was so deafening that many could not hear at all, but as Polycarp came into the arena a voice from heaven came to him: "Be strong, Polycarp, and play the man." No one saw the speaker, but many of our people heard the voice.

His introduction was followed by a tremendous roar as the news went around: "Polycarp has been arrested!" . . . The governor pressed him . . . "I will set you free: Execrate Christ." "For eighty-six years," replied Polycarp, "I have been His servant, and He has never done me wrong: how can I blaspheme my King who saved me?" . . . I have wild beasts," said the proconsul. "I shall throw you to them, if you don't change your attitude." "Call them," replied the old man. "If you make light of the beasts," retorted the governor, "I'll have you destroyed by fire, unless you change your attitude." Polycarp answered: "The fire you threaten burns for a time and is soon extinguished: there is a fire you know nothing about—the fire of the judgement to come and of eternal punishment, the fire reserved for the ungodly. But why do you hesitate? Do what you want."

As he said this and much besides, he was filled with courage and joy, and his features were full of grace. . . . the proconsul was amazed, and sent the crier to stand in the middle of the arena and announce three times: "Polycarp has confessed that he is a Christian." At this announcement the whole mass of Smyrnaeans, Gentiles, and Jews alike, boiled with anger and shouted at the tops of their voices: "This fellow is . . . the father of the Christians, the destroyer of our gods, who teaches numbers of people not to sacrifice or even worship." . . . Then a shout went up from every throat that Polycarp must be burnt alive.

The crowds rushed to collect logs and [bundles of sticks] from the workshop and public baths, the Jews as usual joining in with more enthusiasm than anyone. . . . The instruments prepared for the pyre were put round him, but when they were going to nail him too, he cried: "Leave me as I am: He who enables me to endure the fire will enable me, even if you don't secure me with nails, to remain on the pyre without shrinking." So they bound him without nailing him. . . . Then he prayed: "O Father . . . I bless Thee for counting me worthy of this day and hour, that in the number of the martyrs I may partake of Christ's cup, to the resurrection of eternal life of both soul and body. . . . Among them may I be received into Thy presence today, a rich and acceptable sacrifice. . . ."

When he had offered up the Amen and completed his prayer, the men in charge lit the fire, and a great flame shot up. Then we saw a marvelous sight . . . The fire took the shape of a vaulted room, like a ship's sail filled with wind, and made a wall round the martyr's body, which was in the middle not like burning flesh but like gold and silver refined in a furnace. . . . At last, seeing that the body could not be consumed by the fire, the lawless people summoned [an executioner] to come forward and drive home his sword. When he did so there came out a stream of blood that quenched the fire, so that the whole crowd was astonished. . . .

. . . Nicetes . . . was induced to request the governor not to give up the body "lest they should abandon the Crucified and start worshipping this fellow." These suggestions were made under persistent pressure from the Jews, who watched us when we were going to take him out of the fire, not realizing that we can never forsake Christ.

. . . Such was the story of the blessed Polycarp. Counting those from Philadelphia, he was the twelfth to endure martyrdom at Smyrna.[10]

To a reader at the beginning of the twenty-first century, some of the claims of this letter sound embellished, and maybe they are, but they present no greater miracles than the Apocalypse itself—full of stranger tales than modern philosophy can contain. The letter from Smyrna also describes how the deadly squeeze between Jews and Romans tempted some members of this church to publicly deny their Christian beliefs. What, after all, would it hurt to claim one thing outwardly so long as they retained their beliefs inwardly? Are not beliefs purely an internal matter between oneself and God?

Because Jesus never turned aside from his public teachings in order to spare his life, neither did his true followers. Words were worth everything. They were important enough to make it worth enduring severe persecutions from their own countrymen. It is from Jesus' own experience when the Jewish leaders claimed he was possessed by a satanic spirit that the resurrected Jesus now says in this vision given to John, "I know the blasphemy of them who say they are Jews, and are not." Jesus had called their rejection blasphemy of the Holy Spirit. Now he turns their blasphemy around and proclaims these people are "the synagogue of Satan."

Incidents like the burning of Polycarp revealed that the spirit of John's contemporaries had not abated since the days when Jesus walked the earth. The Apocalypse was written to confront persecution from both Romans and Jews, but its emphasis turns toward the Romans because it is written in a time when Jewish persecution was on the wane.

The Apocalypse reveals a spiritual reality far greater than the physical world in order to encourage the new Christians to overcome their fear of death. The one who first overcame death now appears to John and promises his followers they will not be hurt by the "second death"—the lake of fire shown later in the Apocalypse to be the damnation of the evil. This is both encouragement and a not-so-veiled threat that graver matters are at stake, so hold to the truth. Words can damn your soul.

The Apocalypse is no sunny promise of protection from harm. It does not tell John's congregations they will prosper and experience good health if they live a godly life. On the contrary, it promises them they will die—a hard fact recorded later in history with the many deaths during Polycarp's time. The only promise it gives to the people of Smyrna—and only if they remain faithful to the point of death—is the crown of life hereafter. It is not a once-saved, always-saved promise. They must stay the course. Everything is at stake.

Along these lines, the mysterious statement "ye shall have tribulation ten days" may be attributed figuratively to the ten periods of imperial persecution that were yet to come upon all of Asia Minor.

Finally, the crown was an especially relevant symbol to the Christians in Smyrna. Their city was known as the "Crowned City" because of the majestic public buildings ringing the summit of its central hill.

THE CHURCH AT PERGAMOS

And to the angel of the church in Pergamos write; These things saith he who hath the sharp sword with two edges; I know thy works, and where thou dwellest, even where Satan's throne is: and thou holdest fast my name, and hast not denied my faith, even in those days in which Antipas was my faithful martyr, who was slain among you, where Satan dwelleth. But I have a few things against thee, because thou hast there them that hold the doctrine of Balaam, who taught Balak to cast a stumbling-block before the children of Israel, to eat things sacrificed to idols, and to commit acts of immorality. So hast thou also them that hold the doctrine of the Nicolaitans, which thing I hate. Repent; or else I will come to thee quickly, and will fight against them with the sword of my mouth. He that hath an ear, let him hear what the Spirit saith to the churches; To him that overcometh will I give to eat of the hidden manna, and will give him a white stone, and on the stone a new name written, which no man knoweth except he that receiveth it.

(REVELATION 2:12–17)

The old provincial capital of Pergamos was the earliest place outside the city of Rome to establish an imperial cult. Its temple was dedicated to Augustus and to Rome, probably to make its loyalty to the imperial capital unquestionable. After the Apocalypse was written, Pergamos also acquired a shrine to the emperor Trajan. The reference to Satan's throne, however, may refer to another temple in this city where Aesculapious was worshipped in the form of a serpent, the biblical symbol for Satan. The serpent was so central to the city's culture that its image was even stamped on the city's coins. Pergamos also had a monumental throne-like altar to "Zeus the Savior" and Athena. So, there were many ancient and newer religions vying for ascendancy.

In such a city of religious confusion, the image of the double-edged sword of truth that is drawn or extends from the mouth of Christ is perfect. The primary offense faced by this church is, not surprisingly, false teaching. Only a brazen and determined truth could cut through all the surrounding paganism and imperial arrogance.

The allusion to Balaam refers to a sorcerer/prophet who was summoned by an ancient king to curse God's people, the Jews, as they were being led by Moses into the promised land. It's hard to tell from the Old Testament just what Balaam did that was wrong. He refuses to curse the people and, instead, blesses them just as God instructs. The only thing clear from the Old Testament version of the story is that the king offered Balaam an enormous sum of money if he would curse the Israelites, and Balaam seems all too eager to go to the king in hopes that God will allow him to give the curse and collect the cash.

Perhaps the expression "dumb ass" comes from the story of Balaam, for Balaam's donkey sees the angel of the Lord is trying to stop them from traveling to meet the king; whereas Balaam seems only to see the money that lures him on. The donkey stops, and Balaam beats the donkey for doing so. This happens three times. In the story, it is the poor dumb donkey who finally speaks and pleads for Balaam to stop beating it. Finally, the divine spirit that blocks their path becomes visible to Balaam also and says,

> . . . Wherefore hast thou smitten thine ass these three times? behold, I went out to withstand thee, because thy way is perverse before me: And the ass saw me, and turned from me these three times: unless she had turned from me, surely now also I had slain thee, and saved her alive." (NUMBERS 22:32–33)

Thus, even the "dumb ass" could see what the great seer could not.

The divine being allows Balaam to continue on his way so long as he speaks only what God tells him to. The king's money sounds awfully good, and Balaam eagerly implores God to curse Israel, but God says, "No." Balaam instructs the king to have seven altars built. Balaam, then, offers a sacrifice on each of the seven altars and begs God once more to let him curse Israel. Since the number seven signifies God's interaction with nature—including his judgment against it—these sacrifices represent Balaam's attempt to invoke God's judgment, almost as if by incantation. Because God's judgment is only righteous, Balaam fails repeatedly, but he won't give up (according to Josephus' account). Each time he fails, he moves to other ground, builds seven more altars and implores God again for permission to curse Israel.

In the end, Balaam is disgruntled because he is unable to receive the king's reward. The only things God allows him to say are, first, blessings upon a future king of Israel and, then, curses on the people of Moab and their king, Balaak, and his allies:

> He shall pour the water out of his buckets, and his seed shall be in many waters, and his king shall be higher than Agag, and his kingdom shall be exalted. God brought him forth from Egypt; he hath as it were the strength of an unicorn: he shall eat up the nations his enemies, and shall break their bones, and pierce them through with his arrows. He crouched, he lay down as a lion, and as a great lion: who shall rouse him? Blessed is he that blesseth thee, and cursed is he that curseth thee. . . . I shall see him, but not now: I shall behold him, but not near: there shall come a Star out of Jacob, and a Sceptre shall rise out of Israel, and shall smite the corners of Moab, and destroy all the children of Sheth. And Edom [allies of Moab] shall be a possession, Seir also shall be a possession for his enemies; and Israel shall do valiantly. Out of Jacob shall come he that shall have dominion, and shall destroy him that remaineth of the city.
>
> (NUMBERS 24: 7–9, 17–19)

Here, in fact, could be one of the earliest messianic prophecies in the Old Testament. The star and the scepter indicate David, who is still remembered by the star of David, but some feel this prophecy also envisions to the descendent of David who would reign forever.

If Balaam had stopped here, everything would have been fine, but he didn't. Balaam's passion was for money over truth or justice, and the king, needless to say, was rather nonplussed with Balaam for doing the opposite of what he had been hired to do. According to the Jewish historian Josephus, in his *Antiquities of the Jews,* Balaam wasn't too happy about having to return home without a fattened purse. So, Josephus says, Balaam stopped on his return journey and sent for the king, telling him that even though God would not let him prophesy against Israel, he knew a way Israel could be defeated. Balaam tried to dodge God's intent on a technicality by simply telling the king where Israel was vulnerable:

> The providence of God is concerned to preserve them . . . nor will it permit any such calamity . . . whereby they may all perish; but some small misfortunes, and those for a short time . . . may still befall them. . . . If you have a mind to gain a victory over them for a short space of time, you will obtain it by following my directions: . . . Set out . . . such of your daughters as are most eminent for beauty. . . . Send them to be near the Israelites' camp . . . that when the young men of the Hebrews desire their company, they allow it, and when they see that they are enamored of them, let them take their leaves; and if they [the young men] entreat them to stay, let them not give their consent till they have persuaded them to leave off their obedience to their own [religious] laws and the worship of that God who established them and to worship the gods of the Midianites and Moabites; for by this means God will be angry at them.[11]

According to Josephus, the plan worked precisely as Balaam had laid it out. Just when the men were becoming drunk with passion, the Moabite or Midianite women said it was time for them to go home. The men offered an equal share of all their wealth if these very beautiful women would stay and marry them, but the women said they had plenty of wealth and plenty of affection at home. They protested that they were religious women and could not marry men of another religion:

> . . . nor did we admit of your invitations with design to prostitute the beauty of our bodies for gain. . . . Now seeing you say that you have a great affection for us, and are troubled when you think we are departing, we are not averse to your entreaties; and if we may receive such assurance of your good-will . . . we will be glad to lead our lives with you as your wives. . . . It will be absolutely necessary if you would have us as your wives, that you do withall worship our gods . . . for has any-

one reason to complain that now you are come into this country, you should worship the proper gods of the same country? Especially while our gods are common to all men, and yours such as belong to nobody else but yourselves.[12]

Fools for Eros, the men caved in completely, even to the point of rebelling against Moses later when he implored them to remain faithful to the God who had provided for them on their exodus from Egypt. Moses' opponents argued that the laws of their God were too demanding, and life with the Moabite women was much sweeter, and that Moses was harder upon the Hebrews than the Egyptians had been. This resulted in a battle breaking out between those who had already married Moabite women and those who had refused. Between the battle and a plague (which Josephus credits to God), more than fourteen thousand Israelites died. Moses prevailed and then turned against the king of Moab and his allies the Midianites. In the end, Balaam was stoned to death for his troubles.

Josephus explanation is likely accurate because it squares well with other clues from the New Testament:

[They] have forsaken the right way, and gone astray, following the way of Balaam the son of Beor, who loved the wages of unrighteousness." (2 PETER 2:15)

Woe to them! for they have . . . run greedily after the error of Balaam for reward. . . .
(JUDE 1:11)

This, apparently, was the danger for John's church at Pergamo Although money may not have been the incentive, people like Balaam were persuading new Christians to indulge their passions for women and to eat food sacrificed to the Roman idols. They could enjoy life and avoid needless Roman persecution by fitting in. All they needed to do was pay a little respect to the images of Aesculapious or perhaps of Caesar—either being likely candidates for the "Satan" that dwelled among them. The argument likely ran something like this: "You can honor Christ privately, but publicly live as the Romans do. What good are you to God if you're dead?"

But to those who remain true to their Christian beliefs by turning down temptation in favor of persecution, the Spirit says, "I will give some of the hidden manna" and "a new name."

Manna was the bread that came from heaven to feed the Israelites during their desert sojourn with Moses. This was a reminder that, just as Israel should have stayed true to the God who provided during their exodus (rather than falling to Balaam's temptation), so should these followers remain true to Jesus. The "hidden" manna is spiritual bread—invisible bread—as indicated by Jesus in John's other book:

Our fathers ate manna in the desert; as it is written, He gave them bread from heaven to eat. Then Jesus said to them, Verily, verily, I say to you, Moses gave you not that bread from heaven; but my Father giveth you the true bread from heaven. For the bread of God is he who cometh down from heaven, and giveth life to the world. . . . And Jesus said to them, I am the bread of life: he that cometh to me shall never hunger; and he that believeth on me shall never thirst. . . . Your fathers ate manna in the wilderness, and are dead. . . . I am the living bread which came down from heaven: if any man shall eat of this bread, he shall live for ever: and the bread that I will give is my flesh, which I will give for the life of the world.

(JOHN 6:31–33, 35, 49, 51)

The new name promised by the Spirit is reminiscent of a prophecy in Isaiah:

And ye [those under the old covenant] shall leave your name for a curse to my chosen: for the Lord GOD shall slay thee, and call his servants by another name.

(ISAIAH 65:15)

This new name (possibly a form of the name of the one giving the message, as in "Christian") written on a white stone is meaningful to the people of Pergamos where white marble was used extensively for inscriptions on numerous statues of important gods and people. To be inscribed in white stone was to be immortalized as a person of great significance. The significance of their identity is found in Christ and will one day be recognized by all.

THE CHURCH IN THYATIRA

And to the angel of the church in Thyatira write; These things saith the Son of God, who hath his eyes like a flame of fire, and his feet are like fine brass; I know thy works, and charity, and service, and faith, and thy patience, and thy works; and the last to be more than the first. However I have a few things against thee, because thou allowest that woman Jezebel, who calleth herself a prophetess, to teach and to seduce my servants to commit acts of immorality, and to eat things sacrificed to idols. And I gave her time to repent of her immorality; and she repented not. Behold, I will cast her into a bed, and them that commit adultery with her into great tribulation, except they repent of their deeds. And I will kill her children with death; and all the churches shall know that I am he who searcheth the reins [minds] and hearts: and I will give to each one of you according to your works. But to you I say, and to the rest in Thyatira, as many as have not this doctrine, and who have not known the depths of Satan, as they speak; I will put upon you no other burden. But that which ye have already hold fast till I come. And he that overcometh, and keepeth my works to the end, to him will I give power over the nations: And he shall rule them with a rod of iron; as the vessels of a potter shall they be broken to shivers: even as I received of my Father. And I will give him the morning star. He that hath an ear, let him hear what the Spirit saith to the churches.

(REVELATION 2:18–29)

Here the one John called the "Son of man" clearly identifies himself as "the Son of God." He finishes by quoting a prophecy and stating that the God of the prophets is his father.

The key issues confronted in this letter are idolatry and sexual immorality. The temptation appears to come from a false prophet outside the church. But the Son of God, whose eyes blaze like fire, searches hearts and minds and sees right through these false teachings—and sees which church members are participating in them. Nothing is hidden from him. The feet of bronze probably represent strength—the kind that can stamp out one's enemies. According to the letter, the Son of God will do exactly that. He has patiently allowed time for reform, but no reforms are forthcoming, so he will throw this harlot Jezebel on a bed of tribulation—i.e., a sickbed.

The name "Jezebel" alludes to a story of a wicked Phoenician princess that would have been familiar to Jewish Christians. Wicked Jezebel married Israel's wicked King Ahab—a match made in hell. Similar to events in Balaam's story, she seduced the king of Israel to worship the pagan gods of her homeland. Jezebel also ordered the deaths of Israel's prophets because they didn't have anything good to say about her.

Jezebel's evil brought about a three-year drought upon Israel. In the story, God stopped blessing Israel with water because Jezebel had turned most of his people toward shaman prophets. To end the drought, Elijah, God's true prophet, called down fire from heaven to consume a sacrifice he had prepared and doused symbolically with water three times. When the people of Israel saw fire come down from heaven, they became more than willing to carry out Elijah's orders to kill the false prophets. Elijah then climbed a high mountain and told his servant to go look toward the sea for clouds. But there were no clouds. Elijah tells him to go back and look again, and this is done seven times (the number for God's interaction with nature or for God's judgment). On the seventh time, there is a small cloud. Soon the sky is black and full of wind and rain and fury.

For the death of her prophets, Jezebel swears she will kill Elijah and calls a curse upon herself if she fails to complete her task within one day: "May the gods deal with me ever so severely if I fail." She fails, and eventually she receives her own curse. According to the Old Testament, Elijah prophesied she would die, being eaten by dogs. Some time later, her own eunuchs throw her from a tower, where she is run over by horses with her blood splattering the wall. While the new king of Israel goes inside to eat dinner, what's left of Jezebel is eaten outside by dogs. All that's left are her skull, her feet, and her hands.

THE CHURCH AT SARDIS

And to the angel of the church in Sardis write; These things saith he that hath the seven Spirits of God, and the seven stars; I know thy works, that thou hast a name that thou livest, and art dead. Be watchful, and strengthen the things which remain, that are ready to die: for I have not found thy works perfect before God. Remember therefore how thou hast received and heard, and hold fast, and repent. If therefore thou shalt not watch, I will come on thee as a thief, and thou shalt not know what hour I will come upon thee. Thou hast a few names even in Sardis which have not defiled their garments; and they shall walk with me in white: for they are worthy. He that overcometh, the same shall be clothed in white raiment; and I will not blot out his name out of the book of life, but I will confess his name before my Father, and before his angels. He that hath an ear, let him hear what the Spirit saith to the churches. (REVELATION 3:1–6)

Here the seven Spirits of God are recalled from the original image of the Messiah as he appeared to John, as well as the seven stars, which were defined earlier as the seven angels to the seven churches. One way God makes his Spirit known is through his angels, just as the Apocalypse indicates an angel is speaking to John on Jesus' behalf. This angel (meaning "messenger") of the Lord even takes on an appearance appropriate to the one he represents.

Sardis, the church that had fallen the farthest, gets the sharpest warning: Wake up! You're dead! The spirit of God arrives to wake them up spiritually. The irony is that the Christian community in Sardis has a reputation for being alive. Though they run an active social calendar, the spiritual truth that was once behind their activities is gone. They're instructed to remember their better days, or their end will surprise them like a thief in the night.

"The book of life" that is mentioned will be explained near the end of the Apocalypse. Though the names of Christians had been blotted out of the membership scrolls of the local synagogue, God promises they will not be blotted out of the only membership scroll that really counts.

Being told to "strengthen the things which remain" is a message that had to reverberate in the ears of the saints of Sardis. Their prosperous city had crumbled during a severe earthquake earlier in the century. New buildings had been built out of generous grants from Rome, and those that remained required much shoring up, but the city never recovered its previous financial strength. If a dead city could be resurrected from its rubble, how much more could a dead church be resurrected by the Spirit of God.

THE CHURCH AT PHILADELPHIA

And to the angel of the church in Philadelphia write; These things saith he that is holy, he that is true, he that hath the key of David, he that openeth, and no man shutteth; and shutteth, and no man openeth; I know thy works: behold, I have set before thee an open door, and no man can shut it: for thou hast a little strength, and hast kept my word, and hast not denied my name. Behold, I will make them of the synagogue of Satan, who say they are Jews, and are not, but do lie; behold, I will make them to come and worship before thy feet, and to know that I have loved thee. Because thou hast kept the word of my patience, I also will keep thee from the hour of temptation, which shall come upon all the world, to try them that dwell upon the earth. Behold, I come quickly: hold that fast which thou hast, that no man take thy crown. Him that overcometh will I make a pillar in the temple of my God, and he shall go out no more: and I will write upon him the name of my God, and the name of the city of my God, which is new Jerusalem, which cometh down out of heaven from my God: and I will write upon him my new name. He that hath an ear, let him hear what the Spirit saith to the churches. (REVELATION 3:7–13)

The final elements in John's first image of the Son of God are now alluded to—the keys to death and Hades. The Apocalypse borrowed the name of hell from Greek mythology. Whether the keys were to lock away death and Hades forever, or to lock others up in them, is unclear. But here there is no mention of death or Hades. For this church, those threats are removed. The keys have now become the key of David, whose kingdom on earth typified the eternal "Kingdom of God," a phrase referring to the spiritual realm but including those on earth who were joined to it.

The holy and true "Son of God," in essence, declares that he is the door keeper between the earthly kingdom and the heavenly. Jacob, who gave his new name to his descendants (Israel), once claimed that he had found a door to heaven in the land of Israel. Now that the Apocalypse mentions the giving of a "new name" again, it is made clear that the new name God will give to the people under the New Covenant is the name of Christ: "I will write upon him *my* new name." Those who overcome will be identified with him and with God and with the place of their spiritual dwelling.

The image of an open door is appropriate to this church in another way. Philadelphia lay at an important crossroads to the main continent of Asia. As a church that had remained true through all of their persecutions, they were an open portal between Asia—a world still waiting to hear the news of the New Testament—and the spiritual Kingdom of God. The reference to a "an open door . . . no man can shut" may also be a veiled consolation to those who had been shut out of the synagogue, given the reference to Jewish persecution in the letter.

This church receives only praise and instruction to keep up the good work, but the letter directs more blunt language against those "who say they are Jews, and are not, but do lie." The rejected Messiah says to this weary but good-spirited church, "I will make them come and fall down at your feet and acknowledge that I have loved you." Spiritually, the people of this little church are the *true* Jews, for they acknowledge the Jewish Messiah at great personal cost. Because they have remained completely true to him through much persecution, they are promised they will be kept from the greater peril that is going to come upon the whole world. When the one in whom they have placed their faith reveals his true identity to the world, both unbelieving Jews and unbelieving Romans will fall down at the feet of this small band of believers, acknowledging the truth before them. This is encouragement to hold on.

For that reason, they are promised a crown. Crowns in ancient Rome were not only for kings, they were trophies for victorious athletes. A wreath of laurel was placed upon the head of the victor. This church will receive such a crown.

Gods dwell in temples. So to be made part of the temple of God means they will commune in the eternal presence of God, from which they will never depart. In this context, the vision mentions a new Jerusalem that descends from heaven, which is the first hint from the Apocalypse that the old earthly Jerusalem will not be the *ultimate* fulfillment of Zionist prophecies. The image of a new city and a new name is especially appropriate to Philadelphia, which had also been rebuilt after the major earthquake. In deference to Tiberius Caesar for his generous earthquake relief there was a proposal to rename the city *NeoCaesarea*. Just as Caesar had rebuilt Philadelphia out of new marble, God is building something new—a temple and a spiritual city made, not of stones, but of purified souls:

> . . . coming [to Jesus] as to a living stone, rejected indeed by men, but chosen by God, and precious, Ye also, as living stones, are built up a spiritual house, an holy priesthood, to offer up spiritual sacrifices, acceptable to God by Jesus Christ. Therefore also it is contained in the scripture, *Behold, I lay in Zion [Jerusalem] a chief corner stone, elect, precious: and he that believeth on him shall not be confounded.* To you therefore who believe he is precious: but to them who are disobedient [particularly those who rejected him], the stone which the builders rejected, the same is made the head of the corner, And a stone of stumbling, and a rock of offence, even to them who stumble at the word, being disobedient: to this also they were appointed. But ye are a chosen generation, a royal priesthood, an holy nation, a special people; that ye should show forth the praises of him who hath called you out of darkness into his marvelous light: Who in time past were not a people, but are now the people of God: who had not obtained mercy, but now have obtained mercy.
>
> (1 PETER 2:4–10)

The Apostle Peter brings together two arguments from the prophecies of Hosea: One is that the stone rejected by the chief builders of the nation of Israel (the rejected Messiah) would, in fact, prove to be the ascendant Messiah. He would be placed on top by God, the ultimate builder. The second argument is that because of this rejection, a group of people who had not formerly been known as God's chosen had become the new people of God.

One Fundamentalist view of prophecy mentioned earlier believes that the letter to the church at Philadelphia describes the present age of church history. It's easy to see why this view is popular: It offers comfortable reassurance that today's believers will not have to go through the period of great tribulation described later in the Apocalypse, for the letter to the Philadelphians says: "I also will keep thee from the hour of temptation, which shall come upon all the world, to try them that dwell upon the earth."

It takes a bit of wrenching, however, to fit today's Church with the description of the church at Philadelphia. First, the primary description of this church says it had "little strength." But today's Church has hundreds of millions of believers with billions of dollars worshiping in thousands of elaborate buildings on millions of acres of land. It has thousands of people in high places of government. It owns hundreds of radio and T.V. stations. It even has its own private satellites and private jets and private limousines. How could today's aggregate of believers possibly be called a Church of little strength?

Second, today's Church in North America and Europe does not experience significant conflicts with Jews, as described, and it is not a church that has had to "keep the word of [Christ's] patience" (translated in the New International Version as "since you have kept my command to endure patiently"). Probably half of the Christians on earth today (maybe more) have received almost no persecution for their faith in their lifetimes. Although conflicts still exist between people of different faiths or of no faith, that is true of any age. Being asked to "shut up" or being ridiculed for your beliefs hardly counts as persecution when compared to the perils faced by the little church at Philadelphia.

On the other hand, extreme persecution can be found in a few pockets in the world today, which brings up a significant problem in identifying any of these seven churches as representative of a particular Church age: the Church since the time of Christ has never been homogenous. It has always existed in many cultural situations. While today's Church in Western Europe and North America is mostly wealthy and strong and relatively free of persecution, churches in some countries, such as China, endure life-threatening persecution. The description of the little Philadelphian church perfectly fits scattered groups of Christians, but does not fit the majority. Which group defines the age?

Of course, it's comforting to consider oneself a member of the one age that receives only glowing praise and a promise of freedom from tribulation, but the next church described in the Apocalypse fits today's comfortable church much better—*if* one is going to view these letters as describing periods of Church history.

The Church at Laodicea

And to the angel of the church of the Laodiceans write; These things saith the Amen, the faithful and true witness, the beginning of the creation of God; I know thy works, that thou art neither cold nor hot: I would thou wert cold or hot. So then because thou art lukewarm, and neither cold nor hot, I will spue thee out of my mouth. Because thou sayest, I am rich, and increased with goods, and have need of nothing; and knowest not that thou art wretched, and miserable, and poor, and blind, and naked: I counsel thee to buy of me gold tried in the fire, that thou mayest be rich; and white raiment, that thou mayest be clothed, and that the shame of thy nakedness may not appear; and anoint thy eyes with eyesalve, that thou mayest see. As many as I love, I rebuke and chasten: be zealous therefore, and repent. Behold, I stand at the door, and knock: if any man shall hear my voice, and open the door, I will come in to him, and will sup with him, and he with me. To him that overcometh will I grant to sit with me on my throne, even as I also overcame, and am set down with my Father on his throne. He that hath an ear, let him hear what the Spirit saith to the churches.

(REVELATION 3:14–22)

If there was ever an age that was "rich, and increased with goods, and [had] need of nothing" it would be the present age. So, if one prefers to view these letters as descriptions of an age, the age of Laodicea seems the closest fit for many churches today—especially with so many evangelists preaching a doctrine of divine prosperity. This teaching claims that Christians who live holy lives and give generously to the ministries of evangelists will be blessed by God with considerable wealth. The doctrine sells well in America where prosperity is a possible dream, but it's a tough sell to Christians in Ethiopia.

Paul's letter to Timothy exactly describes such false teachers. They are:

> . . . men of corrupt mind, who have been robbed of the truth and who think that godliness is a means to financial gain. (1 TIMOTHY 6:3–5)

If one thinks wealth is the fruit of a mature spiritual connection to God, one should take special notice of this letter. Christ would say, "Get some salve for your eyes, and you will be able to see that many of the most spiritually mature believers in the world are destitute because they are so busy helping the poor they don't have time to earn much for themselves." John is not criticizing prosperity; he's criticizing the blindness that often comes from too much golden glare.

The prosperous church described at Laodicea is about as satisfying to God as a glass of tepid water. The metaphor of lukewarm water, again, is organic to this particular church. Laodicea is across the River Lycos from a hot springs, which pours into the river.

At the confluence of the river and the springs, the water is neither hot enough for good bathing nor cold enough for good drinking. Water that came into the city by aqueduct would have cooled sufficiently to be equally undesirable. The city may have been rich, but its water was awful.

Apparently there was not much persecution in this leading center of banking, so, the Christians there enjoyed considerable wealth compared to the other churches. They considered their prosperity as proof they were blessed by God. It was proof of righteous living.

Not so! says the vision. This church is stagnant because it rests comfortably on a cushion of wealth. This church is rich like its city, but like its city water, it's undesirable. Persecution would be good for these people. They are going to be refined like gold in fire so they can *become* spiritually rich and pure. (As a noble element, gold is used throughout the Apocalypse and other biblical books as a symbol of spiritual purity.)

Since this church fits today's churches more closely than the church at Philadelphia, there's not much hope here for avoiding the "Great Tribulation" described in the latter chapters of the Apocalypse. Believing that today's Christians are represented by the good church at Philadelphia and, therefore, will all miraculously escape the perilous times ahead may be a leap of logic rather than a leap of faith.

Instead of promising escape from peril, six of the seven letters encourage John's congregations to brave persecution in light of a greater promise. Persecution echoes throughout the Apocalypse, and only once does John offer hope of avoiding it—and that was to a church that had already suffered a great deal.

The promised throne referred to at the end of this letter is symbolic of the power and authority, in which those who overcome persecution and tribulation will share. In the next chapter, John's vision reveals images of that authority being vested in the Son of God.

Finally, this church, instead of being an open door to the Kingdom of God, is a closed door. The one they claim to follow is patiently standing out in the cold and knocking. He would like to come in and commune with them, but it's hard for those who dine in rich company to open the door to someone they don't recognize. This city was renowned for its manufacture of a medicinal eye salve called "collyrium," and the believers here are instructed to use some of it so they can see their shortcomings more clearly and perhaps even see the one they've left standing outside.

John's first vision ends with this church. Some feel the forewarnings given to the church at Laodicea set the tone for most of his revelation to follow. On that basis, they believe Laodicea represents people who will become followers of Christ *during* the Great Tribulation that John describes—the final age of the church. In the broader view, however, *all* of the churches are a prelude to the visions that follow. The seven angels for the seven churches, the seven judgments of God, the seven spirits of God, the persecution faced by all the churches, the perfect union between God and his saints, confrontations with Satanic forces, the victory of the sword of truth, the death of an earthly city, the creation of a new Jerusalem, and the everlasting kingdom of the Messiah—all of these images come back to haunt, inspire, and fulfill John's dreamlike sweep of the intercourse between spiritual heaven and physical earth to the end of time to the end of the universe.

Chapter 9

Visi⊙ns:

Mystical Enco∪nters of
God and Heaven

After John's symbolic vision of Jesus Christ standing among the seven lampstands or churches, John records his own passage through a portal between heaven and earth to a second vision. Since this book follows the order of John's Apocalypse from here on, the prophetic tour now moves to John's visionary encounter with the divine where a voice from his first vision indicates that he is about to be shown events beyond his own time:

> *After this I looked, and, behold, a door was opened in heaven: and the first voice which I heard was as it were of a trumpet talking with me; which said, Come up here, and I will show thee things which must be after this. And immediately I was in the spirit: and, behold, a throne was set in heaven, and one sat on the throne.* (REVELATION 4:1–2)

When John says he was "in the spirit," he is probably indicating he was not physically transported to heaven but experienced heaven in ecstatic rapture. In other words, he was caught up in spirit only. What he is about to see will become the foundation of all the hope he has to offer throughout the rest of his Apocalypse.

The Apostle Paul had a similar experience and even used the term "out of body" to describe it, stating he could not tell from his own perspective whether his body had been transported to heaven or not. He was clearly mystified by his own experience:

> *It is not expedient for me doubtless to glory. I will come to visions and revelations of the Lord. I knew a man in Christ fourteen years ago [Paul, himself], (whether in the body, I cannot tell; or whether out of the body, I cannot tell: God knoweth;) such one caught up to the third heaven. And I knew such a man, (whether in the body, or out of the body, I cannot tell: God knoweth;) How he was caught up into paradise, and heard unspeakable*

words, which it is not lawful for a man to utter. . . . And lest I should be exalted above measure through the abundance of the revelations, there was given to me a thorn in the flesh, the messenger of Satan to buffet me, lest I should be exalted above measure.

(2 CORINTHIANS 12:1–4, 7)

Paul's experience created such ecstasy within him that he was given a physical malady, which he calls a "thorn in the flesh," to keep his feet on the ground and his head out of the clouds. So great were the revelations he received that he might have become arrogant if not for this handicap that he also received. He does not tell his readers specifically what he saw, but clearly it became the bedrock of his hope for the future, which made all the persecutions he suffered in this life worth enduring. He implies this frequently during his ministry. Like John, he had probably seen visions of the Almighty in heaven. Other prophets had similar visions of the Almighty. When Moses saw God, he was told he could not look upon the face of God and live (To see the face of God probably means to be totally in his presence.):

And he [Moses] said, I beseech thee, show me thy glory. And he [God] said, I will make all my goodness pass before thee, and I will proclaim the name of the LORD before thee. . . . And he said, Thou canst not see my face: for there shall no man see me, and live. And the LORD said, Behold . . . it shall come to pass, while my glory passeth by, that I will put thee in a cleft of the rock, and will cover thee with my hand while I pass by: And I will take away my hand, and thou shalt see my back parts: but my face shall not be seen.

(EXODUS 33:18–23)

Other parts of the Bible make similar statements regarding the impossibility of looking directly at God:

. . . the appearing of our Lord Jesus Christ . . . the blessed and only Potentate, the King of kings, and Lord of lords; Who only hath immortality, dwelling in the light which no man can approach; whom no man hath seen, nor can see: to whom be honour and power everlasting. Amen.

(1 TIMOTHY 6:14–16)

No man hath seen God at any time; the only begotten Son, who is in the bosom of the Father, he hath declared him. . . . Not that any man hath seen the Father, except he who is from God, he hath seen the Father. (JOHN 1:18: 6:46)

Jesus saith to him . . . he that hath seen me hath seen the Father; and how sayest thou then, Show us the Father?

(JOHN 14:9)

Jesus made God visible while he was on the earth as a man, but now that he has risen, he exists in eternal communion with God—as John will reveal through his vision. It may be that Jesus can no longer be directly gazed upon any more than God, his Father, can be. This may explain why the Apocalypse states in the beginning that Jesus gave the vision to John *through* an angel. What John saw was a symbolic or angelic representation of Jesus Christ. For this reason, when prophets write about their visions, they often choose words that reflect a little distance between what they saw and what they believe their vision represents, such as "I saw one *like* a son of man" or "I saw the *likeness* of the glory of God":

As the appearance of the bow that is in the cloud in the day of rain [i.e., rainbow], so was the appearance of the brightness all around. This was the appearance of the likeness of the glory of the LORD. And when I saw it, I fell upon my face, and I heard a voice of one speaking. And he said to me, Son of man, stand upon thy feet, and I will speak to thee. And the spirit entered into me when he spoke to me, and set me upon my feet, that I heard him that spoke to me.   (EZEKIEL 1:28; 2:1, 2)

PROPHETIC TECHNIQUE

One cannot induce such divine revelations, for God cannot be invoked as other spirits can. Many parts of the Bible, for example Psalm 38:15 ("I wait for you, O LORD; you will answer, O Lord my God.") indicate that humans must *wait* for God to answer in his own time. There are, however, disciplines that Jewish and Christian prophets have traditionally practiced to put themselves in a state where such revelations can come to them—if they are willing to wait on God and God is willing to speak. The Bible forbids such practices as incantations or astrology or other methods of divining the future. It does not, however, forbid mystical experiences, but neither does it allow the quick-and-easy road of drugs or occult techniques to achieve altered states.

The only path to a direct encounter with God suggested in the Bible is prayer and fasting, along with meditation, though the Bible does not suggest any meditative techniques.

Early Christian mystics were usually monks who often became hermits. Called ascetics, these monks deprived themselves of all food and human company for extensive periods of time and moved to barren landscapes to escape sensory experience. In Judea and Egypt, the place of choice was the wilderness. For later monks, such as those in Ireland in the fourth and fifth centuries, rocky places, like the Skellig Rocks off the Irish coast, served as their isolated Judean wilderness. Even on the Skelligs, the beauty of the sea had to be walled out because it created too much distraction. It's no stretch to suppose that the slave diet and the austerity of John's exile on the Isle of Patmos were similar to the sensory deprivation sought by fasting hermit monks.

Ascetics often added physical discomfort, such as minimal or no clothing and bare feet, though this is never advocated in the Bible. They called this added discipline "mortification of the flesh." This, too, may have been similar to John's torturous work and living conditions in the quarries. But these austere disciplines were not done merely to prove the monk's willingness to make personal sacrifices for God, though that was sometimes an ulterior motive. In fact, such a combination of arduous disciplines had a powerful physiological and psychological effect, inducing an altered state similar to a near-death experience. The lack of food for an extended time (the typical fast recorded in the Bible lasted forty days) would put anybody into the beginning stages of death, traumatizing the body into release its firm grip on the spirit. In fact, John's words, "I was in the Spirit," were often used by Christian mystics who were caught up in a spiritual ecstasy.

The tradition goes back at least as far as Moses, who fasted forty days in complete isolation on a mountain top before he received the Ten Commandments and before he received the vision of the back of God recounted above. The prophet Daniel fasted before receiving his visions. The New Testament describes a prophetess who had been praying and fasting in the temple apparently over a period of about for sixty years before receiving a vision about the Christ child. Jesus fasted forty days in the wilderness before he had a vision of the devil. The Apostles fasted for days when seeking God's guidance on significant questions.

These biblical examples reveal that prayer and fasting are capable of breaking the barrier between physical and spiritual realities. Jesus' experience cautions that one is just as likely to experience demonic spiritual encounters as divine. An altered state of consciousness is no guarantee of truth. As the Apocalypse will reveal, the spirit realm is as full of lies as truth—just like the physical world. Therefore, such fasting was never a practice for the initiate. Even saints well grounded in their faith meditated on God's word in a constant state of prayer in order to condition their minds for truth. Then they questioned whatever they experienced against the word of God. Because Jesus' knowledge of God's word was perfect, he knew how to encounter the devil when the devil came.

Undoubtedly, John was very near death on Patmos, being a man in his nineties. Slaves much younger died under the Roman whip. There's no way of knowing whether or not John's sufferings and deprivation caused his body to release his spirit in anguish and opened his eyes to the spirit world, but suffering and the kingdom of God are interwoven throughout his writing. He had probably been exiled for refusing to worship the Roman emperor Domitian though some scholars believe he was exiled under Nero. Perhaps God took the duress Rome intended for John's harm and used it to release him momentarily from this life so that he might see more clearly into the next. However John's revelation came about, it is certainly the grandest in all of literature.

A VISION OF PARADISE

Just as it is impossible to describe a color that one has never seen or a taste never experienced, human language is limited in describing the divine. There is no human language for paradise. There is no way of truly depicting the appearance of God. That is why Jews were forbidden to make carved images of God (idols). Any image would be nothing more than a human caricature of God.

So writers use metaphors and similes to describe the indescribable in terms of ordinary human experience: Describing color to the blind requires the use of a simile, such as "orange is like the warmth of the sun in summer" or "blue is like the cold of the sea." Even then, the blind person's understanding of color can never rise above an approximation, for if someone tells him later on that a gas flame is blue and he touches it, he will think the description of blue was a lie. It felt nothing like the coldness of the sea.

The prophets faced the same problem when putting their divine encounters into words for the spiritually blind. Any description is only an approximation. Either the prophet must create a likeness of the encounter, or (more likely) what he or she perceived was a *divinely given* likeness of spiritual reality in the first place—a model translated into forms the prophet has experienced and is capable of understanding and sharing:

> And he that sat [on the throne] was in appearance like a jasper and a sardius stone: and there was a rainbow around the throne, in sight like an emerald. And around the throne were four and twenty thrones: and upon the thrones I saw four and twenty elders sitting, clothed in white raiment; and they had on their heads crowns of gold. And out of the throne proceeded lightnings and thunderings and voices: and there were seven lamps of fire burning before the throne, which are the seven Spirits of God. And in front of the throne there was a sea of glass like crystal. . . .
>
> (REVELATION 4:3–6A)

John often uses the word "like," indicating things are not exactly as they appear. God probably does not sit on a throne in heaven. That would imply God, who is spirit, has a human-like body. Therefore, the throne probably visualizes God's authority. The twenty-four elders seated on thrones around the throne of God probably represent the twelve patriarchs of the Jewish race and the twelve apostles of the Church. This is an amazing image because it perfectly unites (using the symbolism of a circle) the leaders of the Old Testament (Old Covenant) with the leaders of the New Testament (New

Covenant). These once-divided people are pictured united around God and centered on his authority and apparently equal in stature.

The twenty-four elders may represent more than just the leadership of the Old and New Testaments. They may represent all of God's people—both Jews and Christians—as they will be in their glorified state, "dressed in white," which represents purity. Later in the Apocalypse, being clothed in white linen is said to symbolize the good deeds or righteous acts of God's people ("the saints"). The crowns and thrones of the elders reveal that God's holy people also have authority, but it is derived from the One in the center. This is made clear later in the vision.

God's Holy Spirit is probably represented as the "*seven* Spirits of God" because John is addressing seven churches, and he wants to make it clear that each church has God's undivided attention—not a part of God's Spirit, but the full presence of his Spirit. (The spiritual realm does not have to follow the laws of division established for the physical world.) To clarify this connection between the realities of heaven and the things of earth, the "seven spirits of God" are uniquely represented as seven lamps—the perfect match for the seven lampstands that represented the seven churches earlier in the vision. The full presence of the Holy Spirit will fill each church with light. Without the Holy Spirit, the churches have nothing to offer the world.

The repeated use of the number *seven* not only provides continuity between the former vision of the seven lampshades and this vision of heaven but also symbolizes the union of God and creation, which is one of the themes of this second vision.

Like Ezekiel, John saw something similar to a rainbow around the one on the throne. He describes it as being similar in appearance to the stones jasper and carnelian. He may have only meant the one on the throne was the color of jasper or carnelian, which is green, or he may have intended the symbolic significance of jasper. Because jasper, when its broken, appears to contain many new stones within itself, like eggs, it symbolized pregnancy or fertility in some cultures. This may be a clue that the one on the throne is none other than the Creator, the source of all life. The emerald halo or rainbow may have the same significance, since emeralds traditionally symbolize new life because of their green vibrancy. A second implication of the rainbow for John's churches is that God will deliver them through the judgments that follow, for the rainbow was a promise given to Noah that God would never again destroy the earth by flood. It is a sign of forgiveness and a reminder of God's covenant with his people.

John's vision also begins with thunder and lightening from the throne of God. Almost all ancient cultures thought thunder and lightening derived directly from God—often as forms of judgment. For Middle-Eastern Jews, who depended on rare storms to fill their cisterns with rain, thunder and lightning were not always judgments. Storms brought life to the desert. They were a sign of power and vitality.

John punctuates each major scene in his poetic vision with thunder and lightning emanating from the throne of God. It is a verbal cue that the curtain is going up on a new act. And, because ephemeral lightning comes down from the heavens to the physical earth, it is a potent reminder of the connection between the spiritual realm and its effects on the physical world. In subsequent scenes of the Apocalypse, the rumbling of the thunder swells to include the rumbling of earthquakes. At that point, it becomes clear that there is an element of judgment in God's thunder and lightning.

The Apocalypse paints a surreal dreamscape. From the throne of God a sea of glass stretches to an undescribed horizon. In literature the sea is often an archetype (a universal symbol) of eternity or the fulness of time because of its vastness and the endless beating of its waves against the shore. It is also used as a symbol of life and death, for life originates out of water, and the waves of the sea sometimes swallow life back into its eternal darkness.

This sea has no waves. It's as calm as glass. Time does not exist here. This sea has no darkness. It's as clear as crystal. Death does not exist here, either. John has transcended time; he stands in the midst of eternity. Beside this placid sea, all of creation was born, for the universe existed eternally in the divine will before it was brought into physical being. John has been transported to the still and perfect center of all being where the thoughts of the All-Knowing are so potent they become a reality on earth below.

(Later in the Apocalypse the sea has a particular meaning, which it may also have here. John is told that the sea represents the nations and languages and people of the earth collectively. It is the sea of humanity. If that sense is also intended here, then the sea of humanity stretches before the eyes of God like a looking glass.)

... and in the midst of the throne, and around the throne, were four living beings full of eyes before and behind. And the first living being was like a lion, and the second living being like a calf, and the third living being had a face as a man, and the fourth living being was like a flying eagle. And the four living beings had each of them six wings about him; and they were full of eyes within: and they rest not day and night, saying, Holy, holy, holy, Lord God Almighty, who was, and is, and is to come.

(REVELATION 4:6B–8)

The four "living beings," often translated "living creatures," are a mystery. Their meaning is never explained. Many scholars have seen them as presenting a special kind of angelic being called the cherubim. John is either borrowing from or seeing something very similar to creatures seen by the prophets Isaiah and Ezekiel. His living creatures seem to be a cross between the "seraphim" in Isaiah's vision (which means something like "fiery ones") and the cherubim in Ezekiel's vision:

In the year that king Uzziah died I saw also the Lord sitting upon a throne, high and lifted up, and his train filled the temple. Above it stood the seraphims: each one had six wings; with two he covered his face, and with two he covered his feet, and with two he flew. And one cried to another, and said, Holy, holy, holy, is the LORD of hosts: the whole earth is full of his glory. And the posts of the door moved at the voice of him that cried, and the house was filled with smoke. Then said I, Woe is me! for I am undone; because I am a man of unclean lips, and I dwell in the midst of a people of unclean lips: for my eyes have seen the King, the LORD of hosts. Then one of the seraphims flew to me, having a live coal in his hand, which he had taken with the tongs from off the altar: And he laid it upon my mouth, and said, Lo, this hath touched thy lips; and thy iniquity is taken away, and thy sin purged.   (ISAIAH 6:1–7)

. . . the heavens were opened, and I saw visions of God. . . . And I looked, and, behold, a whirlwind came out of the north, a great cloud, and a fire infolding itself, and a brightness was about it, and from the midst of it as the colour of amber, from the midst of the fire. Also from the midst of it came the likeness of four living beings. And this was their appearance; they had the likeness of a man. And every one had four faces, and every one had four wings. And their feet were straight feet; and the sole of their feet was like the sole of a calf's foot: and they sparkled like the colour of burnished brass. And they had the hands of a man under their wings on their four sides. . . . As for the likeness of their faces, they four had the face of a man, and the face of a lion, on the right side: and they four had the face of an ox on the left side; they four also had the face of an eagle. Thus were their faces: and their wings were stretched upward; two wings of every one were joined one to another, and two covered their bodies. And they went every one straight forward: wherever the spirit was to go, they went; and they turned not when they went. As for the likeness of the living beings, their appearance was like burning coals of fire, and like the appearance of lamps: it went up and down among the living beings; and the fire was bright, and out of the fire went forth lightning. And the living beings ran and returned as the appearance of a flash of lightning.

(EZEKIEL 1:1, 4–8, 10–14)

In both accounts the creatures are described as fiery—one in name (seraphim), the other by description. Isaiah's have six wings, like John's, but apparently only one face. Ezekiel's have four faces, like John's, but have only four wings. This would either indicate these creatures are symbolic images or that they can change their form. In Ezekiel's vision, each creature has *all* of the four faces, one on each side of its head. In John's vision each of the four creatures has one of the four faces.

The creatures in Ezekiel's vision are around the throne of God and are covered with eyes just as in John's. Ezekiel also repeatedly emphasizes that everything he describes is a "likeness." He is speaking in terms of resemblance:

And above the firmament that was over their heads was the likeness of a throne, as the appearance of a sapphire stone: and upon the likeness of the throne was the likeness as the appearance of a man above upon it. And I saw as the colour of amber, as the appearance of fire around within it, from the appearance of his loins even upward, and from the appearance of his loins even downward, I saw as it were the appearance of fire, and it had brightness on all sides.

. . . And their whole body, and their backs, and their hands, and their wings . . . were full of eyes on every side. . . . (EZEKIEL 1:26, 27; 10:12)

If these are real angelic beings, as many believe, perhaps they take whatever form is appropriate to the message of the vision, since The word "angel" is simply the garden-variety Greek word for "messenger." These could be celestial beings who have authority over different parts of nature; thus, they show themselves in John's vision as covered with physical eyes, for they see everything in nature. In classical symbolism, the eye takes the outer world into the inner world, but it is also capable of projecting the inner world of the soul onto the outer world. In the sense that the eye is the window to the soul, eyes communicate both ways. They receive messages, but they also send out messages.

These creatures appear a little like the Greek or Roman demigods that had charge over the sea and over the underworld, over the lakes and rivers and forests. In Ezekiel's version, they are described as having feet like the hooves of calves. Like the creatures of mythology, the "living creatures" of the Apocalypse have human-like bodies but the faces of animals. Perhaps like demigods these messengers live between the natural world and the spiritual world, communicating more than verbal messages between God and nature.

Pagan cultures may have caught a wisp of truth about the spiritual realm—but only a wisp, for this is not a pantheon. To mere mortals, angelic beings might have *appeared* as gods—especially to those who had mystical encounters without the wisdom to understand what they were seeing. These, however, are called "creatures," which means they are a part of God's creation. They are not gods, even if they have god-like powers when compared to mortals.

These "living creatures" may also be purely symbolic, as the lamps and lampstands seem to be. They may symbolize all living creatures on earth and imply (with their eyes) an awareness between creature and Creator. The creature like a lion may represent all the wild beasts of creation. And the calf (or ox), all domesticated beasts. The one with the face of a man would, of course, represent human beings. And the eagle, birds of the air.

That begs the question, why have the creatures of the sea and the insects beneath the earth been left out? But John may have chosen only the four creatures most familiar to man because the number "four" symbolically represents the whole of creation—the four winds, the four points of the compass, the four corners of the earth, the four ancient elements of earth, wind, fire, and water. To enumerate more kinds of creatures would actually be to represent fewer creatures because without the number "four," the living creatures would no longer symbolize the *universality* of nature. The classic symbolism of the number four and the name "living creatures" provide the strongest basis for connecting these creatures to nature—whether as governing spirits or mere representations.

If the images represent creation on earth, they reflect an intimate and idealized communion between nature and the Creator within the spirit realm—perhaps representing God's spirit within nature. In this ideal state all nature surrounds the throne so that everything is centered on the Creator's authority and not on itself. These creatures are also a reminder that humans are a part of nature. What happens to one kind of creature happens to all:

> *And when those living beings give glory and honour and thanks to him that is seated on the throne, who liveth for ever and ever, The four and twenty elders fall down before him that sat on the throne, and worship him that liveth for ever and ever, and cast their crowns before the throne, saying, Thou art worthy, O Lord, to receive glory and honour and power: for thou hast created all things, and for thy pleasure they are and were created.*
>
> (REVELATION 4:9–11)

Whenever the living creatures honor God, then the twenty-four elders honor him, too, casting their crowns before him as a sign that they yield their authority to the one at the center. All the creatures of earth, together with representatives of the Jewish and Christian saints in heaven, and God, are shown in perfect communion. That's paradise; that's what should exist on earth below. But, as the Apostle Paul describes, the picture on earth is different. Nature suffers for the sins of humanity, and humanity suffers nature's retaliation:

> *For the earnest expectation of the creation waiteth for the revealing of the sons of God. For the creation was made subject to vanity [foolishness], not willingly, but by reason of him [God] who hath subjected the same in hope, Because the creation itself also shall be delivered from the bondage of corruption into the glorious liberty of the children of God. For we know that the whole creation groaneth and travaileth in pain together until now.*
>
> (ROMANS 8:19–22)

Paul appears to be saying that creation suffers the foolishness of man temporarily because out of this whole process will come a greater hope. When humanity is glorified, all of creation will be glorified along with it. Perhaps John's vision is a picture of things to come "on earth as it is in heaven." When humanity is perfected, nature will no longer bear the results of human evil and will, at last, be perfected. That is every culture's utopian dream.

THE MYSTERIOUS SEALED SCROLL

And I saw in the right hand of him that sat on the throne a book written within and on the back, sealed with seven seals. And I saw a strong angel proclaiming with a loud voice, Who is worthy to open the book, and to loose its seals? And no man in heaven, nor in earth, neither under the earth, was able to open the book, neither to look on it. And I wept much, because no man was found worthy to open and to read the book, neither to look on it. (REVELATION 5:1–4)

A book so holy that no one can open it or read what it says. John has witnessed the deaths of many of his followers. He is probably the last of the apostles. Tradition indicates Peter and Paul would have been dead for twenty years or more by the time John receives this vision. What words could be important enough to make a man who has survived torturous slavery and loss of friends now break down and cry—not cry because the words were so powerful, but simply because he could not see them?

This scroll has seven seals that no human has the right to break. The wax seals placed on regal parchments were an ancient method of preventing letters from being secretly read by anyone other than the intended recipient. They were often embossed with royal insignia to prove the authority behind the document. The number seven is a clue that this scroll contains the divine plan for the union of God and humanity—God and nature (three plus four). Because God does not commune with evil, perfect union between the Creator and creation can only happen when creation is purged of evil, so the plan may contain judgment as well.

The scroll does, in fact, prove to contain the final unrolling of the divine plan for earth through the events of the last days. These events lead to perfect union between creation and Creator. The scroll is completely written on, front and back, because nothing will happen during those days that is not already foreseen in the divine plan. There's no room for humans or angels or devils or anything else to make additions. This, it would appear, is God's book of destiny. But the events indicated on each seal must take place *before* earth's final destiny can be unrolled. Among other things, this implies that the prophecy will not be fully understood until all of the events symbolized by the seven seals have taken place.

John has endured his whole life in anticipation of perfect union with and perfect knowledge of God. For him it is a reunion with his beloved teacher, Jesus, who had walked the earth more than forty years earlier. It is a reunion with his closest friends, who had all died for their faith. And now, when the perfect understanding of all this is almost in his hands, it is withheld because no one has the authority to open the seals.

THE REVEALED MESSIAH

And one of the elders saith to me, Weep not: behold, the Lion of the tribe of Judah, the Root of David, hath prevailed to open the book, and to loose its seven seals. And I beheld, and, lo, in the midst of the throne and of the four living beings, and in the midst of the elders, stood a Lamb as it had been slain, having seven horns and seven eyes, which are the seven Spirits of God sent forth into all the earth. (REVELATION 5:5–6)

The "Lion of the tribe of Judah" goes back to one of the oldest prophecies in the Bible. After God made his covenant with Abraham, certain promises were handed down to Abraham's great grandsons, the twelve patriarchs of the twelve tribes of Israel. One of these patriarchs was named Judah. To him the following blessing was given:

Judah, thou art he whom thy brethren shall praise: thy hand shall be on the neck of thy enemies; thy father's children shall bow down before thee. Judah is a lion's whelp: from the prey, my son, thou hast gone up: he stooped down, he crouched as a lion, and as an old lion; who shall rouse him up? The sceptre shall not depart from Judah, nor a lawgiver from between his feet, until Shiloh [probably means "peace" or "the man of peace"] shall come; and to him shall be the obedience of the people. Binding his foal to the vine, and his donkey's colt to the choice vine; he washed his garments in wine, and his clothes in the blood of grapes: His eyes shall be red with wine, and his teeth white with milk. (GENESIS 49:8–12)

The lion, symbol of royalty, will reign forever from the tribe of Judah, but his clothes shall be washed in blood. King David belonged to the tribe of Judah, and he was a king who established his power through bloodshed. But he no longer has a scepter. His kingdom has been gone for two thousand years, and modern Israel has no monarch nor any plans for one.

The Apocalypse provides a key for understanding how this prophecy regarding the eternal King of Judah will be fulfilled. It unlocks the mystery by connecting the Lion of Judah to other prophecies about the "Root of David." The root of King David should be his father, Jesse. Yet all prophecies about Jesse dig down to a deeper root in the family tree. The following prediction pictures the family tree that grew from Jesse as a stump that has been cut off. Though the royal family tree has been severed, a tender shoot (translated "rod" or "branch") will grow up from Jesse's roots. In other words, even though the kingdom of David is severed, a greater king will rise from the same stock:

And there shall come forth a rod out of the stem [stump] of Jesse, and a Branch shall grow out of his [Jesse's] roots: And the spirit of the LORD shall rest upon him, the spirit of wisdom and understanding, the spirit of counsel and might, the spirit of knowledge and of the fear of the LORD; And shall make him of quick understanding in the fear of the LORD: and he shall not judge after the sight of his eyes, neither reprove after the hearing of his ears: But with righteousness shall he judge the poor, and reprove with equity for the meek of the earth: and he shall smite the earth with the rod of his mouth, and with the breath of his lips shall he slay the wicked. And righteousness shall be the belt of his loins, and faithfulness the belt of his reins [mind]. . . . And in that day there shall be a root of Jesse, which shall stand for an ensign of the people; to it shall the Gentiles seek: and his rest shall be glorious.

(ISAIAH 11:1–5, 10)

Since David lived long *before* Isaiah made this prediction, he cannot be the shoot that will grow out of Jesse. Later in Isaiah, there is another description of this mysterious branch, which acknowledges how difficult it will be for God's people to believe in this peaceful Messiah:

Who hath believed our report? and to whom is the arm of the LORD revealed? For he shall grow up before him [God] as a tender plant, and as a root out of a dry ground: he hath no form nor comeliness; and when we shall see him, there is no beauty that we should desire him. He is despised and rejected by men; a man of sorrows, and acquainted with grief: and we hid as it were our faces from him; he was despised, and we esteemed him not. Surely he hath borne our griefs, and carried our sorrows: yet we did esteem him stricken, smitten by God, and afflicted.

(ISAIAH 53:1–4)

One traditional Jewish understanding of this prophecy is that the despised servant of God represents the nation Israel in all their hardships, but the man described cannot represent Israel because Israel is the audience to whom the prophet is writing—the very people the prophecy claims would reject this "man of sorrows." Nor can the man in the prophecy be the prophet, for Isaiah includes himself with Israel by saying "we" instead of "you." Clearly, when he says things like "we esteemed him not," the prophet could not have meant "we did not esteem Israel," for he and his countrymen naturally held themselves and their nation in high esteem (as any people regard themselves and their nation). Nor would it make sense to say they hid their faces from themselves.

Because it will be very difficult for Isaiah's people to recognize their Messiah, the prophet begins by asking "who has believed our report?" The answer is very few of the prophet's own people believed the report. That is why they rejected, even despised, the one predicted. Because the Messiah did not come as a mighty warrior to rally the people against their imperial invaders, he was not recognized as a Messiah. And because he proclaimed a New Covenant, his words sounded foreign to a people saturated in the Old Covenant.

The earlier Isaiah prophecy had said "with the breath of his lips shall he slay the wicked." In other words, he would overcome evil with the truth of his words. This is the image presented earlier in the Apocalypse of one who overcomes by the sword of his mouth. Isaiah implied the only weapon the Messiah would use to strike the world would be the "rod of his mouth." He would come in meekness, unarmed, waging only a war of words. Therefore, those who sought resolution against Rome via insurrection would not recognize him:

> But he was wounded for our transgressions, he was bruised for our iniquities [sins]: the chastisement for our peace was upon him; and with his stripes [the whipping he received] we are healed. All we like sheep have gone astray; we have turned every one to his own way; and the LORD hath laid on him the iniquity of us all. He was oppressed, and he was afflicted, yet he opened not his mouth: he is brought as a lamb to the slaughter, and as a sheep before her shearers is dumb, so he opened not his mouth. He was taken from prison and from judgment: and who shall declare his generation? for he was cut off from the land of the living: for the transgression of my people was he stricken. And he made his grave with the wicked, and with the rich in his death; because he had done no violence, neither was any deceit in his mouth. Yet it pleased the LORD to bruise him; he hath put him to grief: when thou shalt make his soul an offering for sin, he shall see his seed, he shall prolong his days, and the pleasure of the LORD shall prosper in his hand. He shall see of the travail of his soul, and shall be satisfied: by his knowledge shall my righteous servant justify many; for he shall bear their iniquities. Therefore I will divide to him a portion with the great, and he shall divide the spoil with the strong; because he hath poured out his soul to death: and he was numbered with the transgressors; and he bore the sin of many, and made intercession for the transgressors.
>
> (ISAIAH 53:5–12)

In this prophecy, the tender branch Isaiah had predicted earlier turns out to be a meek lamb brought to the slaughter. This is a meaningful symbol to the people of Israel. Salvation from sins had always come through faith carried out in daily sacrifice. If the one described in this prophecy represented Israel, the prophecy would have to mean that the people of Israel would die to provide salvation from their own sins or that their nation would die to provide their salvation. That hardly makes sense. Nor could it be said that Israel had done nonviolence "nor that no deceit" had come from their mouths.

The most famous Jew who ever walked the planet, Jesus, fits all of these descriptions. He was certainly "despised and rejected," "oppressed" and "afflicted" by the people of Israel. "As a sheep before her shearers is dumb, so he opened not his mouth" before the tribunal ready to shear him—except for one crucial moment of proclamation, and then he was "cut off from the land of the living":

> But he held his peace, and answered nothing. Again the high priest asked him, and said to him, Art thou the Christ, the Son of the Blessed? And Jesus said, I am: and ye shall see the Son of man sitting on the right hand of power, and coming in the clouds of heaven.
>
> (MARK 14:61, 62)

Isaiah used the same term found in Daniel: the Messiah would be "cut off." The Isaiah prophecy implies the Messiah would be made into a sacrifice by his own people, yet the Messiah would save them from their sins. The New Covenant the Messiah offered to the Jews went to the Gentiles, which also was predicted:

> And again, Isaiah saith, There shall be a root of Jesse, and he that shall rise to reign over the Gentiles; in him shall the Gentiles trust.   (ROMANS 15:12)

So, according to Isaiah, the root of Jesse would be rejected by his own, yet wind up becoming the Messiah to the Gentiles. It was said the Lion of Judah would wash his clothes in blood. It was also said the salvation of Israel would come from one slaughtered like a lamb. The Apocalypse pulls these prophecies together. The Lion of Judah is announced, but then appears as a lamb that was slain—covered in its own blood. As it turns out, Jesus washed his clothes in blood—his own—unlike King David, who shed the blood of others. The true Lion of Judah turns out to be a lamb of sacrifice:

> Much more then, being now justified by his blood, we shall be saved from wrath through him. For if, when we were enemies, we were reconciled to God by the death of his Son, much more, being reconciled, we shall be saved by his life. . . . so by the obedience of one [before God] shall many be made righteous.
>
> (ROMANS 5:9, 10, 19B)

> Neither by the blood of goats and calves, but by his own blood he entered in once into the holy place, having obtained eternal redemption for us. . . . And for this cause he is the mediator of the new testament [New Covenant], that by means of death, for the redemption [paying off] of the transgressions that were under the first testament [Old Covenant], they who are called may receive the promise of eternal inheritance. . . . For Christ hath not entered into the holy places made with hands, which are the figures [representations] of the true [spiritual places]; but into heaven itself, now to appear in the presence of God for us. . . . And as it is appointed to men once to die, but after this the judgment: So Christ was once offered to bear the sins of many; and to them that look for him he shall appear the second time without sin to salvation.   (HEBREWS 9:12, 15, 24, 27, 28)

Just as it was hard for people steeped in Judaism to understand the New Covenant, it is hard for people today to understand the sacrifices of the Old Covenant. But here is another irony in the way Jesus died: Jesus was crucified during the week of Passover—a Jewish feast that, even today, commemorates the salvation of the Jews by the ancient sacrifice of a lamb. When God freed the Jewish slaves from Egypt, he had to bring judgment in the form of plagues against Egypt in order to get Pharaoh to let them go. The final plague that brought the Jews their freedom was the death of all firstborn male children in Egypt, which included Pharaoh's son. In order to spare their own firstborn male children from the angel of death, the Jews were instructed by God to paint their door posts with the blood of a lamb, and the angel of death would "pass over" their house. What was the purpose of killing an innocent lamb? In the Christian view, the slaughtered lamb that brought the Jews freedom from Egypt and death during that first passover foreshadowed the slaying of the Messiah many Passovers later. Jesus, too, was a firstborn male child.

There is one Old Testament prophecy that ties most of these metaphors and prophecies together—the flight out of Egypt, the eternal king of Judah, the mysterious branch of the family tree. It even indicates, as other prophecies have, that the Messiah will come at a time when the Jews are restored to the land of Israel:

> And I will gather the remnant of my flock [God's people] from all countries where I have driven them, and will bring them again to their folds; and they shall be fruitful and increase. And I will set shepherds over them who shall feed them: and they shall fear no more, nor be dismayed, neither shall they be lacking, saith the LORD. Behold, the days come, saith the LORD, that I will raise to David a righteous Branch, and a King shall reign and prosper, and shall execute judgment and justice upon the earth. In his days Judah shall be saved, and Israel shall dwell in safety: and this is his name by which he shall be called, THE LORD OUR RIGHTEOUSNESS. Therefore, behold, the days come, saith the LORD, that they shall no more say, The LORD liveth, who brought the children of Israel out of the land of Egypt; But, The LORD liveth, who brought and who led the seed [descendants] of the house of Israel out of the north country, and from all countries where I have driven them; and they shall dwell in their own land.
>
> (JEREMIAH 23:3–8)

Another prophecy about "the branch" refers to a historic priest named Joshua, who was commissioned by God to rebuild the temple after Babylon destroyed it. His name, which means "The Lord our Salvation" is the Hebrew form of the name Jesus. Appointed high priest, he is later proclaimed king, but Jews practiced separation of church and state, and no priest ever ruled as king. Besides, a man named Zerubbabel already filled the role of king. So this Joshua may have represented a more important "Joshua" to come.

The following scene takes place when the capstone is being inscribed, which will be ceremonially placed on the top of the temple by Zerubbabel on the day of the temple's completion: (The capstone, in itself, is a literary connection to other messianic prophecies.)

Hear now, O Joshua the high priest, thou, and thy companions that sit before thee: for they are men wondered at [can also mean "they are symbolic men"]: for, behold, I will bring forth my servant the BRANCH. For behold the stone that I have laid before Joshua; upon one stone shall be seven eyes: behold, I will engrave the engraving of it, saith the LORD of hosts, and I will remove the iniquity of that land in one day. In that day, saith the LORD of hosts, shall ye call every man his neighbour under the vine and under the fig tree. . . . For who hath despised the day of small things? for they shall rejoice, and shall see the plummet in the hand of Zerubbabel with those seven; they are the eyes of the LORD, which run to and fro through the whole earth. (ZECHARIAH 3:8–10; 4:10)

Then take silver and gold, and make crowns, and set them upon the head of Joshua the son of Josedech, the high priest; And speak to him, saying, Thus speaketh the LORD of hosts, saying, Behold the man whose name is The BRANCH; and he shall grow up out of his place, and he shall build the temple of the LORD: Even he shall build the temple of the LORD; and he shall bear the glory, and shall sit and rule upon his throne; and he shall be a priest upon his throne: and the counsel of peace shall be between them both. (ZECHARIAH 6:11–13)

The former prophecies regarding the branch indicated that the Messiah, as a slaughtered lamb, would restore perfect union between God and humanity. This prophecy regarding the branch makes a man named "Joshua" king and connects him with the cornerstone or capstone with seven eyes. What does it all mean? The answer to that question will also reveal a deep mystery about the nature of the Messiah, the *root* of David, the Lion who chose the path of the Lamb:

. . . being in the form of God [before he became human], [Christ Jesus] thought it not robbery to be equal with God: But made himself of no reputation, and took upon him the form of a servant, and was made in the likeness of men: And being found in fashion as a man, he humbled himself, and became obedient to death, even the death of the cross. Therefore God also hath highly exalted him, and given him a name which is above every name: That at the name of Jesus every knee should bow, of things in heaven, and things on earth, and things under the earth; And that every tongue should confess that Jesus Christ is Lord, to the glory of God the Father. (PHILIPPIANS 2:6–11)

If spirits can dwell in human bodies, then God's Holy Spirit can dwell in a human body, too, so that his creation might know him. For many Jews this was and is too base an action for God, too undignified. Is becoming a part of his own creation too low for God to stoop? Can the Holy Spirit of God infuse into the common clay in such a way as to become a man?

The Apocalypse reveals the unique identity of Jesus with God's Holy Spirit by describing the Lamb as "having seven horns and seven eyes, which are the seven Spirits of God sent forth into all the earth." This statement corresponds to the capstone mentioned in Zechariah that had seven eyes engraved on it: "the eyes of the Lamb, which run to and fro throughout the earth." The Lamb with seven horns and seven eyes is a highly charged symbol: horns represent power; and eyes, seeing or knowing. Seven is the number for all that exists (the totality of God and creation), so this Lamb is all-powerful and all-seeing or all-knowing. This symbolic image of the Lamb combines the "seven Spirits of God" with one of God's creatures. The spirit and flesh are brought together in what New Testament writers called a "new creation." Spiritually, the Messiah is the "Son of God" and physically, the "Son of Man."

As it turns out, the difficulty for the Jews was not that the Messiah was *less* than expected, but that he was far more. The Apostle Paul said all of this more straightforwardly:

> Moses, who put a veil over his face, that the children of Israel could not steadfastly look [upon his face because of its radiance from being in the presence of God] ... But their minds were blinded: for until this day the same veil remaineth untaken away in the reading of the old testament. . . . Nevertheless when one shall turn to the Lord, the veil shall be taken away. Now the Lord [Jesus Christ] is that Spirit: [of God] and where the Spirit of the Lord is, there is liberty. But we all, with unveiled face beholding as in a mirror the glory of the Lord, are changed into the same image from glory to glory, even as by the Spirit of the Lord.
>
> (2 CORINTHIANS 3:13–18)

The New International Version of the Bible translates the last line: "And we, who with unveiled faces all reflect the Lord's glory, are being transformed into his likeness with ever-increasing glory, which comes from the Lord, [Jesus] *who is the Spirit.*" (2 Corinthians 3:18, emphasis added)

In a prophecy to Jesus' mother, an angel brought the following message regarding her future son:

> *For he shall be great in the sight of the Lord . . . and he shall be filled with the Holy Spirit, even from his mother's womb. . . . And the angel answered and said to her, The Holy Spirit shall come upon thee, and the power of the Highest shall overshadow thee: therefore also that holy one who shall be born of thee shall be called the Son of God.*
>
> (LUKE 1:15, 35)

Elsewhere Paul adds:

But when the fulness of the time was come, God sent forth his Son, made of a woman, made under the law [the Old Covenant], To redeem them that were under the law [the Jews], that we [Jews and Gentiles] might receive the adoption of sons. And because ye are sons, God hath sent forth the Spirit of his Son into your hearts, crying, Abba, Father.

(GALATIANS 4:4–6)

The Spirit itself beareth witness with our spirit, that we are the children of God. (ROMANS 8:16)

This is why Jesus said, in essence, that whoever spoke against his humanity would be forgiven, but there could be no forgiveness for those who spoke against his Spirit, because they failed to recognize the Spirit of God. The unforgivable sin is continuing to reject the Spirit of God, and to reject the divinity of the Messiah is to reject the Spirit of God. (To experience eternal union with God after death, one cannot reject his Spirit, for it is the Spirit of God communing with human spirits that makes union with God possible.) Thus, the Apostle Paul wished for all people . . .

That the God of our Lord Jesus Christ, the Father of glory, may give to you the spirit of wisdom and revelation in the knowledge of him: The eyes of your understanding being enlightened; that ye may know what is the hope of his calling, and what the riches of the glory of his inheritance in the saints, And what is the exceeding greatness of his power toward us who believe, according to the working of his mighty power, Which he wrought in Christ, when he raised him from the dead, and set him at his own right hand in the heavenly places, Far above all principality, and power, and might, and dominion, and every name that is named, not only in this world, but also in that which is to come. (EPHESIANS 1:17–21)

In John's Gospel, Jesus more than hints at his true nature to his disciples before he ascends into heaven. At the beginning of his Gospel, John described Jesus as the "Word of God" made flesh. What is a word but a breath with meaning? "Breath" and "spirit" are the same in the original language of John's Gospel. So, near the end of his Gospel, John writes:

Then said Jesus to them again, Peace be to you: as my Father hath sent me [into the world], even so I send you. And when he had said this, he breathed on them, and saith to them, Receive ye the Holy Spirit. (JOHN 20:21, 21)

It is as though Jesus breathed his own spirit upon them—blew it across the room since "breath" and "spirit" are the same word—just as God breathed the first living spirits into humans in the Garden of Eden.

The final scene of John's second vision in the Apocalypse dramatizes the revelation of the divine nature of the Messiah and the confirmation of his authority over all events on earth. The one who had predicted to the Jewish leaders that he would sit "at the right hand of power" now receives the scroll containing earth's destiny from the right hand of the one on the throne. In Jewish tradition, all blessings are bestowed by the right hand, which symbolizes authority. This scene is the Messiah's investiture by God as the only king with a fully divine right to rule over the events of earth—a right claimed by submission to God in his willingness to die for the truth, but most of all because he is, according to Paul, the Spirit of God indwelling the resurrected body of a human (and humans are seen in biblical terms as the head of God's creation on earth):

> And he came and took the book out of the right hand of him that sat upon the throne. And when he had taken the book, the four living beings and four and twenty elders fell down before the Lamb, having every one of them harps, and golden vials full of odours [incense], which are the prayers of saints. And they sung a new song, saying, Thou art worthy to take the book, and to open its seals: for thou wast slain, and hast redeemed us to God by thy blood out of every kindred, and tongue, and people, and nation; And hast made us to our God kings and priests: and we shall reign on the earth. (REVELATION 5:7–10)

Those who were shown earlier worshiping around the throne of the Almighty Creator now extend the same worship to the Messiah. The Messiah has united both Jews and Gentiles under one New Covenant ("every kindred, and tongue, and people, and nation"). God's two people become one people, forming a single kingdom under the Messiah. Thus, the full prophecy given to Judah will become true: "Judah, thou art he whom thy brethren shall praise: . . . thy father's children shall bow down before thee." (The brothers of Judah were the patriarchs of all the tribes of Israel. These are shown in the Apocalypse as part of the twenty-four elders bowing down before the Lion of Judah.)

The Old Covenant was a covenant of flesh (sacrifice, circumcision, and kosher laws). The New Covenant, as promised in Jeremiah, is a covenant of Spirit, promising humanity's spiritual union with God. In the Christian view, God's spirit did not become base when he entered human flesh; instead, he made flesh holy. God lowered himself to humanity in order to raise humanity to God. Only God could do it.

Even the natural world, which has long suffered because of human evil, will be restored because humans will oversee the world with love and respect for all that has been created. Perfect communion between God and man and nature is depicted in the Apocalypse by concentric circles of creatures centered on God's authority. At last, even the creatures of the sea and the insects under the earth are included. So, all heaven and nature sing:

> *And I beheld, and I heard the voice of many angels around the throne and the living beings and the elders: and the number of them was ten thousand times ten thousand, and thousands of thousands; Saying with a loud voice, Worthy is the Lamb that was slain to receive power, and riches, and wisdom, and strength, and honour, and glory, and blessing. And every creature which is in heaven, and on the earth, and under the earth, and such as are in the sea, and all that are in them, I heard saying, Blessing, and honour, and glory, and power, be to him that sitteth upon the throne, and to the Lamb for ever and ever. And the four living beings said, Amen. And the four and twenty elders fell down and worshipped him that liveth for ever and ever.* (REVELATION 5:11–14)

Chapter 10

S⦿RR⦿WS:

THE SEVEN SEALS AND THE BEGINNING OF THE END

With the Messiah now glorified in heaven, the events of the scroll are ready to unfold. The scene, as it has played out so far, offers total assurance to the members of John's churches and to all of the people of God that the plan of events—no matter how terrible parts of it may be—is in the hand of their trusted Messiah. Regardless of what tribulations may come, the ultimate victory of good is assured to those who are brothers and sisters of the Messiah.

Before earth's final destiny can be revealed—if that is what the scroll contains—the seals must be removed. The seals, then, represent events set into motion by Jesus Christ (since he is the one opening them). They represent the things that must take place before the final events of history begin. They probably do not represent the end itself, because they are not part of the contents of the scroll.

Like the creation story that begins the Bible with its seven days of creation, all of the events of earth's destiny are told in series of seven. The seven seals read like a nightmare of the patterns of evil that will sweep through history from the time of Christ until the last days.

THE FOUR HORSEMEN OF THE APOCALYPSE

The first four seals are distinguished from the final three by being the only ones introduced by each of the four living creatures and by being the only seals containing the images of horsemen. They are probably called out by the four living creatures because they universally plague the four corners of the earth: *four* plagues containing *four* horsemen called out by the *four* living creatures:

And I saw when the Lamb opened one of the seals, and I heard, as it were the noise of thunder, one of the four living beings saying, Come and see. And I saw, and behold a white horse: and he that sat on him had a bow; and a crown was given to him: and he went forth conquering, and to conquer.

And when he had opened the second seal, I heard the second living being say, Come and see. And there went out another horse that was red: and power was given to him that sat on him to take peace from the earth, and that they should kill one another: and there was given to him a great sword. And when he had opened the third seal, I heard the third living being say, Come and see.

And I beheld, and lo a black horse; and he that sat on him had a pair of balances in his hand. And I heard a voice in the midst of the four living beings say, A measure of wheat for a penny, and three measures of barley for a penny; and see thou hurt not the oil and the wine. And when he had opened the fourth seal, I heard the voice of the fourth living being say, Come and see. And I looked, and behold a pale horse: and his name that sat on him was Death, and Hell followed with him. And power was given to them over the fourth part of the earth, to kill with sword, and with hunger, and with death, and with the beasts of the earth.

(REVELATION 6:1–8)

For ancient Jewish readers, horses would have been symbols of war. Most Jews did not use horses for general transport, preferring donkeys and sometimes camels. Horses were for Roman charioteers, and conquering Greeks, Assyrians, and Babylonians. So the horses may indicate that all of the first four events are related to war. The voice that announces these horses rumbles like thunder, calling to mind the thundering hooves of war horses charging into battle.

The horses are represented in *four* colors: white probably signifies victorious conquerors; red for the blood of wars; black for the famines and pestilent diseases that come in the aftermath of war (when the land has been ravaged and strewn with corpses); the fourth is the pallor of death and the grave, which follow famine and disease. Famine also brings high inflation. A penny probably represented a day's wages when the King James Version was written.. As for the deaths that come by wild beasts, these were understood by first-century Christians as referring to the bears and lions of the Roman arenas where Jews and Christians were slaughtered for entertainment, especially after the Jewish rebellion. Others see the deaths by these beasts as a reference to the ongoing conflict between man and nature. There's no reason it can't mean both, since both are reasonable interpretations. That's the beauty of poetry.

War and its casualties, as well as the conflict between humans and nature, are the kinds of general evil that have always plagued the earth—brought on mostly by human imperialism. Christ may be letting his followers know through his prophet that they can expect more of the same until his return. These things are not, in themselves, signs of the end, nor will they come to an end until he returns. This interpretation would seem to make the most sense out of the words of Jesus recorded earlier:

> *And when ye shall hear of wars and ru-*
> *mours of wars, be ye not troubled: for*
> *such things must needs be; but the end*
> *shall not be yet. For nation shall rise*
> *against nation, and kingdom against*
> *kingdom: and there shall be earthquakes*
> *in various places, and there shall be*
> *famines and troubles: these are the be-*
> *ginnings of sorrows.* (MARK 13:7–8)

Since the earth has been plagued by war and famine, disease and death for as long as its been occupied by humans, what is the connection between these four plagues and Jesus?

Many have understood the archer on the white horse (the first seal) as representing the truth of Christ or his Spirit storming through history. The first reason for this view is that, throughout the Apocalypse, white is always a symbol of righteousness. So this horse could represent the advance of righteousness. To see this archer as an evil conqueror, as many others have understood it, would mar the purity of the symbolism in the Apocalypse. Second, if the white horse represents a victorious *evil* conqueror, then the red horse, war, seems redundant. How else do conquerors conquer except by war? Victorinus, an aptly named bishop near Vienna, wrote the following interpretation about two hundred years after John wrote his Apocalypse:

> After the Lord ascended into heaven . . . He sent the Holy Spirit, whose words the preachers sent forth as arrows reaching into the human heart. . . . And the crown on the head is promised to preachers by the Holy Spirit. . . . Therefore the white horse is the . . . Holy Spirit sent into the world. For the Lord says, "This Gospel shall be preached throughout the whole world for a testimony to all nations, and then shall come the end."[1]

The third reason for seeing this as a symbol as the Spirit of Christ is that Christ appears on a white horse at the end of the Apocalypse. The story comes full circle if the first seal shows him riding out on a white horse and the last plague shows him returning on a white horse. Christ on the white horse set the events the Apocalypse into motion and then returns to bring them to a conclusion.

For most people, the difficulty with seeing Christ as the archer on the white horse has been associating him with the remaining six seals, which are all terrible events. How could Christ be the precursor to such evil plagues? But perhaps that is exactly the point. The world has always had war, but not the kind stirred up by the life and death of Jesus Christ. The plagues that follow in the remaining seals may represent rebellion of evil *against* Jesus' advancing truth.

Here is where history is in astounding agreement. Prior to the death of Christ, no wars were fought over religion—with the exception of the Jewish troubles created by Antiochus Epiphanes, who, for that very reason, is seen as a prototype to the Antichrist. But even Antiochus Epiphanes' interest was forcing his *culture* onto the Jews. Jewish religion was simply a hurdle to his culture wars. Before Christ, wars were about power and acquisition of land, or they were about revenge. But after Christ a new kind of war emerged. For the first time in history, wars began over religion alone. First, Jews warred against Romans because the Romans insisted on being worshipped. Then these same Romans slaughtered Jews and Christians in their arenas for refusing to worship them. In later centuries, the Muslims invaded Christian nations to advance their religion by "holy war"; then the tide of battle turned, and Christians drove back into Muslim nations during the "holy crusades." Christians also slaughtered Jews during the crusades *solely* for religious reasons. Most likely Christians even used the white horse of the Apocalypse to rally their knights into action, claiming their crusades advanced the cause of Christ the Conqueror. In that sense, the Apocalypse may have become a self-fulfilling prophecy, plunging history into darkness because people with clouded minds could not comprehend the light it contained. Instead, they used their intrepretation to grant authority for their "holy" wars. In more recent centuries, Catholics slaughtered Protestants and Protestants slaughtered Catholics. (But all of these troubles are for later parts of this narrative.)

The message from the seven seals to John's followers would have been that the truth must continue to be proclaimed in the name of the victorious Christ and to expect the evil plagues of war and persecutions to increase as a result. God will not stop the plagues of the seven seals—even to spare the righteous. This is evident from a prophecy in earlier Jewish history that is similar to the four horsemen of the Apocalypse:

The word of the LORD came again to me, saying, Son of man, when the land sinneth against me by trespassing grievously, then will I stretch out my hand upon it, and will break the staff of its bread, and will send famine upon it, and will cut off man and beast from it: Though these three men, Noah, Daniel, and Job [all renowned for righteousness], were in it, they should deliver their own souls only by their righteousness, saith the Lord GOD. If I cause evil beasts to pass through the land, and they lay it waste, so that it be desolate, that no man may pass through because of the beasts: Though these three men were in it, as I live, saith the Lord GOD, they shall deliver neither sons nor daughters; they only shall be delivered, but the land shall be desolate. Or if I bring a sword upon that land, and say, Sword, go through the land; so that I cut off man and beast from it: Though these three men were in it, as I live, saith the Lord GOD, they shall deliver neither sons nor daughters, but they only shall be delivered themselves. Or if I send a pestilence into that land, and pour out my fury upon it in

blood, to cut off from it man and beast:
Though Noah, Daniel, and Job, were in
it, as I live, saith the Lord GOD, they
shall deliver neither son nor daughter;
they shall deliver their own souls only by
their righteousness. For thus saith the

Lord GOD; How much more when I
send my four grievous judgments upon
Jerusalem, the sword, and the famine,
and the evil beast, and the pestilence, to
cut off from it man and beast?

((EZEKIEL 14:12–21).

Throughout this prophecy, the only surety the righteous are promised is the salvation of their own souls, which leads to the fifth seal.

THE MARTYRS OF RIGHTEOUSNESS

The first four seals seem to represent a long-existing breakdown between human beings that acquired a religious focus overnight after the death of Christ. If one assumes that the invisible gravity of spiritual evil may influence the tide of human events, then history validates a significant change in the spiritual realm following the death of Christ. Whether one can see the moon or not, the change of tides below is evident. Suddenly wars became *in very fact* spiritual battles. For those who believe in a spirit world, this historic transformation evokes an unsettling sense that the death of Christ changed the equilibrium between this universe and another that lies unseen.

The final three seals move away from scenes of human warfare on earth to the spiritual side of the equation. Having introduced the subject of Hades with the fourth seal, the prophet turns to look at the souls of the dead—probably casualties from the preceding conflicts:

And when he had opened the fifth seal, I
saw under the altar the souls of them
that were slain for the word of God, and
for the testimony which they held: And
they cried with a loud voice, saying, How
long, O Lord, holy and true, dost thou
not judge and avenge our blood on them

that dwell on the earth? And white robes
were given to every one of them; and it
was said to them, that they should rest
yet for a little season, until their fel-
lowservants also and their brethren, that
should be killed as they were, should be
fulfilled. (REVELATION 6:9–11)

This scene makes it clear that the religious wars on earth are due to a particular evil that seeks to eradicate the people of God. This means the seven churches and all who follow should expect persecution leading even to death. But such persecutions are no indication the end has come. The souls of the murdered saints—the martyrs—are told they must wait awhile longer. There are more to join their number.

The martyrs are pictured symbolically under the altar because they were sacrificed.

The blood of ancient Jewish sacrifices was poured into a gutter at the base of the altar. So it is with the blood of the martyrs. Because the purpose throughout the Apocalypse is to encourage the persecuted, the apostle's vision reveals that martyrs are given rest and white garments, representing their purity, while they wait for the flow of righteous blood to saturate the dust of a blood-thirsty world.

John offers his suffering congregations no shallow promise of earthly glory, no prosperity as a reward for righteous living. He does not even offer hope that their persecutions will let up or that the flow of righteous blood will be stanched. He practically promises it will continue. Instead, he encourages his followers with the enduring hope of a victorious death. There will be glory on the other side, but all his followers have to carry them through is faith.

A PRELUDE TO THE END

The sixth seal appears to encapsulate the events of earth's final days before the return of Christ a time of great tribulation. (The seventh seal—because it allows the scroll to finally open—should represent the end itself.) The sixth seal comes, as though in answer to the cry of the martyrs. It is vengeance upon a world long drunk with blood.

During this time, the Apocalypse indicates God will permit evil to consume itself, bringing utter destruction upon humanity. The complete removal of God's protection allows the equilibrium of the spiritual realm to shift madly out of control. All of humanity will swing in the gravitational chaos of this change. The resulting increase of evil among humans will upset the equilibrium of nature as well, and nature will retaliate with its own destruction against the earth. All evil will be consumed in the clash of these primal titan forces:

And I beheld when he had opened the sixth seal, and, lo, there was a great earthquake; and the sun became black as sackcloth of hair, and the moon became as blood; And the stars of heaven fell to the earth, even as a fig tree casteth its untimely figs, when it is shaken by a mighty wind. And the heaven departed as a scroll when it is rolled together; and every mountain and isle were moved out of their places. And the kings of the earth, and the great men, and the rich men, and the chief captains, and the mighty men, and every slave, and every free man, hid themselves in the dens and in the rocks of the mountains; And said to the mountains and rocks, Fall on us, and hide us from the face of him that sitteth on the throne, and from the wrath of the Lamb: For the great day of his wrath is come; and who shall be able to stand?

(REVELATION 6:12–17)

Haymo of Halberstadt, a bishop from the mid-ninth century, interpreted this sign of great tribulation upon the earth figuratively. He viewed the sun as Christ, whose light of righteousness during this time will be completely darkened. The church, which reflects his light like the moon, will be red with the blood of martyrs, and the stars of heaven that fall to earth are the righteous saints who are unable to endure the test of their faith during this last great persecution.[2]

But there are also many natural explanations that would justify a literal interpretation of these events. Yet a literal interpretation does not preclude their figurative value at all. Both views can exists side by side and be right. An example of a natural event would be the scorching east wind from the distant deserts of Arabia, sometimes called "the breath of God" or the "scirocco," which occasionally blows death across the land of Israel. Loading the skies with desert sand, this breath of Hades covers the sun and moon and gives them a blood-red cast. It occasionally drives ravenous locusts into the land, which form such a dense cloud they have been known to darken the sun like an eclipse. When they come, they consume every plant and bring famine and pestilence in their wake. Disease ripens in the dead flesh of starving and thirsting animals. These scenes were a familiar horror to the generations of people who lived in the promised land, so John may have been drawing from his own experience.

But the picture in the sixth seal is worldwide, so a sandstorm is not a sufficient answer. Nevertheless, it provides a clue to the kinds of very real disasters, natural or man-made, that are capable of turning the sun black and the moon red from any vantage point on earth.

One of the great strengths of John's vision is the way it pulls so many prophecies of the Bible together in one great cataclysm. It is a monument of apocalyptic writing. In this second-to-the-last seal, John echoes two apocalyptic prophecies given by Isaiah to describe the destruction that would come to Israel from Assyria and Babylon:

Enter into the rock, and hide thee in the dust, for fear of the LORD, and for the glory of his majesty. The lofty looks of man shall be humbled, and the haughtiness of men shall be abased, and the LORD alone shall be exalted in that day. For the day of the LORD of hosts shall be upon every one that is proud and lofty, and upon every one that is lifted up; and he shall be brought low: And upon all the cedars of Lebanon, that are high and lifted up, and upon all the oaks of Bashan, And upon all the high moun-
tains, and upon all the hills that are lifted up, And upon every high tower, and upon every fortified wall, And upon all the ships of Tarshish [a coastal city], and upon all pleasant pictures. And the loftiness of man shall be abased, and the haughtiness of men shall be made low: and the LORD alone shall be exalted in that day. And the idols he shall utterly abolish. And they shall go into the holes of the rocks, and into the caves of the earth, for fear of the LORD, and for the glory of his majesty, when he ariseth to

shake terribly the earth. In that day a man shall cast his idols of silver, and his idols of gold, which they made each one for himself to worship, to the moles and to the bats; To go into the clefts of the rocks, and into the tops of the ragged rocks, for fear of the LORD, and for the glory of his majesty, when he ariseth to shake terribly the earth. Cease ye from man, whose breath is in his nostrils: for why is he to be esteemed?

(ISAIAH 2:10–22)

The burden of Babylon, which Isaiah the son of Amoz saw. . . . I have commanded my sanctified ones, I have also called my mighty ones for my anger, even them that rejoice in my highness. The noise of a multitude in the mountains, as of a great people; a tumultuous noise of the kingdoms of nations gathered together: the LORD of hosts mustereth the host of the battle. They come from a far country, from the end of heaven, even the LORD, and the weapons of his indignation, to destroy the whole land. Wail ye; for the day of the LORD is at hand; it shall come as a destruction from the Almighty. Therefore shall all hands be faint, and every man's heart shall melt: And they shall be afraid: pangs and sorrows shall take hold of them; they shall be in pain as a woman that travaileth: they shall be amazed one at another; their faces shall be as flames. Behold, the day of the LORD cometh, cruel both with wrath and fierce anger, to lay the land desolate: and he shall destroy its sinners out of it. For the stars of heaven and its constellations shall not give their light: the sun shall be darkened in his going forth, and the moon shall not cause her light to shine. And I will punish the world for their evil, and the wicked for their iniquity; and I will cause the arrogance of the proud to cease, and will lay low the haughtiness of the terrible. I will make a man more rare than fine gold; even a man than the golden wedge of Ophir. Therefore I will shake the heavens, and the earth shall remove out of her place, in the wrath of the LORD of hosts, and in the day of his fierce anger. (ISAIAH 13:1, 3–13)

Though Isaiah spoke these words in reference to the destruction of Israel by Babylon, the power of the language begs for greater fulfillment. The scope sounds worldwide, and there is every indication that the pattern of this ancient prophecy is going to repeat on a global scale. Christ, himself, quoted some of these verses when he answered his disciples' question regarding the final time of his return:

But in those days, after that tribulation, the sun shall be darkened, and the moon shall not give her light, And the stars of heaven shall fall, and the powers that are in heaven shall be shaken.

(MARK 13:24, 25)

Men's hearts [shall fail] them for fear, and for expectation of those things which are coming on the earth: for the powers of heaven shall be shaken. And then shall they see the Son of man coming in a cloud with power and great glory. And when these things begin to come to pass, then look up, and lift up your heads; for your redemption draweth near.

(LUKE 21:26–28)

These words were so vital that Christ now repeats them in his final revelation to John, making it clear they apply even beyond the fall of Jerusalem since John is writing after that time. Figurative or literal, there will be great tribulation before the return of Christ. It will introduce an evil solely bent on eradicating God's people, probably both Jews and Christians. Even if the red moon is purely figurative for the blood of martyrs, there must be horrendous times in store for so many martyrs to bloody the moon. What evil could be so dark as to completely eclipse the light of Christ? And if the stars that drop like premature figs out of the sky are only figurative for the saints who are unable to endure the test of their faith, what test could be so severe that such a brilliant host of saints would fall?

To these times that try men's souls, John addresses the rest of his Apocalypse.

Chapter 11

SALVATION:

TRIUMPH OVER TRIBULATION

An interlude between the sixth and seventh seal offers assurance to John's readers before the seventh seal releases terrors of the end times. Against the backdrop of blackened sun and blood-red moon, the vision suddenly opens to a place of serenity, a space of light and calm before the forecast storm is revealed. Four angels, the perfect number for covering all the earth, are seen restraining the elements. Before they are permitted to let it all go, the interlude reveals the people of God receiving a divine seal:

SEALING THE SERVANTS OF GOD

And after these things I saw four angels standing on the four corners of the earth, holding the four winds of the earth, that the wind should not blow on the earth, nor on the sea, nor on any tree. And I saw another angel ascending from the east, having the seal of the living God: *and he cried with a loud voice to the four angels, to whom it was given to hurt the earth and the sea, Saying, Hurt not the earth, neither the sea, nor the trees, till we have sealed the servants of our God in their foreheads.* (REVELATION 7:1–3)

What kind of a mark of identification is this seal, and does it offer protection from the events to come? To the first question, a few hints can be found in the writings of the Apostle Paul when he talks about those who have placed their trust in Jesus Christ:

Now he who establisheth us with you
in Christ, and hath anointed us, is God;
Who hath also sealed us, and given the
earnest of the Spirit in our hearts.

(2 CORINTHIANS 1:21, 22)

In whom [Jesus Christ] ye also trusted, after ye heard the word of truth, the gospel of your salvation: in whom also after ye believed, ye were sealed with that Holy Spirit of promise, Who is the earnest of our inheritance until the redemption of the purchased possession [in other words, until the resurrection], to the praise of his glory. . . . And grieve not the Holy Spirit of God, by whom ye are sealed to the day of redemption.   (EPHESIANS 1:13, 14; 4:30)

Nevertheless the foundation of God standeth firm, having this seal, The Lord knoweth them that are his. . . .
                    (2 TIMOTHY 2:19A)

It was common practice for the apostles to refer to those they had baptized in the name of Jesus as being sealed. St. Clement of Alexandria used the word in the following history about a hundred years after John's writing, showing its common usage around the time John wrote:

[John the Apostle] then returned to Ephesus, and the cleric took home the youngster [John had] entrusted to his care, brought him up . . . and finally gave him the grace of baptism. After this he relaxed his constant care and watchfulness, *having put upon him the seal of the Lord as the perfect protection.* But the youngster snatched at liberty too soon, and was led sadly astray by others. . . . [1]

One possibility, then, is that the people who are about to be sealed are new servants of God—a group of people about to come into the Christian faith who will be receiving God's Holy Spirit as the promise of their eternal salvation. The Spirit of Christ within them is the seal that marks them as his people no matter what events may come.

God's people have always been a marked people. The Jews, for example, had the seal of circumcision marking them as God's people. The high priest wore a gemstone for each tribe of Israel, and each stone was engraved like a signet ring (the kind used for stamping wax seals) with the name of a tribe. In other words, those under the physical covenant had physical seals that marked them as God's people, while those under the spiritual covenant have a spiritual seal that marks them as God's people.

Is this seal more than a spiritual guarantee on their eternal souls? Does it offer physical protection for the times ahead? One of the Psalms promised protection to God's people during times of plague and darkness, but was it referring to the specific times of darkness predicted for the end, or did it simply mean dark times in general?

He that dwelleth in the secret place of the most High shall abide under the shadow of the Almighty. I will say of the LORD, *He is my refuge and my fortress: my God; in him will I trust. Surely he shall deliver thee from the snare of the fowler, and from the perilous pestilence. He shall cover thee with his feathers, and under his wings shalt thou trust: his truth shall be thy shield and buckler. Thou shalt not be afraid for the terror by night; nor for the arrow that flieth by day; Nor for the pestilence that walketh in darkness; nor for the destruction that wasteth at noonday. A thousand shall fall at thy side, and ten thousand at thy right hand; but it shall not come near thee. Only with thy eyes shalt thou behold and see the reward of the wicked. Because thou hast made the LORD, who is my refuge, even the most High, thy habitation; There shall no evil befall thee, neither shall any plague come near thy dwelling. For he shall give his angels charge over thee, to keep thee in all thy ways. They shall bear thee up in their hands, lest thou dash thy foot against a stone. Thou shalt tread upon the lion and adder: the young lion and the dragon shalt thou trample under feet. Because he hath set his love upon me, therefore will I deliver him: I will set him on high, because he hath known my name. He shall call upon me, and I will answer him: I will be with him in trouble; I will deliver him, and honour him. With long life will I satisfy him, and show him my salvation.* (PSALM 91:1–16)

If this Psalm is more than a general comfort, then it could indicate God's people may go through times of tribulation in the end, but they will not be harmed. They will be saved out of those times in the same sense that Noah and his family were saved out of the flood. They endured the flood, but they were given sanctuary in the ark.

In light of the writings above, the seal on the forehead is probably not a visible mark, though it is the counterpart to the mark of the Beast mentioned later in the Apocalypse. If the seal is the Holy Spirit, then certainly a mark on the forehead is purely symbolic—like the old Jewish practice of anointing someone with a clear drop of oil on the forehead as a way of marking them for special service to God. Perhaps, then, the mark of the Beast described later (666 on the forehead) is equally figurative or, in the least, equally invisible.

An ancient prophecy in Ezekiel provides a good example of how this seal may be understood:

And, behold, six men came from the way of the higher gate, which lieth toward the north, and every man a slaughter weapon in his hand; and one man among them was clothed with linen, with a writer's inkhorn by his side: and they went in, and stood beside the brasen altar. And the glory of the God of Israel had gone up from the cherub, on which he was, to the threshold of the house [temple]. And he called to the man clothed with linen, who had the writer's inkhorn by his side; And the LORD said to him, Go through the midst of the city, through the midst of Jerusalem, and set a mark upon the foreheads of the men that sigh and that cry for all the abominations that are done in the midst of it. And to the others he said in my hearing, Go ye after him through the city, and smite: let not your eye spare, neither have ye pity: Slay utterly old and young, both maids, and little children, and women: but come not near any man upon whom is the mark; and begin at my sanctuary. Then they began at the elders who were before the house. And he said to them, Defile the house, and fill the courts with the slain: go ye forth. And they went forth, and slew in the city. . . . And, behold, the man clothed with linen, who had the inkhorn by his side, reported the matter, saying, I have done as thou hast commanded me. (EZEKIEL 9:2–7, 11)

Those who sigh over the abominations and are marked on their foreheads are obviously the righteous—they are people with true hearts for God, or they would not be bothered by the abominations. After the righteous are sealed, the other six angels are sent out to destroy the city, beginning first with the destruction of the temple. Those who have been sealed on their foreheads, however, will be passed over, even though they will be living in the midst of all this destruction. As the psalm had said, "Only with thy eyes shalt [they] behold and see the reward of the wicked."

The Ezekiel prophecy, however, was not about the end of the world but about the end of Israel when Babylon came and destroyed the first temple. No angels of God ran around the city killing people or destroying the temple when the prophecy was fulfilled. Nor did any Jews receive visible marks on their foreheads. The physical judgment against Jerusalem was brought about entirely by the human hands of Babylonians. But the vision was given in advance so the people would recognize that these completely natural events were God's judgment when they happened. The judgment came when God allowed evil Babylon to have its way with Jerusalem. He did not intervene to protect his holy city because of the wickedness that had grown among his own people.

So, too, with the spiritual scenes of the Apocalypse. The scenes in the spiritual realm that influence the events of the physical universe will be invisible to human eyes, but the effects will be devastating. It is reasonable to expect the judgments envisioned may be brought about on the battlefields of earth entirely by humans. As was the case during Jerusalem's assault by Babylon, the calamities will be quite real. Jerusalem and the temple were completely destroyed by Babylon. Tens of thousands died, yet a great many people were spared as prophesied. They were led into Babylonian exile, just as though they had been marked for salvation. Among those taken out after the slaughter was the prophet Daniel, indicating that perhaps it was the righteous who were spared.

God usually does not intervene magically from heaven. Instead, he works from *within* the story, using willing human agents. In essence, Israel only existed because God's spiritual forces restrained the evil all around it. Because Israel lay at the crossroads of the ancient world, it was always in peril. Sometimes, when Israel ignored God, God strategically removed his protection, allowing an evil person or natural forces to exert power over Israel in such a way as to nudge the course of human events in a better direction. Sometimes it was more of a whack than a nudge. God did not cause the evil person to do evil. He simply stopped restraining the evil person from doing what he already wanted to do. In the prophetic view, God is sovereign over human events:

> . . . Thus saith the LORD of hosts, the God of Israel; Thus shall ye say to your masters; I have made the earth, the man and the beast that are upon the ground, by my great power and by my outstretched arm, and have given it to whom it seemed right to me. And now have I given all these lands [around Israel] into the hand of Nebuchadnezzar the king of Babylon, my servant; and the beasts of the field have I given him also to serve him. And all nations shall serve him, and his son, and his son's son, until the very [end] time of his land shall come: and then many nations and great kings shall bring him into subjection. And it shall come to pass, that the nation and kingdom which will not serve the same Nebuchadnezzar king of Babylon, and that will not put their neck under the yoke of the king of Babylon, that nation will I punish, saith the LORD, with the sword, and with the famine, and with the pestilence, until I have consumed them by his hand.
>
> (JEREMIAH 27:4–8)

When God wanted to discipline his people for practicing idolatry, King Nebuchadnezzar's hand applied the whip. If they did not submit to him, God would not prevent him from consuming them. God did not throw lightning bolts from heaven. The extra dose of famine and pestilence were probably the natural results of war because of all the dead bodies lying around. Many empires fought with a scorched-earth policy in those days. King Nebuchadnezzar of Babylon made a suitable agent of discipline because Israel had chosen the gods of Babylon over the true God. Therefore, God let them have their preferred gods, and he let those gods have their way with Israel.

Whenever God removed his hand of protection, the evil lurking on Israel's borders was always ready to swallow them up:

> Remember the former things of old: for I am God, and there is none else; I am God, and there is none like me, declaring the end from the beginning, and from ancient times the things that are not yet done, saying, My counsel shall stand, and I will do all my pleasure: Calling a ravenous bird from the east, the man that executeth my counsel from a far country: yea, I have spoken it, I will also bring it to pass; I have purposed it, I will also perform it. (ISAIAH 46: 9–11)

THE DILEMMA OF EVIL

The four angels of the Apocalypse, ready to release the four winds of destruction, clearly imply that the devastation that comes before the return of Christ is God's judgment. The destruction upon land and sea will potentially be quite real. Only this time it will be worldwide (to the four winds).

All of this raises a terrible question about the nature of God. It is the age-old question of how a loving God can be so judgmental. How can a just God allow evil people and harmful natural forces to prevail—if only for a time? Even if God does not create the evil, doesn't his allowance of it make him somewhat culpable? The interesting thing is that God does not deny his culpability, so to speak. In fact, he directly takes credit for the evil events that bring judgment. God does not use the fact that he employed human agents to distance himself from the responsibility.

One of God's most articulate prophets wrestled with God over this dilemma quite eloquently as he watched Babylon destroy Jerusalem:

> The burden which Habakkuk the prophet saw. O LORD, . . . Why dost thou show me iniquity [evil], and cause me to behold grievance? for plundering and violence are before me. . . . for the wicked doth surround the righteous; therefore judgment goeth forth perverted.
>
> (HABAKKUK 1:1–4)

God's answer as to why he uses evil Babylonian agents to accomplish his will over people who are less evil does not offer much consolation:

> Behold ye among the nations, and regard, and wonder marvellously: for I will work a work in your days, which ye will not believe, though it be told you. For, lo, I raise up the Chaldeans [Babylonians], that bitter and hasty nation, which shall march through the breadth of the land, to possess the dwelling places that are not theirs. They are terrible and dreadful: their judgment and their dignity shall proceed from themselves.
>
> (HABAKKUK 1:5–7)

It does say, however, that the evil they bring is totally from within themselves. God did not plant it there. He is simply letting humans do as they wish to Israel. Because human nature has an evil component, many humans would rather blame God for tolerating the evil than blame their own kind who caused it. The prophet finds this answer insufficient, for God admits to recognizing the evil of the Babylonians yet still says they will judge Israel for lesser sins. Why doesn't he judge Babylon even more harshly? Where's the justice? Habakkuk again implores God with these questions, hinting God should change his ways:

> . . . O LORD, thou hast ordained them for judgment; and, O mighty God, thou hast established them for correction. Thou art of purer eyes than to behold evil, and canst not look on iniquity: why lookest thou on them that deal treacherously, and keepest silence when the wicked devoureth the man that is more righteous than he? (HABAKKUK 1:12, 13)

The most moving aspect of this narrative is that the Creator of the universe actually tolerates such questions and dialogues with his prophet. The prophet is not a mere mouthpiece nor a simple antenna for receiving a vision. The Jewish prophets often speak to God from within their vision. Their engagement with him frequently evokes tension. Much is at stake, but God intends that his prophets understand, so God listens. The prophet Amos said, "Surely the Lord GOD will do nothing, but he revealeth his secret to his servants the prophets" (Amos 3:7).

Fearfully expecting rebuke for having challenged the Creator, Habakkuk, all the same, awaits God's reply with determination. Because he questions God earnestly, God gives him understanding:

> *I will stand upon my watch, and seat myself upon the tower, and will watch to see what he will say to me, and what I shall answer when I am reproved. And the LORD answered me, and said, Write the vision, and make it plain upon tablets, that he may run that readeth it. For the vision is yet for an appointed time, but at the end it shall speak, and not lie: though it may tarry, wait for it; because it will surely come, it will not tarry. . . . For the earth shall be filled with the knowledge of the glory of the LORD, as the waters cover the sea.*
>
> (HABAKKUK 2:1–3, 14)

The broader answer given to Habakkuk reaches to the end of time: Evil will be allowed its time and place, but those who are faithful to God will prevail in the end. There will be justice ultimately, but it will require patience to wait for it. God never gives evil the spur. It lurches ahead of its own accord, but he does hold the reins of restraint. There would be no freedom if God completely restrained human evil, but God will assure good ultimately prevails. To do that he may restrain evil strategically. In his next response, God implies there is equilibrium built into the universe from its conception. The empire established by force will always fall from the very hatred it arouses against itself. Because evil is a destructive force, not a creative force, it is self-canceling. Its center cannot hold. God is the one who holds the center of all things together. So that which denies this center, flies apart. Thus, all the images in the Apocalypse of a utopian universe centered around God's throne.

The one who created the universe is patient to let the balances he has placed in nature work their way. So, concerning Nebuchadnezzar, Emperor of Babylon, God replies:

> *Behold, his soul which is lifted up [arrogant] is not upright in him: but the just shall live by his faith. . . . he is a proud man . . . who enlargeth his desire as hell, and is as death, and cannot be satisfied, but gathereth unto him all nations, and heapeth unto him all people: Shall not all these take up a parable against him, and a taunting proverb against him, and say, Woe to him that increaseth that which is not his! . . .*
>
> *Shall they not rise suddenly that shall*

bite thee [Nebuchadnezzar], and awake that shall oppress thee, and thou shalt be for booty to them? Because thou hast spoiled many nations, all the remnant of the people shall spoil thee; because of men's blood, and for the violence of the land, of the city, and of all that dwell therein. . . . Woe to him that buildeth a town with blood, and establisheth a city by iniquity! Behold, is it not of the LORD of hosts that the people shall labour in the very fire, and the people shall weary themselves for very vanity?

(HABAKKUK 2:4–8, 12, 13)

Imperialism is futile because those who consolidate power around themselves also consolidate their enemies. For this reason, Habakkuk is told, it is always just a matter of time before every human empire falls because all are self-centered. The line that says "is it not of the LORD of hosts that the people shall labour in the very fire" even hints at the warnings given by other prophets that the works of human beings will bring the earth to a fiery end.

The destiny of evil is already written into the laws of the universe. God does not have to stir up evil. It is always pulling at its chains, ready to devour whatever it is permitted to feed upon. The destiny of the faithful lies in the hands of God.

Still, God's answer is not deeply satisfying. It's a little too easy to simply say that all evil is a human creation, a product of free will, for the prophet sees evil in nature, too. The prophet looks out on the surrounding lands ready to devour the small nation of Israel and begins to sense a destiny for the entire earth that is so powerful it becomes superimposed on the misfortunes of the prophet's own time and people.

In his closing vision, Habakkuk sees all power seized in the hand of God, like Thor with his thunderbolts, plagues spreading out at his feet, covering the earth with destruction until it is finally cleansed by fire:

God came from Teman, and the Holy One from mount Paran. . . . His glory covered the heavens, and the earth was full of his praise. And his brightness was as the light; he had horns coming out of his hand: and there was the hiding of his power. Before him went the pestilence, and burning coals went forth at his feet. He stood, and measured the earth: he beheld, and drove asunder the nations; and the everlasting mountains were scattered, the perpetual hills did bow: his ways are everlasting. I saw the tents of Cushan in affliction: and the curtains of the land of Midian trembled. Was the LORD displeased against the rivers? was thy anger against the rivers? was thy wrath against the sea, that thou didst ride upon thy horses and thy chariots of salvation? Thy bow was made quite naked, according to the oaths of the tribes, even thy word. . . . Thou didst cleave the earth with rivers. The mountains saw thee, and they trembled: the overflowing of the water passed by: the deep uttered his voice, and lifted up his hands on high. The sun and moon stood still in their habitation: at the light of thy *arrows they went, and at the shining of thy glittering spear. Thou didst march through the land in indignation, thou didst thresh the nations in anger. Thou wentest forth for the salvation of thy people, even for salvation with thy anointed; thou didst wound the head out of the house of the wicked, by laying bare the foundation to the neck. . . . Thou didst strike through with his staffs the head of his villages: they came out as a whirlwind to scatter me: their rejoicing was as to devour the poor secretly. Thou didst walk through the sea with thy horses, through the mire of great waters.*

When I heard, my belly trembled; my lips quivered at the voice: rottenness entered into my bones, and I trembled in myself, that I might rest in the day of trouble: when he cometh up to the people, he will invade them with his troops. (HABAKKUK 3:3–16)

An end-time prophecy or a figurative representation that human forces and nature are all under God's control? For now the mystery of evil remains, but the prophet has learned that Babylon will be destroyed just as surely as Israel is being destroyed by Babylon. Lesser evils and greater evils will all come to nothing. The demise of evil is seen throughout the Bible as a fact waiting to discover itself. The only difference for Israel was that God protected a small but good remnant, and their descendants live today, while all that remains of Babylon is rubble. Good prevails because God protects, but that does not mean the good do not suffer along with the bad.

Throughout the millennia, the prophets saw evil rise and recorded its fall, often before the event. They seemed to agree that the patterns of evil seen in their local events would reverberate through time, building toward a resounding calamity followed by a long-sustained peace. Evil will not slowly fade out of existence as a new light dawns. According to the biblical prophets, evil grows to a consummation in which it burns itself out. How soon that happens might depend on human choices, but the prophets lay out a path to hope for those who choose truth at all costs.

The counterforce to the justice that is built into the system is God's mercy. God's mercy comes when he protects those who have brought misfortune upon themselves:

Thus saith the LORD against all my evil neighbours, that touch the inheritance [the land] which I have caused my people Israel to inherit; Behold, I will pluck them out of their land, and pluck out the house of Judah from among them. And it shall come to pass, after I have plucked them out I will return, and have compassion on them, and will bring them again, every man to his heritage, and every man to his land. And it shall come to pass, if they will diligently learn the ways of my people, to swear by my name, The LORD liveth; as they taught my people to swear by Baal; then shall they be built in the midst of my people. But if they will not obey, I will utterly pluck up and destroy that nation, saith the LORD. (JEREMIAH 12:14–17)

God, being no respecter of persons, offers mercy even to the enemies of his people—if they will center themselves on him just as he expects his chosen to do.

THE 144,000

So God has ordained that a number of people should be sealed before the mysterious scroll is opened and all hell (perhaps literally) breaks loose on earth. It still remains unclear what this seal offers. The biblical passages that mention a seal of God on his people indicate it is a mark of eternal salvation for the soul, but that has never guaranteed physical protection from the whips and scorns of time or the oppressor's wrong. There is clear mention in one case later on that those who are sealed will be protected like Noah's family in the ark during the flood, but there is also some indication they may be killed. All that can be said for certain is that they are marked as people of Christ.

So who are the people who are sealed?

And I heard the number of them who were sealed: and there were sealed an hundred and forty and four thousand of all the tribes of the children of Israel. Of the tribe of Judah were sealed twelve thousand. Of the tribe of Reuben were sealed twelve thousand. Of the tribe of Gad were sealed twelve thousand. Of the tribe of Asher were sealed twelve thousand. Of the tribe of Naphtali were sealed twelve thousand. Of the tribe of Manasseh were sealed twelve thousand. Of the tribe of Simeon were sealed twelve thousand. Of the tribe of Levi were sealed twelve thousand. Of the tribe of Issachar were sealed twelve thousand. Of the tribe of Zebulun were sealed twelve thousand. Of the tribe of Joseph were sealed twelve thousand. Of the tribe of Benjamin were sealed twelve thousand.

(REVELATION 7:4–8)

The fact that the tribes of Israel are specifically named and counted in a role call indicates the 144,000 who are sealed are all Jewish by race. How could anything be more obvious?

Yet, there is immediately a problem. The list of tribes appears normal at first glance—twelve tribes named for the twelve tribes of Israel. It has two tricky peculiarities, however, which may be why the prophet takes the time to give a role call.

The first peculiarity would be obvious to most modern Jews: A prophecy that appears to list groups of Jews who will become Christians in the end times names *all* the tribes of Israel. Ten of the twelve tribes of Israel dropped permanently out of the historic record when Israel was taken captive by Assyria in 722 B.C. These "lost tribes of Israel" haven't been heard from since, and John would have known that. They were either eradicated, or their descendants assimilated completely with the local population, so their blood is now part of the Gentile races. In fact, any nation that acts kindly toward Jews today is rumored by some Jews to be a descendent of one of the lost tribes.

Even if John knew of some descendants from the ten lost tribes who had escaped Assyria's attack or returned to Israel, that was two thousand years ago. By now, any who had returned to Israel have completely assimilated into the other two tribes or have certainly lost track of their identity. No Jews alive today claim to descend from any of the ten lost tribes. Modern Jews consider themselves descendants from either the tribe of Levi or the tribe of Judah (the only two tribes that avoided capture by Assyria), or they simply don't know their lineage.

The second peculiarity is that only nine of the ten lost tribes appear on John's list; one of ten is even lost in the Apocalypse. The tribe that descended from Dan has been replaced by the tribe of Manasseh, Dan's nephew. Dan's name appears on every Old Testament list of the twelve tribes. So why has it been dropped here? Whenever the name Manasseh appears on the list of tribes, it is in place of his father, Joseph. That's because Joseph had two sons, Manasseh and Ephraim, who split the tribal lands of Joseph between themselves. Therefore, their two names sometimes replace their father's name in order to reflect that split, but in this case Joseph's name remains on the list. It's almost as if the list deliberately manipulates the expected names in order to invite suspicion that something more is intended than the list shows at face value.

That it should happen to be Dan who gets bumped to make room for Manasseh is intriguing because Dan is the only lost tribe that *some* Jews believe *may* have been found. For ages, some rabbis have speculated that all the Jews of Ethiopia descended from Dan. So the only lost tribe that *may* have been found is the one that's lost from this list, and all the tribes that have been long lost are found on this list.

All of this makes a literal interpretation of the 144,000 questionable: Why is Dan left out to make room for Manasseh? Since Manasseh's name *is* on the list, why isn't his brother Ephraim on it, too, and why didn't he take his father's place? Most of all, what people alive today are from the ten lost tribes?

Given that assimilation of the ten lost tribes by their Gentile captors is the most widely accepted view among Jews, two reasonable conclusions emerge: One possibility would be that the 144,000 is a list of Jews *as well as* Gentiles who have a trickle of Jewish blood in them. In that light, the name Manasseh is interesting because of the unique blessing that was given to his tribe by Moses:

> He shall push the peoples [usually means Gentiles], all of them, to the ends of the earth . . . such are the thousands of Manasseh.   (DEUTERONOMY 33:17)

Manasseh, as a branch of the lost tribe of Joseph, may well have dispersed to the ends of the earth and assimilated with Gentiles to the ends of the earth. Perhaps after two thousand years there is no one who doesn't have a drop of Jewish blood in them.

The second possibility would be that this list is not a list of Jews at all, but a list of Christians that intends to show that Christians are now counted as God's chosen people and have taken the place of the former people for good. Those who hold this view believe that the Jews, as a race or nation, are forever out of God's plan, except for those who become Christians. (A popular thought among some Christians.) But, then, why raise the issue of Jewishness in the first place, if Israel as a nation or the Jews as a people have no role in God's plan?

The second view fails to acknowledge that the Old Testament prophets clearly said God would *return* to his original people *after* he had reached out to those who were not his people (the Gentiles). From the very beginning God has said that, should his chosen people reject him, he would bless Gentile nations until his own people returned in jealousy over the Gentile blessing, *but* he has also said he would never completely abandon his first chosen during that process:

And he said, I will hide my face from them [the children of Israel], I will see what their end shall be: for they are a very perverse generation, children in whom is no faith. They have moved me to jealousy with that which is not God; they have provoked me to anger with their vanities: and I will move them to jealousy with those who are not a people [Gentiles]; I will provoke them to anger with a foolish nation. For a fire is kindled in my anger, and shall burn to the lowest hell, and shall consume the earth with her increase, and set on fire the foundations of the mountains.

(DEUTERONOMY 32:20–22)

And yet for all that, when they shall be in the land of their enemies, I will not cast them away, neither will I abhor them, to destroy them utterly, and to break my covenant with them: for I am the LORD their God. But I will for their sakes remember the covenant of their ancestors, whom I brought out of the land of Egypt in the sight of the heathen, that I might be their God: I am the LORD.

(LEVITICUS 26:44, 45)

So the first view (that the ten tribes has assimilated into the Gentile blood) may be a little more generous in the way it pulls the two covenants together. God intends to draw all Jews into the same plan he is working out with Christians—a plan which many Jews have already joined. In the end, he will make the two people one under a covenant that no longer recognizes Jewishness—just belonging by faith. But the Jews were his starting place, and they will not be forgotten.

The absence of the tribe of Dan from the list led a number of early Christians to speculate that the Antichrist would be a Jew from the tribe of Dan. There were a number of reasons for that view having nothing to do with antiSemitism. First, the Antichrist is to be a false Christ—a bad copy of Jesus. Therefore, some felt he had to be a Jew if only to be a racial match. Second, in some views of prophecy, he is to deceive the Jews to their own peril: Who better to win their trust than a wolf in lamb's clothing? The old Jewish Targumim declare that from Dan darkness will spread over the world.[2] Dan was the first tribe to accept idolatry, and the tribal insignia of Dan was the serpent. Thus, many early Christians who wrote on prophecy believed Dan was intentionally left off the list of those who would be saved and sealed.

If the list is not literal, then the number 144,000 may not be either, though many take it to be. It could be intended to symbolize the people of the twelve patriarchs multiplying with the people of the twelve apostles (the product or offspring of the people of the Old Covenant and the people of the new under one umbrella) multiplied numerically by 1,000 to reflect their great number (12x12x1,000). That would be consistent with understanding the twenty-four elders unified around the throne of God as representing the twelve patriarchs plus the twelve apostles. It also fits with later symbolism at the end of the Apocalypse in John's vision of heaven, where both the twelve tribes and the twelve apostles are mentioned. Multiplying these two peoples by 1,000 is also appropriate because it was customary in Old Testament times for Israel to marshal 1,000 troops from each tribe in order to assemble an army. John's vision is built on military metaphors throughout to symbolize the battle between good and evil.

Marked for Martyrdom or Their Fate Is Sealed?

The seal may only mean that God has marked these people as his own in order to secure their souls before the evil powers of this world are allowed to kill them. The brief histories of martyrdom already given clearly reveal that being sealed in the apostles' time was more of a warrant assuring one's death than a mark of protection. For John's seven churches, the cost of eternal life was often temporal death. What was sealed was one's ultimate destiny— so long as he or she "overcame" the temptation to deny the faith in the face of death.

As with all previous periods of persecution, God's people may be killed during the Great Tribulation precisely because they *are* witnesses. Or perhaps they will be protected through the first years of tribulation so they can continue their witness, but may complete their witness as martyrs. That's what happened in John's own time. (The word "martyr" comes from a Greek word meaning "witness." Those who died for their faith were called 'martyrs' because their willingness to die became their ultimate testimony to the truth of their beliefs.)

There are other reasons for believing those who have been sealed will die as martyrs. They are not specifically mentioned by number again in the Apocalypse until they are pictured at the return of Jesus Christ. When they are specifically mentioned later, they are referred to as the "first fruits." Elsewhere in the Bible the first fruits are described as the first to be *resurrected* when Christ returns.

It may even be that the 144,000 is a literal approximation of the number of people who will die *as martyrs*. In other words, there may be many other believers who go into this period of tribulation who will *not* be marked for martyrdom. Because the Apocalypse is not a road map, many things will remain a mystery of possibilities until the end reveals itself.

So, whether the 144,000 represent Jews only or Christians, who include both Jews and Gentiles, and whether or not they are sealed for martyrdom or sealed for protection throughout the end times, God will have a group of witnesses that goes into the period of the Great Tribulation. The important focus of this vision is the next scene, which describes the phenomenal success of the ministry of the 144,000. So many people will center their lives on the true Messiah in those final days that there may be nothing but a minority who remain outside the great communion with God.

The Great White Hope

The number of people who come out of the Great Tribulation and into eternal communion with God includes every race on earth in numbers too great to be counted. Here there is no question that Jews and Gentiles stand united in the same company. The following scene loudly proclaims that, regardless of what happens to those who are sealed during the Great Tribulation (be it life or death), their arrival on the other side will be glorious.

> *After this I beheld, and, lo, a great multitude, which no man could number, of all nations, and kindreds, and people, and tongues, stood before the throne, and before the Lamb, clothed with white robes, and palms in their hands; And cried with a loud voice, saying, Salvation to our God who sitteth upon the throne, and to the Lamb. And all the angels stood around the throne, and about the elders and the four living beings, and fell before the throne on their faces, and worshipped God, Saying, Amen: Blessing, and glory, and wisdom, and thanksgiving, and honour, and power, and might, be to our God for ever and ever. Amen. And one of the elders answered, saying to me, Who are these that are arrayed in white robes? and where did they come from? And I said to him, Sir, thou knowest. And he said to me, These are they who came out of the great tribulation. . . .*
>
> (Revelation 7:9–14a)

People cannot "come out of tribulation," however, unless they were first in it. So again, John's vision offers no light promise that God's saints will be spared suffering. The promise he makes clear is this: For "those who overcome" the severe duress of the final days—for those who cling to their faith—the seal has eternal value. That light of hope will burn through the darkest of nights to guide God's people home, just as it did for the apostles in their times of tribulation. Just as God's people once survived the fires of Rome and the ovens of Hitler, these saints shall rise out of the smoke of earth's final holocaust. Death cannot hold them down. They shall rise above all evil. They shall live eternally in the presence of God:

> . . . These are they who came out of the great tribulation, and have washed their robes, and made them white in the blood of the Lamb. Therefore they are before the throne of God, and serve him day and night in his temple: and he that sitteth on the throne shall dwell among them. They shall hunger no more, neither thirst any more; neither shall the sun light on them, nor any heat. For the Lamb who is in the midst of the throne shall feed them, and shall lead them to living fountains of waters: and God shall wipe away all tears from their eyes. (REVELATION 7:14B–17)

The vision ends with a double oxymoron. This vast sea of humanity has been dressed in robes that are clean and white because they are washed in blood, and the Lamb that was slain has become their Shepherd. The Lamb, of course, is the source of the blood, but being washed in the Lamb's blood could also hint that many of these people shared in his blood quite literally because, like him, they died for truth. They may *all* be martyrs.

Before Jesus was crucified, the mother of two of his disciples (one of whom, John, later wrote the Apocalypse) came up to Jesus and requested,

> . . . Grant that these my two sons may sit, the one on thy right hand, and the other on the left, in thy kingdom. But Jesus answered and said, Ye know not what ye ask. Are ye able to drink of the cup that I shall drink of, and to be baptized with the baptism that I am baptized with? They say to him, We are able. And he saith to them, Ye shall drink indeed of my cup, and be baptized with the baptism that I am baptized with: but to sit on my right hand, and on my left, is not mine to give, but it shall be given to them for whom it is prepared by my Father. (MATTHEW 20:21–23)

Jesus answer clearly implies that sitting with him may require dying like him. At another time, he told all of his disciples that the cup of wine they drank while celebrating Passover was a cup of his blood. He said this, indicating that he was the Passover lamb, the innocent one that would die for truth so that others would have faith to follow. And that is how the Lamb became the Shepherd.

One of the Old Testament prophecies that promised the Jews would be restored to the land indicated this would happen at a time when God's shepherd was present with them. After God let the Jews go into exile under Babylon because of a lack of true spiritual leadership (true shepherds), he raised up the prophet Ezekiel and promised they would return. To a very small degree, the following prophecy was fulfilled when the Jews returned from Babylon—but never to the extent the language implies. Then they were scattered again—for the same lack of true spiritual understanding, according to Jesus. Perhaps this prophecy of their return will be more satisfyingly fulfilled during the end times:

And [my people] were scattered, because there is no shepherd: and they became food to all the beasts of the field, when they were scattered. My sheep wandered through all the mountains, and upon every high hill: yea, my flock was scattered upon all the face of the earth, and none did search or seek for them. . . .

For thus saith the Lord GOD; Behold, I, even I, will both search for my sheep, and seek them out. As a shepherd seeketh out his flock in the day that he is among his sheep that are scattered; so will I seek out my sheep, and will deliver them out of all places where they have been scattered in the cloudy and dark day. And I will bring them out from the people [Gentiles], and gather them from the countries, and will bring them to their own land, and feed them upon the mountains of Israel by the rivers, and in all the inhabited places of the country. I will feed them in a good pasture, and upon the high mountains of Israel shall their fold be: there shall they lie in a good fold, and in a rich pasture shall they feed upon the mountains of Israel. I will feed my flock, and I will cause them to lie down, saith the Lord GOD. I will seek that which was lost, and bring again that which was driven away, and will bind up that which was broken, and will strengthen that which was sick: but I will destroy the fat and the strong [those who profiteered off the flock]; I will feed them with judgment. . . .

And I will set up one shepherd over them, and he shall feed them, even my servant David; he shall feed them, and he shall be their shepherd. And I the LORD will be their God, and my servant David a prince among them; I the LORD have spoken it. And I will make with them a covenant of peace, and will cause the evil beasts to cease out of the land: and they shall dwell safely in the wilderness, and sleep in the woods. And I will make them and the places around my hill a blessing; and I will cause the shower to come down in its season; there shall be showers of blessing. And the tree of the field shall yield her fruit, and the earth shall yield her increase, and they shall be safe in their land, and shall know that I am the LORD, when I have broken the bands of their yoke, and delivered them out of the hand of those that subjected them to service. And they shall no more be a prey to the nations, neither shall the beast of the land devour them; but they shall dwell safely, and none shall make them afraid. And I will raise up for them a plant of renown, and they shall be no more consumed with hunger in the land, neither bear the shame of the nations any more. Thus shall they know that I the LORD their God am with them, and that they, even the house of Israel, are my people, saith the Lord GOD. And ye my flock, the flock of my pasture, are men, and I am your God, saith the Lord GOD.

(EZEKIEL 34:5, 6, 11–16, 23–31)

They shall not hunger nor thirst; neither shall the heat nor sun smite them: for he that hath mercy on them shall lead them, even by the springs of water shall he guide them. And I will make all my mountains a way, and my highways shall be exalted. Behold, these shall come from far: and, lo, these from the north and from the west; and these from the land of Sinim. Sing, O heavens; and be joyful, O earth; and break forth into singing, O mountains: for the LORD hath comforted his people, and will have mercy upon his afflicted. (ISAIAH 49:10–13)

It's interesting to note in Ezekiel's prophecy, written five hundred years after King David's death, that God said *he* (God) would be Israel's shepherd, yet, no sooner did he say that than he also said *David* would be their shepherd. Did God simply mean he would be Isarel's shepherd through the human agency of a resurrected king, or did he (God) mean he would enter humanity through the line of David and become that shepherd, as Christians believe? Jesus, the constant focus of the Apocalypse, certainly proclaimed the latter view in John's earlier book:

I am the good shepherd, and know my [sheep], and am known by mine. As the Father knoweth me, even so I know the Father: and I lay down my life for the sheep. And other sheep I have, which are not of this fold: them also I must bring, and they shall hear my voice; and there shall be one fold, and one shepherd. (JOHN 10:14–16)

Speaking solely to Jews in this instance, Jesus said that he had other sheep (people) who were not of the Jewish flock. The "fold" or "sheep pen" is the protection that surrounds the sheep. To gather both groups of people into the *same* fold under *one* shepherd means the Gentiles will be brought into the same promises God had originally given to the Jews. The Gentiles and Jews will be made one people through one promise (covenant) under one shepherd.

The apocalyptic view is also a picture of one people united under one Jewish Messiah. This union is described in various ways—a circle of the twelve patriarchs plus the twelve apostles, the twelve tribes that descended from the patriarchs multiplying with the spiritual descendants of the twelve apostles, a vast multitude from every nation all wearing the same white gowns, all singing the same song, a single kingdom of priests and kings all centered on the same throne. The Apocalypse promises that, in spite of all the conflict, truth will prevail and unity will be restored.

Chapter 12

TRIBULATION:

THE SEVENTH SEAL AND THE SEVEN TRUMPETS

It was the worst of times, it was the end of time. To assume the catastrophic times that have brought out prophets in the past could never come again seems naive in light of the endless cycles of dark ages human society has brought upon itself. The citizens of Rome thought the times of their prosperity would never end. For a few centuries they were right. In the roaring twenties, people thought the good times would never end. For a decade, they were right. Then came the Great Depression of the thirties, and then came world war, and the naive twenties were gone forever.

Disaster breaks in unexpectedly. Mount Vesuvius gave little warning to the people of Pompeii before it buried them in ash. The forces that make desolate are always lurking—held off perhaps by God's protection (like the four angels holding back the four winds). But when times are good, people also tend to forget about God. It becomes the job of the prophet to ask on God's behalf, "How long will this people provoke me? And how long will it be before they believe me, for all the signs which I have shown among them?" (Numbers 14:11). The time of the end is always waiting.

> Then said I, Lord, how long? And he answered, Until the cities shall be wasted without inhabitant, and the houses without man, and the land be utterly desolate. (ISAIAH 6:11)

One view of prophecy, called amillennialism, states that humanity will progress spiritually until the whole world centers itself on Jesus Christ. Then Christ will return and bring humanity into the eternal presence of God. But the prophets often spoke as though it were naive to think self-centered people would simply go away. The Apocalypse indicates such paradise will not come without a battle: When it is clear to God that the last *willing* person has turned to him, then all God-centered people will be taken out of the world, and all the self-centered will be left in darkness to consume themselves—

the natural end of self-centeredness. The world will be purged with fire, and a new world of light will emerge for those who have chosen the Light:

And I will show wonders in the heavens and on the earth, blood, and fire, and pillars of smoke. The sun shall be turned into darkness, and the moon into blood, before the great and terrible day of the LORD shall come. And it shall come to pass, that whoever shall call on the name of the LORD shall be delivered: for in mount Zion [site of the temple] and in Jerusalem shall be deliverance, as the LORD hath said, and in the remnant whom the LORD shall call.

(JOEL 2:30–32)

WHEN THE HEAVENS SHALL FALL

Now that John has assured his followers of their glorious victory if they overcome evil, his vision returns to where it left off. The Lamb opens the seventh seal, allowing the scroll to unroll and its events to begin. The time of the end has come:

And when he had opened the seventh seal, there was silence in heaven about the space of half an hour. And I saw the seven angels who stood before God; and to them were given seven trumpets. And another angel came and stood at the altar, having a golden censer; and there was given to him much incense, that he should offer it with the prayers of all saints upon the golden altar which was before the throne. And the smoke of the incense, which came with the prayers of the saints, ascended before God out of the angel's hand. And the angel took the censer, and filled it with fire of the altar, and cast it upon the earth: and there were voices, and thunderings, and lightnings, and an earthquake. And the seven angels who had the seven trumpets prepared themselves to sound.

(REVELATION 8:1–6)

After all is quiet, an angel walks up to the altar with a censer, similar perhaps to the type swung on a chain or cord by Orthodox priests as they waft incense over their congregation. The sweet aroma spreading and rising through the air symbolizes the sweet prayers of God's people ascending to heaven. The angel steps up to the altar where the martyrs were seen and fills his censer with fire and hurls it upon the earth. The instrument of prayer becomes the instrument of judgment, and the judgment comes from the altar of God. The seventh seal is the answer to the prayers of the martyrs that were heard under the altar in the fifth seal. From the place where they have cried out to God, judgment rains down on earth.

Just as the seven seals were preceded by thunder and lightning, so the seven trumpets are, too, but now the rumble of an earthquake has been added. The curtain is going up on the second act with a deep tympanic drum roll, but this is more than dramatic addition; it fits the events of the scene to be revealed:

> *The first angel sounded, and there followed hail and fire mixed with blood, and they were cast upon the earth: and the third part of trees was burnt up, and all green grass was burnt up.*
>
> (REVELATION 8:7)

The opening of the second act begins with a scene out of earlier prophecies. It sounds strikingly familiar to one of the plagues God used to deliver the children of Israel out of Egypt so they could begin their journey to the promised land:

> *And the LORD said to Moses, Stretch forth thy hand toward heaven, that there may be hail in all the land of Egypt, upon man, and upon beast, and upon every herb of the field, throughout the land of Egypt. And Moses stretched forth his rod toward heaven: and the LORD sent thunder and hail, and the fire ran along upon the ground; and the LORD rained hail upon the land of Egypt. So there was hail, and fire mingled with the hail, very grievous, such as there had been none like it in all the land of Egypt since it became a nation. Only in the land of Goshen, where the children of Israel were, there was no hail. And Pharaoh sent, and called for Moses and Aaron, and said to them, I have sinned this time: the LORD is righteous, and I and my people are wicked. Entreat the LORD (for it is enough) that there be no more mighty thunderings and hail; and I will let you go, and ye shall stay no longer.*
>
> (EXODUS 9:22–28)

Moses' plague is a reminder that the plagues of the Apocalypse could be averted if the world would turn to God. But, like the ten plagues of Moses, the plagues of the Apocalypse will continue to rain down upon earth until the earth responds or is consumed by them. This, after all, is the end; there is no more time.

This particular plague in Exodus is a good one for the Apocalypse to begin with, for it says the people of God remained safe in a place of sanctuary, though the hail rained down in the land around them. Psalm 91:3 (cited in the previous chapter) indicated God's people would only *see* the "reward of the wicked" come down around them. That was how the plagues of Egypt happened. Whether or not that pattern will repeat, who can say for sure? There have been so many other times when God's people were caught in the line of fire. The emphasis of these particular plagues, however, seems to be a judgment against the earth for all that the people of earth have done to the people of God:

> *Upon the wicked he shall rain snares, fire and brimstone, and an horrible tempest: this shall be the portion of their cup.*
>
> (PSALM 11:6)

O that thou wouldest rend the heavens, that thou wouldest come down, that the mountains might flow down at thy presence, As when the melting fire burneth, the fire causeth the waters to boil, to make thy name known to thy adversaries, that the nations may tremble at thy presence! (ISAIAH 64:1, 2)

The stories of God sparing his people through the exodus may relate to the final exodus of God's people from earth as they prepare to enter the promised land. The story of Noah and his family being spared through the flood in order to be brought into a new earth establishes a similar pattern. Whether one is willing to take these stories literally or not, clearly their intended message is that God *can* save his people even in the middle of their enemies' complete destruction.

The seven trumpets, just like the seven seals, come in a first group of four and then a following set of three. Nothing in the Apocalypse seems arbitrary; that suggests the first four trumpets are uniquely related as the first four seals were (the four horsemen of war and its aftermath). In fact, there is a single completely natural cause that could create the chain of events described in the first four trumpets, which becomes especially evident in the next three:

And the second angel sounded, and as it were a great mountain burning with fire was cast into the sea: and the third part of the sea became blood; And the third part of the creatures which were in the sea, and had life, died; and the third part of the ships were destroyed. And the third angel sounded, and there fell a great star from heaven, burning as it were a lamp [other translations, "a torch"], and it fell upon the third part of the rivers, and upon the fountains of waters; And the name of the star is called Wormwood: and the third part of the waters became wormwood; and many men died from the waters, because they were made bitter. And the fourth angel sounded, and the third part of the sun was smitten, and the third part of the moon, and the third part of the stars; so that the third part of them was darkened, and the day shone not for a third part of it, and the night likewise. (REVELATION 8:8–12)

Perhaps these events are all just spiritual metaphors that will never have a physical reality—as some insist—but they seem like extravagant metaphors for describing the suffering of the human soul among the ordinary evils of life. And they are not even slightly outside the realm of natural possibility. Numerous astronomers, geologists, and paleontologists agree that events exactly fitting these colorful descriptions could be created by the impact of an asteroid or comet (a "mountain" or "star") striking the earth. In fact, this astro-geologic cycle has recurred several times on earth already. All, or very nearly all, scientists agree there is no question *if* such impacts will occur again, but only when:

Halley's comet and the countless others that blaze across the night skies have had a profound effect on history. . . . For centuries comets were widely regarded as harbingers of disaster, omens of death, pestilence, wars, drought, earthquakes and floods. . . . In a bizarre twist, scientists themselves are beginning to attribute great cataclysms of the past to what the ancients called "hairy stars."

. . . On its pass in A.D. 66, Halley's [Comet], in the words of the Jewish historian Flavius Josephus, "hung like a sword in the sky" and presaged the fall of Jerusalem. . . .

During the past few years, evidence has been accumulating to support Physicist Luis Alvarez's theory that a giant comet (or asteroid) struck the earth 65 million years ago . . . spewing so much debris . . . that the skies darkened for months . . . and much of the life on earth—most notably the dinosaurs—perished.

. . . And scientists are certain that it can happen again.   —TIME MAGAZINE[1]

The awesome impact, say the experts, was so powerful that it created fire storms followed by freezing cold and acid rain that killed vegetation—and doomed the dinosaurs that dominated the planet.   —MACLEANS[2]

Many scientists, particularly paleontologists, scoffed at the Alvarez theory. . . . But the discovery in 1990 of a buried crater 112 miles in diameter, centered below the . . . northern tip of Mexico's Yucatan peninsula, gave the doubters pause. And the subsequent confirmation of the crater's age—65 million years—has led most scientists to jump aboard the Alvarez bandwagon.

. . . The blast must have vaporized the sulfur, they say, and spewed more than 100 billion tons of it into the atmosphere, where it mixed with moisture to form tiny drops of sulfuric acid. These drops created a barrier that could have reflected enough sunlight back into space to drop temperatures to near freezing, and could have remained airborne for decades.   —TIME MAGAZINE[3]

"The effects on life on Earth would have been horrendous," says Zdenek Sekanina of the Jet Propulsion Laboratory at Caltech. "It would have been a global catastrophe, comparable to a nuclear winter. The effects on mankind would have been so overwhelming that we could not discuss the topic, because we would not be here."
     —DISCOVER MAGAZINE[4]

The cities [near the site of an impact] are incinerated and millions are killed instantly. But the worst is yet to come. The impact kicks up billions of tons of dust. Much of it stays in the atmosphere for years afterward, blocking the sunlight and causing crop failures all over the world. As billions starve, the very survival of mankind is threatened.

It may not happen in 2005, but as sure as there are stars in the sky, it will happen. . . . Earth has been struck thousands of times by asteroids, comets and other planet-slamming visitors.   —POPULAR MECHANICS[5]

. . . a congressional panel has summoned astronomers and NASA officials to testify today on real- life asteroid hazards.

At issue is whether detection efforts are sufficient and whether enough attention is being paid to ideas about diverting comets and asteroids if that ever becomes necessary.

The hearings before the House Subcommittee on Space and Aeronautics come at a time of heightened public awareness that Planet Earth spins through a rough neighborhood. —CHRISTIAN SCIENCE MONITOR[6]

Also, an improved understanding of . . . cosmic collisions supplies credibility to certain ancient assertions that had seemed completely illogical. A good example . . . can be found in book 5 of *The Sibylline Oracles*. . . . "And then in his anger the immortal God who dwells on high shall hurl from the sky a fiery bolt on the head of the unholy: and summer shall change to winter in that day."

. . . in the light of contemporary knowledge, it is not outrageous to suppose that humanity learned to dread comets as a consequence of direct experience.

—THE WORLD AND I[7]

. . . you could say that we are indeed living in an age of comets.

. . . Weird stuff seems to go with major comets. When a comet appeared in A.D. 60, the people of Rome assumed it meant the impending death of their still new emperor, Nero. . . . When another comet turned up just four years later, ancients say [Nero] ordered the execution of dozens of nobles.

. . . "If you want some idea of the devastation that's possible from a comet," said David Levy, "take a look at what just one of the fragments of [comet] Shoemaker-Levy 9 did to Jupiter. Here's something as long as two or three football fields, and it left a mark bigger than Earth." —NATIONAL GEOGRAPHIC[8]

WHAT ARE THE ODDS?

In July of 1994 the whole world watched as Comet Shoemaker-Levy 9 broke into twenty fragments during a crack-the-whip curve around the sun, then blasted the face of the largest planet in our solar system. It was the first time human beings had ever witnessed a comet hitting another planet. Several of the *fragment* impacts created fireballs the size of earth. Jupiter, being a thousand times larger than earth, was able to absorb the blow.

Shoemaker-Levy 9 is not the first comet astronomers have watched explode as it banked into its tight curve around the sun. In fact, earth bears evidence of an impact from just such a broken comet. If the map of earth is realigned to account for continental drift, five of the major impact craters form a nearly perfect line, indicating a stream of bullets hitting the earth from space like a machine gun. Interestingly the era in which this continental alignment would have existed matches the time of another known period of extinctions in the fossil record, known as the end of the Triassic Period.

About four years after Shoemaker-Levy 9 bombarded Jupiter, news of a similar event headed straight for earth was reported by Brian Marsden, an astronomer for the Harvard-Smithsonian Center for Astrophysics. He discovered that a mile-wide asteroid was on a possible collision course with earth, scheduled to arrive at the station in A.D. 2028. Large enough to disrupt earth's climate, Asteroid 1997 XF11 would pass within 30,000 miles (or closer). In astronomic terms that's not even a stone's throw away. Fortunately, the asteroid arrival was later upgraded to a 600,000-mile miss. A mere bump by another asteroid or a miscalculation in gravity, however, could put 1997 XF11 right back on track for earth.

The odds of a comet impact may be increasing. The twentieth century saw more than its statistical share of comets whiz by (though the increase could be due to better observation and reporting). It's plausible that comets, like many natural phenomena, come in waves. Some comets are on a regular orbit, but others are believed to hover at the edge of the solar system in a formation known as the Oort Cloud, until some gravitational flux invites them in from the outside.

So far, more than 200 mega asteroids have been cataloged with a trajectory that crosses the earth's orbit, though only one is predicted to come close to earth in the twenty-first century. Scientist, however, estimate this number represents less than 10 percent of the actual number of earth-crossing asteroids out there. Earth's crust shows scars from approximately 150 major asteroid and comet impacts. There have probably been even more because the earth's crust is constantly rejuvenating. The team of scientists who are presently cataloging killer asteroids believe major impacts occur on the average of once every 125,000 years. Statistically, however, the odds in any one year are as good (or bad) as the odds in any other. Whatever the likelihood of an earth-shattering impact is for this century or next, it's 100 percent guaranteed eventually.

WHEN FIRE FALLS LIKE RAIN

Asteroids are stony chunks of broken planets, but comets are chunks of frozen gas. If they heat up enough while shooting around the sun, they break apart under the strain of the turn. Smaller fragments may be ejected forward, arriving a few days ahead of the larger pieces. As the comet approached earth, it would come tail first, for the tail of a comet always points directly away from the sun. Thus it would appear to burn like a torch as described in the Apocalypse, the narrow tail being the handle pointing down toward earth, with the head appearing like a flame. The tail is made up of comet fragments and dust. As these fragments rained down upon the earth, they would liquify, then gasify. Some of the gases would ignite from the heat of re-entry, creating streaks of fire falling from the heavens. As the earth rotated, every part of earth at a certain range of latitude would pass through the comet's tail, regardless of where the final impact was to occur. The larger chunks of ice in the comet's tail would survive the atmosphere and crash into the ground, creating the kind of gigantic hail described later in the Apocalypse.

During the evening and morning, the reflected glow of the approaching comet and its tail would fill the sky beside the sun like a great star falling toward the earth. It would almost appear that the sun itself were streaming down upon the earth. Within a day or so (depending on the length of the tail), what was left of the comet's core would appear to fall from the sky like a burning mountain. It would explode as it hit the earth with the force of hundreds of atomic bombs, charring a large part of the earth, blowing down trees, and throwing up a cloud of vaporized earth or steam (depending on whether it hit water or land) that would be thick enough to completely block out the sun and stars and moon across a third or more of the earth's atmosphere.

The concussion if it struck the ocean would kill much of the aquatic life in the ocean and create a tsunami that would destroy most of the ships on that particular sea. The high level of elemental contaminants in the atmosphere (from the burning gases of the comet, its tail, and the vaporized earth) would rain back down over a period years or even of decades. One of the main ingredients of this hellish rain would be high levels of sulfuric acid. ("he shall rain . . . brimstone"). Much of the water on earth would become unfit for human consumption because of this chemical washout, as well as from biological contaminants due to all the dead creatures in the streams and lakes and watersheds that could not withstand the acidic water.

The comet's impact would send shockwaves throughout the earth, destabilizing the earth's plates and distorting its crust with severe earthquakes far beyond anything humans have experienced. Some scientists believe the curvature of the earth would focus this energy through the earth's center into plumes of magma that would erupt on the exact opposite side of the earth from the point (or points) of impact (called the antipode). It could take decades for the crust to stabilize again.

All of this only describes a medium-size impact. A multiple impact similar to Shoemaker-Levy 9 would fill the entire atmosphere with debris and exterminate all life on earth—except perhaps microscopic life. A slightly larger comet would turn the earth itself into an asteroid belt orbiting the sun.

Scientists believe comets are formed of primordial gases that gathered when the solar system was created. So, pristine elements that have remained frozen in space since the beginning of time may bring the end of time. It may even be one of the same comets that appeared as a sign at the birth of Christ or the fall of Jerusalem—offering at the time a little glimmer of what would come again just before Christ came again, a hint from the heavens of two events related across a few brief millennia.

No wonder humans have always seen comets as an omen of doom. Perhaps the human psyche contains an imprint from future time—a future impact so great it reflects backward through time into the human subconscious. According to Einstein, such cosmic events *can* send shockwaves through time because time is not a constant and is altered by major gravitational forces.

How did such an ancient writer as John perceive one of the ways that planetary life dies on a global scale or transforms from one geologic era to another? Though God's judgment may come by such natural means, he telegraphed his word into the future— via a prophet two thousand years ago—so that people will recognize these natural phenomena as God's judgment when they come.

Jove, however, calls to mind the more mythical image of God with his lightning bolts, like Thor. The events are in motion; the earth moves like the perpetual hands of a solar clock, sweeping around its center of light, time after time, and only God knows when the bell will toll at midnight. But he has sent word in advance to help all of humanity find him during their darkest, darkest hour. When this twilight of human history comes, many will recognize his words are true because they were perfectly recorded far in advance of the event. They will seek him in greater numbers than ever before, and they will find him because his Messiah will come.

It is a miracle that life ever happened, and a miracle that life continues in a physical universe fraught with perils. When the end of life on this earth comes, as all scientists agree it will, God has a spiritual universe called heaven, ready to receive the children of the Son. The tired womb of mother earth will yield up her children, and humanity (or much of it) will be born again—spiritually into a spiritual universe. John revealed such a scene as assurance before describing this great cataclysm, and his whole book moves toward a fuller view of that scene at its end.

There may be a real "mountain not carved out with human hands" that is destined to shatter all of earth's governments. It may coincide with the spiritual mountain—the Messiah's kingdom—that arrives to fill the earth as described by the prophet Daniel. The metaphor of a mountain that shatters everything—since it is appears in both the Apocalypse and Daniel—may be aptly chosen because of its literal significance. The result of a major asteroid or comet impact would almost certainly shatter all human governments and drastically transform human history.

For in my jealousy and in the fire of my wrath have I spoken, Surely in that day there shall be a great shaking in the land *of Israel; So that the fishes of the sea, and the fowls of the heaven, and the beasts of the field, and all creeping things that creep upon the earth, and all the men that are upon the face of the earth, shall shake at my presence, and the mountains shall be thrown down, and the steep places shall fall, and every wall shall fall to the ground. And I will call for a sword against him throughout all my mountains, saith the Lord GOD: every man's sword shall be against his brother. And I will plead against him with pestilence and with blood; and I will rain upon him, and upon his bands, and upon the many people that are with him, an over-flowing rain, and great hailstones, fire, and brimstone [sulfur]. Thus will I magnify myself, and sanctify myself; and I will be known in the eyes of many nations, and they shall know that I am the LORD.* (EZEKIEL 38:19–23)

WOE TO THE EARTH: WORLD WAR

And I beheld, and heard an angel flying through the midst of heaven, saying with a loud voice, Woe, woe, woe, to the inhabiters of the earth by reason of the other voices of the trumpet of the three angels, which are yet to sound! (REVELATION 8:13)

Although the first four trumpets appear to describe stages of a single cosmic catastrophe, they are also separated from the last three because those are uniquely described as "woes." (That becomes clearer a little bit later.) The three "woes" appear to describe world wars or different aspects of one world war. After Ezekiel (above) describes the rain of fire and hail and sulfur and an earth-shattering earthquake that will bring down every wall and mountain, the Lord says, "Every man's sword shall be against his brother." Whether or not the Ezekiel passage relates to this same time is unclear, but it certainly fits the details and sequences of the Apocalypse: woe to the earth because global catastrophe has unleashed worldwide anarchy or conflict:

And the fifth angel sounded, and I saw a star fall from heaven to the earth: and to him was given the key of the bottomless pit. And he opened the bottomless pit; and there arose a smoke out of the pit, as the smoke of a great furnace; and the sun and the air were darkened by reason of the smoke of the pit. And there came out of the smoke locusts upon the earth: and to them was given power, as the scorpions of the earth have power. And it was commanded them that they should not hurt the grass of the earth, neither any green thing, neither any tree; but only those men who have not the seal of God in their foreheads. And to them it was given that they should not kill them, but that they should be tormented five months: and their torment was as the torment of a scorpion, when he striketh a man. And in those days shall men seek death, and shall not find it; and shall desire to die, and death shall flee from them. (REVELATION 9:1–6)

The star mentioned here probably is the same fallen star described earlier. The pit it has blasted into the earth has sent up a cloud of smoke that blackens the sun. This establishes a clear cause-and-effect between the catastrophe of the first four trumpets and the battle scenes that follow. The "he" referred to here may be the angel who sounded the trumpet, or it may be the evil leader described shortly thereafter. If it refers to the evil leader, then the image of him rising out of the bottomless pit blasted into the earth by the star is probably a symbolic way of saying his rise to power will be given opportunity by the chaos created from that fallen star.

The trumpet that led off the first four trumpets related to one of the plagues of Moses, and the trumpet that leads off the next three woes relates to the very next plague of Moses:

> And Moses and Aaron came in to Pharaoh, and said to him, Thus saith the LORD God of the Hebrews, How long wilt thou refuse to humble thyself before me? let my people go, that they may serve me. Else, if thou shalt refuse to let my people go, behold, to morrow will I bring the locusts into thy territory: And they shall cover the face of the earth, that one cannot be able to see the earth: and they shall eat the rest of that which hath escaped, which remaineth to you from the hail, and shall eat every tree which groweth for you out of the field. . . .
>
> . . . And the LORD said to Moses, Stretch out thy hand over the land of Egypt for the locusts, that they may come upon the land of Egypt, and eat every herb of the land, even all that the hail hath left. And Moses stretched forth his rod over the land of Egypt, and the LORD brought an east wind upon the land all that day, and all that night; and when it was morning, the east wind brought the locusts. And the locusts went up over all the land of Egypt, and rested in all the territory of Egypt: very grievous were they; before them there were no such locusts as they, neither after them shall be such. For they covered the face of the whole earth, so that the land was darkened; and they ate every herb of the land, and all the fruit of the trees which the hail had left: and there remained not any green thing on the trees, or in the herbs of the field, through all the land of Egypt. (EXODUS 10:3–5, 12–15)

Is it only a coincidence that these two Exodus plagues that correspond to the events of the Apocalypse match in sequence, or did the plagues in Egypt happen in a pattern that foreshadowed events near the end of time? Even the language of Exodus indicates the plague of locusts was to be worldwide, but when the plague happened, it appears it only affected Egypt. Was the prophet exaggerating the first time, or was he seeing events of a later time superimposed on his own?

Just as the hail destroyed most of the plants in Egypt, the hail from the falling star in the Apocalypse destroyed much of the plant life on earth. The locusts of Egypt created a cloud that blackened out the sun, and the smoke out of which the locusts of the Apocalypse descend also blackens the sun. These latter-day locusts are given power to sting all people, except the saints of God, so somehow the seal spoken of earlier has provided protection to God's saints amid the tribulation around them. They are present to "see the reward of the wicked," but they are not personally experiencing it. Since this impact has only incinerated a third of the earth, perhaps they are at a safe distance, as the children of Israel were in Goshen. The fact that there are now seven trumpets blown by seven angels (which matches the seven angels of the seven churches spoken of earlier) may indicate these seven plagues are a judgment on the churches' behalf for all the persecution that has been done against God's people. For that reason, God's people are given sanctuary like Noah in his ark and like the righteous during Jerusalem's fall to Babylon.

The reader is given a hint that these locusts are not actual locusts like those in Egypt. These are told not to harm the trees or plants or grass, which are the only things real locusts eat. Instead, they descend from the sky and inflict horrible stings upon human beings.

What are these near-lethal locusts that descend from the smoke kicked up by the falling star? Are they drops of acidic chemicals that precipitate from the caustic atmosphere and fall upon the people below? The description that follows sounds more militaristic and mechanical than natural. Perhaps they are intended to represent the kind of military action that will precipitate from the impact. Or perhaps both:

> And the shapes of the locusts were like horses prepared for battle; and on their heads were as it were crowns like gold, and their faces were as the faces of men. And they had hair as the hair of women, and their teeth were as the teeth of lions. And they had breastplates, as it were breastplates of iron; and the sound of their wings was as the sound of chariots of many horses running to battle. And they had tails like scorpions, and there were stings in their tails: and their power was to hurt men five months. And they had a king over them, who is the angel of the bottomless pit, whose name in the Hebrew language is Abaddon, but in the Greek language he hath his name Apollyon. (REVELATION 9:7–11)

Nothing here is what it seems. Everything is spoken of as being *like* something, but not the same as. Is this a fighting squadron made up of both men and women in modern military hardware? The use of locusts as a symbol for a great military force has strong biblical precedence. The prophet Joel described a plague of locusts in his own day. It's hard to tell whether he used the locusts as a metaphor for a sweeping military invasion or used military metaphors to describe how potent was the devastation from a very real plague of locusts:

The word of the LORD that came to Joel the son of Pethuel. Hear this, ye old men, and give ear, all ye inhabitants of the land. Hath this been in your days, or even in the days of your fathers? Tell ye your children of it, and let your children tell their children, and their children another generation. That which the palmerworm hath left hath the locust eaten; and that which the locust hath left hath the cankerworm eaten; and that which the cankerworm hath left hath the caterpiller eaten. Awake, ye drunkards, and weep; and wail, all ye drinkers of wine, because of the new wine; for it is cut off from your mouth. For a nation is come up upon my land, strong, and without number, whose teeth are the teeth of a lion, and he hath the cheek teeth of a great lion. He hath laid my vine waste, and barked my fig tree: he hath stripped it bare, and cast it away; its branches are made white.

. . . Sanctify ye a fast, call a solemn assembly, gather the elders and all the inhabitants of the land into the house of the LORD your God, and cry to the LORD, Alas for the day! for the day of the LORD is at hand, and as a destruction from the Almighty shall it come. Is not the food cut off before our eyes, and joy and gladness from the house of our God? The seed hath perished under their clods, the storehouses are laid desolate, the barns are broken down; for the grain is withered. How do the beasts groan! the herds of cattle are perplexed, because they have no pasture; yea, the flocks of sheep are made desolate. O LORD, to thee will I cry: for the fire hath devoured the pastures of the wilderness, and the flame hath burned all the trees of the field. The beasts of the field cry also to thee: for the rivers of waters are dried up, and the fire hath devoured the pastures of the wilderness.

Blow ye the trumpet in Zion, and sound an alarm in my holy mountain: let all the inhabitants of the land tremble: for the day of the LORD cometh, for it is near at hand; A day of darkness and of gloominess, a day of clouds and of thick darkness, as the morning spread upon the mountains: a great people and a strong; there hath not been ever the like, neither shall be any more after it, even to the years of many generations. A fire devoureth before them; and behind them a flame burneth: the land is as the garden of Eden before them, and behind them a desolate wilderness; yea, and nothing shall escape them. The appearance of them is as the appearance of horses; and as horsemen, so shall they run. Like the noise of chariots on the tops of mountains shall they leap, like the noise of a flame of fire that devoureth the stubble, as a strong people set in battle array. Before their face the people shall be much pained: all faces shall gather blackness. They shall run like mighty men; they shall climb the wall like men of war; and they shall march every one on his ways, and they shall not break their ranks: Neither shall one thrust another; they shall walk every one in his path: and when they fall upon the sword, they shall not be wounded. They shall run to and fro in the city; they shall run upon the wall, they shall climb upon the houses; they shall enter in at the windows like a thief. The earth shall quake before them; the heavens shall tremble: the sun and the moon shall be dark, and the stars shall withdraw their shining: And the LORD shall utter his voice be-

fore his army: for his camp is very great: for he is strong that executeth his word: for the day of the LORD is great and very terrible; and who can abide it?

Therefore also now, saith the LORD, turn ye even to me with all your heart, and with fasting, and with weeping, and with mourning: And rend your heart, *and not your garments, and turn to the LORD your God: for he is gracious and merciful, slow to anger, and of great kindness, and repenteth of the evil. Who knoweth if he will return and repent, and leave a blessing behind him; even a meat offering and a drink offering to the LORD your God?* (JOEL 1:1–7, 14–2:14)

Are Joel's locusts described as coming in a day of darkness simply because the cloud of flying insects fills the sky, or was Joel seeing superimposed on the locust plague of his own day another dark day far into the future? The fact that Joel says, "Tell ye your children of it, and let your children tell their children, and their children another generation" indicates he intended his vision for a distant generation. Did John consciously pattern his locusts after Joel's—both having the teeth of a lion—or were both men sensing earth's darkest horizon as though an echo from the far end of time had come back upon them?

Both Joel and John see locusts that look like military horsemen. How is it that Joel's locusts have dried up the streams of water and scorched the land with fire? Is this just the effect of the scirocco wind that drove them in, or is Joel seeing a real military invasion of the future? The prophet doesn't seem to attribute the fire to the wind but to the advancing swarm. If he is describing the advancing fires of war, whose time does he have in mind? John, too, saw a scorched earth. Joel says his locusts are "like" horses, but not that they *are* horses, and that they sound like fiery chariots thundering over the mountaintops. But how do chariots ascend mountains unless they fly? John's locusts also fly with wings that sound like chariots and horses thundering into battle.

Joel says the army he sees is "a great people and a strong; there hath not been ever the like, neither shall be any more after it, even to the years of many generations." There have undoubtedly been greater wars since those fought near Joel's time, so what great war was the prophet seeing? Was he simply exaggerating, or did he foresee the final world war? Strangely, both prophets even speak of people who seem unable to die. Joel says, "When they fall upon the sword, they shall not be wounded." John says, "In those days shall men seek death, and shall not find it; and shall desire to die, and death shall flee from them." If the plight of those who long for death is literal, it remains to be seen how it's possible that people who long for death cannot attain it. If it's figurative, it's still anyone's guess what each prophet meant.

One of the explanations that has been given for John's locusts with iron breastplates and wings that thunder is that they represent modern military attack helicopters, which look like locusts and have tails and "stings." Although John's locusts have stings like scorpions, he does not specifically state the sting is on the tail. The stings could refer to the rockets mounted on the undersides of attack helicopters. That still leaves one grasping to understand how they can sting men but not kill them. That possibility may be too much speculation, but any other explanation equally fails to explain how it is that people would long to die yet be unable to.

Whoever this army is, the name of their king is Apollyon, derived from the same Greek god worshipped by Antiochos Epiphanes whose name means, "destroyer." For a second time, the Apocalypse draws from names out of Greek mythology—first Hades, and now Apollo—though perhaps only because the Apocalypse is written in Greek and those names are the closest parallels to what the prophet is trying to describe.

Both prophets speak of the heavens and the earth quaking, the sun, moon and stars being darkened. Some would argue that John was clearly borrowing from Joel or that his vision was influenced by his years of reading Joel. Perhaps that is true, but it still leaves one wondering how John could have described so perfectly and vividly the kind of cataclysm actually capable of wiping out so much life on earth. How was it possible for him to know that mountains really can fall out of the sky, burn the earth with rain of fire, kill much of its life and make its waters undrinkable, cause the land to shake, and blacken the sun, moon and stars with a cloud of smoke that rises from a deep, deep pit? Such a cascade of events was not even dreamed possible until the last couple of decades, when scientists worked out computer models of major impacts, which reveal events precisely fitting John's poetic description that may have caused most life on earth to perish once already.

> One woe is past; and, behold, there come
> two woes more after this.
>
> (REVELATION 9:12).

Just as the first four trumpets appear to describe a single large event, the last three trumpets do as well—war. The next trumpet apparently depicts war coming over Israel from the Euphrates River. The Euphrates may have had special significance in John's time because it was the far eastern boundary of the Roman empire. For the Romans, it always represented a threat. Attila the Hun eventually came from the other side of the Euphrates and destroyed Rome. In the present time, the river's significance might be that it separates Israel from Baghdad and much of Iraq.

> And the sixth angel sounded, and I heard a voice from the four horns of the golden altar which is before God, Saying to the sixth angel who had the trumpet, Loose the four angels who are bound in the great river Euphrates. And the four angels were loosed, who were prepared for an hour, and a day, and a month, and a year, to slay the third part of men. And the number of the army of the horsemen was two hundred thousand thousand: and I heard the number of them. And

thus I saw the horses in the vision, and them that sat on them, having breast-plates of fire, and of jacinth, and brim-stone: and the heads of the horses were as the heads of lions; and out of their mouths issued fire and smoke and brim-stone. By these three was the third part of men killed, by the fire, and by the smoke, and by the brimstone, which issued out of their mouths. For their power is in their mouth, and in their tails: for their tails were like serpents, and had heads,

and with them they do hurt. And the rest of the men who were not killed by these plagues yet repented not of the works of their hands, that they should not wor-ship demons, and idols of gold, and sil-ver, and brass, and stone, and of wood: which neither can see, nor hear, nor walk: Neither repented they of their murders, nor of their sorceries, nor of their immorality, nor of their thefts.

(REVELATION 9:13–21)

The breastplates of fire and jacinth (a red stone) and brimstone (sulfur) sound like the fire of gunpowder, which is made from sulfur. One could speculate what kind of weaponry this might signify, if it does, but only time will tell. That these scenes do pre-dict actual wars would seem evident from the description of two hundred million mounted troops and the fact that the earlier event was given such a specific duration of five months, a number that doesn't seem to involve any numerologic symbolism.

At the end of Joel's description of these horrible times, he called for people to re-pent. John answers his call from centuries away by saying that, in spite of all that has happened, none of the people who survive these plagues is willing to repent. Their hearts are harder than Pharaoh's. When Pharaoh's heart was hard, God's answer was to send more plagues. That will be his answer here, too. Just as the seventh seal, when it was bro-ken, allowed the seven trumpets to play, the seventh trumpet, when it is sounded, will announce earth's final seven deadly plagues.

The first four seals implied *man-made* disasters (the outfall of war) that were common to history and would continue to the end. The first four trumpets implied *natural* disas-ters on a cosmic scale that bring on the end. Humanity and nature have lost their equi-librium, and the world is whirling into chaos.

With uncanny accuracy an aged prophet on a barren island described the end of life on this world in the exact manner that many of the world's leading scientists are begin-ning to agree *is* this world's most likely end. And the scientific probability of its occur-rence remains equal for any day of the week—this millennium . . . or the next . . . or a thousand millennia away . . .

Chapter 13

MYSTERY:

THE SEVENTH TRUMPET AND THE GREAT REVELATION

A second interlude occurs between the sixth and seventh trumpet just as occurred between the sixth and seventh seal. The interlude explains that the announcement that will follow the seventh trumpet is the revelation of one of God's great mysteries.

And I saw another mighty angel come down from heaven, clothed with a cloud: and a rainbow was upon his head, and his face was as it were the sun, and his feet as pillars of fire: And he had in his hand a little scroll open: and he set his right foot upon the sea, and his left foot on the earth, And cried with a loud voice, as when a lion roareth: and when he had cried, seven thunders uttered their voices. And when the seven thunders had uttered their voices, I was about to write: and I heard a voice from heaven saying to me, Seal up those things which the seven thunders uttered, and write them not. And the angel which I saw stand upon the sea and upon the earth lifted up his hand to heaven, And swore by him that liveth for ever and ever, who created heaven, and the things that are in it, and the earth, and the things that are in it, and the sea, and the things which are in it, that there should be delay no longer:

But in the days of the voice of the seventh angel, when he shall begin to sound, the mystery of God should be finished, as he hath declared to his servants the prophets.

And the voice which I heard from heaven spoke to me again, and said, Go and take the little scroll which is open in the hand of the angel which standeth upon the sea and upon the earth. And I went to the angel, and said to him, Give me the little scroll. And he said to me, Take it, and eat it; and it shall make thy belly bitter, but it shall be in thy mouth sweet as honey. And I took the little scroll out of the angel's hand, and ate it; and it was in my mouth sweet as honey: and as soon as I had eaten it, my belly was bitter. And he said to me, Thou must prophesy again concerning many peoples, and nations, and tongues, and kings.

(REVELATION 10:1–11)

Presumably the little scroll John is given to eat contains the mystery that will be revealed without delay when the seventh trumpet is ready to sound. John is told to digest the words God gives him and then to prophesy again. His message will extend beyond the seven churches to include "many peoples, and nations, and tongues, and kings." Though he prophesies, he is not allowed to tell all. He is commanded to conceal part of the revelation he has learned. Apparently it will not be revealed universally until the end.

The scroll John eats echoes the experience of another prophet who witnessed the destruction of Jerusalem just as John did. Only that prophet, Ezekiel, lived during the first destruction under Babylon:

And the spirit entered into me when he spoke to me, and set me upon my feet, that I heard him that spoke to me.

. . . But thou, son of man, hear what I say to thee; Be not thou rebellious like that rebellious house: open thy mouth, and eat that which I give thee. And when I looked, behold, an hand was sent to me; and, lo, a scroll was in it; And he spread it before me; and it was written within and without: and there was written in it lamentations, and mourning, and woe.

. . . And he said to me, Son of man, cause thy stomach to eat, and fill thy body with this scroll that I give thee. Then did I eat it; and it was in my mouth as honey for sweetness. And he said to me, Son of man, depart, go to the house of Israel, and speak with my words to them. . . . But the house of Israel will not hearken to thee; for they will not hearken to me: for all the house of Israel are impudent and hardhearted. . . . So the spirit lifted me up, and took me away, and I went in bitterness, in the heat of my spirit; but the hand of the LORD was strong upon me.

(EZEKIEL 2:2, 8–10; 3:3, 4, 7, 14)

Like the scroll seen at the beginning of the Apocalypse, the one given to Ezekiel to eat has writing covering both sides, indicating there is no room for anything to be added. Ezekiel is told he must digest the words God gives him. He is not to be rebellious like the nation of Israel, which apparently refused to accept God's word because they did not like what the prophets had spoken.

God's words taste like honey to the prophet, perhaps because of the ecstasy of receiving divine revelations of great mysteries, but afterwards, they bring bitterness to his spirit. No wonder the people have not wanted to hear these words: they are all laments and woe. No one wants to hear a prophet foretelling doom, so prophets like Ezekiel received nothing but bitterness from the people, even though the warnings were intended to help people avert God's judgments. God does not want to judge people; he simply wants them to change. If God gives people a bitter pill to swallow, it's better to get it out of the way, for his mercy will follow more quickly.

Finally, Ezekiel is told,

Therefore say to them, Thus saith the Lord GOD; There shall none of my words be further deferred, but the word which I have spoken shall be done, saith the Lord GOD.

(EZEKIEL 12:28)

John, too, was told there would be no more delay. Once the events of the first six trumpets have taken place, the final revelation of God's mystery will be revealed to the world. This mystery is in the Messiah, and it is revealed at his coming:

> ... there is nothing covered, that shall not be revealed; and hid, that shall not be known. (MATTHEW 10:26)

THE MYSTERY OF GOD REVEALED

The Apostle Paul told the Christian church in Rome that God's mystery was the truth about Jesus Christ. The truth of the Messiah was revealed to those who were willing to receive it at his first coming. It will be revealed to the entire world—whether people are willing to receive it or not—at his second coming (Romans 16:25, 56). One of the things to be revealed at the Messiah's second coming is God's plan to unite his two people, the Jews and Christians, under the New Covenant and to bring all people on earth and all of heaven under that same covenant. For Christians, like Paul, some of that mystery is already understood and experienced:

Having made known to us the mystery of his will, according to his good pleasure which he hath purposed in himself: That in the dispensation of the fulness of times he might gather together in one all things in Christ, both which are in heaven, and which are on earth; even in him: In whom also we have obtained an inheritance, being predestinated according to the purpose of him who worketh all things after the counsel of his own will:

... when ye read, ye may understand my knowledge in the mystery of Christ Which in other ages was not made known to the sons of men, as it is now revealed to his holy apostles and prophets by the Spirit; That the Gentiles should be joint-heirs, and of the same body, and partakers of his promise in Christ by the gospel:

... There is one body, and one Spirit, even as ye are called in one hope of your calling; One Lord, one faith, one baptism, One God and Father of all, who is above all, and through all, and in you all.

(EPHESIANS 1:9–11; 3:4–6; 4:4–6)

Paul says the Gentiles and Jews will become joint heirs to the same promised blessings, which are to be administered by the Messiah Jesus. They will become a single body of people, instead of two distinct groups. Complete unity among Jews and Gentiles is a promise. It will be a union as close as that between the Messiah and his Father in heaven—a deep mystery that lies beyond human comprehension. For Jews, this has always been the major stumbling block in Christianity. How can God be one God and have a son,

Who is the image of the invisible God, the firstborn of all creation: For by him were all things created, that are in heaven, and that are upon earth, visible and invisible, whether thrones, or dominions, or principalities, or powers: all things were created by him, and for him: And he is before all things, and by him all things consist. And he is the head of the body, the church: who is the beginning, the firstborn from the dead; that in all things he may have the preeminence. For it pleased the Father that in him should all fulness dwell; And, having made peace through the blood of his cross, by him to reconcile all things to himself; by him, I say, whether they are things on earth, or things in heaven.

(COLOSSIANS 1:15–20)

This Paul says is the mystery of God that has been hidden for all ages. God revealed to the Jews that he was one. There was no pantheon of many gods ruling the universe in different domains. To the Jews, the one God is a singularity. To Christians, the one God is a unity. These ways of understanding God offer the possibility of a one-to-one communion with God that cannot be found in paganism. But God is greater than any human model of understanding can contain. To this humanly incomprehensible mystery, Paul has been made a minister:

Of which I am made a minister, according to the dispensation of God which is given to me for you, to fulfil the word of God; Even the mystery which hath been hid from ages and from generations, but now is revealed to his saints: To whom God would make known what is the riches of the glory of this mystery among the Gentiles; which is Christ in you, the hope of glory:

... That their hearts may be comforted, being knit together in love, and to all riches of the full assurance of understanding, to the acknowledgement of the mystery of God, and of the Father, and of Christ; In whom are hid all the treasures of wisdom and knowledge. ... For in him dwelleth all the fulness of the Godhead bodily.

(COLOSSIANS 1:25–27; 2:2, 3, 9)

For a spirit to be incarnate means it has a body. The mystery of the incarnation of God says a union will exist, and is being formed already, between the Spirit of God and all of his fleshly people. That is the broader sense in which God becomes incarnate. Paul says elsewhere,

For now we see through a glass, darkly;   *but then shall I know even as also I am*
but then face to face: now I know in part;   *known.*   (1 CORINTHIANS 13:12)

God is forming a perfect union with his people. Even though the prophets of God said no man could look at the face of God, that is to say, fully see God in all his glory, Paul says a time is ordained when men and women and children will see God face to face. A time is coming when people will know God as intimately as God knows them. This means a time of complete spiritual communion between God and his people. This is the meaning of heaven. Because this union with God will be perfect, it is impossible for anyone less than perfect to be brought into this communion. Because there can be no evil in God, no evil can be brought into communion with God.

How, then, is human union with God possible? The mystery of the long-awaited Messiah is that God, himself, somehow reached down into his created world by joining himself to it. Now he draws that world up into himself. That is the ultimate meaning of communion. It is for that reason that Paul calls the Messiah "the firstborn of all creation" and "the firstborn from the dead." In essence, the incarnation of God's Spirit results in the deification of humans in whom his Spirit dwells, for their souls are invited into God's being—into his presence. Therefore, they must be made perfect. So, the New Covenant is far more spectacular than anyone had imagined. The Christian writer C. S. Lewis put it this way:

> The Son of God became a man to enable men to become the sons of God. . . . In the Incarnation, God the Son takes the body and human soul of Jesus, and, through that, the whole environment of Nature . . . into His own being. So that "He came down from Heaven" can almost be transposed into "Heaven drew earth up into it. . . ."
>
> In the Christian story God descends to reascend. He comes . . . down from the heights of absolute being into time and space, down into humanity; down further still . . . to . . . the womb . . . and prehuman phases of life . . . to the very roots and seabed of the Nature He had created . . . rushing down through green and warm water into black and cold water, down through increasing pressure into the death-like region of ooze and slime and old decay; then up again, back to color and light . . . holding in his hand the dripping, precious thing that he went down to recover. He and it are both colored now that they have come up into the light. . . .
>
> . . . he goes down to come up again and bring the whole ruined world up with Him.[1]

It is a serious thing to live in a society of possible gods and goddesses, to remember that the dullest and most uninteresting person you talk to may one day be a creature which, if you saw it now, you would be strongly tempted to worship, or else a horror and a corruption such as you now might meet, if at all, only in a nightmare. All day long we are, in some degree helping each other to one or the other of these destinations. . . . There are no *ordinary* people. You have never talked to a mere mortal. . . . But it is immortals whom we joke with, work with, marry, snub, and exploit—immortal horrors or everlasting splendours. . . . Next to the Blessed Sacrament itself, your neighbour is the holiest object presented to your senses. If he is your Christian neighbour he is holy in almost the same way [as the Blessed Sacrament], for in him also Christ . . . the glorifier and the glorified, Glory Himself, is truly hidden.[2]

If God's Spirit cannot enter human flesh, then God is incapable of intimate spiritual communion with his creation. God cannot know our thoughts if he cannot get inside of us. In full communion, God enters us, and he enables us, in some sense, to enter him. Before humans can gain union with the divine perfection they must be made ready for this union, as a bride prepares herself for her wedding night. That's why God often uses sexual union in marriage as a metaphor to express this mysterious relationship. It is in this sense that Paul calls the Messiah "the hope of glory." What glory? Knowing God and sharing in the glory of God by being made perfectly one with him—knowing God face to face, to use a human metaphor or, to use another, becoming one as a husband and wife become one sexually.

> . . . I will pray the Father, and he shall give you another Comforter, that he may abide with you for ever; Even the Spirit of truth; whom the world cannot receive, because it seeth him not, neither knoweth him: but ye know him; for he dwelleth with you, and shall be in you.
>
> I will not leave you comfortless: I will come to you. Yet a little while, and the world seeth me no more; but ye see me: because I live, ye shall live also. At that day ye shall know that I am in my Father, and ye in me, and I in you. He that hath my commandments, and keepeth them, he it is that loveth me: and he that loveth me shall be loved by my Father, and I will love him, and will reveal myself to him. (JOHN 14:16–21)

When Jesus said this, he meant that he, Jesus, dwelled with them on earth, so they knew him, but when he left the earth physically, he would enter them spiritually and they would know him in a deeper way. His time on earth was the engagement; the marriage, with its deeper way of knowing, was yet to come, and that will be revealed later in the Apocalypse. The reason God commanded that sex be kept holy and enjoyed only under a marriage covenant is because he created it as a sacrament, a physical reminder of the *spiritual* union his people will share with him. That is why he made it such ecstasy.

The mystery of the incarnate God is too great to wrap one's mind around. For the Jewish leaders in Jesus' day, this marriage between God and humanity was blasphemy: the Messiah, himself, was blasphemy. It was beneath God to enter his own creation in order to establish perfect union with it. For many Jews today, it is still beneath God and far too high for humans to hope, with all that it implies. As a result, Paul says this spiritual marriage covenant between God and humans—as spoken of by the prophet Jeremiah—was established between God and the Gentiles first. But the Jews have not been forgotten. As the Jewish prophets, themselves, had implied, God would use this Gentile marriage to make the Jews jealous. Once the news of this covenant has been told to all the Gentile nations on earth, God will draw his former people into this same perfect union, and there will be no more distinction between one people and another:

> For I would not, brethren, that ye should be ignorant of this mystery, lest ye should be wise in your own conceits; that blindness in part hath happened to Israel, until the fulness of the Gentiles shall be come in. And so all Israel shall be saved: as it is written, There shall come out of Zion the Deliverer, and shall turn away ungodliness from Jacob: For this is my covenant to them, when I shall take away their sins.   (ROMANS 11: 25–27)

The mystery of God revealed. The great mystery revealed is God revealed in Jesus the Messiah to those who believe. Believing is seeing.

What perfect union with God means for humans will only be known by experience just as the joys of sexual union can only be known by experience. In Christ, humanity will move into a higher dimension of being. Humans will transcend the dimensions of time and space. In the Christian understanding, eternity does not simply mean "time that goes on and on without end."

What eternity does mean is incomprehensible for now, except by weak analogies. Imagine trying to explain a three-dimensional cube to a two-dimensional creature who had never lived outside a flat two-dimensional world. To describe a three-dimensional cube, all you could say is that it's something like a square. The mystery of cubishness could only be known by expanding (glorifying) this flat creature into the third dimension. So humans can only know God by glorification into his presence. All of this remains God's mysterious destiny for humanity, but all things will be revealed in time.

Or out of time.

THE MYSTERY OF THE LOST TEMPLE

The next part of John's vision is immediately puzzling and a source of debate. He speaks of Jerusalem and the temple as though both remained standing. At the time when John is commonly believed to have written the Apocalypse, Jerusalem was nothing more than flattened rubble. To a few scholars this scene implies that John must have written prior to the fall of Jerusalem (which would mean he was exiled by Nero, contrary to traditional history). Otherwise he would not have spoken of the temple as though it still existed. To others his mention of the city and its temple after they were destroyed is a prophecy that the temple will be rebuilt during the latter days just as the city already has been rebuilt. Yet other scholars have understood the temple here as purely figurative, symbolizing Christ's followers.

There is one small clue that John *did* know the city and temple had fallen. He alluded to Ezekiel's experience eating the sweet words of God that brought bitterness because they were full of woes and laments for the fallen city. Perhaps John's experience with bitterness implies that he, like Ezekiel, is now a captive of the nation that conquered his city, so, the next prophecy, for him, stirs up feelings of lament. Even then, it's still odd he does not acknowledge the destruction of the holy city and its temple, being so ripe with symbolic meaning for the Apocalypse:

> And there was given me a reed like a rod: and the angel stood, saying, Rise, and measure the temple of God, and the altar, and them that worship in it. But the court which is outside the temple leave out, and measure it not; for it is given to the Gentiles: and the holy city shall they tread under foot forty and two months.
> (REVELATION 11:1, 2)

Forty-two months, or three and a half years, is the same length of time that the Romans battled the rebels throughout Israel, as recorded by Josephus. One could interpret this scene as a prophecy that Jerusalem would fall (meaning John did write during Nero's reign), but the Romans did not trample on the city for about forty of those months because they were walled out of the city. Jerusalem was not even under siege during most of the war. So, it's a possible reading, but a loose rendering.

Perhaps there are more hints from parallel experiences by the prophet Ezekiel. John's vision seems to echo another one of Ezekiel's visions, which was given as reassurance to the Jews *after* the first destruction of Jerusalem and its temple. In Ezekiel 40, the prophet describes detailed measurements of a new city and a new temple that presumably would be rebuilt someday. Ezekiel was creating a visual layout of a new city to give the people tangible hope. But Ezekiel's plans were never followed. Though the temple and city were rebuilt after the exile, they were not built in accordance with Ezekiel's envisioned plan. Perhaps John is alluding to that vision as a reminder to the Jewish Christians in his congregations that the city will be rebuilt again *because* Ezekiel's plan still awaited fulfillment, and divine plans never fail. (See Appendix B for the full text of Ezekiel's vision.)

The Romans would not have appreciated John's enthusiasm for the reconstruction of Jerusalem, having just taken great pains to destroy it. They would have considered him an insurgent. But John's message is so encrypted that it could be shouted and still fall on deaf Roman ears because they lacked the prophetic basis for understanding what he was implying. So perhaps John was implying a restoration of the temple without bringing needless danger to his congregations. The forty-two months would have provided the necessary clue to connect the trampling by the "Gentiles" specifically to the Romans.

The present city, which was rebuilt piecemeal after John's Apocalypse was written, does not fit Ezekiel's vision either. Since Jerusalem has been completely rebuilt twice since Ezekiel's prophecy, perhaps it will have to be rebuilt again. Maybe the third time is a charm—the time Ezekiel had in mind all along. In that case, when John talks about the Gentiles trampling the holy city, he may have foreseen *another* three-and-a-half-year period that echoes its last destruction. This would be another case of a prophet seeing a future time superimposed on events of his own day. John does refer to a three-and-a-half-year period several times in other scenes of the Apocalypse that bears no resemblance to the historic fall of Jerusalem. These other events seem to happen during the Great Tribulation already described by the first six trumpets. Those trumpets included a world war, which would likely include Jerusalem, since Jewish prophecies usually center on Jerusalem and Israel. Certainly, modern Jerusalem is a city overrun by Gentiles and always on the verge of war. *If* the three and a half years refers to a future battle in Jerusalem that echoes the last one, then the temple may be given special attention in John's description precisely because the *temple* is the one thing that does *not* exist in the present city.

By the time John wrote the Apocalypse (even if he wrote before Jerusalem was destroyed), "the temple of God" had gained a new meaning for Christians, especially in the area where John's churches were located. The Apostle Paul, who did much of the original missionary work in John's region, used this phrase to mean the collective body of believers in Jesus. Paul maintained that God no longer dwelt in temples made of stone. Nor does he dwell in hearts made of stone. God will dwell in hearts of flesh. This was the meaning of the New Covenant prophesied in the Old Testament:

> *A new heart also will I give you, and a new spirit will I put within you: and I will take away the stony heart out of your flesh, and I will give you an heart of flesh. And I will put my spirit within you, and cause you to walk in my statutes, and ye shall keep my judgments, and do them.* (EZEKIEL 36:26, 27)

So, "Rise, and measure the temple of God" *may* have had ironic meaning to John's listeners: "Measure the old temple of stone and count the worshippers there. You cannot, for God has allowed it to be destroyed. Look for the altar. It is not there, for sacrifice has been abolished, too, and with it the old religion. All that remains is the outer courtyard,

which is overrun by Gentiles, just as the New Covenant has been given to the Gentiles."
This echoes the language of Christ's own prophecy:

> And they shall fall by the edge of the sword, and shall be led away captive into all nations: and Jerusalem shall be trodden down of the Gentiles, until the times of the Gentiles be fulfilled.   (LUKE 21:24)

So, this vision may be another way of making the fall of the old temple an analogy to the fall of the old religion, connecting the spiritual change to the physical events of Jerusalem's destruction.

Even though God no longer dwells in temples of stone, that does not mean there can never be a commemorative temple for God's people to gather in, much as they gather in cathedrals today (perhaps built to the description in Ezekiel). So the temple highlighted because it *will* be rebuilt—against present-day odds; or is it highlighted precisely because it is not there—to underscore the fact that it is gone, and the old ways have gone with it? The beauty of poetic ambiguity is that it even leaves open the possibility that both interpretations are correct for different two. The enigma remains.

THE TWO WITNESSES

> And I will give power to my two witnesses, and they shall prophesy a thousand two hundred and sixty days, clothed in sackcloth. These are the two olive trees, and the two lampstands standing before the God of the earth. And if any man will hurt them, fire proceedeth out of their mouth, and devoureth their enemies: and if any man will hurt them, he must in this manner be killed. These have power to shut heaven, that it rain not in the days of their prophecy: and have power over waters to turn them to blood, and to smite the earth with all plagues, as often as they will.   (REVELATION 11:3-6)

Here, already, is a connection of the three and a half years (1,260 days) to events that have no apparent parallel in the Roman destruction of Jerusalem, so the last mention of three and a half years probably does relate to future events. And here is another enigma that will never be known for certain until the end times come: Who are these two witnesses with such great power? Many Christians believe they are the reincarnation of two ancient prophets. Two great prophets of the Old Testament stand out because they never died, and a third, because of how he died. The first of the three was Enoch, of whom it was said:

And Enoch walked with God: and he
was not; for God took him.

(GENESIS 5:24)

New Testament writers took this to mean that Enoch did not die, but was taken directly into the presence of God (raptured or translated):

By faith Enoch was translated that he should not see death; and was not found, because God had translated him: for before his translation he had this testimony, that he pleased God.

(HEBREWS 11:5)

The second candidate for one of the two witnesses was Elijah:

And it came to pass, as they [Elijah and his disciple Elisha] still went on, and talked, that, behold, there appeared a chariot of fire, and horses of fire, and separated them; and Elijah went up by a whirlwind into heaven. And Elisha saw it, and he cried, My father, my father, the chariot of Israel, and its horsemen. And he saw him no more: and he took hold of his own clothes, and tore them in two pieces. He took up also the mantle of Elijah that fell from him, and went back, and stood by the bank of Jordan.

(2 KINGS 2:11–13)

Elijah also did similar miracles to those described in the Apocalypse, calling down fire from heaven and invoking droughts and famines.

The third candidate is Moses, who died but received a unique burial by God himself. Moses is also a likely candidate because he struck the earth with multiple plagues much like those described above, turning water to blood and calling down fire from heaven:

And the LORD said to him, This is the land which I swore to Abraham, to Isaac, and to Jacob, saying, I will give it to thy seed: I have caused thee to see it with thy eyes, but thou shalt not go over there. So Moses the servant of the LORD died there in the land of Moab, according to the word of the LORD. And he [the LORD] buried him in a valley in the land of Moab, opposite Bethpeor: but no man knoweth of his sepulchre to this day.

(DEUTERONOMY 34:4–6)

Of course the two witnesses do not have to be reincarnated prophets, but one Old Testament prophecy indicates that, at least, one of these three will return:

Behold, I will send you Elijah the prophet before the coming of the great and dreadful day of the LORD: And he shall turn the heart of the fathers to the children, and the heart of the children to their fathers, lest I come and smite the earth with a curse. (MALACHI 4:5, 6)

The New Testament implies that John the Baptist, the evangelist who prepared the way for Jesus' ministry, was the promised reincarnation of Elijah. When Jesus' disciples talked about this prophecy Jesus indicated it was already being fulfilled by John the Baptist during their lifetimes, but he also hints that this same Elijah will precede him at his second coming, too:

> . . . And his disciples asked him, saying, Why then say the scribes that Elijah must first come? And Jesus answered and said to them, Elijah truly shall first come, and restore all things. But I say to you, That Elijah is come already, and they knew him not, but have done to him whatever they desired. Likewise shall also the Son of man suffer by them. Then the disciples understood that he spoke to them concerning John the Baptist.
>
> (MATTHEW 17:9–13)

Jesus says "Elijah truly *shall* come first" and that he will restore everything, which indicates Elijah is yet to come, since all things have not been restored. But he also says Elijah has come already and implies he came as John the Baptist. (King Herod had recently ordered John's head cut off and delivered on a silver platter, which is probably what Jesus meant when he said, "They have done to him whatever they desired.") The scene that Jesus and his disciples are returning from as they have this discussion also provides clues as to who the two witnesses of the Apocalypse may be: They had just come down from a mountaintop experience where Jesus . . .

> was transfigured [changed in appearance] before them: and his face shone as the sun, and his raiment was white as the light. And, behold, there appeared to them Moses and Elijah talking with him. . . . While he was yet speaking, behold, a bright cloud overshadowed them: and behold a voice out of the cloud, which said, This is my beloved Son, in whom I am well pleased; hear ye him. And when the disciples heard it, they fell on their face, and were greatly afraid. And Jesus came and touched them, and said, Arise, and be not afraid. And when they had lifted up their eyes, they saw no man, except Jesus only.
>
> (MATTHEW 17:2, 3, 5–8)

A similar account in the Gospel of Luke also mentions that Moses and Elijah were radiant like Jesus. The disciples were in such awe that they wanted to immediately enshrine the site with a structure for each of the three glorified beings they beheld. The image of Jesus touching them and saying "Arise and be not afraid" is just like the scene at the beginning of the Apocalypse when "one like the Son of Man" does the same thing to John. John, in fact, was one of the disciples who was on the mountain when Jesus was transfigured.

Whether or not the two witnesses in the Apocalypse are reincarnated prophets or just two new prophets who play a similar role, they also may have figurative value. The Apocalypse refers to them as the two lampstands and the two olive trees that stand before the Lord of the earth. This is a reference to another Old Testament vision.

The prophet Zechariah saw a single lampstand with seven lamps upon it. Two olive trees, on each side of the lampstand, fed their oil through pipes directly to the lampstand to keep the lamps *always* burning. When the prophet asked what the two olive trees represented, he was told:

> ... These are the two anointed ones,
> that stand by the Lord of the whole
> earth.   (ZECHARIAH 4:14)

The two anointed ones in Zechariah's time were the king, Zerubbabel, and the high priest, Joshua, mentioned earlier. According to Rabbinic tradition these two leaders *figuratively* represented the physical kingdom and the priesthood. In other words, God was not telling Zechariah that those two *individuals* would light the world forever, but that the two institutions they represented would forever light God's world.

Today, one could say the Old Covenant with the Jews represented the physical kingdom, and the New Covenant represents the spiritual priesthood. In the same sense that Zerubbabel and Joshua stood for the two institutions of kingdom and priesthood, the two witnesses who are called "olive trees" may represent God's chosen people; the Jews (of the old kingdom) and the Christians (of the new priesthood of believers).

Each group, in their own way, has stood as a witness for the Lord to the whole earth. They are also called "two lampstands," a symbol for a group of God's people earlier in the Apocalypse. Since there are two lampstands described in this part of the Apocalypse, the implication may be that the two peoples of God will be working side by side during the Great Tribulation and reunited under the New Covenant where kingdom and priesthood are joined. The language of the New Covenant typically speaks of its members as a "kingdom of priests," bringing both together.

Even if these two witnesses are representatives of God's two chosen peoples, they may still be real individuals, just as Zerubbabel and Joshua were real people, especially given the physical descriptions that follow:

> *And when they shall have finished their testimony, the beast that ascendeth out of the bottomless pit shall make war against them, and shall overcome them, and kill them. And their dead bodies shall lie in the street of the great city, which spiritually is called Sodom and Egypt, where also our Lord was crucified. And they of the people and kindreds and tongues and nations shall see their dead bodies three days and an half, and shall not permit their dead bodies to be put in graves. And they that dwell upon the earth shall rejoice over them, and make*

*merry, and shall send gifts one to an-
other; because these two prophets tormented them that dwelt on the earth.
And after three days and an half the
Spirit of life from God entered into them,
and they stood upon their feet; and great
fear fell upon them who saw them. And
they heard a great voice from heaven
saying to them, Come up here. And they
ascended to heaven in a cloud; and their
enemies beheld them. And the same hour
was there a great earthquake, and the
tenth part of the city fell, and in the
earthquake were killed of men seven
thousand: and the remnant were terrified, and gave glory to the God of heaven.*

*The second woe is past; and, behold,
the third woe cometh quickly.*

(REVELATION 11:7–14)

Here, the two witnesses are connected to the same war monger who ascended out
of the bottomless pit created by the falling star. He has risen to take advantage of the anarchy that has spread across the earth because of this horrific incident (whether a literal
"falling star," i.e., meteor, or something else). Most likely the two witnesses have arrived
to prophesy against this despot. They challenge the tyrant with words of truth and
plagues. Here, the fire from their mouths could be like the sword of truth that proceeds
from the mouth of Christ (or it may be a literal miracle, since the miracles of Elijah and
Moses were quite real). The tyrant offers war in return, and eventually he overcomes
them—but only *after* they have completed their mission.

They die in Jerusalem, here named after two other places devastated by plagues that
came as God's judgment against evil. Two of the plagues of Egypt have already been
shown to be similar to the first four trumpets. The destruction of Sodom alluded to here
also sounds much like the plagues of the trumpets:

Then the LORD rained upon Sodom
and upon Gomorrah brimstone and
fire from the LORD out of heaven;
And he overthrew those cities, and all
the plain, and all the inhabitants of the
cities, and that which grew upon the
ground. . . . And Abraham rose early in
the morning to the place where he
stood before the LORD: And he looked
toward Sodom and Gomorrah, and
toward all the land of the plain, and beheld, and, lo, the smoke of the country
went up as the smoke of a furnace.

(GENESIS 19:24, 25, 27, 28)

The name "Sodom" means "burning" or "scorched." A man named "Lot" and his
children were saved by angels just before Sodom was destroyed. Oddly, the angels
seemed very rushed about getting this man (who was Abraham's nephew) out of the city.
Lot was taking his time, and the angels began dragging him by the hand toward the city
gate. They even told him to flee and not look back. It was as though God's coming judgment was already in motion and could not be stopped.

Of course, Sodom sat at the Dead Sea, and the Dead Sea fills one of the biggest cracks in the earth—the major fault line that separates the African Plate from the Arabian Plate and Asia. It is the site where too great continents collide. In the days of Roman occupation, the Dead Sea was called the "Asphalt Sea" because large globs of tar occasionally oozed up from the crack beneath the sea. So, volcanism is another likely cause of Sodom's demise.

Surprisingly, it is not always easy—even for today's scientists—to distinguish between asteroid impacts and major earthquake sites. That's because asteroids of modest size blow up before impact and do not leave a crater. They create a great fireball like a nuclear explosion that incinerates and flattens everything below. Extremely large earthquakes have also been known to generate bizarre lightning effects along the fault line that could have looked like "fire from heaven."

One of the most famous impact sites in the world is an area in Russia (about equal in size to the plain around Sodom) that was totally flattened by an exploding asteroid. People actually claim to have seen the asteroid pass overhead. Yet, at least one scientist believes this famous Russian site to be an earthquake site:

> If an earthquake hit Tunguska in 1908, it might have released energy . . . as electrical flashes that could have burned the trees. To pursue this notion, Ol'khovatov compared earthquake-related phenomena to the eyewitness accounts of light flashes and sounds at Tunguska. "I was astonished to see such a great resemblance," says Ol'khovatov. Many eyewitness accounts, for example, report discharges of light from the ground, which accord more with earthquake lights than [an asteroid's] descent. . . .
>
> He maintains that all three [suggested asteroid] trajectories closely follow fault lines running through the region, while the epicenter is smack in the middle of an ancient volcanic crater. "Very likely, the locals observed glowing effects set off by awakening tectonic processes. . . ."[3]

The point is that Sodom makes a perfect example for both the earthquake predicted for Jerusalem *and* the plagues of fire that rain down upon the world during the Great Tribulation. Tectonic earthquakes, or earthquakes cause by asteroids—the description of Sodom's destruction works either way.

John subtly connects the predicted destruction of Jerusalem back to the cause (in Christian belief) for its original destruction. After calling Jerusalem "Egypt," he adds, "where also our Lord was crucified." There is a clear implication that the future destruction will be for continued disbelief. When the great earthquake kills seven thousand people after the resurrection of the two witnesses, all the survivors give glory to God. (The number killed could be purely symbolic of God's justice or both literal and symbolic, as real events can have symbolic meanings.) In other words, the Jews living in Jerusalem recognize that the two witnesses were speaking the truth about the Messiah, *and* they recognize that the great earthquake was a judgment against their disbelief. They turn to God, and the seventh trumpet sounds . . .

When he [Christ] shall come to be glorified in his saints, and to be admired by all them that believe (because our testimony among you was believed) in that day. (2 THESSALONIANS 1:10)

THE SEVENTH TRUMPET

And the seventh angel sounded; and there were great voices in heaven, saying, The kingdoms of this world are become the kingdoms of our Lord, and of his Christ; and he shall reign for ever and ever. And the four and twenty elders, who sat before God on their thrones, fell upon their faces, and worshipped God, Saying, We give thee thanks, O Lord God Almighty, who art, and wast, and art to come; because thou hast taken to thee thy great power, and hast reigned. And the nations were angry, and thy wrath is come, and the time of the dead, that they should be judged, and that thou shouldest give reward to thy servants the prophets, and to the saints, and them that fear thy name, small and great; and shouldest destroy them who destroy the earth. And the temple of God was opened in heaven, and there was seen in his temple the ark of his covenant: and there were lightnings, and voices, and thunderings, and an earthquake, and great hail. (REVELATION 11:15–19)

Now that the Jews of Jerusalem have turned to Jesus as their Messiah, the seventh trumpet announces the second coming of Christ. It proclaims that all kingdoms will become one under him, just as all the kingdoms in Nebuchadnezzar's dream were blown away by the One that came out of heaven. It further announces that God's wrath will now come upon the wicked, probably because the last of the Jews have now acquired faith in Christ—many others having already acquired such faith as a result of the ministry of the two witnesses.

This reading confirms the Apostle Paul's belief that the Jews would be the final people to turn to Christ as the Messiah, and their conversion would bring his return and the resurrection of all believers:

I say then, Have [the Jews] stumbled that they should fall? God forbid: but rather through their fall salvation is come unto the Gentiles, for to provoke them [the Jews] to jealousy. Now if the fall of them [the Jews] be the riches of the world, and the diminishing of them [as God's chosen people] the riches of the Gentiles [who became God's newly chosen people]; how much more their fulness? . . . For if the casting away of them be the reconciling of the world, what shall the receiving of them be, but life from the dead? . . . For if thou [the Gentiles] wast cut out of the olive tree which is wild by nature, and wast grafted contrary to nature into a good olive tree: how much more shall these, which are the natural [branches], be grafted into their own olive tree? For I would not, brethren, that ye should be ignorant of this mystery, lest ye should be wise in your own conceits; that blindness in part hath happened to Israel, until the fulness of the Gentiles shall be come in. And so all Israel shall be saved: as it is written, There shall come out of Zion the Deliverer, and shall turn away ungodliness from Jacob: For this is my covenant to them, when I shall take away their sins. As concerning the gospel, they are enemies for your sakes: but as concerning the election, they are beloved for the fathers' [patriarchs'] sakes.

(ROMANS 11:11, 12, 15, 24–28)

Jesus said the Gospel would be preached to all people before he returned, and Paul is adding that the Jews would remain hostile to the Gospel of Jesus Christ until the entire world had received that Gospel. The total conversion of Jews (at least in Jerusalem, if not everywhere) means the last people have come in. Immediately, the seventh trumpet sounds, which heralds the return of Christ and the resurrection of all believers. This is the sense in which the "fulness" of the Jews will bring even greater riches to Gentiles. From that point, "there will be no delay" to the return of Christ.

Behold, I show you a mystery; We shall not all sleep [die], but we shall all be changed, In a moment, in the twinkling of an eye, at the last trumpet: for the trumpet shall sound, and the dead shall be raised incorruptible, and we shall be changed. (1 CORINTHIANS 15:51, 52)

And so the words of Christ are fulfilled:

O Jerusalem, Jerusalem, thou that killest the prophets, and stonest them who are sent to thee, how often would I have gathered thy children together, even as a hen gathereth her chickens under her wings, and ye would not! Behold, your house is left to you desolate. For I say to you, Ye shall not see me henceforth, till ye shall say, Blessed is he that cometh in the name of the Lord.

And Jesus went out, and departed from the temple. . . .

(MATTHEW 23:37-39; 24:1A)

Those who remain after all the Jews of Jerusalem have recognized Jesus as their Messiah are people who will not likely change their ways. So, God's wrath will come to "destroy them who destroy the earth." Here's a strong message for those who think the environment does not matter to God. It is not just the martyrs of Christ who will be avenged; it is all the creatures represented before God by the "four living creatures." God created the earth. He cares about all of his creatures, not just humans, and will harshly judge those who have abused his gift.

The scene of the seven trumpets opened with thunder, rumblings, lightning, and an earthquake. Now it closes with a greater crescendo. First, the spiritual realm of heaven is made visible. ("All things will be revealed.") God's temple is revealed and the long-lost ark of the covenant is seen, perhaps as a reminder of the Old Covenant handed down by Moses that was taken away when Jerusalem was destroyed. Then a "great" hail storm is added to the lightnings and rumblings ("voices") and earthquake. This cacophony is a reprisal of the seven trumpets, recalling even the great chunks of frozen debris that rained down from the sky. This is the music of the former scene coming back up as the curtain closes on another act.

John's vision of the temple of God opening in heaven is reminiscent of Jesus' words when he was choosing his disciples at the beginning of his ministry.

And he saith to him, Verily, verily, I say to you, After this ye shall see heaven open, and the angels of God ascending and descending upon the Son of man.
(JOHN 1:51)

Chapter 14

SATAN:

THE LADY AND THE DRAGON

Before the return of Christ is revealed along with the final wrath of God that pours out upon the earth, John takes another intermission. During this break in the sequence of events, he describes in greater detail a cosmic battle that seems to transcend time. He starts with a mythic tale that brings the whole spiritual battle into focus—the tale of a virtuous lady chased by an evil dragon:

And there appeared a great wonder in heaven; a woman clothed with the sun, and the moon under her feet, and upon her head a crown of twelve stars: And she being with child cried, travailing in birth, and pained to be delivered. And there appeared another wonder in heaven; and behold a great red dragon, having seven heads and ten horns, and seven crowns upon his heads. And his tail drew the third part of the stars of heaven, and cast them to the earth: and the dragon stood before the woman who was ready to be delivered, to devour her child as soon as he was born. And she brought forth a son, who was to rule all nations with a rod of iron: and her child was caught up to God, and to his throne. And the woman fled into the wilderness, where she hath a place prepared by God, that they should feed her there a thousand two hundred and sixty days.

(REVELATION 12:1–6)

One view of this mythic story sees the woman clothed in the sun and crowned with stars as a beautiful representation of Israel. As the lady produced a son, Israel produced the Messiah. This symbolic interpretation comes from Genesis 37, where the patriarch Joseph had a dream. In his dream the sun represented his father Jacob; the moon, his mother Rachel. Jacob's twelve sons (including Joseph), who became the patriarchs of the new nation, were represented by twelve stars. Moving back to John's tale, the seven-headed dragon would represent Rome and its seven emperors up to the time of Jerusalem's destruction (as explained toward the end of this chapter). Thus, the seven heads have seven crowns. At a deeper level, the dragon is Satan. Rome is simply his incarnation.

The Catholic Church has often understood the woman to represent one specific Jew, rather than the entire nation. That woman, of course, was Mary, who literally brought forth the Messiah and who did flee to the deserts of Egypt after Jesus was born because Herod the Great ordered the deaths of all firstborn male children in Bethlehem. He did this because he had heard that a new king of the Jews had been born, and he wanted to protect his throne from this future rival. In this view, as in the last, Satan is the dragon, but in terms of literal history Herod played the role—just as Rome filled the role in the previous view.

Another interpretation of this myth has been that the woman represents the Church, clothed with the glory of Christ (the sun), and crowned with the twelve apostles. A shortcoming to this view is that the Church did not give birth to Christ. Christ brought forth the Church. Through the centuries, the supporters of this view have argued, however, that the Church now brings forth Christ continually in the world through all who are born again spiritually.

Since the symbolism is appropriate in different respects for each view, perhaps these differing interpretations merely support the fractal design of history. God's design played out first on the grand scale of Israel producing the Messiah, then it reproduced itself on the very small scale of a Jewish mother and her hunted son, and finally is seen expanded again through the Church, which continually brings Christ into the world. None of these views are really contradictory; they simply acknowledge the same patterns of evil against good—played out in different times.

THE FALL OF SATAN

At first the dragon is on the offensive, trying to kill the child that is being brought into the world. Satan tried many times to destroy Israel before the Messiah could be produced. Then he tried to destroy the baby Messiah through his agent King Herod. Later in John's lifetime, he tried to destroy the Church that continually brings forth Christ, again using Roman agents. Long after John's death, he even used agents within the Church of Rome itself during the various inquisitions.

But the story turns, and Satan is shown to be on the defensive, fighting a losing battle, trying to recover ground he has already lost. Jesus described this battle to his disciples:

> And he said to them, I beheld Satan as lightning fall from heaven. Behold, I give to you power to tread on serpents and scorpions, and over all the power of the enemy: and nothing shall by any means hurt you. (LUKE 10:18–20)

Jesus was probably describing something he had seen that still lay in the disciples' future, because near his crucifixion he makes it clear that Satan's judgment is *about* to come. Old Testament stories, like Job, showed Satan in heaven speaking with God as a being who had freedom to rove between heaven and earth and who used that freedom to accuse men before God. Apparently, during the time of the Old Testament, Satan had not yet fallen from heaven—at least not in the story of Job. So, Jesus may have been looking toward the future, which is why he tells his disciples they would be given power to crush Satan. At last, the oldest of all biblical prophecies was coming true:

> *And the LORD God said to the serpent, Because thou hast done this, thou art cursed above all cattle, and above every beast of the field; upon thy belly shalt thou go, and dust shalt thou eat all the days of thy life: And I will put enmity between thee and the woman, and between thy seed and her seed; it shall bruise thy head, and thou shalt bruise his heel.*
>
> (GENESIS 3:14, 15)

This prophecy was given the first time Satan accused people before God in the ancient story of the Garden of Eden. John's mythic tale shows the seed of the first woman, Eve, finally being born through Mary. The Messiah has come to earth, and he will crush the serpent as long foretold. Jesus made it clear to his disciples that his crucifixion would be the event that would fix God's judgment against Satan:

> *Now is the judgment of this world: now shall the prince of this world be cast out. And I, if I shall be lifted up from the earth, will draw all men to me. He said this to show the kind of death he was going to die.*
>
> (JOHN 12:31, 32)

So, when Jesus was lifted on the cross, Satan would fall to earth, and the Messiah's followers would rise to heaven. Obviously his followers did not rise at that very moment, but this was the event that secured their resurrection and assured Satan's defeat. Jesus, in his final words to his disciples, said before his crucifixion:

> . . . the prince of this world is judged.
>
> (JOHN 16:11)

The crucifixion marks the time on earth when the dragon's "tail drew the third part of the stars of heaven, and cast them to the earth." When Satan was cast out of heaven, he drew a host of heavenly angels with him. Ezekiel and other prophets had described angels as fiery celestial beings; John now symbolizes them as stars cast out of heaven. At this point, his story focuses on this singular cosmic event, which is the conflict at the heart of his entire vision:

And there was war in heaven: Michael and his angels fought against the dragon; and the dragon fought and his angels, And prevailed not; neither was their place found any more in heaven. And the great dragon was cast out, that old serpent, called the Devil, and Satan, who deceiveth the whole world: he was cast out upon the earth, and his angels were cast out with him. And I heard a loud voice saying in heaven, Now is come salvation, and strength, and the kingdom of our God, and the power of his Christ: for the accuser of our brethren is cast down, who accused them before our God day and night. And they overcame him by the blood of the Lamb, and by the word of their testimony; and they loved not their lives to the death. Therefore rejoice, ye heavens, and ye that dwell in them. Woe to the inhabiters of the earth and of the sea! for the devil is come down to you, having great wrath, because he knoweth that he hath but a short time.

(REVELATION 12:7–12)

Other Old Testament prophecies poetically described this fateful day when Lucifer, whose name means "Light Bearer," became the "Prince of Darkness." As has often been the case, prophets saw this cosmic battle overlaid on events of their own time. Ezekiel, in describing the fall of Israel's enemy, the king of Tyre, ascends to language far higher than befits a king, for Ezekiel recognizes the dragon that breathes behind the king:

Moreover the word of the LORD came to me, saying, Son of man, take up a lamentation upon the king of Tyre, and say to him, Thus saith the Lord GOD; Thou sealest up the sum, full of wisdom, and perfect in beauty. Thou hast been in Eden the garden of God; every precious stone was thy covering, the sardius, topaz, and the diamond, the beryl, the onyx, and the jasper, the sapphire, the emerald, and the carbuncle, and gold: the workmanship of thy tabrets and of thy pipes was prepared in thee in the day that thou wast created. Thou art the anointed cherub that covereth; and I have set thee so: thou wast upon the holy mountain of God; thou hast walked up and down in the midst of the stones of fire. Thou wast perfect in thy ways from the day that thou wast created, till iniquity was found in thee. By the multitude of thy merchandise [trade] they have filled the midst of thee with violence, and thou hast sinned: therefore I will cast thee as profane out of the mountain of God: and I will destroy thee, O covering cherub, from the midst of the stones of fire. Thy heart was lifted up because of thy beauty, thou hast corrupted thy wisdom by reason of thy brightness: I will cast thee to the ground, I will lay thee before kings, that they may behold thee.

(EZEKIEL 28:11–17)

Ezekiel describes a magnificent and innocent angel created by God, but that angel creates a devil out of himself. Given tremendous power, beauty, and freedom from his creation, Lucifer's greatness became his god. Similar to Narcissus in the Greek legend, Lucifer gazed upon his own glory until it blinded him. The "holy mountain of God" refers to heaven, from which Lucifer was cast down. The physical Mount Zion on earth, where God's temple was built in Jerusalem, was to the Jews what Mt Olympus was to the Greeks. Mount Zion became a symbol for heaven, the *spiritual* dwelling place of God, and its temple was the nexus between heaven and earth—God's *physical* dwelling place (until the day of the Messiah, when humanity became God's physical dwelling place and the temple was destroyed).

While recognizing the spiritual evil that lay behind the king of Tyre, Ezekiel speaks of the king's international trade but sees in it the devil's commerce with this world. Lucifer used his freedom to range across the earth and bring destruction, which is what the king of Tyre did. Because the devil's dealings with the world were deceitful, he was cast out of paradise or heaven. This is shown in the Garden of Eden story when the serpent loses its glory and is cast out of the garden to crawl upon the same ground that humans walk upon.

The self-corrupted angel, Lucifer, ultimately becomes lower than humans when humans are raised to heavenly realms. In the present, he is known as "Satan," which means "adversary." Satan desecrates any place that is his sanctuary because he is full of wrath for all that he has lost, and his wrath works itself out in great destruction. And so, John says, "Woe to the inhabiters of the earth . . . for the devil is come down to you, having great wrath, because he knoweth that he hath but a short time."

At the end of Ezekiel's prophecy against the devil, God says,

> *Thou hast defiled thy sanctuaries by the multitude of thy iniquities, by the iniquity of thy merchandise [commerce]; therefore will I bring forth a fire from the midst of thee, it shall devour thee, and I will bring thee to ashes upon the earth in the sight of all them that behold thee. All they that know thee among the people shall be astonished at thee: thou shalt be a terror, and never shalt thou be any more.* (EZEKIEL 28:–19)

Most likely, the city of Tyre was burned during its siege, quite possibly with the king still in it. The prophet sees in this haunting picture a vision of Satan who will be burned along with those he has led. Fire is used throughout the Bible as a symbol for spirit, but also as a symbol for purification or judgment. Whether the fires of hell are literal or symbolic of horrors in the spiritual realm that is under Satan's control, they will be Satan's destruction. Both symbolic meanings of fire—spirit and judgment—are brought together in Ezekiel's picture of spiritual judgment.

It sounds as though Satan will be consumed by a "fire" that comes from within himself—"therefore will I bring forth a fire from the midst of thee." It is God's justice built into the universe that evil should be its own demise. The fruit of evil contains the seeds of its own destruction. By allowing evil to rot itself out over the great span of earth's history, its bitterness and stench becomes evident to all. The "Adversary" creates his own adversaries who will eternally punish him.

This was the kind of end God had also declared for the king of Babylon. When Habakkuk asked God to explain why people of greater evil were allowed to bring punishment on people of lesser evil, God explained that Babylon would soon overextend its evil reach and would accumulate enemies powerful enough to destroy it. God would let evil nature take its course.

The Book of Isaiah contains a prophecy against the last king of Babylon that is strikingly similar to Ezekiel's prophecy against the king of Tyre. Again, one of God's prophets sees through the human mask and recognizes the evil that drives the man who occupies the throne:

> Hell from beneath is moved for thee to meet thee at thy coming: it stirreth up the dead for thee, even all the chief ones of the earth; it hath raised up from their thrones all the kings of the nations. All they shall speak and say to thee, Art thou also become weak as we? art thou become like us? Thy pomp is brought down to the grave, and the noise of thy viols: the worm is spread under thee, and the worms cover thee. How art thou fallen from heaven, O Lucifer, son of the morning! how art thou cut down to the ground, which didst weaken the nations! For thou hast said in thy heart, I will ascend into heaven, I will exalt my throne above the stars of God: I will sit also upon the mount of the congregation, in the sides of the north: I will ascend above the heights of the clouds; I will be like the most High. Yet thou shalt be brought down to hell, to the sides of the pit. They that see thee shall narrowly look upon thee, and consider thee, saying, Is this the man that made the earth to tremble, that shook kingdoms; That made the world as a wilderness, and destroyed its cities; that opened not the house of his prisoners? All the kings of the nations, even all of them, lie in glory, every one in his own house. But thou art cast out of thy grave like an abominable branch, and as the raiment of those that are slain, thrust through with a sword, that go down to the stones of the pit; as a dead body trodden under feet. Thou shalt not be joined with them in burial, because thou hast destroyed thy land, and slain thy people: the seed of evildoers shall never be renowned. (ISAIAH 14:9–20)

A SANCTUARY IN THE DESERT

To this point, John's mythic tale has spoken of the time surrounding Christ's birth and death. It would be appropriate, then, that the conclusion refers to the events that happened right after Christ's death:

And when the dragon saw that he was cast to the earth, he persecuted the woman who brought forth the son. And to the woman were given two wings of a great eagle, that she might fly into the wilderness, into her place, where she is nourished for a time, and times, and half a time, from the face of the serpent. And the serpent cast out of his mouth water as a flood after the woman, that he might cause her to be carried away by the flood. And the earth helped the woman, and the earth opened her mouth, and swallowed up the flood which the dragon cast out of his mouth. And the dragon was enraged with the woman, and went to make war with the remnant of her seed, who keep the commandments of God, and have the testimony of Jesus Christ. (REVELATION 12:13–17)

If the woman is seen as representing the Christian Church, then the place of sanctuary in the desert would be the town of Pella, where the Christians of Jerusalem fled from the armies of Rome during the three and a half years that Rome battled the Jews in Israel. The "great eagle" that carried her into the desert could be Rome. The imperial eagle was the insignia of Rome carried on standards before the Roman armies.

Interpreting the eagle as Rome, however, fits better with the view that the woman represents Israel, for the eagle seems to be a protective force in the desert. Ironically, Rome provided shelter to the Jewish rebels in one of its finest fortresses—a palace built by Herod as a refuge upon a high rock in the desert. The Jews took this luxurious palace as their own fortress during the rebellion. After the fall of Jerusalem, the rebels fled to this place known as Masada, which proved impregnable for three and a half years.

For in the time of trouble he shall hide me in his pavilion: in the secret of his tabernacle shall he hide me; he shall set me up upon a rock. And now shall my head be lifted above my enemies around me: therefore will I offer in his tabernacle sacrifices of joy; I will sing, yea, I will sing praises to the LORD. (PSALM 27:5, 6)

There was, however, no opening of the earth to swallow the flood poured out on those Jews who fled into the desert. In some prophecies, the rising flood of a river has been used to symbolize a great army, which marches across the desert in form like a river, then spreads out at the base of a fortified city and surrounds it like a flood:

Now therefore, behold, the Lord bringeth up upon them the waters of the river, strong and many, even the king of Assyria, and all his glory: and he shall come up over all its channels, and go over all its banks: And he shall pass through Judah; he shall overflow and go over, he shall reach even to the neck; and the spread of his wings shall fill the breadth of thy land, O Immanuel. (ISAIAH 8:7, 8)

Masada offered no final protection from this flood. The only sense in which the earth opened up to swallow the river was that it opened its grave mouth to swallow the

Jews who killed themselves before the Romans could. Once the Romans had swept over all Judea like a flood and put down all rebellion, their attention turned against those "who have the testimony of Jesus Christ." So, following the woman-as-Israel view, once Satan had raised his Roman forces to swallow the woman in the desert, he turned their attention upon the Christians, the woman's "offspring." (Or, as the King James version says, "the remnant of her seed.")

This perfectly closes the poignant story John has to tell, except for that nagging detail about the earth opening its mouth to swallow the river. Perhaps two stories are overlaid here because, while the rebels held out in Masada, another group of Jews chose not to rebel and were carried on Roman wings into a place in the desert.

When Jerusalem was still under siege, an enterprising Rabbi named Jochanan ben Zakkai devised a way to save a number of Jews from the besieged city, and saved Judaism in the process:

> Like Josephus, Jochanan ben Zakkai belonged to the Peace Party. Like Josephus, he was convinced that the stand taken by the Zealots could lead only to tragedy. He deserted the war . . . and, like Josephus, had an encounter with Vespasian. But far from being dubbed a traitor, Jochanan ben Zakkai was acclaimed the savior of Judaism.
>
> Jochanan ben Zakkai was a leading Pharisee intellectual. He foresaw the holocaust which would overtake the Jews, the dispersion the Romans would impose upon his people . . . . He became obsessed with the idea that he must found a Jewish academy which would carry the torch of Jewish learning. . . . He had to get to the ear of Vespasian.
>
> Besieged Jerusalem was a hellhole. People were dying by the thousands of starvation and pestilence. . . . Suspected Peace Party members were thrown over the wall by the Zealots. . . . To outwit the Zealots, Jochanan . . . took a few of his disciples . . . and outlined his plan to them. The disciples went out into the street, tore their clothes according to the plan, and in mournful voices announced that their great rabbi, Jochanan ben Zakkai, had died of the plague. They asked and received permission from the Zealot authorities to bury the revered rabbi outside the gates of Jerusalem to check the spread of pestilence. . . . The disciples carried a sealed coffin with the live Jochanan . . . out of Jerusalem and to the tent of Vespasian, where they opened the coffin and the rabbi stepped out.[1]

Jochanan used the same scheme Josephus had used to gain Vespasian's clemency. He prophesied that Vespasian would soon become emperor (not too difficult since Nero had just died and Vespasian was the strongest general in the empire). And what did Jochanan ask of this great leader, but one small request: that once Vespasian became the emperor of Rome, he grant the rabbi the right to establish a school in some desert Palestinian town. Impressed by the prophecy and the modesty of the request, Vespasian agreed—so long as the prophecy came true.

Perhaps Vespasian felt that killing a prophet who predicts your fortune might upset the gods who had determined that fortune. Or maybe he was just impressed by the audacity and courage of the bearded rabbi as well as the wit he had used to escape his captors. Whatever his reason for granting his promise, Vespasian was true to his word, and when the war ended and he was crowned seventh emperor of Rome, he allowed ben Zakkai to establish the first yeshiva for the development of Jewish studies in the town of Jabneh. The yeshiva at Jabneh became a place of hope and rebirth for Jews in the diaspora and is widely credited for the survival of Talmudic Judaism. In this sense, the woman, Israel, was saved on the wings of the great eagle of Rome, carried to safety by the promise of the one who wore the seventh crown. One could say that the entire diaspora had amounted to salvation in the desert, similar to the forty years that the Jews wandered in the wilderness after leaving Egypt.

Indeed, the story recalls an earlier time when God had brought his people to a promised land in the desert:

> *Ye have seen what I did unto the Egyptians [the plagues mentioned earlier], and how I bare you on eagles' wings, and brought you unto myself. Now therefore, if ye will obey my voice indeed, and keep my covenant, then ye shall be a peculiar treasure unto me above all people: for all the earth is mine: And ye shall be unto me a kingdom of priests, and an holy nation. These are the words which thou shalt speak unto the children of Israel.*
>
> (EXODUS 19:4–6)

The "kingdom of priests" certainly calls to mind the New Covenant. Will God's people, brought into the New Covenant during some future period, be carried to a refuge on eagles' wings? Is this myth, which describes Israel's salvation in the desert, also a prophecy that will play itself out with even greater glory during earth's final days? John gives a hint that it will.

Finally, the river that is swallowed may have no clear connection to the past because it may refer to a parallel time in the future when another great army will flow through the desert like a great river in pursuit of the people of God.

A TIME, TIMES, AND HALF A TIME

A woman is chased by a dragon to her salvation in the desert after her child is caught up to heaven. The story of Israel and her Messiah narrowed to a focus in two people—a young Jewish mother and her Son chased into the deserts of Egypt. Will the greater woman Israel be joined again to her Son during the Great Tribulation of the end times? Does the story of the Woman imply that Israel will find her salvation in a spiritual desert during another three-and-half-year period or perhaps a physical salvation in a physical desert?

John has spoken a few times of a period lasting three and a half years, but in this story he used the peculiar language of Daniel, "a time [year], and times [two years], and half a time." This may be a clue that the three and a half years in the desert also correspond to the time described in Daniel—that the story is more than the history of Israel's preservation at Jabneh. Daniel 12:1–3 describes a future time of deliverance when the cosmic battle of the angels shall resume:

> And at that time shall [the archangel] Michael stand up, the great prince who standeth for the children of thy people: and there shall be a time of trouble, such as never was since there was a nation even to that same time: and at that time thy people shall be delivered, every one that shall be found written in the book.
>
> And many of them that sleep in the dust of the earth shall awake, some to everlasting life, and some to shame and everlasting contempt. And they that are wise shall shine as the brightness of the firmament; and they that turn many to righteousness as the stars for ever and ever . . .

Daniel foretells a period of Great Tribulation such as the world has never seen, which will last three and a half years. The spiritual battle fought at the cross will escalate when the return of Christ the Messiah is near, for the greatly fallen star, Satan, will know his time is short. Like John, Daniel connects this period to the resurrection. "They that are wise" at that time will be those who recognize Christ as their Messiah. These are the ones whose names will be found written in the Book of Life, mentioned here by Daniel and described later by John.

An earlier chapter of this book included some prophecies about an infamous king named Antiochus Epiphanes, who tried to destroy the Jewish religion by corrupting its temple. The prophecies about Antiochus grew out of proportion to the man himself and kept referring to the end. Some of the following part of Daniel's prophecy were quoted earlier to show how it related to Antiochus Epiphanes. By alluding to Daniel's "time, and times and half a time," which appears in the following portion of Daniel's prophesy, John implies Daniel's prophecy will see its ultimate fulfillment in the distant future John is describing. Daniel, too, implied the real fulfillment of this prophecy waited until the end times:

> . . . But thou, O Daniel, shut up the words, and seal the book, even to the time of the end: many shall run to and fro, and knowledge shall be increased. Then I Daniel looked, and, behold, there
>
> stood two others, the one on this side of the bank of the river, and the other on that side of the bank of the river. And one said to the man clothed in linen, who was above the waters of the river, How

long shall it be to the end of these wonders? And I heard the man clothed in
linen, who was above the waters of the
river, when he held up his right hand and
his left hand to heaven, and swore by him
that liveth for ever that it shall be for a
time, times, and an half; and when he
shall have accomplished the breaking up
of the power of the holy people, all these
things shall be finished. And I heard, but
I understood not: then said I, O my Lord,
what shall be the end of these things? And
he said, Go thy way, Daniel: for the words
are closed up and sealed till the time of

the end. Many shall be purified, and
made white, and tried; but the wicked
shall do wickedly: and none of the wicked
shall understand; but the wise shall understand. And from the time that the
daily sacrifice shall be taken away, and
the abomination that maketh desolate set
up, there shall be a thousand two hundred and ninety days. Blessed is he that
waiteth, and cometh to the thousand
three hundred and five and thirty days.
But go thou thy way till the end: for thou
shalt rest, and stand in thy lot at the end
of the days.   (DANIEL 12:1–13)

The last lines were viewed earlier in this book as a reference to the abomination of
desolation set up by Antiochus Epiphanes, who died three and a half years after profaning the altar of God. His death may have come exactly 1,290 days after, which would explain the slight difference between John's 1,260 days and the number mentioned here in
Daniel. And at least one scholar has speculated that it would have taken a month or so
for that news to reach Jerusalem; thus, "Blessed [happy] is he that waiteth, and cometh
to the [1,335] days."

Yet, Daniel has said at several points that his prophecy relates to the end times of
great tribulation. Antiochus brought considerable tribulation, but he was not the end of
anything, except himself. Now that John alludes back to this prophecy, it becomes more
likely that some of what it says—certainly the resurrection—relates to the final events
immediately before the return of Christ.

In the Hebrew Scriptures, the *Tanakh*, the answer to the question "How long shall it
be to the end of these wonders?" is translated "when the breaking of the power of the
holy people comes to an end." Perhaps the restoration of Israel, which gives Jews the opportunity to end the long diaspora, may represent the end of the breaking of Jewish
power, and the beginning of the times the prophecy refers to.

Daniel's reference to many being "purified" may refer to the fiery plagues of the
Great Tribulation that compel many to seek God. They shall quite literally be purified
and tried by fire. But the wicked will also continue to be wicked, as John will soon reveal
in the final plagues of the Apocalypse. Some have suggested that if the Great Tribulation
(the seven trumpets) lasts three and a half years (1,260 days), then the final plagues of
the Apocalypse may all come in a single month, bringing the total number of days to
1,290 and giving greater fulfillment to Daniel's time that was fulfilled first by the death
of Antiochus. The final 45 days that brings Daniel's prophecy to its close at 1,335 days,

then, would be the battle of Armageddon, which winds up the last seven plagues of the Apocalypse. Of course, if the number of days has already been fulfilled perfectly by Antiochus, it is not essential to have any of these days repeat, except that John repeats them. It may be that only parts of the pattern repeat in the final events of earth. Those who like to be adamant about such interpretations should recognize that they will be the first to preserve their belief in biblical inerrancy by jumping to the other man's ship if that's the ship that comes in.

The Second Roman Conflict

Finally, a few words should be said about a view of Daniel's prophecy that has held great sway during the last millennium.

It's only natural that Protestants, who were severely persecuted by the Roman Catholic Church during the Inquisition, would begin to see the Holy Roman Empire as the last and worst of oppressive empires, where imperial power wore a mask of Christian piety. These dark times, when the Catholic Church needed reform, will be discussed later in the book, but one result of this dark age was the development of a new way to understand the numbers given by the prophets John and Daniel. In this view, the 1,260 days (three-and-a-half Babylonian calendar years) are seen as figurative for 1,260 years, measuring the length of the political rule of the pope. Officially, papal authority began in A.D. 533 when Justinian, the emperor of the reunited Roman Empire, declared the bishop of Rome the "head of all the holy churches" and "head of all the holy priests of God." It was not until five years later (538), however, that the last of the bishop's religious contenders (the Ostrogoths) were ousted from Rome, securing the bishop's newly claimed authority.

Perhaps by mere coincidence it was 1,260 years from this date that Napoleon ousted the Pope from Rome, ordering his imprisonment in France in 1798, where he eventually died. Though the papacy as an institution did not perish, respect for the pope's political control continued to decline throughout Europe. Finally, in 1870, what was left of the Holy Roman Empire became the United Kingdom of Italy, a sovereign state separate from the Church. Having held tenuously together for a millennium, the longest-lasting empire in world history was put to rest. Coming close to another coincidence, 1870 ends 1,333 years after the beginning of papal authority for the bishop of Rome—only two years short of Daniel's closing number, 1,335. (A minor error in accounting the years of history could make up the difference.)

This view has a few weaknesses besides being off by two years at the end: The 1,260 years for Rome fits perfectly, except that the bishop did not gain actual *political* authority until a couple of centuries later. And, though the the empire that eventually became known as Holy Roman Empire was extinguished after 1,333 years, the papacy continues, though not with as much political authority.

Also, the establishment of the papacy does not match up in any clear way with the ending of "daily sacrifice" or the "abomination that causes desolation." (The tendered explanation by those Protestants who hold this view is that the papacy, itself, is an abomination of human authority that usurps the position of Jesus Christ. They believe it *is* the abomination because it tried to force religious unity through power, instead of trusting the Holy Spirit to bring unity through his peaceful work in human hearts, which was the way of Christ. Burning heretics was not very Christian.

To many Protestants, it was no wonder that Satan could and would find an incarnation for himself within the Church. Had not the Apostle Paul, himself, foretold such possibilities:

> *For such are false apostles, deceitful workers, transforming themselves into the apostles of Christ.*
> *And no wonder; for Satan himself is transformed into an angel of light.*
>
> *Therefore it is no great thing if his ministers also are transformed as the ministers of righteousness; whose end shall be according to their works.*
>
> (2 CORINTHIANS 11:13–15)

Ultimately, the rise and fall of the Roman Empire (holy or otherwise) is so complicated, it's difficult to post a precise beginning and ending date. But who's to say that all three applications (Antiochus, the Antichrist in the Great Tribulation, and the Holy Roman Empire during the Middle Ages) do not have some merit as interpretations of prophetic fulfillment? Maybe they all represent human incarnations of the same evil, showing variations of the primary pattern.

If God wanted to make Daniel's visions specific and clear, he would have done so. Are the language and the symbols vague in order to conceal—or ambiguous in order to apply to more than one period? Certainly, Daniel's words served the needs of the Jews well when they suffered under Antiochus Epiphanes, and they served the Protestant Reformers' need of an enduring hope. As they tried to clear the Church of some of its darker deeds, they needed to know their deaths were not in vain. If the blood-stained fragments of history are a kaleidoscope of repeating patterns, then the pattern may be seen once more in a grand finale as the fiery dragon is finally overcome.

THE CRUX OF THE BATTLE

There are only a few clues for understanding how this cosmic battle came to a crisis at the cross. They belong to the gray zone of theology, but are summed up in the Apostles' Creed, which says of Jesus Christ:

He suffered under Pontius Pilate, was crucified, died, and was buried. He descended into hell. On the third day he rose again. He ascended into heaven, and is seated at the right hand of the Father. He will come again to judge the living and the dead.

"He descended into hell" is the foggy part of theology, supported by only two ambiguous scriptures, yet it is believed by a majority of Christian churches and found clear expression in some very early Christian writings known as the Odes of Solomon, believed to be songs written in the style of the Psalms. The following is spoken from the view of Christi:

> . . . And I was not rejected though I was reckoned to be so. I did not perish, though they devised it against me. Sheol [the Grave] saw me and was made miserable. Death cast me up and many along with me. I had gall and bitterness, and I went down with him [Death personified] to the utmost of his depth. . . . And I made a congregation of living men amongst his dead men, and I spake with them by living lips: Because my word shall not be void: And those who had died ran towards me: and they cried and said, Son of God, have pity on us, and do with us according to thy kindness, And bring us out from the bonds of darkness: and open to us the door by which we shall come out to thee. For we see that our death has not touched thee. Let us also be redeemed with thee: for thou art our Redeemer. And I heard their voice; and my name I sealed upon their heads: For they are free men and they are mine. Hallelujah.[2]

One of the scriptures that lends shadowy support to this belief was written by the Apostle Paul:

> Wherefore he saith, When he ascended up on high, he led captivity captive, and gave gifts unto men. (Now that he ascended, what is it but that he also descended first into the lower parts of the earth? . . .)   (EPHESIANS 4:8, 9)

Presumably the "lower parts of the earth" could mean hell. Though few people believe hell lies literally under the earth, it is *figuratively* under the earth as a lower level of existence than this one. The figurative description of hell under the earth comes naturally from association with burial. Of course, this verse might only mean Christ descended from heaven to become a man in the lower realm—earth—as Paul taught elsewhere.

If hell *is* the reference here, then Paul taught that Christ descended into it to release its captives when he died on the cross. This hell was not the final place of fire and torment spoken of in the Apocalypse, but simply the spiritual graveyard or repository of human souls who died before the Messiah completed his work on earth.

Victorious in death, the Messiah did not forget the many Jews and others who had lived faithful to God's revelation. Christians often teach that Jews were saved before Christ's crucifixion because they had faith in the *coming* Messiah. But the fact that Jesus had such a difficult time getting anyone to recognize him even when he stood right in front of them certainly indicates that people had many, sometimes opposing, understandings of the Messiah. Jews were saved by faith prior to the arrival of the Messiah, but it was not by faith in the Messiah. It was by faith in the covenant God had revealed. Those who were guaranteed a place in eternity with God were those who were faithful to God's revelation, but the revelation of the Messiah had not happened, and many probably did not understand messianic hope at all. This hope was only hinted at in passages of the Old Testament that seemed obscure at the time.

This does not mean eternity can be entered apart from the Messiah, and here is where these shadowy scriptures play a great role in Christian understanding. Though most of the faithful Jews and Gentiles who died before Christ had only a vague understanding of the Messiah, if any, the tradition of the Odes of Solomon indicates these faithful were all quick to recognize this Messiah as the ultimate object of their faith when he descended into the grave.

To be brought into the New Covenant, they had to transfer their faith, based in the Old Covenant, to the true Messiah. How else could all the faithful, before and after Christ, be joined into one unified kingdom as John has shown in his scenes of the twenty-four elders gathered around the throne of the Lamb? Unity requires that a common center holds, and that is why Lucifer's self-centeredness fractured the unity of the spiritual realm and brought chaos to earth.

Peter also seemed to recognize Christ's mysterious descent into the grave in his writing:

For Christ also hath once suffered for sins, the just for the unjust, that he might bring us to God, being put to death in the flesh, but made alive by the Spirit: By whom also he went and preached to the spirits in prison; Who at one time were disobedient, when once the longsuffering of God waited in the days of Noah, while the ark was preparing, in which few, that is, eight souls were saved by water. . . .

. . . [The Gentiles who lived according to the desires of their flesh] shall give account to him that is ready to judge the quick [living] and the dead. For for this cause was the gospel preached also to them that are dead, that they might be judged according to men in the flesh, but live according to God in the spirit.

(1 PETER 3:18–20; 4:5, 6)

Some newer translations say, "For this is the reason the gospel was preached even to those who are *now* dead." This interpretation implies that these people who *now* are dead were preached to *while* they were living. That attempts to avoid the shadowy belief that Jesus, during the long night of his death, descended into the repository of the dead, but it leaves the first part of Peter's writing unexplained: How did Jesus preach to the *spirits* who had lived in the days of Noah? Since those people had been dead for a couple of millennia before Jesus' birth, that would only be possible in the grave.

Finally, there was evidence above ground that something happened below ground, so to speak, on the day of Jesus' resurrection. One of the New Testament writers states that on the day Jesus rose from the dead, many resurrected souls were seen throughout the city of Jerusalem, as though he *had* descended into the grave and brought a great number back with him:

And the graves were opened; and many bodies of the saints which slept arose, And came out of the graves after his resurrection, and went into the holy city, and appeared unto many.

(MATTHEW 27:52, 53)

So, perhaps the cherished tradition is the true interpretation. The resurrection scene certainly indicates something major happened in the spiritual realm during the time of Jesus' death. Perhaps for the dragon, the end times had begun, regardless of how long they would play out.

If the Messiah presented himself to those who lived in the days of Noah, then he also presented himself to Gentiles, for there were no Jews in Noah's day. To those who had sought divine understanding in their earthly life, Christ's presence in the grave would have been a blazing pathway of light. But to those who had always avoided truth, the light would have been a blinding glare. And so he ascended and, in his train of light, led the captive souls of the righteous out of the grave to everlasting freedom. But

. . . the angels who kept not their proper abode, but left their own habitation, he hath reserved in everlasting chains under darkness to the judgment of the great day.

(JUDE 1:6)

John's Apocalypse reveals that the battle still continues between Satan and the people of God. Christ and his angels cast the devil and his angels out of God's presence, but the battle on earth remains and will grow in fury during the end times. Those who chose in John's time to fight the Prince of Darkness by proclaiming the Light of the World, saw their own small light snuffed by Rome. Those who take up this same battle near the end of time, should expect no less. To all these scattered, but glimmering stars— past and present and future—surrounded by such a dark night, John would say, along with the Apostle Paul,

And the God of peace shall soon crush Satan under your feet. The grace of our Lord Jesus Christ be with you. Amen.

(ROMANS 16:20)

The Dragon and the Saints of God

And the dragon was enraged with the woman, and went to make war with the remnant of her seed, who keep the com- mandments of God, and have the testi- mony of Jesus Christ.

(Revelation 12:17)

Jewish Christians, like John, considered themselves to be the true remnant of Israel's seed—her offspring, the Messiah. They were all that remained. John revealed the battle between Christ and Satan playing itself out in heavenly spheres, and only hints that it now turned against Christians. He didn't have to tell his readers how it played out in real ways on earthly turf; that battle occupied every day of their struggling lives. But for the contemporary reader, a lot of understanding of John's work can be gained from a brief look at this historic battle and the victory foretold by the Apocalypse—history to present readers but future to John's readers.

One advantage of writing in apocalyptic style is the ability to veil your intended meaning from a hostile audience by using language that is accessible only to your intended audience. John wanted to assure his followers that, even though Rome appeared to have absolute power of destruction over the meager Christian churches, the Light of the risen Son would eventually rise over Rome.

To speak directly of the defeat of Roman imperialism would be certain suicide. This may be why John depicts the empire with the literary equivalent of a political cartoon. The dragon, Satan, is used as a figure for the Roman empire, which is identified by its seven heads with seven crowns. The first head probably represented Caesar Augustus, who was the first man to be declared emperor of Rome. Augustus reigned at the birth of Christ, and the dragon is first mentioned as being alive and waiting at the birth of the woman's child. Vespasian would have been the seventh emperor, and he reigned in the time John is describing when Jerusalem was destroyed. Technically, Vespasian is the ninth to actually sit on the throne, but the two who preceded him reigned less than a year between them. The first, named Otho, seized the throne illegitimately by murdering Nero's successor. After only three months, the empire broke into civil war. With a vast part refusing to recognize him as emperor, Otho found himself fighting a losing battle against his contender, Vitellius, and he committed suicide. Vitellius then declared himself emperor. Meanwhile, none of the Eastern half of the empire recognized either Otho or Vitellius. They chose Vespasian, who was busy with his war in the East against the Jews. As a result of Vespasian's detainment, Vitellius was able to briefly occupy the throne in Rome until some of Vespasian's troops arrived to dislodge and kill him. Because neither of the pretenders, Otho nor Vitellius, were recognized by Vespasian or the Eastern half of the empire, John probably does not count them. According to Josephus, Vespasian *did* recognize Nero's successor, Galba, as legitimate emperor. Therefore, after Nero (the fifth emperor) and Galba (the sixth), Vespasian was the next in succession who was recognized by the entire empire. Even if one doesn't count Galba, since he reigned for less than a year and his reign was not recognized by all of Rome either, that would make Vespasian's son Titus the seventh. For either ruler, seven is the perfect number, since both were destroyers of Israel and Jerusalem who brought the prophetic story of ancient Israel to a close.

If John was exiled by Nero as some scholars suggest, then he probably received his apocalypse during the beginning of Vespasian's reign before Vespasian declared an end to Christian and Jewish persecution at the time when John would have been released from exile. But the following historical testimonies all indicate a later period for John's exile to the island of Patmos and his writing.

In the years after Vespasian and Titus, the empire turned its attention against the Christians again. The Church historian Eusebius describes how Vespasian's second son, Domitian, acted just like a reincarnation of Nero:

> . . . he showed himself the successor of Nero in enmity and hostility to God. He was, in fact, the second to organize persecution against us.
>
> There is ample evidence that at the time the apostle and evangelist John was still alive, and because of his testimony to the word of God was sentenced to confinement on the island of Patmos. . . .
>
> . . . Indeed, so brightly shone at that time the teaching of our faith that even historians who accepted none of our beliefs unhesitatingly recorded in their pages both the persecution and the martyrdoms to which it led. They also indicated . . . that in the fifteenth year of Domitian . . . one of the consuls at Rome . . . was with many others, because of their testimony to Christ, taken to the island of Pontia as a punishment.[3]

> After fifteen years of Domitian's rule Nerva succeeded to the throne. By vote of the Roman senate Domitian's honours were removed, and those unjustly banished returned to their homes and had their property restored to them. . . . At that time too [A.D. 96] the apostle John, after his exile on the island, resumed residence at Ephesus, as early Christian tradition records.[4]

The writer of the apocalypse, according to Eusebius and earlier church historians whom he quotes, even outlived Nerva, surviving into the times of the emperor Trajan, who began the third wave of persecutions against the Church:

> In Asia, moreover, there still remained alive the one whom Jesus loved, apostle and evangelist alike, John, who had directed the churches there since his return from exile on the island, following Domitian's death. That he survived so long is proved

by the evidence of two witnesses who could hardly be doubted, ambassadors as they were of the orthodoxy of the Church—Irenaeus and Clement of Alexandria. In Book II of his *Heresies Answered,* Irenaeus writes: "All the clergy who in Asia came in contact with John, the Lord's disciple, testify that John taught the truth to them; for he remained with them till Trajan's time."[5]

The storm of persecutions against Christians that began under Nero raged for two and a half centuries in the iron empire. The clouds broke with intervals of hope and peace under one imperial sun only to close in twice as dark under the next. Though Christians prayed, the heavens were bronze, or so it must have seemed. Prayers for deliverance echoed back without answer. Instead of rescuing his faithful from persecution, God gave them power to stand. Testimonies from the times would indicate God intervened in ways that proved the truth of the Christian faith, but not so as to stop their tribulation. Jesus had warned that the price for following him would be high, but who could have guessed just how relentless it would be, according to Eusebius:

> The arrests went on, and day after day those who were worthy filled up the number of the martyrs. . . . At the soldier's instigation they were falsely accused of . . . Oedipean incest, and things we ought never to speak or think about, or even believe that such things ever happened among human beings. When these rumors spread, people all raged like wild beasts against us, so that even those who because of blood-relationship had previously exercised restraint now turned on us, grinding their teeth with fury. So was proved true the saying of our Lord: "The time will come when whoever kills you will think he is doing a service to God." From then on the holy martyrs endured punishments beyond all description. . . .
>
> When we were all afraid and [a woman named Blandina] was in agony lest she should be unable even to make a bold confession of Christ because of bodily weakness [i.e., inability to withstand her persecution], Blandina was filled with such power that those who took it in turns to subject her to every kind of torture from morning to night were exhausted by their efforts and confessed themselves beaten—they could think of nothing else to do to her. They were amazed that she was still breathing, for her whole body was mangled and her wounds gaped. . . . The blessed woman, wrestling magnificently, grew in strength as she proclaimed her faith . . . uttering the words: "I am a Christian: we do nothing to be ashamed of."
>
> . . . When the tyrant's instruments of torture had been utterly defeated by Christ through endurance of the blessed saints, the devil resorted to other devices—confinement in the darkness of a filthy prison; clamping the feet in the stocks, stretched apart to the fifth hole; and the other agonies which warders when angry and full of the devil are apt to inflict on helpless prisoners. Thus the majority were suffocated in prison—those whom the Lord wished to depart in this way, so revealing his glory. Some, though tortured so cruelly that even if they received

every care it seemed impossible for them to survive, lived on in the prison, deprived of all human attention but strengthened by the Lord and fortified in body and soul, stimulating and encouraging the rest. But the young ones who had been recently arrested and had not previously undergone physical torture could not bear the burden of confinement, and died in prison.

. . . Marturus, Sanctus, Blandina, and Attalus were taken into the amphitheatre to face the wild beasts. . . . Again they ran the gauntlet of whips, in accordance with local custom; they were mauled by beasts, and endured every torment that the frenzied mob on one side or the other demanded and howled for, culminating in the iron chair which roasted their flesh and suffocated them with the reek.

. . . Despite their prolonged and terrible ordeal, life still lingered; but in the end they were sacrificed, after being all day long a spectacle to the world. . . . But Blandina was hung on a post and exposed as food for the wild beasts. . . . She looked as if she was hanging in the form of a cross, and . . . stimulated great enthusiasm in those undergoing their ordeal, who in their agony saw with their outward eyes in the person of their sister the One who was crucified for them, that He might convince those who believe in Him that any man who has suffered for the glory of Christ has fellowship for ever with the living God. As none of the beasts had yet touched her she was taken down from the post and returned to the [jail].

. . . On the last day of the sports Blandina was again brought in, and with her Ponticus, a lad of about fifteen. . . . Ponticus was encouraged by his sister in Christ . . . and he bravely endured every punishment till he gave back his spirit to God. Last of all, like a noble mother who had encouraged her children and sent them before her in triumph to the King, blessed Blandina herself . . . hastened to rejoin them, rejoicing and exulting at her departure as if invited to a wedding supper, not thrown to the beasts. After the whips, after the beasts, after the griddle, she was finally dropped into a basket and thrown to a bull. Time after time the animal tossed her, but she was indifferent now to all that happened to her. Then she, too, was sacrificed, while the heathen themselves admitted that never yet had they known a woman suffer so much or so long.

Not even this was enough to satisfy their insane cruelty to God's people. Goaded by a wild beast [the dragon] . . . the dead bodies became the next object of their vindictiveness. Their defeat did not humble them . . . rather it inflamed their bestial fury, and governor and people vented on us the same inexcusable hatred . . . They threw out the remains left by the beasts and the fire, some torn to ribbons, some burnt to cinders, and set a military guard to watch for days on end the trunks and severed heads of the rest, denying burial to them also. Some raged and ground their teeth at them, longing to take some further revenge on them. . . .

Thus the martyrs' bodies, after six days' exposure to every kind of insult and to the open sky, were finally burnt to ashes and swept by these wicked men into the Rhone which flows near by, that not even a trace of them might be seen on the earth again. . . . "Now let's see if they'll rise again, and if their god can help them and save them from our hands."[6]

Again, the letter above has been greatly abridged, lest the endless chronicling of evil weary the reader. But so went the persecutions of Rome decade after decade, and Christians, Jew or otherwise, experienced the full rage of the dragon just as it had been poured out on their Jewish brethren under Nero and Vespasian. As the Apocalypse had warned, "Woe to the earth, for the devil had been cast down to her." How could the Christians ever have made sense of such times without John's Apocalypse written in advance to give them hope of victory? They would surely have felt God was punishing them for their new beliefs, and the new faith would have died as the mere cult that earlier Jews had claimed it was.

For early Christians, the final decade of their persecutions came under the emperor Diocletian. Eusebius writes:

Everything indeed has been fulfilled in my time; I saw with my own eyes the places of worship torn down from top to bottom, to the very foundations, the inspired holy Scriptures committed to the flames in the middle of the public squares, and the pastors of the churches hiding disgracefully. . . .

Then, then it was that many rulers of the churches bore up heroically under horrible torments. . . . What could I say that would do full justice to them? I could tell of thousands who showed magnificent enthusiasm for the worship of the God of the universe, not only from the beginning of the general persecution, but much earlier when peace was still secure. For at long last the one who had received the authority [alluding to the apocalyptic beast] was . . . awaking from the deepest sleep, after making many attempts—as yet secret and surreptitious—against the churches.

Nothing could be more amazing than the fearless courage of these saints under such duress. . . . You could see a youngster not yet twenty standing without fetters, spreading out his arms in the form of a cross, and with a mind unafraid and unshakable occupying himself in the most unhurried prayers . . . not budging in the least and not retreating from the spot where he stood, though bears and panthers breathing fury . . . almost touched his very flesh. Yet by some supernatural, mysterious power their mouths were stopped, and they ran back again to the rear. . . . At last, when these animals had launched their terrible varied assaults, the martyrs were one and all butchered with the sword, and . . . given to the waves of the sea.

I was in these places, and saw many of the executions for myself. . . . So many were killed on a single day that the axe, blunted and worn out by the slaughter, was broken in pieces, while the exhausted executioners had to be periodically relieved. . . . No sooner had the first batch been sentenced, than others from every side would jump on to the platform in front of the judge and proclaim themselves

Christians. They paid no heed to torture in all its terrifying forms, but undaunted spoke boldly of their devotion to the God of the universe . . . they sang and sent up hymns of thanksgiving to the God of the universe till their very last breath. . . . Throughout the ten-year period of the persecution . . . the seas were unnavigable. . . . Famine and pestilence . . . followed.[7]

And it all ended the way it had begun in the early days under Nero: According to rumor, Diocletian burned his own palace, then blamed Christians for the flames. This began the final ten years of hunting. Whole families were burned in their own homes. In one case, an entire town had declared itself Christian, so it was surrounded by Roman legions and torched. Every citizen either perished in the flames, or they died at the hands of Romans as they tried to escape. When the last smoke settled across the empire, thousands, maybe hundreds of thousands, of Christians had been murdered.

A dragon had, indeed, been hurled down to earth at the crucifixion of the Messiah, and all the dragon's minions joined him. Yet the louder the dragon roared, the more amazed the populous was that mere humans could stand up to him. Greater and greater numbers became Christians—knowing they, too, would face the dragon—until they reached critical mass and a miracle occurred.

Eusebius writes of his own times:

When it became evident that we were in the kindly, beneficent keeping of divine and heavenly grace, an amazing thing happened—our rulers, the very people who had long been the driving force behind the campaign against us, changed their minds . . . and solemnly recanted, extinguishing by means of decrees sympathetic to us . . . the fire of persecution which had raged so fiercely. . . . It was no human initiative that brought this about—no pity, as might be suggested, or humanity on the part of the rulers. . . . It was a manifestation of divine providence, which . . . took action against the perpetrator of these crimes. [Galerius, co-regent of the Eastern empire] . . . was pursued by a divinely ordained punishment, which began with his flesh and went on to his soul. Without warning, suppurative inflammation broke out round the middle of his genitals, then a deep-seated fistular ulcer: these ate their way incurably into his inmost bowels. From them came a teeming indescribable mass of worms, and a sickening smell was given off; for the whole of his hulking body, thanks to over-eating, had been transformed even before his illness into a huge lump of flabby fat, which then decomposed and presented those who came near with a revolting and horrifying sight. Of the doctors, some were unable to endure the overpowering and extraordinary stench, and were executed on the spot. . . .

As he wrestled with this terrible sickness, he was filled with remorse for his cruel treatment of God's servants. So he pulled himself together, and after first making open confession to the God of the universe, he called his court officials and ordered them to lose no time in stopping the persecution of Christians, and by an imperial . . . decree to stimulate the building of churches . . . with the addition of prayers for the Emperor's Majesty. Action immediately followed the word, and imperial ordinances were published in all the cities.[8]

The death of Galerius echoes the death of Antiochus Epiphanes. Evil breeds the worms of its own consumption. Whether it was the hand of God or the natural result of Roman overindulgence and vice that brought the death of Galerius, the political change is a documented fact of history. The decree by Galerius, granting peace to the Christians, ends:

Therefore, in view of this our clemency, they are in duty bound to beseech their own god for our security, and that of the state and of themselves, in order that in every way the state may be preserved in health and they may be able to live free from anxiety in their own homes.[9]

After Diocletian and Galerius passed out of this world, the new emperor, Constantine the Great, in A.D. 313 saw a luminous cross in the sky and declared Christianity the official religion of the Roman empire. With a single decree, Christianity spread throughout the Roman world. And the most important positions of government went to outstanding Christians. When Constantine moved the seat of government from Rome to the new capital, Constantinople, his vacancy of Rome made the most revered position in the ancient capital that of the bishop of Rome—the pope. And so the head of the local church became the head of the city that had long persecuted the people of God throughout the world.

A Revolution in the Understanding of Prophecy

With the door to Christianity wide open, understanding of prophecy began to change, especially later under St. Augustine. Perhaps the world wouldn't end in sudden destruction of evil by the Messiah. The darkness of Rome had ended, and the dawning light of Christianity was now free to sweep round the world until every nation came under that light. With the elements of persecution pertaining to the past, all that remained of the Apocalypse was the bright hope of a new heaven and a new earth. Nothing could stop the followers of Christ from changing the world now that they ruled it. It was their destiny to bring on this new world through the avenues that government afforded.

If the dragon had been seething at his loss, it was not for long. In the marriage of Church and State, he smelled the sweet bouquet of political intoxication all over again. He breathed in the ripe air and could feel the temptations of wealth and power and prestige, ready to be offered anew. Christians were now playing in the dragon's own lair—playing with the stuff he knew best and that they knew not at all.

As power and prestige grew, so did the human will to compromise in order to keep it. Compromises would be made to keep from upsetting the emperor so that Christianity could retain his favor. The imperial power now available presented an easy answer to the spreading of truth. Zeal to transform the world was a noble desire that could be corrupted to rationalize all sorts of evil so long as the end was good. Out of the marriage of Church and State a new kind of imperial beast was born. The Church joined the very imperialism that prophecy condemned.

A radical change occurred in how prophetic destiny was understood. In short, the Apocalypse was seen as proclaiming the right of Christians to rule the world as the rightful heirs to Christ's power and his kingdom. The Church eventually claimed the right to install future emperors and kings, giving kings the divine right to rule, which became the primary pillar that supported all political structure. But the pillar of divine right twisted under the weight of such power and became the divine right for kings and rulers in the Church to do as they pleased, for they were God's authority on earth. If there was any difference between this new form of imperialism and the emperor worship of ancient Rome, it was a subtle shade.

The details of the Dark Ages that ensued are saved for another chapter, but the fact that the world has continued long beyond the days of the Dark Ages and the later Holy Roman Empire shows that the kingdom of this world did not become the kingdom of Christ in the manner Augustine had predicted. The kingdom could never come by the forced conversions of Jews or the burning of heretics—the dragon's own tactics. Pagan Rome was overcome by the blood of the Lamb and the seemingly endless flow of blood from his followers because they did not love life so much as to shrink from death. The dragon and his strongholds of power were overcome by the word of their testimony.

Chapter 15

Antichrist:

A New World Order

After describing his vision of Satan as a seven-headed Roman dragon pursuing the people of God, John describes a similar beast rising out of the sea. His visual clues indicate that he is making a transition to another time entirely—a time which many interpreters understand as referring to the climax of history at Christ's return:

> *And I stood upon the sand of the sea, and saw a beast rise out of the sea, having seven heads and ten horns, and upon his horns ten crowns, and upon his heads the name of blasphemy.*
>
> (REVELATION 13:1)

Some versions of the Bible say that the *dragon* stood upon the sand of the sea, which establishes a clearer connection between the last beast and this present one. (In the original language it's hard to tell who stands on the shore—John or the dragon.)

The similarities between the dragon and the beast which John watches rise from the sea are obvious, yet, there is a subtle but all important difference. When John first saw the dragon with seven heads and ten horns, it had *seven* crowns—one for each head. The seven-headed beast that rises from the sea has *ten* crowns—one for each horn—and this time the horns are mentioned before the heads. This is a strong clue that the image has shifted to a time when the imperial heads of Rome are no longer crowned. Instead of seven rulers, there are now ten, who reign in a time that parallels the previous story of the Lady and the Dragon in Revelation, chapter 12. This parallel is made clear by showing the dragon of the last story looking on from the shore of the sea and by the similarities between the beast and the dragon. The vision has moved from the times near the birth of Christ and his ascension into heaven to the time of his return.

If the exit of the Messiah from this world and his return are parallel times governed by similar beasts, shouldn't God's people expect similar treatment to that which occurred under Rome? If God did not remove his people from tribulation at the dawn of Christianity but, instead, allowed two and a half centuries of testing by fire to refine them and to reveal the underlying truth of their convictions to the world, why should his people today expect to be removed from end-time tribulations?

The one clear theme that plays throughout John's book is the constant reminder that Jesus' followers must conquer evil by remaining true to the faith at all costs. To support that faith, the darkness of John's own times is penetrated over and over by images of a future glory that awaits those who persevere.

The Image of The Beast

And the beast which I saw was like a leopard, and his feet were as the feet of a bear, and his mouth as the mouth of a lion: and the dragon gave him his power, and his throne, and great authority. And I saw one of his heads as it were wounded to death; and his deadly wound was healed: and all the world wondered after the beast. And they worshipped the dragon which gave power to the beast: and they worshipped the beast, saying, Who is like the beast? who is able to make war with him?

(Revelation 13:2–4)

Here the connection between the former dragon and the present beast is made clear. The dragon still plays a role in the story. The spirit of the age in ancient Rome, the *zeitgeist,* was the one who was cast out of heaven. Rome was, so to speak, simply one of the dragon's incarnations.

The image of the seven-headed dragon or serpent came straight out of Babylon. The Jews undoubtedly became familiar with it during their seventy-year exile there. Babylonian mythology says of their god Baal,

Thou didst slay Lotan the primeval serpent, didst make an end of the crooked serpent, the foul-fanged with seven heads.[1]

The Babylonian serpent's name, Lotan, may have been the Jewish source for the mythical beast Leviathan, spoken of in the Bible:

In that day the LORD with his sore and great and strong sword shall punish leviathan the piercing serpent, even leviathan that crooked serpent; and he shall slay the dragon that is in the sea.

(Isaiah 27:1)

For God is my King of old, working salvation in the midst of the earth. Thou didst divide the sea by thy strength: thou didst break the heads of the dragons in the waters. Thou didst break the head of leviathan in pieces, and didst give him to be food to the people inhabiting the wilderness. Thou didst cleave the fountain and the flood: thou didst dry up mighty rivers.

(Psalm 74:12–15)

The seven-headed serpent of the sea is the opposite of the seven spirits of God shown in the Apocalypse, but it is not an equal opposite. For Jews, floods represented God's judgment against the earth as happened in the days of Noah. (It was the dragon in John's mythic tale who spewed out a river to destroy the woman.) But water, as pointed out earlier, is also an archetype for the origin of life. In the Genesis story, God's Spirit hovered over the waters of the deep throughout creation. So, the world and all of its life emerged from water but later was submerged in that same water, which nearly brought its end. The Spirit (whom John describes as seven spirits) was with God at the creation of the world and is the fulness of creative power. But the seven-headed serpent of the sea, Lotan (or perhaps Leviathan in Hebrew), represents a spirit who is the fulness of destructive force, seeking to destroy all the world. God does not create destruction (in fact, "create destruction" is a self-contradicting term), but he does allow evil to burn itself out by consuming all who seek after it.

The similarity between John's dragon or beast and the Babylonian serpent, Lotan, seems deliberate; otherwise, the Apocalypse would not refer later to the dragon's kingdom as "Babylon the Great." For Jews, like John, Babylon was the epitome of destructive evil, especially in connection with the destruction of Jerusalem. The similarity in these mythical beasts reflects the repeated patterns of evil times and points to a common force behind all of those times in Jewish and Christian history.

The beast depicted here in the Apocalypse is a conglomeration of beasts seen by the prophet Daniel during his Babylonian captivity. The prophet Daniel dreamt of a terrible future while lying on his bed. His dream was much like the dream that his king, Nebuchadnezzar, had of the statue with four sections representing four successive empires. Only in Daniel's dream, the four empires were represented by four terrifying beasts. The first three empires were Babylon, Persia, and Greece, represented by a lion, a bear, and a leopard. The fourth is the worst and gives Daniel the most trouble:

After this I saw in the night visions, and behold a fourth beast, dreadful and terrible, and strong exceedingly; and it had great iron teeth: it devoured and broke in pieces, and stamped the remainder with its feet: and it was different from all the beasts that were before it; and it had ten horns. (Daniel 7:7)

This beast represented Rome. The beast John now describes in the Apocalypse sounds similar, but it incorporates elements of all the beasts Daniel saw leading up to Rome—the lion, the bear, and the leopard. It derives its power from the same evil that was behind all these empires. And it has ten horns. Some scholars have seen the beast that comes out of the sea as a symbol of Rome, but John already blended Satan and Rome so perfectly in the image of the seven-headed dragon that he would only cloud his symbolism by coming up with more renditions for the same empire.

It's also hard to find a clear match for the ten horns in any of the emperors of Rome. Rome did not break up into ten kingdoms, nor is there any succession of ten Roman emperors that stands out as a group in Roman history. In fact, much of John's Apocalypse cannot be accounted for by history—clear references to the return of Christ, the resurrection of the dead, the end of the world and even the universe—so that the book forces futuristic interpretations in many places. Given the strongly hinted time change represented by the shifting of the crowns from the heads to the horns and the exchange of power from the dragon to the beast, it's not likely John is referring to any Roman empire he had experienced.

But, then, Daniel's representation of the Roman empire revealed a similar leap in time:

I considered the horns, and, behold, there came up among them another little horn, before whom there were three of the first [ten] horns plucked up by the roots: and, behold, in this horn were eyes like the eyes of a man, and a mouth speaking great things. . . .

I Daniel was grieved in my spirit in the midst of my body, and the visions of my head troubled me. I came near to one of them that stood by, and asked him the truth of all this. So he told me, and made me know the interpretation of the things. These great beasts, which are four, are four kings [kingdoms], which shall arise out of the earth. . . . Then I would know the truth of the fourth beast, which was different from all the others, exceeding dreadful, whose teeth were of iron, and his nails of brass; which devoured, broke in pieces, and stamped the remainder with his feet; And of the ten horns that were in his head, and of the other which came up, and before whom three fell; even of that horn that had eyes, and a mouth that spoke very great things, whose look was more stout than his fellows. I beheld, and the same horn made war with the saints, and prevailed against them; Until the Ancient of days came, and judgment was given to the saints of the most High; and the time came that the saints possessed the kingdom. Thus he said, The fourth beast shall be the fourth kingdom upon earth, which shall be different from all kingdoms, and shall devour the whole earth, and shall tread it down, and break it in pieces. And the ten horns out of this kingdom are ten kings that shall arise: and another shall rise after them; and he shall be different from the first, and he shall subdue three kings.

(DANIEL 7:8, 15–17, 19–24)

So Daniel's vision of Rome as a beast devouring the whole earth, treading upon it, and breaking it to pieces also jumps to the end of time when "the Ancient of days came, and judgment was given to the saints of the most High; and the time came that the saints possessed the kingdom." So, the ten horns arise at the end of days. They appear to be ten kings that rule simultaneously over a confederacy of nations because three of them are pushed out by the little horn that grows more stout than its three predecessors.

In each vision, there is a strong sense of one individual who dominates the ten kings of his time. In John's vision, the dragon that represented the Satan-possessed Roman empire gives his power over to the beast with ten horns, but then the focus shifts to a single ruler, just as it did in Daniel. And, just as Daniel's ruler had "eyes like the eyes of a man, and a mouth speaking great things," John also writes of a leader with a boasting and slanderous mouth:

And there was given to him a mouth speaking great things and blasphemies; and power was given to him to continue forty and two months. And he opened his mouth in blasphemy against God, to blaspheme his name, and his tabernacle, and them that dwell in heaven.

(REVELATION 13:5, 6)

Then, just as Daniel wrote, "I beheld, and the same horn made war with the saints, and prevailed against them," John also writes,

And it was given to him to make war with the saints, and to overcome them: and power was given him over all kindreds, and tongues, and nations. And all that dwell upon the earth shall worship him, whose names are not written in the book of life of the Lamb slain from the foundation of the world. If any man hath an ear, let him hear. He that leadeth into captivity shall go into captivity: he that killeth with the sword must be killed with the sword. Here is the patience and the faith of the saints.

(REVELATION 13:7–10)

Because of a grammatical variations between copies of the original manuscripts, newer versions of the Bible sometimes translate the last sentence quite differently. The New International Version, for example, says,

If anyone is to go into captivity, into captivity he will go. If anyone is to be killed with the sword, with the sword he will be killed.

(REVELATION 13:10A)

THE ANTICHRIST

Here is the one John described earlier who will kill the two witnesses, and here it is made clear that the total number killed will be far more than two. To underscore the seriousness of this final persecution and to clarify that it will happen to the true Church of Christ, John repeats a phrase that he used with all of the seven churches in his own time: "If any man hath an ear, let him hear." Following the newer translations, those who are to go into captivity will be taken into captivity. In other words, they can expect no physical salvation from God in these times. And those who are to be killed by the sword *will* be killed by the sword. It will be for Jesus' followers in those days just as it was for the seven churches in John's own time. Just as Christians were killed for not worshiping the emperor, so they will be killed in these times. History will repeat itself. The same beast looms behind each of these human empires. There will be no reprieve "until the Ancient of days [comes], and judgment [is] given to the saints of the most High." Because there is no help from on high, John writes that this will require "the patience and the faith of the saints."

And here is where the exalted words written by Daniel about Antiochus Epiphanes and perhaps Titus also find their pattern repeating near the end of time:

And out of one of [the horns] came forth a little horn, which became exceeding great, toward the south, and toward the east, and toward the pleasant land. And it grew great, even to the host of heaven; and it cast down some of the host and of the stars to the ground, and stamped upon them. Yea, he magnified himself even to the prince of the host, and by him the daily sacrifice was taken away, and the place of his sanctuary was cast down. . . . And his power shall be mighty, but not by his own power: and he shall destroy wonderfully, and shall prosper, and continue, and shall destroy the mighty and the holy people.

(DANIEL 8:9–11, 24)

The destruction of the temple lasted three and a half years under Antiochus Epiphanes. The destruction of Israel lasted three and a half years under Titus until the second temple was destroyed. Now John talks about a third period lasting three and a half years when the holy people will be overcome. John showed how Satan cast down a third of the hosts from heaven. Daniel said the same for Antiochus in words far bigger than the man could fill. Sacrifice under the old system represented worship, and John shows that worship is taken from God by this beast.

Here, then, is the Antichrist. He is anti-Christ in that he blasphemes (slanders) the name of Christ. He is anti-Christ in that he steals the worship that belongs to Christ and gains the whole world's worship for himself, except, of course, the worship of the true saints. And that is why he is also anti-Christ in that he incarcerates the followers of Christ and kills them.

Daniel says the actual ruler who does these things will not accomplish them by his own power. He will do it by a far greater evil that towers over him. John has said the same thing: The dragon gave his power to the beast. Just as Christ was filled with the Spirit of God, this ruler is possessed by the spirit of Satan, the dragon who cast down the stars of heaven. The implication is that this final ruler is Satan incarnate.

Thus, Daniel finished this part of his vision, saying,

> And he shall speak great words against the most High, and shall wear out the saints of the most High, and think to change times and laws: and they shall be given into his hand until a time and times and the dividing of time. But the judgment shall sit, and they shall take away his dominion, to consume and to destroy it to the end. . . . Here is the end of the matter. As for me Daniel, my thoughts much troubled me, and my countenance changed in me: but I kept the matter in my heart.
>
> (DANIEL 7:25, 26, 28)

These verses may imply that the Antichrist, or the spirit behind him, tries to change the destiny of earth. It is God who determines the timing of world events, so for this beast to try to change the set times and laws of the universe is to rise up against God and usurp the highest authority. But God has already determined his saints will only be subjected to this beast for "a time and times and the dividing of time [i.e., half a time]":

> God that made the world and all things in it, seeing that he is Lord of heaven and earth, dwelleth not in temples made with hands. . . . And hath made of one blood all nations of men to dwell on all the face of the earth, and hath determined the times before appointed, and the bounds of their habitation. . . . And the times of [humanity's sinful] ignorance God overlooked; but now commandeth all men every where to repent: Because he hath appointed a day, when he will judge the world in righteousness by that man whom he hath ordained [Christ Jesus]; of which he hath given assurance to all men, in that he hath raised him from the dead. (ACTS 17:24, 26, 30, 31)

Perhaps the Antichrist seeks to change the short forty-two months allotted to him. Over and over, John and Daniel emphasize three and a half years with reference to the end times. Because the Antichrist is a twisted copy of the real Christ, his public reign is apparently ordained to last for three and a half years, just as Jesus' ministry lasted about that long. This appears to match up perfectly with the three and a half years when the two witnesses walked the earth before they were killed and brings the story back to where John left off. When the two witnesses were killed and resurrected after three and a half days that symbolized their ministry, the seventh trumpet sounded, announcing the return of Christ—the event that determines the Antichrist's appointed end. So perhaps the two witnesses are the last of many saints who will die (or represent the many saints who will die) before the last trumpet sounds.

As to the great words the Antichrist will speak against the Most High, which are his trademark in speech, John gives some clues in his other writings:

> Who is a liar but he that denieth that Jesus is the Christ? He is antichrist, that denieth the Father and the Son.
>
> (1 JOHN 2:22)

> Beloved, believe not every spirit, but try the spirits whether they are of God: because many false prophets have gone out into the world. By this ye know the Spirit of God: Every spirit that confesseth that Jesus Christ hath come in the flesh is from God: And every spirit that confesseth not that Jesus Christ is come in the flesh is not from God: and this is that spirit of antichrist, of which ye have heard that it should come; and even now already it is in the world.
>
> (1 JOHN 4:1–3)

> For many deceivers have entered into the world, who confess not Jesus Christ as coming in the flesh. This is a deceiver and an antichrist.   (2 JOHN 1:7)

And, so, the Antichrist and the two witnesses will be speaking in direct opposition to each other, for the mission of the witnesses is to confess Christ to the world, and the need of the Antichrist is to deny him. For this aggravation, he will finally manage to kill them by the end of his reign, but they will be resurrected at the announced return of Christ by the seventh trumpet.

The spirit of Antichrist has been in the world since he was cast down out of heaven. In the end times, however, one will rise who will be Antichrist incarnate. He will be the fulness of all the antichrists who have ever lived. And his trademark will be his adamant denial of the true Christ.

> Let no man deceive you by any means: for that day [of Christ's return] shall not come, except there come a falling away first, and that man of sin be revealed, the son of perdition; Who opposeth and exalteth himself above all that is called God, or that is worshipped; so that he as God sitteth in the temple of God, showing himself that he is God. Remember ye not, that, when I was yet with you, I told you these things? And now ye know what restraineth that he might be revealed in his time. For the mystery of iniquity doth already work: only he who now restraineth will do so, until he be taken out of the way. And then shall that Wicked be revealed, whom the Lord shall consume with the spirit of his mouth, and shall

destroy with the brightness of his coming: Even him, whose coming is after the
working of Satan with all power and
signs and lying wonders, And with all
deception of unrighteousness in them
that perish; because they received not the
love of the truth, that they might be
saved. And for this cause God shall send
them strong delusion, that they should
believe a lie: That they all may be
damned who believed not the truth, but
had pleasure in unrighteousness.

(2 THESSALONIANS 2:3–12)

If removal of the one that "restraineth" refers to God's Holy Spirit, as some think, then the Holy Spirit will be removed when those he indwells—the two witnesses (and all of God's people)—are taken out of the world by their death or their rapture. Without their interfering Light, the Antichrist will have no opposition to his darkness and will reveal his true identity to the world (or it will be revealed for him), perhaps causing enormous fear among all who have followed him.

During his reign, the Antichrist will polarize the world into those who believe in him and those who believe in Jesus Christ. There will be no others, for John has said all the world will follow him. It is in this sense that God gives the world a lie. He allows Satan to work such great wonders while dwelling in the "temple of God." This phrase may mean inhabiting a human body, as Paul used the term more than once (for God's spirit dwells in human temples); or it may mean the Antichrist is ensconced within a corrupted arm of the Church. Only those who are "written in the Book of Life" will recognize his anti-Christian spirit. However it plays out, the end result on earth is this: the saints will die at his hands, and the living will be damned.

THE RESURRECTION OF THE ANTICHRIST

And I beheld another beast coming up
out of the earth; and he had two horns
like a lamb, and he spoke as a dragon.
And he exerciseth all the power of the
first beast before him, and causeth the
earth and them who dwell in it to worship the first beast, whose deadly wound
was healed. And he doeth great wonders,
so that he maketh fire come down from
heaven on the earth in the sight of men,
And deceiveth them that dwell on the
earth by the means of those miracles
which he had power to do in the sight of
the beast; saying to them that dwell on
the earth, that they should make an image to the beast, which had the wound by
a sword, and lived. And he had power to
give life to the image of the beast, that the
image of the beast should both speak,
and cause that as many as would not
worship the image of the beast should be
killed. (REVELATION 13:11–15)

Twice now, John has mentioned that the first beast has received a mortal wound, yet lived. ("And I saw one of his heads as it were wounded to death; and his deadly wound was healed.") Does this represent the resurrection of an individual or the resurrection of an ancient empire? Of course, John could mean something more figurative—something seemingly more plausible, such as an individual who died politically and then regained power—but, then, why would the whole world be astonished? (". . . his deadly wound was healed: and all the world wondered after the beast. And they worshipped the dragon which gave power to the beast.") The worldwide impact created by the reappearance of the beast leads one to believe in something far more fantastic than mere political revival.

Since Christ was resurrected, and the Antichrist mimics Christ, why shouldn't he or it mimic Christ in every way? Of course, the resurrection of the Antichrist from a mortal wound would likely be counterfeit like everything else about the Antichrist. This so-called miracle could be something much more scientific.

This is the first generation where the stuff of futuristic nightmares, like cloning, has become scientific reality. It is virtually no more difficult to clone one kind of mammal than another. The cloning of sheep in 1997 means all that is necessary to clone a human being is a perfectly preserved specimen of the individual's DNA (genetic code), a live human egg, a surrogate mother, and a laboratory.

Many scientists already see no ethical problem with human cloning. Some even see it as an evolutionary imperative. One American scientist, Richard Seed, announced on National Public Radio on January 6, 1998, that he and his colleagues planned to begin work on human cloning immediately. Seed announced his intentions to establish numerous laboratories that will offer cloning on a commercial basis to interested DNA donors. If the U.S. Congress passes laws to forbid human cloning, Seed said he would simply set up shop offshore. In the words of Richard Seed,

> We are going to become one with God. We are going to have almost as much knowledge and almost as much power as God. Cloning and the reprogramming of DNA is the first serious step in becoming one with God.[2]

Is there any scientific reason to assume human cloning hasn't already been done—if not by Seed then by some other? One company, Advanced Cell Technology in Massachusetts, has already begun cloning human cells. (Cloned in cow eggs, the resulting tissue is 99 percent human and 1 percent cow.)

Will the test tubes and secret refrigerators left behind by Josef Mengele yield the world's future despot—the image of a previous beast revived and made able to speak again?

The early twentieth century provided a bitter foretaste of the very kind of new world order John has described. The first beast represented imperial power and the specific person who rules the final empire. The second beast represents some kind of occult religion and probably the specific representative of that religion. (Its horns are said to be "like a lamb's," calling to mind the earlier image of the Messiah, but it speaks the words of the dragon, so what comes out of it is Satanic. Since lambs have nubbins for horns and the dragon was red, it's not hard to see where the old image of the devil as a red being with nubbin horns came from. But this is not the devil. This is his spokesman, and the horns do not mean he will look evil. Just the opposite. They probably mean that to many he will appear like the Lamb, Jesus Christ. He is the dragon in lamb's clothing in so much as he speaks for the dragon and performs signs and wonders on his behalf.)

The marriage of raw imperial power to occult religion can be found in one of the worst antichrists in history, and it is no wonder that many around the world in the twentieth century claimed he was *the* Antichrist. Adolf Hitler tried to eradicate God's people, the Jews, and likely would have done the same to God's people, the Christians, once his power was consolidated. During the rise of the Third Reich, however, he could not afford to divide his country's unity by arousing the sleeping Lutheran Church since so many Germans were Lutheran.

Hitler's designs for the Jewish people hardly need restating. While the Church in Germany was almost completely silent or even supportive of the führer, a few Christians were deeply disturbed by what was being done to the Jews. Dietrich Bonhoeffer was martyred for opposing the Nazi will. Bonhoeffer was a Protestant pastor who joined the German Resistance against the Nazi Party because he believed Hitler was the Antichrist (or *an* antichrist). Bonhoeffer played a central role in the assassination attempts against Adolf Hitler. He also helped smuggle Jews out of Germany and into Switzerland. Eventually he was imprisoned by the Gestapo and finally killed—about a month before Hitler committed suicide.

Louis Pauwels and Jacques Bergier, in their book, *The Morning of the Magicians,* describe Hitler's own messianic ambitions which eventually would have had to confront the Christian Messiah if he was to claim worldwide supremacy:

> [Hitler's] ambition, and the mission with which he believed himself to be entrusted, reached far beyond the boundaries of politics and patriotism: As he said himself: "I had to encourage 'national' feelings for reasons of expediency. . . . The day will come when even here in Germany what is known as 'nationalism' will practically have ceased to exist. What will take its place in the world will be a universal society of masters and overlords."[3]

> [Hitler's associate and president of the Nazi Danzig Senate, Herman] Rauschning . . . was alarmed by the things Hitler sometimes allowed himself to say. . . . "There would be an upheaval on our planet of which we, the uninitiated, would be unable to understand the full implications." . . . The only way in which he [Hitler] could explain the miracle of his own destiny was by attributing it to the action of unseen forces—the same forces to which he owed his superhuman vocation of having to preach a new Gospel to humanity.[4]

[One of Hitler's] dreams, which was also an obsession, was to change life on Earth everywhere. . . . He once said to Rauschning: "Our revolution is a new stage or, rather, the final stage in an evolution which will end by abolishing history. . . ." Or again, "You know nothing about me; my party comrades have no conception of the dreams which haunt me. . . . The world has reached a turning point. . . . What is happening is something more than the advent of a new religion."[5]

Another book, *The Occult and the Third Reich*, gives the following quotation, also reported by Rauschning:

[Hitler] woke up nights shouting convulsively. . . . Sitting on the edge of his bed, he is as though paralyzed. He is seized with panic which makes him tremble so violently that the bed shakes. He utters confused, unintelligible vociferations. He gasps for breath as though about to suffocate. . . . "It's him! It's him! He's here!" His lips had turned blue. He was dripping with sweat. Suddenly, he uttered some numbers which made no sense, then some words, then bits of sentences. It was frightening. . . . Then, all of a sudden, he screamed: "There! Over there! In the corner! Who is it?" He was jumping up and down, and he was howling.[6]

Were these the ravings of a mad mind or a possessed mind? Had Hitler made a Faustian pact with the devil? Or did the author of *The Occult and the Third Reich* or Rauschning, himself, embellish this tale? Denis de Rougemont, a highly respected Swiss writer who founded the European Cultural Foundation, said of Hitler:

Some people think, from having experienced in his presence a feeling of horror and an impression of some supernatural power, that he is the seat of "Thrones, Dominations and Powers," by which St. Paul meant those secondary spirits which can descend into any ordinary man and occupy him like a garrison. I have heard him pronounce one of his great speeches. Where do the superhuman powers he shows on these occasions come from? It is quite obvious that a force of this kind does not belong to the individual, and indeed could not even manifest itself unless the individual were of no importance except as the vehicle. . . .[7]

Most of the above quotations lean heavily on Rauschning, who said of Hitler's henchman, Himmler:

"I will tell you a secret," said Himmler to Rauschning; "I am founding an Order. . . . It is from there the second stage will emerge—the stage of the Man-God, when Man will be the measure and center of the world. The Man-God, that splendid Being, will be an object of worship."[8]

What Man-God did Himmler have in mind if, in fact, he said this? This sounds remarkably like the serpent's original temptation to Adam and Eve in the Garden of Eden: "And you shall be like God." It also sounds remarkably like a mimic of Jesus Christ.

As for Hitler's poised threat to Christians, Wythe Williams in his book *Riddle of the Reich*, written during World War II, said,

> Christ stands for love, forgiveness, tolerance, equality. For these, the Nazis have not stomach. . . . The conclusion to which the new masters of Germany come is that either Jesus Christ was not wise or divine, or, if he was, Hitler is his reincarnation.

> Deification of Hitler is a very earnest business with the Nazi writers and orators. . . . They are carried away by their own mysticism and exaltation. Said Reverend Dr. Leutheuser in February, 1934: "Adolf Hitler is the voice of Jesus Christ, who desired to become flesh and blood of the German people and did become flesh and blood." Echoed editor of *Der Deutsche Buero und Handelsangestellte*, an official publication of Berlin, in July 1934: "Two thousand years ago the Creator revealed himself to mankind in the person of Jesus Christ. Today God reveals Himself to the German people in the person of His Messiah, Hitler." Herr Spaniol, the Nazi leader in Saarbruecken, exclaimed in January 1935: "The churches will not go on existing in their present form. Its prophet, its pope, its Jesus Christ will be Adolf Hitler."

> The official stamp came from the Minister of Religion, Hanss Kerrl: . . . "The question of the divinity of Christ is ridiculous and inessential. A new answer has risen as to what Christ and Christianity really are: Adolf Hitler."

> . . . Dr. Alfred Rosenburg, one of the earliest . . . "Inspirers" of Hitler . . . decries the Christian churches as "evil powers of the past." Not God, and certainly not that Jew, Christ, can be the essence of a religion. . . . There is no place for Christianity.[9]

> From all of the above, it would appear the dragon had come back to life and was again pursuing the people of God, starting with the Jews and soon to proceed to the Christians.

All of these statements come second-hand through the authors quoted, mostly via Rauschning, but given the worldwide devastation caused by Hitler's obsession with power, it may be hard to doubt their veracity. The presence of an antichrist religion behind Hitler's rise can also be supported from a recent documentary film quoting Hitler, as well as some of his henchmen:

> [Adolf Hitler:] Humanity accomplishes a step up every 700 years. And the ultimate aim is the coming of the sons of God. All created forces will be concentrated in a new species. It will be infinitely superior to modern man.

. . . The party is the selecting ground for German political leaders. . . . Its doctrines will be unchangeable. . . . Its total image . . . will be like a holy order.

[Hienrich Himmler (head of the Nazi S.S.):] Never forget: we are a knightly order—from which one cannot withdraw, to which one is recruited by blood, and within which one remains body and soul.

[Alfred Rosenburg (Nazi Commissioner for Philosophy and Education):] Today a new mythos is dawning, the mythos of the blood—the belief that the godly essence is to be defended through the blood.

[Hitler:] Force without spiritual foundation is doomed to failure. . . .
    . . . The old [pagan] beliefs will be brought back to honor again. The whole secret knowledge of nature, of the divine, the demonic. We will wash off the Christian veneer, and bring out a religion peculiar to our race.
    . . . I want to see again in the eyes of youth the gleam of the beast of prey.

[A German youth song:] Adolf Hitler is our savior and our hero. He is the noblest being in the whole wide world. For Hitler we live. For Hitler we die. Our Hitler is our Lord.[9]

Were those Christians during World War II who were convinced Hitler was the Antichrist far from wrong? Hitler began his quest for power by proclaiming a thousand-year Nazi reign. He coopted Christian rituals and corrupted versions of Christian symbols. Where Christians had the cross, he used its pagan counterpart, the swastika. Where Christians used consecrated wine as a symbol of Jesus' blood, Hitler used real Nazi blood to consecrate political flags as symbols of his empire. Nazi heroes were honored as martyrs of the Reich who were resurrected to eternal life. The first sixteen heroes to die for the Reich were entombed in the "Temple of Honor." Even baptism of infants was conscripted by S.S. warrior priests for dedicating babies to the S.S. These same warrior priests also performed the marriages of S.S. officers.

Under Himmler, twelve chosen members of the S.S. became warrior priests in a replica of the legendary Arthurian Grail Chapel located in Himmler's private castle. (In Christian legend, the grail was the chalice Christ drank from during the Last Supper.) The sacred wine of the grail no longer represented Christ's blood. Himmler believed the grail—if it could be found—held the only pure Aryan blood. He personally sponsored quests for the Holy Grail.

Heeding Hitler's desire to strip away "the Christian veneer," Himmler looked beyond his own Catholic upbringing to early Nordic and Germanic pagan rituals—blood rites, myths of the descent of the Aryans from Nordic gods, and magical runes, such as the double lightning bolt "Ss" that became the emblem of the Nazi "S.S." from the nordic myth of Thor. Ancient pagan temples were restored, and summer solstice became a Nazi rite with bonfire tributes to the führer, instead of to the sun.

Was the *zeitgeist* in Nazi Germany not the same truth-twisting spirit seen centuries ago in the emperor worship of ancient Rome? As will be seen in a later chapter, it was also similar to the Holy Roman Empire, which emerged from the marriage of Church and State. So, once again, under Hitler, the marriage between political aims and corrupted religion and mythology gave birth to worldwide catastrophe and evil. In each of its manifestations—pagan under ancient Rome, "Christian" under Holy Rome, and neo-pagan with a Christian twist under the Third Reich—imperial despotism used religion to acquire emperor worship . . . exactly as the Apocalypse had revealed.

Will the *zeitgeist* of Adolf Hitler rise again? The next reincarnation of Antichrist could be quite literally an apocalyptic beast who died of a mortal head wound and came back to life. Since God is the creator of souls, would God give a soul to a human clone, or would a clone be an abomination before God, open to unhindered spiritual possession? This is the stuff of science fiction and horror films. It's also scientific reality as the seventh millennium of world history begins. Human cloning is now a moral dilemma the world cannot avoid:

> *And then shall that Wicked be revealed . . . Even him, whose coming is after the working of Satan with all power and signs and lying wonders. . . . And for this cause God shall send them strong delusion, that they should believe a lie: That they all may be damned who believed not the truth, but had pleasure in unrighteousness.*
>
> (2 Thessalonians 2:8–12)

Had there been a pure love for the truth in 1920s Germany, Hitler would never have risen to power, but the truth was obscured by racial hatred and human lust for empire. Paul's dire warnings to the Thessalonians and the warnings of the Apocalypse still reverberate in the human consciousness because we have seen in the past century the real prospects of a worldwide Babylon, which almost came into being as the Third Reich. Whatever the revived beast represents, history offers no reason to believe that imperial evil will not widen its pattern toward an ultimate consummation. The lust for a world empire will be continually reborn, and the dragon has proven most dangerous when people are least willing to believe in his presence.

6 6 6

Beyond the possibilities that used to be science fiction—but are science fact today—a literal reincarnation may not be what the author of the Apocalypse had in mind. Perhaps the Apocalypse meant that a leader would arise who would so closely mimic the horrors of an earlier despot as to be his reincarnation figuratively.

The Apocalypse speaks of a mysterious number that will identify the beast. Early Christians noticed that the letters of the name "Nero Caesar" spelled in Hebrew ("Nron Qsar") added up to 666. (Hebrew, like Latin and Greek, used letters to represent numeric values.) When Nero died of a sword wound—like the head of the beast that comes back to life in the Apocalypse—rumors spread that Nero would return to life. It's hard for people to believe human monsters can die of a simple mortal wound so quickly when they have stood so long against great enemies. One only has to look at how long people continued to believe Hitler was alive to recognize that living nightmares are not easily put to rest.

The three main languages of the early Christians were Hebrew, Greek, and Latin. The Hebrew letters for "Roman Kingdom" also added up to 666. Likewise, the Greek name for the Roman Empire, "*Lateinos,*" added up to 666 under the Greek numeral system. So did the Greek words spelling "Latin kingdom." The mysterious number seemed to be written all over Rome. So perhaps the revived head would be a figurative reincarnation of something distinctly Roman.

In later years it was noted that the Greek letters for "Italian church" also added up to 666. And it was probably the reformers who first noticed that the Latin words placed directly in front of the pontiff's forehead when he wears his crown add up to 666 if read as Roman numerals: "*Vicarius Filii Dei*" ("Vicar of the Son of God"). This must have seemed awfully close to the description offered in the Apocalypse:

> *And he causeth all, both small and great, rich and poor, free and bond, to receive a mark in their right hand, or in their foreheads: And that no man might buy or sell, except him that had the mark, or the name of the beast, or the number of his name. Here is wisdom. Let him that hath understanding count the number of the beast: for it is the number of a man; and his number is Six hundred and sixty and six.* (REVELATION 13:16–18)

The emphasis in the Apocalypse, however, seems to be less on the number than on a global economy where all people have this number. And it is here that the vision acquires its clearest significance for modern times. All major players in world markets today recognize that a unified global economy sits on our immediate horizon. Robert Reich, a member of President Clinton's cabinet and a former Harvard professor, has observed:

> The very idea of an American economy is becoming meaningless, as are notions of an American corporation, American capital, American products, and American technology. A similar transformation is affecting every other nation, some faster and more profoundly than others.[11]

President George Bush was fond of proclaiming this new world order:

A new partnership of nations has begun, and we stand today at a unique and extraordinary moment. . . . Out of these troubled times . . . A New World Order can emerge.[12]

And German Chancellor Helmut Kohl has said,

The United States of Europe will form the core of a peaceful order . . . The age prophesied of old, when all shall dwell secure and none shall make them afraid.[13]

Such a utopian order has never resulted from centralized human authority before. Why should anyone believe it will now?

The connection between the number 6 6 6 and universal product codes was described earlier in the book. This connection would seem irrelevant if not for the fact that it may soon be *impossible* to buy or sell items without scanning their UPCs and using electronic cash to complete the transaction. It's all speculation, of course, but not too unlikely according to a leading newspaper article from Seattle, the world's software development mecca:

Cash . . . is becoming trash. It is dirty, cumbersome, easily counterfeited, subject to theft and expensive to track. Even worse, in an American society that worships technology, it is old-fashioned.

Some merchants won't even accept the stuff as legal tender. In Los Angeles and other places, Federal Express outlets don't take cash. . . .

If the people plotting this revolution finish it, cash will completely transmogrify into clean, safe, electronic signals zapped instantaneously through the internet.

Having cut its tether to gold years ago, money would become pure information . . . that moves around on bank-owned computers, which would allow banks to retain control over—and charge for—its transmission.[14]

The article further states that 54 percent of all financial transactions are expected to be electronic by 2005. One of the risks of the world's move toward electronic commerce is the ability for a central authority to shut unwanted players out by denying them access. According to the Apocalypse, that is exactly what will happen to those who claim the name of Christ. Centralized global economies may create just the seat of power the dragon needs in order to raise his head one more time. If history provides any examples, the Antichrist may be a *figurative* reincarnation of earlier despots like Hitler or Nero, though the possibility of a literal reincarnation is not out of the question anymore.

Chapter 16

Return:

The Second Coming,
Resurrection, and the Rapture

And when he [Jesus] had spoken these things, while they [his disciples] beheld, he was taken up; and a cloud received him out of their sight. And while they looked steadfastly toward heaven as he went up, behold, two men stood by them in white apparel; Who also said, Ye men of Galilee, why stand ye gazing up to heaven? this same Jesus, who is taken from you into heaven, shall so come in like manner as ye have seen him go into heaven. (Acts 1:9–11)

The account of the seven-headed beast appears to have been an interlude between the end-time events of the sixth and seventh trumpet, which went back to describe the politics of the times heralded by the first six trumpets.

John's narrative now appears to return to the time when the seventh trumpet sounded to announced the return of Christ, at which time loud voices in heaven proclaimed,

The kingdoms of this world are become the kingdoms of our Lord, and of his Christ; and he shall reign for ever and ever ... and thy wrath is come, and the time of the dead, that they should be judged, and that thou shouldest give reward to thy servants the prophets, and to the saints ... and shouldest destroy them who destroy the earth. (Revelation 11:15, 18)

For the followers of Christ, this moment is everything they've lived and died for. Those who have given their lives to someone they never met will finally see him. He will reward them with the glory that is his to give, and then, in their company, he will deliver the wrath of God against the destroyers of this world. That the Lord's coming would be joy to those who loved him and peril to all others was foretold by the Jewish prophet, Isaiah:

And on this mountain shall the LORD of hosts make to all people a feast of rich things, a feast of wines on the lees, of rich things full of marrow, of wines on the lees well refined. And he will destroy on this mountain the face of the covering cast over all people, and the veil that is spread over all nations. . . . For on this mountain shall the hand of the LORD rest, and Moab [the ancient enemies of God's people] shall be trodden down under him, even as straw is trodden down for the dunghill. And he shall spread forth his hands in the midst of them, as he that swimmeth spreadeth forth his hands to swim: and he shall bring down their pride together with the spoils of their hands. And the fortress of the high fort of thy walls shall he bring down, lay low, and bring to the ground, even to the dust.

(ISAIAH 25:6, 7, 10–12)

The mountain Isaiah speaks of is Mount Zion. From times of old, the prophets have predicted the Messiah would come to Mount Zion in Jerusalem:

And the Redeemer shall come to Zion, and to them that turn from transgression in Jacob, saith the LORD. As for me, this is my covenant with them, saith the LORD; My spirit that is upon thee, and my words which I have put in thy mouth, shall not depart out of thy mouth, nor out of the mouth of thy seed, nor out of the mouth of thy seed's seed, saith the LORD, from henceforth and for ever.

(ISAIAH 59:20, 21)

Mount Zion was one of the last places Jesus visited before he died. It was at Mount Zion that he spoke his parting words to the Jewish leadership at large:

. . . Ye shall not see me henceforth, till ye shall say, Blessed is he that cometh in the name of the Lord.   (MATTHEW 23:39)

It should be no surprise, then, that the Lord, himself, would return to earth at this very spot. One of the oldest books of the Bible proclaimed as much:

For I know that my redeemer liveth, and that he shall stand at the latter day upon the earth: And though after my skin worms destroy this body, yet in my flesh shall I see God: Whom I shall see for myself, and my eyes shall behold, and not another; though my reins [mind or heart] be consumed within me.

(JOB 19:25–27)

Job knew that God would stand on earth in its latter days, and that he would see God with physical eyes, even though worms had long ago reamed out their sockets.

Thus, one of the oldest writings known to mankind brought together two key concepts of prophecy—the arrival of God on earth in the last days and the resurrection of the body—both seen as apparently concurrent events.

A later prophet, Isaiah, had proclaimed a similar thing:

Thy dead men shall live, together with my dead body shall they arise. Awake and sing, ye that dwell in dust: for thy dew is as the dew of herbs, and the earth shall cast out the dead. Come, my people, enter thou into thy chambers, and shut thy doors about thee: hide thyself as it were for a little moment, until the indignation shall be past. For, behold, the LORD cometh out of his place to punish the inhabitants of the earth for their iniquity: the earth also shall disclose her blood, and shall no more cover her slain.

(ISAIAH 26:19–21)

So, Isaiah, too, saw that he would rise from the dead along with the rest of God's dead people at a time when God came out of his heavens to punish the earth. He also hints that God's people would be briefly hidden away during a time of God's wrath. ("Hide thyself as it were for a little moment, until the indignation shall be past.") Perhaps this is a reference to what later he termed the rapture or perhaps it means a place of refuge for Jews during these final and most perilous times. Perhaps both. The prophet goes on to say,

And it shall come to pass in that day, that the LORD shall gather from the channel of the [Euphrates?] river to the stream of Egypt, and ye shall be gathered one by one, O ye children of Israel. And it shall come to pass in that day, that the great trumpet shall be blown, and they shall come who were ready to perish in the land of Assyria, and the outcasts in the land of Egypt, and shall worship the LORD on the holy mount at Jerusalem.

(ISAIAH 27:12, 13)

Such a regathering happened after the Jews were exiled in Assyria, Babylon, and Egypt, but the dead did not live nor did their bodies arise, other than figuratively. A similar regathering from exile has happened in the twentieth century, and this could coincide with the arrival of the Lord that Isaiah has described, which John foresees as he comes to the time of the seventh trumpet:

THE SECOND COMING AND THE RESURRECTION

The next part of John's version hints strongly of the resurrection at the return of the Messiah:

And I looked, and, lo, a Lamb stood on the mount Zion, and with him an hundred and forty and four thousand, having his Father's name written in their foreheads. And I heard a voice from heaven, as the voice of many waters, and as the voice of a great thunder: and I heard the voice of harpers harping with their harps: And they sung as it were a new song before the throne, and before the four beasts, and the elders: and no man could learn that song but the hundred and forty and four thousand, who were redeemed from the earth. These are they who were not defiled with women; for they are virgins. These are they who follow the Lamb wherever he goeth. These were redeemed from among men, being the firstfruits to God and to the Lamb. And in their mouth was found no guile: for they are without fault before the throne of God. (REVELATION 14:1–5)

Since John says that the 144,000 were "redeemed from the earth," that would almost certainly mean they had died. "Redeemed from the earth" was a common expression for the resurrection long before John's time:

None of them [those who boast in their wealth] can by any means redeem his brother, nor give to God a ransom for him: (For the redemption of their soul is precious, and it ceaseth for ever:) That he should still live for ever, and not see corruption. For he seeth that wise men die, likewise the fool and the stupid person perish, and leave their wealth to others. Their inward thought is, that their houses shall continue for ever, and their dwelling places to all generations; they call their lands after their own names. Nevertheless man being in honour abideth not: he is like the beasts that perish. This their way is their folly: yet their posterity approve their sayings. Selah. Like sheep they are laid in the grave; death shall feed on them; and the upright shall have dominion over them in the morning; and their beauty shall consume in the grave from their dwelling. But God will redeem my soul from the power of the grave: for he shall receive me. Selah. (PSALMS 49:7–15)

The psalmist did not particularly mention *physical* resurrection—only spiritual—though the context implies it. Others also used the term "redeem" to imply resurrection of the body from the grave:

I will ransom them from the power of the grave; I will redeem them from death: O death, I will be thy plagues; O grave, I will be thy destruction: repentance shall be hid from my eyes. (HOSEA 13:14)

There are other clues that the 144,000 have died and are now shown resurrected on Mount Zion. (Which, if accurate, reveals that the seal they received on their foreheads did not protect them from the same deaths faced by the two witnesses. In this chapter, that seal is shown as God's name.)

Why are the 144,000 now called virgins when their virginity was not pointed out earlier? Why are they "not defiled by women"? Is it because they are celibate priests or monks? Probably not. This is likely one more way to indicate they have just been resurrected from the dead. They have virginal new bodies.

This concept of virginity fits with other descriptions of life after the resurrection:

> And Jesus answering said to them, The children of this world marry, and are given in marriage: But they who shall be accounted worthy to obtain that world, and the resurrection from the dead, neither marry, nor are given in marriage: Neither can they die any more: for they are equal to the angels; and are the children of God, being the children of the resurrection. (LUKE 20:34–36)

John was probably referring back to this statement by Christ so his own statement is not an antisexual message; it simply points to the change that has happened in their bodies. They are virginal bodies—new, untouched, pristine, and possibly sexless in the same way that we think of angels, though that might not be an accurate assumption about angels either. If John is describing the reclaimed virginity of the resurrected body, then this is not necessarily a pro-celibate argument as some have taken it. It is simply one more evidence that John is writing of the resurrection here—that all things are being made new.

The Apostle Paul also speaks of differences between the present human body and the body that will be resurrected, using the planting of grain as an analogy. The plant that sprouts from the seed is not identical to the seed that was buried and figuratively died in the ground:

> But some man will say, How are the dead raised? and with what body do they come? Thou fool, that which thou sowest is not made alive, except it die: And that which thou sowest, thou sowest not that body that shall be, but bare grain, perhaps of wheat, or of some other grain: But God giveth it a body as it hath pleased him, and to every seed its own body. All flesh is not the same flesh: but there is one kind of flesh of men, another flesh of beasts, another of fishes, and another of birds. There are also celestial bodies, and bodies terrestrial: but the glory of the celestial is one, and the glory of the terrestrial is another. There is one glory of the sun, and another glory of the moon, and another glory of the stars: for one star differeth from another star in glory. So also is the resurrection of the dead. It [the terrestrial body] is sown in corruption; it is raised in incorruption: It is sown in dishonour; it is raised in glory: it is sown in weakness; it is raised in power: It is sown a natural body; it is raised a spiritual body. There is a natural body, and there is a spiritual body. . . . And as we have borne the image of the earthy [being made like Adam, the first man who lived], we shall also bear the image of the heavenly [Christ, being remade like him]. Now this I say,

brethren, that flesh and blood cannot inherit the kingdom of God; neither doth corruption inherit incorruption.

Behold, I show you a mystery; We shall not all sleep, but we shall all be changed, In a moment, in the twinkling of an eye, at the last trumpet: for the trumpet shall sound, and the dead shall be raised incorruptible, and we shall be changed. For this corruptible must put on incorruption, and this mortal must put on immortality. So when this corruptible shall have put on incorruption, and this mortal shall have put on immortality, then shall be brought to pass the saying that is written, Death is swallowed up in victory. O death, where is thy sting? O grave, where is thy victory?
(1 CORINTHIANS 15:35–44, 49–55)

Another ready analogy Paul could have used would be the caterpillar and the butterfly. That which is swallowed up in the chrysalis is not the same as the splendor that emerges. So the resurrected body is clearly different from the present body, and perhaps sex is not one of its joys. Some may wonder, "In that case, why bother? What's a heaven for?" Those who have found sex a rapturous joy in this life may find their dreams of their own heavenly harem quickly disappointed by what is revealed of the resurrected body. That's because all people are limited to understanding the finest joys they have known as being ultimate experience, but what if there's something even greater, something impossible for human minds to conceive of because its completely outside of human experience, something that sex, itself, symbolized?

Aside from what feels like a loss to those who have known nothing better, there are apparently many physical things of which of which a resurrected body *is* capable. After his resurrection, Jesus ate with his disciples. He fried fish on a fire and served them up. He implied to the Apostle Thomas that he could be physically touched. This was so apparent that Thomas did not need to take him up on it. So the resurrected Jesus was more than just a spirit returned from the dead. He also transcended apparent physical laws; he could appear and disappear at will, as one who steps in from another dimension and is free to step out again:

And their eyes were opened, and they knew him; and he vanished out of their sight. (LUKE 24:31)

The 144,000 are also now described by John as being without fault before God. Who can be perfect in this life? So this, too, indicates the 144,000 must be in their perfected (glorified) state before God. They must have died in the Great Tribulation described by the first six trumpets. Now they are raised near the same time as the two witnesses were raised—about the time the seventh trumpet sounded. (Of course, the

144,000 and the two witnesses *could* both be figurative for God's reunited people during the Great Tribulation—Jews and Gentiles.)

The final confirmation that these 144,000 are resurrected from the dead following the Great Tribulation is found in the sentence, "These were redeemed from among men, being the *firstfruits* to God and to the Lamb." The term "firstfruits" was used by the Apostle Paul to describe those who would be the first to be resurrected. In particular, it referred to Jesus Christ, who was the first to die for the New Covenant:

> But now is Christ risen from the dead, and become the firstfruits of them that slept [died]. For since by man came death, by man came also the resurrection of the dead. For as in Adam [the first human] all die, even so in Christ shall all be made alive. But every man in his own order: Christ the firstfruits; afterward they that are Christ's at his coming. Then cometh the end, when he shall have delivered up the kingdom to God, even the Father; when he shall have put down all rule and all authority and power.
>
> (1 CORINTHIANS 15:20–24)

"Firstfruits" is a Hebrew term referring to the first portion of a crop that is given at harvest as an offering to God before the remainder can be taken or used by others. Paul clearly states here that Christ's followers would be resurrected at his second coming, and then the end would follow, at which time all human governments would be destroyed.

So when John says the 144,000 were "redeemed from the earth" and are "firstfruits," he clearly links them to the death, resurrection, and return of the Messiah. Elsewhere, Paul had indicated that those who share in the death of Christ (perhaps implying a martyr's death) or suffer because of Christ would be resurrected:

> That I [being counted righteous by faith] may know him, and the power of his resurrection, and the fellowship of his sufferings, being made conformable to his death; If by any means I may attain to the resurrection of the dead. For our citizenship is in heaven; from which also we look for the Saviour, the Lord Jesus Christ: Who shall change our lowly body, that it may be fashioned like his glorious body, according to the working by which he is able even to subdue all things to himself. (PHILIPPIANS 3:10, 11, 20, 21)

If 144,000 is a symbolic number representing the united people of God, then all the saints who have died in the Great Tribulation are shown as resurrected here. They are perhaps the first to be resurrected because they shared in Christ's death, having been killed for spreading the very words for which Christ was killed. Therefore, they join him in being called "firstfruits"—the portion of earth's harvest sacrificed to God.

That the resurrection would occur in stages is also evident from the New Testament. In the very least, it would occur in three stages—the resurrection of Christ's dead followers, followed by the removal from the earth of those followers who are still alive (called "the rapture"), followed much later by the resurrection of everyone else who has died. Paul describes the first two as happening sequentially:

> But I would not have you to be ignorant, brethren, concerning them who are asleep [dead], that ye sorrow not, even as others who have no hope. For if we believe that Jesus died and rose again, even so them also who sleep in Jesus will God bring with him. For this we say to you by the word of the Lord, that we who are alive and remain to the coming of the Lord shall not precede them who are asleep. For the Lord himself shall descend from heaven with a shout, with the voice of the archangel, and with the trumpet of God: and the dead in Christ shall rise first: Then we who are alive and remain shall be caught up together with them in the clouds, to meet the Lord in the air: and so shall we ever be with the Lord.
>
> (1 THESSALONIANS 4:13–17)

The two things that happen sequentially here are the resurrection of the dead saints, followed by the rapture of the living. John may have shown the first in the form of the 144,000, having been brought with the Lord to Mount Zion. Repeatedly the prophecies of resurrection and rapture happen in the same context, and they repeatedly mention the sounding of a trumpet and the return of Christ (or God) to the earth. The scriptures are consistent in this grouping of the events.

FINAL WARNINGS

Before John describes the second part of this great event—the rapture—he shows that the whole world is given an opportunity to participate. They are not forewarned that a rapture will occur, but they are forewarned that the end is near, and they are warned not to follow the Antichrist:

> And I saw another angel fly in the midst of heaven, having the everlasting gospel to preach to them that dwell on the earth, and to every nation, and kindred, and tongue, and people, Saying with a loud voice, Fear God, and give glory to him; for the hour of his judgment is come: and worship him that made heaven, and earth, and the sea, and the fountains of waters. And there followed another angel, saying, Babylon is fallen, is fallen, that great city, because she made all nations drink of the wine of the wrath of her immorality. And the third angel followed them, saying with a loud voice, If any man worshippeth the beast and his image, and receiveth his mark in his forehead, or in his hand, The same shall drink of the wine of the wrath of God, which is poured out without mix-

ture into the cup of his indignation; and he shall be tormented with fire and brimstone in the presence of the holy angels, and in the presence of the Lamb: And the smoke of their torment ascen-

deth up for ever and ever: and they have no rest day nor night, who worship the beast and his image, and whoever receiveth the mark of his name.

(REVELATION 14:6–11)

The prayers of the saints were shown earlier in the Apocalypse as the smoke of fire and incense. In like manner, the smoke of fire and sulfur (brimstone) described for the Antichrist's followers may represent the fruitless curses at God or cries for mercy howled by the wicked. Since God's agent of discipline for evil has been shown repeatedly to be any evil entity that is allowed to destroy another (until the day all evil consumes itself), perhaps the source of endless torment here is not some fire cooked up by God as punishment, but rather the built-in reality of godless, self-centered souls being abandoned by God to each other's malicious, lying, treacherous, murderous company forever. Having long sought freedom from God, they will now receive all they have sought. Evil people, being completely unleashed upon each other, will continue to bring their own judgment upon their own eternal souls. (In the biblical view *all* souls are eternal.) So while the saints, in the 144,000, were depicted as sending up an eternal harmony of harp music and a song that only they could sing, the evil raise an endless cacophony of screeches, murmurs, cries, and groans because of what they inflict upon one another. The suffering that the good have known in this world that is mixed with evil becomes unadulterated suffering for those who remain when all that is good—all that dilutes the present evil—is taken out of the world.

Nevertheless, the Apocalypse offers some hope that these warnings, along with the impact of the rapture that follows, may cause some to turn to God after it's too late to avoid his wrath against the earth, yet in time to save their souls. They may escape through the flames:

Here is the patience of the saints: here are they that keep the commandments of God, and the faith of Jesus. And I heard a voice from heaven saying to me, Write, Blessed are the dead who die in the Lord

from henceforth: Yea, saith the Spirit, that they may rest from their labours; and their works follow them.

(REVELATION 14:12, 13)

The description of eternal fire and brimstone closes with an emphasis on the patience and endurance this final judgment will require from the saints. John gave that same warning to the saints of God who would have to live through the Great Tribulation. He warned that because of the number who would fall to the sword or be imprisoned for not receiving the mark of the beast, great endurance and faith would be required of God's saints.

Such a strong warning to the saints about the need for endurance right before the rapture *could* indicate that the rapture will *not* be the clean and easy disappearance it is often thought to be. It may, in fact, be a bloody slaughter that brings in the final number of martyrs who refuse the mark—those whose deaths were called "blessed" because they will be resurrected the moment they are killed. Their works will follow them immediately because they are killed after the resurrection has already happened. In other words, immediately upon death they will be resurrected into their glorified bodies and be united with the Messiah. Alternatively, those spoken of here could be those who were not ready for the rapture but who turn to the Messiah after the rapture. Clearly a holocaust is in store for someone, or patience and death would not be re-emphasized.

> *Blessed be the God and Father of our Lord Jesus Christ, who according to his abundant mercy hath begotten us again to a living hope by the resurrection of Jesus Christ from the dead, To an inheritance incorruptible, and undefiled, and that fadeth not away, reserved in heaven for you, Who are kept by the power of God through faith to salvation ready to be revealed in the last time. In this ye greatly rejoice, though now for a season, if need be, ye are in heaviness through various temptations: That the trial of your faith, being much more precious than of gold that perisheth, though tried with fire, might be found to praise and honour and glory at the appearing of Jesus Christ.* (1 Peter 1:3–7)

The Double Harvest

One of the metaphors repeated in New Testament prophecy is that of a double harvest, in which the good (the true followers of the Messiah) will be harvested along with the bad (those who reject God). Only at the time of the harvest will the two be separated:

> *Another parable he put forth to them, saying, The kingdom of heaven is likened to a man who sowed good seed in his field: But while men slept, his enemy came and sowed tares [a type of weed] among the wheat, and went his way. But when the blade had sprung up, and brought forth fruit, then appeared the tares also. So the servants of the householder came and said to him, Sir, didst thou not sow good seed in thy field? how then hath it tares? He said to them, An enemy hath done this. The servants said to him, Wilt thou then that we go and gather them up? But he said, Nay; lest while ye gather up the tares, ye root up also the wheat with them. Let both grow together until the harvest: and in the time of harvest I will say to the reapers, Gather ye together first the tares, and bind them in bundles to burn them: but gather the wheat into my barn. . . . Then Jesus sent the multitude away, and went into the house: and his disciples came to him, saying, Explain to us the parable of the tares of the field. He answered and*

said to them, He that soweth the good seed is the Son of man; The field is the world; the good seed are the children of the kingdom; but the tares are the children of the wicked one; The enemy that sowed them is the devil; the harvest is the end of the world; and the reapers are the angels. As therefore the tares are gathered and burned in the fire; so shall it be in the end of this world. The Son of man shall send forth his angels, and they shall gather out of his kingdom all things that offend, and them who do iniquity; And shall cast them into a furnace of fire: there shall be wailing and gnashing of teeth. Then shall the righteous shine forth as the sun in the kingdom of their Father. Who hath ears to hear, let him hear. (MATTHEW 13:24–30, 36–43)

It is clear in Matthew's Gospel that the children of Christ's kingdom *and* the wicked are harvested at "the end of this world." Jesus even uses the phrase that he used to warn the seven churches at the beginning of the Apocalypse: "Who hath ears to hear, let him hear."

This parable is similar to an image presented by John the Baptist, which comes from a scene that would have been common in Jesus' day. After the harvest, the grain was spread out on clean floor where it was trampled by oxen dragging a threshing sledge over the top of it in order to rub the kernels free from the stalk surrounding chaff. Then the threshed grain was tossed with a pitchfork into the wind in order to blow the lightweight chaff away from the desirable kernels. Finally, the undesirable chaff was burned, while the kernels were scooped up from the floor and stored away safely for the future:

. . . he will thoroughly cleanse his floor, and gather his wheat into the barn; but he will burn the chaff with unquenchable fire. (MATTHEW 3:12)

THE RAPTURE

Only a few prophecies hint that the followers of Christ will be spared from the final hour when God's wrath is brought against all the evil in the world:

The righteous perisheth, and no man layeth it to heart: and merciful men are taken away, none considering that the righteous is taken away from the evil to come. He shall enter into peace: they shall rest in their beds, each one walking in his uprightness. (ISAIAH 57:1, 2)

The above passage, because it mentions "perishing," suggests that the rapture is really a resurrection of the slaughtered children of God who are immediately resurrected to be with God. Such a slaughter by the Antichrist could be the very thing that triggers the final wrath of God when his Spirit completely abandons the evil world to its own catastrophe: (On the other hand, this verse may not be speaking of the rapture at all. It may be speaking of any perilous time when the righteous should be counted blessed for dying, simply because they are spared further torment.)

Two New Testament quotations also lean toward understanding the rapture as a slaughter against all the living saints that happens after the resurrection of the dead:

> *For as the lightning cometh out of the east, and shineth even to the west; so shall also the coming of the Son of man be. For wherever the carcase is, there will the eagles ["vultures" in some translations] be gathered together.*
>
> (MATTHEW 24:27, 28)

> *I tell you, in that night there shall be two [people] in one bed; the one shall be taken, and the other shall be left. Two women shall be grinding together; the one shall be taken, and the other left. Two men shall be in the field; the one shall be taken, and the other left. And they answered and said to him, Where, Lord? And he said to them, Wherever the body is, there will the eagles [or "vultures"] be gathered together.*
>
> (LUKE 17:34–36)

The presence of vultures certainly indicates dead bodies left behind. However the rapture occurs—by death or simply by the righteous floating up from the earth—one thing is clear: the saints are taken up from earth in order to be spared "from the greater evil to come."

> *. . . [They turned to God] to wait for his Son from heaven, whom he raised from the dead, even Jesus, who delivered us from the wrath to come.*
>
> (1 THESSALONIANS 1:10)

John specifically refers to the events that follow in the next chapter as the "wrath of God," but before he reveals the time of the wrath he shows that the believers are resurrected or raptured from the world before the events of God's wrath begin. Early in the Apocalypse, he quoted Jesus or his angel (messenger) as saying:

> *Because thou hast kept the word of my patience, I also will keep thee from the hour of temptation, which shall come upon all the world, to try them that dwell upon the earth.*
>
> (REVELATION 3:10)

Revelation 3:10 (above) appears to mean one of two things—that Christ will spare his followers from the Great Tribulation (already described by John) by the rapture, or he will spare them by the rapture from the wrath to come. It depends on which "hour of temptation" is in view. John, himself, doesn't offer much hope that any of his churches will be spared tribulation. Over and over he has told them to prepare for it, to know that it is coming, and to overcome it. Persecution and martyrdom are a constant drone in the background of John's *magnum opus*. To this point, the Apocalypse has emphasized the need for patient endurance and great faith on the part of God's saints in order to overcome perilous times. So being spared from the "hour of temptation" probably does not refer to the Great Tribulation, especially since John has given no hints of the rapture until the following part of this chapter. More likely the "hour of temptation" from which Christ will keep his Church refers to the final hour of God's wrath, or it simply means they will be given refuge during part of the Great Tribulation like Noah in his ark.

And except the Lord had shortened those days, no flesh should be saved: but for the elect's sake, whom he hath chosen, he hath shortened the days. (MARK 13:20)

This verse may mean that no one would have been saved from the increasing evil of the Great Tribulation if God had not shortened its length by the rapture John is now going to describe, or it could refer to the time of wrath that will be shown in the next chapter.

Like the earlier parable in this chapter, John also describes a double harvest of souls from the earth at its final hour. The first appears to be the harvest of the righteous—those who have placed their faith in Jesus Christ as their Messiah. This is like an image of the rapture The second is clearly the harvest of the unrighteous, which happens through a worldwide holocaust, but the two events are positioned side by side as they were when John the Baptist told of separating the wheat from the chaff as a single event or when Christ told of harvesting the tares and the wheat:

And I looked, and behold a white cloud, and upon the cloud one sat like the Son of man, having on his head a golden crown, and in his hand a sharp sickle. And another angel came out of the temple, crying with a loud voice to him that sat on the cloud, Thrust in thy sickle, and reap: for the time is come for thee to reap; for the harvest of the earth is ripe. And he that sat on the cloud thrust in his sickle on the earth; and the earth was reaped. (REVELATION 14:14–16)

There is one other verse that is often quoted regarding the rapture:

And when these things begin to come to pass, then look up, and lift up your heads; for your redemption draweth near.
(LUKE 21:28)

This is likely the redemption John has shown in the verses above, and the things that "begin to come to pass" preceding that redemption are the events of the Great Tribulation, which John has already described. In other words, Jesus is saying in Luke, "When the Great Tribulation begins to come upon the earth, lift up your head because it simply means the resurrection is near." The one seated on a white cloud like "the Son of man" in John's passage above refers to Jesus Christ or an angel representing him (thus, "like" the Son of man). He arrives on a cloud just as he left on a cloud. That is what the angels promised to his disciples in the Book of Acts quoted at the beginning of this chapter: They would see him return to earth in the same manner as he departed. In the return shown by John, Christ is crowned because he has received his authority from God to begin his reign on earth. Those he reaps are his own—those who are looking to him for redemption from the earth.

THE GRAPES OF WRATH: THE HARVEST OF THE WICKED

So, the resurrection has happened, as depicted by the 144,000 who appear redeemed from the earth on Mount Zion, where the redeemer was prophesied to come by Isaiah. Now, the rapture has occurred, where those who were alive and remaining after the Great Tribulation were caught up to meet Christ in the clouds following the resurrection of the dead, just as Paul had said: ". . . we who are alive and remain to the coming of the Lord shall not precede them who are asleep." Next, the second part of the harvest will begin. This is the third woe brought against the world by the seventh trumpet, which announced salvation for the saints but death to the followers of the Antichrist:

> And another angel came out of the temple which is in heaven, he also having a sharp sickle. And another angel came out from the altar, who had power over fire; and cried with a loud cry to him that had the sharp sickle, saying, Thrust in thy sharp sickle, and gather the clusters of the vine of the earth; for her grapes are fully ripe. And the angel thrust in his sickle into the earth, and gathered the vine of the earth, and cast it into the great winepress of the wrath of God. And the winepress was trodden outside the city, and blood came out of the winepress, even to the horses' bridles, by the space of a thousand and six hundred furlongs. (REVELATION 14:17–20)

The order of the two harvests in John's version is reversed from the order in Christ's parable, where the tares (wicked) were harvested before the wheat, but perhaps Christ was less concerned with the sequence of events than he was with drawing an analogy from everyday life that would link the two harvests.

What John has just described is a prelude to the events that will follow in earth's final days, which culminate in the Battle of Armageddon, where Christ, having established complete union with all of his followers, descends upon the earth to claim it for God and his saints, the true Church. These events are the final woe, which consists of seven deadly plagues. They come after the harvest of Christ's followers (the rapture) because the complete removal of God's people also implies the complete removal of God's Spirit from the earth. This is the dreadful day when evil's unbridled as described by the Old Testament prophet Micah, who spoke from the point of view of one who has been left behind:

Woe is me! for I am as when they have gathered the summer fruits, as the grape-gleanings of the vintage: there is no cluster to eat: my soul desired the firstripe fruit. The good man hath perished from the earth: and there is none upright among men: they all lie in wait for blood; they hunt every man his brother with a net. That they may do evil with both hands earnestly, the prince asketh, and the judge asketh for a reward; and the great man, he uttereth his mischievous desire: so they weave it together. The best of them is as a brier: the most upright is sharper than a thorn hedge: the day of thy watchmen and thy punishment cometh; now shall be their perplexity. Trust ye not in a friend, put ye not confidence in a guide: keep the doors of thy mouth from her that lieth in thy bosom. For the son dishonoureth the father, the daughter riseth up against her mother, the daughter in law against her mother in law; a man's enemies are the men of his own house.

Therefore I will look to the LORD; I will wait for the God of my salvation: my God will hear me. Rejoice not against me, O my enemy: when I fall, I shall arise; when I sit in darkness, the LORD shall be a light to me. I will bear the indignation of the LORD, because I have sinned against him, until he shall plead my cause, and execute judgment for me: he will bring me forth to the light, and I shall behold his righteousness. Then she that is my enemy shall see it, and shame shall cover her who said to me, Where is the LORD thy God? my eyes shall behold her: now shall she be trodden down as the mire of the streets. In the day that thy walls are to be built, in that day shall the decree be far removed. In that day also he shall come even to thee from Assyria, and from the fortified cities, and from the fortress even to the river, and from sea to sea, and from mountain to mountain. Afterwards the land shall be desolate because of them that dwell in it, for the fruit of their doings.

Feed thy people with thy rod, the flock of thy heritage? [those who remain under the Old Covenant?], who dwell solitarily in the forest, in the midst of Carmel: let them feed in Bashan and Gilead, as in the days of old. According to the days of thy departure from the land of Egypt will I show to him marvelous things. The nations shall see and be confounded at all their might: they shall lay their hand upon their mouth, their ears shall be deaf. They shall lick the dust like a serpent, they shall move out of their holes like worms of the earth: they shall be afraid of the LORD our God, and shall fear because of thee. Who is a God like

thee, that pardoneth iniquity, and pas-
seth by the transgression of the remnant
of his heritage? he retaineth not his anger
for ever, because he delighteth in mercy.
He will turn again, he will have compas-
sion upon us; he will subdue our iniqui-

ties; and thou wilt cast all their sins into
the depths of the sea. Thou wilt perform
the truth to Jacob, and the mercy to
Abraham, which thou hast sworn to our
fathers from the days of old.

(MICAH 7:1–20)

Micah may have been describing dark times in his own life, but his words will never ring truer than they will during earth's final hour. (This does not mean that earth ends completely, but that history, as it has been known, is consummated and comes to a close while earth is reborn from its ashes. So earth, too, will have its resurrection in order that the part of creation that has "groaned" and waited in expectation of delivery from human evil will also have its day in Christ.)

If any are to be saved by faith at this time, they will have to endure earth's darkest hour and drink the cup of God's wrath patiently down to its dregs along with all the rest of earth's inhabitants. The wicked will scoff at their apparent foolishness for believing in light within a world that has gone totally dark. Micah ends with hope for the Jews (perhaps any who have not yet believed) that God will give them his truth and mercy, as sworn to their forefathers, Abraham and Jacob. As for the Gentiles, the plauges that follow in John's Apocalypse seem to indicate that none of those who are left are willing to believe.

There is a fair amount of evidence in both Old and New Testaments that a number of Jews will not believe Jesus is their Messiah until the bitter end. As a result, they will endure these most difficult times *after* the full harvest of the Gentiles has come in. (That does not mean there will not be many Jews who will come in with that same harvest.) God will not forget his other people. As Micah says, "He will perform the truth to Jacob and the mercy to Abraham."

In that light, it's possible the verses quoted above regarding two people working side by side (where one will be taken up by Christ and other left behind) may refer to the final end and not the rapture as usually thought. In which case, one will be caught up to Christ when Christ and his saints return, and the other will die; thus the vultures will gather at Armageddon. Some of the verses yet to come in John's Apocalypse indicate none of the wicked will survive the ultimate arrival of Christ at Armageddon, perhaps because those who look upon the face of God shall die if they are not first made perfect—a statement found in the earliest parts of the Bible.

Luke's Gospel, below, indicates that the total destruction of the people of earth happens (or begins) right after God's people are raptured from the earth. It also hints that this destruction will take the same form as the events shown earlier, which *may* have been descriptive of an asteroid or comet impact. This destruction will come unexpectedly for those who have not believed, on a day like any other day, perhaps indicating that the world has recovered from the Great Tribulation. (That would explain why they worship the Antichrist—if they feel he was responsible for the recovery.) The world, in fact, will be rejoicing because the two witnesses have been slain. The last of the Christians—those separatists who would not follow Antichrist—are gone.

> And as it was in the days of Noah, so shall it be also in the days of the Son of man. They ate, they drank, they married wives, they were given in marriage, until the day that Noah entered into the ark, and the flood came, and destroyed them all. Likewise also as it was in the days of Lot; they ate, they drank, they bought, they sold, they planted, they built; But the same day that Lot went out of Sodom it rained fire and brimstone from heaven, and destroyed them all. Even thus shall it be in the day when the Son of man is revealed.   (LUKE 17:26–30)

So when the people of God are removed (as Noah entered his ark or as Lot fled Sodom), then destruction rains down upon the world. Whether these verses refer to the time when God's people are given a place of refuge on earth *during part of the Great Tribulation* (which is how they were quoted earlier) or to the final day when all people on earth are destroyed after God's people are raptured is not clear, but they seem to fit better with the time when the Great Tribulation has ended, then suddenly Christ arrives to bring "God's Wrath":

> But of the times and the seasons, brethren, ye have no need that I write to you. For yourselves know perfectly that the day of the Lord so cometh as a thief in the night. For when they shall say, Peace and safety; then sudden destruction cometh upon them, as travail upon a woman with child; and they shall not escape. But ye, brethren, are not in darkness, that that day should overtake you as a thief. For God hath not appointed us to wrath, but to obtain salvation by our Lord Jesus Christ, Who died for us, that, whether we wake or sleep, we should live together with him.
> (1 THESSALONIANS 5:1–4, 9, 10)

Labor pains come without any *immediate* forewarning, but they do not come unexpectedly. There are months of preparation. Christ's coming will probably be unexpected only by those who have ignored the words of the witnesses, his prophets. Sodom's destruction was not unexpected by Lot, nor was the flood unexpected by Noah. In fact, those around him had certainly seen the ark under construction. They simply chose to ignore the words of a fool who was building a ship in the middle of dry land.

When the earth is ready to give birth to the firstfruits of its womb, its condition will be evident to the followers of Christ, though they will not know the day or hour the birth will happen. Even the year cannot be predicted by some ingenious interpretation of prophecy, but Christ's followers will not be left in darkness either. Once the times become pregnant, the coming spiritual rebirth will be obvious to those who are expecting—those who have the Spirit of God within them as a seal of their fate and a deposit guaranteeing their resurrection.

If anyone has an ear, let him hear.

The Reunion of the Dead

And I saw another sign in heaven, great and marvelous, seven angels having the seven last plagues; for in them is filled up the wrath of God. And I saw as it were a sea of glass mingled with fire: and them that had gained the victory over the beast, and over his image, and over his mark, and over the number of his name, stand on the sea of glass, having the harps of God. And they sing the song of Moses the servant of God, and the song of the Lamb, saying, Great and marvelous are thy works, Lord God Almighty; just and true are thy ways, thou King of saints. Who shall not fear thee, O Lord, and glorify thy name? for thou only art holy: for all nations shall come and worship before thee; for thy judgments are revealed. (Revelation 15:1–4)

Before describing the days of wrath, John returns to the scene near the beginning of his Apocalypse where God's throne was surrounded by a sea of glass. Only now the glassy sea is mingled with fire. It was suggested at the beginning that this sea might represent the people and nations of the world, because later in the Apocalypse the people and nations are referred to as "many waters." If that is the case, the fire of God's wrath has spread out upon the people of earth. Standing on this sea, as though they have risen out of the flames below, are the people of God who have triumphed in the Great Tribulation by not receiving the mark of the beast. As with the 144,000 shown earlier on Mount Zion, they exist in a state of harmony with their Creator, evidenced by the harps they hold and the new song of the Lamb they are singing. The always-imminent end is come, and they have been saved out of it. Many of them—if not all of them—had to lose their lives in order to claim eternal life. It is a principle Jesus taught over and over to his disciples to prepare them for this very end:

. . . fear not them who kill the body, but are not able to kill the soul: but rather fear him who is able to destroy both soul and body in hell. Whoever therefore shall confess me before men, him will I also confess before my Father who is in heaven. But whoever shall deny me before men, him will I also deny before my Father who is in heaven. He that findeth his life shall lose it: and he that loseth his life for my sake shall find it. (Matthew 10:28, 32, 33, 39)

Jesus spoke of dying to one's own needs daily out of service to others. But John has now taken his readers to ultimate times where all truths receive their ultimate test. The seed of Christ cannot be reaped in the first harvest (the rapture) unless they are first buried:

Verily, verily, I say to you, Except a grain of wheat fall into the ground and die, it abideth alone: but if it die, it bringeth forth much fruit. He that loveth his life shall lose it; and he that hateth his life in this world shall keep it to life eternal.

(JOHN 12:24, 25)

Know ye not, that so many of us as were baptized into Jesus Christ were baptized into his death? Therefore we are buried with him by baptism into death: that as Christ was raised from the dead by the glory of the Father, even so we also should walk in newness of life. For if we have been planted together in the likeness of his death, we shall be also in the likeness of his resurrection:

. . . But if the Spirit of him that raised Jesus from the dead dwelleth in you, he that raised Christ from the dead shall also give life to your mortal bodies by his Spirit that dwelleth in you. . . . For we know that the whole creation groaneth and travaileth in pain [as in labor] together until now. And not only they, but ourselves also, who have the firstfruits of the Spirit, even we ourselves groan within ourselves, waiting for the adoption, that is, the redemption of our body. . . . For I am persuaded, that neither death, nor life, nor angels, nor principalities, nor powers, nor things present, nor things to come, Nor height, nor depth, nor any other created thing, shall be able to separate us from the love of God, which is in Christ Jesus our Lord.

(ROMANS 6:3–5; 8:11, 22, 23, 38, 39)

Chapter 17

WRATH:

SEVEN BOWLS OF GOD'S JUDGMENT POURED OUT UPON THE EARTH

And after that I looked, and, behold, the temple of the tabernacle of the testimony in heaven was opened: And the seven angels came out of the temple, having the seven plagues, clothed in pure and white linen, and having their breasts girded with golden bands. And one of the four living beings gave to the seven angels seven golden vials full of the wrath of God, who liveth for ever and ever. And the temple was filled with smoke from the glory of God, and from his power; and no man was able to enter into the temple, till the seven plagues of the seven angels were fulfilled.

(REVELATION 15:5–8)

The first events of the Apocalypse, the seven seals, had power to take a *fourth* of the life from earth. The first four likely stood for the common plague of war that has taken life from earth for centuries, but they led up to the time of the end. Perhaps the numerology of "a fourth" is intended to indicate these were natural plagues, coming from humans that would affect the whole earth. The second set of events, the seven trumpets, presented a great cataclysm that devastated a *third* of the earth. Perhaps the derivative of *three* (the number of God) indicates that these events are not caused by humanity or other earthly sources; they are extraterrestrial in origin, coming down from heaven.

Both the seven seals and the seven trumpets were broken into a group of four followed by a group of three. The four horsemen of the seven seals marked one group from the remaining three. With the trumpets, the three woes marked the final group from the preceding four. Now, looking at the two series together, another shadow of the pattern of four followed by three emerges: The first series had power over a *fourth* of life; the second, over a *third*, revealing how intricately and consistently the symbolism of the Apocalypse is woven together. Now the final set of seven plagues has power over *all* of life on earth.

The saints have risen to be with Christ, and yet no man can enter the temple in heaven until the seven plagues have done their work of destroying evil on earth. The prior plagues, severe as they were, were heralded by trumpets. Trumpets are for official announcements and for signals in ancient battles. These plagues were wake-up calls. They were intended to get the attention of a populace that stubbornly refuses to believe in their own Creator. The final seven bowls (called "vials" in some versions of the Bible) serve a different purpose. They come against those who did not heed the clarion call of the trumpets. They are bowls filled with the wrath of God—like small cauldrons of vile concoctions poured out upon the earth by angels of death. They probably come quickly, one right after the other. They are relentless. Their hunger devours the earth.

If there is an opportunity to repent, no one listens. They are too busy cursing the darkness, cursing the foul things poured out upon them. As a result, God also does not listen to them. As Hosea said, "I will be thy destruction: repentance shall be hid from my eyes" (Hosea 13:14b).

Centuries of history have made clear that some people, no matter how richly blessed they are, refuse their whole lives to see God in their blessings. They give all the credit to themselves. Though they will never use good fortune to acknowledge there is a God, they are surprisingly ready to use bad fortune to prove there is *not* a God, or that if there is, he certainly isn't good. These final plagues have only one lesson to tell. There is a part of humanity that will have nothing to do with God under any condition, so long as they retain the free will to choose. Even when their own evil is allowed to result in an earth so horrible no one can stand it, still they will not turn to God. Instead, they will blame him for not preventing it. Some people simply do not want God to exist because they refuse to acknowledge any authority over their individual sovereignty. For that reason, they are irredeemable, and these plagues reveal who those people are:

> . . . when thy judgments are in the earth, the inhabitants of the world will learn righteousness. Let favour be shown to the wicked, yet he will not learn righteousness: in the land of uprightness he will deal unjustly, and will not behold the majesty of the LORD. LORD, when thy hand is lifted up [probably in judgment], they will not see: but they shall see, and be ashamed for their envy at the people; yea, the fire of thy enemies shall devour them. (ISAIAH 26:9–11)

Isaiah first states the purpose of God's judgments—that people may learn righteousness, as apparently many do during the warnings of the seven trumpets. The prophet implies judgment is necessary because the wicked do not learn when they receive good fortune from God. Then, the prophet says that even when God lifts up his hand (apparently to strike them) they still do not see, but, he concludes, they will see in the very end. The only problem is, in the very end, there may be no opportunity for repentance. They will have seen when it is too late, for the increase of evil around them will devour them. Again, the Bible shows it is not God who devours. The fire that devours the enemies of God, according to Isaiah, comes from the enemies themselves.

THE SEVEN BOWLS OF GOD'S WRATH

And I heard a great voice out of the tem- *pour out the vials [bowls] of the wrath of*
ple saying to the seven angels, Go, and *God upon the earth.* (REVELATION 16:1)

A few of the bowls that follow parallel the plagues God sent against Egypt to get Pharaoh to release his people. The story says that God turned the rivers and ponds and water bowls into blood for seven days. The fish all died, and the river stank. Because Pharaoh's magicians were able to replicate the plague, Pharaoh would not let God's people go. God unleashed a plague of frogs that came up from all the rivers and ponds into the houses and lands of Egypt, yet not in the houses of the Jews, but Pharaoh's magicians repeated that trick, too. Nevertheless, Pharaoh implored Moses to have God get rid of the frogs; then he would let the Jewish people go. So, Moses asked God, and the frogs all died. The Egyptians shovelled them out of the houses into heaps, and the land stank with rotting frogs. But when the frogs were gone, Pharaoh still would not let God's people go. Then the Egyptians were cursed with darkness. The story implies that even their lamps would not burn, but all the Jews had light in their dwellings. All of these are prototypes to the plagues that now cover the entire earth:

And the first went, and poured out his vial upon the earth; and there fell a foul and loathsome sore upon the men who had the mark of the beast, and upon them who worshipped his image. And the second angel poured out his vial upon the sea; and it became as the blood of a dead man: and every living soul died in the sea. And the third angel poured out his vial upon the rivers and fountains of waters; and they became blood. And I heard the angel of the waters say, Thou art righteous, O Lord, who art, and wast, and shalt be, because thou hast judged thus. For they have shed the blood of saints and prophets, and thou hast given them blood to drink; for they are worthy. And I heard another from the altar say, Even so, Lord God Almighty, true and righteous are thy judgments. And the fourth angel poured out his vial upon the sun; and power was given to him to scorch men with fire. And men were scorched with great heat, and blasphemed the name of God, who hath power over these plagues: and they repented not to give him glory. And the fifth angel poured out his vial upon the throne of the beast; and his kingdom was full of darkness; and they gnawed their tongues for pain, And blasphemed the God of heaven because of their pains and their sores, and repented not of their deeds. (REVELATION 16:2–10)

The sea and rivers and springs do not merely turn to blood, they turn to blood like that "of a dead man"; in other words, dark purple, coagulated blood. As for the diseases that come, they only infest those who have received the mark of the beast. Even the darkness only affects the kingdom of the beast. Perhaps this is because *all* of Christ's followers are gone from the earth; not a one remains. There are hints later in the vision that many Jews remain who still do not believe Jesus is their Messiah, but they also have not received the mark of the beast. They have not committed themselves either way. Presumably, because they have not received the mark of the beast, they would not be harmed by these plagues—just as the Jews were not directly harmed by the plagues in Egypt. For them, hope remains. (If that is an accurate reading of later events.)

The plague of darkness is similar to a prophecy against ancient Babylon in the time of its destruction:

> *And they shall pass through it, distressed and hungry: and it shall come to pass, that when they shall be hungry, they shall be enraged, and curse their king and their God, and look upward. And they shall look to the earth; and behold trouble and darkness, dimness of anguish; and they shall be driven to darkness.*
> (ISAIAH 8:21, 22)

Perhaps those words, which were figurative for Babylon, will have literal fulfillment in the end times, for the world in the end times is compared to Babylon throughout the rest of John's Apocalypse. Another part of Isaiah made a similar prediction against Babylon:

> *Behold, the day of the LORD cometh, cruel both with wrath and fierce anger, to lay the land desolate: and he shall destroy its sinners out of it. For the stars of heaven and its constellations shall not give their light: the sun shall be darkened in his going forth, and the moon shall not cause her light to shine. And I will punish the world for their evil, and the wicked for their iniquity; and I will cause the arrogance of the proud to cease, and will lay low the haughtiness of the terrible. I will make a man more rare than fine gold. . . .* (ISAIAH 13:9–12)

Jesus paraphrased this same prophecy from Isaiah when he described the darkness that would precede his second coming, proving (to those who believe he is the Messiah) that the original figurative fulfillment of a prophecy is not always its ultimate or only fulfillment. Jesus clearly saw these ancient prophecies against long-dead Babylon as words awaiting true fulfillment:

> *Immediately after the tribulation of those days shall the sun be darkened, and the moon shall not give her light, and the stars shall fall from heaven, and the powers of the heavens shall be shaken: And then shall appear the sign of the Son of man in heaven: and then shall all the tribes of the earth mourn, and they shall see the Son of man coming in the clouds of heaven with power and great glory.*
> (MATTHEW 24:29–30)

These prophecies are also similar to a prophecy made by Ezekiel against Egypt when he predicted how Babylon would destroy Egypt, the ancient enemy of God's people:

> *And I will lay thy flesh upon the mountains, and fill the valleys with thy height. I will also water with thy blood the land in which thou swimmest, even to the mountains; and the rivers shall be full of thee. And when I shall put thee out, I will cover the heaven, and make its stars dark; I will cover the sun with a cloud, and the moon shall not give her light. All the bright lights of heaven will I make dark over thee, and set darkness upon thy land, saith the Lord GOD. I will also vex the hearts of many people, when I shall bring thy destruction among the nations, into the countries which thou hast not known.*   (EZEKIEL 32: 5–9)

There are two ways of looking at the first part of this prophecy: Since the rivers and mountains were *not* literally filled with the bodies of slain Egyptians, prophecy uses dramatic poetic overstatement to underscore the severity of an event. The other is that the prophet is seeing another time superimposed upon his own, which would be the way Jesus read the prophecies about Babylon. The poetic overstatement is justified, then, by more than affect; it is justified because it sees a time when horror reaches or exceeds the limit of language. The poet reaches to the heights to pick images that are big enough to describe the visions that sweep through his mind—visions so potent they left the prophet Daniel sick in bed. In short, what was fulfilled figuratively in one time, may be fulfilled literally in another.

An example of this kind of poetic dramatization comes from Amos, where he describes the fall of Israel to its ancient enemy Assyria:

> *Thus hath the Lord GOD shown to me: and behold a basket of summer fruit. And he said, Amos, what seest thou? And I said, A basket of summer fruit. Then said the LORD to me, The end is come upon my people of Israel; I will not again pass by them any more. And the songs of the temple shall be wailing in that day, saith the Lord GOD: there shall be many dead bodies in every place; they shall cast them forth with silence.*
>
> *Hear this, O ye that swallow up the needy, even to make the poor of the land to fail, Saying, When will the new moon be gone, that we may sell grain? and the sabbath, that we may set forth wheat, making the ephah [a measurement of dry goods] small, and the shekel great [the price paid for the dry goods], and falsifying the balances by deceit? That we may buy the poor for silver, and the needy for a pair of shoes; and even sell the refuse of the wheat? The LORD hath sworn by the excellency of Jacob, Surely I will never forget any of their works. Shall not the land tremble for this, and every one mourn that dwelleth in it? and it shall rise up wholly as a river; and it shall be cast out and drowned, as by the river of Egypt. And it shall come to pass*

in that day, saith the Lord GOD, that I will cause the sun to go down at noon, and I will darken the earth in the clear day: And I will turn your feasts into mourning, and all your songs into lamentation; and I will bring up sackcloth upon all loins, and baldness upon every head; and I will make it as the mourning of an only son, and the end of it as a bitter day.

Behold, the days come, saith the Lord GOD, that I will send a famine in the land, not a famine of bread, nor a thirst for water, but of hearing the words of the LORD: And they shall wander from sea to sea, and from the north even to the east, they shall run to and fro to seek the word of the LORD, and shall not find it. In that day shall the fair virgins and young men faint for thirst. They that swear by the sin of Samaria, and say, Thy god, O Dan, liveth; and, The manner of Beersheba liveth; even they shall fall, and never rise again.

(AMOS 8:1–14)

This prophecy helps in understanding why God allows such evil destruction. The people of Israel had become corrupt with commercialism. Not only were they anxious for their holy days to end, so they could return to making money, but they used dishonest measures, defrauding the poor in order to make an extra penny or two off each sale. Their greed is so obnoxious that they even sweep the dust off the granary floor to sell it as flour to the poor.

Was there an eclipse in Amos's day that made the darkening literally true, or was he seeing through to ultimate times? Or both? Was Amos speaking only of his own time when he said on behalf of God, "I will make it as the mourning of an only son, and the end of it as a bitter day." Or was he also referring to a time when Israel will mourn for one particular "only son"?

Behold, he cometh with clouds; and every eye shall see him, and they also who pierced him: and all kindreds of the earth shall wail because of him. Even so, Amen.

(REVELATION 1:7)

Either the prophets above were all borrowing from each other's language, or they were showing God's judgment expanding in rings like ripples across the surface of history. Each time humanity has had a chance to turn to God and failed, the judgment became greater than the previous time. In the Apocalypse, it becomes all-encompassing.

When Amos spoke of a famine of God's word in the land, he was speaking of the time of Israel's exile, but his description could not be more true of the times described for earth's end when *all* of the Messiah's people have been removed from the land. The two witnesses have been killed and resurrected from the earth. The 144,000 have joined the Messiah. There is a silence of the Spirit of God throughout the earth. The life-giving breath of God no longer blows across the land. Like a famine brought on when the wind lies dead for months, so the world in silent stillness lies, awaiting its death, but there is no repentance. Does anyone cry to God for help? No, they croak out their parched curses, grovel in the dust, chew on their tongues and wish to die. Or they turn and fight each other. Anything, rather than turning to God. The story of the world does not end with God rejecting humans; it ends with humans rejecting God.

The Apocalypse also speaks of the sun being given the power to burn people prior to the darkness. The prophet Nahum spoke of similar events when God would not relent against the wicked and the earth would burn:

> *The LORD is slow to anger, and great in power, and will not at all acquit the wicked: the LORD hath his way in the whirlwind and in the storm, and the clouds are the dust of his feet. He rebuketh the sea, and maketh it dry, and drieth up all the rivers: Bashan languisheth, and Carmel, and the flower of Lebanon languisheth. The mountains quake at him, and the hills melt, and the earth is burned at his presence, even the world, and all that dwell in it. Who can stand before his indignation? and who can abide in the fierceness of his anger? his fury is poured out like fire, and the rocks are thrown down by him. The LORD is good, a strong hold in the day of trouble; and he knoweth them that trust in him. But with an overrunning flood he will make an utter end of its place, and darkness shall pursue his enemies. . . . There is one come out of thee, that imagineth evil against the LORD, a wicked counsellor. Thus saith the LORD; Though they are quiet, and likewise many, yet thus shall they be cut down, when he shall pass through. Though I have afflicted thee, I will afflict thee no more. . . . Behold upon the mountains the feet of him that bringeth good tidings, that proclaimeth peace! O Judah, keep thy solemn feasts, perform thy vows: for the wicked shall no more pass through thee; he is utterly cut off.*
>
> (NAHUM 1:3–8, 11, 12, 15)

Again, the language used by Nahum grossly overstates the event he prophesied. Nathan spoke against a city called Ninevah, the capital of Assyria. It was utterly destroyed, but the flood was not literal. It was an army. Fire and rocks did not pour down from the sky, unless by catapults. The hills did not melt, and the earth did not burn, and if the ground quaked, it was only with the thunder of horse-drawn chariots. Nahum, of course, did not say the rivers and sea would actually dry up. He merely stated God had the power to do such things.

But if God has the power to do such things, will he always restrain himself? Perhaps Nahum, also, saw a distant time superimposed on his own, for he finishes by saying, "O Judah . . . the wicked shall no more pass through thee." Yet, the wicked have continued to pass through the ancient lands of Judah for millennia. So, while Nahum may have used figurative language to emphasize the terror of Ninevah's destruction, he may also have been describing a time when all prophecy will be "fulfilled" in the absolute meaning of the word—"fully filled"—and history will be "consummated" in the literal meaning of that word, "fully summed up."

PREPARING FOR ARMAGEDDON

Next the plagues of the Apocalypse shift toward preparation for a great war, known as the battle of Armageddon. They start by focusing on a single river:

> And the sixth angel poured out his vial
> upon the great river Euphrates; and its
> water was dried up, that the way of the
> kings of the east might be prepared.
> (REVELATION 16:12)

The drying up of rivers as a preparation for battle is a fairly common theme in prophecy. When the destruction of Assyria and its capital Ninevah were foretold, both Nahum and Zechariah mentioned the drying up of rivers:

> And he shall pass through the sea with affliction, and shall smite the waves in the sea, and all the deeps of the river shall dry up: and the pride of Assyria shall be brought down, and the sceptre of Egypt shall depart. And I will strengthen them in the LORD; and they shall walk up and down in his name, saith the LORD. (ZECHARIAH 10:11, 12)

The river referred to in the prophecy by Zechariah is the Tigris, which separated Ninevah from the lands all around Israel and from Babylon, which conquered Assyria. In days of ancient war, a great river like the Tigris, or its mate the Euphrates, were formidable barriers for an army to cross. The enemy could easily pick off an entire army while it fought the river, so for a river to be dried up meant the army would have easy access to their enemy.

While the Tigris separated Babylon from the capital of Assyria, the Euphrates separated Babylon from Israel. In the days of Rome, when John wrote, the Euphrates also represented the Roman frontier. Rome was never able to extend its empire beyond the Euphrates, and the empire was always under threat from enemies across the Euphrates. It would eventually be from across this river that the Huns would arrive to conquer Rome. But John is now talking about a time far greater than the conquest of Rome. He has made it clear that he is referring to the time of Christ's second coming by showing Christ's coming at the beginning of his description of the plagues.

Whether the drying up of the Euphrates so that the kings of the east can cross into

Israel is literal or figuratively based on the concept that the Euphrates represented the end of the empire is not clear, but many take it literally. In the days of modern warfare, however, a river hardly seems a formidable barrier to cross. Portable bridges, amphibious vehicles, missiles, long-range guns, and airplanes make rivers relatively inconsequential. So it may be the concept of an easy invasion that's most important. In fact, it is as though God makes the opportunity for invasion so easy that the land is begging for its enemies to come. God *wants* the enemies of his people to gather here. It is a trap:

Therefore wait ye upon me, saith the LORD, until the day that I rise up to the prey: for my determination is to gather the nations, that I may assemble the kingdoms, to pour upon them my indignation, even all my fierce anger: for all the earth shall be devoured with the fire of my jealousy. (ZECHARIAH 3:8)

God is going to allow the perfect enticement, represented as the drying up of the Euphrates barrier, so that all the evil armies of the world will gather in one place for their own destruction.

And I saw three unclean spirits like frogs come out of the mouth of the dragon, and out of the mouth of the beast, and out of the mouth of the false prophet. For they are the spirits of demons, working miracles, which go forth to the kings of the earth and of the whole world, to gather them to the battle of that great day of God Almighty. Behold, I come as a thief. Blessed is he that watcheth, and keepeth his garments, lest he walk naked, and they see his shame. And he gathered them together into a place called in the Hebrew tongue Armageddon. (REVELATION 16:13–16)

And the Antichrist walks right into the trap. Here the true natures of the Antichrist and the false prophet are revealed to John's readers. These two leaders are demon possessed. As Nahum had said, "There is one come out of thee, that imagineth evil against the LORD, a wicked counsellor."

Now that the description has broadened, it appears more likely that the importance of the Euphrates is more conceptual than literal, for it is not just the kings of the east who gather, but all the kings of all the world. God allows evil to gather its forces as his agent for its own destruction. The demonic influences are allowed to turn the entire world against Israel in order to gather all the armies of all the nations to a place called "Armageddon."

The word comes from the Hebrew *Har-Megiddo* (Mount of Megiddo), which is a hill overlooking the Valley of Jezreel, where the valley fans out into the vast plain of Megiddo. The ancient walled city of Megiddo was built on top of this hill. This fortified city controlled one of the most important military/trade routes of ancient history. Lying midway along the route between Egypt (to the south) and Assyria (to the north—later, Greece and Rome) at a crossroads less than one hundred miles from Jerusalem, it was also the gateway to Babylon (to the east). As a result, the valley below Megiddo was bathed in blood from one imperial conquest to the next.

It was likely upon *Har-Megiddo* that Elijah the prophet bested the false prophets of Jezebel, calling down fire from heaven to burn a water-sodden sacrifice. A stone's throw up the opposite valley lies Nazareth, the boyhood home of Jesus. And it was here at Megiddo that a young Jewish king wrested control of the land back from the conquering Assyrians. This turnabout led to one of Israel's greatest religious revivals. False prophets were slain, pagan temples demolished, human sacrifice ended. Solar and astral cults and divination were stomped into cinders. *The Book of the Covenant* was again read in the temple, and the one true God worshipped. During this great revival, the prophet Jeremiah began his ministry. And the young king met his defeat here, also, at the hands of Egyptian armies passing through to greater battles against Babylon. Perhaps the king's first great battle, which led to a spiritual victory for Israel, is the reason this site is chosen for the final battle.

Other prophecies indicate that nearby Jerusalem would also be involved in the world's last war:

> *Behold, the day of the LORD cometh, and thy spoil shall be divided in the midst of thee. For I will gather all nations against Jerusalem to battle; and the city shall be taken, and the houses rifled, and the women ravished; and half of the city shall go forth into captivity, and the rest of the people shall not be cut off from the city. Then shall the LORD go forth, and fight against those nations, as when he fought in the day of battle. And his feet shall stand in that day upon the mount of Olives, which is before Jerusalem on the east, and the mount of Olives shall cleave in the midst of it toward the east and toward the west, and there shall be a very great valley; and half of the mountain shall remove toward the north, and half of it toward the south. And ye shall flee to the valley of the mountains; for the valley of the mountains shall reach to Azal [a place near Jerusalem]: yea, ye shall flee, as ye fled from before the earthquake in the days of Uzziah king of Judah: and the LORD my God shall come, and all the saints with thee. And it shall come to pass in that day, that the light shall not be clear, nor dark: But it shall be one day which shall be known to the LORD, not day, nor night: but it shall come to pass, that at evening it shall be light. And it shall be in that day, that living waters shall go out from Jerusalem; half of them toward the former sea, and half of them toward the hinder sea: in summer and in winter shall it be.* (ZECHARIAH 14:1–8)

Over and over the prophets have emphasized the eerie darkness that would cover the earth. Almost every prophet has spoken of it when his language rises to the level of an apocalypse. Obviously, it will be a time of spiritual darkness, but it appears nature will provide her own symbolism of the spirit of the age.

Another feature of this final war that echoes like a refrain throughout prophecy is a great earthquake, such as the world has never seen before, with its epicenter at Jerusalem:

> *For thus saith the LORD of hosts; Yet once, it is a little while, and I will shake the heavens, and the earth, and the sea, and the dry land; And I will shake all nations, and the desire of all nations shall come: and I will fill this house [the temple] with glory, saith the LORD of hosts. . . . Speak to Zerubbabel, governor of Judah, saying, I will shake the heavens and the earth; And I will overthrow the throne of kingdoms, and I will destroy the strength of the kingdoms of the nations; and I will overthrow the chariots, and those that ride in them; and the horses and their riders shall come down, every one by the sword of his brother. In that day, saith the LORD of hosts, will I take thee, O Zerubbabel, my servant, the son of Shealtiel, saith the LORD, and will make thee as a signet: for I have chosen thee, saith the LORD of hosts.*
>
> (HAGGAI 2:6, 7, 21–23)

In the great Day of the Lord, God will shake down the nations. He will shake down the heavens. He will sift the people of earth to remove all evil from the earth. And it will be the sword of brother against brother that accomplishes this. God, however, does not force good upon the world. Jesus did not come as a man of peace, only to return as a man of war–untrue to all that he taught. Evil people will brandish their own swords (and cannons, and missiles, and germ warfare) against each other in earth's final holocaust. And, in the end, God will raise up a king, of whom Zerubbabel was a sign ("signet") in that Zerubbabel reigned when Israel was restored after Babylon.

As the prophet Micah was quoted in the previous chapter: "Afterwards the land shall be desolate because of them that dwell in it, for the fruit of their doings." (Micah 7:13)

> *And the seventh angel poured out his vial into the air; and there came a great voice out of the temple of heaven, from the throne, saying, It is done. And there were voices, and thunders, and lightnings; and there was a great earthquake, such as hath not been since men were upon the earth, so mighty an earthquake, and so great. And the great city was divided into three parts, and the cities of the nations fell: and great Babylon came in remembrance before God, to give to her the cup of the wine of the fierceness of his wrath. And every isle fled away, and the mountains were not found. And there fell upon men a great hail out of heaven, every stone about the weight of a talent: and men blasphemed God because of the plague of the hail; for its plague was exceeding great.*
>
> (REVELATION 16:17–21)

Chapter 18

BABYLON⊙:

BABYLON THE GREAT
AND THE BEASTS

Having introduced the seventh and final bowl of God's judgment, John now writes another interlude, which describes more fully the destruction of Babylon the Great and all that she represents:

And there came one of the seven angels who had the seven vials, and talked with me, saying to me, Come; I will show to thee the judgment of the great harlot that sitteth upon many waters: With whom the kings of the earth have committed acts of immorality, and the inhabitants of the earth have been made drunk with the wine of her immorality. So he carried me away in the spirit into the wilderness: and I saw a woman sit upon a scarlet coloured beast, full of names of blasphemy, having seven heads and ten horns. And the woman was arrayed in purple and scarlet colour, and decked with gold and precious stones and pearls, having a golden cup in her hand full of abominations and filthiness of her immorality: And upon her forehead was a name written, MYSTERY, BABYLON THE GREAT, THE MOTHER OF HAR-LOTS AND ABOMINATIONS OF THE EARTH. And I saw the woman drunk with the blood of the saints, and with the blood of the martyrs of Jesus: and when I saw her, I wondered with great wonder.

And the angel said to me, Why didst thou wonder? I will tell thee the mystery of the woman, and of the beast that carrieth her, which hath the seven heads and ten horns. The beast that thou sawest was, and is not; and shall ascend out of the bottomless pit, and go into perdition: and they that dwell on the earth shall wonder, whose names were not written in the book of life from the foundation of the world, when they behold the beast that was, and is not, and yet is. And here is the mind which hath wisdom. The seven heads are seven mountains, on which the woman sitteth. And there are seven kings: five are fallen, and one is, and the other is not yet come; and when he cometh, he must continue a short time. And the beast that was, and is not, even he is the eighth, and is of the seven, and goeth into perdition.

...And the woman whom thou

sawest is that great city, which reigneth over the kings of the earth.

(REVELATION 17:1–11, 18)

INTERPRETATIONS OF THE SEVEN-HEADED BEASTS

There are more views on who or what the beasts of the Apocalypse represent than there are heads on the beast itself. But maybe that is as it should be. John's vision may deliberately employ symbols that are meaningful to people in more than one time. The answer to the question, "Which interpretation is best?" may simply be, "Yes." Each has been right for its own time.

The one interpretation already presented was that the seven heads represented seven malicious heads of state during John's own life and that the beast represented the empire of Rome governed by these heads at different times. For John's readers, there was probably no question that the beast represented Rome. Which emperors were represented by the first seven heads would have been clear enough to those in that time. Since the prophecy says, "five are fallen, and one is, and the other is not yet come," they could have easily counted back from the emperor alive in their own time to know who the five were, and the one yet to come would reveal himself soon enough. It's more difficult to discern now because of uncertainty as to when the book was written.

Regardless of what the heads represented in John's own day, there is an interpretation that has made sense for all people since those early days. This interpretation views the seven heads as representing seven empires that have come against God's people (of Jewish faith and Christian) across the span of history. Under this view, the beast, itself, is more generalized, representing the evil force that underlies all imperial government. That would also explain why the seven heads are shown in this chapter without any crowns. When the seven heads wore seven crowns, the beast represented imperial Rome under its first seven emperors during the time of Christ and has apostles. When the ten horns wore crowns, the beast represented ten world rulers at the time of Christ's return. Now, when it is shown without any crowns, it transcends any specific time to represent the seven empires that have and will yet persecute God's people. The whole sweep of history is in view, past and future.

If this seven-headed hydra now represents all the imperial governments that have persecuted and will persecute God's people, then each "king" is the figurehead of one empire. The symbolic beast works beautifully on this level because it matches the prophetic vision in Daniel described at the beginning of this book. For Jews like John, Babylon was the epitome of destructive evil. The statue in the Babylonian king's dream began with Nebuchadnezzar as the figurehead for the Babylonian empire and continued to three other empires. Almost all early Church writers believed the remaining three were Persia, Greece, and Rome. Even Josephus, who lived through the fall of Jerusalem, says,

> In the same manner Daniel also wrote about the empire of the Romans and that Jerusalem would be taken by them and the temple laid waste.[1]

That accounts for four of John's seven empires. Two other major empires persecuted God's people *prior* to the time of Nebuchadnezzar and, therefore were not in his dream of the future, but they are included in John's broader overview of historic destiny. The Jews lived in exile under Egypt and much later under Assyria until Babylon conquered Assyria. Adding Egypt and Assyria to the role call of empires accounts for six of the heads. Thus, John writes, "five are fallen" (Egypt, Assyria, Babylon, Persia, and Greece), "one is" (Rome), and one is yet to come. Then he speaks of an eighth that will come after all of these, but in some sense belongs to the first seven.

The Beast of the Dark Ages and the Holy Roman Empire

During the Middle Ages and later, many viewed the one that, in John's time, was "yet to come" as being the Holy Roman Empire. If the legs of iron in Nebuchadnezzar's statue represented Rome, then the feet of iron and clay represent a fractured and weakened Rome—iron states held together by a bond of clay. Rome divided into many states, but the Roman Church managed tenuously to hold the kingdoms of Europe together under its own imperial power.

The image seemed to matched perfectly in other ways. The Catholic Church was headquartered in Rome, a city renowned in ancient times as the city of seven hills and, perfectly fitting the description of the Apocalypse: "The seven heads are seven mountains, on which the woman sitteth." In fact, one Roman coin minted in A.D. 71 depicts Rome as a woman reclining on seven hills. Underneath the woman is the word *Roma*.

Some have gone even farther to see the Holy Roman Empire as the beast that "once was, now is not, and will come up out of the abyss"—the head that died of a mortal wound but was revived, which was shown in Chapter 15 about the Antichrist. The Roman Empire died under Attila the Hun and other invaders but was resurrected as the Holy Roman Empire. This view greatly influenced the Reformation but is probably incorrect for three reasons: If Rome were the empire that died and was resurrected as Holy Rome, John could not have said it "now is not." Rome was much alive in John's day, and its demise came centuries later. Secondly, the *eighth* kingdom was to be the resurrected empire: "And the beast that was, and [now] is not, even he is the *eighth* [king], and is of the seven, and goeth into perdition." The Holy Roman Empire was the seventh in the order of empires that have persecuted God's people. Because the eighth empire is not one of the heads of the beast, its disjunction from it may imply a break in the line of imperial succession—a leap in time from the Holy Roman Empire to the final world empire. Thirdly, when John says this eighth empire will be one that "was" but "is not," he most likely speaks from his own point of reference in time, meaning that the eighth empire or king is revived from a time *before* John's own time and that it no longer existed during his time; so, he is not likely referring to the revival of Rome. (It's possible that the beast that was, is not, and will be again is different from the revived head described earlier by John. In that case, the Holy Roman Empire may have been the revived head.)

Why does all this matter? The view that the Holy Roman Empire was the revived beast and the Catholic Church was the lady that rode upon its back, enjoying its luxuries, held great sway for many centuries. It's not hard to see why that view, which strongly influenced history, has been hard to shake, given John Foxe's description of the death and resurrection of Rome in the times following Constantine (after A.D. 337, when the empire divided into its two legs and Christianity had become the official religion of Rome):

> Although the Christian church continued to grow in power, under the guidance of able bishops, Rome, herself, and the old cities of the empire, began to decline. The people were so idle and pleasure-loving that scarcely one Roman citizen had any longer the courage to fight in battle; but as they still had a great deal of money, they hired Goths, Germans, or Gauls—hardy barbarians from the wild countries of the North—to come and fight for them.
>
> In Rome little was cared for but feasting and display, or looking on the games in the Colosseum. . . . Christianity had not yet put an end to these cruel pastimes, although they were being continually preached against by the clergy.
>
> Much time was also idled away by the Romans at the public baths. . . . The soft, steamy air and warm waters of these baths, which were usually placed in beautiful and richly decorated marble buildings, helped to take away from these once brave and warlike people their ancient valor and resolution. . . . The whole manner of life in the city was as wasteful and self-indulgent as it is possible to imagine. Good and religious people tried to escape from the evil life of the capital.
>
> . . . The Goths rose . . . crossed the Danube under their great leader Alaric. . . . They soon came down from the North [in A.D. 410]. . . . Honorius, the young and almost idiotic emperor, fled to the city of Ravenna, and, safe behind its walls and marshes, thought of nothing but feeding and caring for a favorite flock of chickens. Alaric encamped outside the walls of Rome, thus cutting off all supplies of food, and calmly waited for starvation to bring the people to terms.

... At last not a particle of food remained in the once luxurious city, and the people had either to die or yield. They chose the latter and agreed to pay their enemy the ransom he had asked. ...

Thus Rome for the time escaped the hands of the destroyer. ... Alaric soon returned and entered the gates with his whole army. ... Terrible hardships were suffered by the people of Rome; but on the whole the damage done to the city was less than might have been expected. ...

One good thing came of the Gothic conquest—the pagans were put down for ever by the Arian conquerors. Their temples were utterly destroyed by the Goths, and the heathen idols broken in pieces. The weak and cowardly emperor, Honorius, remained in his refuge at Ravenna, but the bishop of Rome—or, as the Romans had begun to call him, Papa, father or Pope—came back and put the churches in order.

... And now a terrible enemy came against Rome [in A.D. 453]. The Huns, a wild and savage people of Asia, came swarming southward, led by their great chief Attila, leaving every country through which they passed streaming with blood and lurid with flames. Attila led his host into Italy and destroyed all the beautiful cities of the North. Advancing to Rome, no soldiers were there to defend it, but the brave pope, Leo I., went out at the head of his clergy to meet the barbarian, and solemnly threatened him with the wrath of Heaven if he let loose his cruel followers on the city.

Attila, heathen though he was, felt awed by the majestic presence and solemn warning of the head of the Christian church, and contenting himself with a heavy ransom, returned to the Danube.

... [In A.D. 455] Genseric, with his horde of Vandals, fresh from the conquest of the Roman provinces of Africa, was the next assailant of the doomed city. He would take no ransom, but turned his followers loose to plunder for themselves. For fourteen days they pillaged Rome, stripping churches and palaces alike. ... This was the most terrible calamity that Rome, once the queen of cities, had ever suffered from, and a few years later she fell, with the whole empire of the West, and became subject to successive kings or emperors who were merely the victorious leaders of invading armies of Germans, Goths, or Gauls.

This dark age for the great empire which had once ruled the world, lasted over three centuries. But in the year 800, Charles the Great, of France, was chosen emperor according to the old form, and from that time there arose again the Empire of the West.

But it was no longer as an imperial city, but as the home and central state of the Christian church, that Rome was again to dominate the world. The time was to come when the bishops of Rome, or popes, would direct from the papal palace all the affairs of the church in every part of the world. For centuries they were a power for good, directing with matchless ability noble bands of missionaries who carried Christianity to every country in the known world. But with increased strength came worldly pomp. They lived like princes, and came at last to claim not only control over the souls and consciences of men, but authority to rule their every act as well. They sought not only to direct the affairs of the Church, but they governed the nations of the earth.

The popes who came to wield this enormous power, were, naturally, no longer holy men, self-denying, poor, and persecuted; but were rich, arrogant nobles. Many of them were cruel, greedy of gain, and luxurious; hurling against rebellious sovereigns the awful curse of Rome, and dooming thousands of better men than themselves to the rack or the flames.[2]

(It should be noted that Foxe was an ardent Protestant and wrote with the intent of furthering the Protestant cause. His writings catalyzed the Protestant movement by reinforcing a new understanding of the Apocalypse. In many places, Foxe is still part of the Protestant psyche.)

One millennium after the persecutions of ancient Rome had been ended by Constantine, a new and worse period of persecution began under the Holy Roman Empire. Each of the empires in Nebuchadnezzar's dream (and those that inhabited the earth before his dream) sought to exterminate God's people, whether Jew or Christian Jew or Gentile Christian. It would appear the same dark fire that stoked the engine of all the previous empires entered the Church when it became the seventh empire of Judeo-Christian history, for the same pattern ensued. The Church burned disciples of Christ at the stake in a frenzy to eradicate heresies with the same paranoia that had inflamed the heart of Nero and had rekindled in the hearts of his successors. The dragon found within human hearts a smoldering resentment left from the original persecution of Christians by Jews. This passion for vengeance spread until its flames engulfed the Jews in Crusades that swept all the way back to Jerusalem.

When the Crusaders captured Jerusalem, fanatics gathered all the Jews into a synagogue and burned them alive. Estimates of the number of Jews killed in the Crusades run as high as 100,000, but the number of *heretics* killed in the Crusades and later Inquisitions was well over a million. And a heretic could be any Christian who disagreed with Rome. Out of one small group alone (known as the Waldenses), thousands were burned at the stake.

Will Durant, renowed author of the multi-volume *The Story of Civilization*, sums up the Inquisition as follows:

> Compared with the persecution of heresy in Europe . . . the persecution of Christians by Romans in the first three centuries after Christ was a mild and humane procedure. Making every allowance required of an historian and permitted to a Christian, we must rank the Inquisition . . . as among the darkest blots on the record of mankind, revealing a ferocity unknown in any beast.[3]

The Roman beast had been revived—in spirit and in name. It raised its long-dead head, and another incarnation of Babylon was born. That, at least, is how Protestants would come to view the situation, looking back from the Middle Ages:

The Christian Church had, long before [the second millennium], ceased to fear pagan enemies, for it had won in the struggle which had lasted for centuries. The idols were shattered forever throughout Europe, and paganism, except in countries to which the gospel had not yet penetrated, was a thing of the past. . . . A revolution had taken place in the minds of men, and nearly all the world, within the boundaries of the ancient empire, looked to Rome as the earthly citadel of their faith, and to the pope as the visible arbiter of Heaven.

While this high place given to the church and its ceremonies, its bishops and priests, strengthened its power enormously over its converts, and gave it for centuries a beneficial hold upon the minds, the affections, the fears of mankind, it ended by making tyrants of the men—for they were but men—who occupied the papal throne, and who held the highest church offices. The power of the pope and those appointed by him was too great, too absolute for fallible men to wield without becoming worldly, arbitrary, and cruel. . . . Differences in mode of worship or belief practiced by people who were in the main essentials earnest, believing Christians were put down with a merciless hand. "Heretics" they became as soon as they dared to uphold their own opinions against the all-conquering decrees of Rome, and once adjudged heretics they were considered outside the pale of human pity or justice.[4]

When the old Roman Empire split into Eastern and Western halves, it drove a wedge deep into the universal Church. Churches in the Eastern half of the old Roman Empire never went along with the idea of papal authority. The cities in the Eastern Empire considered the bishop of Rome an equal to the bishops of the other four great patriarchates. After all, Peter had never claimed or demonstrated any authority over the other apostles. The fact that St. Peter and St. Paul died in Rome as bishops did not raise Rome to a special level for the people in the Eastern (Byzantine) Empire who could also claim apostles for bishops.

The political division of the empire slowly began to crack the Church in two. Under Constantine, the capital had moved from Rome to the eastern city of Constantinople, undermining any claim to preeminence by the bishop of Rome. Centuries later, Pope Leo III drove the wedge deeper when he crowned Charlemagne as emperor over the Western Empire in A.D. 800. This newly claimed right to crown emperors in the West gave the Roman pope considerable power that was not recognized in the East.

A new kind of political beast was forming. As the Holy Roman Empire slowly evolved after Charlemagne, the crack through the Church could be heard slowly running down to its bottom. Finally, in A.D. 1054, it split the church into the Roman Catholic Church and the Eastern (or Greek) Orthodox Church. This also seemed to aptly fit Nebuchadnezzar's dream. The empire of iron divided into two legs and eventually ended up as two separate feet of iron mixed with baked clay—politics welded together by religion:

> And though thou sawest the feet and toes, part of potters' clay, and part of iron, the kingdom shall be divided; but there shall be in it of the strength of the iron, forasmuch as thou sawest the iron mixed with the miry clay. And as the toes of the feet were part of iron, and part of clay, so the kingdom shall be partly strong, and partly broken. And though thou sawest iron mixed with miry clay, they shall mingle themselves with the seed of men: but they shall not join one to another, even as iron is not mixed with clay.   (DANIEL 2:41–43)

As the popes began to wield their power with a heavier hand, some people in the Western Empire also began to resent papal rule. Where in the Bible, they wondered, did it say anyone was to take the place of Christ on earth? Why did people need to have a priest forgive their sins? Why wasn't believing in and following Jesus enough as it had been for the first three hundred years when the Church had no central authority outside the Bible and Jesus Christ? Was the Eastern Church less Christian because they didn't take orders from the pope? More fractures began forming in the feet of clay. The people did "not join one to another."

By doubting the pope's essential role to forgive the sins of humanity, they struck at the base of papal authority and the priesthood. So long as people needed the pope and his priests for forgiveness, he had absolute power over them—at least if they cared at all about their immortal souls. He could excommunicate them, and they would certainly go to hell, for no one would give them last rites. But the truth wanted to be heard: The pope was simply as human as all other humans. The divisions kept spreading.

A slow splintering could be heard in the great timbers of the Roman Catholic Church. By 1200, Pope Innocent III decided to appoint inquisitors to inspect the timbers for rot. Under papal edict, a priest named Dominic instituted an order called the Dominican friars. Their mission was to probe the empire for those termites called heretics and report back to Rome with their findings. Since the foundation of the papacy was at stake, they were given nearly unlimited power to exterminate any they found.

The dragon, who had long lay low beneath the earth (but not inactive) was warmed by the friction above and raised his smoking nostrils to sniff the surface. Witch hunts always meant there would be burning—at least if he had anything to say about it. The Roman flare for torching towns (and people) was rekindled. The inquisitors even dug up the bones of dead heretics and burned them. The word "bonfire" was invented. It meant "bone fire." One could never have enough bone fires. The last thing an inquisitor wanted to do was leave religious zealots a pile of martyrs' bones they could venerate. So, the bones of martyrs were burned and the ashes were thrown into rivers, where they flowed out to sea and, instead, venerated the whole earth.

The times proved quite inspiring to a writer named Dante Alighieri, who proceeded to expose the wickedness of some of the popes in his *Inferno*. As the power of the papacy had grown, those gravitating toward it were sometimes men who lusted for power, not men of humility and service as the original apostles had been. Places of rank in the Church were given or even sold to people of prestige. If they were well connected and influential, they might even ascend to positions as bishops or cardinals—or even pope. The imperial power of Rome reached its zenith during Dante's life in the person of Pope Boniface VIII. Seated on the former throne of Constantine in the year of our Lord 1300, with a crown on his head and the imperial sword at his side, Boniface waved his scepter and shouted to the people, "I am Caesar. I am Emperor."

Dante compares these imperial popes to a sorcerer from the New Testament named Simon Magus who was impressed with the miraculous powers displayed by the apostles and offered to buy their secrets of power from them. For such foolishness he was cursed by Saint Peter. For the simoniacal popes of his day, Dante reserved the deeper pits of hell.

In Dante's tour of hell, he reaches a level of the Abyss where he sees round holes in the ground with burning, twitching feet sticking out of them. One set of feet seems to be writhing worse than the others. Dante inquires of the man in the hole:

> "O wretched soul . . . that keepest upside down, planted like a stake . . . say a word if thou canst." I was standing like the friar who confesses the . . . assassin, who, after he is fixed, recalls him, in order to delay his death.[5]

Here Dante makes reference to those Dominican inquisitors who tortured confessions out of the Assassins, a secret order of Moslem fanatics who killed Christian Crusaders. Some were recalled for more torture even after their death had been determined ("fixed") by their confession.

The man in the hole identifies himself as Pope Nicholas III and mistakes Dante's voice for that of the reigning pope—Boniface VIII—who seems to have arrived a few years too early:

> "Art thou already standing there, Boniface? By several years the writing lied to me. Art thou so quickly sated with that having, for which thou didst not fear to seize by guile the beautiful Lady [the Church] and then do her outrage?"[6]

Nicholas is obviously greatly concerned at this arrival of another pope who raped the Church, so Dante's guide encourages him to hurry and give his true identity. Upon discovering Dante is not Pope Boniface, Nicholas explains his concern and why he is here in hell:

> "I was . . . so eager to advance . . . up there I put wealth, and here myself, into the purse. Beneath my head are the others that preceded me in simony, [pushed] down flattened through the fissures of the rock. Down there shall I in my turn sink, when he shall come whom I believed that thou wast; but already the time is longer that I have cooked my feet, and that I have been thus upside down, than he will stay planted with his feet red; for after him will come from westward a shepherd without law, of uglier deed. . . . "[7]

In Dante's vision of hell the plight of the evil popes is the eternal misery of knowing the only thing that lies ahead is being wedged upside–down deeper and tighter into their crack by the following pope. Ahead of them, all they hear are the muffled complaints of the pope whose feet presses against their head. Dante feels no mercy for this pitiful pope and says,

> "Pray now tell me, how much treasure did our Lord require of Saint Peter before he placed the keys [of heaven and hell] in his keeping? Surely he asked nothing save: 'Follow thou me.' Nor did Peter or the others take gold or silver of Matthias [the apostle chosen to replace Judas after Judas committed suicide] when he was chosen. . . . Therefore, stay thou, for thou art rightly punished [being pressed tight into a purse-like crack], and guard well the ill-gotten money that made thee bold . . . for your avarice afflicts the world, trampling down the good and exalting the bad. Ye shepherds the Evangelist [writer of the Apocalypse] had in mind, when she that sitteth upon the waters was seen . . . to fornicate with kings: she that was born with the seven heads. . . . Ye have made you a god of gold and silver: and what else is there between you and the idolaters save that they worship one, and ye a hundred?"[8]

Because of papal corruption, some people in Dante's time began to see the Roman Catholic Church as the whore in the Apocalypse who rides upon the seven-headed dragon, just as Dante expressed. Dante, and many like him, saw some of the powers claimed earlier by the medieval papacy as perfectly fulfilling the hubris of Babylon the Great or the apocalyptic beast:

> That the Roman bishop [pope] alone is properly called universal. . . . That the Pope is the only person whose feet are kissed by all princes. . . . That he has the power to depose emperors. . . . That his decree can be annulled by no one, and that he alone may annul the decrees of any one. . . . That he can be judged by no man. . . . That the Roman Church has never erred, nor ever, by the testimony of Scripture, shall err, to all eternity. . . . [9]

Dante was only concerned with the pope's claims on *imperial* power, but from the time the papacy decreed its absolute power and inerrancy, the destructive actions of the imperial Catholic hierarchy had begun to follow the usual litany of plundering and burning and maiming and burning and racking and burning. New tortures were invented, too, such as five-foot cubical rooms lined with spikes—even on the floor—so one could neither sit down, lie down, nor stand up. These rooms were let out for free to heretics as a place to squat until they recanted their heresies. Then they could be killed.

The first sects marked for extinction fled to the mountains and hid among rocks and caves. Their number was too great to round up, so free indulgences for future sin were offered by the pope as a bounty to encourage influential men to join the hunt. Between the Crusades against the Muslims and the Jews, and the Inquisition of Christian heretics, the holy wars had begun. The dragon, who loved nothing so much as the oxymoron of a holy war, flared his nostrils and inhaled deeply.

This opened a new interpretation for the white horse that leads the four horsemen earlier in the Apocalypse. The last three horsemen depicted war, leading to famine, disease, and death. The white horse had been understood alternately as Christ advancing his truth through the world and as the Antichrist because of the wars that follow. The dilemma was that Christ had told his disciple to put down the sword, so how could he establish his kingdom by war? Yet how could the Antichrist be depicted in the white of righteousness? The new interpretation suggested a resolution: Evil had insidiously invaded the Roman Church until the Church, itself, had become the Antichrist, exemplified in the position of the pope. No wonder the horse was white.

The first official on record to refer to the pope as the Antichrist was a Roman Catholic bishop, Arnulf of Orleans. Speaking as prosecutor in a legal trial against another bishop, he recounted some of the noble and true popes of the past, then asked, regarding the pope of his own day,

> What in your eyes, reverend fathers, is that Pontiff, seated on a throne, and clad in purple and gold? If he hath not charity, and be puffed up with his learning only, he is Antichrist, sitting in the temple of God, and demeaning himself as a god. . . . There is, in the words of the apostle, division . . . in the churches, because the time of Antichrist approaches. . . . It is manifest that in the decay of Roman power and the abasement of religion, the name of God is degraded . . . and that the observance of His holy religion is despised by the sovereign pontiffs themselves.[10]

Imperialism proved as ruthless and ungodly under papal control as it had been under old Rome or old Babylon. Because evil did not hesitate to don the white robes of righteousness, it was all the more insidious. From the time the Church first united with the State under Constantine, it had been forewarned by its own leadership that the spirit of Antichrist would be found within. In the middle of the fourth century, Hilary, bishop of Poitiers, had warned the Church:

> Beware of Antichrist. For the evil love of walls has captured you. You wrongly venerate the Church of God in [the form of] roofs and buildings; in these you wrongly find the name of peace. Can it be doubted that in these Antichrist is to be seated? To me mountains and forests and lakes, and prisons and chasms are safer. For the prophets, either dwelling in these or being plunged into them, prophesied in the spirit of God.[11]

Two centuries after Hilary, one of the infallible Catholic popes, Gregory I, had warned,

> Whosoever calls himself, or desires to be called Universal Priest, is in his elation the precursor of Antichrist, because he proudly puts himself above others.[12]

Just before Dante's birth, the pope made exactly that proclamation (as shown earlier). And the pope who said it was none other than Gregory's namesake, Gregory VII, who also made the extravagant claim,

> We desire to show the world that we can give or take away at our will kingdoms, duchies, earldoms, in a word, the possessions of all men.[13]

Yet, according to Gregory VII, *all* popes past and present are inerrant. Now two inerrant popes had made mutually exclusive statements about papal authority. The hubris of Gregory VII even caused one of his archbishops to revolt. Eberhard II, archbishop of Salzburg and counselor to King Frederick II, alluded to a number of prophecies quoted earlier in this book:

> Under the title of Pontifex Maximus, we discern, unless we are blind, a most savage wolf, with the garment of a shepherd; the Roman priests . . . have arms against all Christians; made great by daring, by deceiving, by bringing wars after wars, they slaughter the sheep, they cut them off, they drive away peace and harmony from the earth . . . they devour all, they reduce all to slavery. . . . Those priests of Babylon alone desire to reign, they cannot tolerate an equal, they will not desist until they have trampled all things under their feet, and until they sit in the temple of God, and until they are exalted above all that is worshipped. . . . He [the pope] changes laws, he ordains his own laws, he corrupts, he plunders, he pillages, he defrauds, he kills—that incorrigible man (whom they are accustomed to call Antichrist) on whose forehead an inscription of insult is written: "I am God, I cannot err." He sits in the temple of God, and has dominion far and wide.[14]

Beast on the Prowl: The Inquisition

In time, numerous groups of Christians began trying to reform the Roman Catholic Church and call it back to humility and purity. Many were killed, for they did protest too much. But the number of reformers continued to mount, finding in the pages of the Apocalypse courage to brave death. As a result, these Protestants, as they came to be called, saw the Roman Church as Dante had and began to interpret prophecy accordingly. They viewed the Roman Catholic Church as Babylon the Great and the pope as the Antichrist. If the Apocalypse had not been written, the Catholic Church may not have ever been reformed. Its vivid images were used to place great pressure for reform on the Church hierarchy. The Apocalypse became a blistering attack on the Church.

One did not have to be a free-thinking Christian to be considered a heretic. By the late 1400s, Jews became heretics too. For centuries Jews, Christians, and Muslims had lived in relative peace within the borders of Spain, each enjoying their own share of prosperity. Each usually lived in their own sector of town, and they rarely intermarried, but that was what each group preferred. They mixed regularly in commerce and in public events. Coexistence had its tensions and certainly its inequalities, but there was mutual respect with tension.

All of that ended with the Spanish Inquisition. Now the so-called followers of Christ—who had, centuries earlier, been exiled for their beliefs—begin exiling others, like the Jews, who believed differently. Placing their faith in human power, the Church leadership was not willing to trust the truth to prevail on its own but imposed the truth by violence.

As early as 1349, an entire Jewish community in Strasbourg had been burned under the direction of the Inquisition. Now, with the Spanish Inquisition, the spirit of Antichrist, which had moved both Roman and Jewish leaders to kill Christ and his followers, began moving Christians to kill Jews on a more systematic basis. It was a spirit that revelled most in having the children of God kill each other.

The Inquisition resurrected the deeply buried Christian furor against the Jews. The Catholic doctrine that the bread and wine of Christian communion changes in substance into the body and blood of Jesus Christ was used to substantiate the death of hundreds of Jews. Absurd accusations were leveled that certain Jews had stolen consecrated communion wafers and tortured them to desecrate the body of Christ. Indeed, the wafers were desecrated, but not by the Jews. They became desecrated by the innocent Jewish blood that was shed over them—just as the altar in the Jewish temple had been desecrated by the human blood spilled over it.

Jews were even periodically accused of ritualistic murders, in which they supposedly drank the blood of Christians. Ignorance ruled the day, for anyone knowing anything about Judaism would have known that drinking blood of any kind was anathema to everything Judaism ever stood for. God's law to the Jews was the first light in a pagan world that had forbidden the drinking of blood.

The Catholic Church's concern during the Spanish Inquisition was primarily anti-heretical, rather than anti-Semitic, which is why they killed their own race as well. This can be seen in a papal bull at the time that forcefully declared that Jews who converted to Christianity were to be treated in all respects like all other Christians. (The problem, however, was that not all other Christians were being treated so well.) The archbishop of Spain later reiterated the pope's statement:

> Divisions bring great scandal and schism and divide the seamless garment of Christ who, as the Good Shepherd, gave us a command to love one another in unity and obedience to Holy Mother Church, under one Pontiff and Vicar of Christ, under one baptism, formed under the law into one body, so that whether Jew, Greek or Gentile we are regenerated by baptism and made into new men.[15]

The official word was that Christianity embraced all races, for all people needed re-generation. Blood was not initially the issue for the Inquisition, though it became one later. The goal was to eradicate doctrines that competed with the pope's authority, and if that meant killing a few thousand dissident voices, whether they were Jew or Christian made little difference.

But the outfall was much different. With the Church no longer a fountain of justice, love, forgiveness, and voluntary submission to Christ, the dross naturally rose to the surface of society. Anti-Semitism existed in society in pockets where Jews refused to assimilate with the pre-existing culture. Here the Jews were wedged into a tight place, for their God had commanded them not to assimilate in the Old Testament. The effort of Jews to preserve their nationality, culture, and religion within other sovereign nations, however, created conflict.

The Church's move to expunge heresy and competing doctrines lifted the lid on the social melting pot. Tensions that had been held relatively under control now let off steam. Civility flew apart in all directions: The Jewish community had usually ostracized Jews who converted to Christianity. The Inquisition created opportunity for further re-taliation against the converts. Some Jews bore false witness to the inquisitors—who were ready to believe anything—claiming the Jewish converts to Christianity were still prac-ticing Judaism. (The penalty for such heresy, of course, was burning.) As a result, estab-lishment Christians began ostracizing the new converts because they believed what the other Jews were saying. It was an easy step. Many Spanish Christians were already feeling anti-Semitic jealousy because the new converts had begun to occupy some of their es-tablished positions in society.

Converts who were not deep in their faith also began falsely accusing other converts who wouldn't pay them off. Meanwhile, the old "Christ killer" animosity from the Crusades also raised its head against those who remained of the Jewish faith. Spain became the dragon's playpen.

The Inquisition in Spain got so far out of hand so fast that Pope Sixtus IV wrote:

> ... The Inquisition has for some time been moved not by zeal for the faith and the salvation of souls, but by lust for wealth, and ... many true and faithful Christians, on the testimony of enemies, rivals, slaves and other lower and even less proper persons, have without any legitimate proof been thrust into secular prisons, tortured and condemned as relapsed heretics, deprived of their goods and property and handed over to the secular arm to be executed, to the peril of their souls.[16]

Though the pope rightly summed up the situation, his concern seems to be more that the abuses were coming by *secular* means when it should have been done by the Church. The king and queen of Spain had assumed authority over matters of the Church without consulting him. For years, the Catholic monarchs Isabella and Ferdinand had protected Jews from civil animosity while tolerance for pluralism grew thin, but Ferdinand grew weary of the endless conflicts that surrounded the Jews in Spain. The inquisitors, then, found it easier to obtain their authority to execute punishment from the king than from the pope.

The imperial Ferdinand responded to presumed heresies in the manner of a king. A king quashes insurrections, and since members of the Church were willing to force truth upon people (while not being guided by it themselves), there were no checks and balances. As Ferdinand's weariness over the problem grew, the inquisitors managed to persuade him to exile all people of the Jewish faith—even though a number of his favored court appointees were Jewish. So while Columbus sailed the ocean blue, the Spanish Jews were shipped off to other realms like beggars without a home—again. Alternately, they could convert to Christianity and assimilate. Thus, the dragon, once again chased the woman Israel into the desert.

There were, even in such times, voices of reason from Christians who lived by truth, but they were lost in the din of Church and king and an intolerant populace. Some Christians tried to point out that expulsion of the Jews constituted a tacit invitation to annihilate the Jews, which was contrary to scripture. Others deplored the fact that new converts were treated worse than before they converted. They suggested that perhaps more Jews would be willing to become Christians had they ever actually met a Christian. In the words of one Christian, the inquisitors would "not produce such good Christians with their fire as the bishops ... did with water."[17]

In the early 1500s, Captain General Gonzalo de Ayora wrote,

. . . As for the Inquisition, the method adopted was to place so much confidence in the archbishop of Seville and in Lucero . . . that they were able to defame the whole kingdom, to destroy, without God or justice, a great part of it, slaying and robbing and violating maids and wives to the great dishonour of the Christian religion.

The damage which the wicked officials of the Inquisition have wrought in my land are so many and so great that no reasonable person on hearing of them would not grieve.[18]

The fact that Jews were pressed to convert could be *construed* as evidence that the attacks against them were not racially based. Hitler, by contrast, would never have asked Jews to convert to Naziism. That would have been intolerable (to both). He simply wanted to get rid of them. The Catholic Church, however, desperately wanted Jews to join them—but too desperately. The assumption by both Church and king was that Jews faced with expulsion would choose to convert. They were probably surprised at the number who chose exile.

Of course, branding Jews as "Christ killers" is still bigotry, whether racial or religious. And it's ignorant. Jesus had thousands of followers in his lifetime who were Jews. Some Jews did play a role in the death of Jesus, but another Jew—Mary—gave him his life. Still other Jews wrote his biography. In the very least, it's never fair to blame present people for past blood.

The source of the conflict is neither Christianity nor Judaism. Both teach forgiveness, and Christ never forced his beliefs on anyone. The source is human evil, but there seems to be a deeper, worldwide force driving it. The apocalyptic story of the dragon chasing the woman into the desert reveals an evil in the world that wishes to exterminate God's people or to bring out the worst in them so they exterminate each other. All it has to do is arouse the evil tendencies that are always latent within human beings.

Since the prophecies of Old and New Testaments teach that the salvation of the world lies in the hands of these two groups of people, evil must destroy them or get them to destroy each other. It's perhaps appropriate, then, that the woman chased by the dragon in the Apocalypse has been seen alternately as the Church and as Israel. The dragon has long chased both groups.

REFORMATION

As Protestant reformers emerged from the mayhem, they took some of the heat off the Jews. The Spanish Inquisition broadened under King Charles V's concern that those who would question the authority of the Church would soon question the authority of the king. Power was always the central issue. Charles ordered that all people whose ideas were heretical, regardless of whether they were Jewish heretics or Christian, should "be burnt and their goods confiscated."

Strains of apocalyptic prophecy can be heard in the response to the broadening Inquisition. One priest in Toledo plastered the town with placards saying the Catholic Church was "not the Church of Jesus Christ but the Church of the devil and of Antichrist his son, the Antichrist pope." It almost goes without saying that he was burned. Pamphlets in Seville attacked those "thieves of inquisitors, who rob publicly." The pamphlets also exhorted people to "pray to God for his true Church to be strong and constant in the truth and bear with the persecution from the synagogue of Satan."

In the end, the Roman love of fire was doused by too much blood, and the Church recognized some of its wrongs. It started by adopting many of the reforms the Protestants had sought, but this reformation from within could not overcome the embittered new understanding of the Apocalypse, as expressed by Dante, that Babylon the Great represents the Catholic Church. A major shift in the interpretation of prophecy had occurred. The beast was no longer old imperial Rome.

In spite of reforms, the damage was lasting. The Holy Roman Empire was about to shatter politically and religiously into independent nations and a hundred church denominations. The word of truth from above prevailed against evil, and the dragon's revived empire was broken. The open symbolism of the Apocalypse had accomplished its job one more time. Another group of persecuted Christians found solace in words that fit their situation.

If the majority of Jesus' followers had actually followed him by brandishing the living truth, instead of the killing sword, there would have been no inquisitions, and the Church may not have split. Yet, it may have been the Apocalypse, itself, that fed the Inquisition. It served the purposes of some to read its militaristic portrayal of Christ as a conqueror on a white horse literally. Taken literally, this image seemed to imply that the Church was to march out in Crusades and conquer the world for Christ: It was assured victory in its holy war. Reading the Apocalypse too literally may have justified a world of sin. When the Church in its zeal tried to bring in God's kingdom of light by the methods of darkness, it spread the darkness across the globe.

But the power of the dragon to influence the Church proved no different under Protestants. While the Catholics went through the Counter Reformation, Protestants entered a sort of counter Babylon, returning fire for fire. When British Protestants gained the seat of power with kings and queens as head of the Church of England, they became as severe toward Catholics as the Catholics had been toward the reformers—a conflict that still scars the face of Ireland. It was early *Protestant* rule, not the former Catholic rule, that led to the religious exodus from England to America where a clearer separation of Church and State was eventually established. When those in charge of the truth kneel before the altar wearing helmets and coats of mail, then the sun has truly turned red like blood, and the stars of the sky have fallen.

Ruminating too long on the crimes of history, however, stokes the fire in one's own belly, and the dragon smiles within. Denial of historic crimes, on the other hand, perpetuates the lie that such sins never occurred. If people can look to the past to find their own evil tendencies recorded there, instead of recounting the other group's sins, then looking to the past can lead to confession and healing. The Roman Catholic Church has shown a sincere willingness to confess some of its wrongs in the twentieth century. Pope John XXIII, in the latter half of the century, offered the following confession to Jews in a prayer of atonement:

> We realize now that many, many centuries of blindness have dimmed our eyes, so that we no longer see the beauty of the Chosen People and no longer recognize in their faces the features of our first-born brother. . . . We had forgotten Thy [Jesus'] love. Forgive us the curse which we unjustly laid on the name of the Jews. Forgive us that, with our curse, we crucified Thee a second time.[19]

In his prayer, the Pope expressed the sorry irony than in killing Jews the spirit of the "Christ killers" was to be found in the Church, not in the Jews. Ironically, in protecting itself from heresies, the Church had followed the same spirit that led ancient Jewish leaders to protect Judaism from messianic "heresies" by seeking the death of Jesus. When the medieval fury was ended, the Catholic Church, according to Pope John XXIII, looked down and saw the blood of Christ on its own hands.

In more recent years, Pope John Paul II has also shown himself to be a peaceful man of God, working for reconciliation with the Jewish community and for the end of oppressive Marxist regimes. Having grown up in an elementary school that was one-quarter Jewish, the pope has said,

> . . . anti-Semitism is a great sin against humanity . . . all racial hatred inevitably leads to the trampling of human dignity.
> . . . Two great moments of divine election—the Old and the New Covenants—are drawing closer together.
> . . . As for the recognition of the State of Israel, it is important to reaffirm that I myself never had any doubts in this regard.[20]

In spite of these changes, the existence of a single seat that claims worldwide religious authority over Christians like the Holy See of Rome continues to make many Protestants today wary of the opportunity for the Beast of the Apocalypse to rise there again. The blood of history testifies that the human process of electing a Pope *is* vulnerable to evil, and evil always gravitates toward power.

John's use of poetic language indicates an intentional openness to interpretations that offer assurance of ultimate victory to the followers of Jesus Christ during any major persecution of the Church. Such openness maddens the minds of those who like things to be concrete, but it allows the text to breathe, making Revelation a living word. It can be abused by rallying others to Crusades, or it can overpower evil by giving others courage to die for stating the truth.

THE ULTIMATE BEAST

It may be that John foresaw periods of destruction, with each period serving as a precursor to a greater one to follow. In other words, until humanity yields all power and authority to God, each human empire will only serve to broadened the circle of human destruction. And so the cycles build on each other like fractals until they culminate at the very end of earth history.

Since many prophecies that are applied to end times have already seen fulfillment in former times, it's not necessary for all their parts to be repeated in the future. Patterns usually do not replicate exactly. What could be expected from the patterns of history is that each of the previous downfalls prefigures certain aspects of the ultimate collapse of human empire—the final collapse of the ultimate Babylon.

In some manner, the world will be astonished to see the devil incarnate. The head and beast that was and is no more has to refer to an entity that existed before John's time. So the reincarnation of Hitler, while actually possible under modern science (if living tissue has been frozen or kept alive somewhere by Hitler's own scientists), is not likely the correct interpretation. That head, which is an eighth king, must also come after the Holy Roman Empire, which was the seventh empire to dominate God's people. It may refer to Satan himself, whose visible effects are seen on earth but who is never seen, meaning that he becomes incarnate—possesses a human being. If the revived head is not a human being, but an expired empire, the most likely interpretation would be some kind of revival of Babylon. But does "Babylon the Great" mean that the ancient empire (seated in what is now Iraq) will be physically revived into a worldwide empire in a manner as surprising as the revival that happened to Rome, or does it mean a worldwide empire that will fulfill the prophecies that were originally given to ancient Babylon? Will it be all of these—Satan incarnate, occupying the revived (cloned) body of a former leader, headquartered in the area of ancient Babylon (Iraq) or figurative Babylon (Rome), running an empire that fulfills the grand language of all the prophecies made against ancient Babylon?

Though John's vision in many respects applied to the events of his own day, he clearly intended to predict the future by mentioning a seventh and eighth king beyond his own time, as well as ten kings yet to come (the ten horns on the beast with seven heads):

> And the ten horns which thou sawest are ten kings, who have received no kingdom as yet; but receive power as kings one hour with the beast. These have one mind, and shall give their power and strength to the beast. These shall make war with the Lamb, and the Lamb shall overcome them: for he is Lord of lords, and King of kings: and they that are with him are called, and chosen, and faithful. And he saith to me, The waters which thou sawest, where the harlot sitteth, are peoples, and multitudes, and nations, and tongues. And the ten horns which thou sawest upon the beast, these shall hate the harlot, and shall make her desolate and naked, and shall eat her flesh, and burn her with fire. For God hath put in their hearts to fulfil his will, and to agree, and give their kingdom to the beast, until the words of God shall be fulfilled. And the woman whom thou sawest is that great city, which reigneth over the kings of the earth.
>
> (REVELATION 17:12–18)

Because the book speaks of kings that have not yet come, the historic relevance of the Apocalypse only foreshadows its future visions of worldwide empire and destruction. Such an empire may fulfill every aspect of John's vision—even those that already occurred in localized ways. The final image of a fractal design—wherever it is stopped—contains every pattern that came before.

(Those who insist, however, that the Apocalypse has *only* an end-times scenario in mind should recognize there is chronometric arrogance in assuming God is concerned more about speaking through his prophets to Christians in the present day or the last days than to Christians in earlier times of persecution. Such arrogance assumes that none of the events of history mattered as much to God as our own present or our future. Why wouldn't Christ, the "living word," give his disciple John a book for all seasons?)

Pulling together the visions of John and Daniel, one would expect earth's last empire to be ruled by ten leaders, three of whom will be supplanted by a final leader, the eighth king in John's vision. In other words, it will likely be a federation of nations. The spirit of this ruler will certainly be anti-Christ and related to all of the first seven empires John symbolized, which included the Holy Roman Empire beyond his own time (the seventh head which was yet to come).

Because the feet of baked clay and iron in Nebuchadnezzar's dream (the Holy Roman Empire) divide into ten toes, some have speculated that the ten leaders or nations will descend from the Holy Roman Empire. That is to say, they will be European or even Catholic. Interpreting the next empire as an outgrowth of the last, however, is not necessary. *Most* of the empires in line before Rome were supplanted by entirely unrelated empires that moved in and conquered their predecessor. Some had great gaps of time between them.

A clear view of the end-times beast will emerge out of the mist when its day arrives. Some feel they hear its footsteps in the move toward globalism. Some think it's close enough they can hear its heartbeat in the clocks of computers begging for a common international, electronic currency. They may be right, but the words of the Apocalypse were not given as a road map to know the future in advance. Rather, they are for recognizing it when it happens. Until then, all of these things are speculation.

The climax of earth's history ends in John's Apocalypse with poetic justice. Whether Babylon the Great is Rome (revived for the *second* time) *or* some other last attempt at world empire (as described in the next chapter), it will die from its own flames: "the ten horns which thou sawest upon the beast, these shall hate the harlot, and shall make her desolate and naked, and shall eat her flesh, and burn her with fire. For God hath put in their hearts to fulfil his will, and to agree, and give their kingdom to the beast, until the words of God shall be fulfilled."

Just as satanic evil burned Jerusalem and its temple under the original Babylon, then burned Christians and the Roman capital under Nero, then burned the rebuilt Jerusalem and its temple again under Nero's successor, and later burned Christian reformers and Jews under the revived Holy Rome and finally persecuted Catholics under Protestant rule, so Babylon the Great—the Babylon of all Babylons—will be destroyed with the same fury it has poured out on others. It will be destroyed in a single holocaust of fire.

Chapter 19

HOLOCAUST:

†HE DESTRUCTION OF BABYLON †HE GREAT

John refers to the final imperial power that will dominate the world as "Babylon the Great." In so doing, he connects the ultimate world empire with the first empire in King Nebuchadnezzar's dream. Babylon was the most ancient city in the world, the first city named after the story of Noah's flood. It lay in the heart of the Fertile Crescent, recognized as the cradle of human civilization. In this almost prehistoric city, the infamous tower of Babel was built:

> And they said, come, let us build us a city and a tower, whose top may reach to heaven; and let us make us a name, lest we should be scattered abroad upon the face of the whole earth. And the LORD came down to see the city and the tower, which the children of men were building. And the LORD said, Behold, the people is one, and they have all one language; and this they begin to do: and now nothing will be withheld from them, which they have imagined to do. Come, let us go down, and there confound their language, that they may not understand one another's speech. So the LORD scattered them abroad from there upon the face of all the earth: and they ceased building the city. Therefore is the name of it called Babel; because the LORD there confounded the language of all the earth.... (GENESIS 11:4–9)

The significance of Babel was the human attempt to ascend to the status of God. The Greeks later called this kind of overreaching pride "hubris." In Greek mythology, the gods killed people for this kind of thing. In the Jewish story, God scatters the people across the earth in groups and divides their language. Thus, it was out of Babylon in Mesopotamia that all nationalities descended and to figurative Babylon that all nations shall return. Babylon is the beginning and end of nationalism. In figurative Babylon shall all nations unite and try to reach the heights of God again through their exalted leader, the Antichrist.

What better way to describe the fall of the world's ultimate empire than in terms of the fall of ancient Babylon? The prophets had foretold its fall many times, as when God assured Habakkuk that Babylon would bring its own destruction upon itself. By stirring up so many enemies with its aggression, Babylon would assuredly drink from the same cup of poison from which it had forced the Jews to drink. Other prophets carried a similar message:

> And it [Babylon] shall be as the chased roe, and as a sheep that no man taketh up: they shall every man turn to his own people, and flee every one to his own land. Every one that is found shall be thrust through; and every one that is joined to them shall fall by the sword. Their children also shall be dashed to pieces before their eyes; their houses shall be plundered, and their wives ravished. Behold, I will stir up the Medes against them, who shall not regard silver; and as for gold, they shall not delight in it. Their bows also shall dash the young men to pieces; and they shall have no pity on the fruit of the womb; their eye shall not spare children. And Babylon, the glory of kingdoms, the beauty of the Chaldees' excellency, shall be as when God overthrew Sodom and Gomorrah. It shall never be inhabited, neither shall it be dwelt in from generation to generation: neither shall the Arabian pitch tent there; neither shall the shepherds make their fold there. But wild beasts of the desert shall lie there; and their houses shall be full of doleful creatures; and owls shall dwell there, and satyrs shall dance there. And the wild beasts of the isles shall cry in their desolate houses, and dragons in their pleasant palaces: and her time is near to come, and her days shall not be prolonged. (ISAIAH 13:14–22)

And the prophets were very accurate in what they predicted for Babylon. Although Babylon did not crash into oblivion, it was attacked viciously and declined over the centuries until it eventually ended up in utter desolation. The ruins of Babylon have remained essentially uninhabited to the present day. Once the most glorious city on earth—one of the seven wonders of the ancient world—the site is no longer considered suitable for human habitation. Some have said that even bedouins have avoided its ruins out of superstitious horror. This, then, is the kind of destruction John predicts for the final world empire.

The satyrs and dragons may be allusions to mythical beasts, or they may refer to wild goats and reptiles. ("Dragons" could also be a mistake in the translation since the Hebrew words for "dragon" and "jackal" look similar.) Both allusions, however, may have been intentional—to portray the demonic nature of ancient Babylon, where children were burned as sacrifices to the pagan god Molech.

Babylon, the first to demolish Jerusalem by fire, was seared into the Jewish consciousness much like Auschwitz is today. When Jerusalem was destroyed by fire a second time during John's lifetime, the parallels between Rome, the aggressor, and ancient Babylon would have been obvious to any Jew. The destruction of the temple, the demolition of the Holy City, the forced exile—all of these things repeated events that occurred under Babylon.

ROME AS BABYLON THE GREAT

So, it's not surprising that John's early readers first understood his description of the fall of Babylon the Great as referring to ancient Rome. Saint Jerome, a prolific writer, scholar, and the first translator of the Bible into Latin (the Vulgate), was a man at the heart of the early Catholic Church. His Bible was the only authorized translation used by Catholics until Vatican II in the twentieth century. In A.D. 396, Jerome described the fall of ancient Rome while he lived through it:

> I shudder when I think of the catastrophes of our time. For twenty years and more the blood of Romans has been shed daily . . . pillaged and plundered by Goths and Sarmatians, Quades and Alans, Huns and Vandals and Marchmen. . . . Bishops have been made captive, priests and those in minor orders have been put to death. Churches have been overthrown, horses have been stalled by the altars of Christ. . . . The Roman world is falling: yet we hold up our heads instead of bowing them.
>
> . . . But when the bright light of all the world was put out, or , rather, when the Roman Empire was decapitated, and . . . the whole world perished in one city, "I became dumb and humbled myself."[1]

The death of the great *Pax Romana* (Roman peace) led to anarchy and chaos. The plunge into the Dark Ages cannot be blamed initially on the Roman Catholic Church, for the Inquisitions did not begin for another five hundred years. The Huns and the Vandals brought on a political catastrophe that sent the entire Western world reeling into anarchy. Who could not see in the demise of the world's largest and longest-lasting empire—ever—a fulfillment to the following poetry in John's Apocalypse?

And after these things I saw another angel come down from heaven, having great power; and the earth was made bright with his glory. And he cried mightily with a strong voice, saying, Babylon the great is fallen, is fallen, and is become the habitation of demons, and the hold of every foul spirit, and a cage of every unclean and hateful bird. For all nations have drunk of the wine of the wrath of her immorality, and the kings of the earth have committed acts of immorality with her, and the merchants of the earth have become rich through the abundance of her delicacies. And I heard another voice from heaven, saying,

Come out of her, my people, that ye be not partakers of her sins, and that ye receive not of her plagues. For her sins have reached to heaven, and God hath remembered her iniquities. Reward her even as she rewarded you, and double to her double according to her works: in the cup which she hath filled, fill to her double. How much she hath glorified herself, and lived luxuriously, so much torment and sorrow give her: for she saith in her heart, I sit a queen, and am no widow, and shall see no sorrow. Therefore shall her plagues come in one day, death, and mourning, and famine; and she shall be utterly burned with fire: for strong is the Lord God who judgeth her.

And the kings of the earth, who have committed acts of immorality and lived luxuriously with her, shall bewail her, and lament for her, when they shall see the smoke of her burning, Standing afar off for the fear of her torment, saying, Alas, alas, that great city Babylon, that mighty city! for in one hour is thy judgment come. And the merchants of the earth shall weep and mourn over her; for no man buyeth their merchandise any more: The merchandise of gold, and silver, and precious stones, and of pearls, and fine linen, and purple, and silk, and scarlet, and all thyine wood [citrus wood used as incense and for its beauty], and all kinds of vessels of ivory, and all kinds of vessels of most precious wood, and of brass, and iron, and marble, And cinnamon, and incense, and ointments, and frankincense, and wine, and oil, and fine flour, and wheat, and cattle, and sheep, and horses, and chariots, and bodies, and souls of men. And the fruits that thy soul lusted after have departed from thee, and all things which were luxurious and splendid have departed from thee, and thou shalt find them no more at all. The merchants of these things, who were made rich by her, shall stand afar off for the fear of her torment, weeping and wailing, And saying, Alas, alas, that great city, that was clothed in fine linen, and purple, and scarlet, and decked with gold, and precious stones, and pearls! For in one hour so great riches is come to nought. And every shipmaster, and all the company in ships, and sailors, and as many as trade by sea, stood afar off, And cried when they saw the smoke of her burning, saying, What city is like this great city! And they cast dust on their heads, and cried, weeping and wailing, saying, Alas, alas, that great city, in which were made rich all that had ships in the sea by her wealth! for in one hour is she made desolate. Rejoice over her, thou heaven, and ye holy apostles and prophets; for God hath avenged you on her. And a mighty angel took up a stone like a great millstone, and cast it into the sea, saying, Thus with violence shall that great city Babylon be thrown down, and shall be no more found. And the voice of harpers, and musicians, and of pipers, and trumpeters, shall be no more heard in thee; and no craftsman, of whatever craft he be, shall be found any more in thee; and the sound of a millstone shall be no more heard in thee; And the light of a lamp shall shine no more in thee; and the voice of the bridegroom and of the bride shall be heard no more in thee: for thy merchants were the great men of the earth; for by thy sorceries were all nations deceived. And in her was found the blood of prophets, and of saints, and of all that were slain upon the earth. (REVELATION 18:1–24)

What Christian could not see in this portrait of the luxurious harlot, riding on a seven headed beast, the image stamped on Roman coins of the goddess *Roma*, reclining seductively upon the seven hills of Rome? What city's influence sprawled over so many seas as Rome, which ruled them all and was, itself, a seaport via the Tiber River? What city traded more luxuriously with the merchants of the entire world than Rome? What city traded more in "the bodies, and souls of men"—both Jewish and Christian martyrs—than Rome? What city has ever acted more like a god while torturing the people of God for their refusal to worship the harlot? ("And in her was found the blood of prophets, and of saints, and of all that were slain upon the earth.")

Echoes from the Past

This whole poetic section of the Apocalypse is an echo of all the prophecies spoken against the original Babylon centuries before, clearly showing how prophecies and the history they relate to repeat their patterns. John predicted Babylon the Great would become a haunt for demons, just as Isaiah predicted Babylon would become a haunt for satyrs and dragons. John says the sins of Babylon the Great "reached to heaven" just as the ancient tower of Babel attempted to reach to heaven. Babylon the Great is destroyed for harming God's chosen people the Christians, just as ancient Babylon was destroyed for harming God's chosen people the Jews.

Many echoes can also be heard between John's words and the much earlier voice of Jeremiah who spoke against the original Babylon:

Thus saith the LORD; Behold, I will raise up against Babylon, and against them that dwell in the midst of them that rise up against me, a destroying wind; And will send to Babylon fanners, that shall fan her, and shall empty her land: for in the day of trouble they shall be against her on all sides. . . . Flee from the midst of Babylon, and deliver every man his soul: be not cut off in her iniquity. . . .

[And the Apocalypse said, "Come out of her, my people, that ye be not partakers of her sins, and that ye receive not of her plagues."]

. . . for this is the time of the LORD'S vengeance; he will render to her a recompence. . . .

[And the Apocalypse said, "God hath avenged you on her."]

. . . Babylon hath been a golden cup in the LORD'S hand, that made all the earth drunk: the nations have drunk of her wine; therefore the nations are mad: . . .

[And the Apocalypse said, "For all nations have drunk of the wine of the wrath of her immorality."]

... *Babylon is suddenly fallen and destroyed.* . . .

["In one hour is she made desolate."]

... *wail for her; take balm for her pain,*
it may be she may be healed. . . .

["And the kings of the earth, who have committed acts of immorality and lived luxuriously with her, shall bewail her, and lament for her."]

... *We would have healed Babylon, but she is not healed: forsake her, and let us go every one into his own country: for her judgment reacheth to heaven, and is lifted even to the skies.* . . .

["For her sins have reached to heaven, and God hath remembered her iniquities."]

... *O thou that dwellest upon many waters, abundant in treasures, thy end is come, and the measure of thy covetousness.* . . .

["How much she hath glorified herself, and lived luxuriously, so much torment and sorrow give her. . . . "]

... *Surely I will fill thee with men, as with caterpillers; and they shall raise a shout against thee. . . . And I will render to Babylon and to all the inhabitants of Chaldea all their evil that they have done in Zion in your sight, saith the LORD. Behold, I am against thee, O destroying mountain, saith the LORD, which destroyest all the earth: and I will stretch out my hand upon thee, and roll thee down from the rocks, and will make thee a burnt mountain.* . . .

[". . . . she shall be utterly burned with fire. . . . they shall see the smoke of her burning. . . . "]

... *And they shall not take of thee a stone for a corner, nor a stone for foundations; but thou shalt be desolate for ever, saith the LORD. . . . And the land shall tremble and sorrow: for every purpose of the LORD shall be performed against Babylon, to make the land of Babylon a desolation without an inhabitant.* . . .

[And the Apocalypse said "And the voice of harpers, and musicians, and of pipers, and trumpeters, shall be no more heard in thee . . . and the voice of the bridegroom and of the bride shall be heard no more in thee. . . . "]

. . . The mighty men of Babylon have ceased to fight, they have remained in their strong holds: their might hath failed; they became as women: they have burned her dwellingplaces; her bars are broken. . . . The violence done to me and to my flesh be upon Babylon, shall the inhabitant of Zion say; and my blood upon the inhabitants of Chaldea, shall Jerusalem say. Therefore thus saith the LORD; Behold, I will plead thy cause, and take vengeance for thee; and I will dry up her sea, and make her springs dry. And Babylon shall become heaps, a dwellingplace for dragons, an horror, and an hissing, without an inhabitant. . . .

[" . . . Babylon the great is fallen, is fallen, and is become the habitation of demons, and the hold of every foul spirit. . . . "]

. . . They shall roar together like lions: they shall yell as lions' whelps. In their heat I will make their feasts, and I will make them drunk, that they may rejoice, and sleep a perpetual sleep, and not wake, saith the LORD. How is Sheshach [a cryptic word for Babylon] taken! and how is the praise of the whole earth surprised! how is Babylon become an horror among the nations! . . .

["And the kings of the earth . . . shall see the smoke of her burning, Standing afar off for the fear of her torment, saying, Alas, alas, that great city Babylon, that mighty city! . . . "]

. . . The sea is come up upon Babylon: she is covered with the multitude of its waves. Her cities are a desolation, a dry land, and a wilderness, a land in which no man dwelleth, neither doth any son of man pass by it. . . .

["And every shipmaster . . . and as many as trade by sea, stood afar off, And cried . . . alas, alas, that great city, in which were made rich all that had ships in the sea by her wealth! for in one hour is she made desolate."]

And I will punish Bel [the god whose name is the root of Belzebub] in Babylon, and I will bring forth out of his mouth that which he hath swallowed: and the nations shall not flow together any more to him: even the wall of Babylon shall fall. My people, depart from the midst of her, and deliver ye every man his soul from the fierce anger of the LORD. . . .

["Come out of her, my people, that ye be not partakers of her sins, and that ye receive not of her plagues."]

. . . And lest your heart should faint, and ye should fear for the rumour that shall be heard in the land; a rumour shall both come one year, and after that in another year shall come a rumour, and violence in the land, ruler against ruler. Therefore, behold, the days come, that I will execute judgment upon the graven images of Babylon: and her whole land shall be confounded, and all her slain shall fall in the midst of her. Then the heaven and the earth, and all that is in them, shall sing for Babylon: for the spoilers shall come to her from the north, saith the LORD. As Babylon hath caused the slain of Israel to fall, so at Babylon shall fall the slain of all the earth.

(JEREMIAH 51:1, 2, 6–10, 13, 14, 24–26, 29, 30, 35–49)

["And in her was found the blood of prophets, and of saints, and of all that were slain upon the earth."]

Other parts of Jeremiah are also echoed in the Apocalypse' description of the fall of Babylon the Great. Only, these parts did not describe the fall of ancient Babylon but, rather, the destruction that Babylon would bring against Israel and the rest of the world, showing that other nations are engulfed in the flood of Babylon's evil. But in the middle of his prophecy, the prophet makes it clear that even Babylon—God's agent of punishment—would drink from the cup of its own poison:

Behold, I will send and take all the families of the north, saith the LORD, and Nebuchadnezzar the king of Babylon, my servant, and will bring them against this land [Israel], and against the inhabitants thereof, and against all these nations round about, and will utterly destroy them, and make them an astonishment, and an hissing, and perpetual desolations.

Moreover I will take from them the voice of mirth, and the voice of gladness, the voice of the bridegroom, and the voice of the bride, the sound of the millstones, and the light of the candle. And this whole land shall be a desolation, and an astonishment . . .

For thus saith the LORD God of Israel to me [Jeremiah]; Take the wine cup of this fury at my hand, and cause all the nations, to whom I send thee, to drink it. And they shall drink, and be moved, and go mad, because of the sword that I will send among them. Then I took the cup at the LORD'S hand, and made all the nations to drink, to whom the LORD had sent me: . . . And all the kings of the north [Babylon], far and near, one with another, and all the kingdoms of the world, which are upon the face of the earth: and the king of Sheshach [Babylon] shall drink after them. Therefore thou shalt say to them, Thus saith the LORD of hosts, the God of Israel; Drink ye, and be drunk, and vomit, and fall, and rise no more, because of the sword which I will send among you. And it shall be, if they refuse to take the cup at thy hand to drink, then shalt thou say to them, Thus saith the LORD of hosts; Ye shall certainly drink. For, lo, I begin to bring evil on the city which is called by my name [Jerusalem], and should ye be utterly unpunished? Ye shall not be unpunished: for I will call for a sword upon all the inhabitants of the earth, saith the LORD of hosts.

Therefore prophesy thou against them all these words, and say to them, The LORD shall roar from on high, and utter his voice from his holy habitation; he shall mightily roar upon his habitation; he shall give a shout, as they that tread the grapes, against all the inhabitants of the earth. A noise shall come even to the ends of the earth; for the LORD hath a controversy with the nations, he will plead with all flesh; he will give them that are wicked to the sword, saith the LORD. Thus saith the LORD of hosts, Behold, evil shall go forth from na-

tion to nation, and a great whirlwind shall be raised from the ends of the earth. And the slain of the LORD shall be at that day from one end of the earth even to the other end of the earth: they shall not be lamented, neither gathered, nor buried; they shall be refuse upon the ground. Wail, ye shepherds, [i.e., leaders of the people] and cry; and wallow yourselves in the ashes, ye chief of the flock: for the days of your slaughter and of your dispersions are accomplished; and ye shall fall like a pleasant vessel. And the shepherds shall have no way to flee, nor the chief of the flock to escape. A voice of the cry of the shepherds, and a wailing of the chief of the flock, shall be heard: for the LORD hath laid waste their pasture. And the peaceable habitations are cut down because of the fierce anger of the LORD. He hath forsaken his covert [lair], as the lion: for their land is desolate because of the fierceness of the oppressor, and because of his fierce anger.
(JEREMIAH 25:9–11, 16, 17, 26–38)

How much of this whirlwind of words that swirl around Babylon and the nations that surrounded it related only to Jeremiah's time? Was this torrent of prophecies against Babylon and the nations of the earth a stream of prophetic consciousness that overflowed it banks, spilling into a more distant future? The fact that these prophecies against ancient Babylon are echoed so thoroughly in John's vision of future destruction could indicate that even the oldest words against Babylon will see their ultimate fulfillment in a time that still lay in John's future. The fact that he chose the name "Babylon" makes the connection pointedly obvious. John was clearly making the whole rise and fall of Babylon a pattern for the times he foresaw. How much was fulfilled by the fall of Rome three hundred or more years after his life, and how much is yet to come?

HOLY ROME AS BABYLON THE GREAT

Though the fall of Rome led to a millennium of great tribulation mostly known as the Dark Ages, the world did not end as many thought it would. Nor was Rome destroyed in a day as depicted in the Apocalypse. It took nearly half a century for the Vandals and Huns to thoroughly beat it down. Neither was Rome ever left uninhabited, for it quickly rose again.

Meanwhile the eastern half of the old Roman Empire continued through the Dark Ages as the Byzantine Empire. So the destruction of imperial Rome was not complete. The fall of Rome, great as it was, does not adequately fulfill the permanent and complete holocaust of Babylon the Great as it is lamented in the Apocalypse. Nevertheless, when the great Roman Empire, which had so recently declared itself Christian, crumbled into rubble, the Apocalypse served the followers of Jesus well. In times that surely seemed like the end of the world, they experienced the assurance of the return of Jesus Christ and read of apocalyptic visions of a new earth.

This assurance did not make them fatalistic about the end. In fact, just the opposite. Rome rose quickly from its ashes as the bishop of the Roman Church filled the empty throne. The pope's new claim to the former throne of the Emperor Constantine was diminished only by the contentions of feudal kings. The Catholic Church, however many its medieval faults, did save the world from anarchy.

When it was clear that the destruction of ancient Rome did not bring about the end of the world, nor even the end of Rome, those who questioned the Roman Church's legitimacy began to look toward the destruction of the revived Unholy Roman Empire. Surely, its fall would be the fulfillment of the Apocalypse.

Many, such as Dante, had identified the Church with Babylon the Great, and some had come to see the pope as the Antichrist. Dante is considered by many scholars to be the last writer of the Middle Ages. Francesco Petrarch, the celebrated poet laureate of Rome, is the harbinger of the Renaissance. As a man of social prominence, Petrarch knew the Roman Catholic hierarchy from close association. He joined Dante's chorus, inveighing against the Roman Church, for having acquired abundance of worldly goods while becoming impoverished of spiritual values:

> Vengeance must fall on thee, thou filthy whore
> Of Babylon, thou breaker of Christ's fold . . .
> Art rich become with making many poor.
> . . . Slave to delights that chastity hath sold
> For wine and ease which settith all thy store
> Upon whoredom and none other lore.
> In thy palace of strumpets young and old
> There walks Plenty, and Belzebub thy Lord
> Guides thee and them and doth thy reign uphold.
> It was but late, as writing will record,
> That poor thou wert without land or gold;

Yet how hath gold and pride, by one accord
In wickedness so spread thy life abroad
That it doth stink before the face of God?[2]

Like Dante, Petrarch alluded to the Apocalypse in criticizing the depravity of the Catholic Church during the brief time the pope was living at Avignon:

Thou Babylon, seated on the wild banks of the Rhone, shall I call thee famous or infamous, O harlot, who has committed harlotry with the kings of the earth? Truly thou are the same that the holy Evangelist [John] saw in the spirit . . . sitting upon many waters. Either literally, being surrounded by three rivers, or, in the profusion of this world's goods, among which thou sittest wanton and secure, unmindful of eternal riches; or, in the sense . . . that the waters on which you the harlot sit are peoples and nations and languages. Recognize thine own features. A woman clothed in purple and scarlet, decked with gold and precious stones and pearls, having a golden cup in her hand, full of abomination in the impurity of her fornication—Dost though not know thyself, O Babylon? Unless perhaps what is written upon her forehead is wrong, Babylon the great, you indeed are Babylon the little.[3]

The Church rose as a world power—as much at the center of world commerce and luxury as ancient Rome. Being both an empire *and* a Church that had turned away from its true love, the humble Jesus Christ of Nazareth, it fit the description of a harlot even better than the earlier Roman Empire.

With such notable voices as Dante and Petrarch joining in the recognition of the Catholic Church as Babylon the Great, the pressure against the Church grew, driving toward the Reformation. The crisis established itself in 1378 when two popes were elected at the same time. Each claimed to be the universal bishop of the universal Church, and each, along with his supporting cardinals, labelled the other pope as the Antichrist and as anathema to the Church. Now that even popes were identifying popes as the Antichrist, evil had followed its usual pattern of rising like the tower of Babel to its own fall.

The Reformation began. During the latter years of the Reformation, many poured from the Roman Catholic Church, resulting in a great loss of worldly influence for the imperial Church. To stanch the rapid flow, the Catholic hierarchy in time granted some of the changes requested by the reformers, but the loss of its preeminence was permanent.

By no means, however, did the Roman Church die in the manner predicted in John's Apocalypse. It did not die at all, and its decline in worldly power did not happen in an hour—not even figuratively. Like the earlier Rome, it declined over several centuries. In many parts of the world it remained as strong as ever, right to the present day. The evil that burned within burned itself out, and the truer aspects of the Church remained, considerably purified by fire.

And, as was the case with the first Roman fall, the world did not end. If the numerous critics of Catholicism were correct in seeing the Church as Babylon the Great and some of those distant popes as the Antichrist, the end of the Reformation still left the Apocalypse wanting a greater fulfillment. This has led many Fundamentalists to speculate that the Roman Church will still fall. They believe the Antichrist will rise from Rome again to meet his ultimate end.

JERUSALEM VERSUS ROME AS BABYLON THE GREAT

Others speculate that the Antichrist will not rise in Rome at all, but in Jerusalem. After all, Babylon the Great is called the "great city" in the Apocalypse, and so is Jerusalem. Both cities are said to be places that killed the saints and prophets and would be judged for it. Both cities have been referred to as harlots by the prophets, and Jerusalem was even compared to Sodom and Gomorrah, whose destruction compares to the plagues of the Apocalypse:

The vision of Isaiah the son of Amoz, which he saw concerning Judah and Jerusalem. . . . Except the LORD of hosts had left to us a very small remnant, we should have been as Sodom, we should have been like Gomorrah. Hear the word of the LORD, ye rulers of Sodom; give ear to the law of our God, ye people of Gomorrah. . . .

How is the faithful city become an harlot! it was full of judgment [justice]; righteousness lodged in it; but now murderers. . . . Therefore saith the Lord, the LORD of hosts, the mighty One of Israel, Ah, I will rid myself of my adversaries, and avenge me of my enemies: And I will turn my hand upon thee, and thoroughly purge away thy dross, and take away all thy tin: And I will restore thy judges as at

the first, and thy counsellors as at the beginning: afterward thou shalt be called, The city of righteousness, the faithful city. Zion shall be redeemed with judgment, and her converts with righteousness. And the destruction of the transgressors and of the sinners shall be together, and they that forsake the LORD shall be consumed. For they shall be ashamed of the oaks which ye have desired, and ye shall be confounded for the gardens that ye have chosen. For ye shall be as an oak whose leaf fadeth, and as a garden that hath no water. And the strong shall be as a wick, and its maker as a spark, and they shall both burn together, and none shall quench them.

(ISAIAH 1:1A, 9, 10, 21, 24–31)

Both Rome and Jerusalem have also played a central role in Christian history. Both are called holy cities. Both revived after their prophesied destruction. Jerusalem's second destruction probably occurred *before* John wrote the Apocalypse, in which case the Apocalypse wouldn't have made sense to John's listeners if he had spoken of Jerusalem's final destruction as something yet to come; so, it would make a great deal of sense to give the future Jerusalem a metaphoric name like "Babylon the Great."

Aside from these obvious parallels, the belief that the final Antichrist will rise in Jerusalem, not Rome, comes from a statement written by the Apostle Paul. Consoling the followers of Jesus who had been misled into believing Christ had already returned, Paul made the following statement regarding the Antichrist and the return of the true Christ:

> *Now we beseech you, brethren, by the coming of our Lord Jesus Christ, and by our gathering together to him, that ye be not soon shaken in mind, or be troubled, neither by spirit, nor by word, nor by letter as from us, as that the day of Christ has come.*
>
> *Let no man deceive you by any means: for that day shall not come, except there come a falling away first, and that man of sin be revealed, the son of perdition; who opposeth and exalteth himself above all that is called God, or that is worshipped; so that he as God sitteth in the temple of God, showing himself that he is God.* (2 THESSALONIANS 2:1–4)

Recently, this statement has caused some scholars to believe the temple in Jerusalem must be rebuilt before the Antichrist can be revealed there. However, in every other part of the Bible where Paul uses the phrase "the temple of God" he uses it figuratively to refer to the individual bodies of Jesus' followers, in whom God's Spirit dwells, or to refer to the entire congregation of Jesus' followers that constitutes the Church. Unless this passage is an exception, in no place does Paul use "the temple of God" to refer to the building in Jerusalem. Rebuilding such a temple today would certainly result in world war, as it would require tearing down the third-most holy mosque of Islam, which now sits on the temple site. Insisting that the temple must be rebuilt for the Antichrist to arise there is probably reading Paul's words too literally.

By saying that Jesus will not return until "the son of perdition" is revealed "in the temple of God," Paul may be implying that the end times will not occur until Satan possesses a human being who is in a position of ultimate authority within the Church of God. This man of sin, or possessed person, will set himself up to be worshipped as God. And that view takes some Fundamentalists back to keeping an eye on the papal seat.

The demonic possession of a Church authority who would set himself up to be worshipped as God is, of course, exactly how the Reformers understood this passage. The papal claim that all popes are infallible and are the vicars of Jesus Christ on earth, became untenable to many when two popes both made the same claim of inerrancy while both contradicted each other to the extreme.

The Eastern Orthodox Church and the Protestant reformers believed that the same antichrist spirit possessed any pope who oppressed and killed lowly followers of Christ when they challenged his authority. So, it didn't matter that several popes at different times fit this description of the Antichrist, even though the Apocalypse seemed to refer to only one. All popes who did such things were of one spirit. After all, the Apostle John had also written,

Little children, it is the last time: and as ye have heard that antichrist cometh, even now are there many antichrists; by which we know that it is the last time. They went out from us, but they were not of us; for if they had been of us, they would no doubt have continued with us: but they went out, that they might be shown that they were not all of us.

(1 JOHN 2:18, 19)

If there had been many antichrists in the days of the apostle under ancient Rome—all of whom sprang up from among the followers of Jesus—then why couldn't that pattern repeat itself under the revived Rome?

The Apostle Paul had also taught that the Antichrist could not be "revealed" until that which withholds him was taken out of the way:

And now ye know what restraineth that he might be revealed in his time. For the mystery of iniquity doth already work: only he who now restraineth will do so, until he be taken out of the way. And then shall that Wicked be revealed, whom the Lord shall consume with the spirit of his mouth, and shall destroy with the brightness of his coming: Even him, whose coming is after the working of Satan with all power and signs and lying wonders. (2 THESSALONIANS 2:6–9)

"He who now restraineth" has been understood in two ways: Originally, it was received as a reference to the Holy Spirit of God, who restrains evil in the world through his followers. Many Fundamentalist scholars today have returned to that interpretation. There is another view, however, that places the emphasis on Holy Rome.

Early on, the Greek Orthodox Church understood the restrainer as a reference to ancient Roman rule. In other words, the Antichrist could not be revealed until the Roman caesars got out of the way. A vacuum of power in the Roman capital would open the door for the Antichrist to step up to the Roman throne and make himself evident. One of the early Orthodox Patriarchs of Constantinople, John Chrysostom, wrote:

One may naturally enquire, what is that which withholdeth, and . . . why Paul expresses it so obscurely. Some indeed say, the grace of the Spirit, but others the Roman empire, to whom I most of all accede. Wherefore? Because if he meant to say the Spirit, he would not have spoken obscurely, but plainly. . . . But because he said this of the Roman empire, he naturally glanced at it, and speaks covertly and darkly. For he did not wish to bring upon himself superfluous enmities, and useless dangers. For if he had said that after a little while the Roman empire would be dissolved, they would immediately have even overwhelmed him, as a pestilent person. . . . [4]

In the very least, Chrysostom proved right for his own time and many centuries that followed. Once secular Roman power was taken out of the way, the spirit of Antichrist was free to use worldly power to corrupt the Church—the "temple of God."

Before the Church came into power, it had been almost universally believed that evil would rise to a climax in the world, Christ would come and destroy it, and then he and his saints would establish a reign of peace. Because of a passage near the end of the Apocalypse, many believed this era of peace would last a thousand years. Though others thought the thousand years was figurative in length, they still believed this utopian era would come only after the return of Christ.

But when the last of the old order of Roman emperors was removed and Christ still had not come and the Church took the throne, Saint Augustine took previous prophetic understanding and stood it on its head. He argued that the establishment of power within the Church meant the millennial reign of peace and enlightenment had begun— that it would gradually dawn across the world as the imperial Church of Rome spread the Gospel light along with its spreading influence.

The hope for such a millennium endured for almost a thousand years. In retrospect, it failed miserably. This new belief, in fact, became the fuel for the crusades. Seeing its own ascendancy as the means to prophetic fulfillment, the Church tried to establish its prophetic destiny by forcing the conversions of Jews, Muslims, and Christian heretics as described in the last chapter. Obviously, it did not work. The Church could not restrain evil (or even perceived evil) by the use of power. The utter failure of imperialism to bring on an era of peace—even when dressed in religious clothing—is a central theme of prophecy—especially John's. Augustine's misunderstanding of prophetic destiny contributed to years of discord throughout the world.

It would be unfair, however, to say the Dark Ages were all the fault of the imperial church. Would the world have been any brighter if the church had not stepped into limit the anarchy of Attila?

THE LAST BABYLON

All of this begs the question, where will the final beast of the Apocalypse arise? Perhaps Babylon and Rome were both prototypes of the final empire. At the very least, they are examples of how the pattern will play out in the future, or John would not have drawn so many parallels between those two city states and the future toward which he ultimately moves at the end of his Apocalypse.

As for Jerusalem, it bears many similarities to Babylon the Great but lacks other key traits. It is not a city that sits on many waters, nor has it ever ruled many waters. It is not even a port city, nor has it ever been the center of worldwide commerce or power or luxury. Few "ships on the sea" have become rich through trade with Jerusalem. Nor is it a city that sits on seven hills.

The unholy union of political and religious power raised its head in the emperor worship of pagan Rome and then again at times under the Holy Roman Empire and again under Hitler and his Nazi Blood Cult. So, it could rise anywhere in the future. Babylon the Great would seem to represent imperial religion *wherever* it raises its head and by whatever religion it uses. Those seeking to establish world government may someday feel the need to impose their views by eradicating "separatists"—people like Christians and Jews who absolutely refuse to assimilate into the new global order under its Orwellian dictator. Why would Christians refuse to join this global union? Because many already believe the Apocalypse forbids this unholy allegiance. In which case, the Apocalypse, itself, becomes the final driver of world destiny, creating the very response that leads to the persecutions and wars it predicts.

Some people think the United States fits the description of Babylon the Great. It's not hard to see why. As the capital of world commerce, the U.S. consumes the goods of all the world's merchants—just as the Apocalypse describes. Without its market, most of those merchants would go broke and lament their loss—just as the Apocalypse describes. It's culture has spread throughout the world as described in the Apocalypse. At the same time, it's often as hated, just as the Apocalypse describes the hatred that the ten kings will have for the prostitute when they turn against her.

Its dominant religion, Christianity, has become corrupted in a few pockets of the Church by a slick-looking doctrine that offers prosperity as the guaranteed reward of righteousness. This divine right to prosperity is the ultimate self-centered religion for a self-preoccupied culture. It's also not unlike the situation Petrarch described for the Catholic Church. It's a religious belief that serves the luxurious harlot well. In theme, if not in fact, the religion and the politics of the U.S. are married. Their union is becoming so close, one almost expects a new political party will emerge that places the name "Christian" directly on its forehead.

Given the historic debate, between Protestants and Catholics over the joining of Church and state, it seems ironic that some Protestants are currently allured to political power as the means to convert the wayward soul of America. Curiously, Christ stayed out of politics altogether, yet converted the world by simple truth. He changed the human soul in order to right the world, instead of changing the world in order to right human souls. This should not be taken as a criticism against Christians who are individually involved in politics. In a democracy, all citizens need to be involved at some level. Alexis de Tocqueville, a French political scientist during the Napoleonic years, said:

> Not until I went into the churches of America and heard her pulpits flame with righteousness did I understand the secret of her genius and power. America is great because America is good, but if America ever ceases to be good, America will cease to be great.[5]

A democracy is only as good as its people, so good people are needed in politics—Christian or otherwise. Good people are the only thing that can keep the U.S. from becoming Babylon the Great, but if a party emerges that bears the name "Christian," then abuse of the name may not be far behind. One only has to look around the world and to history to find abundant examples of "Christian" political parties that have long ceased to act very Christian. Power corrupts, and such parties often become well-intentioned dragons, using their power to force their understanding of God's will upon the rest of the world.

Politically, the United States holds the world together by a combination of diplomacy and good ol' style Roman might. The world is now united by a *Pax Americana*, a softer form of the old Roman peace:

> "When Japan looks at the world, it sees a 'Pax Americana' that will last through the first decades of the twenty-first century," according to Takashi Inoguchi, a political scientist at the University of Tokyo. "The supremacy of the United States is felt even more strongly than in the past."
>
> Said former [U.S.] national-security adviser, Zbigniew Brzesinski: "We have no rivals. Not Europe within the next twenty-five years. Russia will be a regional power at most."
>
> . . . "Never before in modern history has a country dominated the Earth so totally as the United States does today," said *Der Spiegel*, a German news magazine.
>
> . . . Part of this . . . power is military. The U.S. Defense budget is nearly as big as those of the next six most powerful nations combined; it is double the defense budgets of all its conceivable enemies put together.
>
> . . . Part of it is institutional. The United States either is host to major global organizations . . . or dominates them. . . .[6]

The U.S. helped create many of these global institutions—NATO, the U.N., the World Bank, the World Trade Organization, and the International Monetary Fund—serving its own interests by serving the interests of others. Unlike Rome, the U.S. has developed and protected its interests without attempting to acquire land and build a world empire. It is a nation built on world dominance, but not on conquest.

While it's natural to compare the U.S. to Babylon the Great because of numerous similarities, one probably has to look further to find the last Babylon. Most of Christianity in the U.S. does not ascribe to the idea of divinely guaranteed prosperity, and the minority that does abhors global government anyway. They, of all people, would be the first to refute the Antichrist. And a separate "Christian" political party may be a fear of some which never becomes reality.

In spite of how U.S. consumer culture is prostituted throughout the world (just as the Apocalypse describes for Babylon the Great), the U.S. may be just one of several players leading the world toward the last Babylon. Balances of power can change abruptly as was proven when the Berlin wall came down—in spite of what Tokyo political scientists say. More likely, Babylon the Great represents a new global economy that will emerge after the next worldwide economic collapse, which could leave the U.S. greatly diminished. Some believe this new economic and political power will ascend from the old Roman states of the new European Community—given evil's past infatuation with Rome.

Superpower supremacy built on nuclear virility and a strong economy offers no protection from small germ or chemical bombs carried in suitcases by terrorists. Biologic viruses or computer viruses can turn an economy into chaos. (So can extraterrestrial objects, which the Apocalypse more than hints at.) The amazing thing is not that the terrorism of tiny germs can undermine a massive national economy but that it hasn't already. In a world with a large number of power-driven people, widespread nuclear and biologic technology raises the individual's capacity to create anarchy. You can't fight terrorism with armies or missiles. Thus, the U.S. may be the last dinosaur from the nuclear age of power.

The final political hope for security in the face of anarchy will have to be worldwide cooperation. Though John may have used Babylon as a metaphor for the imperial city of Rome, the metaphor may evolve in the days of Christ's coming to where the great "city" represents the global village. In that case, the seven hills on which the harlot sits may come to represent the seven continents, which quite literally sit upon the seven seas or "many waters."

But the hope of peace through worldwide cooperation is a façade, because cooperation cannot overcome the underlying problem of human evil empowered by technology nor the desire of one human being to become the focus of power. The fall of Babylon the Great may represent a holocaust that will come upon the entire earth in its last "hour":

Behold, the LORD maketh the earth empty, and maketh it waste, and turneth it upside down, and scattereth abroad its inhabitants. And it shall be, as with the people, so with the priest; as with the servant, so with his master; as with the maid, so with her mistress; as with the buyer, so with the seller; as with the lender, so with the borrower; as with the taker of interest, so with the giver of in-

terest to him. *The land shall be utterly emptied, and utterly spoiled: for the LORD hath spoken this word. The earth mourneth and fadeth away, the world languisheth and fadeth away, the haughty people of the earth do languish. The earth also is defiled under its inhabitants; because they have transgressed the laws, changed the ordinance, broken the everlasting covenant. Therefore hath the curse devoured the earth, and they that dwell in it are desolate: therefore the inhabitants of the earth are burned, and few men left. The new wine mourneth, the vine languisheth, all the merry-hearted do sigh. The mirth of tabrets ceaseth, the noise of them that rejoice endeth, the joy of the harp ceaseth. They shall not drink wine with a song; strong drink shall be bitter to them that drink it. The city of confusion is broken down: every house is shut up, that no man may enter. There is a crying for wine in the streets; all joy is darkened, the mirth of the land is gone. In the city is left desolation, and the gate is smitten with destruction. When thus it shall be in the midst of the land among the people, there shall be as the shaking of an olive tree, and as the gleaning grapes when the vintage is done. They shall lift up their voice, they shall sing for the majesty of the LORD, they shall cry aloud from the sea. Therefore glorify ye the LORD in the fires, even the name of the LORD God of Israel in the isles of the sea.*

From the uttermost part of the earth have we heard songs, even glory to the righteous. But I said, My leanness, my leanness, woe to me! the treacherous dealers have dealt treacherously; yea, the treacherous dealers have dealt very treacherously. Fear, and the pit, and the snare, are upon thee, O inhabitant of the earth. And it shall come to pass, that he who fleeth from the noise of the fear shall fall into the pit; and he that cometh up out of the midst of the pit shall be taken in the snare: for the windows from on high are open, and the foundations of the earth do shake. The earth is utterly broken down, the earth is all dissolved, the earth is exceedingly moved. The earth shall reel to and fro like a drunkard, and shall be removed like a cottage; and the transgression of it shall be heavy upon it; and it shall fall, and not rise again. And it shall come to pass in that day, that the LORD shall punish the host of the high ones that are on high, and the kings of the earth upon the earth. And they shall be gathered together, as prisoners are gathered in the pit, and shall be shut up in the prison, and after many days shall they be visited. Then the moon shall be confounded, and the sun ashamed, when the LORD of hosts shall reign on mount Zion, and in Jerusalem, and before his ancients gloriously. (ISAIAH 24:1–23)

Certainly, the last lines of this prophecy, which describes the time of Christ's coming, fit the scenario of a world economy changed by an event like an asteroid or comet impact. Something of that magnitude could tip the earth on its axis, causing it to reel "to and fro" literally. It would also explain the severe earthquake (more severe than any in human history) described in the Apocalypse for the destruction of Babylon the Great. How aptly chosen, in that light, is the celestial metaphor used for Babylon the Great's destruction, which described a mighty angel picking up "a stone like a great millstone" and casting it down into the sea. With such violence the great city would be thrown down and found no more.

The Apocalypse, however, was not written to enable an enlightened few to forecast world events; it was written to help Jesus' followers keep the true faith when evil times are ready to devour them and when false doctrines corrupt the truth. That's why it begins with letters to encourage seven persecuted churches and to correct them for wandering from the perfect truth.

So, until the course of human events reveals the correct understanding of these prophecies, the identity of Babylon the Great and the Antichrist and all doomsday scenarios are mere speculation. Whether Babylon the Great represents a cosmopolitan city or the entire world, its fall could come by comet or asteroid or the descent of a nuclear missile, all of which would bring a quick end by fire from the sky. The important concept to recognize is that Babylon the Great will be more than a world economy; it represents another marriage of religion with political power. This unholy alliance will lead, as such combinations always have, to a new form of emperor worship around a single charismatic individual—an apparent world savior. As Hitler, the world's last notorious Antichrist, recognized, "Force without spiritual foundation is doomed to failure."

Chapter 20

C⊙ΠSUᛖᛖATi⊙Π:

THE WEDDiΠG OF THE LAᛖB

John has described the second coming of the Messiah from the perspective of people on earth. He now turns from the destruction that came in the wake of the resurrection and rapture to show what the resurrection means for the saints of God. He uses the metaphor of marriage to reveal their new and perfect union with Christ. While Babylon the Great is consumed with fire on earth, the long-awaited marriage between Jesus Christ and his Bride, the Church, is consummated ceremonially in heaven.

THE CEREMONY

And after these things I heard a great voice of many people in heaven, saying, Hallelujah; Salvation, and glory, and honour, and power, to the Lord our God: For true and righteous are his judgments: for he hath judged the great harlot, who corrupted the earth with her immorality, and hath avenged the blood of his servants at her hand. And again they said, Hallelujah. And her smoke rose up for ever and ever. And the four and twenty elders and the four living beings fell down and worshipped God who sat on the throne, saying, Amen; Hallelujah. And a voice came out of the throne, saying, Praise our God, all ye his servants, and ye that fear him, both small and great. And I heard as it were the voice of a great multitude, and as the voice of many waters, and as the voice of mighty thunderings, saying, Hallelujah: for the Lord God omnipotent reigneth. Let us be glad and rejoice, and give honour to him: for the marriage of the Lamb is come, and his wife hath made herself ready. And to her was granted that she should be arrayed in fine linen, clean and white: for the fine linen is the righteousness of saints. And he saith to me, Write, Blessed are they who are called to the marriage supper of the Lamb. And he saith to me, These are the true sayings of God. And I fell at his feet to worship him. And he said to me, See thou do it not: I am thy fellowservant, and of thy brethren that have the testimony of Jesus: worship God: for the testimony of Jesus is the spirit of prophecy.

(REVELATION 19:1–10)

An eternity could have taken place in heaven during the hour of the harlot's destruction on earth. In that sense, the smoke of Babylon the Great rises up for ever and ever, even though on earth it may have only lasted a month, a year, or a millennium. An eternity as exists in the gaze between two lovers.

The perfect union between Christ and his Bride is described in terms of a marriage that contrasts with the unholy union between the Antichrist and his harlot. The saints of God, like the last bright leaves of fall, are borne upward to the sun by the breath of God's Spirit. Rising above the smoke of Babylon, they leave the naked earth to face alone the winter of its discontent. They rise to meet the sun, which imbues their natural colors with the radiance of its light until they glow like a bride dressed in white linen.

The scene becomes a wedding banquet. The twenty-four elders re-enter the picture to remind everyone that this is the company of Jew and Gentile joined. The four living creatures are present because all of creation benefits from this new harmony.

The attention is focused on the bride. The righteousness of the people—of God— not the self-righteousness, but the love of truth and justice and mercy (love, itself, and all that is good)—shines to their glory because everything that was false and selfish and spiteful and all that was bad, all the ignorance that diminished their light below, has been stripped away. Only that which was pure in spirit has been resurrected to shine with the light of God, and the dross has been left in the ashen earth where it is purged with fire. This purification is what the Apostle Paul had in mind when he revealed that human marriage is a sacrament because it symbolizes a deep spiritual reality. It celebrates in advance the perfect union with God.

> Husbands, love your wives, even as Christ also loved the church, and gave himself for it; That he might sanctify and cleanse it with the washing of water by the word, That he might present it to himself a glorious church, not having spot, or wrinkle, or any such thing; but that it should be holy and without blemish.
>
> (EPHESIANS 5:25–27)

That is also why the 144,000 were described as celibate at the resurrection and why Christ said there would be no giving in marriage after the resurrection. In heaven, the union that was symbolized and celebrated by marriage on earth finds its full, ultimate realization. Everything that marriage has meant is consummated in God. The children of earth and the God of heaven become one. Those marriages on earth that were true to God glowed like candles lit in a New Year's vigil, but the vigil ceremonies end when the end itself comes. The symbol of holy communion is lost when perfect communion is found.

Though John has focused on the Bride, other scriptures focus on the Bridegroom. An ancient wedding song, written for the king of Israel upon his marriage to the queen, rises to the kind of lofty language that uses things temporal to allude to things eternal, which is what marriage is all about:

(. . . A Song of loves.) My heart is overflowing with a good matter: I speak of the things which I have made concerning the king: my tongue is the pen of a skilful writer. Thou art fairer than the children of men: grace is poured into thy lips: therefore God hath blessed thee for ever. Gird thy sword upon thy thigh, O most mighty, with thy glory and thy majesty. And in thy majesty ride prosperously because of truth and meekness and righteousness; and thy right hand shall teach thee terrible things. Thy arrows are sharp in the heart of the king's enemies; by which the people fall under thee. Thy throne, O God, is for ever and ever: the sceptre of thy kingdom is a sceptre of justice. Thou lovest righteousness, and hatest wickedness: therefore God, thy God, hath anointed thee with the oil of gladness above thy companions. All thy garments smell of myrrh, and aloes, and cassia, out of the ivory palaces, by which they have made thee glad. Kings' daughters were among thy honourable women: upon thy right hand stood the queen in gold of Ophir. Hearken, O daughter, and consider, and incline thy ear; forget also thy own people, and thy father's house; So shall the king greatly desire thy beauty: for he is thy Lord; and worship thou him. And the daughter of Tyre shall be there with a gift; even the rich among the people shall entreat thy favour. The king's daughter is all glorious within: her clothing is of wrought gold. She shall be brought to the king in raiment of needlework: the virgins her companions that follow her shall be brought to thee. With gladness and rejoicing shall they be brought: they shall enter into the king's palace. Instead of thy fathers shall be thy children, whom thou mayest make princes in all the earth. I will make thy name to be remembered in all generations: therefore shall the people praise thee for ever and ever. (PSALM 45:1–17)

The opening image of the king riding forth in righteousness with sword at his side and with sharpened arrows is picked up in the twin images seen by John—first, of Christ riding on a white horse with a bow and arrow; later, in the scene to come, Christ riding with his sword of truth. The king will prosper because of his love of truth and meekness and righteousness. But prosperity is not the goal. This is not the cheap promise that all who live righteously will prosper in this life regardless of the circumstances they are born into. It is not a carrot offered for good behavior or to increase tithes to the local church or some televised ministry. This is the inevitable product of a kingdom where the king at the top loves truth and lives meekly. When the king and his people love, honor, and serve each other like bride and groom and the earth is treated like a cherished wedding gift, how can such a kingdom not prosper? When times are low, they bear each other up, and when times are high, they prudently put away for the future so that meager times will be no more. There will be no poor in God's kingdom because all serve to their fullest capacity, and all share in the fulness of the bounty without greed.

How different from the harlot who only consumed. How different from the harlot who used the people and the kings of the earth to lavish herself with luxuries, who drank until she was drunk and toppled over in her stupor. When prosperity is the goal, consumption is its end.

True religion is a daily wedding ceremony, celebrating the union of God with his people. It is rich communion. False religion is a means to pomp and power. It is cheap commerce. In the kingdom of God, the children of God are princes and princesses; whereas the union between the Antichrist and the harlot produces no children. It only consumes them.

And so John shows the people of God singing over the horrible destruction of the child-eating harlot with her cup of blood—singing because her end means the salvation of many:

> *Therefore my people shall know my name: therefore they shall know in that day that I am he that doth speak: behold, it is I. How beautiful upon the mountains are the feet of him that bringeth good tidings, that proclaimeth peace; that bringeth good tidings of good, that proclaimeth salvation; that saith to Zion, Thy God reigneth! Thy watchmen shall lift up the voice; with the voice together shall they sing: for they shall see eye to eye, when the LORD shall bring again Zion. Break forth into joy, sing together, ye waste places of Jerusalem: for the LORD hath comforted his people, he hath redeemed Jerusalem. The LORD hath made bare his holy arm in the eyes of all the nations; and all the ends of the earth shall see the salvation of our God.*
>
> (ISAIAH 52:6–10)

But what is salvation? At its lowest level, it is freedom from Babylon the Great. Those who have been persecuted will find this alone is more than cause for celebration. But the biblical concept of salvation is much loftier than mere escape from hell or from hell on earth. It has less to do with what one is saved from than what one is saved for.

SALVATION AND ETERNAL LIFE

> *The Spirit of the Lord GOD is upon me; because the LORD hath anointed me to preach good tidings to the meek; he hath sent me to bind up the brokenhearted, to proclaim liberty to the captives, and the opening of the prison to them that are bound; To proclaim the acceptable year of the LORD, and the day of vengeance of our God; to comfort all that mourn; To appoint to them that mourn in Zion,*

to give to them beauty for ashes, the oil of joy for mourning, the garment of praise for the spirit of heaviness; that they may be called trees of righteousness, the planting of the LORD, that he may be glorified.

. . . I will greatly rejoice in the LORD, my soul shall be joyful in my God; for he hath clothed me with the garments of salvation, he hath covered me with the robe of righteousness, as a bridegroom decketh himself with ornaments, and as a bride adorneth herself with her jewels. For as the earth bringeth forth her bud, and as the garden causeth the things that are sown in it to spring forth; so the Lord GOD will cause righteousness and praise to spring forth before all the nations.

(ISAIAH 61:1–3, 10, 11)

Pope John Paul II has beautifully expressed the full meaning of salvation in his book *Crossing the Threshold of Hope:*

To accept the Gospel's demands means to affirm all of our humanity, to see in it the beauty desired by God. . . . God desires the salvation of man, He desires that humanity find that fulfillment to which He Himself has destined it. . . .[1]

And what is this eternal life? It is happiness that comes from union with God. Christ affirms: "Now this is eternal life, that they should know you, the only true God, and the one whom you sent, Jesus Christ" (Jn 17:3) Union with God is realized in the vision of the Divine Being "face to face" . . . a vision called "beatific" because the vision of God "face to face" allows enjoyment of the absolute fullness of truth. In this way man's aspiration to truth is ultimately satisfied.

Salvation, however, is not reducible to this. In knowing God "face to face," man encounters the absolute fullness of good . . . Not union with the idea of good, but rather union with Good itself. God is this Good.

. . . This is life that has no limits in time or space . . . Participation in the life of God Himself. . . . The death of Christ gives life, because it allows believers to share in His Resurrection.

. . . Man is saved in the Church by being brought into the Mystery of the Divine Trinity, into the mystery of the intimate life of God. . . . "The one People of God is present among all nations on earth, since he takes its citizens from every race."[2]

As for me, I will behold thy face in righteousness: I shall be satisfied, when I awake, with thy likeness. (PSALM 17:15)

The One People of God

This, too, is the meaning of the wedding—that all people shall become one.

Just as monogamous marriage was a sacrament, bigamy was declared sacrilege in the New Testament. Even in that declaration of a sacrilege something is revealed of the ultimate consummation. The Messiah will not have two brides. He will not have the Church (composed of Christian Gentiles and Christian Jews) as one bride under one covenant and the Jews as another bride under a former covenant. There will be no divisions between God's people and no distinctions. There are no degrees of oneness. The people under both covenants will be brought under the greater umbrella of the New Covenant that was promised by Jeremiah.

Jesus explained this mystery to his disciples. He began by telling them how the kingdom of God would, first, be taken away from the Jews:

Jesus saith to them, Did ye never read in the scriptures, The stone which the builders rejected, the same is become the head of the corner: this is the Lord's doing, and it is marvelous in our eyes?

Therefore I say to you, The kingdom of God shall be taken from you, and given to a nation bringing forth the fruits of it.
(Matthew 21:42, 43)

And then telling them the same thing in a parable:

The kingdom of heaven is like a certain king, who made a marriage for his son, And sent his servants to call them that were invited to the wedding: and they would not come. Again, he sent other servants, saying, Tell them who are invited, Behold, I have prepared my dinner: my oxen and my fatlings are killed, and all things are ready: come to the marriage. But they made light of it, and went their ways, one to his farm, another to his merchandise: And the remnant took his servants, and treated them spitefully, and slew them. But when the king heard of it, he was angry: and he sent his armies, and destroyed those murderers, and burned up their city. Then he saith to his servants, The wedding is ready, but they who were invited were not worthy. Go ye therefore into the highways, and as many as ye shall find, invite to the marriage. So those servants went out into the highways, and gathered together all as many as they found, both bad and good: and the wedding was furnished with guests. And when the king came in to see the guests, he saw there a man who had not a wedding garment: And he saith to him, Friend, how camest thou in here not having a wedding garment? And he was speechless. Then said the king to the servants, Bind him hand and foot, and take him away, and cast him into outer darkness; there shall be weeping and gnashing of teeth. For many are called, but few are chosen.
(Matthew 22:2–14)

The king, of course, is God, who established a marriage covenant for his son, who is Jesus Christ. The first people in the parable to be invited to the wedding of the king's son represent the nation of Israel, invited to be the Messiah's chosen under God's covenant with the Jews. The servants who invited them were God's prophets, some of whom were killed by those they invited. The rejection of the invitation by the first people invited represents the rejection the Messiah's by many Jews at his first coming. Because of this rejection, their city, Jerusalem, was destroyed. Then the king prepares a new invitation, a New Covenant, to be offered to others. The servants who are then sent out into the highways are the Messiah's disciples, who travelled abroad to call others—even Gentiles—to join in the Messiah's wedding. They proclaimed the New Covenant, just as the prophets had proclaimed the old. Both good and bad people are welcomed into the New Covenant if they will receive the invitation. Both are made perfect people, which is represented by the linen wedding garments they are given to wear. Those who have not entered the wedding through the New Covenant of Jesus Christ do not have such perfect clothes to wear and are cast back out into the dark night.

But if God has one people, not two, what happens to those Jews who came in under the terms of the Old Covenant? Scriptures quoted earlier in this book along with early Church writings indicate these souls converted to the New Covenant after death when Christ descended into the grave. Jesus' answer is that the first people of God, the Jews of the Old Covenant, will receive everything that was promised to them, but they should not be surprised to discover that later people called by God under new terms will be the first to receive the same reward promised to them:

> But many that are first shall be last; and the last shall be first. For the kingdom of heaven is like a man that is an householder [homeowner], who went out early in the morning to hire labourers into his vineyard. And when he had agreed with the labourers for a penny a day [a typical day's wages when the Bible was first translated into English], he sent them into his vineyard. And he went out about the third hour, and saw others standing idle in the marketplace, And said to them; Go ye also into the vineyard, and whatever is right I will give you. And they went. Again he went out about the sixth and ninth hour, and did the same. And about the eleventh hour he went out, and found others standing idle, and saith to them, Why stand ye here all the day idle? They say to him, Because no man hath hired us. He saith to them, Go ye also into the vineyard; and whatever is right, that shall ye receive. So when evening was come, the lord of the vineyard saith to his steward, Call the labourers, and give them their hire, beginning from the last to the first. And when they came that were hired about the eleventh hour, they received every man a penny. But when the first came, they supposed that they should receive more; and they likewise received every man a penny. And when they had received it, they murmured against the master of the house, Saying, These last have worked but one hour, and thou hast

made them equal to us, who have borne
the burden and heat of the day. But he
answered one of them, and said, Friend,
I do thee no wrong: didst thou not agree
with me for a penny? Take that which is
thine, and go thy way: I will give to this

last, even as to thee. Is it not lawful for
me to do what I will with my own? Is thy
eye evil, because I am good? So the last
shall be first, and the first last: for many
are called, but few chosen.

(MATTHEW 19:30; 20:1–16)

The meaning of the message is that the people who come into God's kingdom under the unspecified promises of the New Covenant will receive exactly the same reward as the people who came earlier under the specific promises of God's covenant with Abraham. God will make them equal. To those who murmur this is not fair—the Jews bore a heavier burden for so much longer—the Messiah responds, "How is it not fair if they receive everything they were promised? If I want to give just as generously to others who were chosen later, is it not mine to give?"

The two people will be made one, but the courtship for this ultimate marriage has been filled with strife. In the end, however, the oneness between God's people, who are joined from all races, is probably far deeper and more mystical than simply belonging to the same kingdom and receiving the same rewards. But that, again, is material for a later chapter.

This part of John's vision closes with the statement that "the testimony of Jesus is the spirit of prophecy." This statement implies that all the prophecies of the Bible, Old Testament and New, ultimately have one theme. They form a multi-faceted revelation that Jesus is the Messiah, Son of Man, Son of God, rightful ruler of earth, and king of all kings.

But until the day of the Lord arrives, the wedding banquet is set and still waiting for the peoples of God to come together:

And he said to them, I have earnestly de-
sired to eat this passover with you before
I suffer: For I say to you, I will not any
more eat of it, until it shall be fulfilled in
the kingdom of God. And he took the
cup, and gave thanks, and said, Take

this, and share it among yourselves: For I
say to you, I will not drink of the fruit of
the vine, until the kingdom of God shall
come. . . . This cup is the new testament
[covenant] in my blood, which is shed
for you. (LUKE 22:15–18, 22B)

Chapter 21

Armageddon:

The War to End All Wars

The interlude concerning the destruction of Babylon the Great now comes to a close, and John moves to the final event—the appearance of Christ that establishes the end. When John described the two harvests earlier, he started with the rapture of Christ's followers, represented by the Son of Man arriving on a cloud with a sickle. Then he described a second harvest, which gave rise to the expression "the grapes of wrath." There he gave a figurative preview of a bloody battle scene, described as crushing the blood out of the grapes as they are gathered into a vat. That vat is the Valley of Armageddon where the armies of the world gather. After previewing the second harvest, John proceeded to describe the kinds of catastrophes that would lead up to that battle. Now he comes to the ultimate battle itself:

> And I saw heaven opened, and behold a white horse; and he that sat upon him was called Faithful and True, and in righteousness he doth judge and make war. His eyes were as a flame of fire, and on his head were many crowns; and he had a name written, that no man knew, but he himself. And he was clothed with a vesture dipped in blood: and his name is called The Word of God. And the armies which were in heaven followed him upon white horses, clothed in fine linen, white and clean. And out of his mouth goeth a sharp sword, that with it he should smite the nations: and he shall rule them with a rod of iron: and he treadeth the winepress of the fierceness and wrath of Almighty God. And he hath on his vesture and on his thigh a name written, KING OF KINGS, AND LORD OF LORDS.
>
> (REVELATION 19:11–16)

Trampling out the Vintage

John uses one of his favorite names for Jesus Christ, "the Word of God." This was how he introduced Christ in his gospel:

In the beginning was the Word, and the Word was with God, and the Word was God. . . . All things were made by him; and without him was not any thing made that was made. In him was life; and the life was the light of men. . . .

And the Word was made flesh, and dwelt among us, (and we beheld his glory, the glory as of the only begotten of the Father,) full of grace and truth.

(JOHN 1:1, 3–4, 14)

The Word that became flesh is the mystery that, according to John's vision, will be made known to everyone in the end times. The revealing of Christ before the world is the event John now describes. The Word that became flesh returns, and everyone recognizes the truth of his being, the meaning of the mystery. He comes with many crowns because he will be the king who rules over all kings. He is the sovereign to whom all the rulers of all nations will answer.

He returns with all his saints, who were resurrected or raptured from the earth, and with all the angels of heaven, just as described in other New Testament prophecies:

. . . Behold, the Lord cometh with ten thousands of his saints, To execute judgment upon all, and to convict all that are ungodly among them of all their ungodly deeds which they have impiously committed, and of all their hard speeches which ungodly sinners have spoken against him. (JUDE 14B, 15)

For the Son of man shall come in the glory of his Father with his angels; and then he shall reward every man according to his works. (MATTHEW 16:27)

And then they shall see the Son of man coming in the clouds with great power and glory. And then he shall send his angels, and shall gather together his elect from the four winds, from the uttermost part of the earth to the uttermost part of heaven. (MARK 13:26, 27)

Jesus returns to put an end to evil. John has already shown that the only people left on earth are those who refuse to repent under any condition. No matter how much the prophets have warned them, no matter how great or horrible the signs of heaven have been, the more they are judged, the more they are filled with anger and hatred. If earth is ever to enjoy goodness and peace and prosperity for all, it cannot happen as long as evil people remain in the world. Evil destroys peace and prosperity because it lusts after power and is full of greed.

It is not fair that innocent people and even animals suffer endlessly from the evil around them just because pity for the wicked keeps the wicked from being destroyed. And so the hoofbeats of the white horse of the Apocalypse are heard approaching once again, just as they were heard at the beginning of John's visions. Only this time there is a growing thunder of hoofbeats racing behind him, coming down upon the world to trample out all evil:

> For, behold, the day cometh, that shall burn as an oven; and all the proud, and all that do wickedly, shall be stubble [remains of a harvested field]: and the day that cometh shall burn them up, saith the LORD of hosts, that it shall leave them neither root nor branch. But to you that fear my name shall the Sun of right-eousness arise with healing in his wings; and ye shall go forth, and grow up as calves of the stall. And ye shall tread down the wicked; for they shall be ashes under the soles of your feet in the day that I shall do this, saith the LORD of hosts. (MALACHI 4:1–3)

The image of God's anointed trampling out evil doers as though they were grapes in a winepress occurs in several Old Testament prophecies. When Isaiah spoke of the destruction of one of Israel's enemies to the east, Edom, he used language that may have also foreshadowed this great day of God's wrath against the world. Edom was an enemy that had allied itself with Babylon in the destruction of Israel, but the pattern of evil against evil again came to play, and Babylon turned on Edom and devoured it. Since the name "Edom" means "red," the image of red-stained clothes would have come readily to mind for Isaiah. The one who tramples the grapes in a great wine vat gets his clothes completely stained with the blood of the grapes. It's a mad image:

> Who is this that cometh from Edom, with dyed garments from Bozrah [a city in Edom]? this that is glorious in his apparel, travelling in the greatness of his strength? I that speak in righteousness, mighty to save. Why art thou red in thy apparel, and thy garments like him that treadeth in the winepress? I have trodden the winepress alone; and of the people there was none with me: for I will tread them in my anger, and trample them in my fury; and their blood shall be sprinkled upon my garments, and I will stain all my raiment. For the day of vengeance is in my heart, and the year of my redeemed is come. And I looked, and there was none to help; and I wondered that there was none to uphold: therefore my own arm brought salvation to me; and my fury, it upheld me. And I will tread down the people in my anger, and make them drunk in my fury, and I will bring down their strength to the earth. (ISAIAH 63:1–6)

As demonstrated before, God used one evil nation as his agent to destroy another, though Babylon acted of its own free will. The destruction of Edom was amazingly complete. No people remain in the land today who descend from that nation. In fact, few people of any kind remain. Even the language is dead. The entire land is a barren waste, a haunt for jackals. It suffered the same death that later came to city of Babylon. And so Edom is a good example of what will happen to earth in the end times. God destroyed Israel's enemies without any help from Israel. He let mad Babylon have its way with Edom. That probably establishes a pattern that will be true for the arrival of the Messiah. He will come with his hosts from heaven but will destroy the enemies of Israel without any help from those Jews who remain on earth after the rapture. He will be their help; they will not be his. He will be their salvation.

For, behold, in those days, and in that time, when I shall bring again the captivity of Judah and Jerusalem, I will also gather all nations, and will bring them down into the valley of Jehoshaphat, and will judge them there for my people and for my heritage Israel, whom they have scattered among the nations, and divided my land. . . .

Proclaim ye this among the Gentiles; Prepare war, wake up the mighty men, let all the men of war draw near; let them come up: Beat your plowshares into swords, and your pruninghooks into spears: let the weak say, I am strong. Assemble yourselves, and come, all ye nations, and gather yourselves together all around: there cause thy mighty ones to come down, O LORD. Let the nations be awakened, and come up to the valley of Jehoshaphat: for there will I sit to judge all the nations on every side. Put ye in the sickle, for the harvest is ripe: come, go down; for the press is full, the vats overflow; for their wickedness is great. Multitudes, multitudes in the valley of decision: for the day of the LORD is near in the valley of decision. The sun and the moon shall be darkened, and the stars shall withdraw their shining. The LORD also shall roar out of Zion, and utter his voice from Jerusalem; and the heavens and the earth shall shake: but the LORD will be the hope of his people, and the strength of the children of Israel. So shall ye know that I am the LORD your God dwelling in Zion, my holy mountain: then shall Jerusalem be holy, and there shall no strangers pass through her any more. . . . Egypt shall be a desolation, and Edom shall be a desolate wilderness, for the violence against the children of Judah, because they have shed innocent blood in their land. But Judah shall dwell for ever, and Jerusalem from generation to generation. For I will cleanse their blood that I have not cleansed: for the LORD dwelleth in Zion.

(JOEL 3:1, 2, 9–17, 19–21)

Although there was a Jehoshaphat in Israel's history, there is no known valley with his name. The Valley of Jehoshaphat could refer to a valley near Edom where the king and his people celebrated the defeat of Edom, or the meaning of the name, itself, may be all that matters. "Jehoshaphat" means "God judges." So, this is the valley where God judges. The description of the scene when king Jehoshaphat and his people arrived to view Edom's destruction is one of total desolation:

> When the men of Judah came to the place that overlooks the desert and looked towards the vast army, they saw only dead bodies lying on the ground; no-one had escaped.
>
> (2 CHRONICLES 20:24)

In the Apocalypse, the valley to which God gathers the nations of the earth in order to judge them is the Valley of Armageddon. Perhaps he calls this the Valley of Decision because this is where the fate of all who remain will be decided. That is why the prophet twice emphasizes the multitudes who will be gathered here.

Regardless of where this scene plays out, the significant theme is the regathering of the Jews into Israel along with the other nations of the world. The nations, of course, have gathered to destroy Israel, but God, himself, will be the one who saves Israel—God in the person of his anointed.

When John introduced the image of the harvest, he picked up on some of the language used by Joel, probably to forge a connection between the two visions:

> *... Thrust in thy sharp sickle, and gather the clusters of the vine of the earth; for her grapes are fully ripe. And the angel thrust in his sickle into the earth, and gathered the vine of the earth, and cast it into the great winepress of the wrath of God.* (REVELATION 14:18B, 19)

That the same times are in view is also implied by the setting. Like so many other prophecies of the end times, Joel describes a time when the sun, moon, and stars are darkened and the earth and heavens shake. The shaking of the heavens may imply that the unstable conditions on earth comes from above. It may even imply the tilting of the earth on its axis, which was implied in another part of the Bible. Again, it reinforces the possibilities of an asteroid or comet impact.

So, while Joel was predicting the destruction of ancient Edom, the similarity between his description and John's indicates he was perceiving something of earth's great judgment in the horrific view of Edom's desolation.

GOD REMEMBERS THE PEOPLE OF HIS COVENANT

Armageddon is about destruction *and* salvation. Over and over, the Jewish prophets foresaw a day when God would strike evil from the earth. Almost always they used images of fire. In John's Apocalypse, the horseman rides with fire in his eyes. The plagues that have preceded him brought fire to the earth from the sky. In spite of this great conflagration, the hearts of the survivors grow harder and colder toward God. In the final battle, they have gathered of their own accord into Israel to destroy the people of God. Therefore, the salvation of God's people has to mean destruction of these relentless enemies. The seven bowls of wrath have revealed that the enemies will not simply walk away or reform.

God will not forget the people of his first covenant, and the battle at Armageddon is where any Jews who have not recognized their Messiah will meet him:

> (A Psalm) O sing to the LORD a new song; for he hath done marvelous things: his right hand, and his holy arm, hath gotten him the victory. The LORD hath made known his salvation: his righteousness hath he openly shown in the sight of the nations. He hath remembered his mercy and his truth toward the house of Israel: all the ends of the earth have seen the salvation of our God. Make a joyful noise to the LORD, all the earth: make a loud noise, and rejoice, and sing praise. . . . Let the sea roar, and all it containeth; the world, and they that dwell in it. Let the floods clap their hands: let the hills be joyful together Before the LORD; for he cometh to judge the earth: with righteousness shall he judge the world, and the people with equity.
>
> (PSALM 98:1–4, 7–9)

The psalmist spoke as though the event had already happened because the vision was as real to him as fact. The nations will all see the salvation of the people of Israel because they have all gathered to destroy Israel. They shall not prevail. They have a surprise coming. Israel is not as helpless as they think:

> Out of Zion, the perfection of beauty, God hath shined. Our God shall come, and shall not keep silence: a fire shall devour before him, and it shall be very tempestuous around him. He shall call to the heavens from above, and to the earth, that he may judge his people. Gather my saints together to me; those that have made a covenant with me by sacrifice. And the heavens shall declare his righteousness: for God is judge himself. Selah. Hear, O my people, and I will speak; O Israel, and I will testify against thee: I am God, even thy God. . . . And call upon me in the day of trouble: I will deliver thee, and thou shalt glorify me.
>
> (PSALM 50:2–7, 15)

The covenant made by sacrifice is the covenant God made with the Jews and Moses. It is the Mosaic Law. The people of the law are those whose salvation is now in view. The fire that devours before their deliverer comes was seen in the plagues of the Great Tribulation, which created an environmental and political storm around the world before the Messiah's coming. The poet writes that God shall call to the heavens above for judgment.

Why would God call to the heavens in which he lives? Why would he call to himself? Perhaps the poet implies he is calling for objects from heaven to bring judgment on earth.

For the Gentiles, the opportunity for repentance is past. If the Jews call to God, however, he will answer them. He will save them out of peril. An example of God's people needing to find him anew can be found in the prophet Jeremiah:

> *My heart, my heart! I am pained at my very heart; my heart maketh a noise in me; I cannot hold my peace, because thou hast heard, O my soul, the sound of the trumpet, the alarm of war. Destruction upon destruction is cried; for the whole land is laid waste: suddenly are my tents ruined, and my curtains in a moment. How long shall I see the standard, and hear the sound of the trumpet? For my people are foolish, they have not known me; they are silly children, and they have no understanding: they are wise to do evil, but to do good they have no knowledge. I beheld the earth, and, lo, it was without form, and void; and the heavens, and they had no light. I beheld the mountains, and, lo, they trembled, and all the hills moved lightly. I beheld, and, lo, there was no man, and all the fowls of the heavens had fled. I beheld, and, lo, the fruitful place was a wilderness, and all its cities were broken down at the presence of the LORD, and by his fierce anger. For thus hath the LORD said, The whole land shall be desolate; yet will I not make a full end. For this shall the earth mourn, and the heavens above be black: because I have spoken it, I have purposed it, and will not repent, neither will I turn back from it.*
>
> (JEREMIAH 4:19–28)

Was Jeremiah speaking only of the trumpets of war as Babylon marched against Jerusalem with its standards raised, or was he hearing the distant trumpets of the Apocalypse as well? Again, the earth is shaken and the heavens are dark. When the prophet said he "beheld and . . . there was no man," was he speaking only of his situation or was he witnessing the ultimate destruction of earth? He may only have been referring to the desolation of Israel as a result of Babylon's judgment against it, but there is an implication at the end that, because of this kind of evil, the whole earth will pay.

It's not hard to see why a prophet or two was killed by his own people. The prophets had to speak such judgmental words on God's behalf as, "For my people are foolish, they have not known me; they are silly children, and they have no understanding." Not something that is likely to engender popularity unless a people are humble enough to listen without becoming defensive—rare in any human being receiving criticism. When God said his people did not know him, he may have meant they did not know his anointed.

The God who led his people out of exile in Babylon promises he will lead them out of their worldwide exile in the future:

> *As I live, saith the Lord GOD, surely with a mighty hand, and with an outstretched arm, and with fury poured out, will I rule over you: And I will bring you*

out from the people, and will gather you out of the countries in which ye are scattered, with a mighty hand, and with an outstretched arm, and with fury poured out. And I will bring you into the wilderness of the people, and there will I enter into judgment with you face to face. As I entered into judgment with your fathers in the wilderness of the land of Egypt, so will I enter into judgment with you,

saith the Lord GOD. And I will cause you to pass under the rod, and I will bring you into the bond of the covenant: And I will purge out from among you the rebels, and them that transgress against me: I will bring them forth out of the country where they sojourn, and they shall not enter into the land of Israel: and ye shall know that I am the LORD.

(EZEKIEL 20:33–38)

Here is the key phrase that Pope John Paul II used to describe perfect union with God. The Jews will be brought out of all the lands of the diaspora, just as they were brought out of Babylon. The pattern will repeat, and they will meet God "face to face." God's face is seen in his anointed, and his judgment burns in the Anointed One's eyes. The prophet warns that this meeting will not be without discipline. He uses the phrase "pass under the rod"; i.e., the whipping rod. That rod probably refers to the gathering of nations that will come against Israel.

Through this peril, God will bring his people into the bond of his covenant. In the days of Babylon, the covenant was the Old Covenant. In the days ahead, it can only be the New Covenant, predicted by the prophet Jeremiah. The return from Babylon reminded the Jews their God was Lord of the earth. How else could deliverance from such a powerful enemy come with no effort on the part of the Jews? If the prophecy speaks of a similar deliverance from the diaspora and from the extreme anti-Semitism of the end times, then their deliverer will be their Messiah, and they will know that he is the Lord. This is not an easy message, but it conveys hard-won hope all the same. What hope for the Jews was ever anything but hard-won?

TRIBULATION FORCES

The prophecies regarding God's salvation of the Jews are almost always spoken in the context of a great battle and great cataclysm that shall befall the earth. The battle is the battle to end all battles.

. . . God is our refuge and strength, a very present help in trouble. Therefore will we not fear, though the earth shall be removed, and though the mountains shall be carried into the midst of the sea;

Though its waters shall roar and be troubled, though the mountains shake with its swelling. Selah. There is a river, the streams of which shall make glad the city of God [Jerusalem], the holy place of the *tabernacles of the most High. God is in the midst of her; she shall not be moved: God shall help her, and that right early. The nations raged, the kingdoms were moved: he uttered his voice, the earth melted. The LORD of hosts is with us; the God of Jacob is our refuge. Selah. Come, behold the works of the LORD, what desolations he hath made in the*

earth. He maketh wars to cease to the end of the earth; he breaketh the bow, and cutteth the spear asunder; he burneth the chariot in the fire. Be still, and know that I am God: I will be exalted among the nations, I will be exalted in the earth. The LORD of hosts is with us; the God of Jacob is our refuge. Selah.

(Psalm 46:1–11)

Though the nations gather against Jerusalem, the city will be saved. God is their warrior. They do not depend on walls. God is their fortress. When God restores his people, the earth shall shake and the skies shall bleed with fire:

The LORD reigneth; let the earth rejoice; let the multitude of isles be glad. Clouds and darkness surroundeth him: righteousness and judgment are the habitation of his throne. A fire goeth before him, and burneth up his enemies on every side. His lightnings enlightened the world: the earth saw, and trembled. The hills melted like wax at the presence of the LORD, at the presence of the Lord of the whole earth. The heavens declare his righteousness, and all the people see his glory. Confounded be all they that serve graven images, that boast themselves of

idols: worship him, all ye gods. Zion heard, and was glad; and the daughters of Judah rejoiced because of thy judgments, O LORD. For thou, LORD, art high above all the earth: thou art exalted far above all gods. Ye that love the LORD, hate evil: he preserveth the souls of his saints; he delivereth them out of the hand of the wicked. Light is sown for the righteous, and gladness for the upright in heart. Rejoice in the LORD, ye righteous; and give thanks at the remembrance of his holiness. (Psalm 97:1–12)

Again, the fire is said to precede the arrival of God when he saves his people and brings judgment against earth. Fire and darkness are spoken of over and over. Of course, these can be purely metaphoric of spiritual darkness and God's spirit—as some insist they are. Yet, the fire the Jews saw on Mount Sinai when God first dwelled with his people was real. At least, it is portrayed as real. It had the power to stream down and kill people who touched the holy mountain. All evidence from the Apocalypse indicates the fire will be just as real when God returns to dwell with his people and just as dangerous. But God's people rejoice in these judgments because they bring the end of evil, an end humans have never been able to accomplish. The Lion of Judah is good, but he is not safe. He is not a pet god:

Come near, ye nations, to hear; and hearken, ye people: let the earth hear,

and all that is in it; the world, and all things that spring from it. For the indig-

nation of the LORD is upon all nations, and his fury upon all their armies: he hath utterly destroyed them, he hath delivered them to the slaughter. Their slain also shall be cast out, and their foul odour shall come up from their dead bodies, and the mountains shall be melted with their blood. And all the host of heaven shall be dissolved, and the heavens shall be rolled together as a scroll: and all their hosts shall fall down, as the leaf falleth from the vine, and as a falling fig from the fig tree. For my sword shall be bathed in heaven: behold, it shall come down upon Edom [the enemies of God's people], and upon the people of my curse, to judgment. The sword of the LORD is filled with blood, it is made fat with fatness, and with the blood of lambs and goats, with the fat of the kidneys of rams: for the LORD hath a sacrifice in Bozrah, and a great slaughter in the land of Edom. And the unicorns [usually translated "oxen"] shall come down with them, and the young bulls with the bulls; and their land shall be soaked with blood, and their dust made fat with fatness. For it is the day of the LORD'S vengeance, and the year of recompences for the controversy of Zion.

And its streams shall be turned into pitch, and its dust into brimstone, and its land shall become burning pitch. It shall not be quenched night nor day; the smoke of it shall ascend for ever: from generation to generation it shall lie waste; none shall pass through it for ever and ever. But the cormorant and the bittern shall possess it; the owl also and the raven shall dwell in it: and he shall stretch out upon it the line of confusion, and the stones of emptiness. They shall call its nobles to the kingdom, but none shall be there, and all her princes shall be nothing. And thorns shall come up in her palaces, nettles and brambles in its fortresses: and it shall be an habitation of dragons [or possibly jackals], and a court for owls. The wild beasts of the desert shall also meet with the wild beasts of the isle, and the satyr shall cry to his companion; the screech owl also shall rest there, and find for herself a place of rest. There shall the great owl make her nest, and lay, and hatch, and gather under her shadow: there shall the vultures also be gathered, every one with her mate. Seek ye out of the book of the LORD, and read: no one of these shall fail, none shall lack her mate: for my mouth it hath commanded, and his spirit it hath gathered them [the animals]. And he hath cast the lot [like throwing dice] for them, and his hand hath divided it to them by line: they shall possess it for ever, from generation to generation shall they dwell in it.   (ISAIAH 34:1–17)

In this prophecy, *all* armies are finally destroyed by God. The smoke of figurative Edom, like that of figurative Babylon, shall ascend forever. And, as always, the light of the heavenly bodies fails as they fall like figs from the sky. The earth is consumed by fire and brimstone from the heavens and bathed in the blood of war. Neither in the New Testament nor in the Old is God ever presented as safe. In Hebrews, he's called "a living fire."

Frequent mention of animals occupying human cities occurs in prophecies regarding the destruction of the enemies of God's people. On one level, this may be nothing more than a colorful way of showing the desolation of a place after its judgment has fallen. On another level, it speaks of the restoration that nature receives when evil humans are removed. It is not just humanity that will benefit from the removal of those who practice evil. All of creation rests securely. Even the fortresses of the wicked are converted into lairs and nests for wild beasts and birds to inhabit. God gives the spoils of war back to nature. When God comes to destroy the destroyers of earth, their loss is salvation to animals. So, there is justice at all levels.

ᴀʀᴍᴀɢᴇᴅᴅᴏɴ

What was described by John as a wedding banquet in heaven turns out to be a supper of human flesh on earth:

And I saw an angel standing in the sun; and he cried with a loud voice, saying to all the fowls that fly in the midst of heaven, Come and gather yourselves together to the supper of the great God; That ye may eat the flesh of kings, and the flesh of captains, and the flesh of mighty men, and the flesh of horses, and of them that sit on them, and the flesh of all men, both free and bond, both small and great. And I saw the beast, and the kings of the earth, and their armies, gathered together to make war against him that sat on the horse, and against his army. And the beast was taken, and with him the false prophet that wrought miracles before him, with which he deceived them that had received the mark of the beast, and them that worshipped his image. These both were cast alive into a lake of fire burning with brimstone. And the remnant were slain with the sword of him that sat upon the horse, which sword proceedeth out of his mouth: and all the fowls were filled with their flesh.

(ʀᴇᴠᴇʟᴀᴛɪᴏɴ 19:17–21)

The horses here are war horses, of course. Outside of those that die in war, the animals benefit from the spoils of war when human evil is consumed—both spiritually and literally. Spiritually, the end of evil is seen in the demise of the beast. Physically, of course, it is seen in the utter desolation of the desolators of earth.

The battle at Armageddon may just be another way of describing the destruction of Babylon the Great, for Armageddon is world war. World War III (or IV or V) amounts to all the nations of the world—or what remains of them after the Great Tribulation—attacking Israel. But those who try to remove Jerusalem from the face of the earth will find themselves removed, though they outnumber the Jews a thousand to one:

The burden of the word of the LORD for Israel, saith the LORD, who stretcheth forth the heavens, and layeth the foundation of the earth, and formeth the spirit of man within him. Behold, I will make Jerusalem a cup of trembling to all the surrounding people, when they shall be in the siege both against Judah and against Jerusalem. And in that day will I make Jerusalem a burdensome stone for all nations: all that burden themselves with it shall be cut in pieces, though all the people of the earth be gathered against it. In that day, saith the LORD, I will smite every horse with astonishment, and his rider with madness: and I will open my eyes upon the house of Judah, and will smite every horse of the people with blindness. And the governors of Judah shall say in their heart, The inhabitants of Jerusalem shall be my strength in the LORD of hosts their God. In that day will I make the governors of Judah like an hearth of fire among the wood, and like a torch of fire in a sheaf; and they shall devour all the surrounding people, on the right hand and on the left: and Jerusalem shall be inhabited again in her own place, even in Jeru-salem. The LORD also shall save the tents of Judah first, that the glory of the house of David and the glory of the inhabitants of Jerusalem may not magnify themselves against Judah. In that day shall the LORD defend the inhabitants of Jerusalem; and he that is feeble among them at that day shall be as David; and the house of David shall be as God, as the angel of the LORD before them.

And it shall come to pass in that day, that I will seek to destroy all the nations that come against Jerusalem. And I will pour upon the house of David, and upon the inhabitants of Jerusalem, the spirit of grace and of supplications: and they shall look upon me whom they have pierced, and they shall mourn for him, as one mourneth for his only son, and shall be in bitterness for him, as one that is in bitterness for his firstborn. In that day shall there be a great mourning in Jerusalem, as the mourning of Hadadrimmon in the valley of Megiddon.

(ZECHARIAH 12:1–11)

Early in the Apocalypse, John quoted a line of this prophecy to indicate a time would come when those who killed the Messiah would recognize him and bitterly mourn the loss. Now it is clear where that event happens in John's description of the end times. It is the final event that happens in the Valley of Har Megiddo:

Awake, awake; put on thy strength, O Zion; put on thy beautiful garments, O Jerusalem, the holy city: for henceforth there shall no more come into thee the uncircumcised and the unclean. Behold, my servant shall deal prudently, he shall be exalted and extolled, and be very high. As many were astonished at thee; his visage was so marred more than any man, and his form more than the sons of men: So shall he sprinkle many nations [with sacrificial blood]; the kings shall shut their mouths at him: for that which had not been told them shall they see; and that which they had not heard shall they consider.   (ISAIAH 52:1, 13–15)

When destruction for Jerusalem seems assured, the skies open, and the Messiah is revealed—the one formerly disfigured upon the cross. With him are all his resurrected followers and the angels, who are also revealed. Out of nowhere, Jerusalem's destroyers find they are now the ones outnumbered a thousand to one. The siege is ended as soon as it has begun. History, as it has been know, has come to its close.

> And the LORD shall be king over all the earth: in that day shall there be one LORD, and his name one. All the land shall be turned as a plain from Geba to Rimmon south of Jerusalem: and it shall be lifted up, and inhabited in her place, from Benjamin's gate to the place of the first gate, to the corner gate, and from the tower of Hananeel to the king's wine-presses. And men shall dwell in it, and there shall be no more utter destruction; but Jerusalem shall be safely inhabited. And this shall be the plague with which the LORD will smite all the people that have fought against Jerusalem; Their flesh shall consume away while they stand upon their feet, and their eyes shall consume away in their holes, and their tongue shall consume away in their mouth. And it shall come to pass in that day, that a great tumult from the LORD shall be among them; and they shall lay hold every one on the hand of his neigh-bour, and his hand shall rise up against the hand of his neighbour. And Judah also shall fight at Jerusalem; and the wealth of all the nations on every side shall be gathered together, gold, and sil-ver, and apparel, in great abundance. And so shall be the plague of the horse, of the mule, of the camel, and of the don-key, and of all the beasts that shall be in these tents, as this plague.
>
> (ZECHARIAH 14:9–15)

The holocaust described could be nuclear or celestial; it could come from incendiary chemical bombs or germs engineered by evil people to devour human flesh in minutes; or it could be supernatural. One thing is certain: It is complete.

HOW THE WORLD IS WON

So, is God like the angry Thor, who throws down lightning bolts from heaven? Does peace and truth fail so that even the Messiah must use war to prevail? If Jesus was a man of peace, does he not betray his own truth by resorting in the end to the same tactics used by all the empires he is supposed to overcome? What happened to the Messiah who told his disciple to lay down the sword? Is Christ's truth in the end not sufficient for victory? Were all the previous empires right?

For those who believe truth prevails, this is a deeply disturbing scene, but take a second look at the Apocalypse. The white horse and its rider who gallop into Armageddon are most likely just as symbolic of the Messiah as they were at the beginning of the Apocalypse. The sword from the rider's mouth may still be the sword of truth. There's no sign of actual blades being lifted. The Messiah comes. The nations attack him; he does not attack them. The evil leaders are captured and overthrown (but not struck), and then all the people of earth are killed by the sword that comes out of the *mouth* of the rider. The sword of truth alone shall slay the wicked.

> And there shall come forth a rod out of the stem of Jesse, and a Branch shall grow out of his roots: And the spirit of the LORD shall rest upon him, the spirit of wisdom and understanding, the spirit of counsel and might, the spirit of knowledge and of the fear of the LORD; And shall make him of quick understanding in the fear of the LORD: and he shall not judge after the sight of his eyes, neither reprove after the hearing of his ears: But with righteousness shall he judge the poor, and reprove with equity for the meek of the earth: and he shall smite the earth with the rod of his mouth, and with the breath of his lips shall he slay the wicked. And righteousness shall be the belt of his loins, and faithfulness the belt of his reins. (ISAIAH 11:1–5)

This passage certainly seems to say that the judgment that strikes the wicked comes from the mouth of the one John calls "the Word." It comes from the breath, which is the words that he speaks. The militaristic images of the Apocalypse are merely to emphasize the conquering power of truth. Without those images, truth seems too small to overturn the powers of this world.

Remember, also, that whenever God spoke of judging a nation for it wrongs—whenever he said he would come against them like a flood—the flood was the army of another evil empire. God spoke as though Babylon was his agent against Jerusalem and then as though the Medes were his agent against Babylon. Fish swallowed fish. Evil consumed evil.

Zechariah said "that a great tumult from the LORD shall be among them; and they shall lay hold every one on the hand of his neighbour, and his hand shall rise up against the hand of his neighbour." Perhaps the overwhelming appearance of the saints and especially the Messiah—the truth revealed in all its splendor—is all it takes to turn the ten kings of the end times against the great harlot in self-destruction. Evil ambition rushes in to fill the power vacuum when the beast at the top is captured, and anarchy breaks out in the ranks of the evil. Because everyone wants to be leader, each man turns against the other, as Zechariah proclaimed. The melting of their flesh from their faces like hot wax may quite literally be the effect of the kings of earth turning their own nuclear arsenals upon each other as they vie for the top position in the empire and have to fight off their own people below. God calls this a plague from himself, because, like all plagues, he has allowed it—even foreseen it. The self-destruction of evil is an immutable pattern of nature, a safety feature God built into the original design. That which goes wrong, self-destructs.

One of the apocryphal books reveals a similar kind of end at the Messiah's return:

After this I looked, and behold, all who had gathered together against him [the Messiah], to wage war with him, were much afraid, yet dared to fight. And behold, when he saw the onrush of the approaching multitude, he neither lifted his hand nor held a spear or any weapon of war; but I saw only how he sent forth from his mouth as it were a stream of fire, and from his lips a flaming breath, and from his tongue shot forth sparks. All these were mingled together . . . and fell on the on-rushing multitude which was prepared to fight and burned them all up so that suddenly nothing was seen of the innumerable multitude but only the dust of ashes and the smell of smoke. . . .

After this I saw the same man come down from the mountain and call to him another multitude which was peaceable. Then many people came to him, some of whom were joyful and some sorrowful; some of them were bound, and some were bringing others as offerings.[1]

Was the melting of their flesh from nuclear or chemical war, or does Christ spew fire from his mouth like a dragon to melt the flesh off his self-proclaimed enemies? Perhaps the fire from his mouth is no different than the sword from his mouth in the Apocalypse—both symbolizing the truth of his words. John has called him "The Word of God" in the section of the Apocalypse quoted at the beginning of this chapter. By his word the heavens were created. So, perhaps by his word they will also end.

The multitude with which the Messiah has arrived is described as "peaceable." And those who greet them are both happy and mournful. Happiness and mourning—that's the same way John described the Jews' meeting the Messiah. (The book of 2 Esdras, where this prophecy comes from, purports to be written by the priest Ezra in Old Testament times. Most scholars, however, believe much of it was written by Christians. Whether or not the book is legitimately prophetic, it does reflect the understanding of early Christians.)

It turns out the prophecy of 2 Esdras is self-interpreting, with the following explanation given, showing that, indeed, that God's people will be protected:

He who brings the peril at that time will himself protect those who fall into peril, who have works and have faith in the Almighty. . . . This is he whom the Most High has been keeping for many ages, who will himself deliver his creation; and he will direct those who are left. And as for your seeing wind and fire and a storm coming out of his mouth, and as for his not holding a spear of weapon of war, yet destroying the onrushing multitude which came to conquer him, this is the interpretation: . . . The Most high will deliver those who are on the earth [the rapture?]. And bewilderment of mind shall come over those who dwell on the earth. And they shall plan to make war against one another, city against city . . . and kingdom against kingdom. . . . Then my Son will be revealed, whom you saw . . . and when all the nations hear his voice, every man shall leave his own land and the warfare that they have against one another; and an innumerable multitude shall be gathered together, as you saw, desiring to come and conquer him. But he will stand on top of Mount Zion. And Zion will come and be made manifest to all people, prepared and built . . . the mountain carved out without hands. And he, my Son, will reprove the assembled nations for their ungodliness . . . and will reproach them to their face with their evil thoughts and the torments with which they are to be tortured (which were symbolized by the flames), and will destroy them without effort by the law (which was symbolized by the fire).[2]

According to 2 Esdras, the sword that issues from the Messiah's mouth will be the absolute and clear revelation of the eternal death (called the "second death" in the Apocalypse) that awaits the evil. Hearing this truth as well as the truth of their own evil in the presence of the Messiah's undeniable glory, after seeing their own leaders overcome, will destroy the foundations of every belief the wicked ever had. They will be devoured with terror. What 2 Esdras describes as "city against city . . . and kingdom against kingdom" is complete world anarchy. And, though 2 Esdras doesn't make the following step, it seems probable that the anarchy that has seized them will cause them to rage against each other in blame. Already hot for blood, they will fight what they are able fight (each other) in the face of what they cannot fight. They will slaughter each other like sharks in a feeding frenzy. In the end, evil contains the spark that ignites its own cremation.

Evil shall slay the wicked: and they that hate the righteous shall be desolate. The LORD redeemeth the soul of his ser- *vants: and none of them that trust in him shall be desolate.* (PSALM 34:21, 22)

Then, there is also the spiritual fact that no one can see God face to face and live—except those resurrected into his glory. Perhaps God has turned his face to shine upon the evil and melt away their darkness.

MORE ON THE 144,000

Second Esdras concludes prophetic interpretation of Armageddon with the following account related to the 144,000 and the ten lost tribes of Israel:

And as for your seeing him gather to himself another multitude that was peaceable, these are the ten tribes which were led away from their own land into captivity in the days of . . . the Assyrians. . . . They were taken into another land. But they formed this plan for themselves, that they would leave the multitude of the nations and go to a more distant region, where mankind had never lived, that there at least they might keep their statutes which they had not kept in their own land. . . . For at that time, the Most High . . . stopped the channels of the [Euphrates] river until they had passed over. . . .

Then they dwelt there until the last times; and now, when they are about to come again, the Most High will stop the channels of the river again, so that they may be able to pass over. Therefore you saw the multitude gathered together in peace. But those who are left of your people, who are found within my holy borders, shall be saved. Therefore, when he destroys the multitude of the nations that are gathered together, he will defend the people [Jews] who remain. . . .

So no one on earth can see my Son or those who are with him, except in the time of his day.[3]

Could it be that the lost tribes did, indeed, break from the Assyrians (at least a part of them) and escape to a distant eastern land? It seems highly unlikely, given present knowledge of geography, that a multitude of Jews remains as a separate nation, but might they have migrated through Russian and back across northern Europe over the centuries and assimilated with other pagan cultures, so that a trickle of their blood is in every Gentile?

This passage from 2 Esdras clearly equates the 144,000 with the multitude that arrives with the Messiah, yet, John has described those who arrive with him as the armies of heaven, which in his Christian view would presumably include all the resurrected saints who live in communion with him. A literal 144,000 would not be much of an army.

WHERE DOES IT ALL LEAD?

The purpose of letting evil rise to its own destruction is to clear the way for paradise:

Why do the nations rage, and the people imagine a vain thing? The kings of the earth set themselves, and the rulers take counsel together, against the LORD, and against his anointed, saying, Let us break their bands asunder, and cast away their cords from us. He that sitteth in the heavens shall laugh: the Lord shall have them in derision. Then shall he speak to them in his wrath, and trouble them in his great displeasure. Yet have I set my king upon my holy hill of Zion. I will declare the decree: the LORD hath said to me, Thou art my Son; this day have I begotten thee. Ask of me, and I shall give thee the nations for thine inheritance, and the uttermost parts of the earth for thy possession. Thou shalt break them with a rod of iron; thou shalt dash them in pieces like a potter's vessel. Be wise now therefore, O ye kings: be instructed, ye judges of the earth. Serve the LORD with fear, and rejoice with trembling. Kiss the Son, lest he be angry, and ye perish from the way, when his wrath is kindled but a little. Blessed are all they that put their trust in him. (PSALM 2:1–12)

God sends his Messiah (anointed) to earth to purge it of evil and establish a worldwide reign of peace.

Chapter 22

Millennium:

The Fulfillment of Utopia

The Bible begins with the seven days of creation and ends with a book of sevens about the ultimate destiny of creation. As will be seen near the close of the Apocalypse, the Bible also ends with the same symbolic images used in the beginning of the Bible for the Garden of Eden story.

The seven letters to the seven churches have been read; the seven seals have been opened; the seven trumpets have sounded; and the seven bowls of judgment have been poured out. The seven heads of three beasts have raised themselves and fallen. In the course of his visions, John has relayed seven blessings to his readers and seven images of the Messiah. Seven stars, seven lamps and seven lampstands, seven mountains, seven kings, seven angels, seven spirits of God, seven thunders, and a lamb with seven horns and seven eyes and seven crowns. The seven theme is so intricately repeated throughout the Apocalypse that there can be no a doubt the writer is calling attention to it for a highly significant purpose. But what purpose?

To the Jewish mind, seven is the sabbath—a concept established by God himself according to the writings of the Jews:

> Remember the sabbath day, to keep it holy. Six days shalt thou labour, and do all thy work: But the seventh day is the sabbath of the LORD thy God . . . For in six days the LORD made heaven and earth, the sea, and all that in them is, and rested the seventh day: wherefore the LORD blessed the sabbath day, and hallowed it. (Exodus 20:8–11)

And how important was this sacramental day?

> Ye shall keep the sabbath therefore; for it is holy unto you: every one that de- fileth it shall surely be put to death: for whosoever doeth any work therein,

that soul shall be cut off from among his people. Wherefore the children of Israel shall keep the sabbath, to observe the sabbath throughout their generations, for a perpetual covenant.

(EXODUS 31:14, 16)

The seventh day represented the completion of creation—the day on which all of God's creating was finished. There was also a sabbath month after the harvest was brought in, which celebrated some of the most significant Jewish holy days, including *Yom Kippur* and *Sukkot* (also known as the Feast of Tabernacles or Feast of Booths):

... In the seventh month, in the first day of the month, shall ye have a sabbath, a memorial of blowing of trumpets, an holy convocation. Ye shall do no servile work in it: but ye shall offer an offering made by fire to the LORD. . . . Also on the tenth day of this seventh month there shall be a day of atonement: it shall be an holy convocation to you; and ye shall afflict your souls, and offer an offering made by fire to the LORD. . . . Ye shall do no manner of work: it shall be a statute for ever throughout your generations in all your dwellings. It shall be to you a sabbath of rest, and ye shall afflict your souls: in the ninth day of the month at evening, from evening to evening, shall ye celebrate your sabbath. . . . Also in the fifteenth day of the seventh month, when ye have gathered in the fruit of the land, ye shall keep a feast to the LORD seven days: on the first day shall be a sabbath, and on the eighth day shall be a sabbath. . . . And ye shall keep it a feast to the LORD seven days in the year. It shall be a statute for ever in your generations: ye shall celebrate it in the seventh month.

(LEVITICUS 23:24, 25, 27, 31, 32, 39, 41)

Every seventh year was a sabbath year to be observed by letting all of the natural world enjoy its rest by letting agricultural lands lie fallow:

And the LORD spoke to Moses in mount Sinai, saying, Speak to the children of Israel, and say to them, When ye come into the land which I give you, then shall the land keep a sabbath to the LORD. Six years thou shalt sow thy field, and six years thou shalt prune thy vineyard, and gather in its fruit; But in the seventh year shall be a sabbath of rest to the land, a sabbath for the LORD: thou shalt neither sow thy field, nor prune thy vineyard.

(LEVITICUS 25: 1–4)

After every seventh sabbath year (i.e., every forty-nine years) came a special celebration called the Year of Jubilee:

And thou shalt number seven sabbaths of years to thee, seven times seven years; and the space of the seven sabbaths of years shall be to thee forty and nine years. Then shalt thou cause the trumpet of the jubilee to sound on the tenth day of the seventh month, in the day of atonement shall ye make the trumpet sound throughout all your land. And ye shall hallow the fiftieth year, and proclaim liberty throughout all the land to all its inhabitants: it shall be a jubilee to you; and ye shall return every man to his possession, and ye shall return every man to his family.

(LEVITICUS 25:8–10)

THE SABBATH MILLENNIUM

Since sabbath days, months, and years became increasingly grand in scope as the unit of time increased, what would be the magnitude of a sabbath millennium? Would it be the fulfillment of all sabbaths? The observance of the sabbath day was a sacrament to commemorate the completion of God's creation at the beginning of the world. Could it also be a sacrament intended to foreshadow earth's final destiny? Could seven, which traditionally represents the fulness of God and nature (i.e., all that is), also represent the fulness of time, measured in millennia of human experience?

What if the sabbath really was intended to make God's people aware not just of their origins but of their destiny? Another theme repeatedly emphasized in the Apocalypse is "the beginning and the end" or "the first and the last."

According to the *biblical* record of human history, humanity is just entering its seventh millennium. ("History," by definition, does not necessarily cover the length of human existence on the planet; history is the recorded *story* of human existence, and if one is interpreting biblical prophecies, one would naturally measure that time by the biblical record.)

This Feast of Tabernacles, mentioned above, was the seventh of seven holy festivals on the Jewish calendar. It celebrated Israel's delivery out of Egypt following all the plagues. Could it also have been a sacrament anticipating the Jews' future delivery in the seventh millennium from the similar plagues of the Great Tribulation? John has shown throughout that the plagues of both times, as well as the deliverance of both times, parallel each other.

Just as the Feast of Tabernacles strongly connects the number seven to the Jewish exodus, the number seven is also strongly connected to the Jews' entry a generation after the exodus into the promised land. To enter the promised land, the children of Israel had to march around the pagan city of Jericho seven days. On the seventh day, they marched around the city seven times with seven priests blowing seven trumpets, not unlike the seven angels blowing seven trumpets in the Apocalypse. The walls of the pagan city crumbled and all its evil occupants were killed, not unlike Armageddon in the Apocalypse. Then the children of Israel began their lives in the promised land.

It may be more than coincidence that the next event in the Apocalypse after the seven trumpets and the battle at Armageddon is the ultimate promised land on earth:

And I saw an angel come down from heaven, having the key of the bottomless pit and a great chain in his hand. And he laid hold on the dragon, that old serpent, who is the Devil, and Satan, and bound him a thousand years, And cast him into the bottomless pit, and shut him up, and set a seal upon him, that he should deceive the nations no more, till the thousand years should be fulfilled: and after that he must be loosed a little season. And I saw thrones, and they sat upon them, and judgment was given to them: and I saw the souls of them that were beheaded for the witness of Jesus, and for the word of God, and who had not worshipped the beast, neither his image, neither had received his mark upon their foreheads, or in their hands; and they lived and reigned with Christ a thousand years. But the rest of the dead lived not again until the thousand years were finished. This is the first resurrection. Blessed and holy is he that hath part in the first resurrection: on such the second death hath no power, but they shall be priests of God and of Christ, and shall reign with him a thousand years.

(REVELATION 20:1–6)

Are all the ancient Jewish sabbaths a divine foreshadowing of the day when humanity will enter a sabbath millennium—a holy millennium of rest in the ultimate promised land? There are some hints of this in the New Testament.

... the sabbaths ... are a shadow of things to come. ...

(COLOSSIANS 2:16B, 17)

They [scoffers] deliberately ignore this fact, that by the word of God heavens existed long ago, and an earth formed out of water and by means of water, through which the world that then existed was deluged with water and perished. But by the same word the heavens and earth that now exist have been stored up for fire, being kept until the day of judgment and destruction of ungodly men.

But do not ignore this one fact, beloved, that with the Lord one day is as a thousand years, and a thousand years as one day. (2 PETER 3:5–8)

Could it be that when God said, "Six days shalt thou labor, and do all thy work: But the seventh day is the sabbath of the LORD thy God," he also meant, "Six thousand years shalt mankind labor upon the earth, but the seventh thousand is the Day of the Lord—a time that is to be hallowed and blessed, a time of peace and rest"? Certainly Peter connects the first seven days with the final days of judgment by putting them back-to-back. He says the earth began by water and will end by fire. And he says that both events—the seven days of the beginning and the days of the end—come "by the same word." In that very context, he emphasizes that days may be counted as millennia on God's scale of time.

The Apocalypse shows that human imperial government will end by fire when God's Holy One returns—the "word" who was at the beginning and will come at the end. If the millennium mentioned in the Apocalypse is meant to be taken literally, it could be the last of seven millennia—a seventh "day" that is the Lord's, following the six "days" in which humans have attempted self-rule.

If this is what the Apocalypse is hinting at by repeating the number seven, there should be other consistent evidence within the book. There should be a way to test the hypothesis.

What about the peculiar structure of the book? The series of seven seals and the series of seven trumpets were each divided into sub-groups of four events followed by a group of three. The original creation story that provides the basis for the sabbath also shows an important division between the fourth day and the last three. It is on the fourth day that the sun is created to bring life into the world. So, the first four days of creation were without life, but in the last three life springs forth, is sustained, and, ultimately, finds its rest. The fourth day is also the first day that time could be measured by the sun. (Which may imply that the days mentioned were not solar days at all, but were figurative division of the eras of creation intended for religious significance. What, then, would be their significance?)

Was there a counterpart in the millennia of human history to the first four days of creation? Follow biblical history via its genealogies through the first four millennia, one arrives at the birth of Christ exactly between the fourth and fifth millennium, which to this day remains the turning point of our calendar (B.C. to A.D.). One can hardly state any date in history without inadvertently referencing it to this singular event.

So, the great divide in human history also came after the fourth "day"—if a day is as a thousand years. This is when the oldest of the world's great religions, Judaism, divided into two primary branches—Christianity and the branch that became Talmudic Judaism. For Christians, this great historic divide represents the fulfillment of the Old Covenant (Old Testament) and beginning of the New Covenant (New Testament).

That modern calendars still revolve around this event may be more than a happenstance of Christian heritage—*if* one believes in destiny. When the sun was created on the fourth day, a new light dawned on the world. The Anointed One who was born after the fourth millennial day said, "I am the light of the world," The sun brought physical life, and the Son brought spiritual life, claiming, "I have come that you may have life and have it more abundantly." At creation, God breathed the breath of life into man, and he became a living physical being. At Jesus' resurrection, Jesus breathed his Holy Spirit into the heart of each disciple, and each one received spiritual life. So, in the Christian view, there is a clear spiritual correlation between the fourth day of creation and the close of the fourth millennium.

Regarding Jesus Christ, the same John who wrote the Apocalypse said, "without him was not any thing made," and the Apostle Paul said, "he is before all things, and by him all things consist." That a hypothetical time line based purely on the structure of the Apocalypse perfectly "predicts" the first advent (arrival) of the same person the Apocalypse repeatedly refers to as "the beginning and the end" seems more than coincidental. That it gives a mystical meaning to the story of the seven days of creation compounds the coincidence.

Jesus is also the one Christians believe is ultimately referred to in the earlier quote about the sabbath month, which says, "the priest, whom he [God the Father] shall anoint [the Messiah], and whom he shall consecrate to minister in the priest's office in his father's [God's] stead shall make the atonement, and shall put on the linen clothes [the clothes of righteousness placed on the saints repeatedly in the Apocalypse]."

Is there more within the Apocalypse that might support the idea that seven millennia (by biblical accounting) represent the fulness of human and divine history on earth?

John also interrupts both the series of seals and the series of trumpets with a major interlude between the sixth and seventh event. Both of these series describe times of great tribulation on earth that precede the return of Jesus Christ. If the structure of the Apocalypse is intentionally patterned after some divine structure of history, the placement of these interludes should indicate some significant event in history. Perhaps John's predictable interludes between the sixth and seventh events signify the *second* coming of Jesus Christ occurring between the sixth and seventh millennia.

In other words, not only did the first four millennia of biblical history come before Christ's first advent, but there will only be three millennia of history following his advent (*if* the hypothesis is correct) to make a total of seven. Moreover, his second coming will occur between the sixth and seventh millennia (corresponding to John's interludes between the sixth and seventh events in each series). He has to come after the sixth *if* he's going to reign throughout the seventh.

As though to back this up, the final series of events, the bowls of judgment, are not grouped into fours and threes, nor is there any interruption between the sixth and seventh bowl. *After* the seventh bowl is poured, the destruction of Babylon the Great is described briefly, then an interlude explains the destruction in detail for two chapters, then Armageddon brings the destruction to an end. So, the interlude is contained within the description of the seventh bowl.

But this may be the proverbial exception that proves the rule. The seven seals and seven trumpets described events *leading up to* and culminating in Christ's return. But the seven bowls *are* his return. They are the judgment he brings to earth when he comes, which culminates at Armageddon. At the beginning of the seven bowls, Christ has re-united with his saints, but he does not yet reign on earth, even though his reign has been announced. First, his saints, dead or alive, were caught up to meet him as he returned; then judgment began to pour out upon the earth. At the end of the bowls of judgment, he and his saints made themselves visible at Armageddon to all who were left. This short period is an interlude in history, during which Christ has come, but his kingdom is not yet established. It is an overlap between the period of imperial government and the thousand years of Christ's reign when both are in power. It is a time when the two powers must meet and one will prevail. As though to indicate the seven bowls *are* the inter-lude in history, they do not have any divisions or groupings.

Will the sixth millennium of history (the one just passing) be followed by an inter-lude of great tribulation in which evil is defeated and a new age of peace dawns? If hu-manity stands at the edge of the ultimate promised land today, the evil of Jericho still lies between and must be overcome. The seven bowls are earth's final Jericho.

All of this is speculation, of course. Though the modern calendar measures years from the birth of Christ ("The year of our Lord," *anno Domini*, A.D.), it is probably not accurate enough to show exactly when the seventh millennium would begin, but most historians would agree the calendar is within a decade of being accurate on the birth of Christ. Many historians believe the birth of Christ actually happened in about 4 B.C. In which case, the millennium of Christ's reign would have begun in 1996, by the above reasoning, and obviously that did not happen.

There's a second caveat: Many historians would insist more than four thousand years occurred between the beginning of human history and Jesus Christ's birth. That may be irrelevant to interpreting the Apocalypse, however, given that the appropriate calendar to use for biblical revelation would be the biblical calendar. Even then, there are discrepancies in the biblical chronologies between various ancient manuscripts where two manuscripts each have different time spans for the same event. The first year on the Jewish Calendar, for example is -3760, which would place the beginning of the seventh millennium near the year 2240. Nevertheless, many historians agree biblical genealogies count back very close to four thousand years before Christ. (Some would say exactly four thousand years.)

Then why didn't the seventh millennium begin in 1996? Perhaps Christ's first ad-vent should also be considered an interlude in the time line, so the prophetic clock may not have started ticking again until he left the earth. Jesus' life was certainly an interrup-tion in the flow of human history. Small as the events of his life seemed in his own time, it's not hard to argue they were the biggest interruption history has ever seen in terms of their consequence.

It could also be that millennia are not exact time spans. John's thousand years may be a round figure. People don't commonly measure decades precisely, so, why millennia?

When people talk about the "sixties," for example, they don't usually mean 1961–1970. They usually mean the period of the social revolution that took place roughly during that decade, but didn't end until the U.S. began to pull out of the Vietnam War in 1973, which diffused the revolution. Major divisions of human history into millennia may not be the kind of thing one can set one's watch by. Christ clearly taught that his followers would not know the day or hour of his return, and it is overly literal to say, "Ah, but that still allows we can know the month or year." His point was simply, you will never *know* when he is going to come.

The most important question may not be chronological but theological: Is it even right to take a general statement like "with the Lord one day is as a thousand years, and a thousand years as one day" and apply it as a formula for establishing a prophetic time line? To the affirmative side of the argument, this statement *is* made in the context of the original days of creation *and* the final days of earth's judgment, yet that does not necessarily make it a formula for earth's destiny. It could be nothing more than a figure of speech, meaning the eternal God does not reckon time as man does.

THE SECRETS OF ENOCH AND THE SEVENTH MILLENNIUM

These objections considered, John is not the only prophet to speak in terms of millennia with hints that seven millennia may be the full measure of human history. A mysterious work, known as *The Book of Enoch,* was not accepted as part of the Bible, though it was sometimes quoted by early Church writers. It may not have made the list simply because people tend to read its descriptions of heaven and other events literally. In which case, they sometimes sound like a child's daydreams. No matter how one regards it, *Enoch* retains the distinction of being the only non-biblical book quoted word-for word within the Bible. Jesus' brother Jude quotes from *Enoch* in his little book, which comes right before the Apocalypse:

> *And Enoch also, the seventh from Adam, prophesied of these, saying, Behold, the Lord cometh with ten thousands of his saints, To execute judgment upon all, and to convict all that are ungodly among them of all their ungodly deeds which they have impiously committed, and of all their hard speeches which ungodly sinners have spoken against him.*
>
> (JUDE 1:14–15)

(Of course, Jude, like the *Book of Enoch* almost didn't make it into the Bible, and the Apocalypse also nearly missed inclusion.)

Three versions of the *Book of Enoch* exist, two of which appear to be fragments from larger manuscripts. They have significant differences, which may account for why they were not included in the Bible. The original from which these three versions theoretically derived is believed to have been put into writing before the time of Christ. Though none of Enoch the prophet's words are found in the Old Testament, the man is mentioned by name in the book of Genesis:

> And Enoch walked with God after he begat Methuselah three hundred years, and begat sons and daughters: And all the days of Enoch were three hundred sixty and five years: And Enoch walked with God: and he was not; for God took him. (GENESIS 5:22–24)

Unfortunately there is no way of knowing whether or not the *Book of Enoch* actually contains the knowledge of this ancient prophet who was so holy he avoided death—except that Jesus' brother believed it did, or he wouldn't have quoted from it. The version containing the words quoted by Jude is an Ethiopian version. The quote that follows is from the Slavonic version known as the *Secrets of Enoch*. Though this fragment of a manuscript does not include the section quoted by Jude (to authenticate its acceptance by Jude), it does contain an interesting description of earth's historic time line beginning with God's curse upon Adam. It indicates that history, from Adam on, will run seven thousand years, corresponding to the seven days of creation, and that the seventh millennium will follow the Messiah's second coming:

> I [God] said to him [Adam]: "Earth thou art, and into the earth whence I took thee thou shalt go, and I will not ruin thee, but send thee whence I took thee. Then I can again take thee [by resurrection] at My second coming." . . . And I blessed the seventh day, which is the sabbath on which he [Adam] rested from all his works.
>
> And I appointed the eighth day also, that the eighth day should be the first-created after my work, and that the first seven revolve in the form of the seventh thousand, and that at the beginning of the eighth thousand there should be a time of not-counting, endless with neither years, nor months nor weeks nor days nor hours.[1]

Since this was written before the word "millennium" was coined to mean a thousand years, wouldn't "the seventh thousand" mean the seventh millennium? The words clearly leap from talking in terms of the seven days of creation to talking in terms of thousands. The length of each day is to be measured in terms of the seventh day, which is called the "seventh thousand." God seems to be telling Enoch that each of the seven days of his creation prefigures a thousand revolutions of the earth around the sun. (Note that the mention of revolutions puts this prophecy way ahead of its time in terms of knowledge.) The *Secrets of Enoch*, then, implies the seventh thousand will be blessed as a time of rest after the Messiah's return when Adam and his kind are resurrected from the earth. As for Enoch's mysterious eighth day, John's Revelation fits perfectly there, too, but that part of the Apocalypse is yet to come.

What's particularly interesting about this prophecy is that people creating their own time lines for the end of the world always find a way to align the end with their own generation. (It's almost a rule of thumb for creating prophetic time lines.) This prophet is as unlikely as a Chinese pope because he placed the end times centuries beyond his own. His timing happens to line up with the present millennial change and fits perfectly with the structure of the Apocalypse, and it matches perfectly with the quote from Peter that placed "a day to the Lord is as a thousand years" in the context of earth's creation *and* final judgment.

The larger version of *Enoch,* which contains the material quoted by Jude, also describes the total history of earth in terms of seven thousand years, but, instead of dividing earth's destiny into seven periods of a one thousand years, it divides it into ten periods of seven hundred years (called weeks of centuries), describing a key event for each week of centuries. By its accounting, something much like the Great Tribulation occurs sometime between A.D. 1600 and A.D. 2300, when . . .

> . . . the judgment of righteousness [shall] be revealed to the whole world. Every work of the ungodly shall disappear from the whole earth; the world shall be marked for destruction; and all men shall be on the lookout for the path of integrity.[2]

This final period of righteousness lasts seven hundred years, then comes the tenth period, which is eternity. In dealing with this version, it should be pointed out that the description of historic periods before Christ match up with actual events in history, but the description of the seven hundred-year periods after the time of Christ do not appear to match up with historic events. Thus, the "prophet" did a better job looking backward in time than he did looking forward (since he wrote his book very near the time when Christ lived on earth).

Discrepancies aside, both versions taken together reveal a clear belief among ancient Jews and Christians that earth's total history will encompass seven thousand years. And both use the number seven as the key to earth's destiny, as does the Apocalypse.

EZEKIEL AND THE SEVENTH MILLENNIUM

One doesn't have to look outside the Bible to find mystical connections between the number seven and a period of glory and peace for the earth. An unusual, prophecy in the book of Ezekiel describes in elaborate detail, down to the very measurements, a temple that was never built. Supposedly the new design was intended to replace Solomon's temple, which was destroyed by the Babylonians, but the replacement temple that was actually built was not to Ezekiel's specifications. Since the replacement temple was destroyed by Rome, many people believe Ezekiel's temple will be built in the end times as it should have been built originally. Others feel Ezekiel's temple is purely figurative. (See Appendix B for the full prophecy.)

Regardless of whether the temple is ever intended to be built, no scholar would deny that its details are in some way symbolic. The details of *all* Jewish temples have had mystical importance. In Ezekiel's temple, one has to ascend seven steps to enter any one of the three gates leading into the temple courtyard. What is the symbolic meaning, if any, that the seventh step places one in the holy court? Travelling one hundred cubits across this outer courtyard, one comes to the walls of the inner courtyard. Here, eight steps are required to enter the gates and see the actual holy temple itself. Could the steps, like the seventh and eighth days in *the Secrets of Enoch,* be intended to count the days of history (in millennia) that are necessary for humanity to enter the presence of God? Another interesting feature of Ezekiel's prophecy is that it describes Jews and Gentiles as inheriting the land of Israel with the right to enter the temple courts as equals. In Israel's past, only Jews were able to enter the inner courtyard. So, it shows the people of God united as equals.

EARLY CHRISTIAN BELIEF IN THE SEVENTH MILLENNIUM

Many early Church fathers believed that Christ would come and reign at the beginning of the seventh millennium of human history. One of the first on record was the companion and fellow preacher with the Apostle Paul, a man named Barnabas. His belief is quoted below. Two others were bishops: Irenaeus was bishop of Lyons (A.D. 177), and Hippolytus was an antipope bishop near Rome. He challenged Pope Callistus I in his teaching about the readmission to the Church of repentant Christians who had apostatized during time of persecution. Yet another, Lactantius, was tutor to Emperor Constantine's son. Even Jerome (translator of the Vulgate Bible) believed the seventh millennium would be the reign of Christ. These early Christians used various calendars for accounting the years, placing the time a few hundred years beyond themselves.

Whether the Epistle of Barnabas was the inspired word of God or not, many early Church Fathers and later scholars were certain that it was written by the Apostle Paul's companion. Numerous early Church fathers have attested to its authorship, including Origen, Clement, Eusebius, and Jerome. The Epistle of Barnabas says:

... And elsewhere he saith: If thy children shall keep my sabbaths, then will I put my mercy upon them. And even in the beginning of creation he makes mention of the sabbath. And God made in six days the works of his hands; and he finished them on the seventh day, and he rested the seventh day, and sanctified it.

Consider, my children, what that signifies, he finished them in six days. The meaning of it is this: that in six thousand years the Lord God will bring all things to an end. For with him one day is a thousand years; as himself testifieth, saying, Behold this day shall be as a thousand years. Therefore, children, in six days, that is, in six thousand years, shall all things be accomplished.

And what is that he saith, And he rested the seventh day; he meaneth this: that when his Son shall come, and abolish the season of the Wicked One, and judge the ungodly; and shall change the sun and the moon and the stars; then he shall gloriously rest in that seventh day. . . . Behold therefore he will then truly sanctify it with blessed rest, when we (having received the righteous promise, when iniquity [sin] shall be no more, all things being renewed by the Lord) shall be able to sanctify it, being ourselves first made holy.[3]

Another mystical form of the symbolism of "days" can be found in the death and resurrection of Jesus Christ. For two days Jesus lay dead to the earth, but he arose from the dead at the dawn of the third day. Could this foreshadow his being dead to the world for two millennia followed by his return and the resurrection of his saints from the dead at the dawn of the third millennium? It would seem odd that the three days for the most important event in Christian history should be purely arbitrary, lacking any symbolic value. Not only are these three days counted in more than one part of the New Testament, but they are celebrated in the form of Easter as regularly as the Jews celebrated the sabbath month. It would be entirely consistent, on the other hand, for the three days of the new creation in Christ to have the same sacramental value as the seven days of the old creation story:

Come, and let us return to the LORD: for he hath torn, and he will heal us; he hath smitten, and he will bind us up. After two days will he revive us: in the third day will he raise us up, and we shall live in his sight. Then shall we know, if we follow on to know the LORD: his going forth is prepared as the morning; and he shall come to us as the rain, as the latter and former rain to the earth.

(HOSEA 6:1–3)

These verses were quoted earlier as being a hidden prophecy about the death and resurrection of Christ, the firstfruits. In light of all that's been said, might these verses have a second hidden meaning: that Israel was torn apart for rejecting the Messiah but the Jews will return to him after two millennia and God will revive them, and in the morning of the third millennium, he will resurrect them and live with them face-to-face and bless them like the blessing of freshly fallen rain—along with all of his other saints?

Like a fractal, the days of the crucifixion may be a pattern that spreads across all of history since the time of Christ, a divine imprint on the events of humankind.

THE MILLENNIAL CONTROVERSY

There is virtually no disagreement among Christians regarding the belief that Christ will return some day, but the question of whether or not John's millennium was meant to be taken literally has been debated since the third- or fourth-generation of believers. Shortly after A.D. 300, Eusebius wrote about a bishop named Papias, who had listened to "John the Elder" directly (whom Papias refers to as a "disciple of the Lord") and had listened to the pupils of the other Apostles. After quoting Papias favorably on various stories, Eusebius argues against him on his literal understanding of the millennium:

> He says that after the resurrection of the dead there will be a period of a thousand years, when Christ's kingdom will be set up on this earth in material form. I suppose he got these notions by misinterpreting the apostolic accounts and failing to grasp what they had said in mystic and symbolic language. For he seems to have been a man of very small intelligence, to judge from his books. But it is partly due to him that the great majority of churchmen after him took the same view, relying on his early date.[4]

Could it be that *Eusebius* has failed to grasp what is being said in mystic and symbolic language? Elsewhere, he quotes Papias as a reliable source of direct information regarding the author of the Apocalypse, but he dismisses Papias as a man of small intelligence when it comes to understanding the Apocalypse. So long as Papias agrees with Eusebius, he's highly reliable. When he disagrees, he's an idiot.

One more book, believed to have been written by a Jew before the time of Christ, reinforces a literal understanding of John's one thousand years. That book is the Book of Jubilees, found among the Dead Sea Scrolls:

> And the days shall begin to grow many and increase among those children of men [in the end times] till their days grow nigh to one thousand years. . . . And there shall be no old man nor one who is satisfied with days, for all shall be children and youths. And all their days they shall complete and live in peace and joy, and there shall be no Satan nor any evil destroyer; for all their days shall be blessing and healing.[5]

It would make sense that the children born during the utopian age would almost reach one thousand years in age if the period described is a literal millennium. The description above fits a period described in the Old Testament that seems to match John's millennium and the times that follow his millennium. The prophet indicates a time when someone who dies at a hundred years old will be considered a mere child:

> For, behold, I create new heavens and a new earth: and the former shall not be remembered, nor come into mind. But be ye glad and rejoice for ever in that which I create: for, behold, I create Jerusalem a rejoicing, and her people a joy. And I will rejoice in Jerusalem, and joy in my people: and the voice of weeping shall be no more heard in her, nor the voice of crying. There shall be no more there an infant of days, nor an old man that hath not filled his days: for the child shall die an hundred years old; but the sinner being an hundred years old shall be accursed. And they shall build houses, and inhabit them; and they shall plant vineyards, and eat the fruit of them. They shall not build, and another inhabit; they shall not plant, and another eat: for as the days of a tree are the days of my people, and my elect shall long enjoy the work of their hands. They shall not labour in vain, nor bring forth for trouble; for they are the seed of the blessed of the LORD, and their offspring with them. And it shall come to pass, that before they call, I will answer; and while they are yet speaking, I will hear. The wolf and the lamb shall feed together, and the lion shall eat straw like the ox: and dust shall be the serpent's food. They shall not hurt nor destroy in all my holy mountain, saith the LORD.
>
> (ISAIAH 65:17–25)

Until the time of Augustine near the fall of Rome (about A.D. 400), almost all Christians believed Christ would literally reign on earth for a thousand years at the close of history, though they had varying views as to what that time would be like. Many believed this would be a sabbath millennium—a time of rest from human labor. Augustine changed all that, stating that John's millennium was a figurative time period that began from the time of Christ's ministry. The one thousand years in the Apocalypse when the saints would rule with Christ did not mean Christ would physically return as regent. It meant that the spirit of Christ would rule the world through the Church hierarchy for a long but indefinite period until Jesus returned to judge the earth and take his saints to heaven. Satan was seen as being bound by Christ in the sense of being cast out of the believer's heart, but still very much present in the unbeliever's heart.

The majority took to Augustine's views that John was not referring to a literal reign of Christ, but the reign of the Church, yet many of these still thought the rule of the Church would last a literal thousand years, at which point Christ's followers would be taken into God's eternal presence. That created considerable angst and turmoil beginning near the year A.D. 1000 and lasting until about 1033 (which would have been about one thousand years after Christ's death). When the world did not stop going around the sun, the "amillennialists," as they became known (because they didn't believe in a millennium when Christ would reign on earth *in person*), accepted Augustine's figurative interpretation of the time span and continued to believe the one thousand-year reign referred to earthly rule by the Church hierarchy.

Because Augustine lived in an age of monumental political transition, his reshaping of prophetic interpretation reshaped the world, especially five hundred years later (A.D. 1000) when the glacial force of a millennial change came up behind it. Entire nations converted to Christianity—at least nominally. As explained earlier, the belief that Christ would reign *through the Church* gave the Church manifest destiny to become an imperial power.

Interestingly, Augustine, himself, had believed in a literal sabbath millennium *until* he decided it had to be rejected because many of those who believed in a sabbath millennium thought it would be graced with abundant physical pleasures. That couldn't be good. (Augustine tended to be hard on himself that way, and on others, to the point of self-loathing.) Under Augustine's influence Christianity developed a kind of dualistic philosophy, where everything physical was evil, and the only true good was spiritual good.

> [Some people], on the strength of [the millennial passage in the Apocalypse], . . . have been moved, among other things, specially by the number of a thousand years, as if it were a fit thing that the saints should thus enjoy a kind of sabbath-rest during that period, a holy leisure after the labours of the six thousand years since man was created . . . so that thus, as it is written, "One day is with the Lord as a thousand years, and a thousand years as one day," there should follow on the completion of six thousand years . . . a kind of seventh-day sabbath in the succeeding thousand years; and that it is for this purpose the saints rise, viz., to celebrate this sabbath. And this opinion would not be objectionable, if it were believed that the joys of the saints in that sabbath shall be spiritual . . . for I myself, too, once held this opinion. But, as they assert that those who then rise again shall enjoy the leisure of immoderate carnal banquets . . . such assertions can be believed only by the carnal.[6]

Augustine further taught that it was not possible for the Church to be seduced by evil because the devil had already been bound for the figurative thousand years during which the Church was reigning. If the Church could not be seduced by evil, it only followed that the Church could do no evil. The Roman Catholic Church became its own standard. The logic, of course, was entirely circular: How did one know the actions of the Church were infallible? Because it was the *Church* that did them. Originally an advocate of religious liberty, Augustine became one of the first bishops to assert the principle of religious coercion and to put his name behind civil persecution by the Church. Augustine cast a long shadow across the Age of the Church. When Charlemagne formed what became known as the Holy Roman Empire, his most-loved book was Augustine's *City of God,* which led him to pursue Augustine's dream of "one God, one emperor, one pope, one city of God."

THE ETERNAL DREAM

Whether or not John's millennium is meant to be literal—and regardless of whether the structure of his Apocalypse conveys hints of its timing—the hope of an Aquarian age is universal. It has gone by many names: Xanadu, Utopia, Shangri-la, the Millennium. It is a dream that perpetually rises from the human subconscious, which makes it reasonable to think it will someday be realized. Most universal hopes and archetypal symbols have a basis in reality. Every desire God created seems to have its object. Would such a strong dream exist in the collective unconscious of humanity if it were not to find the object of its fulfillment? Perhaps it is a dream planted by God through the visions of his holy men and women and through his Holy Spirit awakening each human subconscious into awareness of God.

If there were never going to be a period of earthly perfection when Christ would literally reign on earth, how could the Apostle Paul say that all creation hopes to be restored when mankind is redeemed? If redemption is purely spiritual, there would be no hope for the physical creation and no need for resurrected bodies. What would be the purpose of physical resurrection if Christ's followers pass directly into heaven? And what would be the purpose of Christ's return? Is he just stopping by to pick up his followers and survey the damages?

There are probably more prophecies in the Bible about a utopian age than there are of any other kind. (Most of them have been put in Appendix A of this book.) The day of doom predicted in apocalyptic prophecies is a mere interlude between the years of humanity's daily turmoil and the years of promised rest for the faithful who will inherit the earth. Does any good story come to its resolution without a crisis? The Great Tribulation is simply the crisis in the dynamic drama that develops between God and humans. It is not the end of the story. It is the turning point that leads to a glorious end.

If there were no such world to come, would the writer of the New Testament Book of Hebrews have spoken of a world to come in the following statement regarding Jesus Christ:

For to the angels he hath not put in subjection the world to come, concerning *which we speak. But one in a certain place testified, saying, What is man, that thou art mindful of him? or the son of man, that thou visitest him? Thou madest him a little lower than the angels; thou didst crown him with glory and honour, and didst set him over the works of thy hands: Thou hast put all things in subjection under his feet. For in that he put all in subjection under him, he left nothing that is not made subject to him. But now we see not yet all things made subject to him. But we see Jesus, who was made a little lower than the angels for the suffering of death, crowned with glory and honour; that he by the grace of God should taste death for every man.*

(HEBREWS 2:5–9)

The writer of Hebrews quotes a Psalm about humans in general but implies it will be ideally fulfilled by Jesus Christ in particular. Not only does he imply a better world when all things will be entirely subjected to Christ. He also states that the present world is *not* subjected to Christ. In other words, his idealized Psalm has not been fulfilled. Later, when he talks about the time of its fulfillment, he calls this time the "seventh day," a time of "rest," comparing it to the time the Jews were kept out of the promised land because of their disbelief:

And to whom did he [God] swear that they should not enter into his rest, but to them [the Jews under Moses] that believed not? So we see that they could not enter in [to the promised land] because of unbelief. . . . For he spoke in a certain place of the seventh day on this wise, And God rested the seventh day from all his works. . . . Seeing therefore it remaineth that some must enter into [his rest], and they to whom it was first preached [the Jews in Moses' day] entered not because of unbelief: . . . There remaineth therefore a rest to the people of God.

(HEBREWS 3:18, 19; 4:4, 6, 9)

The writer speaks of a time when humans will cease to *strive* for perfection because they *rest* in perfection. Their faith will have brought them home to the promised land. The concept of the millennium affirms the destiny and value of God's physical creation. It says that God's care is broader than just restoring the human soul; he intends to restore all of nature to Garden-of-Eden perfection. The cursed earth will be redeemed, and the story will come full circle, yet all will have changed. The story of creation will have gained a depth and complexity that Eden never knew. It's perfect ending will be genuine—organically fashioned over centuries of time out of the clay of earth and dust of turmoil in a setting where God had to play by the rules he created.

The millennium and the resurrection are concepts that stand squarely against the ascetic view of Augustine and others that the physical world is entirely corrupt—that human flesh is a shell to be cast off so the spirit within can be released. All things shall be perfected.

THE ULTIMATE PROMISED LAND

In describing this place of rest, the Old Testament prophets said,

The wolf also shall dwell with the lamb, and the leopard shall lie down with the kid; and the calf and the young lion and the fatling together; and a little child shall lead them. And the cow and the bear shall feed; their young ones shall lie down together: and the lion shall eat straw like the ox. And the nursing child shall play on the hole of the asp, and the weaned child shall put his hand on the den of the adder. They shall not hurt nor destroy in all my holy mountain: for the earth shall be full of the knowledge of the LORD, as the waters cover the sea. And in that day there shall be a root of Jesse, which shall stand for an ensign of the people; to it shall the Gentiles seek: and his rest shall be glorious.

(ISAIAH 11:6–10)

Throughout the Apocalypse, the root of Jesse has been revealed as Jesus Christ. Certainly there has been no Jew in history who so completely fulfills Isaiah's words, "to [him] shall the Gentiles seek." That the Messiah would be someone the Gentiles believe in should come as no surprise to Jews, for the Old Testament clearly prophesied that the true Messiah and the God of Israel would be followed by many Gentile nations, which would all declare Jerusalem their capital and would bring their wealth into it:

But in the last days it shall come to pass, that the mount of the house of the LORD shall be established on the top of the mountains, and it shall be exalted above the hills; and people shall flow to it. And many nations shall come, and say, Come, and let us go up to the mountain of the LORD, and to the house of the God of Jacob; and he will teach us of his ways, and we will walk in his paths: for the law shall go forth from Zion, and the word of the LORD from Jerusalem. And he shall judge among many people, and rebuke strong nations afar off; and they shall beat their swords into plowshares, and their spears into pruninghooks: nation shall not lift up a sword against nation, neither shall they learn war any more. But they shall sit every man under his vine and under his fig tree; and none shall make them afraid: for the mouth of the LORD of hosts hath spoken it. For all people will walk every one in the name of his god, and we will walk in the name of the LORD our God for ever and ever. In that day, saith the LORD, I will assemble her that is lame, and I will gather her that is driven out, and her that I have afflicted; And I will make her that limped a remnant, and her that was cast far off a strong nation: and the LORD shall reign over them in mount Zion from henceforth, even for ever. And thou, O tower of the flock, the strong hold of the daughter of Zion, to thee shall it come, even the first dominion; the kingdom shall come to the daughter of Jerusalem.

(MICAH 4:1–8)

So, as the Gospel of Christ spreads throughout the earth, it prepares the way for the Jewish Messiah to reign over all the earth. Millions throughout the world have already submitted to this Jewish Messiah. All that remains is for Jews to submit to him, also.

I lifted up my eyes again, and looked, and behold a man with a measuring line in his hand. Then said I, Where goest thou? And he said to me, To measure Jerusalem, to see what is its breadth, and what is its length. And, behold, the angel that talked with me went forth, and another angel went out to meet him, And said to him, Run, speak to this young man, saying, Jerusalem shall be inhabited as towns without walls for the multitude of men and cattle in it: For I, saith the LORD, will be to her a wall of fire on every side, and will be the glory in the midst of her.

Sing and rejoice, O daughter of Zion: for, lo, I come, and I will dwell in the midst of thee, saith the LORD. And many nations shall be joined to the LORD in that day, and shall be my people: and I will dwell in the midst of thee, and thou shalt know that the LORD of hosts hath sent me to thee. And the LORD shall inherit Judah his portion in the holy land, and shall choose Jerusalem again. Be silent, O all flesh, before the LORD: for he is raised up out of his holy habitation.

(ZECHARIAH 2:1–5, 10–13)

The man in the above prophecy was measuring the city in order to draw up plans for its walls, but he is told by divine revelation that Jerusalem will be a city without walls. It will be without walls because its people are too many to contain, and it will be without walls because protection of city walls is unnecessary. God will give protection to all the earth.

It will be to the Lord as Messiah that all nations come. The God of Israel becomes their Messiah through his birth in the world as Jesus, the Messiah—the Christ. How else could Zechariah the prophet say, "I come, and I will dwell in the midst of thee, saith the LORD . . . and thou shalt know that the LORD of hosts hath sent me to thee." How can God send God, except in the mysterious incarnation of Jesus Christ?

What other candidate among all of the Jewish people who ever lived is more likely to unite numerous Gentile nations to Israel than Jesus? How else could God come "out of his holy habitation" and truly live among his people, except in the flesh? In the days of Moses, God's Spirit dwelled among his people within an elaborate box called the Ark of the Covenant. This ark symbolized God's covenant with the Jews through the laws of Moses, ten of which were written on stone tablets stored within the ark. It was the Spirit of Law. But the prophet Jeremiah clearly stated that the Ark of the Covenant would be no more. That this most revered object in Jewish history would no longer be remembered shows that the Old Covenant of Law given to Moses, which it contained in the form of the tablets, is to forgotten and shall be no more:

And it shall come to pass, when ye shall be multiplied and increased in the land, in those days, saith the LORD, they shall say no more, The ark of the covenant of the LORD: neither shall it come to mind: neither shall they remember it; neither shall they miss it; neither shall that be done any more. At that time they shall call Jerusalem the throne of the LORD; and all the nations shall be gathered to it, to the name of the LORD, to Jerusalem: neither shall they walk any more after the imagination of their evil heart. In those days the house of Judah shall walk with the house of Israel, and they shall come together from the land of the north to the land that I have given for an inheritance to your fathers. But I said, How shall I put thee among the children, and give thee a pleasant land, a beautiful heritage of the hosts of nations? and I said, Thou shalt call me, My father; and shalt not turn away from me. Surely as a wife treacherously departeth from her husband, so have ye dealt treacherously with me, O house of Israel, saith the LORD. (JEREMIAH 3:16–20)

When Jesus Christ returns, Jerusalem shall be called the throne of the Lord because the Messiah will occupy the throne of Jerusalem. He is the presence of God. Through him, the Spirit of God is made visible to all flesh. Those who have communion with the Messiah under the New Covenant will have not the stone tablets of Law within but the Spirit of God wherever they dwell on earth. And the two peoples—Jew and Gentile—will be made one by virtue of their one God, who is one ruler on the throne of the world's one capital, Jerusalem. The international Holy City will become the international capital city. How else could Isaiah have said the following words in one of the most famous of all prophecies:

For to us a child is born, to us a son is given: and the government shall be upon his shoulder: and his name shall be called Wonderful, Counsellor, The mighty God, The everlasting Father, The Prince of Peace. Of the increase of his government and peace there shall be no end, upon the throne of David, and upon his kingdom, to order it, and to establish it with judgment and with justice from henceforth even for ever. The zeal of the LORD of hosts will perform this. (ISAIAH 9:6, 7)

What other child could rightfully be called "The mighty God" and "The Prince of Peace"? Through this ultimate prince, the words of Daniel at the beginning of this book will finally have their fulfillment. Through him, Nebechadnezzar's dream about the empires of earth comes to its close:

And in the days of these kings [the final empires to be destroyed] shall the God of heaven set up a kingdom, which shall never be destroyed: and the kingdom shall not be left to other people, but it shall break in pieces and consume all these kingdoms, and it shall stand for ever. (DANIEL 2:44)

In this kingdom, the disciples of Jesus, who were all Jews, will reign over the former lands of the twelve tribes. That, in part, is why Jesus chose twelve disciples—because he knew the role that would be cut out for them in the distant future:

Then answered Peter and said to him, Behold, we have forsaken all, and followed thee; what shall we have therefore? And Jesus said to them, Verily I say to you, That ye who have followed me, in the regeneration when the Son of man shall sit on the throne of his glory, ye also shall sit upon twelve thrones, judging the twelve tribes of Israel. And every one that hath forsaken houses, or brethren, or sisters, or father, or mother, or wife, or children, or lands, for my name's sake, shall receive an hundredfold, and shall inherit everlasting life. (MATTHEW 19:27–29)

If earth is never going to be regenerated, why did Jesus speak of the "regeneration"? Later, the same message was also given to the Gentiles through the Apostle Paul:

Do ye not know that the saints shall judge the world? . . . Know ye not that we shall judge angels? how much more things that pertain to this life?

. . . For he [Christ] must reign, till he hath put all enemies under his feet. (1 CORINTHIANS 6:2A, 3; 15:25)

This, too, fulfills the words of the prophet Daniel:

But the saints of the most High shall take the kingdom, and possess the kingdom for ever, even for ever and ever. . . . And the kingdom and dominion, and the greatness of the kingdom under the whole heaven, shall be given to the people of the saints of the most High, whose kingdom is an everlasting kingdom, and all dominions shall serve and obey him. (DANIEL 7:18, 27)

Chapter 23

JUDGMENT:

THE TWILIGHT OF AN AGE

And when the thousand years have ended, Satan shall be loosed from his prison, And shall go out to deceive the nations which are in the four quarters of the earth, Gog and Magog, to gather them together to battle: the number of whom is as the sand of the sea. And they went up on the breadth of the earth, and surrounded the camp of the saints, and the beloved city: and fire came down from God out of heaven, and devoured them. And the devil that deceived them was cast into the lake of fire and brimstone, where the beast and the false prophet are, and shall be tormented day and night for ever and ever.

(REVELATION 20:7–10)

A nd so a thousand years of peace comes to an end. Apparently even utopia cannot last forever. Was it too good to be true? What went wrong? How could people live through a thousand years of peace and prosperity and still be incited to rebellion?

GOG AND MAGOG

The prophecy of Gog and Magog comes from the Old Testament, where a great battle is described against a legendary leader named Gog and his empire, Magog:

And the word of the LORD came to me, saying, Son of man, set thy face against Gog, the land of Magog, the chief prince of Meshech and Tubal, and prophesy against him, And say, Thus saith the Lord GOD; Behold, I am against thee, O Gog, the chief prince of Meshech and Tubal: And I will turn thee back, and put hooks into thy jaws, and I will bring thee forth, and all thy army, horses and horsemen, all of them clothed with all sorts of armour, even a great company with bucklers and shields, all of them handling swords: Persia, Cush, and Libya *with them; all of them with shield and helmet: Gomer, and all his troops; the house of Togarmah of the north quarters, and all his troops: and many people with thee. Be thou prepared, and prepare for thyself, thou, and all thy company that are assembled to thee, and be thou a guard to them.* (EZEKIEL 38:1–7)

The names "Gog" and "Magog" have no known counterpart in history, nor do the descriptions of the battle that follows. Likewise the identity of the lands of Meshech and Tubal is unclear, though many think these names refer to lands north of Israel that were occupied by Israel's ancient enemies. Many have tried to equate this legendary empire with Russia because the Hebrew word that is translated here as "*chief* prince" is "rosh," which is similar to the slavic word "Rus" for "Russia." By the same reasoning, some have found "Meshech" similar to "Moscow." Likewise "Tubal," an unknown land, is similar to "Tobolsk," an insignificant Russian city.

But the name "Rus" did not enter the slavic language until the Vikings introduced it about A.D. 850. It has nothing to do with the Hebrew "rosh," which means "head," as in "head (or chief) prince." Likewise, Tobolsk was not founded until two thousand years after Ezekiel's writing. Any similarity between the Russian words and the Hebrew has nothing to do with the origins of the words. So, the Russian interpretation may be nothing more than cold-war theology. Most likely Ezekiel created fictitious names to keep his prophecy from becoming self-defeating. The names are place holders until their identity becomes obvious through the actual events predicted.

The Apocalypse indicates that Gog is Satan, himself, brought back from his captivity in the bottomless pit. Perhaps this is what Ezekiel had in mind when he wrote, "I will turn thee back, and put hooks into thy jaws, and I will bring thee forth, and all thy army." The next part of Ezekiel's prophecy does seem to indicate its fulfillment would come after a utopian era—after a time when Israel has recovered from war and dwelled long in peace without fortified walls:

After many days thou [Gog] shalt be visited: in the latter years thou shalt come into the land that is brought back from the sword, and is gathered out of many people, against the mountains of Israel, which have been always waste: but it is brought forth out of the nations, and they shall all dwell in safety. Thou shalt ascend and come like a storm, thou shalt be like a cloud to cover the land, thou, and all thy troops, and many people with thee. Thus saith the Lord GOD; It shall also come to pass, that at the same time shall things come into thy mind, and thou shalt think an evil thought: And thou shalt say, I will go up to the land of unwalled villages; I will go to them that are at rest, that dwell safely, all of them dwelling without walls, and having neither bars nor gates, To take a spoil, and to take a prey; to turn thy hand upon the desolate places that are now inhabited, and upon the people that are gathered out of the nations, which have gotten cattle and goods, that dwell in the midst of the land. Sheba, and Dedan, and the merchants of Tarshish, with all its young lions, shall say to thee, Art thou come to take a spoil? hast thou gathered thy company to take a prey? to carry away silver and gold, to take away cattle and goods, to take a great spoil? Therefore, son of man, prophesy and say to Gog, Thus saith the Lord GOD; In that day when my people of Israel dwelleth safely, shalt thou not know it? And thou shalt come from thy place out of the north parts, thou, and many people with thee, all of them riding upon horses, a great company, and a mighty army: And thou shalt come against my people of Israel, as a cloud to cover the land; it shall be in the latter days, and I will bring thee against my land, that the nations may know me, when I shall be sanctified in thee, O Gog, before their eyes. Thus saith the Lord GOD; Art thou he of whom I have spoken of old by my servants the prophets of Israel, who prophesied in those days many years that I would bring thee against them? (EZEKIEL 38:8–17)

"The land that is brought back from the sword" could easily refer to the land that recovered from Armageddon. That this land should be visited by evil "after many days" could imply that Gog will rise after the thousand years of peace. Thus, the prophecy says, "I will go to them that are at rest, that dwell safely." "And thou shalt say, I will go *up* to the land of unwalled villages" could imply that Gog will ascend from the bottomless pit. Gog will rise against an unsuspecting people, many of whom have never known evil because they were born after the millennium began. They are a people who live in resettled ruins—"desolate places that are now inhabited."

Then the language of the prophecy shifts. Suddenly it sounds like a description of the Great Tribulation and Armageddon, which according to the Apocalypse occurred before Gog's uprising. Are these horrible times to repeat themselves, or does the prophet, seeing so far into the future, superimpose the events of the last days? Perhaps Ezekiel saw the events of the Great Tribulation and Armageddon and the final uprising of evil, called Gog and Magog, overlaying certain events of his own time because each of these periods represent days of judgment against the same evil:

And it shall come to pass at the same time when Gog shall come against the land of Israel, saith the Lord GOD, that my fury shall come up in my face. For in my jealousy and in the fire of my wrath have I spoken, Surely in that day there shall be a great shaking in the land of Israel; So that the fishes of the sea, and the fowls of the heaven, and the beasts of the field, and all creeping things that creep upon the earth, and all the men that are upon the face of the earth, shall shake at my presence, and the mountains shall be overturned, and the steep places shall fall, and every wall shall fall to the ground. And I will call for a sword against him [Gog] throughout all my mountains, saith the Lord GOD: every *man's sword shall be against his brother. And I will enter into judgment against him with pestilence and with blood; and I will rain upon him, and upon his troops, and upon the many people that are with him, an overflowing rain, and*

great hailstones, fire, and brimstone. Thus will I magnify myself, and sanctify myself; and I will be known in the eyes of many nations, and they shall know that I am the LORD. (EZEKIEL 38:18–23)

Because this description fits the events of an asteroid or comet impact and sounds like the other descriptions of the Great Tribulation, it was quoted once already in the context of the seven trumpets. Was Ezekiel seeing the events of the seven trumpets (the Great Tribulation) and seven bowls (leading to Armageddon), or is the scene of Gog and Magog the actual end of earth? It would not be surprising if the end of earth repeats many of the patterns seen in the Tribulation. In fact, the event described in the Apocalypse after the scene of Gog and Magog *is* the final passing away of the heavens and the earth.

One concept that favors understanding Ezekiel's prophecy in terms of the Great Tribulation and Armageddon is that God says he "will be known in the eyes of many nations" as a result of the events Ezekiel describes. In the Apocalypse, it is the Great Tribulation and Armageddon that clear the way for the millennium when God is known by all nations:

Therefore, thou son of man, prophesy against Gog, and say, Thus saith the Lord GOD; Behold, I am against thee, O Gog, the chief prince of Meshech and Tubal: And I will turn thee back, and leave but the sixth part of thee, and will cause thee to come from the north parts, and will bring thee upon the mountains of Israel: And I will strike thy bow out of thy left hand, and I will cause thy arrows to fall from thy right hand. Thou shalt fall upon the mountains of Israel, thou, and all thy troops, and the people that are with thee: I will give thee to the ravenous birds of every sort, and to the

beasts of the field to be devoured. Thou shalt fall upon the open field: for I have spoken it, saith the Lord GOD. And I will send a fire on Magog, and among them that dwell securely in the isles: and they shall know that I am the LORD. So will I make my holy name known in the midst of my people Israel; and I will not let them profane my holy name any more: and the nations shall know that I am the LORD, the Holy One in Israel. Behold, it is come, and it is done, saith the Lord GOD; this is the day of which I have spoken. (EZEKIEL 39:1–8)

The description of ravenous birds feasting on the carnage of war certainly sounds like the apocalyptic descriptions of Armageddon, and the scene that follows could very well be the clean-up after Armageddon, which leads into the millennium. Given the ancient weapons described, it could also describe a clean-up after a local battle in Ezekiel's own day. Even so, the prophet's local scene may have become a screen upon which the future was projected:

> *And they that dwell in the cities of Israel shall go forth, and shall set on fire and burn the weapons, both the shields and the bucklers, the bows and the arrows, and the javelins, and the spears, and they shall burn them with fire seven years: So that they shall take no wood out of the field, neither cut down any out of the forests; for they shall burn the weapons with fire: and they shall lay waste those that wasted them, and rob those that robbed them, saith the Lord GOD. And it shall come to pass in that day, that I will give to Gog a place there of graves in Israel, the valley of the travellers on the east of the sea: and it shall stop the noses of the travellers: and there shall they bury Gog and all his multitude: and they shall call it The Valley of Hamongog [means "multitude of Gog"]. And seven months shall the house of Israel be in burying them, that they may cleanse the land. Yea, all the people of the land shall bury them; and it shall be to them a renown in the day that I shall be glorified, saith the Lord GOD. And they shall set apart men for the continual task of passing through the land to bury with the travellers those that remain upon the face of the land, to cleanse it: after the end of seven months shall they search. And as travellers pass through the land, when any seeth a man's bone, then shall he set up a sign by it, till the buriers have buried it in the valley of Hamongog. And also the name of the city shall be Hamonah ["multitude"]. Thus shall they cleanse the land. And, thou son of man, thus saith the Lord GOD; Speak to every feathered fowl, and to every beast of the field, Assemble yourselves, and come; gather yourselves on every side to my sacrifice that I do sacrifice for you, even a great sacrifice upon the mountains of Israel, that ye may eat flesh, and drink blood. Ye shall eat the flesh of the mighty, and drink the blood of the princes of the earth, of rams, of lambs, and of goats, of bulls, all of them fatlings of Bashan. And ye shall eat fat till ye are full, and drink blood till ye are drunk, of my sacrifice which I have sacrificed for you. Thus ye shall be filled at my table with horses and chariots, with mighty men, and with all men of war, saith the Lord GOD. And I will set my glory among the nations, and all the nations shall see my judgment that I have executed, and my hand that I have laid upon them.*
>
> (EZEKIEL 39:9–21)

Quite likely the aftermath of a war in Ezekiel's own time described a pattern that will recur after Armageddon and perhaps a third time after the final battle with Gog and Magog. The scene certainly sounds like the description of the "supper of God" following Armageddon. It's hard to imagine why any clean-up would be necessary following the scene in the Apocalypse where Gog and Magog are consumed by fire from God. There is no battle in the Apocalypse. There is an uprising put down by God, and the next event is the passing away of the physical universe. So, why clean up afterward?

Another indicator that Armageddon and the millennium are in view in Ezekiel's prophecy comes from what the Hebrew prophet said about Israel prior to Gog's attack:

So the house of Israel shall know that I am the LORD their God from that day and forward. And the nations shall know that the house of Israel went into captivity for their iniquity: because they trespassed against me, therefore I hid my face from them, and gave them into the hand of their enemies: so they all fell by the sword. According to their uncleanness and according to their transgressions have I done to them, and hidden my face from them.

(EZEKIEL 39:22–24)

None of the events of these two chapters from Ezekiel have any clear match with events following the Jewish exile in Babylonia, so the exile in view must be the present diaspora, for the prediction is yet to be fulfilled. In that case, the Hebrew prophet clearly says the diaspora resulted as a judgment by God against Israel.

O Israel, return to the LORD thy God; for thou hast fallen by thy iniquity. . . . I will heal their backsliding, I will love them freely: for my anger is turned away from him. I will be as the dew to Israel: he shall grow as the lily, and cast forth his roots as Lebanon. His branches shall spread, and his beauty shall be as the olive tree, and his fragrance like Lebanon. They that dwell under his shadow shall return; they shall revive as the grain, and grow as the vine: the scent of it shall be as the wine of Lebanon. Ephraim [part of Israel] shall say, What have I to do any more with idols? I have heard him, and observed him: I am like a green fir tree. From me is thy fruit found. Who is wise, and he shall understand these things? prudent, and he shall know them? for the ways of the LORD are right, and the just shall walk in them: but the transgressors shall fall in them.

(HOSEA 14:1, 4–9)

This prophecy probably had the return from Babylon in view, but God's patience is long, and he is as willing to forgive, heal, and restore now as much as he ever was, and so the prophecy may be fulfilled again in the millennium to come. Yet, judgment remains for all—Jew or Gentile—who will not submit to the Messiah, for he is the union of God and humanity.

However one unthreads the predictions of Ezekiel, John clearly alludes to the prophecy of Gog and Magog in the Apocalypse as relating, at least in part, to a final uprising that will come after the millennium. But why would a people of peace be raised again to follow evil? Does this mean free choice will always reign, and, given the opportunity, there will always be some who, like Adam and Eve, will repeat the story of human sin? Do humans, in the end, learn nothing from their history? Does eternal judgment become the only answer?

There is an alternative reading: The wording of the Apocalypse could indicate the people of Magog, who follow their leader Gog, are armies that rise out of hell: "And they went *up on* the breadth of the earth, and surrounded the camp of the saints." Since the next scene in the Apocalypse is another resurrection, this army could be the great multitude who are raised to be judged at the end of time. They are given one last chance to repent, which implies one last chance to rebel. They choose rebellion. They rise from the grave with nothing but their anger and self-centered ambition intact. Come hellfire or the high waters of Noah's flood, they will never submit to the Messiah. They make war and are judged as in the following verses. Their eternal judgment is just because they have already known hell and yet choose hell over righteousness.

JUDGMENT DAY AND THE END OF TIME

And I saw a great white throne, and him that sat on it, from whose face the earth and the heaven fled away; and there was found no place for them. And I saw the dead, small and great, stand before God; and the books were opened: and another book was opened, which is the book of life: and the dead were judged out of the things which were written in the books, according to their works. And the sea gave up the dead which were in it; and death and hell delivered up the dead which were in them: and they were judged every man according to their works. And death and hell were cast into the lake of fire. This is the second death. And whoever was not found written in the book of life was cast into the lake of fire. (REVELATION 20:11–15)

"From [God's] face the earth and heaven fled away." What a beautiful description of the end of time, the final passing of the physical universe. And so the Apocalypse reaches to the most remote events that humans can fathom—the end of the universe. How far away this time is cannot be guessed or known. Even if the millennium is a literal thousand years, the Apocalypse may skip thousands or even millions of years between the destruction of Gog and Magog and the brief mention of earth's passing. In the prophetic foreshortening of time, a million years may lie between the space of two paragraphs.

Most scientists place the end of the universe, billions of years into the future. Even the sun is believed to hold millions of years of fire in its belly. Though we are not accustomed to thinking in such distant terms, the end of our solar system, or even the end of this present universe, is an eventual reality for all of humankind. It's not unreasonable, on the other hand, to think that the predictions of science, in its astronomic youth, are based on incomplete information. Science may not comprehend all the cataclysms that can end a solar system or a universe before the prime of its life. The end may be surprisingly soon:

> See that ye refuse not him that speaketh. For if they escaped not who refused him that spoke on earth, much more shall not we escape, if we turn away from him that speaketh from heaven: Whose voice then shook the earth: but now he hath promised, saying, Yet once more I shake not the earth only, but also heaven. And this word, Yet once more, signifieth the removing of those things that are shaken, as of things that are made, that those things which cannot be shaken may remain. Therefore we receiving a kingdom which cannot be moved, let us have grace, by which we may serve God acceptably with reverence and godly fear: For our God is a consuming fire.
>
> (HEBREWS 12:25–29)

> Seeing then that all these [material] things shall be dissolved, what manner of persons ought ye to be in all holy conduct and godliness, Looking for and hasting to the coming of the day of God, when the heavens being on fire shall be dissolved, and the elements shall melt with fervent heat? Nevertheless we, according to his promise, look for new heavens and a new earth, in which dwelleth righteousness.
>
> (2 PETER 3:11–13)

Whenever time ticks its last tock, the material world shall pass away, leaving only the spiritual, which cannot be removed. Then the immortal spirits of mankind must be judged to determine what role they will have in the eternity that remains forever unshaken. While some may despise the thought of eternal punishment, Jesus repeated it frequently as a necessity and a reality to be considered now:

> When the Son of man shall come in his glory, and all the holy angels with him, then shall he sit upon the throne of his glory: And before him shall be gathered all nations: and he shall separate them one from another, as a shepherd divideth his sheep from the goats: And he shall set the sheep on his right hand, but the goats on the left. Then shall the King say to them on his right hand, Come, ye blessed of my Father, inherit the kingdom prepared for you from the foundation of the world: For I was hungry, and ye gave me food: I was thirsty, and ye gave me drink: I was a stranger, and ye took me in: Naked, and ye clothed me: I was sick, and ye visited me: I was in prison, and ye came to me. Then shall the righteous answer him, saying, Lord, when saw we thee hungry, and fed thee? or thirsty, and gave thee drink? When saw we thee a stranger, and took thee in? or naked, and clothed thee? Or when saw we thee sick, or in prison, and came to thee? And the King shall answer and say to them, Verily I say to you, Inasmuch as ye have done it to one of the least of these my brethren, ye have done it to me. Then shall he say also to them on the left hand, Depart from me, ye cursed, into everlasting fire, prepared for the devil and his angels: For I was hungry, and ye gave me

no food: I was thirsty, and ye gave me no drink: I was a stranger, and ye took me not in: naked, and ye clothed me not: sick, and in prison, and ye visited me not. Then shall they also answer him, saying, Lord, when saw we thee hungry, or thirsty, or a stranger, or naked, or sick, or in prison, and did not minister to thee? Then shall he answer them, saying, Verily I say to you, Inasmuch as ye did it not to one of the least of these, ye did it not to me. And these shall go away into everlasting punishment: but the righteous into life eternal.

(MATTHEW 25:31–46)

According to this scene, the judgment happens after Christ arrives with his heavenly host at Armageddon with no intervening millennium. It may be Christ's predictions also shortened the time between events in order to connect his coming with the judgment that eventually follows because Armageddon, itself, represents judgment of evil in the presence of Christ. Armageddon, however, appears to be only physical, as the evil people who remain alive turn on each other and destroy each other. The completion of this judgment follows at the end of time when those long dead are also judged.

What is important is not the timing, but the basis of judgment. Those whom Jesus condemns in his prophecy are condemned because of how they treated Christ's followers—"these my brethren"—which would include his followers of every generation. Here, the martyrs of the Apocalypse, who cried for justice from beneath the altar of God, have their prayers answered. The issue, however, is not vengeance. Jesus is saying that anyone who did not give his followers a good reception will not be allowed into his kingdom because, in rejecting the messengers, they were really rejecting the message. In rejecting his disciples, they were really rejecting him. The same reasoning would apply in future generations. Ultimately, the great divide of eternity falls at the acceptance or rejection of Christ:

Verily I say to you, All sins shall be forgiven to the sons of men, and whatever blasphemies they shall blaspheme: But he that shall blaspheme against the Holy Spirit never hath forgiveness, but is in danger of eternal damnation:

(MARK 3:28, 29)

That Spirit is the Spirit of Christ, as pointed out earlier in this book. According to the New Testament, it was for rejecting the divinity of Christ that all Israel was burned by Rome and the diaspora began. (To follow this line of thought one of the books of the New Testament, see Matthew 9:1–8; 10:14–23, 40; 11:20–27; 12:6–8, 22–32, 42–45; 13:14, 15, 54–58; 15:1, 2, 7–9, 12, 13; 16:1–4, 20–21; 17:22–23; 20:17–19; 21:23–27, 42–45; 22:41–46; 23:1–7, 13–15, 23–39; 24:1–3, 15–20 [probably alluding to the destruction of Jerusalem and the beginning of the disaspora]; 26:1–5, 47–67; 27:1, 2, 11–18, 20–25,

35–43.) That was a physical and temporal judgment, but there will also be *eternal* judgment for rejecting the Spirit of God in Christ Jesus:

> But I will forewarn you whom ye shall fear: Fear him, who after he hath killed hath power to cast into hell; yea, I say to you, Fear him. . . . Also I say to you, Whoever shall confess me before men, him shall the Son of man also confess before the angels of God: But he that denieth me before men shall be denied before the angels of God. And whoever shall speak a word against the Son of man, it shall be forgiven him: but to him that blasphemeth against the Holy Spirit it shall not be forgiven.   (LUKE 12:5, 8–10)

The one who has "power to cast into hell" is Jesus Christ. He makes that clear in the sentences that follow. So, when it is time for all souls to pass from temporal existence into eternity, salvation goes not to those who are perfect, but to those who submit to Christ in faith. Without such submission, paradise would retain the endless rebellion of earth, and paradise could not be paradise.

These who shall stand on his right—the hand of blessing and authority through which inheritance is passed down—are those who have received his messengers and their message with grace:

> For whoever shall give you [the disciples] a cup of water to drink in my name, because ye belong to Christ, verily I say to you, he shall not lose his reward.
>
> (MARK 9:41)

The books in the judgment scene (Revelation 20:11–15) that are used to judge the works of every human reveal no one was perfect, and none are able to enter into God's perfection of their own merit. All would be judged and condemned, except that the names of some are found in a book of exceptions—the book of those who have chosen submission to Christ, even though their lives lacked perfection—called The Book of Life. These are the saints who have been given a new name—sealed with the name Christ. That name, in fact, may be the only name written in the Book of Life. But if they have made it their own name, then life eternal is also theirs.

Exactly what the Lake of Fire represents can only be guessed at, but most likely it is symbolic of some spiritual but very horrible reality, just as the crowns and thrones and lampstands and stars in the hand of Christ were all symbolic of spiritual realities.

Hell: A Place of its Own Making

In the Greek Orthodox view, hell is a chosen reality:

> Judgement, as St. John's Gospel emphasizes, is going on all the time throughout our earthly existence. Whenever, consciously or unconsciously, we choose the good, we enter already by anticipation into eternal life; whenever we choose evil, we receive a foretaste of hell. The Last Judgement is best understood as the *moment of truth* when everything is brought to light . . . when we realize with clarity who we are and what has been the deep meaning of our life . . .
>
> Christ is the judge; and yet, from another point of view, it is we who pronounce judgement upon ourselves. If anyone is in hell, it is not because God has imprisoned him there, but because that is where he himself has chosen to be. The lost in hell are self-condemned, self-enslaved; it has been rightly said that the doors of hell are locked *on the inside.*[1]

For that reason, the Apocalypse emphasized, after each bowl of judgment was poured upon the earth, that those who remained refused to repent. They remain forever angry at God for asking them to submit, for denying their self-actualization, and ultimately for their final demise. Perhaps they feel tricked or cheated because they continue to believe their delusions and self-aggrandizement were real hopes. Evil at its heart is nothing more than self-centeredness, and those who remain self-centered shall wither forever into their own small soul like a dry leaf curling in on itself. Hell is not large. Because it is inward, it is infinitely small and lonely.

> *And seekest thou great things for thyself? seek them not: for, behold, I will bring vil upon all flesh, saith the LORD: but thy life will I give to thee for a prize in all places where thou goest.*
>
> (Jeremiah 45:5)

Heaven, on the other hand, is outward and infinitely large. It is a green leaf, forever opening and growing. It is eternal life for those who go in the path of the Lord. But the evil shall fall forever into the bottomless pit of their own making:

> *Thou hast rebuked the nations, thou hast destroyed the wicked, thou hast put out their name for ever and ever. O thou enemy, destructions are come to a perpetual end: and thou hast destroyed cities; their memorial hath perished with them. But the LORD shall endure for ever: he hath prepared his throne for judgment. And he shall judge the world in righteousness, he shall minister judgment to the people in uprightness.*
>
> *The nations are sunk down in the pi that they made: in the net which they hid is their own foot taken. The LORD is*

known by the judgment which he exe-
cuteth: the wicked is snared in the work
of his own hands. Higgaion [a musical
term]. Selah. The wicked shall be turned
into hell, and all the nations that forget
God. For the needy shall not always be
forgotten: the expectation of the poor

shall not perish for ever. Arise, O LORD;
let not man prevail: let the nations be
judged in thy sight. Put them in fear, O
LORD: that the nations may know
themselves to be but men. Selah.

(PSALM 9:5–8, 15–20)

"The wicked shall be turned into hell." It is almost as though hell is not a *place* to which they go, but a *state* in which they become ensnared. They have proven by their final uprising that eternity will never be paradise so long as the wicked are allowed to share in it. Their removal is essential to the concept of paradise, itself.

But why does a repository for the eternal souls of the wicked require eternal punishment? Is eternal exile not enough? But, then, who says the punishment is of God's making? Even when God shouldered the blame for evil on earth, saying he would bring his agent of judgment, that human agent always appeared to be acting of his own free will. If hell has real fire, it is not too hard to figure out who actually ignited it, given evil's historic penchant for flames. Since the dragon loved playing with fire so much, he will spend eternity in his own conflagration, enjoying poetic justice: The dragon burns in his own sea of fire—the surrounding company of all his Neros, Attilas, and Hitlers—in the junkyard of derelict souls.

In fact, the image of hell as a burning waste pit for derelict souls came from an actual garbage dump in Jerusalem. The word often translated "hell" in the New Testament (including several of the quotes used in this chapter) is "Gehenna." Gehenna does not mean "hell." Gehenna was a real dump on the edge of a real valley at the south end of real Jerusalem. At Gehenna, human waste and dead animals were cast out of the city and burned. Because this constantly smoldering, stinking pit was familiar to all in Jerusalem, it became a fitting symbol for Jesus to use in conveying the concept of eternal death for the wicked:

And if thy hand causeth thee to stumble,
cut it off: it is better for thee to enter life
maimed, than having two hands to go
into hell [Gehenna], into the fire that
never shall be quenched: Where their
worm dieth not, and the fire is not
quenched. And if thy foot causeth thee to
stumble, cut it off: it is better for thee to
enter lame into life, than having two feet
to be cast into hell, into the fire that
never shall be quenched: Where their

worm dieth not, and the fire is not
quenched. And if thy eye causeth thee to
stumble, pluck it out: it is better for thee
to enter into the kingdom of God with
one eye, than having two eyes to be cast
into hell fire: Where their worm dieth
not, and the fire is not quenched. For
every one shall be salted with fire, and
every sacrifice shall be salted with salt.

(MARK 9:43–49)

If the above words show nothing else, they certainly show that Jesus took the doctrine of hell with utmost seriousness. Obviously the "Gehenna" of future judgment is not the literal Gehenna on the south side of old Jerusalem. So, many of the Bible's references to hell are symbolic images taken from everyday life. Symbolically, evil and judgment are often portrayed as fire because fire consumes itself. Evil becomes its own judgment and its own destruction. Sometimes hell is called a "fiery furnace," but not all the images of hell involve fire. Hell is also called the "blackness of darkness forever" and a "mist of darkness" and "chains of darkness," which hold the fallen angels. These are the demons that haunt hell.

These fallen angels stoke the figurative fires of hell. When the Pharisees accused Jesus of casting out demons by the power of Satan, his response indicated the torments of hell are created by the fallen angels who naturally dwell there:

> And if I by Beelzebub cast out demons,
> by whom do your children cast them out?
> therefore they shall be your judges.
> (MATTHEW 12:27)

Some scholars have said that hell is the only part of eternity where God's Spirit does not dwell. Therefore, there are no limits placed on the evil that does dwells there— angelic or human. If souls like Hitler and Nero created such hell on earth, what will they do when relegated to each other's company in eternity with no limitations by God? But what about those whose sins do not reach the depths of a Hitler or a Nero? Is their destiny the same?

> But these [the ungodly who have crept into the local churches with false teachings] speak evil of those things which they know not: but what they know naturally, as brute beasts, in those things they corrupt themselves. . . . These are spots in your feasts of charity, when they feast with you, feeding themselves without fear: clouds they are without water, carried about by winds; late autumn trees, without fruit, twice dead, plucked out by the roots; Raging waves of the sea, foaming out their own shame; wandering stars, to whom is reserved the blackness of darkness for ever.
> (JUDE 10, 12, 13)

The big and the small who choose their own small hell over submission to Christ, both choose eternal death. Yet, Jesus' statements about the punishments of hell also include a sense of proportionality in the punishments of those who enter hell. In a parable about a servant who became lazy because his master was a long time in returning home, Jesus said:

The lord of that servant will come in a day when he looketh not for him, and at an hour when he is not aware, and will cut him in two, and will appoint him his portion with the unbelievers. And that servant, who knew his lord's will, and prepared not himself, neither did according to his will, shall be beaten with many stripes. But he that knew not, and committed things worthy of stripes, shall be beaten with few stripes. For to whomever much is given, of him shall much be required: and to whom men have committed much, from him they will ask the more. I am come to send fire on the earth; and what will I, if it is already kindled? (LUKE 12:46–49)

It would seem from Jesus' words that people will be held accountable only for what they know. The darkness and smallness of one's own soul may define the walls of one's own hell. Those who have been given much opportunity for spiritual understanding will face high expectations on Judgment Day. From those who have been given very little opportunity to understand, less will be expected and their eternity—if they continue in rebellion against God's Messiah—will be less severe. Deliberate ignorance, however, provides no cover.

In this respect, Jesus told the Pharisees, who had much opportunity to gain spiritual understanding, to make themselves right with him before they died, before the end should come, for it would go better with their souls if they did:

When thou goest with thy adversary to the magistrate, as thou art in the way [i.e., "in route"], give diligence that thou mayest be delivered from him; lest he drag thee before the judge, and the judge deliver thee to the officer, and the officer cast thee into prison. I tell thee, thou shalt not depart from there, till thou hast paid the very last mite. (LUKE 12:58, 59)

Jesus also made it clear to the Jewish leaders that their Jewishness would not get them into the kingdom of heaven. He said that on the day of judgment he would see some of the very people with whom he had walked the streets of Jerusalem and would choose not to recognize them because they had not recognized who he was:

Then said one to him, Lord, are there few that are saved? And he said to them, Strive to enter in at the narrow gate: for many, I say to you, will seek to enter in, and shall not be able. When once the master of the house hath risen up, and hath shut the door, and ye begin to stand without, and to knock at the door, saying, Lord, Lord, open to us; and he shall answer and say to you, I know you not where ye are from: Then ye shall begin to say, We ate and drank in thy presence, and thou hast taught in our streets. But he shall say, I tell you, I know you not where ye are from; depart from me, all ye workers of iniquity. There shall be weep-

ing and gnashing of teeth, when ye shall see Abraham, and Isaac, and Jacob, and all the prophets, in the kingdom of God, and you yourselves thrust out. And they shall come from the east, and from the west, and from the north, and from the south, and shall sit down in the kingdom of God. And, behold, there are last who shall be first, and there are first who shall be last. (LUKE 13:23–30)

Though Jesus was a Jew, he made it clear that on the day of Judgment one is not counted among God's people by virtue of race, but by virtue of faith in him. The Jewish patriarchs and the prophets will be in his kingdom, as will many Gentiles from every direction; but, because the Jewish Messiah will be judge of the whole earth, he must use a standard in which everyone can participate, and one cannot choose to be Jewish.

Jesus told the story another way in a parable:

There was a certain rich man, who was clothed in purple and fine linen, and fared sumptuously every day: And there was a certain beggar named Lazarus, who was laid at his gate, full of sores, And desiring to be fed with the crumbs which fell from the rich man's table: moreover the dogs came and licked his sores. And it came to pass, that the beggar died, and was carried by the angels into Abraham's bosom [the resting place of the faithful dead]: the rich man also died, and was buried; And in hell he lifted up his eyes, being in torments, and seeth Abraham afar off, and Lazarus in his bosom. And he cried and said, Father Abraham, have mercy on me, and send Lazarus, that he may dip the tip of his finger in water, and cool my tongue; for I am tormented in this flame. But Abraham said, Son, remember that thou in .hy lifetime didst receive thy good things, and likewise Lazarus evil things: but now he is comforted, and thou art tormented. And besides all this, between us and you there is a great gulf fixed: so that they who would pass from here to you cannot; neither can they pass to us, that would come from there. Then he [the rich man] said, I pray thee therefore, father, that thou wouldest send him [Lazarus] to my father's house: For I have five brethren; that he may testify to them, lest they also come into this place of torment. Abraham saith to him, They have Moses and the prophets; let them hear them. And he said, Nay, father Abraham: but if one went to them from the dead, they will repent. And he said to him, If they hear not Moses and the prophets, neither will they be persuaded, though one rose from the dead. (LUKE 16:19–31)

Lazarus, the beggar, may have been a Gentile. At the very least, he had no social standing, but the rich man clearly called Abraham his father, and Abraham called him "son." Still accustomed to being waited on, the rich man asked Abraham to send Lazarus as a servant. The story implies that neither racial belonging nor social status have any relevance for inclusion in the kingdom of heaven and that the time to choose is now, not later. The last statement, "If they hear not Moses and the prophets, neither will they be persuaded, though one rose from the dead," was, of course, an allusion to Jesus' own resurrection, which was not believed by many Jews in his own day.

Throughout the New Testament, the message is that Jesus is humanity's only gate to eternity, and he does not wish to see any condemned:

Then Peter opened his mouth, and said, In truth I perceive that God is no respecter of persons [i.e., race or status]: But in every nation he that feareth him, and worketh righteousness, is accepted with him.... And he [Jesus] commanded us to preach to the people, and to testify that it is he who was ordained by God to be the Judge of the living and the dead. To him give all the prophets witness, that through his name whoever believeth in him shall receive remission of sins.

(ACTS 10:34, 35, 42, 43)

For God so loved the world, that he gave his only begotten Son, that whoever believeth in him should not perish, but have everlasting life. For God sent not his Son into the world to condemn the world; but that the world through him may be saved. He that believeth on him is not condemned: but he that believeth not is condemned already, because he hath not believed in the name of the only begotten Son of God.... The Father loveth the Son, and hath given all things into his hand. He that believeth on the Son hath everlasting life: and he that believeth not the Son shall not see life; but the wrath of God abideth on him.

(JOHN 3:16–18, 35, 36)

For [God] the Father judgeth no man, but hath committed all judgment to the Son: That all men should honour the Son, even as they honour the Father. He that honoureth not the Son honoureth not the Father who hath sent him. . . . For as the Father hath life in himself; so hath he given to the Son to have life in himself; And hath given him authority to execute judgment also, because he is the Son of man.

(JOHN 5:22, 23, 26, 27)

[Jesus said] And if any man hear my words, and believe not, I judge him not: for I came not to judge the world, but to save the world. He that rejecteth me, and receiveth not my words, hath one that judgeth him: the word that I have spoken, the same shall judge him in the last day.   (JOHN 12:47, 48)

And so, as was said earlier by a priest of the Greek Orthodox Church, "Last Judgement is best understood as the *moment of truth* when everything is brought to light . . . when we realize with clarity who we are and what has been the deep meaning of our life . . . Christ is the judge; and yet, from another point of view, it is we who pronounce judgement upon ourselves."

That the Jewish Messiah should become the judge of the whole earth should have come as no surprise to the Pharisees, for Daniel prophesied a judgment scene five hundred years before Christ that is nearly identical to the judgment scene in the Apocalypse. The dead are judged, and the beast and false prophet thrown into the lake of fire. In Daniel's scene, the son of a man judges the earth and is given glory from God and eternal dominion over all people:

I beheld till the thrones were cast down, and the Ancient of days did sit, whose garment was white as snow, and the hair of his head like the pure wool: his throne was like the fiery flame, and his wheels [of his throne] as burning fire. A fiery stream issued and came forth from before him: thousand thousands ministered to him, and ten thousand times ten thousand stood before him: the judgment was set, and the books were opened. I beheld then because of the voice of the great words which the horn [the beast or Antichrist] spoke: I beheld even till the beast was slain, and his body destroyed, and given to the burning flame. As concerning the rest of the beasts, they had their dominion taken away: yet their lives were prolonged for a season and time. I saw in the night visions, and, behold, one like the Son of man came with the clouds of heaven, and came to the Ancient of days, and they brought him near before him. And there was given him dominion, and glory, and a kingdom, that all people, nations, and languages, should serve him: his dominion is an everlasting dominion, which shall not pass away, and his kingdom that which shall not be destroyed. (DANIEL 7:9–14)

Chapter 24

PARADISE:

WHEN TIME SHALL BE NO MORE

And I saw a new heaven and a new earth: for the first heaven and the first *earth had passed away; and there was no more sea.* (REVELATION 21:1)

Science indicates this present universe may be neither the first nor the last. There may have been many end times for the cosmos as it has expanded and collapsed and expanded again. Some scientists speculate that multiple universes may coexist in different dimensions under different sets of physical laws—a single universe being defined by its own laws. The physical laws of *this* universe indicate that the elements from which all life is fabricated were forged in the furnaces of stars, which exploded long ago and cast their spore throughout the galaxy. This star dust rains down upon the earth endlessly, so we are made of such stuff as stars are made of.

When this world has produced all the life it was destined for, will the human story end? When this present universe finally implodes, will all of humanity be dragged into the oblivion of the black hole?

The prophets foresaw the physical end of the universe yet boldly answer "no." There is a part of each man and woman that is not made of star dust and is not bound by physical laws—a spirit that seeks reunion with its source.

Of old hast thou laid the foundation of the earth: and the heavens are the work of thy hands. They shall perish, but thou [God] shalt endure: yea, all of them shall grow old like a garment; as a vesture shalt thou change them, and they shall *be changed: But thou art the same, and thy years shall have no end. The children of thy servants shall continue, and their seed shall be established before thee.* (PSALM 102:25–28)

Lift up your eyes to the heavens, and look upon the earth beneath: for the heavens *shall vanish away like smoke, and the earth shall become old like a garment,*

and its inhabitants shall die in like man-
ner: but my salvation shall be for ever,

and my righteousness shall not be abol-
ished. (ISAIAH 51:6)

Nevertheless we, according to his
[Christ's] promise, look for new heavens

and a new earth, in which dwelleth
righteousness. (2 PETER 3:13)

It is a testimony to the inspiration of the prophets that they could see an end to something so seemingly eternal as the universe, an end that science only began to grasp in this past century. Jesus also recognized the inevitable end of the substantial universe yet proclaimed that something as seemingly insubstantial as a breath would endure forever:

Heaven and earth shall pass away, but
my words shall not pass away.
(MATTHEW 24:35)

THE EIGHTH DAY: BEYOND THE SABBATH MILLENNIUM

And I John saw the holy city, new Jeru-
salem, coming down from God out of
heaven, prepared as a bride adorned for
her husband. And I heard a great voice
out of heaven saying, Behold, the taber-
nacle of God is with men, and he will
dwell with them, and they shall be his
people, and God himself shall be with
them, and be their God. And God shall

wipe away all tears from their eyes; and
there shall be no more death, neither sor-
row, nor crying, neither shall there be
any more pain: for the former things
have passed away. And he that sat upon
the throne said, Behold, I make all things
new. And he said to me, Write: for these
words are true and faithful.
(REVELATION 21:2–5)

If the millennium is represented by the seventh or Sabbath day, is there a counterpart in Old Testament symbolism for a time *beyond* the millennium? The Old Testament also spoke of an eighth day that was holy like the seventh, but in a completely different way. The celebration of this day occurred in the latter part of the seventh month at the end of the seventh Jewish holy festival: (By modern Jews, it is celebrated as *Smini Atzeret*, a day of praying for rain from God for Jerusalem.)

For seven days present offerings made
to the LORD by fire, and on the eighth
day hold a sacred assembly and present
an offering made to the LORD by fire.

It is the closing assembly; do no regular
work. . . . the eighth day also is a day of
rest.

(LEVITICUS 23:36, 39)

The eighth day in Leviticus may foreshadow the eighth day mentioned earlier in this book by *the Secrets of Enoch,* which predicted a seventh millennium of rest like the millennium described by John in the Apocalypse. Enoch goes on to predict an eighth, eternal day, just as John has moved on to describe the passing of humans from the millennium into the timeless presence of God:

And I appointed the eighth day also, that the eighth day should be the first-created *after* my work . . . and that at the beginning of the eighth thousand there should be a time of not-counting, endless with neither years, nor months nor weeks nor days nor hours.[1]

So, there are two days of rest—the millennium and an eternal day to follow. In *the Book of Enoch,* earth's seven-thousand-year history ends as follows:

There shall be an everlasting judgment, which shall be executed upon the Watchers [certain angels]; and a spacious eternal heaven shall spring forth in the midst of the angels. The former heaven shall depart and pass away; a new heaven shall appear; and all the celestial powers shine with sevenfold splendour for ever . . . which shall eternally exist in goodness and in righteousness. Neither shall sin be named there for ever and for ever.[2]

Even Barnabas in his epistle finishes his description of the sabbath millennium by mentioning an eighth day:

Lastly, he saith unto them: Your new moons and your sabbaths I cannot bear them. Consider what he means by it: the sabbaths, says he, which ye now keep are not acceptable unto me; . . . when resting from all things [in the seventh millennium] I shall begin the eighth day, that is, the beginning of the other world. For which cause we observe the eighth day with gladness, in which Jesus rose from the dead; and having manifested himself to his disciples ascended unto heaven.[3]

People are mistaken in thinking early Christians observed Sunday as the *first* day of the week. Because it follows the sabbath (the seventh day), they observed it sacramentally as the *eighth* day—the first day of the *new* week. And they called it the "Lord's Day" instead of the sabbath, because it summed up the apocalyptic "Day of the Lord" spoken of in ancient prophesies. Many early Christians, like Barnabas, believed the eighth day was holy because Christ's resurrection happened on Sunday during the eight-day celebration of Passover. They believed his resurrection foreshadowed the new creation, which many believed would follow the seventh millennium.

The apocryphal Book of 2 Esdras may also have something to say about the end of the physical universe following the seventh millennium:

> For behold, the time will come, when the signs which I have foretold to you will come to pass, that the city [the New Jerusalem] which now is not seen shall appear, and the land which now is hidden shall be disclosed. And everyone who has been delivered from the evils that I have foretold shall see my wonders. For my son the Messiah shall be revealed with those who are with him, and those who remain shall rejoice four hundred years. And after these years my son the Messiah shall die, and all who draw human breath. And the world shall be turned back to primeval silence for seven days, as it was at the first beginnings; so that no one shall be left. And after seven days the world, which is not yet awake, shall be roused, and that which is corruptible shall perish. And the earth shall give up those who are asleep in it, and the dust those who dwell silently in it; and the chambers shall give up the souls which have been committed to them. And the most high shall be revealed upon the seat of judgment, and compassion shall pass away, and patience shall be withdrawn, but only judgment shall remain, truth shall stand, and faithfulness shall grow strong. And recompense shall follow, and the reward shall be manifested. . . . Then the pit of torment shall appear, and opposite it shall be the place of rest; and the furnace of hell shall be disclosed, and opposite it the paradise of delight. Then the Most High will say to the nations that have been raised from the dead, "Look now, and understand whom you have denied, whom you have not served, whose commandments you have despised! Look on this side and that; here are delight and rest, and there are fire and torments! Thus he will speak to them on the day of judgment—a day that has no sun or moon or stars, or cloud or thunder or lightning or wind or water or air, or darkness or evening or morning . . . but only the splendor of the glory of the Most High.[4]

Although this vision places the death of the Messiah after he reigns on earth for four hundred years, in all it's quite an amazing summary of the final events described by later prophets. It's amazing because most textual critics believe the author of this portion of 2 Esdras was a Palestinian Jew, not a Christian. (A Christian would not likely have had the Messiah die after a four-hundred year reign. Yet, a non-Christian Jew would not likely have had him die at all.)

In 2 Esdras, the judgment and the end of the physical universe ("all that is corruptible") happen after a period of seven days of silence. Could these seven days be commemorative of the seven millennia of human history (including the last under the Messiah's reign) described by other prophets? If they are, then the period that follows the "seven days" in 2 Esdras would be the eighth day when "the land which now is hidden [the promised land or paradise] shall be disclosed."

It implies there are, indeed, multiple universes that exist in different dimensions. It implies there is a universe already made, waiting to be disclosed to the people of God.

Had not Jesus said to his disciples,

> In my Father's house are many mansions: if it were not so, I would have told you. I go to prepare a place for you. And if I go and prepare a place for you, I will come again, and receive you to myself; that where I am, there ye may be also.
>
> (JOHN 14:2, 3)

The mansions Jesus described may have been figurative for life in the eternal glory of God.

Even Ezekiel's vision of the temple may have contained mystical hints of God's new creation on the "eighth day." Ezekiel describes eight steps leading into the inner courtyard. Since the temple represents the place where God dwells with humanity, do the eight steps to the entrance of God's dwelling signify the eighth day mentioned by Enoch and Barnabas and Ezra (Esdras) and hinted at in the book of Leviticus? Eight steps before God "will dwell with [humanity], and they shall be his people, and God himself shall be with them"?

After Ezekiel's temple has been built and is still in its virginal state, Ezekiel gives the following description as to how God's people are to make themselves ready to enter God's presence:

> Seven days shall they purge the altar and purify it; and they shall consecrate themselves. And when these days are fulfilled, it shall be, that upon the eighth day, and so onward, the priests shall make your burnt offerings upon the altar, and your peace offerings; and I will accept you, saith the Lord GOD.
>
> (EZEKIEL 43:26, 27)

Again, do the seven days of purging signify the millennia of history that humans must pass through before they are ready to enter the eternal presence of God, which shall last from then "onward"? As though to emphasize that this ceremony is a sacred rite of passage, Ezekiel says:

> Then he brought me back the way of the gate of the outward sanctuary which looketh toward the east; and it was shut. Then said the LORD unto me; This gate shall be shut, it shall not be opened, and no man shall enter in by it; because the LORD, the God of Israel, hath entered in by it, therefore it shall be shut. It is for the prince; the prince, he shall sit in it to eat bread before the LORD; he shall enter by the way of the porch of that gate, and shall go out by the way of the same.
>
> (EZEKIEL 44:1–3)

How is it that the prince in this ceremony can enter the gate that no man can open or enter—a gate reserved for God alone—and yet the prince dines there with God? Remember the words of John's Messiah to the seven churches in the Apocalypse?

> *These things saith he that is holy, he that*
> *is true, he that hath the key of David, he*
> *that openeth, and no man shutteth; and*
> *shutteth, and no man openeth.*
>
> (REVELATION 3:7)

Perhaps those words, which identify the Messiah as one who holds the key held by the ancient King David of Israel, are key to understanding Ezekiel's words about the prince who will enter the gate with God. Since no man could enter in by the east outer gate, the prince who stands within the gate with God must not be a man as we think of men. He is the Messiah, the one who holds the key that opens a gate no man can open. He is man to man, God to God. The gate is where God and man come together through the God-Man.

Within Ezekiel's temple courtyard is a second court reserved for priests. On sabbaths, the Messiah prince stands in the gate to this holy area of the temple and worship's with his priests—possibly foreshadowing the sabbath millennium when the Messiah shall be present on earth. He enters it again in a new way with a new kind of sacrifice on the day of the new moon, possibly foreshadowing God's new universe:

> *Thus saith the Lord GOD; The gate of the inner court that looketh toward the east shall be shut the six working days; but on the sabbath it shall be opened, and in the day of the new moon it shall be opened. And the prince shall enter by the way of the porch of that gate without, and shall stand by the post of the gate, and the priests shall prepare his [the prince's] burnt offering and his peace offerings, and he shall worship at the threshold of the gate: then he shall go forth; but the gate shall not be shut until the evening. Likewise the people of the land shall worship at the door of this gate before the LORD in the sabbaths and in the new moons. And the burnt offering that the prince shall offer unto the LORD in the sabbath day shall be six lambs without blemish, and a ram without blemish. . . . And in the day of the new moon it shall be a young bullock without blemish, and six lambs, and a ram: they shall be without blemish.*
>
> (EZEKIEL 46:1–4, 6)

Ezekiel's sabbath celebration contained six of one kind of sacrifice (six lambs) and then a seventh of a different kind (a ram). Could the ancient sacrificial language foreshadow six millennia of common human experience (the "six working days" with ordinary sacrifices), then a seventh millennium of a different kind represented by a different kind of sacrifice? Finally, on the festival of the new moon, an *eighth* kind of sacrifice is introduced, signifying the old heavens and old earth that must be sacrificed to make way for an existence that transcends the physical limits of time and space. Whether or not Ezekiel intended to communicate these things, the patterns of worship resonate with the times and destiny described in the other writings above.

> *And he said to me, It is done. I am Alpha and Omega, the beginning and the end. I will give to him that is thirsty of the fountain of the water of life freely. He that overcometh shall inherit all things; and I will be his God, and he shall be my son. But the fearful, and unbelieving, and the abominable, and murderers, and immoral persons, and sorcerers, and idolaters, and all liars, shall have their part in the lake which burneth with fire and brimstone: which is the second death.*
>
> (REVELATION 21:6–8)

These words of the Apocalypse echo the final words of Christ on the cross: "It is finished." At the beginning of the Apocalypse, the person in John's vision said he was "the beginning and the end," and now, as the Apocalypse comes to a close, he repeats that refrain and recalls to mind something that he had said while he walked the earth:

> In the last day, that great day of the feast [the eighth day of the Feast of Tabernacles], Jesus stood and cried [out], saying, If any man thirsteth, let him come to me, and drink. He that believeth on me, as the scripture hath said, out of his heart shall flow rivers of living water. (JOHN 7:37, 38)

Having shown the trials that will come upon the earth and even upon the faithful churches, he proclaims life to the faithful who *overcome* these persecutions—another refrain of the Apocalypse. But why shall the "fearful" die in the second death along with the immoral? Because they would not brave the first death, the death of martyrs. Fearful instead of faithful, they chose to preserve their own finite lives on earth over choosing God.

The Apocalypse reveals that all souls are immortal and will either go to be with God—the source from which all life flows eternally like a river—or they will be forever separated from God, in essence, dying eternally (the "second death") because they are cut off from the only original source of life.

KNOWING GOD FACE TO FACE

But what does it mean to live eternally in the presence of God if God is not bound by time? Paradise is more than a place. Like hell, it is a state of eternal existence. Yet, it's impossible for humans to understand how physical laws and time can be transcended. Nevertheless, time is not the constant people commonly think it is. According to Albert Einstein, time is relative. It changes, depending on the velocity at which one is moving and on the gravitational mass of nearby objects. Thus, time bends around a planet and sucks right into the extreme gravity of a black hole. Peculiar as Einstein's theory of relativity seems to ordinary perception, it has been scientifically established by placing an atomic clock in high-velocity orbit around the earth. The orbiting clock slowed out of synchronization with atomic clocks on the earth by exactly the amount Einstein's theory predicted. Time changes, and at the speed of light, according to Einstein, time ceases to exist.

Throughout the Bible, God uses light as a metaphor for himself. God is often described as a being of light:

> *They shall be abundantly satisfied with the fatness of thy house; and thou shalt make them drink of the river of thy plea-sures. For with thee is the fountain of life: in thy light shall we see light.*
>
> (PSALM 36:8, 9)

So, God is life and light, but what does seeing the light of God really mean?

> *For we know in part, and we prophesy in part. But when that which is perfect is come, then that which is in part shall be done away. . . . For now we see in a mir-ror, darkly; but then face to face: now I know in part; but then shall I know even as also I am known.*
>
> (1 CORINTHIANS 13:9, 10, 12)

When this present universe is "done away," those who have joined themselves to the Messiah will be joined to God completely without limits. Knowing God "face to face" expresses communion with God that knows no barriers in knowledge or time or space. It is the greatest of all miracles:

> Christ has risen, and so we shall rise. St. Peter for a few seconds walked on water; and the day will come when there will be a re-made universe, infinitely obedient to the will of glorified and obedient men, when we can do all things, when we shall be those gods that we are described as being in Scripture. To be sure, it feels wintry enough still: but often in the very early spring it feels like that. Two thousand years are only a day or two by this scale.[5]

> *One thing have I desired of the LORD, that will I seek after; that I may dwell in the house of the LORD all the days of my life, to behold the beauty of the LORD, and to enquire in his temple.*
>
> (PSALM 27:4)

Surely goodness and mercy shall follow
me all the days of my life: and I will dwell
in the house of the LORD for ever.

(PSALM 23:6)

Eternity does not mean time that goes on and on—duration without limit. Within God's eternal being, time ceases—just as time ceases when travelling at the speed of light. These eternal concepts, however, are too vast for humans to wrap their minds around, so John gives a tangible description of eternal life in the presence of God:

And there came to me one of the seven angels who had the seven vials full of the seven last plagues, and talked with me, saying, Come, I will show thee the bride, the Lamb's wife. And he carried me away in the spirit to a great and high mountain, and showed me that great city, the holy Jerusalem, descending out of heaven from God, Having the glory of God: and her light was like a stone most precious, even like a jasper stone, clear as crystal; And had a wall great and high, and had twelve gates, and at the gates twelve angels, and names written on them, which are the names of the twelve tribes of the children of Israel: On the east three gates; on the north three gates; on the south three gates; and on the west three gates. And the wall of the city had twelve foundations, and on them the names of the twelve apostles of the Lamb.

(REVELATION 21:9–14)

The "bride of the Lamb" is now called the "wife of the Lamb." If the resurrection and rapture were represented by the wedding banquet, this is the consummation of the marriage, where the two, God and humanity, are made one, where the bride's veil is lifted and the two finally see each other face to face. The angel tells John he will reveal the wife of the lamb to him, yet what John sees is a city called the New Jerusalem. So, the city symbolizes the wife of the Lamb, the people of God. The angel presents a visual metaphor of a great city in order to describe the perfect union that now exists between God and his people, for a city is the greatest thing man can create or imagine. A city also represents community, and this is the community of believers.

When John describes the city shining with the glory of God, he means the people now shine with the glory of God in the afterglow of their union. They share in the divinity of God through a union as close as husband and wife. That this grand miracle is only possible by an act of God is shown by having the city descend out of heaven. This is what it means to see God face to face.

THE NEW HEAVEN AND NEW EARTH

There is a twist to understanding such spiritual metaphors: heaven is not a metaphor; heaven *is* the ultimate reality. Rather, the physical universe that we have known is a metaphor for that which is to come. To think of heaven as a literal floating city with streets of gold hovering above Mount Zion, as many do, is to ignore all the elements in John's description. Every element represents a spiritual truth, and Mount Zion is not even mentioned. For example, the city shines like jasper, "clear as crystal." Real jasper is never clear. The streets of gold described later are transparent as glass, but real gold is never transparent like glass. Jasper, because it looks like it contains many stone-like eggs, symbolizes life and fertility, as mentioned earlier; and gold symbolizes refined purity. And, of course, both are beautiful; and whatever union with God is like, it must certainly be beautiful. John must describe what no human can conceive by using terms with which every human is familiar:

> But as it is written, Eye hath not seen,
> nor ear heard, neither have entered into
> the heart of man, the things which God
> hath prepared for them that love him.
> (1 CORINTHIAN 2:9)

In other words, the reality John is describing is completely outside human comprehension, but he (or the one giving this vision to him) wants his readers to understand something of its nature and beauty. Objects of the real world are the only metaphor available. In the end, we must always come back to thinking of heaven in physical terms, or we are unable to think of it at all.

The New Jerusalem represents the perfect restoration of God's two chosen peoples. It is founded on the twelve foundations of the apostles, representing Christians, and it has gates for each of the tribes of Israel, representing access to all Jews. Using cities and buildings as metaphors for the community of God's saints is, in fact, common in the New Testament.

Such a metaphor was even used earlier in the Apocalypse in a verse that referred ahead to the present section:

> Him that overcometh will I make a pillar the city of my God, which is new Jeru-
> in the temple of my God, and he shall go salem, which cometh down out of heaven
> no more out: and I will write upon him from my God: and I will write upon him
> the name of my God, and the name of my new name. (REVELATION 3:12)

Since the temple of God is not a structure that is literally built out of human pillars, there's no reason to think the New Jerusalem mentioned in the same verse is any more literal.

By faith Abraham, when he was called to move into a place which he should later receive for an inheritance, obeyed; and he went out, not knowing where he was going. By faith he sojourned in the land of promise, as in a foreign country, dwelling in tents with Isaac and Jacob, the heirs with him of the same promise: For he looked for a city which hath foundations, whose builder and maker is God. . . . These all died in faith, not having received the promises, but having seen them afar off, and were persuaded of them, and embraced them, and confessed that they were strangers and pilgrims on the earth. For they that say such things declare plainly that they seek a country. And truly, if they had been mindful of that country from which they came, they might have had opportunity to return. But now they desire a better country, that is, an heavenly [country]: therefore God is not ashamed to be called their God: for he hath prepared for them a city.

. . . But ye are come to mount Zion, and to the city of the living God, the heavenly Jerusalem, and to an innumerable company of angels, To the general assembly and church of the firstborn, who are written in heaven, and to God the Judge of all, and to the spirits of just men made perfect, And to Jesus the mediator of the new covenant. . . . For here [in this life on earth] we have no continuing city, but we seek one to come.

(HEBREWS 11:8–10, 13–16; 12:22–24; 13:14)

The Book of Hebrews emphasizes that entrance into the promised land comes by faith in the promise. There is no other way. Yet, Abraham, Isaac, and Jacob all died without having received the land that was promised to them. The land did not belong to the Jews until hundreds of years later, but Israel and Jerusalem were really only metaphors for the ultimate promised land, which was "afar off," and which Abraham and Isaac and Jacob did receive. They lived for a land that could not be found on earth. Dying in such faith, they entered it. Thus, all the saints of God feel like strangers on the earth, for "they desire a better country." Their desire will find its object, and John paints a picture of the object of their desire. It is the city of God, built of the saints of the Church and the angels and Jesus Christ and the Holy Spirit and God the Father—just like the one described above in Hebrews.

Other New Testament passages have also used the metaphor of a building to describe the union between God and his people:

For we are labourers together with God: . . . ye are God's building. According to the grace of God which is given to me, as a wise masterbuilder, I have laid the foundation, and another buildeth upon it. But let every man take heed how he buildeth upon it. For other foundation can no man lay than that which is laid, which is Jesus Christ

(1 CORINTHIANS 3:9–11)

Therefore remember, that ye being in time past Gentiles in the flesh, who are called Uncircumcision by that which is called the Circumcision in the flesh made by hands [i.e., Gentiles versus Jews, for whom circumcision is the identifying mark]; That at that time [past] ye were without Christ, being aliens from the commonwealth of Israel, and strangers from the covenants of promise, having no hope, and without God in the world: But now in Christ Jesus ye who once were far off are made near by the blood of Christ. For he is our peace, who hath made both one, and hath broken down the middle wall of partition between us;

Having abolished in his flesh the enmity, even the law of commandments contained in ordinances; to make in himself of two one new man, so making peace; And that he might reconcile both to God in one body by the cross, having by himself slain the enmity. . . . Now therefore ye are no more strangers and aliens, but fellowcitizens with the saints, and of the household of God; And are built upon the foundation of the apostles and prophets, Jesus Christ himself being the chief corner stone; In whom all the building fitly framed together groweth to an holy temple in the Lord: (EPHESIANS 2:11–16, 19–21)

Paul is saying that at one time Gentiles were aliens to God's covenant, which he had made by the Jews and signified by the mark of circumcision. He says that God's covenant created a commonwealth among the Jews in which Gentiles had no part. The Gentiles, who did not know the God of the Jews, however, came to know him through Jesus Christ under a new covenant that was open to all people. This is represented by the breaking down of the partition wall that existed in the old Jewish temple to keep worshiping Gentiles removed from Jews. God's new temple (his new dwelling place) is the people themselves, so there is no dividing wall. The two now intermingle even in the holiest parts of life like the many stones that go into building a temple. They have been made one. They are "fellowcitizens," which means they share equally in all the inherent privileges of citizenship. Everything that was promised to the Jews under the first covenant is now also promised to the Gentiles. As Christ was quoted earlier, those who came into the picture later will be given the same wages as those who came earliest. The new Jerusalem weds both of God's people into one.

John continues his description of this perfect union between God and all his people by elaborating on his metaphor of the New Jerusalem:

And he that talked with me had a golden reed to measure the city, and its gates, and its wall. And the city lieth foursquare, and the length is as large as the breadth: and he measured the city with the reed, twelve thousand furlongs.

The length and the breadth and its height are equal. And he measured its wall, an hundred and forty four cubits, according to the measure of a man, that is, of the angel. And the building of its wall was of jasper: and the city was pure

gold, like clear glass. And the founda-
tions of the wall of the city were gar-
nished with all manner of precious stones.
The first foundation was jasper; the sec-
ond, sapphire; the third, a chalcedony;
the fourth, an emerald; The fifth, sar-
donyx; the sixth, sardius; the seventh,
chrysolite; the eighth, beryl; the ninth, a
topaz; the tenth, a chrysoprasus; the
eleventh, a jacinth; the twelfth, an
amethyst. And the twelve gates were
twelve pearls; each one of the gates was of
one pearl: and the street of the city was
pure gold, as it were transparent glass.

(REVELATION 21:15–21)

Because union with God is more beautiful than can be imagined, the city that represents that union is larger and more beautiful than any ever seen. In fact, if it were a literal city, it would be 1,400 miles high and equally wide and long. The New Jerusalem would be more than a hundred times larger in surface area than the entire nation of Israel, and it would extend far beyond the earth's atmosphere. People on its upper levels would be essentially weightless, except for the gravity created by the city itself. In fact, if the city were a literal city, earth would have a bump protruding from its side, or hovering only a few feet above it, equal to one-sixth of the earth's diameter. The upperatmospheric gulf stream would pound its side at 400 miles per hour. Being two-thirds the size to the moon, its own gravitational forces would react with the earth's at such close range, causing one or both to explode. All of which speaks rather strongly against a literal interpretation, though who knows what's possible in a new universe.

Even the 144,000 who lived in the Great Tribulation are included in the description of the New Jerusalem. They are called to mind by the wall that is 144 cubits thick. To be sure the point is not lost, these walls are 12,000 furlongs in length and height, recalling the 12,000 from each tribe that made up the original 144,000. So, it turns out, the importance of the city's dimensions was not just to create a sense of immense grandeur; its dimensions have symbolic meaning. They reinforce the idea expressed earlier that the 144,000 represented *all* the united people of God, for now those same numbers represent the full measure of the city of God—only instead of 12,000 times twelve tribes, the number is 12,000 cubed. Twelve traditionally represents the product of God and nature in numerology (three times four). This city has very big twelves written all over it. This is the ultimate product of God and humanity joined. God has become a city by joining other souls to his own divine self.

The stones that are mentioned for the foundations are practically identical to stones mentioned early in the Book of Exodus that represent the twelve tribes of Israel. One of the priestly garments had unique gemstones fastened on it to represent each tribe of Israel. Here, each of the foundations of the apostles has a unique gemstone. (It's hard to get a perfect match between the Greek names of the stones listed in the Apocalypse and the Hebrew names listed in Exodus because their English equivalents are not always certain. Likely all twelve stones are intended to match those listed in Exodus.)

O thou afflicted, tossed with tempest, and not comforted, behold, I will lay thy stones with fair colours, and lay thy foundations with sapphires. And I will make thy windows of agates, and thy gates of carbuncles, and all thy borders of pleasant stones.

(ISAIAH 54:11, 12)

So, again, the twelve Jewish tribes are seen joined to the twelve Christian apostles. From every angle, the New Jerusalem symbolizes the people of God united into a magnificent new creation.

And I saw no temple in it: for the Lord God Almighty and the Lamb are its temple. (REVELATION 21:22)

If the Lord and the Lamb are its temple and the people of God are pillars in that temple, then all are the temple.

Know ye not that ye are the temple of God, and that the Spirit of God dwelleth in you? If any man defileth the temple of God, him shall God destroy; for the temple of God is holy, which temple ye are.

(1 CORINTHIANS 3:16, 17)

And what agreement hath the temple of God with idols? for ye are the temple of the living God; as God hath said, I will dwell in them, and walk in them; and I will be their God, and they shall be my people. . . . And I will be a Father to you, and ye shall be my sons and daughters, saith the Lord Almighty.

(2 CORINTHIAN 6:16, 18)

So, the Apocalypse says the Lord is the temple of his people, and the Apostle Paul says the people are the temple of God. Taken together, these statements express the mutual nature of communion with God. As Jesus said,

At that day [the resurrection] ye shall know that I am in my Father, and ye in me, and I in you. (JOHN 14:20)

For we know that if our earthly house of this tabernacle [referring figuratively to our bodies] were dissolved, we have a building of God, an house not made with hands, eternal in the heavens. For in this we groan, earnestly desiring to be clothed with our house which is from heaven . . . that mortality might be swallowed up in life. Now he that hath wrought us [fashioned us] for this very thing is God, who also hath given to us the earnest of the Spirit. (2 CORINTHIANS 5:1, 2, 4B, 5)

In the end, images are the only way we can understand heaven at all, but they serve us better when we understand them poetically. The Apocalypse is a poetic masterpiece, but its complexity often creates a sense of chaos, appropriate to the turmoil it describes. Whenever numerous intricate patterns converge, chaos is the apparent result. But chaos is an illusion. There is no chaos in the Apocalypse; only complexity. It is, in fact, perfectly formed around its own numerology. There is no chaos in heaven, either, where everything is ultimately centered on the one throne of God, while everything that refuses to completely join that center is completely excluded:

And the city had no need of the sun, neither of the moon, to shine in it: for the glory of God lightened it, and the Lamb is its lamp. And the nations of them who are saved shall walk in its light: and the kings of the earth bring their glory and honour into it. And its gates shall not be shut by day: for there shall be no night there. And they shall bring the glory and honour of the nations into it. And there shall by no means enter into it any thing that defileth, neither whoever worketh abomination, or maketh a lie: but they who are written in the Lamb's book of life.

(REVELATION 21:23–27)

Awake, awake; put on thy strength, O Zion; put on thy beautiful garments, O Jerusalem, the holy city: for henceforth there shall no more come into thee the uncircumcised and the unclean.

(ISAIAH 52:1)

There, again, the real holy city was a metaphor for the surreal city of God:

And the Lord shall deliver me from every evil work, and will preserve me unto his heavenly kingdom: to whom be glory for ever and ever. Amen. (2 TIMOTHY 4:18)

FROM PARADISE TO PARADISE: THE STORY COMES FULL CIRCLE

And he showed me a pure river of water of life, clear as crystal, proceeding out of the throne of God and of the Lamb. In the midst of its street, and on each side of the river, was there the tree of life, which bore twelve kinds of fruits, and yielded her fruit every month: and the leaves of the tree were for the healing of the nations. And there shall be no more curse: but the throne of God and of the Lamb shall be in it; and his servants shall serve him: And they shall see his face; and his name shall be in their foreheads. And there shall be no night there; and they need no lamp, neither light of the sun; for the Lord God giveth them light: and they shall reign for ever and ever.

(REVELATION 22:1–5)

In the beginning, humans lived in a garden paradise, and at the center of this garden grew a tree that could give eternal life. Humans chose to eat from another tree—the tree of knowledge of good and evil, which means, essentially, conscience. They wanted to be like God and were told by the serpent this would make them like God. What they really wanted was self-aggrandizement, and they chose not to trust God in order to get it. So God cast them out of the garden to prevent them from eating fruit from the tree of life; otherwise, they might live forever in their newfound sin.

The Apocalypse brings the human story back to its beginning, back to paradise, yet everything has changed. Humans now have a conscience. They understand good and evil. It has been a long and painful lesson, but they got what they reached out for in naivete. It even appears they will be like God, being brought into the unity of God. Thus, the tree of knowledge of good and evil is no longer in the story. The humans have eaten from that tree long enough.

But the tree of life, which was never eaten from, has returned. It stands on both sides of the river of life—a river that flows out of a place called heaven and that waters the universe. Here, again, the symbolism unites Jews and Christians through the Messiah. This is shown by having two trees of life now—one on each side of the river of life, which is Christ. The original Garden of Eden only had one tree of life. There is a tree for each of God's chosen people—a tree for each covenant. The tree on one side of the life that flows from Christ has twelve kinds of the fruit for the people of the twelve tribes, and the tree on the other side has twelve kinds for the people of the twelve apostles. They yield their fruit for twelve months. And, yet, it's spoken of as a single tree.

The people see God face to face. They walk in heaven by the light of God, just as the first humans walked in the garden with God. Thy share his name, just as a bride traditionally acquires the name of her spouse. So, the people of God, as his bride, acquire the name of God and all that goes with that name. For names in the Bible always have meaning. The peoples of God share equally in his identity, which is their new identity.

And the Messiah reigns from his throne which he shares with God Almighty.

For he [God the Father] hath put all things under his [Christ's] feet. But when he saith all things are put under him, it is evident that he [the Father] is excepted, who did put all things under him. And when all things shall be subdued to him [Christ], then shall the Son also himself be subject to him that put all things under him, that God may be all in all. (1 Corinthians 15:27, 28)

Look to me, and be ye saved, all the ends of the earth: for I am God, and there is none else. I have sworn by myself, the word is gone out of my mouth in righteousness, and shall not return, That to me every knee shall bow, every tongue shall swear. Surely, shall one say, in the LORD have I righteousness and strength: even to him shall men come; and all that are incensed against him shall be ashamed. In the LORD shall all the seed of Israel be justified, and shall glory. . . . For the mountains shall depart, and the hills be removed; but my kindness shall not depart from thee, neither shall the covenant of my peace be removed, saith the LORD that hath mercy on thee.

(ISAIAH 45:22–25; 54:10)

Everything is back in its proper order, but humanity has gained infinite complexity. The story that began in a rural garden paradise ends in a cosmopolitan paradise. A city has grown up around Eden, but the innocense, perfection, and beauty of Eden still wait at the city's heart, which is the throne of God and the Lamb. Because the children of God—the brothers and sisters of the Lamb—are back where the tree of life is found, the curse of death that began in Eden is also removed, just as the prophets promised:

He will swallow up death in victory; and the Lord GOD will wipe away tears from off all faces; and the rebuke of his people shall he take away from off all the earth: for the LORD hath spoken it. And it shall be said in that day, Lo, this is our God; we have waited for him, and he will save us: this is the LORD; we have waited for him, we will be glad and rejoice in his salvation.

(ISAIAH 25:8, 9)

And so, for the followers of God's anointed, the end is only the beginning.

Chapter 25

FULFILLMENT:

LIVING IN THE
LIGHT OF REVELATION

Therefore, O thou son of man, speak to the house of Israel; Thus ye speak, saying, If our transgressions and our sins are upon us, and we pine away in them, how should we then live? Say to them, As I live, saith the Lord GOD, I have no pleasure in the death of the wicked; but that the wicked should turn from his way and live: turn ye, turn ye from your evil ways; for why will ye die, O house of Israel?

Therefore, thou son of man, say to the children of thy people, The righteousness of the righteous shall not deliver him in the day of his transgression: as for the wickedness of the wicked, he shall not fall by it in the day that he turneth from his wickedness; neither shall the righteous be able to live for his righteousness in the day that he sinneth.

(EZEKIEL 33:10–12)

PROPHET WITH A PURPOSE

Prophecy was not given in a vacuum. In most cases, the words were spoken to the prophet's own people before they were written down. Like all people, the prophets were more concerned about their own times than the end times. During good times, they roared in order to shake people out of their complacency, to awaken them to an awareness of God. In the bad times, the prophets saw beyond the present gloom and encouraged the overwrought—not with flighty hopes of an easier road but with insights on how to make a difficult road worthwhile. In all cases, the prophets clearly intended to change the course of human events, not merely predict them.

God's prophets were never just a mouth piece. Though they chastised their own people, they also implored God for mercy on behalf of the people. God inscribed very few of his words on stone. Most were impressed upon human minds and spoken with human tongues, for a man can speak with compassion, where stone is cold. A man can speak with anger, where stone is unmoved. A man can even speak back to God, reasoning with the words of prophets who preceded him, where a stone can only echo the voice of God mindlessly:

And I prayed to the LORD my God, and made my confession, and said, O Lord, the great and dreadful God, keeping the covenant and mercy to them that love him, and to them that keep his commandments; We have sinned, and have committed iniquity. . . . Neither have we hearkened to thy servants the prophets, who spoke in thy name to our kings, our princes, and our fathers, and to all the people of the land. . . . And all Israel have transgressed thy law, even by departing, that they might not obey thy voice; therefore the curse is poured upon us, and the oath that is written in the law of Moses the servant of God, because we have sinned against him.

(DANIEL 9:4–6, 11)

The prophet Daniel recalled the curse spoken earlier by the prophet Moses when the story of God and the chosen people of his covenant began:

But if ye will not hearken unto me . . . so that ye will not do all my commandments, but that ye break my covenant: . . . I will set my face against you, and ye shall be slain before your enemies: they that hate you shall reign over you; and ye shall flee when none pursueth you. And if ye will not yet for all this hearken unto me, then I will punish you seven times more for your sins. . . . And if ye will not be reformed by me by these things, but will walk contrary unto me; . . . I will bring a sword upon you, that shall avenge the quarrel of my covenant: and when ye are gathered together within your cities, I will send the pestilence among you; and ye shall be delivered into the hand of the enemy. And I will make your cities waste, and bring your sanctuaries unto desolation, and I will not smell the savour of your sweet odours. And I will bring the land into desolation: and your enemies which dwell therein shall be astonished at it.

(LEVITICUS 26:14, 15, 17, 18, 23, 25, 31, 32)

The prophet Daniel saw the fulfillment of this prophecy in his own lifetime when Babylon destroyed Jerusalem, and he acknowledged the guilt of his people before God. He acknowledged that their sin against God's covenant with Moses brought the destruction of Jerusalem. He acknowledged these things in order to implore God for mercy on their behalf:

And he hath confirmed his words [to Moses], which he spoke against us . . . by bringing upon us a great evil: for under the whole heaven it hath not been done as it hath been done upon Jerusalem. As it is written in the law of Moses, all this evil is come upon us: yet we have not made our prayer before the LORD our God, that we might turn from our iniquities, and understand thy truth. . . . O Lord, according to all thy righteousness, I beseech thee, let thy anger and thy fury be turned away from thy city Jerusalem, thy holy mountain: because for our sins, and for the iniquities of our fathers, Jerusalem and thy people have become a reproach to all that are about us.

(DANIEL 9:12, 13, 16)

In speaking of reproach, Daniel acknowledged the fulfillment of Moses' prophecy as though Moses had spoken directly to him across time:

. . . So that the generation to come of your children that shall arise after you, and the stranger that shall come from a distant land, shall say, when they see the plagues of that land, and the sicknesses which the LORD hath laid upon it; And that its whole land is brimstone, and salt, and burning . . . like the overthrow of Sodom, and Gomorrah . . . which the LORD overthrew in his anger, and in his wrath: Even all the nations shall say, Why hath the LORD done thus to this land? what meaneth the heat of this great anger? Then men shall say, Because they have forsaken the covenant of the LORD God of their fathers, which he made with them when he brought them forth from the land of Egypt.

(DEUTERONOMY 29:22–25)

Yet, Moses had also prophesied that God would forgive Israel if they returned to him and to the covenant he had made with them. Guided by the prophetic faith of his forefather, Daniel seized this ancient promise to Israel and asked God to make the prophesied forgiveness as real as the predicted destruction had been:

Now therefore, O our God, hear the prayer of thy servant, and his supplications, and cause thy face to shine upon thy sanctuary that is desolate, for the Lord's sake. O my God, incline thy ear, and hear; open thy eyes, and behold our desolations, and the city which is called by thy name: for we do not present our supplications before thee for our righteousnesses, but for thy great mercies.

(DANIEL 9:17, 18)

Who could make a better guide as to how prophecy is to be used than one who was, himself, a prophet? Daniel recognized that the changes sought and the catastrophes predicted if changes were not made were recorded for a future people, even more than for the people of Moses' own time. Though they were true for all times, they had been expressly stated in order to guide people of a distant future back to God.

The words of the prophets are not esoteric glimmers of future knowledge. They are deliberate echoes into the future, inspired by God and breathed out by men and women, intended to influence the patterns of history as it develops.

Like the driving equation in a fractal, they keep emerging in our chaos to recreate meaningful change. They push us out of our complacency or compel us through our suffering toward the bright belief that good and truth prevail. Their future counters the wisdom of the world, which says, "Live only for yourself in the present, for that is all you can be certain of." The prophecies are a bias in the fabric of time, a cross current to the flow of events. They challenge us to live as eternal souls—as people unbound by time. Those who know they are eternal will suffer visible disgrace if necessary in order to proclaim invisible truth, just as the prophets did. They will endure present humiliation to proclaim future glory, just as the prophets did. They will forego revenge now in belief of divine justice later. They will die now that others might live after them. Just as the prophets did.

PROPHETIC FAITH TO INCREASE THE HARVEST

The words of the prophets—Christian Jew and non-Christian Jew—have changed the world. Their light has penetrated nearly every nation on earth through the spread of Christianity and the diaspora of Judaism. They have also inspired exploration of the world and of science. And, unfortunately, they have been misused as a flag to wave for ignoble causes, such as wars for acquisition of land or even ministries for acquisition of wealth.

One might think that belief in prophecy borders on superstition and is incompatible with the age of science, yet the father of modern science himself, Isaac Newton, devoted as much interest and time to biblical prophecy as he did to scientific discovery—a part of history that is usually ignored. To Isaac Newton, prophecy and science were both means to enlightenment that ran a parallel course. Newton wrote extensively on prophecy.

A good example of how prophecy both hindered scientific exploration and impelled it can be found in Christopher Columbus. Some ignorant churchmen believed the earth was flat because of their overly literal readings of the Bible's poetry, which occasionally spoke of the earth as resting upon pillars:

> . . . Which shaketh the earth out of her
> place, and the pillars thereof tremble.
> (JOB 9:6)

And the Bible occasionally spoke of the sun moving through the sky, rather than the earth revolving around the sun. This was taken to be further proof that a flat earth lay at the center of the universe. In light of fact, however, the same book of the Bible that speaks of the earth resting upon pillars shows itself to be far more enlightened than its ancient time, for it also says,

> He stretcheth out the north over the
> empty place, and hangeth the earth
> upon nothing.   (Job 26:7)

So, even Job did not really ascribe to the primitive view that a flat earth rested on pillars or was held up on the shoulders of a god. He was speaking poetically, as prophets do. When the Bible spoke of the sun moving through the sky, it did so in the same manner in which well enlightened scientific minds continue to do in common speech today. From a human point of view, the sun does move through the sky.

The clinching argument against a rotund earth had been espoused nearly a millennium before Columbus in a writing titled *Christian Topography*. The argument was based on the prophecy that Christ would descend from heaven at his return, when every eye would see him. How could every eye see him descend if the earth was round and some people lived on the side of the globe? Obviously, it had to be flat so all could look up. With that stroke of argumentative brilliance, a millennium of astronomical darkness covered the earth.

When Columbus, a devout Catholic, sought to enlighten the prevailing darkness by exploration, his mission and his life were endangered by the Spanish Inquisition, even though learned people had believed in a round earth for centuries. The argument that prevailed in his request for financing from Isabella and Ferdinand was this: If Columbus' belief was heresy, it was wrong. If Columbus was wrong, he would sail off the edge of the world. *Ergo,* those who fervently believed he was a heretic should allow him to sail to his own death, and the problems of both parties would be solved.

The irony in all of this is that prophecy was also the very force that compelled Columbus to make his journeys. Prophetic faith made Columbus a man of discovery. Prophetic faith meant destiny, and destiny meant reason to explore. In one of his letters Columbus wrote:

> God made me the messenger of the new heaven and the new earth, of which He spoke in the Apocalypse by St. John, after having spoken of it by the mouth of Isaiah; and He showed me the spot where to find it.[1]

And, thus, Columbus named his discovery the "New World," being a little misguided, himself, as to what the new earth of the Apocalypse really implied.

A decade after discovering the "New World," Columbus completed his *Book of Prophecies,* in which he credits God and the prophets—more than science—for all his explorations. In this book, Columbus followed many who came before him in advocating the belief that earth would end after seven thousand years of human history. By prophetic faith, Columbus envisioned that it was his duty to prepare for that end by completing the conversion of all the people in the New World. Columbus' vision and prophetically inspired name for the new hemisphere quickly caught on, and, for better or worse, much of Europe jumped to Columbus's conclusion that the Americas were the final missionary frontier, ending for good the Inquisition's resistance to exploration. Columbus wrote:

> Our Redeemer said that before the consummation of this world all that was written by the prophets is to be accomplished. . . . I said above that much remained for the completion of the prophecies, and I say that . . . the sign is that Our Lord is hastening them; the preaching of this gospel in so many lands, in recent times, tells it to me.[2]

This had been Columbus' sense of mission from his first voyage, after which he wrote:

> Let Christ rejoice upon Earth as He rejoices in heaven, as He foresees that so many souls of so many people heretofore lost are to be saved.[3]

The desire to save the primitive New World with the Gospel of Christ moved the Church and society forward in unison. The Augustinian view of prophecy, which claimed the Church should and must reign on earth, mated itself to the aspirations of every king or queen who wished to extend his or her temporal share of that reign. Once again, the unholy marriage of religion and politics fed each other's worst side. Conquistador and missionary set out together, giving rise to more centuries of conquest on behalf of Christ and King. Religion gave moral authority to conquest, and conquest gave worldly power to religion.

A belief in prophetic destiny emboldened the disciples of Christ throughout history to explore and push beyond the known frontiers of the earth in quest of unreached people. Many of their efforts were noble, intended only to preach Christ's words as he had commanded in one of his own prophecies:

> *And he [Jesus] said to them, Go ye into all the world, and preach the gospel to every creature. He that believeth and is baptized shall be saved; but he that believeth not shall be damned.*
> (MARK 16:15–16)

The Apostle Paul also anchored his encouragements to preach the words of Christ in the prophetic hope of Christ's second coming:

I charge thee therefore before God, and the Lord Jesus Christ, who shall judge the living and the dead at his appearing and his kingdom; Preach the word; be dili- *gent in season, out of season; reprove, rebuke, exhort with all longsuffering [patient endurance] and doctrine.*

(2 TIMOTHY 4:1, 2)

In fact, the whole reason Christ would wait so long to make his second coming was to ensure that *all* the nations of earth would have a chance to hear the gospel of his salvation:

And account that the longsuffering of our Lord is salvation. (2 PETER 3:15A)

PROPHETIC FAITH IN THE FACE OF PERSECUTION

While the prophets' purpose was often to elicit change in times of moral decline, some prophets, like John, wrote in times when change was hopeless. Instead, they prophesied to encourage the faithful to remain faithful and overcome their persecutions. John's work certainly triumphed in giving courage to future missionaries squeezed in the dragon's mouth, as did the earlier words of Jesus spoken to John and the other disciples when they were young:

And he [Jesus] lifted up his eyes on his disciples, and said, Blessed are ye poor: for yours is the kingdom of God. Blessed are ye that hunger now: for ye shall be filled. Blessed are ye that weep now: for ye shall laugh. Blessed are ye, when men shall hate you, and when they shall separate you from their company, and shall reproach you, and cast out your name as evil, for the Son of man's sake. Rejoice ye in that day, and leap for joy: for, behold, *your reward is great in heaven: for in the like manner did their fathers to the prophets. But woe to you that are rich! for ye have received your consolation. Woe to you that are full! for ye shall hunger. Woe to you that laugh now! for ye shall mourn and weep. Woe to you, when all men shall speak well of you! [because you preach only what they want to hear] for so did their fathers to the false prophets.* (LUKE 6:20–26)

For whoever will save his life shall lose it: but whoever will lose his life for my sake, the same shall save it. For what is a man profited, if he shall gain the whole world, and lose himself, or be cast away? For *whoever shall be ashamed of me and of my words, of him shall the Son of man be ashamed, when he shall come in his own glory, and in that of his Father, and of the holy angels.* (LUKE 9:24–26)

Jesus, living up to his own words, did not seek to save his life, but continued preaching words that would bring his death. He preached them because they were true, regardless of who did not want to hear them. Anticipating his own death, he said at the Passover supper,

I am the living bread which came down from heaven: if any man shall eat of this bread, he shall live for ever: and the bread that I will give is my flesh, which I will give for the life of the world.

(JOHN 6:51)

When his disciples wished to claim a place for themselves at his throne in the kingdom of heaven, Jesus implied they must also suffer a death similar to his own before they could claim such a prize. The world would treat them no better than it did him if they continued to preach his words:

. . . Then Peter began to say to him, Lo, we have left all, and have followed thee. Jesus answered and said, Verily I say to you, There is no man that hath left house, or brethren, or sisters, or father, or mother, or wife, or children, or lands, for my sake, and the gospel's, But he shall receive an hundredfold now in this time, houses, and brethren, and sisters, and mothers, and children, and lands, with persecutions; and in the world to come eternal life. But many that are first shall be last; and the last first.

. . . And James and John, the sons of Zebedee, come to him, saying, Master, we would that thou shouldest do for us whatever we shall desire. And he said to them, What would ye that I should do for you? They said to him, Grant to us that we may sit, one on thy right hand, and the other on thy left hand, in thy glory. But Jesus said to them, Ye know not what ye ask: can ye drink of the cup that I drink of? and be baptized with the baptism that I am baptized with? And they said to him, We can. And Jesus said to them, Ye shall indeed drink of the cup that I drink of; and with the baptism that I am baptized with shall ye be baptized: But to sit on my right hand and on my left hand is not mine to give; but it shall be given to them for whom it is prepared.

(MARK 10:28–31, 35–40)

These two wanted the glory without the grief. They had no idea what they were saying when they claimed they could drink of the same cup that Jesus drank of. The cup of wine at the Passover supper (*seder*) would come to represent the blood of the innocent one slain during the Passover celebration. They would drink of the cup of his blood, which would be their own blood, poured out for the truth of his words. They would share in his death. Truth is expensive, but not living for the truth is even more expensive:

If we suffer, we shall also reign with him:
if we deny [him], he also will deny us.
(2 Timothy 2:12)

So, prophecy is both warning and hope—hope that, for all that one loses, infinitely more will eventually be gained. The prophecies provide a carrot and prod incentive to living and spreading the truth of Christ. They hold out glory as a promise but remind of judgment. The man who knows glory lies ahead, while an open pit lies right behind, is not as likely to step backward from the face of death as the man who is only aware of the glory ahead. The two combined provide strength to keep the faithful advancing into danger with the truth so that the truth can overcome evil:

And let us consider one another to stir up to love and to good works: Not forsaking the assembling of ourselves [in churches and homes], as the manner of some is; but exhorting one another: and so much the more, as ye see the day approaching. For if we sin wilfully after we have received the knowledge of the truth, there remaineth no more sacrifice for sins, But a certain fearful expectation of judgment and fiery indignation, which shall devour the adversaries. He that despised Moses' law died without mercy under two or three witnesses: Of how much more severe punishment, suppose ye, shall he be thought worthy, who hath trodden under foot the Son of God, and hath counted the blood of the covenant, by which he was sanctified, an unholy thing, and hath done despite to the Spirit of grace? For we know him that hath said, Vengeance belongeth to me, I will recompense, saith the Lord. And again, The Lord shall judge his people. It is a fearful thing to fall into the hands of the
living God. But call to remembrance the former days, in which, after ye were illuminated, ye endured a great fight of afflictions; Partly, while ye were made a gazingstock both by reproaches and afflictions; and partly, while ye became companions of them that were so used. For ye had compassion of me in my bonds, and took joyfully the plundering of your goods, knowing in yourselves that ye have in heaven a better and an enduring substance. Cast not away therefore your confidence, which hath great recompence of reward. For ye have need of patience, that, after ye have done the will of God, ye may receive the promise. For yet a little while, and he that is coming will come, and will not tarry [delay]. Now the just shall live by faith: but if any man shall draw back, my soul shall have no pleasure in him. But we are not of them who draw back to perdition; but of them that believe to the saving of the soul. (Hebrews 10:24–39)

Here was warning from behind (the fire that will devour the evil) coupled with encouragement to what lies ahead. The writer of Hebrews warns those who have accepted Jesus as the Son of God not to ever reject him out of fear of death or temptation to evil. It will go no better for a Christian who rejects his faith than it did for a Jew who rejected the revelation received from Moses. Both Moses and Christ established a covenant between God and humanity, laying out conditions for living in the presence of God.

The Book of Hebrews also acknowledges that "it is a fearful thing to fall into the hands of the living God." Being a chosen people of God has always meant standing in the line of fire, whether as a Jew or as a Christian. As Tevye was quoted earlier from *Fiddler on the Roof*: "I'm tired of being one of the chosen. Could you choose someone else for a while?"

Life has never been easy for the people of God under either covenant. Since it was not easy right after Jesus' first coming, his followers should not expect it will be easy preceding his second coming. Those who fail, do so to their own despair, for they have tasted that which is good and have spit it out. It will be worse for them than for any.

The character Tevye spoke as one who had lost sight of the glory that lies ahead. The Apostle Paul, a man of the New Covenant, acknowledged the same sense of struggle expressed by Tevye but never lost sight of the glory:

> I have fought a good fight, I have finished my course, I have kept the faith: Henceforth there is laid up for me a crown of righteousness, which the Lord, the righteous judge, shall give me at that day: and not to me only, but to all them also that love his appearing.   (2 TIMOTHY 4:7, 8)

The difference is hope. Jesus' brother James, who died for his faith at the hands of the Pharisees when he was thrown from the temple parapet, had expressed much the same thing:

> Blessed is the man that endureth temptation [especially the temptation to turn from the truth]: for when he is tried, he shall receive the crown of life, which the Lord hath promised to them that love him.   (JAMES 1:12)

Clearly, James did not receive that crown during his life. How ironic that this same James, who was renowned as "James the Just," wrote the following words about people like the Pharisees. Unwittingly, he may have foretold his own death:

> Ye have condemned and killed the just; and he doth not resist you. [And, then, to followers:] Be patient therefore, brethren, until the coming of the Lord. Behold, the farmer waiteth for the precious fruit of the earth, and hath long patience for it, until he receiveth the early and the latter rain. Be ye also patient; establish your hearts: for the coming of the Lord draweth near.   (JAMES 5:6–8)

James refers to "the just" in the singular as though he meant one particular person killed by rich oppressors.

Peter, one of Jesus' first disciples, also predicted the persecution that would come to the followers of Christ. Like other prophets, he encouraged his followers with predictions of the glory that would come to those who persevered. They, like James, would share in Christ's death:

> Beloved, think it not strange concerning the fiery trial which is to try you, as though some strange thing happened to you: But rejoice, seeing ye are partakers of Christ's sufferings; that, when his glory shall be revealed, ye may be glad also with exceeding joy. . . . For the time is come that judgment must begin at the house of God: and if it first beginneth with us, what shall be the end of them that obey not the gospel of God?
>
> (1 PETER 4:12, 13, 17)

Never in all the New Testament prophecies was there a promise of prosperity in this life for those who follow Christ and live righteously. Over and over again the true followers of Christ were promised hardship. In fact, those who were leaders in ministry were especially warned not to seek personal prosperity from donations that were given for ministry:

> The elders who are among you I exhort, who am also an elder, and a witness of the sufferings of Christ, and also a partaker of the glory that shall be revealed: Feed the flock of God which is among you, taking the oversight of it, not by constraint, but willingly; not for dishonest gain, but from a ready mind; Neither as being lords over God's heritage, but being examples to the flock. And when the chief Shepherd shall appear, ye shall receive a crown of glory that fadeth not away. . . . Be sober, be vigilant; because your adversary the devil, as a roaring lion, walketh about, seeking whom he may devour: Whom resist steadfast in the faith, knowing that the same afflictions are accomplished in your brethren that are in the world. But the God of all grace, who hath called us to his eternal glory by Christ Jesus, after ye have suffered a while, make you perfect, establish, strengthen, settle you.
>
> (1 PETER 5:1–5, 8–10)

Here the prophet indicates that the underlying cause of persecution is the dragon, himself, firing up the world against the people of God. Yet, the people of God are guaranteed the ultimate victory:

> Who is he that overcometh the world, but he that believeth that Jesus is the Son of God? (1 JOHN 5:5)

One would think that such an austere message would never have won the world, for prophecy looks at the future through a cold glass eye. Who would come to a faith that promised a life of persecution even if it does gleam with distant hope?

PROPHETIC FAITH AND FATALISM

Both the gloom and the gleam sometimes lead people to inaction, rather than to the bold action the prophecies intend to inspire. Too much interest in end-time prophecies can become nothing more than a Christian form of escapism, even fatalism. For example: Christians, more than anyone, should respect the environment, since Christians believe God created the environment and put people in the garden to take care of it. Yet, it's easy, if one believes God is going to destroy the earth with fire and plagues, to consume the world recklessly with the attitude that it's all going to hell anyway.

The Apostle Paul, however, warned against dark and fatalistic ways of thinking, saying that anticipation of the end should motivate one to positive action, not complacency:

> *And this, knowing the time, that now it is high time to awake out of sleep: for now is our salvation nearer than when we believed. The night is far spent, the day is at hand: let us therefore cast off the works of darkness, and let us put on the armour of light.* (ROMANS 13:11, 12)

If the tribulation that comes upon the earth is a direct effect of unrestrained human evil, then environmental or political or spiritual fatalism is going with the wrong flow. The one who wants to be found ready when Christ returns will be found caring for Christ's household. He or she will recall the warning of the Apocalypse that foretells God will "destroy them who destroy the earth." He or she will be a good steward of God's earth, physically and spiritually, as Jesus forewarned in a parable about being dressed and ready for his return:

> *Let your loins be girt, and your lamps burning; And ye yourselves like men that wait for their lord, when he will return from the wedding; that when he cometh and knocketh, they may open to him immediately. Blessed are those servants, whom the lord when he cometh shall find watching: verily I say to you, that he shall gird himself, and make them to sit down to eat, and will come forth and serve them. And if he shall come in the second watch, or come in the third watch, and find them so, blessed are those servants. And this know, that if the master of the house had known what hour the thief would come, he would*

have watched, and not have allowed his house to be broken into. Be ye therefore ready also: for the Son of man cometh at an hour when ye think not.

Then Peter said to him, Lord, speakest thou this parable to us, or even to all? And the Lord said, Who then is that faithful and wise steward, whom his lord shall make ruler over his household, to give them their portion of food in due season? Blessed is that servant, whom his lord when he cometh shall find so doing.

Truly I say to you, that he will make him ruler over all that he hath. But if that servant shall say in his heart, My lord delayeth his coming; and shall begin to beat the male and female servants, and to eat and drink, and to be drunk; The lord of that servant will come in a day when he looketh not for him, and at an hour when he is not aware, and will cut him in two, and will appoint him his portion with the unbelievers.

(LUKE 12:35–46)

This warning explicitly to his own disciples can hardly be considered a call to let the earth and society go to hell in the last days while one sits around and hopes for the coming of Christ. Some almost seem to *hope* society will grow worse, so that Christ will return more quickly. They are ready even to speed it along. It is to such people that Isaiah warned,

Woe unto them that draw iniquity with cords of vanity [futility], and [draw] sin as it were with a cart rope: That say, Let him [God] make speed, and hasten his work, that we may see it: and let the counsel of the Holy One of Israel draw nigh and come, that we may know it! Woe unto them that call evil good, and good evil; that put darkness for light, and light for darkness; that put bitter for sweet, and sweet for bitter! . . . Therefore is the anger of the LORD kindled against

his people, and he hath stretched forth his hand against them, and hath smitten them: and the hills did tremble, and their carcasses were torn in the midst of the streets. For all this his anger is not turned away, but his hand is stretched out still. And he will lift up an ensign to the nations from far, and will hiss unto them from the end of the earth: and, behold, they shall come with speed swiftly.

(ISAIAH 5:18–20, 25, 26)

Spoken of earlier times when God would draw Israel's enemies upon his people, this prophecy could apply equally to any time when God's people are hastening the Lord's doom by watching their society become corrupt, believing any attempt to steer it in a better direction is futile because prophesy has predestined the end.

PROPHETIC FAITH AND PREDESTINATION

It is not always true that prophetic statements predestine events. This may be one more reason the prophets use poetic ambiguity. More than one possible interpretation allows for more than one outcome—like an escape clause. Since the prophet's function is not primarily one of seeing into the future but one of appealing to God's people for change, that very change may change the outcome of the prophecy. Some prophecies are conditional, even though they don't state they are conditional. Other prophecies were made within God's covenants and were explicitly conditioned upon obedience of those covenants.

The Bible has several examples of prophecies that were not fulfilled precisely as indicated by prophet because humans changed their ways. Sometimes the predicted doom was *delayed* because people changed: Micah prophesied that Jerusalem would turn into a heap of ruins and be plowed as a field, but King Hezekiah and his people repented, and God held back his judgment for a later generation. Yet, there was nothing conditional in how the prophecy was stated as it is recounted later by Jeremiah:

Then Jeremiah spoke to all the princes and to all the people, saying, The LORD sent me to prophesy against this house and against this city all the words that ye have heard. Therefore now amend your ways and your doings, and obey the voice of the LORD your God; and the LORD will repent him of the evil that he hath pronounced against you. ["Repent him" means "change his mind regarding," not "feel sorry because."]

. . . Then arose certain of the elders of the land, and spoke to all the assembly of the people, saying, Micah the Morasthite prophesied in the days of Hezekiah king of Judah, and spoke to all the people of Judah, saying, Thus saith the LORD of hosts; Zion shall be plowed like a field, and Jerusalem shall become heaps, and the mountain of the house as the high places of the forest. Did Hezekiah king of Judah and all Judah put him to death? did he not fear the LORD, and beseech the LORD, and the LORD repented of the evil which he had pronounced against them? Thus might we procure great evil against our souls.

(JEREMIAH 26:12, 13, 17–19. Compare to MICAH 3:12 AND 2 KINGS 20:1–5.)

If changing the hearts of God's people is one of the prophet's primary objectives, what would be the point if the outcome were inevitable anyway? Change can happen because God is not impersonal. His relationship with his creation is dynamic. God will reciprocate to the response of a human heart. God's decrees and his nature do not change, but humans do, and God's decrees are designed to take that into account. His goal is always to guide his creation into communion with himself:

At what instant I shall speak concerning a nation, and concerning a kingdom, to pluck up, and to pull down, and to destroy it; If that nation, against which I have pronounced, shall turn from their evil, I will repent of the evil that I thought to do to them. And at what instant I shall speak concerning a nation, and concerning a kingdom, to build and to plant it; If it shall do evil in my sight, that it obey not my voice, then I will repent of the good, with which I said I would benefit them.

(JEREMIAH 18:7–10. Compare also to EZEKIEL 18:27, 28; 33:13–20.)

The words "at what instant" seem to indicate that *anytime* God predicts something there is an implicit condition within *each* prediction. Whether good or evil is predicted for a nation, God will relent of that which he predicted if people change. For that reason, one cannot say with absolute assurance that a prophecy will be fulfilled in the future simply because it has not yet been fulfilled. These words indicate that even good prophecies, such as those regarding Israel as a nation in the millennium, will not be fulfilled if the nation chooses selfish policies over justice.

Given enough time, however, the right conditions for a prophecy's fulfillment are bound to return. Typically, the repentance of one generation has only delayed a prophecy until such time as another generation returns to the nation's former wickedness. The words "at what instant" could also imply that the ability to change the course of action exist only at the time the prophecy is spoken and only when the prophecy regards a specific situation. If that's the case, the words of the Apocalypse, which do not identify any specific nations or people or times, will meet their fulfillment no matter what, but they are still open enough that we cannot know exactly what their fulfillment will be. There is still room for human choice. Once the events happen, we may never know what the alternative futures were.

One of the best examples of a prophecy that was not fulfilled precisely as it was stated is found in the book of Jonah. Jonah prophesied the destruction of Nineveh, the capital of Assyria:

. . . Yet forty days, and Nineveh shall be overthrown. [But] the people of Nineveh believed God, and proclaimed a fast, and put on sackcloth, from the greatest of them even to the least of them.

(JONAH 3:5)

Jonah's straightforward prediction did not offer any apparent conditions by which Nineveh might be saved, yet the city was not destroyed in forty days. Instead, the king of Nineveh said,

Who can tell if God will turn and repent, and turn away from his fierce anger, that we perish not? And God saw their works, that they turned from their evil way; and God repented of the evil, that he had said that he would do to them; and he did it not. (JONAH 3:9–10)

So, Nineveh was not destroyed in forty days, nor in forty years, but it *was* destroyed about 150 years later. When the people of Nineveh no longer believed the lesson of their ancestors, the city was destroyed forever. Perhaps the actual destruction took forty days, but history does not say. Jonah, however, was really annoyed that the fireworks he had predicted did not happen, and God was annoyed with Jonah for being so selfish. The prophet missed the point: His prophecy was not an opportunity for God to show off; it was supposed to elicit change in the people. God prophesied doom because he *wanted* to spare them. God was moved by their sincere response, whereas his minister, Jonah, was still slavering to see the great demise:

> Say unto them, As I live, saith the Lord GOD, I have no pleasure in the death of the wicked; but that the wicked turn from his way and live: turn ye, turn ye from your evil ways; for why will ye die, O house of Israel? (Ezekiel 33:11)

Even the very wicked King Ahab repented when Elijah the prophet predicted Israel's doom. And, in spite of how wicked he had been, God says,

> *Seest thou how Ahab humbleth himself before me? because he humbleth himself before me, I will not bring the evil in his days: but in his son's days will I bring the evil upon his house.* (1 Kings 21:29)

The punishment, apparently, passed on to the sons because they did not repent as their father had.

Sometimes God did not do as he had predicted because the prophets acted as mediators between God and his people. When God told Moses he would destroy the people of Israel because they had turned to worshiping an idol cast out of gold right after God had delivered them from Egypt, Moses implored God to repent of that promise, and God did repent (i.e., change). Likewise, when Amos asked God to repent from carrying out the vision of Israel's destruction, which God had given Amos, God did repent (Exodus 32:7–14 and Amos 7:1–6). These events portray beautifully the dynamic relationship between God and his people. It is true relationship—true give and take—and the smaller party is given respect by the Almighty.

Even those New Testament prophecies that relate to the end times give some hint that God may repent regarding the doom he has predicted. In predicting the fall of Jerusalem and the end of the world, Jesus said,

> *Watch ye therefore, and pray always, that ye may be accounted worthy to escape all these things that shall come to pass, and to stand before the Son of man.* (Luke 21:36)

Why pray for a certain outcome if the outcome is entirely predetermined? Though the events, themselves, may not be stopped, some individuals may escape them, whether by death or sanctuary or maybe even rapture. When Jerusalem fell, some did escape, not by death nor by rapture, but by the ordinary method of running. And perhaps that's all this means for the future, if it still has a future reference.

Even the original prophecy Jesus alludes to when he describes the darkening of the sun, moon, and stars in the end times indicates that repentance on the part of the people may change the course of events:

> Blow the trumpet in Zion, sanctify a fast, call a solemn assembly: Gather the people, sanctify the congregation, assemble the elders, gather the children, and those that nurse at the breasts: let the bridegroom go forth from his chamber, and the bride out of her room. Let the priests, the ministers of the LORD, weep between the porch and the altar, and let them say, Spare thy people, O LORD, and give not thy heritage to reproach, that the nations should rule over them: why should they say among the people, Where is their God? Then will the LORD be jealous for his land, and pity his people. And the LORD will answer and say to his people, Behold, I will send you grain, and wine, and oil, and ye shall be satisfied with it: and I will no more make you a reproach among the nations: But I will remove far from you the northern army, and will drive him into a land barren and desolate, with his face toward the east sea, and his rear toward the west sea, and his stink shall come up, and his ill savour shall come up, because he hath done great [arrogant] things.
>
> (JOEL 2:15–20)

Jesus also said,

> But pray ye that your flight be not in the winter, neither on the sabbath day [because Jews could not run on the sabbath].
>
> (MATTHEW 24:20)

Why pray if the time of their flight was already prescheduled?

There appears to be much room for human choice within God's plans. The mere breath of prayer and repentance will influence the patterns of destiny, just as a butterfly flapping its wings might conceivably change the weather patterns of the world.

The dynamic of human choice in connection with God's choice over human destiny is particularly evident in verses regarding the human soul and its individual destiny:

> . . . God hath from the beginning chosen you to salvation through sanctification [making holy by means] of the Spirit and belief of the truth: To which he called you by our gospel, to the obtaining of the glory of our Lord Jesus Christ.
>
> (2 THESSALONIANS 2:13B, 14)

For whom he did foreknow, he also did predestinate to be conformed to the image of his Son, that he might be the firstborn among many brethren. Moreover whom he did predestinate, them he also called: and whom he called, them he also justified: and whom he justified, them he also glorified.

(ROMANS 8:29, 30)

It all begs the question, "If God foreknows all events, how can humans have any choice?" If God cannot be wrong, then anything God knows in advance must happen. Major theological battles have been fought over this conundrum. Until we understand time, however, we are not likely to understand the relationship between destiny (or predestination) and human choice. Suffice it to say that the Bible says much more about human choice—as though it truly matters—than it does about predestination. Some solve the dilemma by claiming that God does *not* foreknow all events. Others are content to live with the mystery and accept it as a matter of incomplete knowledge.

PROPHETIC FAITH TO LIVE BY

As John comes to the close of his vision, he makes it clear that one of the most basic purposes of prophecy is to guide people into a present life that evolves into eternity. The message of the prophet is that eternity begins now:

And he said to me, These words are faithful and true: and the Lord God of the holy prophets sent his angel to show to his servants the things which must shortly be done. Behold, I come quickly: blessed is he that keepeth the words of the prophecy of this book. And I John saw these things, and heard them. And when I had heard and seen, I fell down to worship before the feet of the angel who showed me these things. Then saith he to me, See thou do it not: for I am thy fellowservant, and of thy brethren the prophets, and of them who keep the words of this book: worship God. And he saith to me, Seal not the words of the prophecy of this book: for the time is at hand. He that is unjust, let him be unjust still: and he who is filthy, let him be filthy still: and he that is righteous, let him be righteous still: and he that is holy, let him be holy still. (REVELATION 22:6–11)

The kingdom of God has already begun like a seed planted in the human soul. John is told to let the seed grow. Let the wheat and the tares (the good and the bad) continue to grow side by side right up to the end, just as Jesus said in his parable. John is not told to eradicate heresy or evil by force in order bring on the kingdom of God. Taking violence against evil—or even forcing another's choice—is not the way. Trust the good to prevail in the end. Deliberate ignorance, however, is no excuse.

Imperial Christianity darkened the ages of history when its leaders failed to understand the non-violent heart of Christ. Instead of humility, they worshipped hierarchy. Instead of peace, they reached for power. Real Christianity, on the other hand, is what Renaissance scholar C. S. Lewis called "mere" Christianity. It is not concerned with personal power but with personal transformation.

> . . . Verily I say unto you, Except ye be converted, and become as little children, ye shall not enter into the kingdom of heaven. Whosoever therefore shall humble himself as this little child, the same is greatest in the kingdom of heaven. . . . Take heed that ye despise not one of these little ones; for I say unto you, That in heaven their angels do always behold the face of my Father which is in heaven. . . . But Jesus said, Permit the little children, and forbid them not, to come to me: for of such is the kingdom of heaven.
>
> (MATTHEW 18:3, 4, 10; 19:14)

> But he that is greatest among you shall be your servant. And whoever shall exalt himself shall be abased; and he that shall humble himself shall be exalted.
>
> (MATTHEW 23:11, 12)

Humility comes from confidence in the goodness and justice and love of God. Mere Christianity is not intimidated by the vast darkness surrounding it because it trusts the truth to prevail. It splits the darkness with light. Mere Christianity warms and enlightens souls with its spark of divine revelation. Mere Christians can be confident good will prevail against all odds because the Apocalypse has revealed that much to them in advance.

> Being confident of this very thing, that he who hath begun a good work in you will perform it until the day of Jesus Christ: . . . And this I pray, that your love may abound yet more and more in knowledge and in all [good] judgment; That ye may approve things that are excellent; that ye may be sincere and without offence till the day of Christ.
>
> (PHILIPPIANS 1:6, 9, 10)

One side of the entire prophetic story, starting with the statue in Nebuchadnezzar's dream, is of the quest for power—for world dominion—all that opposes mere Christianity. Most of the time this battle is as small as one individual trying to dominate another—on the play field, in the home, or in the marketplace. The root of human evil knows no foreign soil. When all is said and done, the final goal of all prophecy is to call individuals out of their self-preoccupation to true religion and to a true revelation of God within themselves—which is the spirit of Jesus Christ dwelling within those who give themselves to him as a bride gives herself to her husband and a husband to his bride.

And what is true religion?

Pure religion ... before God and the Father is this, To visit the fatherless and widows in their affliction, and to keep [oneself] unspotted from the world.

(JAMES 1:27)

Is not this the fast [the religious act] that I have chosen? to loose the bands of wickedness, to undo the heavy burdens, and to let the oppressed go free, and that ye break every yoke? Is it not to deal thy bread to the hungry, and that thou shouldest bring the poor that are cast out to thy house? when thou seest the naked, that thou shouldest cover him; and that thou shouldest not hide thyself from thy own flesh?

Then shall thy light break forth as the morning, and thy health shall spring forth speedily: and thy righteousness shall go before thee; the glory of the LORD shall be thy rear guard. Then shalt thou call, and the LORD shall answer; thou shalt cry, and he shall say, Here I am. If thou shalt take away from the midst of thee the yoke, the putting forth of the finger, and speaking vanity; And if thou shalt draw out thy soul to the hungry, and satisfy the afflicted soul; then shall thy light rise in obscurity, and thy darkness be as the noonday: And the

LORD shall guide thee continually, and satisfy thy soul in drought, and make fat thy bones: and thou shalt be like a watered garden, and like a spring of water, whose waters fail not. And they that shall be of thee shall build the old waste places: thou shalt raise up the foundations of many generations; and thou shalt be called, The repairer of the breach [in the wall], The restorer of paths to dwell in.

If thou shalt turn away thy foot from the sabbath, from doing thy pleasure on my holy day; and call the sabbath a delight, the holy of the LORD, honourable; and shalt honour him, not doing thy own ways, nor finding thy own pleasure, nor speaking thy own words: Then shalt thou delight thyself in the LORD; and I will cause thee to ride upon the high places of the earth, and feed thee with the heritage of Jacob thy father: for the mouth of the LORD hath spoken it.

(ISAIAH 58:6–14)

True religion opens the heart outward to others. Instead of an endless inner searching of the soul, it is an opening of the soul to a light from beyond that shines within. The insecure soul cannot reach out to others. It is too concerned about clutching what it has and grasping for a little more. The soul illuminated by faith is freed to feed the hungry and help the afflicted, to share what it has with others. Thus, the kingdom begins bringing light to earth today and continues into a more glorious eternity. The sabbath millennium is always as imminent as the willingness of all people to turn to such noble selfless principles. Yet, the prophets recognized that not everyone will turn. So, let evil continue until it brings its own destruction. Meanwhile, let the righteous focus on doing what is right, instead of shaking their fingers at evil.

This does not mean being complacent about evil when it is in one's power to protect others from it. The prophets were never complacent about evil, but too much "putting forth of the finger," allows evil to distract one from true righteous living and usually comes across as self-righteous anyway. The "mere" Christian lives by the proverb, "It's better to light one candle than stand and curse the darkness."

> Depart from evil, and do good; and dwell for evermore. For the LORD loveth judgment, and forsaketh not his saints; they are preserved for ever: but the seed of the wicked shall be cut off. The righteous shall inherit the land, and dwell therein for ever. . . . Wait on the LORD, and keep his way, and he shall exalt thee to inherit the land: when the wicked are cut off, thou shalt see it. . . . Mark the perfect man, and behold the upright: for the end of that man is peace. But the transgressors shall be destroyed together: the end of the wicked shall be cut off. But the salvation of the righteous is of the LORD: he is their strength in the time of trouble. And the LORD shall help them, and deliver them: he shall deliver them from the wicked, and save them, because they trust in him.
>
> (PSALM 37:27–29, 34, 37–40)

The end is always as near as the present, for how we live today shapes the end and, especially, our own particular place in it:

> And whatever ye do, do it heartily, as to the Lord, and not to men; Knowing that from the Lord ye shall receive the reward of the inheritance: for ye serve the Lord Christ. But he that doeth wrong shall receive for the wrong which he hath done: and there is no respect of persons.
>
> (COLOSSIANS 3:23–25)

In other words, Jew or Gentile, rich or poor, male or female, God will judge the works of each person impartially. If one does good for praise from his or her fellow human beings, he or she may fail when the praise is not forthcoming. Those who live by the light of prophecy do what they do because they know it is right before God, regardless of whether anyone notices:

> Take heed that ye do not your alms before men, to be seen by them: otherwise ye have no reward from your Father who is in heaven. Therefore when thou doest thy alms, do not sound a trumpet before thee, as the hypocrites do in the synagogues and in the streets, that they may have glory from men. Verily I say to you, They have their reward. But when thou doest alms, let not thy left hand know what thy right hand doeth: That thy alms may be in secret: and thy Father who seeth in secret himself shall reward thee openly. And when thou prayest,

thou shalt not be as the hypocrites are: for they love to pray standing in the synagogues and in the corners of the streets, that they may be seen by men. Verily I say to you, They have their reward. But thou, when thou prayest, enter into thy closet, and when thou hast shut thy door, pray to thy Father who is in secret; and thy Father who seeth in secret shall reward thee openly.

. . . if ye forgive men their trespasses, your heavenly Father will also forgive you: But if ye forgive not men their trespasses, neither will your Father forgive your trespasses. Moreover when ye fast, be not, as the hypocrites, of a sad countenance: for they disfigure their faces, that they may appear to men to fast. Verily I say to you, They have their reward. But thou, when thou fastest, anoint thy head, and wash thy face; That thou mayest not appear to men to fast, but to thy Father who is in secret: and thy Father, who seeth in secret, shall reward thee openly. Lay not up for yourselves treasures upon earth, where moth and rust doth corrupt, and where thieves break through and steal: But lay up for yourselves treasures in heaven, where neither moth nor rust doth corrupt, and where thieves do not break through nor steal: For where your treasure is, there will your heart be also. (MATTHEW 6:1–6, 14–21)

When someone receives evil in return for the good they have done, the only thing that will strengthen them to persevere in the good is faith in the revealed end. That's living in the light of prophecy. If one lives for the end times all the time, one needn't be concerned about the end:

And behold, I come quickly; and my reward is with me, to give to every man according as his work shall be.
(REVELATION 22:12)

Behold, the Lord GOD will come with strong hand, and his arm shall rule for him: behold, his reward is with him, and his work before him. He shall feed his flock like a shepherd: he shall gather the lambs with his arm, and carry them in his bosom, and shall gently lead those that are with young.
(ISAIAH 40:10, 11)

More important than doing good, however, is being good. God cares more about who we are than what we do, and sustainable good deeds are the overflow of a good heart:

And besides this, giving all diligence, add to your faith virtue; and to virtue knowledge; And to knowledge self-control; and to self-control patience; and to patience godliness; And to godliness brotherly kindness; and to brotherly kindness charity. For if these things are in you, and abound, they make you that ye shall neither be barren nor unfruitful in the knowledge of our Lord Jesus Christ. But he that lacketh these things is blind, and cannot see afar off, and hath forgotten that he was purified from his old sins. Therefore the rather, brethren, give diligence to make your calling and election sure: for if ye do these things, ye shall never fall: For so an entrance shall be ministered to you abundantly into the everlasting kingdom of our Lord and Saviour Jesus Christ.

. . . Therefore, beloved, seeing that ye look for such things, be diligent that ye may be found by him in peace, without spot, and blameless.

(2 PETER 1:5–10; 3:14)

CHRIST THE MESSIAH:
THE LIGHT OF PROPHETIC FAITH

John's vision closes, as it began, with an image of the Messiah standing before him:

I am Alpha and Omega, the beginning and the end, the first and the last. Blessed are they that do his commandments, that they may have right to the tree of life, and may enter in through the gates into the city. For outside are dogs, and sorcerers, and immoral persons, and murderers, and idolaters, and whoever loveth and maketh a lie. I Jesus have sent my angel to testify to you these things in the churches. I am the root and the offspring of David, and the bright and morning star. (REVELATION 22:13–16)

Even more important than who you are is whose you are. Ultimately, only those who have messianic faith will enter into communion with God, for the Messiah is the gate. Those who choose to remain outside of God's covenant with humanity will remain outside of his presence:

Then Peter said to them, Repent ye, and each one of you be baptized in the name of Jesus Christ for the remission of sins, and ye shall receive the gift of the Holy Spirit. For the promise is to you, and to your children, and to all that are afar off, even as many as the Lord our God shall call.

. . . Neither is there salvation in any other: for there is no other name under heaven given among men, by which we must be saved. (ACTS 2:38, 39; 4:12)

That if thou shalt confess with thy mouth the Lord Jesus, and shalt believe in thy heart that God hath raised him from the dead, thou shalt be saved. For with the heart man believeth to righteousness; and with the mouth confession is made to salvation. For the scripture saith, Whoever believeth on him shall not be ashamed. . . . For whoever shall call upon the name of the Lord shall be saved. (ROMANS 10:9–11, 13)

The ultimate mystery and revelation of prophecy is the Messiah, whom John describes as being from the beginning with God and in the end with God—the Alpha and Omega. Those who join the Messiah shall be joined with God. For God originally spoke about the Messiah through his Jewish prophets, but in the end he spoke about himself through the Jewish Messiah, who became the last of those prophets whose words are still regarded as sacred:

God, who at many times and in many ways spoke in time past to the fathers by the prophets, Hath in these last days spoken to us by his Son, whom he hath appointed heir of all things, by whom also he made the worlds; Who being the brightness of his glory, and the express image of his person, and upholding all things by the word of his power, when he had by himself made purification for our sins, sat down on the right hand of the Majesty on high; Being made so much better than the angels, as he hath by inheritance obtained a more excellent name than they. For to which of the angels said he at any time, Thou art my Son, this day have I begotten thee? And again, I will be to him a Father, and he shall be to me a Son? And again, when he bringeth in the firstbegotten into the world, he saith, And let all the angels of God worship him. And of the angels he saith, Who maketh his angels spirits, and his ministers a flame of fire. But to the Son he saith, Thy throne, O God, is for ever and ever: a sceptre of righteousness is the sceptre of thy kingdom. Thou hast loved righteousness, and hated iniquity; therefore God, even thy God, hath anointed thee with the oil of gladness above thy companions. And, Thou, Lord, in the beginning hast laid the foundation of the earth; and the heavens are the works of thy hands: They shall perish; but thou remainest; and they all shall become old as doth a garment; And as a vesture shalt thou fold them up, and they shall be changed: but thou art the same, and thy years shall not fail.

(HEBREWS 1:1–12)

Under the laws of Moses, the Jews were forbidden to make images of God, for no human hands could craft an image of God, but the writer of Hebrews claims Jesus is the express image of God. He is that which was made without human hands—the one who was prophesied by Daniel to come from heaven to destroy all corrupt earthly empires. The God who inscribed his words into stone tablets for Moses to give to the Jewish people breathed himself into Jewish flesh for all people—to become a light that his people had not been. He chose a human voice of his own because he desires human relationship.

Jesus described his unique role in fulfilling Jewish prophecy at the last Passover supper he ate with his disciples prior to his death:

. . . he took the cup, when he had supped, saying, This cup is the new testament [New Covenant] in my blood: this do ye, as often as ye drink it, in remembrance of

me. For as often as ye eat this bread, and drink this cup, ye do show the Lord's death till he shall come. Therefore whoever shall eat this bread, and drink this cup of the Lord, unworthily, shall be guilty of the body and blood of the Lord. But let a man examine himself, and so let him eat of that bread, and drink of that cup. For he that eateth and drinketh unworthily, eateth and drinketh judgment to himself, not discerning the Lord's body. (1 CORINTHIANS 11:25–29)

Jesus' claim before his disciples was that *he* is the fulfillment of the Jewish Passover celebration. Like the lamb that was traditionally sacrificed for the Jewish Passover meal to commemorate Israel's salvation from death in Egypt, he would be sacrificed for the salvation of the people during their Passover week. He also is implying that rejection of the Messiah is rejection of the New Covenant that abolished sacrifice forever. Earlier prophets had claimed Jerusalem would always be protected by God, *unless* its people rejected God or his covenant. Prophecy and later events would seem to favor Jesus' statement that he was God's New Covenant.

The Old Testament prophet Isaiah forewarned,

Ho, every one that thirsteth, come ye to the waters, and he that hath no money; come ye, buy, and eat; yea, come, buy wine and milk without money and without price. Why do ye spend money for that which is not bread? and your labour for that which satisfieth not? hearken diligently to me, and eat ye that which is good, and let your soul delight itself in fatness. And now, O inhabitants of Jerusalem, and men of Judah, judge, I pray you, between me and my vineyard [Israel]. What more could have been done to [cultivate] my vineyard, that I have not done in it? Why, when I expected that it should bring forth grapes, brought it forth wild grapes? And now come; I will tell you what I will do to my vineyard: I will take away its hedge [protection], and it shall be eaten up; and break down the wall of it, and it shall be trodden down: Seek ye the LORD while he may be found, call ye upon him while he is near: Let the wicked forsake his way, and the unrighteous man his thoughts: and let him return to the LORD, and he will have mercy upon him; and to our God, for he will abundantly pardon. For my thoughts are not your thoughts, neither are your ways my ways, saith the LORD. For as the heavens are higher than the earth, so are my ways higher than your ways, and my thoughts than your thoughts. For as the rain cometh down, and the snow from heaven, and returneth not there, but watereth the earth, and maketh it bring forth and bud, that it may give seed to the sower, and bread to the eater: So shall my word be that proceedeth from my mouth: it shall not return to me void, but it shall accomplish that which I please, and it shall prosper in the thing for which I sent it. (ISAIAH 55:1–11)

The Apocalypse refers to Jesus as both the Word of God and the Lamb. The Lamb that was slain continually holds out the olive branch of peace and restoration for those who will respond and accept the New Covenant on its own terms. As his coming draws near and the full number of Gentiles joins him, he will have only one people left to reach out to. The people who were first shall be last, but in the end, *all* shall be restored as one new creation:

> *And the Spirit and the bride say, Come.*
> *And let him that heareth say, Come. And*
> *let him that is thirsty come. And whoever*
> *will, let him take the water of life freely.*
> (REVELATION 22:17).

AFTERWORD:

THE END IS NEAR

The end of the *world* may or may not be near, but the end of this book is. And so it seems most appropriate to close by acknowledging the final warning of the Apocalypse:

> For I testify to every man that heareth the words of the prophecy of this book, If any man shall add to these things, God shall add to him the plagues that are written in this book: And if any man shall take away from the words of the book of this prophecy, God shall take away his part out of the book of life, and out of the holy city, and from the things which are written in this book.
>
> (REVELATION 22:18–19)

The Apocalypse is perfect in form and function. The simple changing of a number from four to five would destroy the entire meaning of a passage because numbers in the Apocalypse mean much more than their mathematical value. Even the misplaced name of a Jewish tribe could be intentional to trigger deeper study. The apparent mistake must not be corrected by later copyists. And so the author made it clear that nothing—no matter how puzzling—was to be adjusted for clarification. The book was to be copied from generation to generation precisely as it had been written. Because even the structure of the Apocalypse appears to convey meaning, it has been presented in this book in its original order as found in the Bible, and all other prophecies have been woven around it.

AUTHOR'S DISCLAIMER

The prophecies recorded in this book contain mysteries too deep for a human mind to sound their bottom. One easily gets lost merely staring into their unfathomed depths.

Because this book was intended to pull together as many of the end-time prophecies of the Bible as could be identified, it has not been possible to fully develop all major positions regarding their interpretation. In the end, only God's revelation has the final word on what his prophecies mean.

Simply linking passages together as I've done in this book can distort meaning if the wrong links are forged. If the reader sees a more natural fit for any prophecy than where it has been placed, he or she should explore that connection. With that in mind, the greatest benefit from this book may come from being able to reread all (or, at least, most) of the Bible's end-time revelations by browsing through the italicized text. Hopefully some of my own commentary in between provides beneficial insights about the spiritual realm that surrounds us and is within us, but any insight into mysteries so deep is bound to prove shortsighted in the distant scope of time.

It's best to keep one's opinions about God's revelation fluid and allow the God who makes all things new to shape one's opinions over time and to reshape oneself in the process. A dogmatic stance on words the Bible, itself, describes as ultimate mysteries belittles the greatness of God. It presumptuously assumes that the human mind can fully comprehend God's mysteries.

The ambiguities of apocalyptic symbolism are not intended so much for answering questions as for stimulating them. Reading and rereading these poetic images keeps the mind fluid and alive, spiritually and intellectually. They are living words, which is to say moving words, just as "living water" means "flowing water." They may not be intended to map out the future so much as they are intended to influence the future by influencing us.

Thus, John ends his book much as he began it: "Do not seal up the words of the prophecy of this book, because the time is near," and "Blessed is he who keeps the words of the prophecy in this book." There are answers to be found in the Apocalypse and in the other prophecies of the Bible, but never enough answers to fill all our questions. In this garden of verses, every stone one turns over reveals two or more stones beneath. Every answer leads to more questions. As nature abhors a vacuum, so human nature abhors unanswered questions. Constantly digging up more questions may cause the timid to give up in despair; alternately, it can drive us on an eternal quest. That is what makes these living words: they keep the mind engaged. It is the eternal quest that John hopes the reader will begin.

Revelation is neither sealed in the sense of being completely impossible to understand, nor is it sealed in the sense of being possible to completely understand. It is an open book for open minds. Its images have haunted and perplexed people for millennia. Images, by nature, refuse finite definitions and leave room for interpretation, which is a problem for the twentieth-century mind, impatient for answers, short on attention, and accustomed to hard scientific fact.

Prophetic images go beyond doctrine. They are for meditating upon. They work in the domain of the subconscious. The mind that meditates on these images meditates on the indefinable God. Do not expect this God to come into perfect resolution. If you understand him completely, you do not understand him at all, for you have made him much too small. Though he communes with the human soul, he cannot be contained by it. Trying to fit God into a human brain will burst the brain. No one can "see the face of God" and live.

> Our glib . . . distinctions are . . . defeated by the seamless yet ever-varying texture of reality, the liveness, the elusiveness, the intertwined harmonies of the multidimensional fertility of God.[1]

So let the reader be clear as to which words in this book are God's revelation and which are the words of this writer. Meditate on the prophecies in this book until you dream about them. Let them rearrange themselves before you like a kaleidoscope of infinite pieces of revelation, fragments of history and future tumbling together in new, yet familiar, patterns, infinite fractal designs that trace the fingerprint of God on human events. Let them pool in the shadowy eddies of your mind. Let them well up unexpectedly in your sleeping and in your waking. They are living water for the soul.

Despise not prophesyings. Examine all things; hold fast that which is good. . . . And the very God of peace sanctify you wholly; and I pray God your whole spirit and soul and body may be preserved blameless to the coming of our Lord Jesus Christ. (1 THESSALONIANS 5:20, 21, 23)

He which testifieth these things saith, Surely I come quickly. Amen. Even so, come, Lord Jesus. The grace of our Lord Jesus Christ be with you all. Amen.

(REVELATION 22:20–21)

MORE END-TIME PROPHECIES

Some of the prophecies relating to end times have been included in this appendix for three reasons: First, some themes related to the end times receive more coverage in the Bible than could be dealt with in the preceding chapters. In cases where there were too many prophecies on a given theme to include all of them in their appropriate chapter, those that seemed most representative were placed in the chapter, and the additional material was kept for this appendix. Second, some prophecies are virtual repeats of others that were already used in a chapter. Third, Appendix A also includes a number of prophetic passages that may have already seen the only fulfillment they're going to, yet their language hints at broader possibilities. The following prophecy, which opens the book of Zephaniah, is a good example:

I [God] will utterly consume all things from off the land, saith the LORD. I will consume man and beast; I will consume the fowls of the heaven, and the fishes of the sea, and the stumblingblocks with the wicked; and I will cut off man from off the land, saith the LORD. I will also stretch out my hand upon Judah, and upon all the inhabitants of Jerusalem; and I will cut off the remnant of Baal from this place, and the name of the Chemarims with the priests; And them that worship the host of heaven upon the housetops; and them that worship and that swear by the LORD, and that swear by Malcham; And them that have turned back from the LORD; and those that have not sought the LORD, nor enquired for him.

Hold thy peace at the presence of the Lord GOD: for the day of the LORD is at hand: for the LORD hath prepared a sacrifice, he hath invited his guests. And it shall come to pass in the day of the LORD'S sacrifice, that I will punish the princes, and the king's children, and all such as are clothed with foreign apparel. In the same day also will I punish all those that leap on the threshold, who fill their masters' houses with violence and deceit. And it shall come to pass in that day, saith the LORD, that there shall be the noise of a cry from the fish gate, and a wailing from the second, and a great crashing from the hills. Wail, ye inhabitants of Maktesh, for all the merchant people are cut down; all they that bear silver are cut off. And it shall come to pass at that time, that I will search Jerusalem with lamps, and punish the men that are settled on their lees: that say in their heart, The LORD will not do good, neither will he do evil. Therefore their goods shall become a booty, and their houses a desolation: they shall also build houses, but not inhabit them; and they shall plant vineyards, but not drink the wine of them.

The great day of the LORD is near, it is near, and hasteneth greatly, even the voice of the day of the LORD: the mighty man shall cry there bitterly. That day is a day of wrath, a day of trouble and distress, a day of wasting and desolation, a day of darkness and gloominess, a day of clouds and thick darkness, A day of the trumpet and alarm against the fortified cities, and against the high towers. And I will bring distress upon men, that they shall walk like blind men, because they have sinned against the LORD: and their blood shall be poured out as dust, and their flesh as the dung. Neither their silver nor their gold shall be able to deliver them in the day of the LORD'S wrath; but the whole land shall be devoured by the fire of his jealousy: for he shall make even a speedy riddance of all them that dwell in the land.   (ZEPHANIAH 1:2–18)

This prophecy specifically describes the fall of Jerusalem and its surrounding land to Babylonian invaders, but it speaks in such sweeping language it seems to indicate that the doom of Israel would encompass the whole world. The word translated "land" may also be translated "earth" where the prophecy says, " I will utterly consume all things from off the *land* [earth], saith the LORD. . . . Neither their silver nor their gold shall be able to deliver them in the day of the Lord's wrath; but the whole *land* [earth] shall be devoured by the fire of his jealousy: for he shall make even a speedy riddance of all them that dwell in the *land* [earth]." Though this prophecy could speak of global destruction (foreshadowed by Israel's own destruction), its language is not as elevated as most apocalyptic language, including that which comes later in Zephaniah; therefore, it is placed in the back of the book.

All the prophecies that follow have been organized thematically to correspond to the preceding chapters. Each group is subtitled with the leading word of the chapter title it corresponds to so that themes of specific chapters can be explored further, according to individual interest. Where there is no subtitle corresponding to a previous chapter, all the identifiable prophecies on that theme are already in the main body of the book. Some of the early chapters of the book supplied background information that is essential for understanding end-time prophecies but is not specifically end-time prophecy; for example, the destruction of Jerusalem. No additional prophecies related to those background topics are included in this appendix, which is intended solely to make the book comprehensive in its coverage of the *end times*.

Because this is the self-guided part of the journey, there is very little commentary to interrupt or guide the reader's own musings. What brief commentary seemed necessary to establish context is included in brackets inserted into or just preceding the prophetic text.

COVENANTS AND CONFLICT

[The first prophecy below actually refers to a covenant made between the ancient Israelite king, Hezekiah, and the king of Assyria; but some recent interpreters think it applies to a covenant that will be formed between the Antichrist and modern Israel. Josephus records its fulfillment in *Antiquities of the Jews*, X.I.]

Therefore hear the word of the LORD, ye scornful men, that rule this people who are in Jerusalem. Because ye have said, We have made a covenant with death, and with hell are we in agreement; when the overflowing scourge shall pass through, it shall not reach us: for we have made lies our refuge, and under falsehood have we hid ourselves: Therefore thus saith the Lord GOD, Behold, I lay in Zion for a foundation a stone, a tried stone, a precious corner stone, a sure foundation: he that believeth shall not make haste. Judgment also will I lay to the line, and righteousness to the plummet: and the hail shall sweep away the refuge of lies, and the waters shall overflow the hiding place. And your covenant with death shall be broken, and your agreement with hell shall not stand; when the overflowing scourge shall pass through, then ye shall be trodden down by it. From the time that it goeth forth it shall take you: for morning by morning shall it pass over, by day and by night: and it shall be a vexation only to understand the report. (ISAIAH 28:14–19)

And now, saith the LORD that formed me from the womb to be his servant, to bring Jacob again to him, Though Israel be not gathered, yet shall I be glorious in the eyes of the LORD, and my God shall be my strength. And he said, It is a light thing that thou shouldest be my servant to raise up the tribes of Jacob, and to restore the preserved of Israel: I will also give thee for a light to the Gentiles, that thou mayest be my salvation to the end of the earth. Thus saith the LORD, the Redeemer of Israel, and his Holy One, to him whom man despiseth, to him whom the nation abhorreth, to a servant of rulers, Kings shall see and arise, princes also shall worship, because of the LORD that is faithful, and the Holy One of Israel, and he shall choose thee. Thus saith the LORD, In an acceptable time have I heard thee, and in a day of salvation have I helped thee: and I will preserve thee, and give thee for a covenant of the people, to establish the earth, to cause to inherit the desolate heritages; That thou mayest say to the prisoners, Go forth; to them that are in darkness, Show yourselves. They shall feed in the ways, and their pastures shall be in all high places. (ISAIAH 49:5–9)

Hearken to me, my people [Israel]; and give ear to me, O my nation: for a law shall proceed from me, and I will make my judgment to rest for a light of the people. My righteousness is near; my sal- *vation is gone forth, and my arms shall judge the people; the isles [or distant coastlands] shall wait upon me, and on my arm shall they trust.*

(ISAIAH 51:4–5)

Then he [Jesus] began to upbraid the cities in which most of his mighty works had been done, because they repented not: Woe to thee, Chorazin! woe to thee, Bethsaida! for if the mighty works, which had been done in you, had been done in Tyre and Sidon [Israel's ancient enemies], they would have repented long ago in sackcloth and ashes. But I say to you, It shall be more tolerable for Tyre *and Sidon at the day of judgment, than for you. And thou, Capernaum, which art exalted to heaven, shalt be brought down to hell: for if the mighty works, which have been done in thee, had been done in Sodom, it would have remained until this day. But I say to you, That it shall be more tolerable for the land of Sodom in the day of judgment, than for thee.* (MATTHEW 11:20–24)

[The following passages are also statements made by Jesus to his fellow Jews.]

The men of Nineveh shall rise in judgment with this generation, and shall condemn it: because they repented at the preaching of Jonah; and, behold, a greater than Jonah is here. The queen of the south shall rise up in the judgment *with this generation, and shall condemn it: for she came from the ends of the earth to hear the wisdom of Solomon; and, behold, a greater than Solomon is here.*

(MATTHEW 12:41, 42)

The queen of the south shall rise up in the judgment with the men of this generation, and condemn them: for she came from the utmost parts of the earth to hear the wisdom of Solomon; and, behold, a greater than Solomon is here. The *men of Nineveh shall rise up in the judgment with this generation, and shall condemn it: for they repented at the preaching of Jonah; and, behold, a greater than Jonah is here.*

(LUKE 11:31, 32)

O Jerusalem, Jerusalem, that killest the prophets, and stonest them that are sent to thee; how often would I have gathered thy children together, as a hen gathereth her brood under her wings, and ye would not! Behold, your house [temple] is left *to you desolate: and verily I say to you, Ye shall not see me, until the time shall come when ye shall say, Blessed is he that cometh in the name of the Lord.*

(LUKE 13:34, 35)

And when one of them [the disciples] that sat eating with him heard these things, he said to him [Jesus], Blessed is he that shall eat bread in the kingdom of *God. Then said he to him, A certain man gave a great supper, and invited many: And sent his servant at supper time to say to them that were invited, Come; for* all things are now ready. And they all with one consent began to make excuse. The first said to him, I have bought a piece of ground, and I must needs go and see it: I pray thee have me excused. And another said, I have bought five yoke of oxen, and I go to try them out: I pray thee have me excused. And another said, I have married a wife, and therefore I cannot come. So that servant came, and showed his lord these things. Then the master of the house being angry said to his servant, Go out quickly into the streets and lanes of the city, and bring in here the poor, and the maimed, and the lame, and the blind. And the servant said, Lord, it is done as thou hast commanded, and yet there is room. And the lord said to the servant, Go out into the highways and hedges, and compel them to come in, that my house may be filled. For I say to you, That none of those men who were invited shall taste my supper.

(LUKE 14:15–24)

[The following words of Paul particularly address his fellow Jews who had become Christians.]

For as many as are led by the Spirit of God, they are the sons of God. For ye have not received the spirit of bondage again to fear [under the laws of Moses with all their penalties]; but ye have received the Spirit of adoption [into the New Covenant], by which we cry, Abba, Father. The Spirit himself beareth witness with our spirit, that we are the children of God: And if children, then heirs; heirs of God, and joint-heirs with Christ; if so be that we suffer with him, that we may be glorified together. For I reckon that the sufferings of this present time are not worthy to be compared with the glory which shall be revealed in us.

(ROMANS 8:14–18)

Brethren, my heart's desire and prayer to God for Israel is, that they may be saved. For I bear them witness that they have a zeal of God, but not according to knowledge. . . . For the scripture saith, Whoever believeth on him shall not be ashamed. For there is no difference between the Jew and the Greek: for the same Lord over all is rich to all that call upon him. For whoever shall call upon the name of the Lord shall be saved.

(ROMANS 10:1, 2, 11–13)

For finding fault with them [the Jews of ancient Israel], he [God] saith [in the prophecies of Jeremiah], Behold, the days come, saith the Lord, when I will make a new covenant with the house of Israel and with the house of Judah: Not according to the covenant that I made with their fathers in the day when I took them by the hand to lead them out of the land of Egypt; because they continued not in my covenant, and I regarded them not, saith the Lord. For this is the covenant that I will make with the house of Israel after those days, saith the Lord; I will put my laws into their mind, and write them in their hearts: and I will be to them a God, and they shall be to me a people: And they shall not teach every man his neighbour, and every man his brother, saying, Know the Lord: for all *shall know me, from the least to the greatest. For I will be merciful to their unrighteousness, and their sins and their iniquities will I remember no more. In that he saith, A new covenant, he hath made the first old. Now that which decayeth and groweth old is ready to vanish away.* (HEBREWS 8:8–13)

RESTORATION

[Although many of the following prophecies predicted Israel's first restoration after its fall to Assyria and Babylon, they include statements that had no apparent fulfillment in Israel's historic return from exile and that relate to events described in other end-time prophecies, such as Armageddon. There is much within them that would indicate the prophets had another period of restoration in mind than the less fulfilling return from Babylon, which was on their immediate horizon.]

For God will save Zion, and will build the cities of Judah: that they may dwell there, and have it in possession. The seed also of his servants shall inherit it: and they that love his name shall dwell in it. (PSALMS 69:35, 36)

And it shall come to pass in that day, that the Lord shall set his hand again the second time to recover the remnant of his people, which shall be left, from Assyria, and from Egypt, and from Pathros, and from Cush, and from Elam, and from Shinar, and from Hamath, and from the isles of the sea. And he shall set up an ensign for the nations, and shall assemble the outcasts of Israel, and gather together the dispersed of Judah from the four corners of the earth. The envy also of Ephraim shall depart, and the adversaries of Judah shall be cut off: Ephraim shall not envy Judah, and Judah shall not distress Ephraim. But they shall fly upon the shoulders of the Philistines toward the west; they shall spoil them of the east together: they shall lay their hand upon Edom and Moab; and the children of Ammon shall obey them. And the LORD shall utterly destroy the tongue of the Egyptian sea; and with his mighty wind shall he shake his hand over the river, and shall smite it in the seven streams, and make men go over dryshod. And there shall be an highway for the remnant of his people, which shall be left, from Assyria; as it was to Israel in the day that he came up from the land of Egypt. (ISAIAH 11:11–16)

Thus saith the Lord GOD, Behold, I will lift up my hand to the Gentiles, and set up my standard to the people: and they shall bring thy sons in their arms, and thy daughters shall be carried upon their shoulders. And kings shall be thy nursing fathers, and their queens thy nursing mothers: they shall bow to thee with their face toward the earth, and lick up the dust of thy feet; and thou shalt know that I am the LORD: for they shall not be ashamed that wait for me. Shall the prey be taken from the mighty, or the lawful captive delivered? But thus saith the LORD, Even the captives of the mighty shall be taken away, and the prey of the terrible shall be delivered: for I will contend with him that contendeth with thee, and I will save thy children. And I will feed them that oppress thee with their own flesh; and they shall be drunk with their own blood, as with sweet wine: and all flesh shall know that I the LORD am thy Saviour and thy Redeemer, the mighty One of Jacob.

(ISAIAH 49:22–26)

For, lo, the days come, saith the LORD, that I will bring again the captives of my people Israel and Judah, saith the LORD: and I will cause them to return to the land that I gave to their fathers, and they shall possess it. And these are the words that the LORD spoke concerning Israel and concerning Judah. For thus saith the LORD; We have heard a voice of trembling, of fear, and not of peace. Ask ye now, and see whether a man doth travail with child? Why do I see every man with his hands on his loins, as a woman in travail, and all faces are turned into paleness? Alas! for that day is great, so that none is like it: it is even the time of Jacob's trouble; but he shall be saved out of it. For it shall come to pass in that day, saith the LORD of hosts, that I will break his yoke from off thy neck, and will burst thy bonds, and strangers shall no more bring him into subjection: But they shall serve the LORD their God, and David their king, whom I will raise up to them.

Therefore fear thou not, O my servant Jacob, saith the LORD; neither be dismayed, O Israel: for, lo, I will save thee from afar, and thy seed from the land of their captivity; and Jacob shall return, and shall be in rest, and quiet, and none shall make him afraid. For I am with thee, saith the LORD, to save thee: though I make a full end of all nations where I have scattered thee, yet will I not make a full end of thee: but I will correct thee in measure, and will not leave thee altogether unpunished. . . . Therefore all they that devour thee shall be devoured; and all thy adversaries, every one of them, shall go into captivity; and they that plunder thee shall be a spoil, and all that prey upon thee will I give for a prey. For I will restore health to thee, and I will heal thee of thy wounds, saith the LORD; because they called thee an Outcast, saying, This is Zion, whom no man seeketh after.

Thus saith the LORD; Behold, I will bring again the captives of Jacob's tents, and have mercy on his dwellingplaces; and the city shall be built upon her own heap, and the palace shall remain after its manner. And out of them shall proceed thanksgiving and the voice of them that make merry: and I will multiply them, and they shall not be few; I will also glorify them, and they shall not be small. Their children also shall be as in former time, and their congregation shall be established before me, and I will punish all that oppress them. And their nobles shall be from themselves, and their governor shall proceed from the midst of them; and I will cause him to draw near, and he shall approach to me: for who is this that engaged his heart to approach to me? saith the LORD. And ye shall be my people, and I will be your God. Behold, the whirlwind of the LORD goeth forth with fury, a continuing whirlwind: it shall fall with pain upon the head of the wicked. The fierce anger of the LORD shall not return, until he hath done it, and until he hath performed the intents of his heart: in the latter days ye shall consider it.

(JEREMIAH 30:3–11, 16–24)

Behold, I will bring them from the north country, and gather them from the ends of the earth, and with them the blind and the lame, the woman with child and her that travaileth with child together: a great company shall return there. They shall come with weeping, and with supplications will I lead them: I will cause them to walk by the rivers of waters in a straight way, in which they shall not stumble: for I am a father to Israel, and Ephraim is my firstborn. Hear the word of the LORD, O ye nations, and declare it in the isles afar off, and say, He that scattered Israel will gather him, and keep him, as a shepherd doth his flock. For the LORD hath redeemed Jacob, and ransomed him from the hand of him that was stronger than he. Therefore they shall come and sing in the height of Zion, and shall flow together to the goodness of the LORD, for grain, and for wine, and for oil, and for the young of the flock and of the herd: and their soul shall be as a watered garden; and they shall not sorrow any more at all. Then shall the virgin rejoice in the dance, both young men and old together: for I will turn their mourning into joy, and will comfort them, and make them rejoice from their sorrow. And I will abundantly satisfy the soul of the priests with fatness, and my people shall be satisfied with my goodness, saith the LORD. Thus saith the LORD; A voice was heard in Ramah, lamentation, and bitter weeping; Rachel weeping for her children refused to be comforted for her children, because they were not. Thus saith the LORD; Restrain thy voice from weeping, and thy eyes from tears: for thy work shall be rewarded, saith the LORD; and they shall come again from the land of the enemy. And there is hope in thy end, saith the LORD, that thy children shall come again to their own border. . . .

Set thee up waymarks, make thee high heaps: set thy heart toward the highway, even the way which thou wentest: turn again, O virgin of Israel, turn again to these thy cities. How long wilt thou wander about, O thou backsliding daughter? for the LORD hath created a new thing in the earth, A woman shall encompass a man. Thus saith the LORD of hosts, the God of Israel; As yet they shall use this speech in the land of Judah and in its cities, when I shall bring again their captives; The LORD bless thee, O habitation of justice, mountain of holiness. And there shall dwell in Judah itself, and in all its cities together, farmers, and they that go forth with flocks. For I have abundantly satisfied the weary soul, and I have replenished every sorrowful soul. Upon this I awoke, and beheld; and my sleep was sweet to me.

Behold, the days come, saith the LORD, that I will sow the house of Israel and the house of Judah with the seed of man, and with the seed of beast. And it shall come to pass, that as I have watched over them, to pluck up, and to break down, and to throw down, and to destroy, and to afflict; so will I watch over them, to build, and to plant, saith the

LORD. In those days they shall say no more, The fathers have eaten a sour grape, and the children's teeth are set on edge. But every one shall die for his own iniquity: every man that eateth the sour grape, his teeth shall be set on edge.

(JEREMIAH 31:8–17, 21–30)

Behold, I will gather them out of all countries, where I have driven them in my anger, and in my fury, and in great wrath; and I will bring them again to this place, and I will cause them to dwell in safety: And they shall be my people, and I will be their God: And I will give them one heart, and one way, that they may fear me for ever, for the good of them, and of their children after them: And I will make an everlasting covenant with them, that I will not turn away from them, to do them good; but I will put my fear in their hearts, that they shall not depart from me. Yea, I will rejoice over them to do them good, and I will plant them in this land assuredly with my whole heart and with my whole soul. For thus saith the LORD; As I have brought all this great evil upon this people, so will I bring upon them all the good that I have promised them. And fields shall be bought in this land, of which ye say, It is desolate without man or beast; it is given into the hand of the Chaldeans. Men shall buy fields for money, and sign deeds, and seal them, and take witnesses in the land of Benjamin, and in the places about Jerusalem, and in the cities of Judah, and in the cities of the mountains, and in the cities of the valley, and in the cities of the south: for I will cause their captives to return, saith the LORD. (JEREMIAH 32:37–44)

Moreover the word of the LORD came to Jeremiah, saying, Considerest thou not what this people have spoken, saying, The two families which the LORD hath chosen, he hath even cast them off? thus they have despised my people, that they should be no more a nation before them. Thus saith the LORD; If my covenant is not with day and night, and if I have not appointed the ordinances of heaven and earth; Then will I cast away the seed of Jacob, and David my servant, so that I will not take any of his seed to be rulers over the seed of Abraham, Isaac, and Jacob: for I will cause their captives to return, and have mercy on them.

(JEREMIAH 33:23–26)

But fear not thou, O my servant Jacob, and be not dismayed, O Israel: for, behold, I will save thee from afar, and thy seed from the land of their captivity; and Jacob shall return, and be in rest and at ease, and none shall make him afraid. Fear thou not, O Jacob my servant, saith the LORD: for I am with thee; for I will make a full end of all the nations where I have driven thee: but I will not make a full end of thee, but correct thee in measure; yet will I not leave thee wholly unpunished. (JEREMIAH 46:27, 28)

Therefore say, Thus saith the Lord GOD; Although I have cast them far off among the nations, and although I have scattered them among the countries, yet will I be to them as a little sanctuary in the countries where they shall come. Therefore say, Thus saith the Lord GOD; I will even gather you from the people, and assemble you out of the countries where ye have been scattered, and I will give you the land of Israel. And they shall come there, and they shall take away from there all its detestable things and all its abominations. And I will give them one heart, and I will put a new spirit within you; and I will take the stony heart out of their flesh, and will give them an heart of flesh: That they may walk in my statutes, and keep my ordinances, and do them: and they shall be my people, and I will be their God. (EZEKIEL 11:16–20)

I will overturn, overturn, overturn, it [Israel, as happened under Titus]: and it shall be no more, until he [the Messiah] cometh whose right it is; and I will give it him. (EZEKIEL 21:27)

[The following prophecy, though it is sometimes quoted as an end-time prophecy, may have already seen its only fulfillment in the return from Babylonian exile. Yet, there are verses within it that would appear not to have been fulfilled. It promises a time when the land will no longer be a source of wars and a cause for the loss of Israel's children. So far, such a time has not come.]

But ye, O mountains of Israel, ye shall shoot forth your branches, and yield your fruit to my people of Israel; for they are soon to come. For, behold, I am for you, and I will turn to you, and ye shall be tilled and sown: And I will multiply men upon you, all the house of Israel, even all of it: and the cities shall be inhabited, and the wastes shall be built: And I will multiply upon you man and beast; and they shall increase and bring fruit: and I will settle you according to your old estates, and will do better to you than at your beginnings: and ye shall know that I am the LORD. Yea, I will cause men to walk upon you, even my people Israel; and they shall possess thee, and thou shalt be their inheritance, and thou shalt no more henceforth bereave them of men. Thus saith the Lord GOD; Because they say to you, Thou land devourest men, and hast bereaved thy nations; Therefore thou shalt devour men no more, neither bereave thy nations any more, saith the Lord GOD. Neither will I cause men to hear in thee the shame of the nations any more, neither shalt thou bear the reproach of the people any more, neither shalt thou cause thy nations to fall any more, saith the Lord GOD. (EZEKIEL 36:8–15)

Therefore thus saith the Lord GOD; Now will I bring again the captivity of Jacob [actually meaning "bring back from the captivity of Jacob/Israel"], and have mercy upon the whole house of Israel, and will be jealous for my holy name; After they have borne their shame, and all their trespasses by which they have tres- passed against me, when they dwelt safely in their land, and none made them afraid. When I have brought them again from the people, and gathered them out of the lands of their enemies, and am sanctified in them in the sight of many nations; Then shall they know that I am the LORD their God, who caused them to be led into captivity among the nations: but I have gathered them to their own land, and have left none of them there any more. Neither will I hide my

face any more from them: for I have poured out my spirit upon the house of Israel, saith the Lord GOD.

(EZEKIEL 39:25–29)

In that day will I raise up the tabernacle [tent (or house)] of David that is fallen, and close up its breaches; and I will raise up its ruins, and I will build it as in the days of old: That they may possess the remnant of Edom, and of all the nations, who are called by my name, saith the LORD that doeth this. Behold, the days come, saith the LORD, that the plowman shall overtake the reaper, and the treader of grapes him that soweth seed; and the mountains shall drop sweet

wine, and all the hills shall melt. And I will bring again the captivity of my people of Israel [meaning "bring back from captivity"], and they shall build the waste cities, and inhabit them; and they shall plant vineyards, and drink the wine of them; they shall also make gardens, and eat the fruit of them. And I will plant them upon their land, and they shall no more be pulled up out of their land which I have given them, saith the LORD thy God.   (AMOS 9:11–15)

I will surely assemble, O Jacob, all of thee; I will surely gather the remnant of Israel; I will put them together as the sheep of Bozrah, as the flock in the midst of their fold: they shall make great noise by reason of the multitude of men. The

breaker is come up before them: they have broken up, and have passed through the gate, and have gone out by it: and their king shall pass before them, and the LORD on the head of them.

(MICAH 2:12, 13)

And I will sow them among the people: and they shall remember me in far countries; and they shall live with their children, and turn again. I will bring them again also out of the land of Egypt, and

gather them out of Assyria; and I will bring them into the land of Gilead and Lebanon; and place shall not be found for them.   (ZECHARIAH 10:9, 10)

And they [the Jews] shall come from the east, and from the west, and from the north, and from the south, and shall sit down in the kingdom of God.

(LUKE 13:29)

[The following event is Jesus' final scene with his disciples after his resurrection. It clearly shows the disciples did not consider Israel to be restored as the earlier prophecies (above) regarding Israel's return from Babylon had said it would be. Jesus' answer also implies the restoration of Israel predicted by the prophets still lay ahead.]

To whom [his disciples] . . . he [Jesus] showed himself alive after his passion by

many infallible proofs, being seen by them forty days, and speaking of the things pertaining to the kingdom of God: . . . When they therefore were come together, they asked of him, saying, Lord, wilt thou at this time restore again the kingdom to Israel? And he said to them, It is not for you to know the times or the seasons, which the Father hath put in his own power. (ACTS 1:3, 6, 7)

SIGNS

[The following prophecy is not so much a sign preceding the last days as it is a general condition that will prevail during those times. The context is Jesus predicting the persecutions that would be faced by his own disciples, but it seems likely the times preceding his return will repeat many of the patterns that surrounded his first coming.]

And the brother shall deliver up the brother to death [because one had converted to Christianity], and the father the child: and the children shall rise up against their parents, and cause them to be put to death. And ye shall be hated by all men for my name's sake: but he that endureth to the end shall be saved. But when they persecute you in this city, flee ye into another: for verily I say to you, Ye shall not have gone over the cities of Israel, till the Son of man shall have come. (MATTHEW 10:21–23)

[Much of the following prophecy by Jesus may refer to the time of Jerusalem's fall, but many parts are often quoted as referring to the end times, too. Parts of this prophecy that were included in the main body of the book are omitted here.]

And as he sat upon the mount of Olives opposite the temple, Peter and James and John and Andrew asked him privately, Tell us, when shall these things be? and what shall be the sign when all these things shall be fulfilled?

And Jesus answering them began to say, Take heed lest any man deceive you: For many shall come in my name, saying, I am Christ; and shall deceive many. . . . And the gospel must first be proclaimed among all nations. . . .

But when ye shall see the abomination of desolation, spoken of by Daniel the prophet, standing where it ought not, (let him that readeth understand,) then let them that are in Judaea flee to the mountains: And let him that is on the housetop not go down into the house, neither enter it, to take any thing out of his house: And let him that is in the field not turn back again to take up his garment. But woe to them that are with child, and to them that nurse infants in those days! And pray ye that your flight be not in the winter. For in those days shall be affliction, such as hath not been from the beginning of the creation which God created to this time, neither shall be. And except the Lord had shortened those days, no flesh should be saved: but for the elect's sake, whom he hath chosen, he hath shortened the days. And then if any man shall say to you, Lo, here is Christ; or, lo, he is there; believe him not: For false Christs and false prophets shall rise, and shall show signs and wonders, to seduce, if it were possible, even the elect. But take ye heed: behold, I have foretold you all things. . . .

Now learn a parable of the fig tree; When its branch is yet tender, and putteth forth leaves, ye know that summer is near: So ye in like manner, when ye shall see these things come to pass, know that it is near, even at the doors. . . . For the Son of man is as a man taking a long journey, who left his house, and gave authority to his servants, and to every man his work, and commanded the porter to watch. Watch ye therefore: for ye know not when the master of the house cometh, at evening, or at midnight, or at the cockcrowing, or in the morning: Lest coming suddenly he should find you sleeping. And what I say to you I say to all, Watch.

(MARK 13:3–6, 10, 14–23, 28, 29, 34–37)

For the time will come when they [people in general] will not endure sound doctrine; but after their own lusts shall they heap up to themselves teachers, having itching ears; And they shall turn away their ears from the truth, and shall be turned to fables. (2 TIMOTHY 4:3, 4)

But, beloved, remember ye the words which were spoken before by the apostles of our Lord Jesus Christ; How that they told you there should be mockers in the last time, who should walk after their own ungodly lusts. These are they who separate themselves, sensual, having not the Spirit. (JUDE 1:17–19)

RETURN (INCLUDING RESURRECTION AND RAPTURE)

I have set the LORD always before me: because he is at my right hand, I shall not be moved. Therefore my heart is glad, and my glory rejoiceth: my flesh also shall rest in hope. For thou wilt not leave my soul in hell; neither wilt thou permit thy Holy One to see corruption. Thou wilt show me the path of life: in thy presence is fulness of joy; at thy right hand are pleasures for evermore.

(PSALM 16:8–11)

The hand of the LORD was upon me, and carried me out in the spirit of the LORD, and set me down in the midst of the valley which was full of bones, And caused me to pass by them on every side: and, behold, there were very many in the open valley; and, lo, they were very dry. And he said to me, Son of man, can these bones live? And I answered, O Lord GOD, thou knowest. Again he said to me, Prophesy upon these bones, and say to them, O ye dry bones, hear the word of the LORD. Thus saith the Lord GOD to these bones; Behold, I will cause breath to enter into you, and ye shall live: And I will lay sinews upon you, and will bring up flesh upon you, and cover you with skin, and put breath in you, and ye shall live; and ye shall know that I am the LORD. So I prophesied as I was commanded: and as I prophesied, there was a noise, and behold a shaking, and the bones came together, bone to his bone. And when I beheld, lo, the sinews and the flesh came up upon them, and the skin covered them above: but there was no breath in them. Then said he to me, Prophesy to the wind, prophesy, son of man, and say to the wind, Thus saith the Lord GOD; Come from the four winds, O breath, and breathe upon these slain, that they may live. So I prophesied as he commanded me, and the breath came into them, and they lived, and stood up upon their feet, an exceeding great army. Then he said to me, Son of man, these bones are the whole house of Israel: behold, they say, Our bones are dried, and our hope is lost: we are cut off on our part. Therefore prophesy and say to them, Thus saith the Lord GOD; Behold, O my people, I will open your graves, and cause you to come out of your graves, and bring you into the land of Israel. And ye shall know that I am the LORD, when I have opened your graves, O my people, and brought you out of your graves, And shall put my spirit in you, and ye shall live, and I shall place you in your own land: then shall ye know that I the LORD have spoken it, and performed it, saith the LORD.

(EZEKIEL 37:1–14)

[The following seems to be a promise that those who became true to God during Israel's first restoration from the fall to Babylon would be a part of the resurrection.]

And they shall be mine, saith the LORD of hosts, in that day when I make up my jewels; and I will spare them, as a man spareth his own son that serveth him.

The same day came to him the Sadducees, who say that there is no resurrection, and asked him [a question regarding marriage after the resurrection, to which Jesus answered,] . . . in the resurrection they neither marry, nor are given in marriage, but are as the angels of God in heaven. But as concerning the resurrection of the dead, have ye not read that which was spoken to you by God, saying, I am the God of Abraham, and the God of Isaac, and the God of Jacob? God is not the God of the dead, but of the living.

Then shall ye return, and discern between the righteous and the wicked, between him that serveth God and him that serveth him not. (MALACHI 3:17, 18)

(MATTHEW 22:23, 29–32)

[Concerning the time of Jesus' return.]

Then shall two be in the field; the one shall be taken, and the other left. Two women shall be grinding at the mill; the one shall be taken, and the other left.

(MATTHEW 24:40, 41)

And he [Jesus] said, So is the kingdom of God, as if a man should cast seed into the ground; And should sleep, and rise night and day, and the seed should spring and grow up, he knoweth not how. For the earth bringeth forth fruit of itself; first the blade, then the ear, after that the ripe grain in the head. But when the fruit is brought forth, immediately he putteth in the sickle, because the harvest is come.
(MARK 4:26–29)

[Another version of Jesus' comment to Sadducees regarding marriage after the resurrection.]

For when they shall rise from the dead, they neither marry, nor are given in marriage; but are as the angels who are in heaven. And concerning the dead, that they rise: have ye not read in the book of Moses, how in the bush God spoke to him, saying, I am the God of Abraham, and the God of Isaac, and the God of Jacob? He is not the God of the dead, but the God of the living: ye therefore do greatly err.
(MARK 12:25–27)

Now that the dead are raised, even Moses showed at the bush, when he calleth the Lord the God of Abraham, and the God of Isaac, and the God of Jacob. For he is not a God of the dead, but of the living: for all live to him.
(LUKE 20:37, 38)

... the hour is coming, in which all that are in the graves shall hear his voice, And shall come forth; they that have done good, to the resurrection of life; and they that have done evil, to the resurrection of damnation.
(JOHN 5:28, 29)

And Jesus said to them, I am the bread of life: he that cometh to me shall never hunger; and he that believeth on me shall never thirst. . . . For I came down from heaven, not to do my own will, but the will of him that sent me. And this is the Father's will who hath sent me, that of all which he hath given me I should lose nothing, but should raise them up again at the last day. And this is the will of him that sent me, that every one who seeth the Son, and believeth on him, may have everlasting life: and I will raise him up at the last day. . . . No man can come to me, except the Father who hath sent me draw him: and I will raise him up at the last day. . . . Whoever eateth my flesh, and drinketh my blood, hath eternal life; and I will raise him up at the last day. . . . As the living Father hath sent me, and I live by the Father: so he that eateth me, even he shall live by me. This is that bread which came down from heaven: not as your fathers ate manna, and are dead: he that eateth of this bread shall live for ever.
(JOHN 6:35, 38–40, 44, 54, 57, 58)

Jesus saith to her, Thy brother shall rise again. Martha saith to him, I know that he shall rise again in the resurrection at the last day. Jesus said to her, I am the resurrection, and the life: he that believeth in me, though he were dead, yet shall he live: And whoever liveth and believeth in me shall never die. Believest thou this?
(JOHN 11:23–26)

. . . there shall be a resurrection of the dead, both of the just and unjust.

(ACTS 24:15)

And God hath both raised up the Lord, and will also raise up us by his own power. (1 CORINTHIANS 6:14)

Now if Christ is preached that he rose from the dead, how say some among you that there is no resurrection of the dead? But if there is no resurrection of the dead, then is Christ not risen: And if Christ is not risen, then is our preaching vain, and your faith is also vain. And indeed, we are found false witnesses of God; because we have testified concern-ing God that he raised up Christ: whom he raised not, if in fact the dead rise not. For if the dead rise not, then is not Christ raised: And if Christ is not raised, your faith is vain; ye are yet in your sins. Then they also who have fallen asleep in Christ have perished. If in this life only we have hope in Christ, we are of all men most miserable. (1 CORINTHIANS 15:12–19)

. . . he who raised the Lord Jesus shall raise us [the apostles] also by Jesus, and shall present us with you [Paul's follow-ers—presented like a bride on her wedding day before God and all of creation].

(2 CORINTHIANS 4:14

When Christ, who is our life, shall appear, then shall ye [Paul's followers] also appear with him in glory.

(COLOSSIANS 3:4)

For what is our hope, or joy, or crown of rejoicing? Are not even ye [Paul's follow-ers when they shall be presented] in the presence of our Lord Jesus Christ at his coming? (1 THESSALONIANS 2:19)

Therefore I endure all things [even mar-tyrdom] for the sake of the elect, that they may also obtain the salvation which is in Christ Jesus with eternal glory. . . . For if we are dead with him, we shall also live with him: (2 TIMOTHY 2:11)

Beloved, now are we the sons of God, and it doth not yet appear what we shall be: but we know that, when he shall appear, we shall be like him; for we shall see him as he is. (1 JOHN 3:2)

CONSUMMATION

But I say to you, I will not drink hence-forth of this fruit of the vine, until that day when I drink it new with you in my Father's kingdom. (MATTHEW 26:29)

Verily I say unto you, I will drink no more of the fruit of the vine, until that day that I drink it new in the kingdom of God. (MARK 14:25)

ARMAGEDDON

See now that I, even I [God], am he, and there is no god with me: I kill, and I make alive; I wound, and I heal: neither is there any that can deliver out of my hand. For I lift up my hand to heaven, and say, I live for ever. If I shall whet my glittering sword, and my hand take hold on judgment; I will render vengeance to my enemies, and will reward them that hate me. I will make my arrows drunk with blood, and my sword shall devour flesh; and that with the blood of the slain and of the captives, from the beginning of revenges upon the enemy. Rejoice, O ye nations, with his people: for he will avenge the blood of his servants, and will render vengeance to his adversaries, and will be merciful to his land, and to his people. (DEUTERONOMY 32:39–43)

He raiseth the poor out of the dust, and lifteth the beggar from the dunghill, to set them among princes, and to make them inherit the throne of glory: for the pillars of the earth are the LORD'S, and he hath set the world upon them. He will keep the feet of his saints, and the wicked shall be silent in darkness; for by strength shall no man prevail. The adversaries of the LORD shall be broken to pieces; out of heaven shall he thunder upon them: the LORD shall judge the ends of the earth; and he shall give strength to his king, and exalt the horn of his anointed. (1 SAMUEL 2:8–10)

Be ye afraid of the sword: for wrath bringeth the punishments of the sword, that ye may know there is a judgment. (JOB 19:29)

[The following psalm was probably composed originally for the arrival of the Ark of the Covenant into the temple on Mt. Zion in Jerusalem, but also fits the New Testament images of Christ arriving on Mt. Zion before Armageddon.]

(To the chief Musician, A Psalm or Song of David.) Let God arise, let his enemies be scattered: let them also that hate him flee before him. As smoke is driven away, so drive them away: as wax melteth before the fire, so let the wicked perish at the presence of God. But let the righteous be glad; let them rejoice before God: yea, let them exceedingly rejoice. Sing to God, sing praises to his name: extol him that rideth upon the heavens by his name JAH [shortened form of "Jehovah" (or "Yahweh" in Hebrew)], and rejoice before him. . . .

Why leap ye, ye lofty hills? this is the hill which God desireth to dwell in; yea, the LORD will dwell in it for ever. The chariots of God are twenty thousand, even thousands of angels: the Lord is among them, as in Sinai, in the holy place. Thou hast ascended on high [probably said of King David originally, but anticipating the Messiah who would descend from David], thou hast led captivity captive: thou hast received gifts for men; yea, for the rebellious also, that the LORD God might dwell among them. Blessed be the Lord, who daily loadeth us with benefits, even the God of our salva-tion. Selah. He that is our God is the God of salvation; and to GOD the Lord belong the issues from death. But God shall wound the head of his enemies, and the hairy scalp of such one as goeth on still in his trespasses.

The Lord said, I will bring again from Bashan, I will bring my people again from the depths of the sea: That thy foot may be dipped in the blood of thy enemies, and the tongue of thy dogs in the same. (PSALM 68:1–4, 16–23)

They gather themselves together against the soul of the righteous, and condemn the innocent blood. . . . And he [God] shall bring upon them their own iniq-uity, and shall cut them off in their own wickedness; yea, the LORD our God shall cut them off. (PSALM 94:21, 23)

[From the modern Jewish perspective, this psalm has the voice of one speaking to King David, telling him what God, the Lord, says to the king; from that perspective, it's appropriate the speaker refers to David as "my Lord." The psalm, however, states things that would never have been true about David, and in ancient times the Jews considered it a messianic psalm; that is, one anticipating David's offspring, God's anointed (Messiah).]

(A Psalm of David.) The LORD said to my Lord, Sit thou at my right hand, until I make thine enemies thy footstool. The LORD shall send the rod of thy strength out of Zion: rule thou in the midst of thy enemies. Thy people shall be willing in the day of thy power, in the beauties of holiness from the womb of the morning: thou hast the dew of thy youth. The LORD hath sworn, and will not repent, Thou art a priest for ever after the order of Melchizedek. [Never true of David or any Jewish king.] The Lord at thy right hand shall strike through kings in the day of his wrath. He shall judge among the nations, he shall fill the places with the dead bodies; he shall wound the heads over many countries. He shall drink of the brook in the way: therefore shall he lift up the head.

(PSALM 110:1–7)

[The psalmist speaking on behalf of Israel:]

All nations surrounded me: but in the name of the LORD will I destroy them. They surrounded me; yea, they sur-rounded me: but in the name of the LORD I will destroy them. They surrounded me like bees; they are quenched as the fire of thorns: for in the name of the LORD I will destroy them. Thou hast violently thrust at me that I might fall: but the LORD helped me. The LORD is my strength and song, and is become my salvation. The voice of rejoicing and salvation is in the tabernacles of the righteous: the right hand of the LORD doeth valiantly. The right hand of the LORD is exalted: the right hand of the LORD doeth valiantly. I shall not die, but live, and declare the works of the LORD. The LORD hath chastened me greatly: but he hath not given me over to death.

(PSALM 118:10–18)

[A prophecy likely referring to Jesus of Galilee, who will bring enlightenment to earth with his second coming, just as he did with his first.]

Nevertheless the dimness [darkness of the end] shall not be such as was in her [Jerusalem's] distress [under Babylon], when at the first he lightly afflicted the land of Zebulun and the land of Naphtali, and afterward did more grievously afflict her by the way of the sea, beyond Jordan, in Galilee of the nations. The people that walked in darkness have seen a great light: they that dwell in the land of the shadow of death, upon them hath the light shined. Thou hast multiplied the nation, and to him increased the joy: they rejoice before thee according to the joy in harvest, and as men rejoice when they divide the spoil. For thou hast broken the yoke of his burden, and the staff of his shoulder, the rod of his oppressor, as in the day of Midian. For every battle of the warrior is with confused noise, and garments rolled in blood; but this shall be with burning and fuel of fire.

(ISAIAH 9:1–5)

[The following two prophecies were prophesied originally against Israel's enemy Assyria.]

Moreover the multitude of thy [Jerusalem's] strangers shall be like small dust, and the multitude of the terrible ones shall be as chaff that passeth away: yea, it shall be at an instant suddenly. Thou shalt be visited by the LORD of hosts with thunder, and with earthquake, and great noise, with storm and tempest, and the flame of devouring fire. And the multitude of all the nations that fight against Ariel [Jerusalem], even all that fight against her and her strong hold, and that distress her, shall be as a dream of a night vision. It shall even be as when an hungry man dreameth, and, behold, he eateth; but he awaketh, and his soul is empty: or as when a thirsty man dreameth, and, behold, he drinketh; but he awaketh, and, behold, he is faint, and his soul hath appetite: so shall the multitude of all the nations be, that fight against mount Zion.

(ISAIAH 29:5–8)

And there shall be upon every high mountain, and upon every high hill, rivers and streams of waters in the day of the great slaughter, when the towers fall. Moreover the light of the moon shall be as the light of the sun, and the light of the sun shall be sevenfold, as the light of seven days, in the day that the LORD bindeth up the breach of his people, and healeth the stroke of their wound. Behold, the name of the LORD cometh from far, burning with his anger, and the burden of it is heavy: his lips are full of indignation, and his tongue as a devouring fire: And his breath, as an overflowing stream, shall reach to the midst of the neck, to sift the nations with the sieve of vanity: and there shall be a bridle in the jaws of the people, causing them to err.

Woe to thee [imperial Gentile nations] that layest waste, and thou wast not laid waste; and dealest treacherously, and they [other nations, including Israel] dealt not treacherously with thee! when thou shalt cease to lay waste, thou shalt be wasted; and when thou shalt make an end of dealing treacherously, they shall deal treacherously with thee. O LORD,

Strengthen ye the weak hands, and confirm the feeble knees. Say to them that are of a fearful heart, Be strong, fear not: be-

Behold, all they that were incensed against thee [Israel] shall be ashamed and confounded: they shall be as nothing; and they that contend with thee shall perish. Thou shalt seek them, and shalt not find them, even them that contended with thee: they that war against thee shall be as nothing, and as a thing of nought. For I the LORD thy God will hold thy right hand, saying to thee, Fear

The LORD shall go forth as a mighty man, he shall stir up jealousy like a man of war: he shall cry, yea, roar; he shall prevail against his enemies. I have long time held my peace; I have been still, and restrained myself: now will I cry like a

Ye shall have a song, as in the night when a holy solemnity is kept; and gladness of heart, as when one goeth with a pipe to come upon the mountain of the LORD, to the mighty One of Israel. And the LORD shall cause his glorious voice to be heard, and shall show the lighting down of his arm, with the indignation of his anger, and with the flame of a devouring fire, with scattering, and tempest, and hailstones. (ISAIAH 30:25–30)

be gracious to us; we have waited for thee: be thou their arm every morning, our salvation also in the time of trouble. At the noise of the tumult the people fled; at the lifting up of thyself the nations were scattered. And your spoil shall be gathered like the gathering of the caterpiller: as the running to and fro of locusts shall he run upon them. (ISAIAH 33:1–4)

hold, your God will come with vengeance, even God with a recompence; he will come and save you. (ISAIAH 35:3–4)

not; I will help thee. Fear not, thou worm Jacob, and ye men of Israel; I will help thee, saith the LORD, and thy redeemer, the Holy One of Israel. Behold, I will make thee a new sharp threshing instrument having teeth: thou shalt thresh the mountains, and beat them small, and shalt make the hills as chaff.

(ISAIAH 41:11–15)

travailing woman; I will destroy and devour at once. I will make waste mountains and hills, and dry up all their herbs; and I will make the rivers isles, and I will dry up the pools.

(ISAIAH 42:13–15)

Thus saith the LORD, The labour of Egypt, and merchandise of Cush and of the Sabeans, men of stature, shall come over to thee, and they shall be thine: they shall come after thee; in chains they shall come over, and they shall fall down to thee, they shall make supplication to thee, saying, Surely God is in thee; and there is none else, there is no God. Verily thou art a God that hidest thyself, O God of Israel, the Saviour. They shall be ashamed, and also confounded, all of them: they shall go to confusion together that are makers of idols. But Israel shall be saved in the LORD with an everlasting salvation: ye shall not be ashamed nor confounded world without end.

(ISAIAH 45:14–17)

According to their deeds, accordingly he will repay, fury to his adversaries, recompence to his enemies; to the isles he will repay recompence. So shall they fear the name of the LORD from the west, and his glory from the rising of the sun. When the enemy shall come in like a flood, the Spirit of the LORD shall lift up a standard against him.

(ISAIAH 59:18, 19)

[In the following prediction of Egypt's destruction by Babylon, was the prophet seeing through the Egypt of this own day, almost as though it were already a ghost, to the Egypt of some distant point on his event horizon—a point he would have called "the end of the earth?"]

Son of man, take up a lamentation for Pharaoh king of Egypt, and say to him, Thou art like a young lion of the nations, and thou art as a whale in the seas: and thou didst come forth with thy rivers, and didst trouble the waters with thy feet, and didst foul their rivers. Thus saith the Lord GOD; I will therefore spread out my net over thee with a company of many people; and they shall bring thee up in my net. Then will I leave thee upon the land, and I will cast thee forth upon the open field, and will cause all the fowls of the heaven to remain upon thee, and I will fill the beasts of the whole earth with thee. And I will lay thy flesh upon the mountains, and fill the valleys with thy height. I will also water with thy blood the land in which thou swimmest, even to the mountains; and the rivers shall be full of thee. And when I shall put thee out, I will cover the heaven, and make its stars dark; I will cover the sun with a cloud, and the moon shall not give her light. All the bright lights of heaven will I make dark over thee, and set darkness upon thy land, saith the Lord GOD. I will also vex the hearts of many people, when I shall bring thy destruction among the nations, into the countries which thou hast not known. Yea, I will make many people astonished at thee, and their kings shall be horribly afraid for thee, when I shall brandish my sword before them; and they shall tremble at every moment, every man for his own life, in the day of thy fall.

(EZEKIEL 32:2–10)

For the day of the LORD is near upon all the nations: as thou [the imperial nation] hast done, it shall be done to thee: thy reward shall return upon thy own head. For as ye drank upon my holy mountain, so shall all the nations drink continually, yea, they shall drink, and they shall swallow down, and they shall be as though they had not been. But upon mount Zion shall be deliverance, and there shall be holiness; and the house of Jacob shall possess their possessions. And the house of Jacob shall be a fire, and the house of Joseph a flame, and the house of Esau for stubble, and they shall kindle in them, and devour them; and there shall not be any remaining of the house of Esau; for the LORD hath spoken it. And they of the south shall possess the mount of Esau; and they of the plain the Philistines: and they shall possess the fields of Ephraim, and the fields of Samaria: and Benjamin shall possess Gilead. And the captives of this host of the children of Israel shall possess that of the Canaanites, even to Zarephath; and the captives of Jerusalem, which is in Sepharad, shall possess the cities of the south. And deliverers shall come upon mount Zion to judge the mount of Esau; and the kingdom shall be the LORD'S.

(OBADIAH 1:15–21)

Now gather thyself in troops, O daughter of troops: he hath laid siege against us: they shall smite the judge of Israel with a rod upon the cheek. But thou, Bethlehem Ephratah, though thou art little among the thousands of Judah, yet out of thee shall he come forth to me that is to be ruler in Israel; whose goings forth have been from of old, from everlasting. Therefore will he give them up, until the time that she who travaileth hath brought forth: then the remnant of his brethren shall return to the children of Israel. And he shall stand and feed in the strength of the LORD, in the majesty of the name of the LORD his God; and they shall abide: for now shall he be great to the ends of the earth. And this man shall be the peace, when the Assyrian shall come into our land: and when he shall tread in our palaces, then shall we raise against him seven shepherds, and eight principal men. And they shall waste the land of Assyria with the sword, and the land of Nimrod in its entrances: thus shall he deliver us from the Assyrian, when he cometh into our land, and when he treadeth within our borders. And the remnant of Jacob shall be in the midst of many people as a dew from the LORD, as the showers upon the grass, that tarrieth not for man, nor waiteth for the sons of men. And the remnant of Jacob shall be among the Gentiles in the midst of many people as a lion among the beasts of the forest, as a young lion among the flocks of sheep: who, if he goeth through, both treadeth down, and teareth in pieces, and none can deliver. Thy hand shall be lifted up upon thy adversaries, and all thy enemies shall be cut off.

(MICAH 5:1–9)

For thus saith the LORD of hosts; After the glory hath he sent me to the nations which wasted you [Jerusalem]: for he that toucheth you toucheth the apple of his eye. For, behold, I will shake my hand upon them, and they shall be a spoil to their servants: and ye shall know that the LORD of hosts hath sent me.

(ZECHARIAH 2:8–9).

And shall not God avenge his own elect, who cry day and night to him, though he beareth long with them? I tell you that he will avenge them speedily. Nevertheless when the Son of man cometh, shall he find faith on the earth?   (LUKE 18:7, 8)

MILLENNIUM

[A promise made by God through his prophet to King David, partially realized in his son Solomon.]

Moreover I will appoint a place for my people Israel, and will plant them, that they may dwell in a place of their own, and move no more; neither shall the children of wickedness afflict them any more, as in times past, And as since the time that I commanded judges to be over my people Israel, and have caused thee to rest from all thy enemies. Also the LORD telleth thee that he will make thee an house. And when thy days shall be fulfilled, and thou shalt sleep with thy fathers, I will set up thy seed after thee, who shall proceed out of thy own body, and I will establish his kingdom. He shall build an house for my name, and I will establish the throne of his kingdom for ever. And thine house and thy kingdom shall be established for ever before thee: thy throne shall be established for ever.   (2 SAMUEL 7:10–13, 16)

The meek shall eat and be satisfied: they shall praise the LORD that seek him: your heart shall live for ever. All the ends of the world shall remember and turn to the LORD: and all the kindreds of the nations shall worship before thee. For the kingdom is the LORD'S: and he is the governor among the nations. All the prosperous of the earth shall eat and worship: all they that go down to the dust shall bow before him: and none can keep alive his own soul.   (PSALM 22:26–29)

[Though the earth is already the Lord's, Charles Spurgeon wrote in regard to this Psalm: "We look also for a sublimer fulness when the true ideal of a world for God shall have been reached in millennial glories."]

(A Psalm of David.) The earth is the LORD'S, and all it containeth; the world, and they that dwell in it. For he hath founded it upon the seas, and established it upon the floods. Who shall ascend upon the hill of the LORD? and who shall stand in his holy place? He that hath clean hands, and a pure heart; who hath not lifted up his soul to vanity, nor sworn deceitfully. He shall receive the blessing from the LORD, and righteousness from the God of his salvation. This is the generation of them that seek him, that seek thy face, O Jacob. Selah. Lift up your heads, O ye gates; and be ye lifted up, ye everlasting doors; and the King of glory shall come in. Who is this King of glory? The LORD strong and

mighty, the LORD mighty in battle. Lift up your heads, O ye gates; even lift them up, ye everlasting doors; and the King of glory shall come in. Who is this King of glory? The LORD of hosts, he is the King of glory. Selah. (PSALMS 24:1–10)

(To the chief Musician, A Psalm for the sons of Korah.) O clap your hands, all ye people; shout to God with the voice of triumph. For the LORD most high is terrible; he is a great King over all the earth. He shall subdue the people under us, and the nations under our feet. He shall choose our inheritance for us, the excellency of Jacob whom he loved. Selah. God is gone up with a shout, the LORD with the sound of a trumpet. Sing praises to God, sing praises: sing praises to our King, sing praises. For God is the King of all the earth: sing ye praises with understanding. God reigneth over the nations: God sitteth upon the throne of his holiness. The princes of the people are gathered together, even the people of the God of Abraham: for the shields of the earth belong to God: he is greatly exalted. (PSALM 47:1–9)

[This psalm, which rhapsodizes about Jerusalem, could anticipate an idealized Jerusalem in the Millennium of Christ's reign?]

(A Song and Psalm for the sons of Korah.) Great is the LORD, and greatly to be praised in the city of our God, in the mountain of his holiness. Beautiful for situation, the joy of the whole earth, is mount Zion, on the sides of the north, the city of the great King. God is known in her palaces for a refuge. For, lo, the kings were assembled, they passed by together. They saw it, and so they wondered; they were troubled, and hasted away. . . . Fear took hold upon them there, and pain, as of a woman in travail. . . . As we have heard, so have we seen in the city of the LORD of hosts, in the city of our God: God will establish it for ever. Selah. . . . According to thy name, O God, so is thy praise to the ends of the earth: thy right hand is full of righteousness. Let mount Zion rejoice, let the daughters of Judah be glad, because of thy judgments. . . . For this God is our God for ever and ever: he will be our guide even to death. (PSALM 48:1–6, 8, 10,11, 14)

O let the nations be glad and sing for joy: for thou shalt judge the people righteously, and govern the nations upon earth. Selah. (PSALM 67:4)

[Originally a song of prayer for King Solomon, possibly at his coronation. This prayer is thought by some to anticipate the Messiah who comes from Solomon's line and who will fulfill the prayer perfectly during his own reign—since it was never realized in Solomon's own life.]

(A Psalm for Solomon.) Give the king thy judgments, O God, and thy righteousness to the king's son. He shall judge thy people with righteousness, and thy poor with judgment. The mountains shall bring peace to the people, and the little hills, by righteousness. He shall judge the poor of the people, he shall save the children of the needy, and shall break in pieces the oppressor. They shall fear thee as long as the sun and moon endure, throughout all generations. He shall come down like rain upon the mown grass: as showers that water the earth. In his days shall the righteous flourish; and abundance of peace so long as the moon endureth. He shall have dominion also from sea to sea, and from the river to the ends of the earth. They that dwell in the wilderness shall bow before him; and his enemies shall lick the dust. The kings of Tarshish and of the isles shall bring presents: the kings of Sheba and Seba shall offer gifts. Yea, all kings shall fall down before him: all nations shall serve him. For he shall deliver the needy when he crieth; the poor also, and him that hath

no helper. He shall spare the poor and needy, and shall save the souls of the needy. He shall redeem their soul from deceit and violence: and precious shall be their blood in his sight. And he shall live, and to him shall be given of the gold of Sheba: prayer also shall be made for him continually; and daily shall he be praised. There shall be an handful of grain in the earth upon the top of the mountains; its fruit shall shake like Lebanon: and they of the city shall flourish like grass of the earth. His name shall endure for ever: his name shall be continued as long as the sun: and men shall be blessed in him: all nations shall call him blessed. Blessed be the LORD God, the God of Israel, who only doeth wondrous things. And blessed be his glorious name for ever: and let the whole earth be filled with his glory; Amen, and Amen. The prayers of David the son of Jesse are ended.   (PSALM 72:1–20)

And of Zion it shall be said, This and that man was born in her: and the Highest himself shall establish her. The LORD shall count, when he writeth up the

people, that this man was born there. Selah. As well the singers as the players on instruments shall be there: all my springs are in thee.   (PSALM 87:5–7)

For a thousand years in thy sight are but as yesterday when it is past, and as a watch in the night.   (PSALM 90:4)

[This song for the sabbath day may anticipate a sabbath millennium.]

(A Psalm or Song for the sabbath day.) It is a good thing to give thanks to the LORD, and to sing praises to thy name, O most High:
    . . . When the wicked spring as the grass, and when all the workers of iniquity do flourish; it is that they shall be destroyed for ever: But thou, LORD, art most high for evermore. For, lo, thy ene-

mies, O LORD, for, lo, thy enemies shall perish; all the workers of iniquity shall be scattered. But my horn shalt thou exalt like the horn of an unicorn: I shall be anointed with fresh oil. My eye also shall see my desire on my enemies, and my ears shall hear my desire of the wicked that rise up against me. The righteous shall flourish like the palm tree: he shall grow like a cedar in Lebanon. Those that are planted in the house of the LORD shall flourish in the courts of our God. They shall still bring forth fruit in old age; they shall be fat and flourishing; To show that the LORD is upright: he is my rock, and there is no unrighteousness in him.　(PSALM 92:1, 7–15)

O worship the LORD in the beauty of holiness: fear before him, all the earth. Say among the nations that the LORD reigneth: the world also shall be established that it shall not be moved: he shall judge the people righteously. Let the heavens rejoice, and let the earth be glad; let the sea roar, and all it containeth. Let the field be joyful, and all that is in it: then shall all the trees of the forest rejoice Before the LORD: for he cometh, for he cometh to judge the earth: he shall judge the world with righteousness, and the people with his truth.　(PSALM 96:9–13)

But thou, O LORD, shalt endure for ever; and thy remembrance to all generations. Thou shalt arise, and have mercy upon Zion: for the time to favour her, yea, the set time, is come. For thy servants take pleasure in her stones, and favour her dust. So the nations shall fear the name of the LORD, and all the kings of the earth thy glory. When the LORD shall build up Zion, he shall appear in his glory. He will regard the prayer of the destitute, and not despise their prayer. This shall be written for the generation to come: and the people which shall be created shall praise the LORD. For he hath looked down from the height of his sanctuary; from heaven hath the LORD beheld the earth; To hear the groaning of the prisoner; to loose those that are appointed to death; To declare the name of the LORD in Zion, and his praise in Jerusalem; When the people are gathered together, and the kingdoms, to serve the LORD.　(PSALM 102:12–22)

For the LORD hath chosen Zion; he hath desired it for his habitation. This is my rest for ever: here will I dwell; for I have desired it. I will abundantly bless her provision: I will satisfy her poor with bread. I will also clothe her priests with salvation: and her saints shall shout aloud for joy. There will I make the horn of David to bud: I have ordained a lamp for my anointed. His enemies will I clothe with shame: but upon himself shall his crown flourish.

(PSALM 132:13–18)

The word that Isaiah the son of Amoz saw concerning Judah and Jerusalem. And it shall come to pass in the last days, that the mount of the LORD'S house shall be established on the top of the mountains, and shall be exalted above the hills; and all nations shall flow to it. And many people shall go and say, Come ye, and let us go up to the mountain of the LORD, to the house of the God of Jacob; and he will teach us of his ways, and we will walk in his paths: for out of Zion shall go forth the law, and the word of the LORD from Jerusalem. And he shall judge among the nations, and shall rebuke many people: and they shall beat their swords into plowshares, and their spears into pruninghooks: nation shall not lift up sword against nation, neither shall they learn war any more.

(ISAIAH 2:1–4)

In that day shall the branch of the LORD be beautiful and glorious, and the fruit of the earth shall be the pride and glory of them that have escaped of Israel. And it shall come to pass, that he that is left in Zion, and he that remaineth in Jerusalem, shall be called holy, even every one that is written among the living in Jerusalem: When the Lord shall have washed away the filth of the daughters of Zion, and shall have purged the blood of Jerusalem from the midst of it by the spirit of judgment, and by the spirit of burning. And the LORD will create upon every dwelling place of mount Zion, and upon her assemblies, a cloud and smoke by day, and the shining of a flaming fire by night: for upon all the glory shall be a defence. And there shall be a tabernacle for a shade in the daytime from the heat, and for a place of refuge, and for a covert from storm and from rain.

(ISAIAH 4:2–6)

And in that day [following Israel's restoration] thou shalt say, O LORD, I will praise thee: though thou wast angry with me, thy anger is turned away, and thou didst comfort me. Behold, God is my salvation; I will trust, and not be afraid: for the LORD JEHOVAH is my strength and my song; he also is become my salvation. Therefore with joy shall ye draw water out of the wells of salvation. And in that day shall ye say, Praise the LORD, call upon his name, declare his doings among the people, make mention that his name is exalted. Sing to the LORD; for he hath done excellent things: this is known in all the earth. Cry aloud and shout, thou inhabitant of Zion: for great is the Holy One of Israel in the midst of thee.

(ISAIAH 12:1–6)

For the LORD will have mercy on Jacob, and will yet choose Israel, and set them in their own land: and the strangers shall be joined with them, and they shall unite with the house of Jacob. And the people shall take them, and bring them to their place: and the house of Israel shall possess them in the land of the LORD for servants and handmaids: and they shall take them captives, whose captives they were; and they shall rule over their oppressors. And it shall come to pass in the day that the LORD shall give thee rest from thy sorrow, and from thy fear, and from the hard bondage in which thou wast made to serve,

(ISAIAH 14:1–3)

And in mercy shall the throne be established: and he shall sit upon it in truth in the tabernacle of David, judging, and seeking judgment, and swiftly executing righteousness.

(ISAIAH 16:5)

In that day shall there be an altar to the LORD in the midst of the land of Egypt, and a pillar at its border to the LORD. And it shall be for a sign and for a witness to the LORD of hosts in the land of Egypt: for they shall cry to the LORD because of the oppressors, and he shall send them a saviour, and a great one, and he shall deliver them. And the LORD shall be known to Egypt, and the Egyptians shall know the LORD in that day, and shall do sacrifice and oblation; yea, they shall vow a vow to the LORD, and perform it. And the LORD shall smite Egypt: he shall smite and heal it: and they shall return even to the LORD, and *he shall be entreated by them, and shall heal them. In that day shall there be a highway from Egypt to Assyria, and the Assyrian shall come into Egypt, and the Egyptian into Assyria, and the Egyptians shall serve with the Assyrians. In that day shall Israel be the third with Egypt*

and with Assyria, even a blessing in the midst of the land: Whom the LORD of hosts shall bless, saying, Blessed be Egypt my people, and Assyria the work of my hands, and Israel my inheritance.

(ISAIAH 19:19–25)

In that day shall this song be sung in the land of Judah; We have a strong city; salvation will God appoint for walls and bulwarks. Open ye the gates, that the righteous nation which keepeth the truth may enter in. . . . LORD, thou wilt or-

dain peace for us: for thou also hast wrought all our works in us. . . . Thou hast increased the nation, O LORD, thou hast increased the nation: thou art glorified: thou hadst removed it far to all the ends of the earth. (ISAIAH 26:1, 2, 12, 15)

In that day sing ye to her [Israel], A vineyard of red wine. I the LORD do keep it; I will water it every moment: lest any hurt it, I will keep it night and day. Fury is not in me: who would set the briers and thorns against me in battle? I would go through them, I would burn them together. Or let him take hold of my strength, that he may make peace with

me; and he shall make peace with me. He shall cause them that descend from Jacob to take root: Israel shall blossom and bud, and fill the face of the world with fruit. Hath he smitten him, as he smote those that smote him? or is he slain according to the slaughter of them that are slain by him? (ISAIAH 27:2–7)

The meek also shall increase their joy in the LORD, and the poor among men shall rejoice in the Holy One of Israel. For the terrible one is brought to nought, and the mocker is consumed, and all that watch for iniquity are cut off: That make a man an offender for a word, and lay a snare for him that reproveth in the gate, and turn aside the just for a thing of nought. Therefore thus saith the LORD, who redeemed Abraham, concerning the

house of Jacob, Jacob shall not now be ashamed, neither shall his face now become pale. But when he seeth his children, the work of my hands, in the midst of him, they shall sanctify my name, and sanctify the Holy One of Jacob, and shall fear the God of Israel. They also that erred in spirit shall come to understanding, and they that murmured shall learn doctrine. (ISAIAH 29:19–24)

Behold, a king shall reign in righteousness, and princes shall rule in judgment. And a man shall be as an hiding place from the wind, and a covert from the tempest; as streams of water in a dry place, as the shadow of a great rock in a weary land. And the eyes of them that see shall not be dim, and the ears of them

that hear shall hearken. The heart also of the rash shall understand knowledge, and the tongue of the stammerers shall be ready to speak plainly. The vile person shall be no more called noble, nor the churl said to be bountiful. . . .

Because the palaces shall be forsaken; the multitude of the city shall be left; the forts and towers shall be for dens for ever, a joy of wild donkeys, a pasture of flocks; Until the spirit shall be poured upon us from on high, and the wilderness shall be a fruitful field, and the fruitful field shall be counted for a forest. Then judgment shall dwell in the wilderness, and right-eousness remain in the fruitful field. And the work of righteousness shall be peace; and the effect of righteousness quietness and assurance for ever. And my people shall dwell in a peaceable habitation, and in sure dwellings, and in quiet rest-ing places; When it shall hail, coming down on the forest; and the city shall be low in a low place. Blessed are ye that sow beside all waters, that send forth there the feet of the ox and the donkey.

(ISAIAH 32:1–5, 14–20)

The LORD is exalted; for he dwelleth on high: he hath filled Zion with judgment and righteousness. And wisdom and knowledge shall be the stability of thy times, and strength of salvation: the fear of the LORD is his treasure. . . .

Thy eyes shall see the king in his beauty: they shall behold the land that is very far off. Thy heart shall meditate ter-ror. Where is the scribe? where is the re-ceiver? where is he that counted the towers? Thou shalt not see a fierce people, a people of deeper speech than thou canst perceive; of a stammering tongue, that thou canst not understand. Look upon Zion, the city of our solemni-ties: thy eyes shall see Jerusalem a quiet habitation, a tabernacle that shall not be taken down; not one of its stakes shall ever be removed, neither shall any of its cords be broken. But there the glorious LORD will be to us a place of broad rivers and streams; in which shall go no galley with oars [i.e., war ships], neither shall gallant ship pass through it. For the LORD is our judge, the LORD is our lawgiver, the LORD is our king; he will save us. Thy tacklings are loosed; they could not well strengthen their mast, they could not spread the sail: then is the prey of a great spoil divided [the spoils of Armageddon?]; the lame take the prey. And the inhabitants shall not say, I am sick: the people that dwell in it shall be forgiven their iniquity.

(ISAIAH 33:5, 6, 17–24)

The wilderness and the solitary place shall be glad for them; and the desert shall rejoice, and blossom as the rose. It shall blossom abundantly, and rejoice even with joy and singing: the glory of Lebanon shall be given to it, the excel-lency of Carmel and Sharon, they shall see the glory of the LORD, and the excel-lency of our God. Strengthen ye the weak hands, and confirm the feeble knees. Say to them that are of a fearful heart, Be strong, fear not: behold, your God will come with vengeance, even God with a recompence; he will come and save you. Then the eyes of the blind shall be opened, and the ears of the deaf shall be un-stopped. Then shall the lame man leap as an hart, and the tongue of the dumb shall sing: for in the wilderness shall wa-ters break out, and streams in the desert. And the parched ground shall become a pool, and the thirsty land springs of wa-ter: in the habitation of dragons [or rep-tiles/serpents], where each lay, shall be grass with reeds and rushes. And an highway shall be there, and a way, and it shall be called The way of holiness; the unclean shall not pass over it; but it shall be for those: the wayfaring men, though fools, shall not err in it. No lion shall be there, nor any ravenous beast shall go up on it, it shall not be found there; but the redeemed shall walk there: And the ran-

somed of the LORD shall return, and come to Zion with songs and everlasting joy upon their heads: they shall obtain joy and gladness, and sorrow and sighing shall flee away.   (ISAIAH 35:1, 2, 5–10)

When the poor and needy seek water, and there is none, and their tongue faileth for thirst, I the LORD will hear them, I the God of Israel will not forsake them. I will open rivers in high places, and fountains in the midst of the valleys: I will make the wilderness a pool of water, and the dry land springs of water. I will plant in the wilderness the cedar, the

shittah tree, and the myrtle, and the oil tree; I will set in the desert the fir tree, the pine, and the box tree together: That they may see, and know, and consider, and understand together, that the hand of the LORD hath done this, and the Holy One of Israel hath created it.

(ISAIAH 41:17–20)

Remember ye not the former things, neither consider the things of old. Behold, I will do a new thing; now it shall spring forth; shall ye not know it? I will even make a way in the wilderness, and rivers in the desert. The beast of the field shall

honour me, the dragons and the owls: because I give waters in the wilderness, and rivers in the desert, to give drink to my people, my chosen. This people have I formed for myself; they shall show forth my praise.   (ISAIAH 43:18–21)

For the LORD shall comfort Zion: he will comfort all her waste places; and he will make her wilderness like Eden, and her desert like the garden of the LORD; joy and gladness shall be found in it, thanksgiving, and the voice of melody. . . .

Therefore the redeemed of the LORD shall return, and come with singing to Zion; and everlasting joy shall be upon their head: they shall obtain gladness and joy; sorrow and mourning shall flee away.   (ISAIAH 51:3, 11)

[Isaiah 54, which follows, must refer to the millennium, for at no time after Isaiah's writing did Israel dispossess nations and settle in their desolate cities. It was barely able to reclaim its own land.]

Sing, O barren, thou that didst not bear; break forth into singing, and cry aloud, thou that didst not travail with child: for more are the children of the desolate than the children of the married wife, saith the LORD. Enlarge the place of thy tent, and let them extend the curtains of thy habitations: spare not, lengthen thy cords, and strengthen thy stakes; For thou shalt break forth on the right hand

and on the left; and thy seed shall inherit the Gentiles, and make the desolate cities to be inhabited. Fear not; for thou shalt not be ashamed: neither be thou confounded; for thou shalt not be put to shame: for thou shalt forget the shame of thy youth, and shalt not remember the reproach of thy widowhood any more. For thy Maker is thy husband; the LORD of hosts is his name; and thy Redeemer the Holy One of Israel; The God of the whole earth shall he be called.

For the LORD hath called thee as a woman forsaken and grieved in spirit, and a wife of youth, when thou wast refused, saith thy God. For a small moment have I forsaken thee; but with great mercies will I gather thee. In a little wrath I hid my face from thee for a moment; but with everlasting kindness will I have mercy on thee, saith the LORD thy Redeemer. For this is as the waters of Noah to me: for as I have sworn that the waters of Noah shall no more overflow the earth; so have I sworn that I will not be angry with thee, nor rebuke thee. For the mountains shall depart, and the hills be removed; but my kindness shall not depart from thee, neither shall the covenant of my peace be removed, saith the LORD that hath mercy on thee.

For ye shall go out with joy, and be led forth with peace: the mountains and the hills shall break forth before you into singing, and all the trees of the field shall clap their hands. Instead of the thorn

When thou criest, let thy companies deliver thee; but the wind shall carry them all away; vanity shall take them: but he that putteth his trust in me shall possess the land, and shall inherit my holy mountain; And shall say, Cast ye up, cast ye up, prepare the way, take up the stumblingblock out of the way of my people. For thus saith the high and lofty One that inhabiteth eternity, whose name is Holy; I dwell in the high and holy place, with him also that is of a contrite and humble spirit, to revive the spirit of the humble, and to revive the heart of the

. . . And all thy children shall be taught from the LORD; and great shall be the peace of thy children. In righteousness shalt thou be established: thou shalt be far from oppression; for thou shalt not fear: and from terror; for it shall not come near thee. Behold, they shall surely gather together, but not by me: whoever shall gather together against thee shall fall for thy sake. Behold, I have created the smith that bloweth the coals in the fire, and that bringeth forth an instrument for his work; and I have created the waster to destroy. No weapon that is formed against thee shall prosper; and every tongue that shall rise against thee in judgment thou shalt condemn. This is the heritage of the servants of the LORD, and their righteousness is from me, saith the LORD.

(ISAIAH 54:1–10, 13–17)

shall come up the fir tree, and instead of the brier shall come up the myrtle tree: and it shall be to the LORD for a name, for an everlasting sign that shall not be cut off. (ISAIAH 55:12, 13)

contrite ones. For I will not contend for ever, neither will I be always angry: for [if I did] the spirit should fail before me, and the souls whom I have made. For the iniquity of his covetousness I was angry, and smote him: I hid myself, and was angry, and he went on backsliding in the way of his heart. I have seen his ways, and will heal him: I will lead him also, and restore comforts to him and to his mourners. I create the fruit of the lips; Peace, peace to him that is far off, and to him that is near, saith the LORD; and I will heal him. (ISAIAH 57:13–19)

And the Redeemer shall come to Zion, and to them that turn from transgression in Jacob, saith the LORD. As for me, this is my covenant with them, saith the LORD; My spirit that is upon thee, and my words which I have put in thy mouth, shall not depart out of thy mouth, nor out of the mouth of thy seed, nor out of the mouth of thy seed's seed, saith the LORD, from henceforth and for ever.

(ISAIAH 59:20, 21)

Arise, shine; for thy light is come, and the glory of the LORD is risen upon thee. For, behold, the darkness shall cover the earth, and gross darkness the people: but the LORD shall arise upon thee, and his glory shall be seen upon thee. And the Gentiles shall come to thy light, and kings to the brightness of thy rising. Lift up thy eyes around, and see: all they gather themselves together, they come to thee: thy sons shall come from far, and thy daughters shall be nursed at thy side. Then thou shalt see, and flow together, and thy heart shall fear, and be enlarged; because the abundance of the sea shall be converted to thee, the forces of the Gentiles shall come to thee. The multitude of camels shall cover thee, the dromedaries of Midian and Ephah; all they from Sheba shall come: they shall bring gold and incense; and they shall show forth the praises of the LORD. All the flocks of Kedar shall be gathered together to thee, the rams of Nebaioth shall minister to thee: they shall come up with acceptance on my altar, and I will glorify the house of my glory. Who are these that fly as a cloud, and as doves to their windows? Surely the isles shall wait for me, and the ships of Tarshish first, to bring thy sons from far, their silver and their gold with them, to the name of the LORD thy God, and to the Holy One of Israel, because he hath glorified thee. And the sons of foreigners shall build up thy walls, and their kings shall minister to thee: for in my wrath I smote thee, but in my favour have I had mercy on thee. Therefore thy gates shall be open continually; they shall not be shut day nor night; that men may bring to thee the forces of the Gentiles, and that their kings may be brought. For the nation and kingdom that will not serve thee shall perish; yea, those nations shall be utterly wasted. The glory of Lebanon shall come to thee, the fir tree, the pine tree, and the box together, to beautify the place of my sanctuary; and I will make the place of my feet glorious. The sons also of them that afflicted thee shall come bending to thee; and all they that despised thee shall bow themselves down at the soles of thy feet; and they shall call thee, The city of the LORD, The Zion of the Holy One of Israel.

Though thou hast been forsaken and hated, so that no man went through thee, I will make thee an everlasting pride, a joy of many generations. Thou shalt also suck the milk of the Gentiles, and shalt suck the breast of kings: and thou shalt know that I the LORD am thy Saviour and thy Redeemer, the mighty One of Jacob. For brass I will bring gold, and for iron I will bring silver, and for wood brass, and for stones iron: I will also make thy officers peace, and thy exactors righteousness. Violence shall no more be heard in thy land, wasting nor destruction within thy borders; but thou shalt call thy walls Salvation, and thy gates Praise. The sun shall be no more thy light by day; neither for brightness shall the moon give light to thee: but the LORD shall be to thee an everlasting light, and thy God thy glory. Thy sun shall no more go down; neither shall thy moon withdraw itself: for the LORD shall be thy everlasting light, and the days of thy mourning shall be ended. Thy

But ye shall be named the Priests of the LORD: men shall call you the Ministers of our God: ye shall eat the riches of the Gentiles, and in their glory shall ye boast yourselves. For your shame ye shall have double; and for confusion they shall rejoice in their portion: therefore in their land they shall possess the double: everlasting joy shall be to them. For I the

For Zion's sake I will not hold my peace, and for Jerusalem's sake I will not rest, until its righteousness shall go forth as brightness, and its salvation as a lamp that burneth. And the Gentiles shall see thy righteousness, and all kings thy glory: and thou shalt be called by a new name, which the mouth of the LORD shall name. Thou shalt also be a crown of glory in the hand of the LORD, and a royal diadem in the hand of thy God. Thou shalt no more be termed Forsaken; neither shall thy land any more be termed Desolate: but thou shalt be called Hephzibah [means "my delight"], and thy land Beulah ["my bride"]: for the LORD delighteth in thee, and thy land shall be married. For as a young man marrieth a virgin, so shall thy sons marry thee: and as the bridegroom rejoiceth over the bride, so shall thy God rejoice over thee.

I have set watchmen upon thy walls, O Jerusalem, which shall never hold their peace day nor night: ye that make mention of the LORD, keep not silence,

people also shall be all righteous: they shall inherit the land for ever, the branch of my planting, the work of my hands, that I may be glorified. A little one shall become a thousand, and a small one a strong nation: I the LORD will hasten it in its time.   (ISAIAH 60:1–22)

LORD love judgment, I hate robbery for burnt offering; and I will direct their work in truth, and I will make an everlasting covenant with them. And their seed shall be known among the Gentiles, and their offspring among the people: all that see them shall acknowledge them, that they are the seed which the LORD hath blessed.   (ISAIAH 61:6–9)

And give him no rest, till he shall establish, and till he shall make Jerusalem a praise in the earth. The LORD hath sworn by his right hand, and by the arm of his strength, Surely I will no more give thy grain to be food for thy enemies; and the sons of the foreigner shall not drink thy wine, for which thou hast laboured: But they that have gathered it shall eat it, and praise the LORD; and they that have brought it together shall drink it in the courts of my holiness.

Go through, go through the gates; prepare ye the way of the people; cast up, cast up the highway; gather out the stones; lift up a standard for the people. Behold, the LORD hath proclaimed to the end of the world, Say ye to the daughter of Zion, Behold, thy salvation cometh; behold, his reward is with him, and his work before him. And they shall call them, The holy people, The redeemed of the LORD: and thou shalt be called, Sought out, A city not forsaken.   (ISAIAH 62:1–12)

O LORD, my strength, and my fortress, and my refuge in the day of affliction, the Gentiles shall come to thee from the ends of the earth, and shall say, Surely our fa-

At the same time, saith the LORD, I will be the God of all the families of Israel, and they shall be my people. Thus saith the LORD, The people who were left by the sword found grace in the wilderness; even Israel, when I went to cause him to rest. The LORD appeared of old to me, saying, I have loved thee with an everlasting love: therefore with lovingkindness have I drawn thee. Again I will build thee, and thou shalt be built, O virgin of Israel: thou shalt again be adorned with thy tabrets [tambourines], and shalt go forth in the dances of them that make merry. Thou shalt yet plant vines upon the mountains of Samaria: the planters shall plant, and shall eat them as common things. For there shall be a day, that the watchmen upon the mount Ephraim shall cry, Arise ye, and let us go

Behold, I will bring it health and cure, and I will cure them, and will reveal to them the abundance of peace and truth. . . . And it shall be to me a name of joy, a praise and an honour before all the nations of the earth, which shall hear all the good that I do for them: and they shall fear and tremble for all the goodness and for all the prosperity that I procure for it. Thus saith the LORD; Again there shall be heard in this place, which ye say shall be desolate without man and without beast, even in the cities of Judah, and in the streets of Jerusalem, that are desolate, without man, and without inhabitant, and without beast, The voice of joy, and the voice of gladness, the voice of the bridegroom, and the voice of the

thers have inherited lies, vanity, and things in which there is no profit.

(JEREMIAH 16:19)

up to Zion to the LORD our God. For thus saith the LORD; Sing with gladness for Jacob, and shout among the chief of the nations: proclaim ye, praise ye, and say, O LORD, save thy people, the remnant of Israel. . . .

Behold, the days come, saith the LORD, that the city shall be built to the LORD from the tower of Hananeel to the gate of the corner. And the measuring line shall yet go forth straight forward over the hill Gareb, and shall turn toward Goath. And the whole valley of the dead bodies, and of the ashes, and all the fields to the brook of Kidron, to the corner of the horse gate toward the east, shall be holy to the LORD; it shall not be plucked up, nor thrown down any more for ever.

(JEREMIAH 31:1–7, 38–40)

bride, the voice of them that shall say, Praise the LORD of hosts: for the LORD is good; for his mercy endureth for ever: and of them that shall bring the sacrifice of praise into the house of the LORD. For I will cause to return the captives of the land, as at the first, saith the LORD. Thus saith the LORD of hosts; Again in this place, which is desolate without man and without beast, and in all its cities, shall be an habitation of shepherds causing their flocks to lie down. In the cities of the mountains, in the cities of the vale, and in the cities of the south, and in the land of Benjamin, and in the places about Jerusalem, and in the cities of Judah, shall the flocks pass again under the hands of him that counteth them, saith the LORD. Behold, the days come, saith the LORD, that I will perform that good thing which I have promised to the house of Israel and to the house of Judah. In those days, and at that time, will I cause the Branch of righteousness to grow up to David; and he shall execute judgment and righteousness in the land. In those days shall Judah be saved, and Jerusalem shall dwell in safety: and this is the name by which she shall be called, The LORD our righteousness. For thus saith the LORD; David shall never lack a man to sit upon the throne of the house of Israel; Neither shall the priests the Levites lack a man before me to offer burnt offerings, and to kindle meat offerings, and to do sacrifice continually.

(JEREMIAH 33:6, 9–18)

And there shall be no more a pricking brier to the house of Israel, nor any grieving thorn of all that are around them, that despised them; and they shall know that I am the Lord GOD. Thus saith the Lord GOD; When I shall have gathered the house of Israel from the people among whom they are scattered, and shall be sanctified in them in the sight of the nations, then shall they dwell in their land that I have given to my servant Jacob. And they shall dwell safely in it, and shall build houses, and plant vineyards; yea, they shall dwell with confidence, when I have executed judgments upon all those that despise them around them; and they shall know that I am the LORD their God.

(EZEKIEL 28:24–26)

[The following prophecy may have only referred to Israel's restoration from Babylonian captivity, since the language doesn't push much beyond that, but it immediately follows a prophecy that promises the New Covenant. Also, Israel has never looked remotely like a Garden of Eden, as predicted here, since the time of Ezekiel's writing.]

And ye shall dwell in the land that I gave to your fathers; and ye shall be my people, and I will be your God. I will also save you from all your uncleannesses: and I will call for the grain, and will increase it, and lay no famine upon you. And I will multiply the fruit of the tree, and the increase of the field, that ye shall receive no more reproach of famine among the nations. Then shall ye remember your own evil ways, and your doings that were not good, and shall lothe yourselves in your own sight for your iniquities and for your abominations. Not for your sakes do I this, saith the Lord GOD, be it known to you: be ashamed and confounded for your own ways, O house of Israel. Thus saith the Lord GOD; In the day that I shall have cleansed you from all your iniquities I will also cause you to dwell in the cities, and the wastes shall be built. And the desolate land shall be tilled, though it lay desolate in the sight of all that passed by. And they shall say, This land that was desolate is become like the garden of Eden; and the waste and desolate and ruined cities are become fortified, and are inhabited. Then the nations that are left around you shall know that I the LORD build the ruined places, and plant that which was desolate: I the LORD *have spoken it, and I will do it. Thus saith the Lord GOD; I will yet for this be enquired of by the house of Israel, to do it for them; I will increase them with men like a flock. As the holy flock, as the flock of Jerusalem in her solemn feasts; so shall the waste cities be filled with flocks of men: and they shall know that I am the LORD.* (EZEKIEL 36:28–38)

[The following prophecy may have only referred to a period of restoration after a locust plague, symbolic of military invasion, described by the prophet Joel. New Testament writers claimed part of it referred to the time immediately after Christ dwelled in Jerusalem. Some elements seem to reach further ahead. The global cataclysmic parts were quoted earlier in the book, so they're omitted here.]

Fear not, O land; be glad and rejoice: for the LORD will do great things. Be not afraid, ye beasts of the field: for the pastures of the wilderness do spring, for the tree beareth its fruit, the fig tree and the vine do yield their strength. Be glad then, ye children of Zion, and rejoice in the LORD your God: for he hath given you the former rain moderately, and he will cause to come down for you the rain, the former rain, and the latter rain in the first month. And the floors shall be full of wheat, and the vats shall overflow with wine and oil. And I will restore to you the years that the locust hath eaten, the cankerworm, and the caterpiller, and the palmerworm, my great army which I sent among you. And ye shall eat in plenty, and be satisfied, and praise the name of the LORD your God, that hath dealt wondrously with you: and my people shall never be ashamed. And ye shall know that I am in the midst of Israel, and that I am the LORD your God, *and none else: and my people shall never be ashamed. And it shall come to pass afterward, that I will pour out my spirit upon all flesh; and your sons and your daughters shall prophesy, your old men shall dream dreams, your young men shall see visions: And also upon the servants and upon the handmaids in those days will I pour out my spirit. . . .*

And it shall come to pass in that day, that the mountains shall drop down new wine, and the hills shall flow with milk, and all the rivers of Judah shall flow with waters, and a fountain shall come forth from the house of the LORD, and shall water the valley of Shittim. Egypt shall be a desolation, and Edom shall be a desolate wilderness, for the violence against the children of Judah, because they have shed innocent blood in their land. But Judah shall dwell for ever, and Jerusalem from generation to generation.

(JOEL 3:18–20). (JOEL 2:21–29; 3:18–20)

The LORD will be terrible to them [Israel's enemies to the east]: for he will famish all the gods of the earth; and men *shall worship him, every one from his place, even all the isles of the nations.*

(ZEPHANIAH 2:11)

For then will I turn to the people [probably Jews and Gentiles] a pure language [one people, one language?], that they may all call upon the name of the LORD, to serve him with one consent. From beyond the rivers of Cush [Ethiopia] my suppliants, even the daughter of my dispersed, shall bring my offering. In that day shalt thou not be ashamed for all thy doings, when thou hast transgressed against me: for then I will take away out of the midst of thee them that rejoice in thy pride, and thou shalt no more be haughty in my holy mountain. I will also leave in the midst of thee an afflicted and poor people, and they shall trust in the name of the LORD. The remnant of Israel shall not do iniquity, nor speak lies; neither shall a deceitful tongue be found in their mouth: for they shall feed and lie down, and none shall make them afraid.

Sing, O daughter of Zion; shout, O Israel; be glad and rejoice with all the heart, O daughter of Jerusalem. The LORD hath taken away thy judgments, he hath cast out thy enemy: the king of Israel, even the LORD, is in the midst of thee: thou shalt not see evil any more. In that day it shall be said to Jerusalem, Fear thou not: and to Zion, Let not thy hands be slack. The LORD thy God in the midst of thee is mighty; he will save, he will rejoice over thee with joy; he will rest in his love, he will joy over thee with singing. I will gather them that are sorrowful for the solemn assembly, who are of thee, to whom the reproach of it was a burden. Behold, at that time I will undo all that afflict thee: and I will save her that is lame, and gather her that was driven out; and I will get them praise and fame in every land where they have been put to shame. At that time will I bring you again, even in the time that I gather you: for I will make you a name and a praise among all people of the earth, when I turn back your captivity before your eyes, saith the LORD.

(ZEPHANIAH 3:9–20)

Again the word of the LORD of hosts came to me, saying, Thus saith the LORD of hosts; I was jealous for Zion with great jealousy, and I was jealous for her with great fury. Thus saith the LORD; I have returned to Zion, and will dwell in the midst of Jerusalem: and Jerusalem shall be called a city of truth; and the mountain of the LORD of hosts the holy mountain. Thus saith the LORD of hosts; There shall yet old men and old women dwell in the streets of Jerusalem, and every man with his staff in his hand for very age. And the streets of the city shall be full of boys and girls playing in its streets. Thus saith the LORD of hosts; If it is marvelous in the eyes of the remnant of this people in these days, should it also be marvelous in my eyes? saith the LORD of hosts. Thus saith the LORD of hosts; Behold, I will save my people from the east country, and from the west country; And I will bring them, and they shall dwell in the midst of Jerusalem: and they shall be my people, and I will be their God, in truth and in righteousness.

. . . Thus saith the LORD of hosts; It shall yet come to pass, that there shall come people, and the inhabitants of many cities: And the inhabitants of one city shall go to another, saying, Let us go speedily to pray before the LORD, and to seek the LORD of hosts: I will go also.

And many people and strong nations shall come to seek the LORD of hosts in Jerusalem, and to pray before the LORD. Thus saith the LORD of hosts; In those days it shall come to pass, that ten men out of all languages of the nations, shall take hold, shall even take hold of the skirt of him that is a Jew, saying, We will go with you: for we have heard that God is with you.   (ZECHARIAH 8:1–8, 20–23)

And I will cut off the chariot from Ephraim, and the horse from Jerusalem, and the battle bow shall be cut off: and he [the messianic king] shall speak peace to the nations: and his dominion shall be from sea to sea, and from the river to the ends of the earth.   (ZECHARIAH 9:10)

And it shall come to pass, that every one that is left of all the nations which came against Jerusalem shall even go up from year to year to worship the King, the LORD of hosts, and to keep the feast of tabernacles. And it shall be, that whoever will not come up of all the families of the earth to Jerusalem to worship the King, the LORD of hosts, even upon them shall be no rain. And if the family of Egypt shall not go up, and shall not come, that have no rain; there shall be the plague, with which the LORD will smite the nations that come not up to keep the feast of tabernacles. This shall be the punish-ment of Egypt, and the punishment of all nations that come not up to keep the feast of tabernacles. In that day there shall be upon the bells of the horses, HO-LINESS TO THE LORD; and the pots in the LORD'S house shall be like the bowls before the altar. Yea, every pot in Jeru-salem and in Judah shall be holiness to the LORD of hosts: and all they that sac-rifice shall come and take of them, and boil in them: and in that day there shall be no more the Canaanite [the people originally driven out of the land by the children of Israel] in the house of the LORD of hosts.   (ZECHARIAH 14:16–21)

Ye [the disciples] are they who have con-tinued with me [Jesus] in my tempta-tions. And I appoint to you a kingdom, as my Father hath appointed to me; That ye may eat and drink at my table in my kingdom, and sit on thrones judging the twelve tribes of Israel.

(LUKE 22:28–30).

JUDGMENT

Therefore the ungodly shall not stand in the judgment, nor sinners in the congre-gation of the righteous. For the LORD knoweth the way of the righteous: but the way of the ungodly shall perish.

(PSALM 1:5, 6)

[Regarding the following psalm, commentator Charles Spurgeon wrote: "As 'Sheminith' signifies the eighth, the Arabic version says it is concerning the end of the world, which shall be the eighth day, and refers it to the coming of the Messiah." Actually, the eighth day would follow the millennium, which could make this a reference to the final judg-ment or the battle of Gog and Magog—if it's even a prophecy.]

(To the chief Musician upon Sheminith, A Psalm of David.) Help, LORD; for the godly man ceaseth; for the faithful fail from among the children of men. They speak vanity every one with his neighbour: with flattering lips and with a double heart do they speak. The LORD shall cut off all flattering lips, and the tongue that speaketh proud things: Who have said, With our tongue will we prevail; our lips are our own: who is lord over us? For the oppression of the poor, for the sighing of the needy, now will I arise, saith the LORD; I will set him in safety from him that puffeth at him. The words of the LORD are pure words: as silver tried in a furnace of earth, purified seven times. Thou shalt keep them, O LORD, thou shalt preserve them from this generation for ever. The wicked walk on every side, when the vilest men are exalted. (PSALMS 12:1–8)

For God shall bring every work into judgment, with every secret thing, whether it is good, or whether it is evil. (ECCLESIASTES 12:14)

[Written regarding the devastation brought upon Israel by Assyria, but possibly alluding to ultimate judgment.]

And the people shall be as the burnings of lime: as thorns cut up shall they be burned in the fire. . . . The sinners in Zion are afraid; fearfulness hath surprised the hypocrites. Who among us shall dwell with the devouring fire? who among us shall dwell with everlasting burnings? He that walketh righteously, and speaketh uprightly; he that despiseth the gain of oppressions, that keepeth his hands from accepting of bribes, that stoppeth his ears from hearing of blood, and shutteth his eyes from seeing evil; He shall dwell on high: his place of defence shall be the strong holds of rocks: bread shall be given him; his waters shall be sure. (ISAIAH 33:12, 14–16)

Behold my servant, whom I uphold; my elect, in whom my soul delighteth; I have put my spirit upon him: he shall bring forth judgment to the Gentiles. . . . he shall bring forth judgment to truth. He shall not fail nor be discouraged, till he hath set judgment in the earth: and the isles shall wait for his law. (ISAIAH 42:1, 3, 4)

O LORD, the hope of Israel, all that forsake thee shall be ashamed, and they that depart from me shall be written in the earth, [i.e., "written in the dust"] because they have forsaken the LORD, the fountain of living waters. (JEREMIAH 17:13)

And I will come near to you [Israel] to judgment; and I will be a swift witness against the sorcerers, and against the adulterers, and against false swearers, and against those that oppress the hireling in his wages, the widow, and the fatherless, and that turn aside the stranger

from his right, and fear not me, saith the LORD of hosts.　　(MALACHI 3:5)

For I [Jesus] say to you, That except your righteousness shall exceed the righteousness of the scribes and Pharisees, ye shall in no way enter into the kingdom of heaven.

Ye have heard that it was said to them of old time, Thou shalt not kill; and whoever shall kill shall be in danger of the judgment: But I say to you, That whoever is angry with his brother without a cause shall be in danger of the judgment: and whoever shall say to his brother, Raca, shall be in danger of the council: but whoever shall say, Thou fool, shall be in danger of hell fire. . . . Agree with thy adversary quickly, while thou art in the way with him; lest at any time the adver-

sary deliver thee to the judge, and the judge deliver thee to the officer, and thou be cast into prison. Verily I say to thee, Thou shalt by no means come out from there, till thou hast paid the uttermost farthing. . . .

And if thy right eye shall cause thee to sin, pluck it out, and cast it from thee: for it is profitable for thee that one of thy members should perish, and not that thy whole body should be cast into hell. And if thy right hand shall cause thee to sin, cut it off, and cast it from thee: for it is profitable for thee that one of thy members should perish, and not that thy whole body should be cast into hell.

(MATTHEW 5:20–22, 25, 26, 29, 30)

Not every one that saith to me [Jesus], Lord, Lord, shall enter into the kingdom of heaven; but he that doeth the will of my Father who is in heaven. Many will say to me in that day, Lord, Lord, have we not prophesied in thy name? and in

thy name have cast out demons? and in thy name done many wonderful works? And then will I profess to them, I never knew you: depart from me, ye that work iniquity.　　(MATTHEW 7:21–23)

But I [Jesus] say to you, That for every idle word that men shall speak, they shall give account for it in the day of judg-

ment. For by thy words thou shalt be justified, and by thy words thou shalt be condemned.　　(MATTHEW 12:36, 37).

Again, the kingdom of heaven is like a net, that was cast into the sea, and gathered of every kind: Which, when it was full, they drew to the shore, and sat down, and gathered the good into vessels, but cast away the bad. So shall it be

at the end of the world: the angels shall come forth, and separate the wicked from among the righteous, And shall cast them into the furnace of fire: there shall be wailing and gnashing of teeth.

(MATTHEW 13:47–50)

[In the following excerpt from Jesus' parable, a wicked servant—representing any person who will stand before God's judgment—was forgiven an unpayable debt by his master (representing God). Later this same servant would not forgive one of his fellow servants for an insignificant debt. When his master heard of this, the master responded as follows:]

And his lord was angry, and delivered him to the torturers, till he should pay all that was due to him. So likewise shall my heavenly Father do also to you, if ye from your hearts forgive not every one his brother their trespasses.

(MATTHEW 18:34, 35)

[Spoken by John the Baptist regarding Christ.]

Whose [threshing] fan is in his hand, and he will thoroughly cleanse his floor, and will gather the wheat into his barn; but the chaff he will burn with fire unquenchable.

(LUKE 3:17)

[Spoken by Jesus, regarding any cities in Israel that would reject his disciples message.]

But I say to you, that it shall be more tolerable in that day [judgment day] for Sodom, than for that city. Woe to thee, Chorazin! woe to thee, Bethsaida! for if the mighty works had been done in Tyre and Sidon [Israel's enemies], which have been done in you, they had a great while ago repented, sitting in sackcloth and ashes. But it shall be more tolerable for Tyre and Sidon at the judgment, than for you. And thou, Capernaum, which art exalted to heaven, shall be thrust down to hell.

(LUKE 10:12–15)

For there is nothing covered, that shall not be revealed; neither hid, that shall not be known. Therefore whatever ye have spoken in darkness shall be heard in the light; and that which ye have spoken in the ear in closets shall be proclaimed upon the housetops.

(LUKE 12:2, 3)

Beware of the scribes [Jewish religious leaders], who desire to walk in long robes, and love greetings in the markets, and the highest seats in the synagogues, and the best places at feasts; Who devour widows' houses, and for a show make long prayers: the same shall receive greater condemnation.

(LUKE 20:46, 47)

[The following is by the Apostle Paul to an audience of mixed Jews and Gentiles. In essence, his argument states that Jews will be judged by the standards of the religious laws of Moses, and Gentiles will be judged by their intuitive knowledge of right and wrong, which they display every time they criticize someone else's behavior.]

For the wrath of God is revealed from heaven against all ungodliness and unrighteousness of men, who hold [know] the truth [but act] in unrighteousness. . . . Therefore thou art inexcusable, O man, whoever thou art that judgest [anyone]: for in that thou judgest another, thou condemnest thyself; for thou that judgest doest the same things. But we are sure that the judgment of God is according to truth against them who commit such things. And thinkest thou this, O man, that judgest them who do such things, and doest the same, that thou shalt escape the judgment of God? Or despisest thou the riches of his goodness and forbearance and longsuffering [patience]; not knowing that the goodness of God leadeth thee to repentance? But after thy hardness and impenitent heart treasurest up to thyself wrath in the day of wrath and revelation of the righteous judgment of God; Who will render to every man according to his deeds: To them who by patient continuance in well doing seek for glory and honour and immortality, eternal life: But to them that are contentious, and do not obey the truth, but obey unrighteousness, indignation and wrath, Tribulation and anguish, upon every soul of man that doeth evil, of the Jew first, and also of the Gentile; But glory, honour, and peace, to every man that worketh good, to the Jew first, and also to the Gentile: For there is no respect of persons with God. For as many as have sinned without law [i.e., Gentiles who live in ignorance of the religious laws of Moses] shall also perish without law: and as many as have sinned in the law [i.e., Jews] shall be judged by the law; (For not the hearers of the law are just before God, but the doers of the law shall be justified. . . . In the day when God shall judge the secrets of men by Jesus Christ according to my gospel. . . .

shall not uncircumcision [Gentiles] which is by nature, if it keepeth the law, judge thee [Jews], who by the letter and circumcision dost transgress the law?

(ROMANS 1:18; 2:1–13, 16, 27)

Dearly beloved, avenge not yourselves, but rather give place to wrath: for it is written, Vengeance is mine; I will repay, saith the Lord. (ROMANS 12:19)

But why dost thou judge thy brother? or why dost thou show contempt for thy brother? for we shall all stand before the judgment seat of Christ. For it is written, As I live, saith the Lord, every knee shall bow to me, and every tongue shall confess to God. So then every one of us shall give account of himself to God. Let us not therefore judge one another any more: but judge this rather, that no man put a stumblingblock or an occasion to fall in his brother's way. (ROMANS 14:10–13)

Therefore judge nothing before the time, until the Lord shall come, who will both bring to light the hidden things of darkness, and will reveal the counsels of the hearts: and then shall every man have praise from God. (1 CORINTHIANS 4:5)

For what have I [Paul] to do to judge them also that are outside the church? do ye not judge them that are within? But them that are outside God judgeth. . . .

(1 CORINTHIANS 5:12, 13)

Know ye not that the unrighteous shall not inherit the kingdom of God? Be not deceived: neither fornicators, nor idolaters, nor adulterers, nor effeminate, nor abusers of themselves with mankind, Nor thieves, nor covetous, nor drunkards, nor revilers, nor extortioners, shall inherit the kingdom of God.

(1 CORINTHIANS 6:9, 10)

The last enemy that shall be destroyed is death. (1 CORINTHIANS 15:26)

For we must all appear before the judgment seat of Christ; that every one may receive the things done in his body, according to what he hath done, whether good or bad. (2 CORINTHIANS 5:10)

That no man . . . defraud his brother in any matter: because the Lord is the avenger of all such, as we also have forewarned you and testified. (1 THESSALONIANS 4:6)

Seeing it is a righteous thing with God to recompense tribulation to them that trouble you; And to you who are troubled rest with us, when the Lord Jesus shall be revealed from heaven with his mighty angels, In flaming fire taking vengeance on them that know not God, and that obey not the gospel of our Lord Jesus Christ: Who shall be punished with everlasting destruction from the presence of the Lord, and from the glory of his power; When he shall come to be glorified in his saints, and to be admired by all them that believe (because our testimony among you was believed) in that day. (2 THESSALONIANS 1:6–10)

. . . those who have been once enlightened [by Christ], and have tasted of the heavenly gift, and have been made partakers of the Holy Spirit . . . If they shall fall away [from Christ] are like . . . the earth which drinketh in the rain that cometh often upon it . . . But . . . which beareth thorns and briers [and] is rejected, and is close to being cursed; whose end is to be burned. (HEBREWS 6:4, 6, 7, 8 ABRIDGED)

. . . it is appointed to men once to die, but after this the judgment: (HEBREWS 9:27)

So speak ye, and so do, as they that shall be judged by the law of liberty. For he shall have judgment without mercy, that hath shown no mercy; and mercy rejoiceth against judgment. (JAMES 2:12, 13)

Come now, ye rich men, weep and wail for your miseries that shall come upon you. Your riches are corrupted, and your garments are motheaten. Your gold and silver is rusted; and its rust shall be a witness against you, and shall eat your flesh as it were fire. Ye have heaped up treasure for the last days. Behold, the hire of the labourers who have reaped your fields, which is by you kept back by fraud, crieth: and the cries of them who have reaped have entered into the ears of the Lord of sabaoth. Ye have lived in pleasure on the earth, and been wanton; ye have nourished your hearts, as in a day of slaughter. Ye have condemned and killed the just; and he doth not resist you. . . . the coming of the Lord draweth near. . . . behold, the judge standeth before the door. (JAMES 5:1–6, 8B, 9B)

Therefore gird up the loins of your mind [i.e., be ready for decisive action], be sober, and hope to the end for the grace that is to be brought to you at the revelation of Jesus Christ; . . . Having your be-

For the time past of our life may suffice us to have wrought [done] the will of the Gentiles, when we walked in lasciviousness [outrageous loose behavior], lusts, excess of wine, revellings, drinking parties, and abominable idolatries: In which they think it strange that ye run not with them to the same flood of dissipation,

For if God spared not the angels that sinned, but cast them down to hell, and delivered them into chains of darkness, to be reserved to judgment; And spared not the old world [before Noah's flood], but saved Noah the eighth person, a preacher of righteousness, bringing the flood upon the world of the ungodly; And turning the cities of Sodom and Gomorrah into ashes condemned them with an overthrow, making them an example to those that afterwards should live ungodly lives;

And delivered just Lot, grieved with the immoral behavior of the wicked [out of Sodom]: . . . [then] The Lord knoweth how to deliver the godly out of temptations, and to reserve the unjust to the day of judgment to be punished:

But chiefly them that walk after the flesh in the lust of uncleanness, and despise government [authority]. Presumptuous are they, selfwilled, they are not afraid to speak evil of dignities [or "celestial beings"]. Though angels, who are greater in power and might, bring not a railing accusation against them before the Lord. But these, as natural brute beasts, made to be taken and destroyed,

havior honest among the Gentiles: that, though they speak against you as evildoers, they may by your good works, which they shall behold, glorify God in the day of visitation.   (1 PETER 1:13; 2:12)

speaking evil of you: Who shall give account to him that is ready to judge the living and the dead. . . . But the end of all things is at hand: be ye therefore sober minded, and watch to prayer. And above all things have fervent charity among yourselves: for charity shall cover a multitude of sins.   (1 PETER 4:3–5, 7, 8)

speak evil of the things that they understand not; and shall utterly perish in their own corruption; And shall receive the reward of unrighteousness, as they that count it pleasure to riot in the day time. Spots they are and blemishes, sporting [amusing] themselves with their own deceivings while they feast with you; Having eyes full of adultery, and that cannot cease from sin; beguiling unstable souls: they have an heart exercised with covetous practices; cursed children: . . . These [boisterous people] are wells without water, clouds that are carried with a tempest; to whom the mist of darkness is reserved for ever. For when they speak great swelling words of vanity, they allure through the lusts of the flesh, through much wantonness, those that are just escaping from them who live in error. While they promise them liberty, they themselves are the servants of corruption: for by whom a man is overcome, by the same is he brought into bondage. For if after they [the ones who are overcome by boisterous deceivers] have escaped the pollutions of the world through the knowledge of the Lord and Saviour Jesus Christ, they are again en-

tangled in them, and overcome, the latter end is worse with them than the beginning. For it had been better for them not to have known the way of righteous-

ness, than, after they have known it, to turn from the holy commandment delivered to them.

(2 PETER 2:4–7, 9–14, 17–21)

And the world passeth away, and its lust: but he that doeth the will of God abideth for ever. (1 JOHN 2:17)

And the angels who kept not their proper abode, but left their own habitation, he hath reserved in everlasting chains under darkness to the judgment of the great day. Even as Sodom and Gomorrah, and

the cities about them in like manner, giving themselves over to gross immorality, and going after strange flesh, are set forth for an example, suffering the vengeance of eternal fire. (JUDE 6, 7)

FULFILLMENT (LIVING IN THE LIGHT OF REVELATION)

Blessed is the man whom thou chastenest, O LORD, and teachest him out of thy law; That thou mayest give him rest from the days of adversity, until the pit is dug for the wicked. For the LORD will not

cast off his people, neither will he forsake his inheritance. But judgment shall return to righteousness: and all the upright in heart shall follow it.

(PSALM 94:12–15)

Thus saith the LORD, Keep ye judgment, and do justice: for my salvation is near to come, and my righteousness to be revealed. Blessed is the man that doeth

this, and the son of man that layeth hold on it; that keepeth the sabbath from profaning it, and keepeth his hand from doing any evil. (ISAIAH 56:1, 2)

Gather yourselves together, yea, gather together, O nation not desired; Before the decree bringeth forth, before the day passeth as the chaff, before the fierce anger of the LORD cometh upon you, before the day of the LORD'S anger

cometh upon you. Seek ye the LORD, all ye meek of the earth, who have performed his judgment; seek righteousness, seek meekness: it may be ye shall be hidden in the day of the LORD'S anger.

(ZEPHANIAH 2:1–3)

Blessed are the poor in spirit: for theirs is the kingdom of heaven. Blessed are they that mourn: for they shall be comforted. Blessed are the meek: for they shall inherit the earth. Blessed are they who hunger and thirst for righteousness: for they shall be filled. Blessed are the merci-

ful: for they shall obtain mercy. Blessed are the pure in heart: for they shall see God. Blessed are the peacemakers: for they shall be called children of God. Blessed are they who are persecuted for righteousness' sake: for theirs is the kingdom of heaven. Blessed are ye, when men *shall revile you, and persecute you, and shall say all manner of evil against you falsely, for my sake. Rejoice, and be exceeding glad: for great is your reward in heaven: for so they persecuted the prophets who were before you.*

(MATTHEW 5:3–12)

He that receiveth a prophet in the name of a prophet shall receive a prophet's reward; and he that receiveth a righteous man in the name of a righteous man shall receive a righteous man's reward. And whoever shall give to drink to one of these little ones [probably meaning to his disciples] a cup of cold water only in the name of a disciple, verily I say to you, he shall by no means lose his reward.

(MATTHEW 10:41, 42)

Then said Jesus to his disciples, If any man will come after me, let him deny himself, and take up his cross, and follow me. For whoever will save his life shall lose it: and whoever will lose his life for my sake shall find it.

(MATTHEW 16:24,25)

Jesus said to him, If thou wilt be perfect, go and sell what thou hast, and give to the poor, and thou shalt have treasure in heaven: and come and follow me.

(MATTHEW 19:21)

And he saith to them . . . to sit [in heaven] on my right hand, and on my left, is not mine to give, but it shall be given to them for whom it is prepared by my Father.

(MATTHEW 20:23)

For the kingdom of heaven is as a man travelling into a far country, who called his own servants, and delivered to them his goods. And to one he gave five talents, to another two, and to another one; to every man according to his own ability; and immediately took his journey. Then he that had received the five talents went and traded with the same, and gained [an]other five talents. And likewise he that had received two, he also gained [an]other two. But he that had received one went and dug in the earth, and hid his lord's money. After a long time the lord of those servants cometh, and reckoneth with them. And he that had received five talents came and brought [an]other five talents, saying, Lord, thou didst deliver to me five talents: behold, I have gained besides them five talents more. His lord said to him, Well done, thou good and faithful servant: thou hast been faithful over a few things, I will make thee ruler over many things: enter thou into the joy of thy lord. He also that had received two talents came and said, Lord, thou didst deliver to me two talents: behold, I have gained two other talents besides them. His lord said to him, Well done, good and faithful servant; thou hast been faithful over a few things, I will make thee ruler over many things:

enter thou into the joy of thy lord. Then he who had received the one talent came and said, Lord, I knew thee that thou art an hard man, reaping where thou hast not sown, and gathering where thou hast not scattered seed: And I was afraid, and went and hid thy talent in the earth: lo, there thou hast what is thine. His lord answered and said to him, Thou wicked and slothful servant, thou knewest that I reap where I have not sown, and gather where I have not scattered seed: Thou oughtest therefore to have put my money in the bank, and then at my coming I should have received my own with interest. Take therefore the talent from him, and give it to him who hath ten talents. For to every one that hath shall be given, and he shall have abundance: but from him that hath not shall be taken away even that which he hath. And cast ye the unprofitable servant into outer darkness: there shall be weeping and gnashing of teeth. (MATTHEW 25:14–30).

And when he had called the people to him with his disciples also, he said to them, Whoever will come after me, let him deny himself, and take up his cross, and follow me. For whoever wishes to save his life shall lose it; but whoever shall lose his life for my sake and the gospel's, the same shall save it. For what shall it profit a man, if he shall gain the whole world, and lose his own soul? Or what shall a man give in exchange for his soul? Whoever therefore shall be ashamed of me and of my words in this adulterous and sinful generation; of him also shall the Son of man be ashamed, when he cometh in the glory of his Father with the holy angels. (MARK 8:34–38)

And they [the people of the town Jesus was in] brought young children to him, that he should touch them: and his disciples rebuked those that brought them. But when Jesus saw it, he was much displeased, and said to them, Permit the little children to come to me, and forbid them not: for of such is the kingdom of God. Verily I say to you, Whoever shall not receive the kingdom of God as a little child, he shall not enter it. (MARK 10:13–15)

For whoever exalteth himself shall be abased; and he that humbleth himself shall be exalted. Then said he[Jesus] . . . When thou givest a dinner or a supper, call not thy friends, nor thy brethren, neither thy kinsmen, nor thy rich neighbours; lest they also bid thee again, and a recompence be made thee. But when thou givest a feast, call the poor, the maimed, the lame, the blind: And thou shalt be blessed; for they cannot recompense thee: for thou shalt be recompensed at the resurrection of the just. (LUKE 14:11–14)

But Jesus called them [his disciples] to him, and said, Permit the little children to come to me, and forbid them not: for of such is the kingdom of God. Verily I say to you, Whoever shall not receive the kingdom of God as a little child shall by no means enter into it. (LUKE 18:16, 17)

And he said to them, Verily I say to you, There is no man that hath left house, or parents, or brethren, or wife, or children, for the sake of the kingdom of God, Who shall not receive much more in this present time, and in the world to come life everlasting. (LUKE 18:29, 30)

... [Jesus] spoke a parable, because he was near to Jerusalem, and because they [the people of the area] thought that the kingdom of God should immediately appear. He said therefore, A certain nobleman went into a far country to receive for himself a kingdom, and to return. And he called his ten servants, and delivered them ten pounds, and said to them, Occupy till I come. But his citizens hated him, and sent a message after him, saying, We will not have this man to reign over us. And it came to pass, that when he had returned, having received the kingdom, then he commanded these servants to be called to him, to whom he had given the money, that he might know how much every man had gained by trading. Then came the first, saying, Lord, thy pound hath gained ten pounds. And he said to him, Well, thou good servant: because thou hast been faithful in a very little, have thou authority over ten cities. And the second came, saying, Lord, thy pound hath gained five pounds. And he said likewise to him, Be thou also over five cities. And another came, saying, Lord, behold, here is thy pound, which I have kept laid up in a napkin: For I feared thee, because thou art an austere man: thou takest up what thou didst not lay down, and reapest what thou didst not sow. And he saith to him, Out of thy own mouth will I judge thee, thou wicked servant. Thou knewest that I was an austere man, taking up what I laid not down, and reaping what I did not sow: Why then gavest thou not my money into the bank, that at my coming I might have required my own with interest? And he said to them that stood by, Take from him the pound, and give it to him that hath ten pounds. (And they said to him, Lord, he hath ten pounds.) For I say to you, That to every one who hath shall be given; and from him that hath not, even what he hath shall be taken away from him. But those my enemies, who would not that I should reign over them, bring here, and slay them before me. (LUKE 19:11–27)

And take heed to yourselves, lest at any time your hearts be overcharged with dissipation, and drunkenness, and cares of this life, and so that day [of the Messiah's return] come upon you unawares. For as a snare shall it come on all them that dwell on the face of the whole earth. (LUKE 21:34, 35)

... in every thing ye are enriched by him [Jesus Christ], in all utterance [speech], and in all knowledge ... so that ye come behind in no gift; waiting for the coming of our Lord Jesus Christ: Who shall also confirm you to the end, that ye may be blameless in the day of our Lord Jesus Christ. (1 CORINTHIANS 1:5, 7, 8)

Now if any man buildeth upon this foundation [laid by Jesus Christ] gold, silver, precious stones, wood, hay, stubble; Every man's work shall be made manifest [apparent for what it is]: for the day shall declare it, because it shall be revealed by fire; and the fire shall try every man's work of what sort it is. If any man's work abideth [endures times of trial or God's judgment] which he hath built upon it, he shall receive a reward. If

any man's work shall be burned, he shall suffer loss: but he himself shall be saved; yet so as by fire.

(1 CORINTHIANS 3:12–15)

But when we are judged [in the present life], we are chastened by the Lord, that we should not be condemned with the world. (1 CORINTHIANS 11:32)

Be not deceived; God is not mocked: for whatever a man soweth, that shall he also reap. For he that soweth to his flesh shall from the flesh reap corruption; but he that soweth to the Spirit shall from

the Spirit reap life everlasting. And let us not be weary in well doing: for in due season we shall reap, if we faint not.

(GALATIANS 6:7–9)

With good will doing service, as to the Lord, and not to men: Knowing that whatever good thing any man doeth, the

same shall he receive from the Lord, whether he be bond [slave] or free.

(EPHESIANS 6:7, 8)

Let your moderation be known to all men. The Lord is at hand.

(PHILIPPIANS 4:5)

Mortify therefore your members which are upon the earth [i.e., be as though you are dead to the word when it comes to the following]; immorality, uncleanness, inordinate affection, evil desire, and cov-

etousness, which is idolatry: For which things' the wrath of God cometh on the children of disobedience:

(COLOSSIANS 3:5, 6)

And the Lord make you to increase and abound in love one toward another, and toward all men, even as we do toward you: To the end he may establish your

hearts unblameable in holiness before God, even our Father, at the coming of our Lord Jesus Christ with all his saints.

(1 THESSALONIANS 3:12, 13)

Fight the good fight of faith, lay hold on eternal life, to which thou art also called, and hast professed a good profession before many witnesses. I command thee in the sight of God, who maketh alive all things, and before Christ Jesus, who before Pontius Pilate witnessed a good con-

fession; That thou keep this commandment without spot, unrebukeable, until the appearing of our Lord Jesus Christ: Who in his times he shall show, who is the blessed and only Potentate, the King of kings, and Lord of lords;

(1 TIMOTHY 6:12–15)

Teaching us that, denying ungodliness and worldly lusts, we should live soberly,

righteously, and godly, in this present world; Looking for that blessed hope, and the glorious appearing of the great God and our Saviour Jesus Christ; Who gave himself for us, that he might redeem us from all iniquity, and purify to himself his own special people, zealous of good works. (TITUS 2:12–14)

Follow peace with all men, and holiness, without which no man shall see the Lord: (HEBREWS 12:14)

And now, little children, abide in him; that, when he shall appear, we may have confidence, and not be ashamed before him at his coming. (1 JOHN 2:28)

And we have known and believed the love that God hath to us. God is love; and he that dwelleth in love dwelleth in God, and God in him. In this is our love made perfect, that we may have boldness in the day of judgment: because as he is, so are we in this world. (1 JOHN 4:16, 17)

Look to yourselves, that we lose not those things which we have wrought [worked for], but that we receive a full reward. (2 JOHN 8)

Keep yourselves in the love of God, looking for the mercy of our Lord Jesus Christ to eternal life. . . . Now to him that is able to keep you from falling, and to present you faultless before the presence of his glory with exceeding joy, To God the only wise, our Saviour, be glory and majesty, dominion and power, both now and ever. Amen. (JUDE 21, 24, 25)

Ezekiel's Temple

The descriptions from the Book of Ezekiel (chapters 40–48), which follow, describe a temple that was never built and the reinstitution of temple sacrifice. They occur right after Ezekiel prophesies about the millennium. Therefore, many people feel Ezekiel intended to describe a temple that is yet to be built—perhaps during the period of the Great Tribulation, which precedes the millennium, or perhaps during the millennium. Other parts of the Bible, however, indicate there will be no sacrifices during the reign of Jesus the Messiah, for all sacrifice ended after his death on the cross. Such a restored temple with the sacrifice Ezekiel describes would seem to be an abomination to Christianity, as well as to Reformed Judaism. Going back to rituals that were meaningful communication in a pagan world would imply that the endless burning of blood and flesh is necessary to appease an angry God. In response to this, some maintain that the sacrifices would be purely commemorative, having nothing to do with the continued forgiveness for sin.

Nevertheless, Ezekiel's writings says that God, himself, ordains the sacrifices at this temple. Therefore, other scholars of prophecy believe Ezekiel was not prophesying at all here but giving an ordinance for the temple as it *should have been rebuilt* after the first temple fell to Babylon—just as Moses gave instructions on how to build God's tabernacle, which were not prophetic but instructive (". . . show the [temple] to the house of Israel, that they may be ashamed of their iniquities: and let them measure the pattern . . . that they may keep its whole form, and all its ordinances, and do them" [Ezekiel 43:10,11]).

That God's instructions given through Ezekiel were not followed by those who built the final temple was a failure on the part of that generation, not on the part of the prophet. Israel ignored the words of many of its prophets. One has to wonder, however, how the builders would have materialized the great river described at the end, which flows out of the temple to water the land. Perhaps that would have been a consecration of the temple provided miraculously by God in response to the completed work. (Just as it would have to be if the temple were actually built in the Great Tribulation or the millennium.)

Finally, some see the description of this temple as purely symbolic—that Ezekiel was creating an elaborate allegory for the present and/or future kingdom of God, much like the symbol of the New Jerusalem at the end of the Apocalypse. The exacting detail given by Ezekiel, however, makes this an unlikely (even tedious) literary symbol if literary symbolism was his intention. The level of mechanical detail supports the view that Ezekiel was giving architectural directions for something actually intended for construction. Of course, the temple is symbolic in its features because all temples are.

The prophecy does say, "This is where I will live among the Israelites for ever," though it's hard to imagine God intended to live in a temple made of stone forever. That would petrify religious practice for eternity.

Yet, at least one prophecy that is clearly messianic indicates the Messiah would reign from his temple and that sacrifices would be reinstituted:

> Behold, I will send my messenger [thought to be John the Baptist], and he shall prepare the way before me [Jesus Christ, God in the flesh]: and the Lord, whom ye seek, shall suddenly come to his temple, even the messenger of the covenant, whom ye delight in: behold, he shall come, saith the LORD of hosts. But who may abide the day of his coming? and who shall stand when he appeareth? for he is like a refiner's fire, and like fullers' soap: And he shall sit as a refiner and purifier of silver: and he shall purify the sons of Levi, and purge them as gold and silver, that they may offer to the LORD an offering in righteousness. [All accomplished in the ministry of Jesus Christ] Then shall the offering of Judah and Jerusalem be pleasant to the LORD, as in the days of old, and as in former years.
>
> (MALACHI 3:1–4)

Malachi wrote after the temple had been rebuilt and just a few hundred years before the advent of Jesus Christ. He was clearly writing about something in his future, and Jesus seems the most likely fulfillment. But was the offering Malachi spoke of related to animal sacrifice that would be restored *after* the time of Christ, or the offering of pure hearts and actions before the Lord?

So, Ezekiel's final writing remains an enigma. While many do not believe it is a prophecy, many others believe it speaks prophetically of a temple that will be built during the Great Tribulation or the millennium, so it is included here as being potentially a part of the end times.

Ezekiel starts by saying he was taken up on a very high mountain. He says the location of the temple he is about to describe is on the south side of this mountain. This is not too far removed from John's description of the New Jerusalem descending upon a great high mountain in the Apocalypse:

EZEKIEL 40

1 In the five and twentieth year of our captivity, in the beginning of the year, in the tenth day of the month, in the fourteenth year after the city was smitten, in the same day the hand of the LORD was upon me, and brought me there. 2 In the visions of God he brought me into the land of Israel, and set me upon a very high mountain, by which was a structure like a city on the south. 3 And he brought me there, and, behold, there was a man, whose appearance was like the appearance of brass, with a line of flax in his hand, and a measuring reed; and he stood in the gate. 4 And the man said to me, Son of man, behold with thy eyes, and hear with thy ears, and set thy heart upon all that I shall show thee; for to the intent that I might show them to thee art thou brought here: declare all that thou seest to the house of Israel. 5 And behold a wall on the outside of the house all around, and in the man's hand a measuring reed of six cubits long by the cubit and an hand breadth: so he measured the breadth of the building, one reed; and the height, one reed. 6 Then he came to the gate which looketh toward the east, and ascended its steps, and measured the threshold of the gate, which was one reed broad; and the other threshold of the gate, which was one reed broad. 7 And every little chamber was one reed long, and one reed broad; and between the little chambers were five cubits; and the threshold of the gate by the porch of the gate within was one reed. 8 He measured also the porch of the gate within, one reed. 9 Then he measured the porch of the gate, eight cubits; and its posts, two cubits; and the porch of the gate was inside. 10 And the little chambers of the gate eastward were three on this side, and three on that side; they three were of one measure: and the posts had one measure on this side and on that side. 11 And he measured the breadth of the entrance of the gate, ten cubits; and the length of the gate, thirteen cubits. 12 The space also before the little chambers was one cubit on this side, and the space was one cubit on that side: and the little chambers were six cubits on this side, and six cubits on that side. 13 He measured then the gate from the roof of one little chamber to the roof of another: the breadth was five and twenty cubits, door against door. 14 He made also posts of sixty cubits, even to the post of the court around to the gate. 15 And from the face of the gate of the entrance to the face of the porch of the inner gate were fifty cubits. 16 And there were narrow windows to the little chambers, and to their posts within the gate on every side, and likewise to the arches: and windows were all around inside: and upon each post were palm trees. 17 Then he brought me into the outer court, and, lo, there were chambers, and a pavement made for the court all around: thirty chambers were upon the pavement. 18 And the pavement by the side of the gates was as wide as the length of the gates; was to the lower pavement. 19 Then he measured the breadth from the front of the lower gate to the front of the inner court on the other side, an hundred cubits eastward and northward. 20 And the gate of the outer court that looked toward the north, he measured its length, and its breadth. 21 And its little chambers were three on this side and three on that side; and its posts and its arches were after the measure of the first gate: its length was fifty cubits, and its breadth five and twenty cubits. 22 And their windows, and their arches, and their palm trees, were after the measure of the gate that looketh toward the east; and they went up to it by seven steps; and its arches were before them. 23 And the gate of the inner court was opposite the gate toward the north, and toward the east; and he measured from gate to gate an hundred cubits. 24 After that he brought me toward the south, and behold a gate toward the south: and he measured its posts and its arches according to these measures. 25 And there were windows in it and in its arches all around, like those windows: the length was fifty cubits, and the breadth five and twenty cubits. 26 And there were seven steps to go up to it, and its arches were before them: and it had palm trees, one on this side, and another on that side, upon its posts. 27 And there was a gate in the inner court toward the south: and he measured from gate to gate toward the south an hundred cubits. 28 And he brought me to the inner court by the south gate: and he measured the south gate according to these measures; 29 And its little chambers, and its posts, and its arches, according to these measures: and there were windows in it and in its arches all around: it was fifty cubits long, and five and twenty cubits broad. 30 And the arches all around were five and twenty cubits long, and five cubits broad. 31 And its arches were toward the outer court; and palm trees were upon its posts: and the ascent to it had eight steps.

32 And he brought me into the inner court toward the east: and he measured the gate according to these measures. 33 And its little chambers, and its posts, and its arches, were according to these measures: and there were windows in it and in its arches all around: it was fifty cubits long, and five and twenty cubits broad. 34 And its arches were toward the outer court; and palm trees were upon its posts, on this side, and on that side: and the ascent to it had eight steps. 35 And he brought me to the north gate, and measured it according to these measures; 36 Its little chambers, its posts, and its arches, and the windows all around: the length was fifty cubits, and the breadth five and twenty cubits. 37 And its posts were toward the outer court; and palm trees were upon its posts, on this side, and on that side: and the ascent to it had eight steps. 38 And the chambers and its entrances were by the posts of the gates, where they washed the burnt offering. 39 And in the porch of the gate were two tables on this side, and two tables on that side, to slay on it the burnt offering and the sin offering and the trespass offering. 40 And on the outside, as one goeth up to the entrance of the north gate, were two tables; and on the other side, which was at the porch of the gate, were two tables. 41 Four tables were on this side, and four tables on that side, by the side of the gate; eight tables, upon which they slew their sacrifices. 42 And the four tables were of hewn stone for the burnt offering, of a cubit and an half long, and a cubit and an half broad, and one cubit high: upon which also they laid the instruments with which they slew the burnt offering and the sacrifice. 43 And within were hooks, an hand broad, fastened all

around: and upon the tables was the flesh of the offering. 44 And outside the inner gate were the chambers of the singers in the inner court, which was at the side of the north gate; and their prospect was toward the south: one at the side of the east gate having the prospect toward the north. 45 And he said to me, This chamber, whose prospect is toward the south, is for the priests, the keepers of the charge of the house. 46 And the chamber whose prospect is toward the north is for the priests, the keepers of the charge of the altar: these are the sons of Zadok among the sons of Levi, who come near to the LORD to minister to him. 47 So he measured the court, an hundred cubits long, and an hundred cubits broad, foursquare; and the altar that was before the house. 48 And he brought me to the porch of the house, and measured each post of the porch, five cubits on this side, and five cubits on that side: and the breadth of the gate was three cubits on this side, and three cubits on that side. 49 The length of the porch was twenty cubits, and the breadth eleven cubits; and he brought me by the steps by which they went up to it: and there were pillars by the posts, one on this side, and another on that side.

EZEKIEL 41

1 Afterward he brought me to the temple, and measured the posts, six cubits broad on the one side, and six cubits broad on the other side, which was the breadth of the tabernacle. 2 And the breadth of the door was ten cubits; and the sides of the door were five cubits on the one side, and five cubits on the other side: and he measured the length of it, forty cubits: and the breadth, twenty cubits. 3 Then he went inward, and measured the post of the door, two cubits; and the door, six cubits; and the breadth of the door, seven cubits. 4 So he measured the length of it, twenty cubits; and the breadth, twenty cubits, before the temple: and he said to me, This is the most holy place. 5 Afterward he measured the wall of the house, six cubits; and the breadth of every side chamber, four cubits, round the house on every side. 6 And the side chambers were three, one over another, and thirty in order; and they entered into the wall which was of the house for the side chambers all around, that they might have hold, but they had not hold in the wall of the house. 7 And there was an enlarging, and a winding about still upward to the side chambers: for the winding about of the house went still upward on all side of the house: therefore the breadth of the house was still upward, and so ascended from the lowest chamber to the highest by the middle chamber. 8 I saw also the height of the house all around: the foundations of the side chambers were a full reed of six great cubits. 9 The thickness of the wall, which was for the side chamber on the outside, was five cubits: and that which was left was the place of the side chambers that were within. 10 And between the chambers was the width of twenty cubits all around the house on every side. 11 And the doors of the side chambers were toward the place that was

left, one door toward the north, and another door toward the south: and the breadth of the place that was left was five cubits all around. 12 Now the building that was before the separate place at the end toward the west was seventy cubits broad; and the wall of the building was five cubits thick all around, and its length ninety cubits. 13 So he measured the house, an hundred cubits long; and the separate place, and the building, with its walls, an hundred cubits long; 14 Also the breadth of the face of the house, and of the separate place toward the east, an hundred cubits. 15 And he measured the length of the building in front of the separate place which was behind it, and its galleries on the one side and on the other side, an hundred cubits, with the inner temple, and the porches of the court; 16 The door posts, and the narrow windows, and the galleries on every side on their three stories, opposite the door, panelled with wood all around, and from the ground up to the windows, and the windows were covered; 17 To that above the door, even to the inner house, and outside, and by all the wall all around within and without, by measure. 18 And it was made with cherubim and palm trees, so that a palm tree was between a cherub and a cherub; and every cherub had two faces; 19 So that the face of a man was toward the palm tree on the one side, and the face of a young lion toward the palm tree on the other side: it was made through all the house all around. 20 From the ground to above the door were cherubim and palm trees made, and on the wall of the temple. 21 The posts of the temple were squared, and the face of the sanctuary; the appearance of the one as the appearance of the other. 22 The altar of wood was three cubits high, and its length was two cubits; and its corners, and its length, and its walls, were of wood: and he said to me, This is the table that is before the LORD. 23 And the temple and the sanctuary had two doors. 24 And the doors had two leaves each, two turning leaves; two leaves for the one door, and two leaves for the other door. 25 And there were made on them, on the doors of the temple, cherubim and palm trees, as were made upon the walls; and there were thick planks upon the face of the porch outside. 26 And there were narrow windows and palm trees on the one side and on the other side, on the sides of the porch, and upon the side chambers of the house, and thick planks.

EZEKIEL 42

1 Then he brought me forth into the outer court, the way toward the north: and he brought me into the chamber that was opposite the separate place, and which was before the building toward the north. 2 Before the length of an hundred cubits was the north door, and the breadth was fifty cubits. 3 Opposite the twenty cubits which were for the inner court, and opposite the pavement which was for the outer court, was gallery against gallery in three stories. 4 And before the chambers was a walk of ten cubits breadth inward, a way of one cubit; and their doors toward the north. 5 Now the upper chambers were narrower: for

the galleries were higher than these, than the lower, and than the middle ones of the building. 6 For they were in three stories, but had not pillars as the pillars of the courts: therefore the upper chambers were set back more than the lower and the middle ones from the ground. 7 And the wall that was outside by the side of the chambers, toward the outer court on the forepart of the chambers, the length of it was fifty cubits. 8 For the length of the chambers that were in the outer court was fifty cubits: and, lo, before the temple were an hundred cubits. 9 And from under these chambers was the entrance on the east side, as one goeth into them from the outer court. 10 The chambers were in the thickness of the wall of the court toward the east, opposite the separate place, and opposite the building. 11 And the way before them was like the appearance of the chambers which were toward the north, as long as they, and as broad as they: and all their exits were both according to their fashions, and according to their doors. 12 And according to the doors of the chambers that were toward the south was a door in the head of the way, even the way directly before the wall toward the east, as one entereth into them. 13 Then said he to me, The north chambers and the south chambers, which are before the separate place, they are holy chambers, where the priests that approach to the LORD shall eat the most holy things: there shall they lay the most holy things, and the meat offering, and the sin offering, and the trespass offering; for the place is holy. 14 When the priests enter in it, then shall they not go out of the holy place into the outer court, but there they shall lay their garments in which they minister; for they are holy; and shall put on other garments, and shall approach to those things which are for the people. 15 Now when he had finished measuring the inner house, he brought me forth toward the gate whose prospect is toward the east, and measured it all around. 16 He measured the east side with the measuring reed, five hundred reeds, with the measuring reed on every side. 17 He measured the north side, five hundred reeds, with the measuring reed on every side. 18 He measured the south side, five hundred reeds, with the measuring reed. 19 He turned about to the west side, and measured five hundred reeds with the measuring reed. 20 He measured it by the four sides: it had a wall all around, five hundred reeds long, and five hundred broad, to make a separation between the sanctuary and the common place.

EZEKIEL 43

1 Afterward he brought me to the gate, even the gate that looketh toward the east: 2 And, behold, the glory of the God of Israel came from the way of the east: and his voice was like a noise of many waters: and the earth shined with his glory. 3 And it was according to the appearance of the vision which I saw, even according to the vision that I saw when I came to destroy the city: and the visions were like the vision that I saw by the river Chebar; and I fell upon my face. 4 And the glory of the LORD came into the house by the way of the gate whose

prospect is toward the east. 5 So the spirit took me up, and brought me into the inner court; and, behold, the glory of the LORD filled the house. 6 And I heard him speaking to me out of the house; and the man stood by me. 7 And he said to me, Son of man, the place of my throne, and the place of the soles of my feet, where I will dwell in the midst of the children of Israel for ever, and my holy name, shall the house of Israel no more defile, neither they, nor their kings, by their harlotry, nor by the dead bodies of their kings in their high places. 8 In their setting of their threshold by my thresholds, and their post by my posts, and the wall between me and them, they have even defiled my holy name by their abominations that they have committed: therefore I have consumed them in my anger. 9 Now let them put away their harlotry, and the dead bodies of their kings, far from me, and I will dwell in the midst of them for ever. 10 Thou son of man, show the house to the house of Israel, that they may be ashamed of their iniquities: and let them measure the pattern. 11 And if they will be ashamed of all that they have done, show them the form of the house, and the fashion of it, and its exits, and its entrances, and all its forms, and all its ordinances, and all its forms, and all its laws: and write it in their sight, that they may keep its whole form, and all its ordinances, and do them. 12 This is the law of the house; Upon the top of the mountain its whole limit all around shall be most holy. Behold, this is the law of the house. 13 And these are the measures of the altar after the cubits: The cubit is a cubit and an hand breadth; even the bottom shall be a cubit, and the breadth a cubit, and the

border of it by its edge on every side shall be a span: and this shall be the higher place of the altar. 14 And from the bottom upon the ground even to the lower ledge shall be two cubits, and the breadth one cubit; and from the smaller ledge even to the greater ledge shall be four cubits, and the breadth one cubit. 15 So the altar shall be four cubits; and from the altar and upward shall be four horns. 16 And the altar shall be twelve cubits long, twelve broad, square in its four sides. 17 And the ledge shall be fourteen cubits long and fourteen broad in its four sides; and the border about it shall be half a cubit; and the bottom of it shall be a cubit about; and its stairs shall look toward the east. 18 And he said to me, Son of man, thus saith the Lord GOD; These are the ordinances of the altar in the day when they shall make it, to offer burnt offerings on it, and to sprinkle blood on it. 19 And thou shalt give to the priests the Levites that are of the seed of Zadok, who approach to me, to minister to me, saith the Lord GOD, a young bull for a sin offering. 20 And thou shalt take of his blood, and put it on its four horns, and on the four corners of the ledge, and upon the border on every side: thus shalt thou cleanse and purge it. 21 Thou shalt take the bull also of the sin offering, and he shall burn it in the appointed place of the house, outside of the sanctuary. 22 And on the second day thou shalt offer a kid of the goats without blemish for a sin offering; and they shall cleanse the altar, as they cleansed it with the bull. 23 When thou hast finished cleansing it, thou shalt offer a young bull without blemish, and a ram out of the flock without blemish. 24 And thou shalt offer them before the LORD, and the priests shall cast salt upon them, and they shall offer them for a burnt offering to the LORD. 25 Seven days shalt thou prepare every day a goat for a sin offering: they shall also prepare a young bull, and a ram out of the flock, without blemish. 26 Seven days shall they purge the altar and purify it; and they shall consecrate themselves. 27 And when these days are fulfilled, it shall be, that upon the eighth day, and so onward, the priests shall make your burnt offerings upon the altar, and your peace offerings; and I will accept you, saith the Lord GOD.

EZEKIEL 44

1 Then he brought me back the way of the gate of the outer sanctuary which looketh toward the east; and it was shut. 2 Then said the LORD to me; This gate shall be shut, it shall not be opened, and no man shall enter in by it; because the LORD, the God of Israel, hath entered in by it, therefore it shall be shut. 3 It is for the prince; the prince, he shall sit in it to eat bread before the LORD; he shall enter by the way of the porch of that gate, and shall go out by the way of the same. 4 Then he brought me the way of the north gate before the house: and I looked, and, behold, the glory of the LORD filled the house of the LORD: and I fell upon my face. 5 And the LORD said to me, Son of man, mark well, and behold with thy eyes, and hear with thy ears all that I say to thee concerning all the ordinances of the house of the LORD, and all its laws; and mark well the entrance of the house, with every exit from the sanctuary. 6 And thou shalt say to the rebellious, even to the house of Israel, Thus saith the Lord GOD; O ye house of Israel, let it suffice you of all your abominations, 7 In that ye have brought into my sanctuary strangers, uncircumcised in heart, and uncircumcised in flesh, to be in my sanctuary, to pollute it, even my house, when ye offer my bread, the fat and the blood, and they have broken my covenant because of all your abominations. 8 And ye have not kept the charge of my holy things: but ye have set keepers of my charge in my sanctuary for yourselves. 9 Thus saith the Lord GOD; No stranger, uncircumcised in heart, nor uncircumcised in flesh, shall enter into my sanctuary, of any stranger that is among the children of Israel. 10 And the Levites that have gone away far from me, when Israel went astray, who went astray from me after their idols; they shall even bear their iniquity. 11 Yet they shall be ministers in my sanctuary, having charge at the gates of the house, and ministering to the house: they shall slay the burnt offering and the sacrifice for the people, and they shall stand before them to minister to them. 12 Because they ministered to them before their idols, and caused the house of Israel to fall into iniquity; therefore have I lifted up my hand against them, saith the Lord GOD, and they shall bear their iniquity. 13 And they shall not come near to me, to do the office of a priest to me, nor to come near to any of my holy things, in the most holy place: but they shall bear their shame, and their abominations which they have committed. 14 But I will make them keepers of the charge of

the house, for all its service, and for all that shall be done in it. 15 But the priests the Levites, the sons of Zadok, that kept the charge of my sanctuary when the children of Israel went astray from me, they shall come near to me to minister to me, and they shall stand before me to offer to me the fat and the blood, saith the Lord GOD: 16 They shall enter into my sanctuary, and they shall come near to my table, to minister to me, and they shall keep my charge. 17 And it shall come to pass, that when they enter in at the gates of the inner court, they shall be clothed with linen garments; and no wool shall come upon them, while they minister in the gates of the inner court, and within. 18 They shall have linen headdresses upon their heads, and shall have linen breeches upon their loins; they shall not gird themselves with any thing that causeth sweat. 19 And when they go forth into the outer court, even into the outer court to the people, they shall put off their garments in which they ministered, and lay them in the holy chambers, and they shall put on other garments; and they shall not sanctify the people with their garments. 20 Neither shall they shave their heads, nor allow their locks to grow long; they shall only cut the hair of their heads. 21 Neither shall any priest drink wine, when they enter into the inner court. 22 Neither shall they take for their wives a widow, nor her that is put away: but they shall take maidens

of the seed of the house of Israel, or a widow that had a priest before. 23 And they shall teach my people the difference between the holy and profane, and cause them to discern between the unclean and the clean. 24 And in controversy they shall stand in judgment; and they shall judge it according to my judgments: and they shall keep my laws and my statutes in all my assemblies; and they shall hallow my sabbaths. 25 And they shall come near no dead person to defile themselves: but for father, or for mother, or for son, or for daughter, for brother, or for sister that hath had no husband, they may defile themselves. 26 And after he is cleansed, they shall reckon to him seven days. 27 And in the day that he goeth into the sanctuary, to the inner court, to minister in the sanctuary, he shall offer his sin offering, saith the Lord GOD. 28 And it shall be to them for an inheritance: I am their inheritance: and ye shall give them no possession in Israel: I am their possession. 29 They shall eat the meat offering, and the sin offering, and the trespass offering; and every dedicated thing in Israel shall be theirs. 30 And the first of all the firstfruits of all things, and every oblation of all, of every sort of your oblations, shall be the priest's: ye shall also give to the priest the first of your dough, that he may cause the blessing to rest in thy house. 31 The priests shall not eat of any thing that is dead of itself, or torn, whether of fowl or beast.

EZEKIEL 45

1 Moreover, when ye shall divide by lot the land for inheritance, ye shall offer an oblation to the LORD, an holy portion of

the land: the length shall be the length of five and twenty thousand reeds, and the breadth shall be ten thousand. This shall be holy in all its borders on every side. 2 Of this there shall be for the sanctuary five hundred in length, with five hundred in breadth, square on every side; and fifty cubits on every side for its common lands. 3 And of this measure shalt thou measure the length of five and twenty thousand, and the breadth of ten thousand: and in it shall be the sanctuary and the most holy place. 4 The holy portion of the land shall be for the priests the ministers of the sanctuary, who shall come near to minister to the LORD: and it shall be a place for their houses, and an holy place for the sanctuary. 5 And the five and twenty thousand of length, and the ten thousand of breadth, shall also the Levites, the ministers of the house, have for themselves, for a possession for twenty chambers. 6 And ye shall appoint the possession of the city five thousand broad, and five and twenty thousand long, beside the oblation of the holy portion: it shall be for the whole house of Israel. 7 And a portion shall be for the prince on the one side and on the other side of the oblation of the holy portion, and of the possession of the city, before the oblation of the holy portion, and before the possession of the city, from the west side westward, and from the east side eastward: and the length shall be the same as one of the portions, from the west border to the east border. 8 In the land shall be his possession in Israel: and my princes shall no more oppress my people; and the rest of the land shall they give to the house of Israel according to their tribes. 9 Thus saith the Lord GOD; Let it suffice you, O princes of Israel: remove violence and spoil, and execute judgment and justice, take away your exactions from my people, saith the Lord GOD. 10 Ye shall have just balances, and a just ephah, and a just bath. 11 The ephah and the bath shall be of one measure, that the bath may contain the tenth part of an homer, and the ephah the tenth part of an homer: the measure of it shall be after the homer. 12 And the shekel shall be twenty gerahs: twenty shekels, five and twenty shekels, fifteen shekels, shall be your maneh. 13 This is the oblation that ye shall offer; the sixth part of an ephah of an homer of wheat, and ye shall give the sixth part of an ephah of an homer of barley: 14 Concerning the ordinance of oil, the bath of oil, ye shall offer the tenth part of a bath out of the cor, which is an homer of ten baths; for ten baths are an homer: 15 And one lamb out of the flock, out of two hundred, out of the rich pastures of Israel; for a meat offering, and for a burnt offering, and for peace offerings, to make reconciliation for them, saith the Lord GOD. 16 All the people of the land shall give this oblation for the prince in Israel. 17 And it shall be the prince's part to give burnt offerings, and meat offerings, and drink offerings, in the feasts, and in the new moons, and in the sabbaths, in all solemnities of the house of Israel: he shall prepare the sin offering, and the meat offering, and the burnt offering, and the peace offerings, to make reconciliation for the house of Israel. 18 Thus saith the Lord GOD; In the first month, in the first day of the month, thou shalt take a young bull without blemish, and cleanse the sanctuary: 19 And the priest shall take of the blood of the sin offering, and put it upon the posts of the house, and upon the four corners of the ledge of the altar, and upon the posts of the gate of the inner court. 20 And so thou shalt do the seventh day of the month for every one that erreth, and for him that is simple: so shall ye reconcile the house. 21 In the first month, in the fourteenth day of the month, ye shall have the passover, a feast of seven days; unleavened bread shall be eaten. 22 And upon that day shall the prince prepare for himself and for all the people of the land a bull for a sin offering. 23 And seven days of the feast he shall prepare a burnt offering to the LORD, seven bulls and seven rams without blemish daily the seven days; and a kid of the goats daily for a sin offering. 24 And he shall prepare a meat offering of an ephah for a bull, and an ephah for a ram, and an hin of oil for an ephah. 25 In the seventh month, in the fifteenth day of the month, shall he do likewise in the feast of the seven days, according to the sin offering, according to the burnt offering, and according to the meat offering, and according to the oil.

EZEKIEL 46

1 Thus saith the Lord GOD; The gate of the inner court that looketh toward the east shall be shut the six working days; but on the sabbath it shall be opened, and in the day of the new moon it shall be opened. 2 And the prince shall enter by the way of the porch of that gate from outside, and shall stand by the post of the gate, and the priests shall prepare his burnt offering and his peace offerings, and he shall worship at the threshold of the gate: then he shall go forth; but the gate shall not be shut until the evening. 3 Likewise the people of the land shall worship at the door of this gate before the LORD in the sabbaths and in the new moons. 4 And the burnt offering that the prince shall offer to the LORD in the sabbath day shall be six lambs without blemish, and a ram without blemish. 5 And the meat offering shall be an ephah for a ram, and the meat offering for the lambs as he shall be able to give, and an hin of oil to an ephah. 6 And in the day of the new moon it shall be a young bull without blemish, and six lambs, and a ram: they shall be without blemish. 7 And he shall prepare a meat offering, an ephah for a bull, and an ephah for a ram, and for the lambs according as his hand shall be able, and an hin of oil to an ephah. 8 And when the prince shall enter, he shall go in by the way of the porch of that gate, and he shall go forth by the way of it. 9 But when the people of the land shall come before the LORD in the solemn feasts, he that entereth in by the way of the north gate to worship shall go out by the way of the south gate; and he that entereth by the way of the south gate shall go forth by the way of the north gate: he shall not return by the way of the gate by which he came in, but shall go forth opposite it. 10 And the prince in the midst of them, when they go in, shall go in; and when they go forth, shall go forth. 11 And in the feasts and in the solemnities the meat offering shall be an ephah to a bull, and an ephah to a ram, and to the lambs as he is able to give, and an hin of oil to an ephah. 12 Now when the prince shall prepare a voluntary burnt offering or peace offerings voluntarily to the LORD, one shall then open to him the

gate that looketh toward the east, and he shall prepare his burnt offering and his peace offerings, as he did on the sabbath day: then he shall go forth; and after his going forth one shall shut the gate. 13 Thou shalt daily prepare a burnt offering to the LORD of a lamb of the first year without blemish: thou shalt prepare it every morning. 14 And thou shalt prepare a meat offering for it every morning, the sixth part of an ephah, and the third part of an hin of oil, to moisten the fine flour; a meat offering continually by a perpetual ordinance to the LORD. 15 Thus shall they prepare the lamb, and the meat offering, and the oil, every morning for a continual burnt offering. 16 Thus saith the Lord GOD; If the prince shall give a gift to any of his sons, the inheritance of it shall be to his sons'; it shall be their possession by inheritance. 17 But if he will give a gift of his inheritance to one of his servants, then it shall be his to the year of liberty; afterward it shall return to the prince: but his inheritance shall be to his sons for them. 18 Moreover the prince shall not take of the people's inheritance by oppression, to thrust them out of their possession; but he shall give his

sons inheritance out of his own possession: that my people be not dispossessed every man from his possession. 19 Afterward he brought me through the entrance, which was at the side of the gate, into the holy chambers of the priests, which looked toward the north: and, behold, there was a place on the two sides westward. 20 Then said he to me, This is the place where the priests shall boil the trespass offering and the sin offering, where they shall bake the meat offering; that they bear them not out into the outer court, to sanctify the people. 21 Then he brought me forth into the outer court, and caused me to pass by the four corners of the court; and, behold, in every corner of the court there was a court. 22 In the four corners of the court there were courts joined of forty cubits long and thirty broad: these four corners were of one measure. 23 And there was a row of building all around in them, around the four of them, and it was made with boiling places under the rows on every side. 24 Then said he to me, These are the places of them that boil, where the ministers of the house shall boil the sacrifice of the people.

EZEKIEL 47

1 Afterward he brought me again to the door of the house; and, behold, waters issued out from under the threshold of the house eastward: for the front of the house stood toward the east, and the waters came down from under from the right side of the house, at the south side of the altar. 2 Then he brought me out of the way of the gate northward, and led me about the way outside to the outer gate

by the way that looketh eastward; and, behold, there ran out waters on the right side. 3 And when the man that had the line in his hand went forth eastward, he measured a thousand cubits, and he brought me through the waters; the waters were to the ankles. 4 Again he measured a thousand, and brought me through the waters; the waters were to the knees. Again he measured a thousand, and brought me through; the waters were to the loins. 5 Afterward he measured a thousand; and it was a river that I could not pass over: for the waters had risen, waters to swim in, a river that could not be passed over. 6 And he said to me, Son of man, hast thou seen this? Then he brought me, and caused me to return to the brink of the river. 7 Now when I had returned, behold, at the bank of the river were very many trees on the one side and on the other. 8 Then said he to me, These waters issue out toward the east country, and go down into the desert, and go into the sea: which being brought forth into the sea, the waters shall be healed. 9 And it shall come to pass, that every thing that liveth, which moveth, wherever the rivers shall come, shall live: and there shall be a very great multitude of fish, because these waters shall come there: for they shall be healed; and every thing shall live where the river cometh. 10 And it shall come to pass, that the fishermen shall stand upon it from Engedi even to Eneglaim; they shall be a place to spread forth nets; their fish shall be according to their kinds, as the fish of the great sea, very many. 11 But its miry places and its marshes shall not be healed; they shall be given to salt. 12 And by the river upon its bank, on this side and on that side, shall grow all trees for food, whose leaf shall not fade, neither shall its fruit be consumed: it shall bring forth new fruit according to its months, because their waters they issued out of the sanctuary: and its fruit shall be for food, and its leaf for medicine. 13 Thus saith the Lord GOD; This shall be the border, by which ye shall inherit the land according to the twelve tribes of Israel: Joseph shall have two portions. 14 And ye shall inherit it, one as well as another: concerning which I lifted up my hand to give it to your fathers: and this land shall fall to you for inheritance. 15 And this shall be the border of the land toward the north side, from the great sea, the way of Hethlon, as men go to Zedad; 16 Hamath, Berothah, Sibraim, which is between the border of Damascus and the border of Hamath; Hazarhatticon, which is by the border of Hauran. 17 And the border from the sea shall be Hazarenan, the border of Damascus, and the north northward, and the border of Hamath. And this is the north side. 18 And the east side ye shall measure from Hauran, and from Damascus, and from Gilead, and from the land of Israel by Jordan, from the border to the east sea. And this is the east side. 19 And the south side southward, from Tamar even to the waters of strife in Kadesh, the river to the great sea. And this is the south side southward. 20 The west side also shall be the great sea from the border, till a man cometh opposite Hamath. This is the west side. 21 So shall ye divide this land to you according to the tribes of Israel. 22 And it shall come to pass, that ye shall divide it by lot for an inheritance to you, and to the strangers that sojourn among you, who shall beget children among you: and they shall be to you as born in the country among the children of Israel; they shall have inheritance with you among the tribes of Israel. 23 And it shall come to pass, that in what tribe the stranger sojourneth, there shall ye give him his inheritance, saith the Lord GOD.

EZEKIEL 48

1 Now these are the names of the tribes. From the north end to the border of the way of Hethlon, as one goeth to Hamath, Hazarenan, the border of Damascus northward, to the border of Hamath; for these are his sides east and west; a portion for Dan. 2 And by the border of Dan, from the east side to the west side, a portion for Asher. 3 And by the border of Asher, from the east side even to the west side, a portion for Naphtali. 4 And by the border of Naphtali, from the east side to the west side, a portion for Manasseh. 5 And by the border of Manasseh, from the east side to the west side, a portion for Ephraim. 6 And by the border of Ephraim, from the east side even to the west side, a portion for Reuben. 7 And by the border of Reuben, from the east side to the west side, a portion for Judah. 8 And by the border of Judah, from the east side to the west side, shall be the offering which ye shall offer of five and twenty thousand reeds in breadth, and in length as one of the other parts, from the east side to the west side: and the sanctuary shall be in the midst of it. 9 The oblation that ye shall offer to the LORD shall be of five and twenty thousand in length, and of ten thousand in breadth. 10 And for them, even for the priests, shall be this holy oblation; toward the north five and twenty thousand in length, and toward the west ten thousand in breadth, and toward the east ten thousand in breadth, and toward the south five and twenty thousand in length: and the sanctuary of the LORD shall be in the midst of it. 11 It shall be for the priests that are sanctified of the sons of Zadok; who have kept my charge, who went not astray when the children of Israel went astray, as the Levites went astray. 12 And this oblation of the land that is offered shall be to them a thing most holy by the border of the Levites. 13 And next to the border of the priests the Levites shall have five and twenty thousand in length, and ten thousand in breadth: all the length shall be five and twenty thousand, and the breadth ten thousand. 14 And they shall not sell of it, neither exchange, nor alienate the firstfruits of the land: for it is holy to the LORD. 15 And the five thousand, that are left in the breadth next to the five and twenty thousand, shall be a common place for the city, for dwelling, and for common lands: and the city shall be in the midst of it. 16 And these shall be the measures of it; the north side four thousand and five hundred, and the south side four thousand and five hundred, and on the east side four thousand and five hundred, and the west side four thousand and five hundred. 17 And the common lands of the city shall be toward the north two hundred and fifty, and toward the south two hundred and fifty, and toward the east two hundred and fifty, and toward the west two hundred and fifty. 18 And the remainder in length next to the oblation of the holy portion shall be ten thousand eastward, and ten thousand westward: and it shall be next to the oblation of the holy portion; and its increase shall be for food to them that serve the city. 19 And they that serve the city shall serve it out of all the tribes of Israel. 20 All the oblation shall be five and twenty thousand by five and twenty

thousand: ye shall offer the holy oblation foursquare, with the possession of the city. 21 And the remainder shall be for the prince, on the one side and on the other of the holy oblation, and of the possession of the city, next to the five and twenty thousand of the oblation toward the east border, and westward next to the five and twenty thousand toward the west border, next to the portions for the prince: and it shall be the holy oblation; and the sanctuary of the house shall be in the midst of it. 22 Moreover from the possession of the Levites, and from the possession of the city, being in the midst of that which is the prince's, between the border of Judah and the border of Benjamin, shall be for the prince. 23 As for the rest of the tribes, from the east side to the west side, Benjamin shall have a portion. 24 And by the border of Benjamin, from the east side to the west side, Simeon shall have a portion. 25 And by the border of Simeon, from the east side to the west side, Issachar a portion. 26 And by the border of Issachar, from the east side to the west side, Zebulun a portion. 27 And by the border of Zebulun, from the east side to the west side, Gad a

portion. 28 And by the border of Gad, at the south side southward, the border shall be even from Tamar to the waters of strife in Kadesh, and to the river toward the great sea. 29 This is the land which ye shall divide by lot to the tribes of Israel for inheritance, and these are their portions, saith the Lord GOD. 30 And these are the exits of the city on the north side, four thousand and five hundred measures. 31 And the gates of the city shall be after the names of the tribes of Israel: three gates northward; one gate of Reuben, one gate of Judah, one gate of Levi. 32 And at the east side four thousand and five hundred: and three gates; one gate of Joseph, one gate of Benjamin, one gate of Dan. 33 And at the south side four thousand and five hundred measures: and three gates; one gate of Simeon, one gate of Issachar, one gate of Zebulun. 34 And the west side four thousand and five hundred, with their three gates; one gate of Gad, one gate of Asher, one gate of Naphtali. 35 The circumference was eighteen thousand measures: and the name of the city from that day shall be, The LORD is there.

Πotes

Introduction

1. Walter Brueggemann, *Finally Comes the Poet: Daring Speech for Proclamation* (Minneapolis, Minnesota: Fortress Press, 1988).

Chapter 1

1. See 2 Chronicles 28:1–3. **2.** Flavius Josephus, *The Wars of the Jews* from *The Works of Flavius Josephus*, Trans. William Whiston, 4 vols. (1738 rpt. Grand Rapids, Michigan: Baker Book House, 1984). **3.** Josephus, *Wars*, II.XIV.2 (p. 168). **4.** Josephus, *Wars*, II.XIII.4 (p. 165). **5.** Josephus, *Wars*, III.IX.1 (p. 263). **6.** Josephus, *Wars*, II.VIII.7 (p. 197). **7.** Josephus, *Wars*, II.XX.1 (p. 206). **8.** Josephus, *Wars*, IV.III.2–7 (pp. 292–294). **9.** Josephus, *Wars*, IV.III.10 (pp. 296–297). **10.** Josephus, *Wars*, IV.III.13 (p. 300). **11.** Josephus, *Wars*, IV.IV.3 (p. 307). **12.** Josephus, *Wars*, IV.IV.5 (p. 310). **13.** Josephus, *Wars*, IV.V.1–2 (p. 313). **14.** Josephus, *Wars*, IV.V.2 (p. 313). **15.** Josephus, *Wars*, IV.V.2 (p. 314). **16.** Josephus, *Wars*, IV.VI.2 (pp. 319, 320). **17.** Josephus, *Wars*, IV.VI.3 (p. 321). **18.** Josephus, *Wars*, V.I.1 (p. 351). **19.** Josephus, *Wars*, V.I.3 (p. 353). **20.** Josephus, *Wars*, V.I.5 (p. 355). **21.** Josephus, *Wars*, V.X.2–3 (pp. 402, 403). **22.** Josephus, *Wars*, V.XII.3 (p. 412). **23.** Josephus, *Wars*, V.XIII.4 (p. 416). **24.** Josephus, *Wars*, V.XIII.6 (p. 418). **25.** Josephus, *Wars*, VI.I.1 (p. 421). **26.** Josephus, *Wars*, VI.II.4 (p. 434). **27.** Josephus, *Wars*, VI.IV.4 (p. 444). **28.** Josephus, *Wars*, VI.V.1 (pp. 451, 452). **29.** Josephus, *Wars*, VI.IX.2 (p. 469). **30.** Josephus, *Wars*, VI.IX.2 (p. 469). **31.** Josephus, *Wars*, VII.I.1 (p. 473).

Chapter 2

1. Josephus, *Wars*, V.I.3 (p. 353). **2.** Josephus, *Wars*, VI.II.1 (p. 430). **3.** Josephus, *Wars*, VI.II.1 (p. 431). **4.** Josephus, *Wars*, VI.II.1 (pp. 431–432). **5.** Josephus, *Wars*, V.VIII.1 and V.IX.1,2 (pp. 390, 392, 393). **6.** Josephus, *Wars*, V.IX.4 (p. 399). **7.** Josephus, *Wars*, VI.II.2,3 (p. 433). **8.** Josephus, *Wars*, VI.IV.2 (p. 446). **9.** Josephus, *Wars*, VI.V.3 (p. 453). **10.** *The Oxford Annotated Apocrypha: Revised Standard Version* (New York: Oxford University Press, 1977), 1. Maccabees 1:20–24;

41–48; 54–64; 3:45; 4:38. **11.** See 2 Maccabees 6:2. **12.** *The Oxford Annotated Apocrypha,* 1 Maccabees 1:11–15. **13.** *The Oxford Annotated Apocrypha,* note p. 231. **14.** *The Oxford Annotated Apocrypha,* 1 Maccabees 4:38, 42, 47, 52–54. **15.** *The Oxford Annotated Apocrypha,* 1 Maccabees 6:8–16. **16.** *The Oxford Annotated Apocrypha,* 2 Maccabees 9:5–10, 28.

CHAPTER 4

1. Eusebius, *The History of the Church from Christ to Constantine,* Trans. G.A. Williamson (New York: Dorset Press, 1984), II.23. **2.** Josephus, *Antiquities of the Jews,* Trans. William Wiston (Grand Rapids, Michigan: Baker Book House, 1984), XVIII.III.3 (p. 11). **3.** Eusebius, pp. 66, 67. **4.** Eusebius, p. 67. **5.** Josephus, *Wars,* VII.VIII.6,7 (pp. 507, 508, 512). **6.** Josephus, *Wars,* VII.IX.1 (p. 514). **7.** Eusebius, IV.8.

CHAPTER 5

1. William F. Albright as quoted by H.L. Wilmington, *Signs of the Times: Current Events Point to the Imminent Return of Jesus Christ* (Wheaton, Illinois: Tyndale, 1981).

CHAPTER 6

1. Josephus, *Wars,* VI.V.2 (p. 453). **2.** Alfred Tennyson, "Crossing the Bar," in *English Poems from Chaucer to Kipling,* ed. Thomas Marc Parrott and Augustus White Long (Boston: Ginn & Company, 1902), p. 245. **3.** David Stipp, "Disaster Bets: A New Way to Bet on Disasters," *Fortune,* September 8, 1997, pp. 124 ff. **4.** Neil Winton, "Insurers Tremble Before Climate Change Threat," *Reuters Business Report,* March 19, 1997. **5.** Lani Luciano and Beth Kobliner (Reporter Associate: Kelly Smith), "Your Property: The Insurance Squeeze on Homeowners," *Money,* May 1, 1994. **6.** "Disasters: What Will It Take? Need for a national insurance program is increasingly apparent," Home Edition, *Los Angeles Times,* April 28, 1997, p. B–4. **7.** David Stipp, "Disaster Bets: A New Way to Bet on Disasters," *Fortune,* September 8, 1997, pp. 124 ff. **8.** Bill Gates with Nathan Myhrvold and Peter Rinearson, *The Road Ahead* (New York: Viking, 1995), pp. 74–77. **9.** Gates, pp. 6, 7, 158, 159, 181.

CHAPTER 7

1. G. K. Chesterton, *Orthodoxy* (New York: John Lane Co., 1908), p. 29.

CHAPTER 8

1. P. Cornelius Tacitus, *The Annals* and *The Histories* Trans. Alfred John Church and William Jackson Brodribb (Chicago: Encyclopedia Britannica, Inc., 1952), XV.37. **2.** Tacitus, *The Annals,* XV.44. **3.** Rutherford H. Platt, ed., *The Lost Books of the Bible and the Forgotten Books of Eden* (Iowa Falls, Iowa: World Bible Publishers, 1963), p. 98. **4.** Tacitus, *Annals,* XVI.13. **5.** Tacitus, *Annals,* XVI.16. **6.** Tacitus, *The Histories,* I.2,3. **7.** Eusebius, III.17,18. **8.** Eusebius, IV.8. **9.** Eusebius, III.29. **10.** Eusebius, IV.15. **11.** Josephus, *Antiquities* IV.VI.6 (pp 252–253). **12.** Josephus, *Antiquities,* IV.VI.8 (p. 254).

CHAPTER 10

1. LeRoy Edwin Froom, *The Prophetic Faith of Our Fathers,* 4 vols. (Washington, D.C.: Review and Herald, 1950), vol. I, p. 339.   **2.** Froom, vol. I, p. 554.

CHAPTER 11

1. Eusebius, III.23.   **2.** *Midrash Rabbah* on Genesis 49:14–17.

CHAPTER 12

1. Leon Jaroff with reporting by Mary Wormley, "Historic Cometary Tales," *Time,* 12–16–1985, pp 63ff.   **2.** Mark Nichols and Warren Caragata, "Celestial Mysteries: Some Fear a Collision Between a Comet and the Earth," *Macleans,* July 18, 1994, vol. 107, pp. 40 ff.   **3.** Leon Jaroff with reporting by David Bjerklie, "A Double Whammy? After the Comet Hit, a Second Jolt from Volcanoes May Have Helped Send the Dinosaurs to Their Doom," *Time,* January 9, 1995, pp. 59 ff.   **4.** Richard Stone, "The Last Great Impact on Earth," *Discover Magazine,* September 1, 1996, vol. 17, pp. 60 ff.   **5.** Mark Alpert, "Killing asteroids: Once-Secret Data Shows that Earth gets Hit More Often than we Thought," *Popular Mechanics,* April 1,1997, vol. 174, pp. 40 ff.   **6.** Peter N. Spotts, "If Asteroids Drop In, Will We See Them Coming?" *The Christian Science Monitor,* May 21, 1998, p. 1.   **7.** Bob Kobres, "The Path of a Comet and Phaèthon's Ride," *The World and I,* February 1, 1995.   **8.** William R. Newcott, "The Age of Comets," *National Geographic,* December 1997, pp. 95–109.   **9.** Dr. David Morrison on *Asteroids: Deadly Impact.*

CHAPTER 13

1. C. S. Lewis, *The Joyful Christian: 127 Readings* (New York: Macmillan Publishing Company, 1984), pp. 50, 52, 54, 55.   **2.** C. S. Lewis, *The Seeing Eye* (New York: Ballantine Books, 1992), pp. xi–xii.   **3.** Richard Stone, "The Last Great Impact on Earth," *Discover Magazine,* vol. 17, September 1, 1996, pp. 60ff.

CHAPTER 14

1. Max I. Dimont, *Jews, God, and History* (New York: Signet Books, 1962), pp. 102–103.   **2.** Odes of Solomon 42:13–17, 19–26 (*The Lost Books of the Bible and The Forgotten Books of Eden,* p. 140.)   **3.** Eusebius, III.17,18.   **4.** Eusebius, III.20.   **5.** Eusebius, III.23.   **6.** Eusebius, V.1.   **7.** Eusebius, VIII.2,7,9.   **8.** Eusebius, VIII.16.   **9.** Eusebius, VIII.17.

CHAPTER 15

1. D. Winton Thomas, *Documents from Old Testament Times* (London: Harper TorchBooks, 1958), p. 129.   **2.** Richard Seed, *All Things Considered,* National Public Radio, January 6, 1998.   **3.** Louis Pauwels and Jacques Bergier, *The Morning of the Magicians,* Trans. Rollo Myers (New York: Dorset Press, 1988), p. 172.   **4.** Pauwels and Bergier, p. 176.   **5.** Pauwels and Bergier, p. 195.   **6.** Jean-Michel Angebert, *The Occult and the Third Reich,* Trans. Lewis A.M. Sumberg (New York: Macmillan, 1974), p. 234. **7.** Pauwels and Bergier, p. 202. **8.** Pauwels and Bergier, p. 204. **9.** Wythe Williams and Albert Parry, *Riddle of the Reich* (New York: Prentice Hall, 1941), pp. 142–144. **10.** *Nazis: the Occult Conspiracy;* Produced and directed by Tracy Atkinson and Joan Baran; Executive Producer, Gaynelle Evans; Cinnabar Pictures, Inc. © Discovery Communications, Inc., 1998. **11.** Ed Hindson, *Final Signs* (Eugene, Oregon: Harvest House Publishers, 1996), p. 93, quoting from Robert Reich, *The Work of Nations* (New York: Alfred Knopf, 1991), p. 8. **12.** Hindson, p. 104, quoting from George Bush, "Address to the Nation," September 16, 1990. **13.** Hindson, p. 107. **14.** Patricia Lamiell, "Is Cash Dead?" *The Seattle Times,* July 20, 1998, pp. D-1,4.

CHAPTER 18

1. Josephus, *Antiquities,* X.11.7. **2.** John Foxe, *Foxe's Christian Martyrs of the World* (Chicago: Moody Press), pp. 153–162. **3.** Will Durant, *The Story of Civilization,* vol. IV, *The Age of Faith* (New York: Simon and Schuster, 1950), p. 784. **4.** Foxe, pp. 178–179. **5.** Dante Alighieri, *The Divine Comedy,* Trans. Charles Eliot Norton (Chicago: Encyclopedia Britannica, Inc., 1952), "Inferno," Canto XIX.46. **6.** Dante, "Inferno," XIX.52. **7.** Dante, "Inferno," XIX.61. **8.** Dante, "Inferno," XIX.88. **9.** Froom, vol. I, pp. 669–670, quoting from *Dictatus Papae.* **10.** Froom, vol. I, p. 542, quoting from Abel François Villemain, *Life of Gregory the Seventh,* vol. I, pp. 175,176. **11.** Froom, vol. I, pp. 409–410. **12.** Froom, p. 527, quoting from Pope Gregory I, *Epistles,* book 5, Epistle 33 (To Mauricius). **13.** Froom, vol. I, p. 539, quoting from Döllinger, *The Pope and the Council,* by Janus [pseudonym]. 3rd, ed. (London, Rivingtons, 1870), p. 110. **14.** Froom, vol I, p. 799, quoting from Ioannes Aventinus, *Annales Boiorum Libri Septem.* **15.** Henry Kamen, *The Spanish Inquisition: A Historical Revision* (London: Weidenfeld & Nicolson, 1997), p. 35. **16.** Kamen, p. 49. **17.** Kamen, p. 69. **18.** Kamen, p. 73. **19.** Rabbi Joseph Telushkin, *Jewish Literacy* (New York: William Morrow and Company, 1991), p. 417. **20.** Pope John Paul II, *Crossing the Threshold of Hope,* ed. Vittorio Messori (New York: Alfred A. Knopf, 1994), pp, 97, 99, 100.

CHAPTER 19

1. Froom, vol. I, p. 445. **2.** Petrarch's 105th Sonnet. **3.** Froom, vol. II, p. 30, quoting from Petrarch, *Epistolarum Sine Titulo, Liber.* **4.** Froom, vol. I, pp. 428–429. **5.** Alexis de Tocqueville, *Democracy in America,* 1835. **6.** R. C. Longworth (reporting for the *Chicago Tribune*), "800-Pound Gorilla? Like it or not, U.S. is the powerhouse of world affairs," *The Seattle Times,* April 15, 1998, p. 1 ff.

CHAPTER 20

1. Pope John Paul II, *Crossing the Threshold* (New York: Alfred A. Knopf, 1994), p. 223. **2.** Pope John Paul II, p. 71, 72, 137, 138, quoting from the *Lumen Gentium.*

CHAPTER 21

1. 2 Esdras 13:8–13. **2.** 2 Esdras 13:23–38. **3.** 2 Esdras 13:39–52.

CHAPTER 22

1. Secrets of Enoch 32:1, 2, 4; 33:1.   **2.** The Book of Enoch 92:14,15.   **3.** Barnabas 13:2–8 (*The Lost Books of the Bible and The Forgotten Books of Eden,* pp. 160, 161).   **4.** Eusebius, III.39.   **5.** Book of Jubilees 23:27–29.   **6.** Augustine, *The City of God,* XX.7.

CHAPTER 23

1. Fr. Kallistos Ware, *The Orthodox Way* (Crestwood, New York: St. Vladimir's Seminary Press, 1979), p. 181.

CHAPTER 24

1. Secrets of Enoch 33:1, 2.   **2.** Enoch 92:16–18.   **3.** Barnabas 13:9–10.   **4.** 2 Esdras 7:26–42.   **5.** C. S. Lewis, *God in the Dock: Essays on Theology and Ethics* (Grand Rapids, Michigan: William B. Eerdmans Publishing Company, 1970), p. 87.

CHAPTER 25

1. Froom, vol. II, p. 170, quoting from Columbus, *Selected Letters,* p. 148.   **2.** Froom, vol. II, pp. 174,175, quoting from Columbus, *Libro de las Profecías,* in *Scritti,* vol. I, pp. 81–83.   **3.** Froom, vol. II, p. 175, quoting from the first letter of Christopher Columbus to the Noble Lord Raphael Sanchez, dated Lisbon, March 14, 1493.

AFTERWORD

1. C. S. Lewis, *God in the Dock,* p. 37.

BIBLIOGRAPHY

BOOKS

Abbott, Lyman, ed. *The Book of Enoch the Prophet.* Trans. Richard Laurance. San Diego: Wizards Bookshelf, 1995.

Aligheri, Dante. *The Divine Comedy.* Trans. Charles Eliot Norton. Chicago: Encyclopedia Britannica, Inc., 1952.

Archer, Gleason L. *Encyclopedia of Bible Difficulties.* Grand Rapids, Michigan: Zondervan Publishing House, 1982.

Armerding, Carl E. and W. Ward Gasque, eds. *A Guide to Biblical Prophecy* (originally published as *Dreams, Visions and Oracles*). Peabody, Massachusetts: Hendrickson Publishers, 1992.

Augustine. *The City of God.* Trans. Marcus Dods. Chicago: Encyclopaedia Britannica, Inc., 1952.

Brown, Colin, ed. *The New International Dictionary of New Testament Theology.* 3 vols. Grand Rapids, Michigan: Zondervan Publishing House, 1981.

Buursma, Dirk R., Ed. *The NIV Topical Study Bible: New International Version.* Grand Rapids, Michigan: Zondervan Bible Publishers, 1989.

Court, John M. *Myth and History in the Book of Revelation.* Atlanta: John Knox Press, 1979.

Demaray, Donald E. *Cowman Handbook of the Bible.* Los Angeles: Cowman Publishing Co., 1964.

Dimont, Max I. *Jews, God and History.* New York: Signet Books, 1962.

Duncan, David Ewing. *Calendar: Humanity's Epic Struggle to Determine a True and Accurate Year.* New York: Avon Books, 1998.

Erdman, Charles R. *An Exposition: The Revelation of John.* Philadelphia, Pennsylvania: The Westminster Press, 1929.

Eusebius. *The History of the Church from Christ to Constantine.* Trans. G. A. Williamson. New York: Dorset Press, 1984.

Fee, Gordon D., and Douglas Stuart. *How to Read the Bible For All Its Worth: A Guide to Understanding the Bible.* Grand Rapids, Michigan: Academie Books, 1982.

Foxe, John. *Foxe's Christian Martyrs of the World.* Chicago: Moody Press. No copyright or publishing date stated.

Froom, LeRoy Edwin. *The Prophetic Faith of Our Fathers.* 4 vols. Washington, D.C.: Review and Herald, 1950.

Fruchtenbaum, Arnold G. *Israelology: The Missing Link in Systematic Theology.* Tustin, California: Ariel Ministries, 1996.

Goodspeed, Edgar J. *An Introduction to the New Testament.* Chicago: University of Chicago Press, 1950.

Halley, Henry H. *Halley's Bible Handbook.* 25th ed. Grand Rapids, Michigan: Zondervan Publishing House, 1965.

Hindson, Ed. *Final Signs.* Eugene, Oregon: Harvest House Publishers, 1996.

John Paul II. *Crossing the Threshold of Hope.* Ed. Vittorio Messori. New York: Alfred A. Knopf, 1994.

Josephus, Flavius. *The Works of Flavius Josephus.* 4 vols. Trans. William Whiston. Grand Rapids, Michigan: Baker Book House, 1984.

Kamen, Henry. *The Spanish Inquisition: A Historical Revision.* London: Weidenfeld & Nicolson, 1997.

Lace, O. Jessie, ed. *The Cambridge Bible Commentary on the New English Bible: Understanding the New Testament.* Cambridge, England: Cambridge University Press, 1979.

Larson, David L. *Jews Gentiles and the Church: A New Perspective on History and Prophecy.* Grand Rapids, Michigan: Discovery House, 1995.

Levin, Meyer. *The Story of Israel.* New York: G. P. Putnam's Sons, 1966.

Lewis, C. S. *God in the Dock: Essays on Theology and Ethics.* Grand Rapids, Michigan: William B. Eerdmans Publishing Company, 1970.

———. *The Joyful Christian: 127 Readings.* New York: Macmillan Publishing Company, 1984.

———. *The Seeing Eye.* New York: Ballantine Books, 1992.

Ludwigson, R. *A Survey of Bible Prophecy.* Grand Rapids, Michigan: Academie Books, 1975.

Martin, Ralph. *Is Jesus Coming Soon? A Catholic Perspective on the Second Coming.* San Francisco: Ignatius Press, 1997.

Metzger, Bruce M., ed. *The Oxford Annotated Apocrypha: Revised Standard Version, Expanded Edition.* New York: Oxford University Press, 1977.

Nichol, Francis D., ed. *The Seventh-day Adventist Bible Commentary.* 7 vols. Washington, D.C.: Review and Herald Publishing Association, 1978.

Oxford Family Encyclopedia. New York: Oxford University Press, 1997.

Patricius, Magonus. *Saint Patrick.* Ed. Iain MacDonald. Trans. Ludwig Bieler. Edinburgh: Floris Books, 1992.

Pauwels, Louis, and Jacques Bergier. *The Morning of the Musicians.* Trans. Rollo Myers. New York: Dorset Press, 1988.

Payne, J. Barton. *Encylopedia of Biblical Prophecy: The Complete Guide to Scriptural Predictions and Their Fulfillment.* Grand Rapids, Michigan: Baker Book House, 1980.

Peterson, Eugene H. *Reversed Thunder: The Revelation of John and the Praying Imagination.* HarperSanFrancisco, 1988.

Platt, Rutherford H., ed. *The Lost Books of the Bible and the Forgotten Books of Eden.* Iowa Falls, Iowa: World Bible Publishers, 1963.

Scofield, C. I., ed. *Oxford NIV Scofield Study Bible.* New International Version. New York: Oxford University Press, 1978.

Spurgeon, Charles Haddon, ed. *Treasury of David.* 2 vols. Guardian Press, 1976.

Tacitus, P. Cornelius. *The Annals and The Histories.* Trans. Alfred John Church and William Jackson Brodribb. Chicago: Encyclopedia Britannica, Inc., 1952.

Telushkin, Rabbi Joseph. *Jewish Literacy.* New York: William Morrow and Company, 1991.

The Holy Bible: Old Testament. 2 vols. New York: Thomas Nelson & Sons, 1952.

Thomas, D. Winton. *Documents from Old Testament Times.* London: Harper Torch Books, 1958.

Vanderwaal, C.; *Hal Lindsey and Biblical Prophecy;* St Catharines, Ontario: Paideia Press, 1978.

Van Kampen, Robert. *The Sign.* Wheaton, Illinois: Crossway Books, 1993.

Walvoord, John F. *The Prophecy Knowledge Handbook.* Wheaton, Illinois: Victory Books, 1973.

Ware, Fr. Kallistos. *The Orthodox Way.* Crestwood, New York: St. Vladimir's Orthodox Theological Seminary, 1979.

Williams, Wythe, and Albert Parry. *Riddle of the Reich.* New York: Prentice Hall, 1941.

Willmington, H. L. *The Book of Bible Lists.* Wheaton, Illinois: Tyndale House Publishers, 1987.

ARTICLES

Alpert, Mark. "Killing Asteroids: Once-Secret Data Shows that Earth Gets Hit More Often than We Thought." *Popular Mechanics,* April 1, 1997, pp. 40 ff.

Anonymous. "Disasters: What Will It Take? Need for a National Insurance Program is Increasingly Apparent." *Los Angeles Times,* Home Edition, April 28, 1997, p. B-4.

Barnes-Svarney, Patricia. "Killer Rocks." *Popular Science,* June 1, 1998.

Finkelstein, Israel, and David Ussishkin. "Back to Megiddo." *Biblical Archeology Review,* January/February 1994, pp. 28–43.

Friesen, Steven. "Ephesus: Key to a Vision in Revelation." *Biblical Archeology Review,* May/June 1993, pp. 24–37.

Jaroff, Leon (with reporting by Mary Wormley). "Historic Cometary Tales." *Time,* December 16, 1985, pp. 63 ff.

Jaroff, Leon (with reporting by David Bjerklie). "A Double Whammy? After the Comet Hit, a Second Jolt from Volcanoes May Have Helped Send the Dinosaurs to Their Doom." *Time,* January 9, 1995, pp. 59 ff.

Kobres, Bob. "The Path of a Comet and Phaèthon's Ride." *The World and I,* February 1, 1995.

Lamiell, Patricia. "Is Cash Dead?" *The Seattle Times,* July 20, 1998, pp. D-1,4.

Longworth, R. C. (reporting for the *Chicago Tribune*). "800-Pound Gorilla? Like it or Not, U.S. is the Powerhouse of World Affairs." *The Seattle Times,* April 15, 1998, p. 1.

Luciano, Lani, and Beth Kobliner (Reporter Associate: Kelly Smith). "Your Property: The Insurance Squeeze on Homeowners." *Money,* May 1, 1994.

Macdonald, Sally. "Israel at 50: Beloved Country." *The Seattle Times,* April 19, 1998. Section M.

Newcott, William R. "The Age of Comets." *National Geographic,* December 1997, pp. 95-109.

Nichols, Mark, and Warren Caragata. "Celestial Mysteries: Some Fear a Collision Between a Comet and the Earth." *Maclean's,* July 18, 1994, pp. 40 ff.

Spotts, Peter N. "If Asteroids Drop In, Will We See Them Coming?" *The Christian Science Monitor,* May 21, 1998, p. 1.

Stipp, David. "Disaster Bets: A New Way to Bet on Disasters." *Fortune,* September 8, 1997, pp. 124 ff.

Stone, Richard. "The Last Great Impact on Earth" *Discover Magazine,* September 1, 1996, pp. 60 ff.

Vanderkam, James C. "Implications for the History of Judaism and Christianity." *The Dead Sea Scrolls After Forty Years.* (Lectures from a 1990 symposium at the Smithsonian Institute, available in book form by the Biblical Archeology Society, Washington, D.C., 1992.)

Winton, Neil. "Insurers Tremble Before Climate Change Threat." *Reuters Business Report,* March 19, 1997.

MAPS & CHARTS

Hull, Edward. *The Wall Chart of World History.* London: Studio Editions, 1988.

Pritchard, James B., ed. *Harper Collins Atlas of the Bible.* London: Harper Collins, 1997.

FILMS AND OTHER MEDIA

Atkinson, Tracy and Joan Baran, Producers/Directors. *Nazis: the Occult Conspiracy.* Executive Producer, Gaynelle Evans. Cinnabar Pictures, Inc. © Discovery Communications, Inc, 1998.

Palca, Joe, reporting. *All Things Considered.* National Public Radio. January 6, 1998.

Parmee, Nina, Producer. *Asteroids: Deadly Impact.* Written and directed by Eitan Weinreich. National Geographic Video, 1997.

İ П D E X

allow 6 pages

TK